FOURTH EDITION

NATIVE PEOPLES IN CANADA

Contemporary Conflicts

JAMES S. FRIDERES

with **Lilianne Ernestine Krosenbrink-Gelissen**

Prentice Hall Canada Inc., Scarborough, Ontario

Canadian Cataloguing in Publication Data

Frideres, James S., 1943-
        Native peoples in Canada: contemporary conflicts
4th ed.
Second ed. published under title: Native people in Canada..
1st ed. published under title: Canada's Indians
Includes bibliographical references and index.

ISBN 0-13-012204-1

1. Native peoples - Canada.* 2. Native peoples -
Canada- Social conditions.* I. Title
E78.C2F75 1993   971'.00497   C93-093269-2

© 1993, 1988 Prentice-Hall Canada Inc., Scarborough, Ontario

Previous editions were published as *Native People in Canada*
© 1983 and as *Canada's Indians* © 1974.

Prentice-Hall, Inc., Englewood Cliffs, New Jersey
Prentice-Hall International (UK) Limited, London
Prentice-Hall of Australia, Pty. Limited, Sydney
Prentice-Hall Hispanoamericana, S.A., Mexico City
Prentice-Hall of India Private Limited, New Delhi
Prentice-Hall of Japan, Inc., Tokyo
Simon & Schuster Asia Private Limited, Singapore
Editora Prentice-Hall do Brasil, Ltda., Rio de Janeiro

ISBN 0-13-012204-1

Acquisitions Editor: Michael Bickerstaff
Developmental Editor: Maryrose O'Neill
Copy Editor: Deborah Burrett
Production Editor: William Booth
Production Coordinator: Anita Boyle
Cover Image & Design: Carole Giguère

1 2 3 4 5   97 96 95 94 93

Printed and bound in the U.S.A.

Every reasonable effort has been made to obtain permissions for all articles and data used in this
edition. If errors or omissions have occurred, they will be corrected in future editions provided
written notification has been received by the publisher.

CONTENTS

7. NATIVE URBANIZATION   257

8. NATIVE ORGANIZATIONS   281

PART 3 • 333

9. THE NATIVE WOMEN'S ASSOCIATION OF CANADA   335

Lilianne Ernestine Krosenbrink-Gelissen

13. POLITICAL ECONOMY OF NATIVES   464

PREFACE

This book is about Native-White relations in Canadian society. It traces the relationship from the time of contact and how it has evolved over time. In this revision, I have followed the general format of the original work. It incorporates new materials produced in a variety of academic disciplines and provides up to date social and demographic information about Native people. People say that if you work on an enterprise long enough, you will eventually gain some perspective on it. As someone also noted, the gain in perspective will be offset by failing eyesight. I have no doubts that as I enter the fourth edition, both events have occurred, particularly since I now wear glasses. Even though my eyesight may have dimmed, I am convinced that the perspective I offer the reader will illuminate their intellectual world and provide for a better appreciation of native people in Canadian society. Hopefully I will have given the reader a lens to view our society of considerable complexity, variety, conflict and dynamism, so that a more complete understanding of Native-White relations can take place.

Novelists, academics and politicians have been inspired for years to write about their observations of Native people. Social scientists have conducted research to better understand Native people and their relations with the dominant society. During your life, you will have few encounters with Native people, yet you will speak about and listen to others thousands of times about them; their plight and place in Canadian society. From them you will develop an understanding about how and why they behave. Sometimes you will be in agreement, on other occasions you will differ. My goal in writing this book is to provide a critical interpretation of "the person on the street's" thinking about Native people in our society. Most textbooks are written from the point of view of the dominant majority. They generally advocate a universalistic view that reflects the dominant perspective. The material presented in the present book looks at ethnic relations from another position—that of the minority groups. Using an historical structural perspective, the material presented attempts to provide a macro theory of Native-White relations.

This fourth edition, like previous ones, has been written for individuals who have a minimal understanding of Natives and their place in our society. It is primarily for the neophyte reader, but one who would like as panoramic a view as possible. For the more advanced reader, the book presents up to date statistical material and incorporates the latest research on Native issues.

Over the past five years, a number of national and international events have occurred that have an impact on Native-White relations. At the national level, the Meech Lake Accord failed to receive the required unanimous consent when Elijah Harper, a Native MLA from Manitoba, blocked its passage. The Charest Committee

(1990) was established to bring about changes in the position of Native people. Many will point to the failure of the above domestic proposals and, while we acknowledge the lack of passage of such proposed legislation, we must also note that the discussion of the issues has brought about some change in how Native people are dealt with in our society. Whether these changes will produce structural changes that will alter the relationships between Natives and non-Natives remains to be seen.

The proliferation of new material on Native people has been phenomenal. During the past year, nearly one hundred scholarly works have been written on Native issues. An equally impressive amount of non-scholarly material has been produced. This later material has contained useful insights and some empirical data that are useful in understanding Native-White relations. Using the above material, I have tried to strike a balance between description, and explanation and theory. I have tried to place Native-White relations in the context of an ideological and philosophical perspective that has taken more than three centuries to emerge. It is hoped that the material presented will help the reader achieve a basic understanding of how and why Native people behave the way they do.

ACKNOWLEDGEMENTS

Those who know the subject will recognize that I owe a large debt to those who have already worked on and written about Native people. As such, regardless of what the copyright law says, this book is not the sole product of one author. I have drawn heavily on the works of my colleagues across Canada and they have shared their thoughts and ideas with me. Their trust for understanding and criticisms of old ideas made me search constantly for new conceptualizations and hopefully, new solutions. I thank them for their insightful comments.

I owe a great deal to Dr. Roy Bowles, whose intellectual influence began when I first took a course from him while in graduate school. Don Whiteside and Katie Cook have, over the years, shared with me their philosophical perspectives as well as the materials I requested, some of which were provided at considerable cost to themselves. I would also like to thank those Native people who have, over the years, shared with me their views and interpretations of Native-White relations in this country. The citations at the end of this volume should be regarded as further acknowledgments to a number of scholars who have written on the subject.

At Prentice Hall, I am grateful to William Booth for the strong support he has given this project and for his outstanding work in preparing the manuscript for publication. I would also like to thank Michael Bickerstaff and Maryrose O'Neill for their support, as well as Deborah Burrett, who copy-edited the manuscript, Carole Giguère, who designed the book, and Anita Boyle, who shepherded it through the production process. I owe a special word of appreciation to Joey Dyrholm for her typing of the manuscript.

James S. Frideres
Calgary, Alberta
1993

P A R T 1

Over the past five years, considerable changes in Native-White relations have taken place. Important legal and political decisions were made over the past few years that have added to the more militant stance taken by Native people; e.g., the passage of *Bill C-31*, self-government, Aboriginal rights, unity negotiations. The nature and extent of conflict has escalated, culminating in the armed conflict between Mohawks and the Canadian army in 1990. The death of the Meech Lake Accord was partially a product of Native resistance and has brought the country to the crossroads of its destiny.

The first section of this book provides the historical context essential to a full understanding of the issues faced by Native people. Over the years there has been a continuing evolution of the idea of who is a Native, and Chapter 1 focuses on these definitions. Part I also reviews the legal and political negotiations that have been concluded between Natives and the government. This section concludes with an up-to-date discussion of the land claims now being presented by Native people. Some of these claims have been finalized, others are being negotiated and still others are in the preparation stage. This proliferation of claims now being presented demonstrates the freedom of action Native people have achieved over the past two decades.

COLONIALISM, NATIVES AND HISTORY

INTRODUCTION

The social and economic problems facing Native people in our country as they enter the twenty-first century have not emerged overnight. Nor are they the result of random factors impinging upon these groups. What is important to note is that Aboriginal people in other parts of the world have experienced similar fates and face similar problems today. This suggests that there are processes that have affected Aboriginal peoples in historical times as well as in the present. These structural impacts began to affect Aboriginal people at the time of contact with Europeans and became increasingly influential as the immigrant population grew. As the world political economy began to integrate with the Canadian domestic economy, these structural effects relegated Aboriginal peoples—in Canada and throughout the world—to a peripheral position in society.

What are these processes? How have they impacted upon Aboriginal people? We begin our long and complex analysis of Native-White relations and Native participation in our society by moving our analysis from a micro (individual) analysis to a macro (structural) analysis. For too long, social scientists have viewed Native-White relations through a micro model, focusing exclusively on individual actions, e.g., prejudice, discrimination. Not surprisingly, these models see solutions to the problems Native people face as being brought about through individual action, e.g., individual enhancement, individual entrepreneurship. We wish to approach the problems from a different perspective—structural. While we will not deny that Aboriginal people are exposed to a great deal of prejudice and discrimination, their greatest obstacle is the very structure of our society itself, which prevents Native people from effectively participating in the social, economic and political structure of our society. Furthermore, we feel that there is a linkage between the structural effects (the institutional arrangements of our society) and the behaviour of individuals.

The analytical model presented here has as its forerunners those offered by Cumming (1967), Carstens (1971) and Patterson (1972). Drawing heavily on these authors, the macro-model used here presents the Indian reserve as an internal colony that is exploited by the dominant group in Canada. Canadians are seen as the colonizing people, while Natives are considered the colonized people.

By conceptualizing the reserve as an internal colony of a larger nation, it is possible to see beyond the individual factors involved in inter-group behaviour. While the individualized approach has offered much to the study of Native-White relations, it has not really produced any cogent explanation of those relations. Nor has it produced any meaningful improvement in the Native's position in our society. If anything, that position has worsened.

Many social scientists have rejected the colonial analysis as misleading, claiming that our social and political patterns are significantly different from those in, for example, Africa or India. Although there have certainly been differences, these do not obscure the fact that the indigenous peoples of Canada were unquestionably colonized and that their position in Canada today is a direct result of the colonization process.

Tabb has described conditions in a typical underdeveloped country as follows:

> ...low per capita income; high birthrate; a small, weak middle class; low rates of increase in labour productivity, capital formation, and domestic savings; and a small monetized market. The economy of such a country is heavily dependent on external markets where its few basic exports face an inelastic demand (that is, demand is relatively constant regardless of price, and so expanding total output may not mean higher earnings). The international demonstration effect (the desire to consume the products enjoyed in wealthier nations) works to increase the quantity of foreign goods imported, putting pressure on the balance of payments as the value of imports exceeds the value of exports. Much of the small modern sector of the economy is owned by outsiders. Local entrepreneurship is limited, and in the absence of inter-governmental transfers, things might be still worse for the residents of these areas (1970:22).

This is a relatively accurate description of a reserve in Canada today.

The colonization process can be considered in seven parts (Kennedy, 1945; Blauner, 1969). The first concerns the incursion of the colonizing group into a geographical area. Usually, this takes the form of forced-voluntary entry; acting in its own interests, the colonizing group forces its way into an area. In Canada, both French and English settlement followed this pattern. At present, many Northern Natives argue that forced-voluntary colonization is occurring in the North.

The second attribute of colonization is its destructive effect on the social and cultural structures of the indigenous group. In Canada's case, White colonizers destroyed the Natives' political, economic, kinship and, in most cases, religious systems. The values and norms of Native people were either ignored or violated. For example, after the War of 1812, when a large number of White settlers arrived, the colonial government decided that Natives should be forced to surrender their traditional lifestyles. Official programs were developed, and between 1830 and 1875 legislation was enacted to carry out this destructive policy (Surtees, 1969).

As Titley (1986) points out, the federal government's policies were in harmony with the non-Native demands. Native protests were futile and when Natives took action to support their claims in the late 1860s, harsh repression followed, including the bombardment of coastal villages by British warships (Tobias, 1976). By the late 1890s, the federal government had amended the *Indian Act* (of 1876) so that "surplus" or "idle" Indian land could be available for the use of non-Indians. In 1911, amendments to the *Indian Act* gave even greater coercive powers to the federal government. For example, Section 46 allowed portions of reserves to be taken by municipalities or companies for roads or similar public purposes with the consent of the Governor-in-Council, (today called the Cabinet) but without a surrender (Carter, 1990).

Canadian officials have, since the early nineteenth century, viewed Natives as inferior. Education and religious groups have been instrumental in attempting to bring about Native social change in order to "civilize" and "Christianize" them. A symbiotic relationship emerged between various churches and the state. The best example of this was when the churches were being frustrated in their efforts to Christianize Natives. Church officials felt that because certain Native cultural components were incompatible with Christianity, they should be eradicated. They therefore convinced the state to pass legislation outlawing a variety of dances and other ceremonies that were an integral component of the Native culture, for example, the potlatch.

The third and fourth aspects of colonization are the interrelated processes of external political control and Native economic dependence. In the standard practice of colonization, the mother country sends out representatives through which it indirectly rules the newly conquered land. In our model, the representative ruler is DIAND (the Department of Indian Affairs and Northern Development). Until 1940, Indian Affairs decided which Natives could and couldn't leave reserve lands. Native self-government has been effectively prevented. Until recently, band funds could not be used by Natives to develop social and political organizations of their own (Whiteside, 1972). In some cases, Natives have been allowed to elect their own chiefs and band councils, but these are advisory only, with no real power.

Council recommendations continue to be subject to acceptance or rejection by DIAND.

The Minister of DIAND can suspend almost any right set forth in the *Indian Act*. For example, Section 80 of the Indian Act authorizes band councils to pass by-laws for public health and traffic regulation. However, to date, the Minister has granted fewer than two-thirds of band councils permission to do so.

Acting through the Governor-in-Council, DIAND can also veto any decisions of band councils. For example, section 82 of the *Indian Act* allows a band to enact money by-laws. However, first the Governor-in-Council must find that the band has reached a "high state of development." At present, fewer than 50 bands have been so defined, and these have mostly used their powers to build sewers, wells and so on. Section 68 of the Act allows a band to "control, manage, and expand in whole or in part its revenue moneys." No band was actually permitted to do so until 1959, and to date fewer than 20 percent have received permission. Section 60 allows a band "the right to exercise such control and management over lands in the reserve occupied by that band as the Governor-in-Council considers desirable." To date, the Governor-in-Council has found this desirable for less than ten reserves.

Section 35 of the *Act* explicitly states that reserve land can be expropriated by the federal government at any time. In 1971, the National Indian Brotherhood (NIB) announced that the federal government had redrawn treaty maps and stripped titles to a number of land parcels claimed by Natives. Natives were not consulted before or during the redrawing of the maps. Significantly, the federal government did not refute the accusations. Moreover, the National Indian Brotherhood uncovered a classified government memo ordering that all copies of previous treaty maps be destroyed.

In the initial stages of colonization, the colonized people generally accept their fate. Only later do they reject their powerless position. Native leaders on reserves today tend to be considerably more militant than those who initially signed treaties. But even if Natives no longer accept their subordinate status, there is little they can do to change it. Although, as Bolt (1980) has shown, many Native leaders are currently viewing extra-legal activity as a viable method of pressing their claims, other Natives have surrendered to a general apathy and dispiritedness. The process of acculturation and the demise of indigenous Native tribal associations have eroded Native self-identification. Communal bonds have broken down among individual Natives and among bands, contributing to the continued failure of Native organizations. Leadership responsibilities on the reserves have become further divided and poorly defined, exacerbating the disorganization of Native groups. The success rate for Native organizations is very low; most are dissolved soon after they are created.

In the political arena, Natives have been ineffectual for several reasons. Most importantly, they have been prevented from voting or running for office until recently. Except for Nova Scotia, Natives did not receive the right to vote in provincial elections until after World War II. They did not receive the federal franchise until 1960. Needless to say, this severely restricted their ability to make political demands. Those with no voice in the political structure that governs their lives have no means of influencing or sanctioning the policies that affect them.

After receiving the vote, Natives were initially sceptical of their new rights and failed to exercise them to any great extent. This attitude is changing however. For example, in the 1968 federal election, nearly 90 percent of the Native population that voted in a Saskatchewan riding cast their vote for a Red Power candidate. In the 1982 provincial election, an Aboriginal Party was established in Saskatchewan.

Natives remain economically dependent on White society because their reserves are treated as geographical and social hinterlands for White exploitation. White-controlled businesses exploit nonrenewable primary resources such as oil, minerals, water and forest products, and ship them to urban industrial centres for processing. This practice has two important results for reserve Natives: the development of Native-owned industries is pre-empted and Native occupational activities remain at a primary level. As the treaties and the *Indian Act* show, federal policy has always tried to orient Native occupations toward agriculture and primary industries (Carter, 1990).

In the colonization process, a two-level system develops in which the White colonizers own, direct and profit from industries that depend upon exploitation of colonized Natives, who provide an unskilled, seasonal work force. On the reserves, the long-term result has been a Native population that lives at subsistence level, working at unskilled, seasonal jobs in primary industries and practising subsistence agriculture to survive. Although the profits from raw material production are based on reserve resources and cheap Native labour, they disappear from the reserve into the pockets of White entrepreneurs.

Reserve hinterlands are at a low level of economic development. Economic development is not the same as economic growth. Economic growth refers to an increase in the productive capacity of an areas's economy, while economic development reflects a change in the structure of an area's economy, such as a movement from primary extractive or agricultural industries to secondary or processing industries. For example, Alberta reserves and Métis colonies have experienced considerable short-term economic growth due to oil and mineral discoveries but no real economic development.

As Boldt points out, this lack of economic development has a profound effect on Native leadership and political organization.

> Most striking is the statistic relative to leaders who derive their influence from the economic sector. Not a single Indian leader could be classified as exercising his influence in the economic sector. This provides evidence of the degree to which Indians generally have been excluded from the Canadian economic sector and hence the power structure (1980:18).

The federal government had effectively discouraged the economic development of reserves, as the *Income Tax Act* and the *Indian Act* show. Fields and Stanbury find that:

> If Indians choose to undertake economic development of their reserves utilizing the form of a limited company, then they lose the benefit of exemption from taxation as individuals or as a band. Income earned by a corporation wholly owned by Indians is subject to taxation the same as any corporation—even if the income is derived solely from activities on a reserve (1975:203).

The structural complexities involved in the payment of property taxes on reserve lands also prevent Natives from profitably leasing their lands. To exemplify this, Fields and Stanbury posit an example in which a developer decides to build a warehouse on a piece of rented property. Two similarly suitable locations are available; one is on an Indian reserve, the other is not. The firm discovers that it can rent either the reserve or the off-reserve land for $3000 per year. When it approaches the band, however, it finds that it must agree to pay taxes to the municipality assessed at $1500 per year, as though it owned the land. In order then, to compete with the owner of the off-reserve land, the band must reduce its rent to $1500 per year to absorb the taxes. As Fields and Stanbury point out, by leasing its land instead of developing and occupying it itself, the band incurs an opportunity cost of $1500.

A fifth characteristic of colonization is the provision of low-quality social services for the colonized Natives in such areas as health and education. A recent survey by DIAND confirms a desperate need for adequate social services. For example, the report points out:

- Life expectancy, a reflection of health standards, is still ten years less than that for the general population.
- In 1964, an estimated 36 percent of the Indian population received social assistance; by 1977-78, between 50 and 70 percent received social assistance; by 1988 these figures remained stable.
- One in three families lives in crowded conditions. 11 000 new houses are required and 9000 need repair. Less than 50 percent of Indian houses are properly serviced, compared to the national level of over 90 percent (1980:3).

Although Native living conditions have improved in some material ways, social problems, including alcohol abuse and welfare dependency, have increased.

The last two aspects of colonization relate to social interactions between Natives and Whites and refer to racism and the establishment of a colour-line. Racism is a belief in the genetic superiority of the colonizing Whites and the inferiority of the colonized Natives. With a colour-line, indicators such as skin pigmentation and body structure are established to become the basis for determining superiority and inferiority. Interaction then goes on only among members of the same group: Whites interact with Whites and Natives with Natives. In Canada, for example, Indians have the highest rate of marriage within their own ethnic group—93.6 percent.

The ultimate consequence of colonization is to weaken the resistance of the colonized Natives to the point at which they can be controlled. Whether the motives for colonization are religious, economic or political, the rewards are clearly economic. White Canada has gained far more than it has lost in colonizing its Natives. Although Wuttnee (1973) claims that the federal government has spent $2 billion on Natives over the past century, he fails to point out that it has profited by about $60 billion. For example, the federal government spends $530 per treaty Native per year and $740 per non-Native. From that source alone, the result is a saving of $210 per Native per year or a total of $52 million per year (Fidler, 1970).

Currently, Métis in Alberta are suing the federal government over nonpayment of royalties on the extraction of natural resources from Métis colonies. The Métis began a legal battle to win the mineral rights to their land in 1938. They estimate that the royalties on the 200 producing oil and gas wells on their land amount to $60 million.

Like any model, the colonization approach has certain limitations. The world is complex: people, social structures and cultures change with time. Of necessity, however, a model is frozen in time, a static recreation of what occurs around us. In order to construct a portrait that corresponds closely to the real world, we select and incorporate certain variables, discard others as unimportant, and make assumptions about how people behave.

If the resulting model produces accurate explanations and predictions, it can be considered successful. It may then become a useful tool in finding solutions to social problems and in developing social action programs. If, however, a model proves incapable of providing accurate predictions or explanations, it must be revised or discarded.

Nevertheless, we must still answer the central question: why are Natives in such a dependent position in Canadian society? Several explanations have been proffered. Usually these explanations point to a single cause. However, it would seem more realistic to accept the position that several reasons contribute to the low standing Natives hold in Canadian society. All seem to fall within and stem from the historical colonialism that has characterized our society.

First of all, Natives have become economically redundant over time because of changes in the structure and technology of the economy. After the buffalo hunts ended and the fur trade all but ceased, Natives were largely unable to participate in the economy. As Canadian society moved to agriculture and then to an urban-industrial base, Native peoples did not possess, and were not in a position to acquire, new technologies or skills. The result is that Natives find themselves operating a subsistence economy parallel to that of the more modern economy. In other words, there are two economies in our society. The industrial and technologically based modern sector of the economy is dynamic—change promotes further change. The traditional, subsistence sector of the economy, however, resists change—it clings to the old ways and refuses to adopt new technology (Wien, 1986). This of course suggests that as our economy becomes more "high-tech," barriers are created that hinder or stop entrance of Natives into the modern economy. Certain technical and social skills are now prerequisites to entering the labour force. People without these skills will be kept from participating as full-time members in the modern labour market.

As individuals are prevented from entering the modern economy, a cultural ethos emerges which is quite different from that expressed in the social mainstream. Anthropologists have referred to this distinctive ethos as the "culture of poverty." When the goals of higher status are denied to people, other forms of adaptations are created—for example, withdrawal and rebellion—in order to deal with the despair and hopelessness that are central to the culture of poverty. This encourages individuals to develop a different perspective on life and on how to deal with everyday occurrences.

Once an individual is placed within the traditional culture of poverty, it is almost impossible for him or her to get out. As we have seen, the lack of certain technical and social skills keeps Natives from entering the modern labour market. And, as that market becomes increasingly segmented into a primary and a secondary market, there is greater difficulty moving from the secondary to the primary market.[1] As a result, Natives are increasingly shut out of the primary market.

Natives played an important role in the development of Canada. However, as the twentieth century emerged, the lack of technological skills relegated Native people to second class citizens. While many history books acknowledge the interaction of Natives and Europeans, they tend to characterize Natives as passive, always responding to actions taken by Europeans. In short, the interaction between the two parties usually portrayed Europeans as the proactive agents, asserting their vision of Canada onto Native people. There are some exceptions to this general pattern (Miller, 1989), but the history of Native-White relations in Canada has generally been told from the perspective of non-Natives.

When Natives and Europeans first came into contact, two different cultures came into contact. Aboriginals were hunters and gatherers (although there were some agricultural tribes) who lived in harmony with their physical environment. Their limited technological developments placed few constraints on the ecology, and the small numbers of people meant that population pressures were light (Miller, 1989). Europeans, on the other hand, were continually developing their technology to achieve superiority over nature. They were ethnocentric in outlook and had a mission to Christianize the world. The clash of these two cultures was resounding, and while there is no doubt that Natives have taken the brunt of this collision, they have, surprisingly, retained considerable elements of their culture. They have, when possible, tried to adopt a "controlled acculturation" perspective, adapting certain behaviours and actions of Euro-American culture while retaining other valued mental constructs from their own culture. Perhaps the creation of reserves and the high level of isolation of many Natives has allowed this selective retention to be carried on.

The underlying basis which characterizes Native-White relations in our history is that Europeans have always assumed a superiority over Native people. As was noted in the discussion of the characteristics of colonization, this is racism—the belief that one group is biologically inferior to another group.

As the British secretary of state for war and the colonies noted in 1830:

> It appears to me that the course which has hitherto been taken in dealing with these people [Indians], has had reference to the advantages which might be derived from their friendship in times of war, rather than to any settled purpose of gradually reclaiming them from a state of barbarism, and of introducing amongst them the industrious and peaceful habits of civilized life (Sir G. Murray, 1834).

Although some people may object to this claim, racism is undeniably the underlying ideology of the manifest policies regarding Native-White relations throughout the history of Canada. To choose just one indicator, the proceedings of the federal Parliament with regard to Native issues are shot through with racist dogma. The Commission appointed to enquire into the conditions of Indians of the Northwest Coast noted that "the Indians having acquired a little mental activity and a very partial knowledge of some of the things about which they are agitating, probably imagine that they know a great deal and are thoroughly able to say what is good for them" (1888, pp. 32-33). As another example, Dosman (1972) has shown that the Agents' Reports of Native life have historically been inundated with racist comments. The following is an example from Alexander Morris, who arranged the initial treaties with Native peoples:

> Let us have Christianity and civilization to leaven the masses of heathenism and paganism among the Indian Tribes; let us have a wise and paternal government faithfully carrying out the provisions of our treaties.... They [Native people] are wards of Canada, let us do our duty to them...(1880:296-97).

And here is a statement by the Minister of the Interior, in 1902:

> Our position with reference to the Indian is this: We have them with us, and we have to deal with them as wards of the country. There is no question that the method we have adopted [will bring] these people to an improved state.... There is a difference between the savage and a person who has become civilized, though perhaps not of a high type. (Debate of the House of Commons, 2nd sess., 9th Parl., 1902:3046).

The reader may claim that these are isolated examples from a different era. However, these statements are representative of the widely prevailing legal, academic and literary attitudes of the time. The reader might also claim that people are far more enlightened today.

To be sure, most people today would not argue that one group of people are biologically inferior to another. However, this biological racism has been supplanted with a new form of social/cultural racism which focuses on the inferiority of a group's way of life, their ethos and their assumptions about the world. In taking this view, people may escape being accused of racism: they are prepared to accept the biological similarities of different groups of people. However, they are not prepared to accept cultural equality. Individual racism has given way to structural racism. Examining structural racism allows one to focus on the way discrimination is built into systems of power and institutions in Canada.

Over time, non-Native Canadians have revealed contradictory attitudes and behaviour toward Native people. They have publicly proclaimed respect for Natives' rights while at the same time denying them such basic rights as voting and the right to choose their reserves (Anderson and Wright, 1971; Washburn, 1965). For those wishing to examine a more detailed historical review of Native-White relations in Canada, the following sources should be consulted: *Report on the Affairs of the Indians in Canada*, 1844; Jenness, 1937; Stanley, 1952; Patterson, 1972; Miller, 1989.

Although it may never be possible to quantify the degree of racism that exists in a given society, the evidence unmistakably reveals that racism widely distorts the attitudes of White Canadians toward Native peoples. Whether blatantly or covertly, most Canadians still believe that Natives are inferior; as a result, these people believe that there is a sound rational basis for discrimination against Natives at both the individual and institutional level.

The hostility and conflict established historically between Aboriginals and political and legal enforcement bodies has contributed to the contemporary relationships, which are based on suspicion, disrespect and mistrust from both sides. Through a history of enactments legislated through colonial Parliament, the institutions in this country have been used to segregate Native people from the dominate culture and to legitimize paternalistic control over all aspects of their lives. Having been excluded from recognition as human beings, it was not until after World War II that Aboriginals were granted a social identity as Canadians in the full sense of the word. However, whilst being granted Native rights (in their own country) may have helped to alleviate some of the consequences that emanated from the horrific colonial era, no attempts were made by political or judicial quarters to address the discriminatory and biased legal provisions that were used to deny them parity and equality with their dominant counterparts. The historical situation provided the initial conditions, and by apathy and indifference, rather than intentional exploitation, those conditions have continued to exist. While the introduction of the *Charter of Rights and Freedoms* in 1982 was assessed as a significant step toward enacting a degree of reform in this area, the Native population found little comfort in it because of the inadequacies that were attached to its legislative jurisdictional powers.

[marginal handwritten notes: "Old vs. new view on Native / non Native Relations"]

The old ways of non-Natives looking at and relating to Natives have been reflected in the way government has treated Natives. However, some of these old views are now coming under scrutiny and being challenged. Weaver (1991) points out that the *Penner Report* on Indian self-government (1983) and the *Coolican Report* on comprehensive land claims (1986) broke new ground in conceptualizing issues involving Native people. What is this new conceptualization? First, the findings in the two reports brought into the public forum a new idea about the relationship between Natives and non-Natives. Whereas previously non-Natives tended to view the linkages as eventually resulting in the "termination" of Natives and/or the full integration of Natives into non-Native society (i.e., assimilation), these two reports view the relationship as parallel over time, the two cultures adjusting to each other as the time and context change. In other words, they see the relationship as flexible and evolving.

[marginal handwritten note: "Sanctioned rights"]

A second new conceptualization identified by Weaver (1991) is the notion of sanctioned rights, which she defines as those rights recognized by the state as justified claims against its actions toward a particular group. Related to this is a new political ethic developed in government with regard to how it deals with Natives. There is a new commitment to be direct, honest and honourable in government dealings with Native people. This new ethic has been brought to the forefront as a result of a number of court decisions which have gone against the government. This also means that partnership is the relationship government will have with Native people. Out of this partnership, jointly formulated policies will emerge which will lead to some form of Native empowerment (Weaver, 1991).

All of the above reveal a new ethos regarding the relationship between Natives and the government. If it is to be accepted, then the relationship must be restructured. These new ideas have begun to challenge the old views, but before they become dominant in government thinking, old conceptualizations will have to be dropped. Therefore, during the current transitional period, the Department of Indian Affairs is undergoing turbulent times as proponents of each perspective try to make their position the basis for action. This is one reason why government seemingly has taken contradictory stands in dealing with Native people. For example, Sanders (1991) points out that even the Supreme Court has not been consistent in its rulings with regard to Native people. In some cases the inconsistencies reflect the evolution of doctrine, while others defy explanation. Yet the changes seem to reflect the emergence of a new perspective and a new place for Natives in Canadian society. However, whether or not this new view of Natives will become the dominant one remains to be seen.

Confrontations between Natives and Whites noted in the press tend to focus on specific complaints, overlook broader issues, and reflect an old definition of Natives and their role in Canadian society. Hence, in many cases where conflict emerges, Natives are labelled as malcontents, troublemakers and opportunists, labels that can only be defended through a distorted and abbreviated view of history. As Weaver

(1991) points out, the federal government's response to Oka was that the situation was a "law and order" problem which, when defined in this manner, required the harsh and extraordinary measures taken.

As at Oka, the stage for clashes between Natives and Whites has generally been set by historical facts and existing structural relations, though few people are interested in examining these. For example, the Lubicon Indians in Alberta who blockaded roads and shut down oil pumps also were depicted as irresponsible troublemakers. Yet surely the reasons for their protest were linked to the fact that the band has been fighting for land to be set aside for a reserve promised 50 years ago, for compensation for energy and forestry development which had taken well over $5 billion of natural resources from the area, for the Native children who die before their first birthday, for the Native people who are unable to get jobs, and for the large number of Natives who are unable to secure adequate housing. Nevertheless, when confrontations erupt, the implication is that the fault lies largely with Native people. This assumption reveals a biased and short-term perspective. Such an assumption ignores the subtle violence that has been perpetrated against Natives since the arrival of the White explorers. It also serves those who want to remain in power and maintain the status quo that excludes Native Canadians from a share in their country's bounty and that allows them to remain hungry, uneducated and inadequately housed in the midst of plenty.

Some readers will be angered by these statements and indignant that their society should be labelled racist. They will say that other history books do not make such claims. But history is humanity's way of recording past behaviour; historians are extremely susceptible to the political and social forces that govern while their histories are actually being written. What Natives have been encouraged to write histories? And when Native histories have been written, why have they been dismissed as fabrications?

An author's explanation of social events depends on an individual point of view. Because overt social behaviour can be interpreted in many different ways, the historian must always infer the actors' motives. Historians infer motives for groups as well as for individuals. Unfortunately, until recently, our historians have largely been Euro-Canadians; as a result, they have largely based their inferences on the same primary assumptions and therefore have presented similar views of social reality.

Throughout recorded time, empowered groups have been able to define history and provide an explanation of the present. A good example is the portrayal of wars between Indians and Whites by Canadian historians. White historians have concentrated on these wars partly because of the "enemy concept": as Pelletier (1970) has pointed out, White endeavours are continually described in terms of fighting an enemy, whether the war is waged against crime, inflation or cancer.

In the history books, when Indians attacked a White village or fort and won, the result was called a massacre. If Whites attacked an Indian village and won, it was

Power of History

described as a victory. Because the dominant group was able to make these interpretations and definitions, it was also able to keep others from initiating alternative explanations or definitions. History gives credence and legitimacy to a society's normative structure; to legitimize its power, the dominant groups must reconstruct social history whenever necessary. The early reconstructions of Canadian history were effective: today, most Canadians continue to associate "savage" and "heinous" behaviour with Canadian Natives.

An example of the reconstruction of history can be found in the comparison by Trudel and Jain (1970) of French-Canadian and English-Canadian history textbooks. Anyone who reads, for example, about the battle of the Plains of Abraham in both an English and a French text, comes away feeling that the two books are not discussing the same event. As Patterson (1972) points out, alien history is pulled down and discredited, and national history replaces it. Continuity of tradition for any group is truncated when the communication channels are taken over by others who wish to transmit different information (Lindesmith and Strauss, 1968). How often have we known something to be true only to find out many years later that the government, or some other group, distorted information that might had led us to believe something quite different? Brown (1971) and Andrist (1964) have vividly portrayed American-Indian history from an alternative point of view. Their information concerning Indian-White relations is quite dissimilar to that provided by "established" historians.

Readers have reacted quite differently to books by Cardinal (1969), Pelletier (1970) and Waubageshig (1970) than they have to books by Morton (1963), McInnes (1959) and Lower (1957). The layperson typically rejects the conclusion of the first three authors as the products of bias. But the same layperson tends to accept the explanations provided by the second group of "established academic" authors. I am not suggesting that the first are right or the second wrong. But both groups deserve to be read and judged fairly.

It is essential to realize that the history of Canada that is taught from Grade Five through university has been written mainly by English-speaking Euro-Canadians, specifically of British ethnicity. The Ontario Education Commission, in a study of elementary Canadian history books, has discovered that many historical events involving Native people have not even been recorded. In fact, the commission found that many history books did not discuss the role of Indians in Canadian history at all. In a preliminary study, I have found the same omission from university history texts.

Walter (1971) characterized Canadian historians in their analysis of Indians in Canada as ignorant, prejudiced and, in some cases, dishonest. But we do not have to attribute deliberate falsification to historians. In any reconstruction of the past, the author shapes an interpretation of events according to individual perceptions, memories, analytical preferences and social background. Whether deliberately or unconsciously, a reshaping of the past occurs. No historian is free of bias, no history is capable of presenting only the facts.

History of Relations between Euro-Canadians and Native Peoples

The balance of this chapter will provide an overview of the history of the relations between the two dominant Canadian groups and Native peoples. First the French policy will be considered, then the British. Conclusions have been based on documents and histories written during the time of contact; this gathering of information through historical documents is known as a content analysis. Analysis has been limited to formal and informal documents relevant to the times, including personal correspondence between government officials.

Before discussing Native-White relations, we should point out that Native-Native relations are also an important component in the way Canada has developed. For those concerned with this issue, we suggest reading the work of Trigger (1985), who points out that Europeans were able to establish themselves in Canada partially due to the fact that a large number of Natives wished them to do so. He makes it very clear that since Natives in the beginning controlled the fur trade and were militarily superior to the newcomers, European entry into the land could not have been accomplished without the cooperation of the Native groups.

In the study of Native-White relations, there have been many critical historical periods which have shaped the structural linkages between them. These links determined the distribution of power, the opportunities to participate in the dominant structure and the eventual position of subordination for the Natives. In short, the actions of the government influenced the political development and incorporation of Native people. The most recent critical period was the 1960s, when the community development ideology began to emerge. At the turn of the century, the political links between Natives and Whites were extremely limited. Non-Indians had taken over Native communities and were accountable to other non-Indians. Power was unilateral in this relationship which excluded Natives from participating in the larger socio-political structure. However, in the 1960s the federal government and other dominant agencies began to promote individualization as an antidote to what they saw as the problem of tribalism. This action would forever change the structure of the relationship between Natives and the government.

A movement for reform in Indian policy had been gaining momentum since after World War II. The new "human rights" awareness, the belief in social justice and the interest in cultural diversity began to influence government policy. In the mid-1960s, the federal government commissioned a national study of the Indians' position in Canadian society—the *Hawthorn Report*. This document reported, in specific style, the appalling conditions under which Natives were forced to live. It suggested support for community development and promoted the implementation of major new initiatives in the area of health and education. Nevertheless, the central assumption of the *Hawthorn Report* was for Natives to assimilate.

FRENCH-NATIVE RELATIONS

Initially, the French were interested in the New World as a source of wealth capable of financing wartime activities. It was hoped that the land would hold precious metals that would rival in worth those found in Spanish America (Trigger, 1985). Throughout the sixteen century, fishing and whaling were the major economic activities that attracted more and more Europeans to North America. It was only at the end of the sixteenth century that the fur trade began to grow into an important economic activity.

French-Native relations must first be considered in the context of North America as a whole before we can turn specifically to Canada. A thorough review of the documents available on the attitudes of French settlers to the Indians reveals that no well-defined policy was established to govern French-Native relations. Generally, the French were attempting to exploit the land and to continue "pseudo-colonization" of North America. However, initially, they did not intend to settle New France with any large stable population. Moreover, only a small number of French people wished to emigrate to New France; this fact, combined with France's mercantilistic philosophy[2] and the strong influence of Roman Catholicism, meant that no policy of cultural or physical genocide was invoked.

Initially the French were totally dependent on the Indians, but the relationship between the two soon changed to a symbiotic one. Intermarriage, or "wintering in," between French trappers and Indian women soon became common practice and was encouraged by French authorities who wanted to strengthen Indian relations so that the fur trade would continue. These marriages between French men and Indian women were not meant to be exploitive; the relationships were stable, and the father was considered legally responsible for his wife and offspring.

In general, the French tried to expand their territories in North America by peaceful means. Usually they succeeded, because their agricultural style of life only minimally disrupted Native life.[3] After they had settled a territory, the French then asked the Indians to join in a treaty to acknowledge submission to the King of France. In this way, the French usually won territory without actually expropriating it. However, the process was not always so peaceful, and the French were certainly prepared to use force when they found it expedient to do so. When the Marquis de Tracy was placed in charge of Canada in 1663, his commissions included a provision for the use of arms to subjugate the Natives if necessary.[4]

The two strongest ideological influences in seventeenth-century New France were Roman Catholicism and mercantilism, which was popular as an economic theory. French policy, rather than treating Indians as distinct and inferior, tried to make them over into French citizens, at least in Canada.[5] This ideology of "Frenchification" is illustrated in various exchanges of letters between religious and state leaders of the day. For example, on April 6, 1666, Colbert wrote to Talon that:

> In order to strengthen the Colony in the manner you propose, by bringing the isolated settlements into parishes, it appears to me, without waiting to depend on the new colonists who may be sent from France, nothing would contribute more to it than to endeavour to civilize the Algonkians, the Hurons, and other Indians who have embraced Christianity, and to induce them to come and settle in common with the French, to live with them and raise their children according to our manners and customs (O'Callaghan, 1856-1857:184).

Talon replied, some seven months later, that he had tried to put Colbert's suggestions into practical operation under police regulations. Colbert then wrote, on April 9, 1667, as follows.

> Recommendation to mould the Indians, settled near us, after our manners and language.
>   I confess that I agreed with you that very little regard had been paid, up to the present time, in New France, to the police and civilization of the Algonkians and Hurons (who were a long time ago subjected to the King's domination) through our neglect to detach them from their savage customs and to obligate them to adopt ours, especially to become acquainted with our language. On the contrary, to carry on some traffic with them, our French have been necessitated to attract those people, especially such as have embraced Christianity, to the vicinity of our settlements, if possible to mingle there with them, in order that through course of time, having only but one law and one master, they might likewise constitute only one people and one race.

Another exchange of letters from the period demonstrates that this policy of assimilation was expressly favoured by the king. Duchesneau, in his letter to de Signelay, November, 10, 1679, writes:

> I communicated to the Religious communities, both male and female, and even to private persons, the King's and your intentions regarding the Frenchification of the Indians. They all promised me to use their best efforts to execute them, and I hope to let you have some news thereof next year. I shall begin by setting the example and will take some young Indians to have them instructed (Cole, 1939:864).

In another letter to de Signelay, dated November 13, 1681, Duchesneau states:

> Amidst all the plans presented to me to attract the Indians among us and to accustom them to our manners, that from which most success may be anticipated,

without fearing the inconveniences common to all the others, is to establish villages of those people in our midst.

Thomas, commenting on this letter, says:

That the same policy was in vogue as late as 1704 is shown by the fact that at this time the Abnaki was taken under French protection and placed, as the records say, "in the centre of the colony" (1896:544).

Through a policy, then, of assimilation, rather than genocide, the French were able to maintain relatively amiable relations with the Native population for quite some time.

When war broke out with England in the eighteenth century, the demand for fur decreased, and the French mercantilistic philosophy came to an end. War also brought a change in the French policy toward the Indians. Native land rights began to be systematically ignored (Harper, 1947:131). Letters signed by Louis XV at this time gave companies headed for New France full ownership of the land, coasts, ports and havens of New France, and full right to dispose of these properties in any way they desired (French, 1851). Similar provisions can be found in the privileges, power and requirements given to the Company of One Hundred Associates by Cardinal Richelieu nearly a century earlier.[6]

BRITISH-NATIVE RELATIONS

The Natives' experience with the English was considerably more negative than that with the French. This was partly due to the operation of different structural variables when the English made a serious bid to control New France. Mercantilism as an economic theory had been discarded, and the importance of the fur trade was dwindling; colonization in the true sense was now important. In addition, the religious ideology of the British had a very different basis than that of the French. Manifest destiny and the Hamlite rationalization[7] pervaded the British secular way of life, exemplified in the Protestant ethic that hard work and no play would bring salvation.

A review of the documents relevant to the initial contact period between the English and the Indians in Canada reveals that Native concerns were completely ignored. Little control was exerted over the British settlers as they expanded westward. As Thomas points out, the Indians were not even mentioned in discussions when land was given to companies.

For example, the letters patent of James I to Sir Thomas Gage and others for "two several colonies," dated April 10, 1606, although granting away two vast areas of territory greater than England, inhabited by thousands of Indians, in fact of which the King had knowledge both officially and unofficially, do not contain therein the slightest allusion to them (1972:550).

Although later charters recognized the existence of Natives, they did so in extremely racist fashion. In the charters of Charles I, this statement, typical of several, authorizes the state to

> ... collect troops and wage wars on the barbarians, and to pursue them even beyond the limits of their province and if God shall grant it, to vanquish and captivate them; and the captive put to death....

Until 1755, the English followed a policy of expediency. At first they chose to ignore the Native population. When this was no longer feasible due to the need for westward expansion, the English chose to isolate Indians through the reserve system or to annihilate them, as they did the Beothuk Indians of Newfoundland. In 1755, Indian agents, today called superintendents, were appointed, formally establishing Canada's policy of treating Native people as wards of the state. Significantly, the Indian agents initially placed in control of the reserves were always military men.

By 1830, the federal government was questioning the value of the Indian for Canada's future. Although it remained a concern for some, invasion from the south by the United States was no longer an immediate and direct threat. Because there were no other potential attackers, Indians were not likely to be needed for support in battle. Without their status as military allies, the Indians had no value for White Canada. Thus, in 1830, Indian Affairs was removed from military control and became a branch of the public service (Surtees, 1969). This change of jurisdiction allowed the British to adopt a more humanitarian attitude towards Natives.

Native-White Relations since Confederation

The first *Indian Act* after Canadian Confederation, was passed in 1876. It was first revised in 1880, and received minor alterations in 1884 and 1885. For the next 65 years, the *Act* underwent annual minor changes. However, in 1951, the *Act* underwent a major revision which left it essentially in its present form. Interestingly enough, the 1880 version of the *Act* and the present one are remarkably similar, indicating that Indian Affairs has not yet undergone any major ideological shifts in the past hundred years of dealing with the Native population.

Our analysis of Native-White relations shows that explanations based on a "national character" are not only inadequate but highly suspect. As Trigger (1985) notes, one must go well beyond the old stereotypical trait analysis to explain why the French treated Natives differently than the English did. To adequately understand how Native-White relations unfolded over time, we must look at the activities and attitudes of different European social classes, the regions of Europe they represented and the political factions that emerged. It is only then that we will have an adequate understanding of how an initial symbiotic relationship turned into one of overt hostility leading to the genocidal policies that have been carried out against the Natives.

In addition, Native affairs have long been thought of in terms of domestic affairs of little import in the operation of most of our institutional spheres, e.g., education, economics, politics. Recently it has become clear that they have taken on greater domestic importance and, as well, have entered the international scene. Furthermore, the impact of Native issues on Canadians is no longer limited to local areas. For example, in 1984, the Lubicon Indians in Northern Alberta approached the United Nations, claiming they were being denied the right of self-determination. Six years later, the Human Rights Subcommittee of the United Nations concluded that the Canadian government had not respected the civil and political rights of the Lubicons. The committee noted that the historical inequities and more recent developments threaten the way of life and culture of the Lubicons and constitute a violation of Article 27 of the *International Covenant on Civil and Political Rights*. Canada first had tried to get the case dismissed but was not successful and now has found itself the centre of attention in the international arena. The U.N. committee's report, which is critical of a member country, is embarrassing to Canada. Furthermore, the government, arguing that its $45 million settlement is sufficient, sees the Lubicons' rejection of their offer as solely an issue of money.[8] Lubicons, on the other hand, argue that the federal government is haggling over a few dollars, while they are fighting over the matter of their own future for all time. From this example it is clear that as we move into the twenty-first century, Native issues can no longer be viewed as unique to one community or area of Canada. What happens in one part of this country has substantive impacts on Native affairs in other parts. It is also clear that Native issues are no longer the concern solely of Natives. All Canadians are affected by a variety of issues—both directly and indirectly. For example, the settlement of land claims bears directly upon non-Natives in the area where the claims are being dealt with. Indirectly, land claim decisions have an impact upon businesses and potential land users.

Native Identity

Along with the globalization of Native issues, there is a cohesiveness among Native people that is emerging. The strand that links Native people is the general sense of betrayal and injustice that they believe has been meted out over the past century. A sense of solidarity and identity is slowly bringing various factions together. The continued failure of the government to consult with Natives reinforces their sense of isolation within Canada. The inability of governments (federal or provincial) to act in a prudent manner to protect Native peoples continues to reinforce the belief that the achievement of any goals will have to come from within Native communities.

What do Native people want? What are they looking for? How do they plan to achieve their goals? Native people would like to see a power-sharing arrangement with the federal and provincial governments. Whether this sharing emerges out of the existing political structure or requires a new arrangement is irrelevant. They feel they must be able to participate in the power arrangements if they are to develop economically and become part of the larger economic system of Canada. They also feel that they must be in a position to protect what few rights they now have. There has been a continual erosion of Native rights and there is a sense that these rights will become nonexistent if Natives themselves are not vigilant in protecting them. Therefore, there is a feeling that power sharing is a minimal condition which will allow Native people to integrate without assimilating.

Before continuing, we need to address the question as to who is a Native? Who is an Indian? And what are the differences? In other words, we must begin by addressing the age old question of identity. There are two major ways of establishing identity—using objective or subjective criteria. In the objective approach, a number of attributes are established which identify the boundaries of identity. These attributes establish indicators which are "visible" to all observers. Then each individual under question is matched with these attributes. Thus, if skin pigmentation, hair texture, bone structure, language and eye colour are used, one would assess each individual in terms of these attributes to determine whether or not he or she would fall into the category of "Native" (or, similarly, "Indian," "Inuit," "Métis").

The second approach, the subjective, is a more fluid one that flows from intrinsic self-definition. There are no measurable, objective criteria which establish the boundaries of inclusion and/or exclusion. In short, if others define you as a Native and you agree (or in certain circumstances your agreement or disagreement is irrelevant), then you are Native. If you "feel" Native, then, under the subjective approach, you are Native. In other words, the identity of the individual lies in his/her conceptualization of self. We can attempt to measure this self-conceptualization in some form, but all it tells us is the degree to which an individual feels Native. It does not identify the defining attributes nor the relative importance of each of these attributes.

We will not solve this problem in this book because it is not solvable. It is a question which has two answers, depending upon the perspective used. Nor are the two perspectives independent of each other. How have these perspectives been used? The Department of Indian Affairs has chosen the former, while some Natives have chosen the latter. As a result, there has been considerable conflict over who is a Native. In addition, government has, on occasion, allowed for the subjective approach in determining who is a Native. Needless to say this has generated considerable confusion for all Canadians in terms of trying to define who is a Native, Indian, Métis or Inuit.

A second issue regarding definitions centres on whose definition is used. Again, this is not to say that one definition is correct. It simply refers to a power relation which enables one party or another to employ a certain definition. The use of any definition also implies certain consequences. In the present case, the federal government has used its power to create a definition of Natives which has been incorporated into the legal structure of our political, social and economic world. Thus, it should be clear that the dominant definition of Native (or any subgroup definition) has been created by the federal government. Over time, many Natives have come to accept this definition. This definition has come to be associated with certain rights and privileges. Hence it is important that we clarify the boundaries of the various terms and the social consequences that emanate from this definition.

CONCLUSION

The policy governing Native-White relations was administered differently throughout Canada. In Ontario and Québec, until 1860, the imperial government handled all the affairs and expenses of Native Canadians. At that time, a Crown Lands Department was established and a commissioner appointed to assume the role of chief superintendent of Indian Affairs. In other areas of Canada, the Indian Affairs office was administered directly by the various provincial or colonial governments.

Included in the *British North America Act* of 1867 was a special provision allowing for the administration of Indian Affairs to come under the control of the government of Canada. Initially, Indian Affairs was the responsibility of the Department of the Secretary of State, but, in 1873, it was transferred to the Department of the Interior. In 1880, a separate Department of Indian Affairs was formed. In 1936, it was shifted to the jurisdiction of the Department of Mines and Resources, and, in 1950, it was shifted again to the Department of Citizenship and Immigration. From 1953 to 1966, Indian Affairs was handled by the Northern Affairs and National Resources Department. Since 1966, this had been called the Department of Indian Affairs and Northern Development or Indian and Northern Affairs Canada. Hence, the administration of Indian Affairs had been shunted from one department to another and never been allowed to develop consistent, humane policies. Furthermore, the definition of who is a Native has changed considerably over the past two centuries. This issue will be discussed in more detail in the next chapter.

NOTES

1. The primary labour market includes all those jobs that require skilled workers. The secondary market involves all unskilled labour.

2. Mercantilism was the economic theory that prevailed in Europe during the eighteenth century. Mercantilism held two basic tenets: the mother country was entitled to accumulate wealth in any form, and the mother country was entitled to

exploit its colonies as a source for raw materials and a market for finished products, thereby maintaining a favourable balance of trade.

3. Because they used the seigneur system of agriculture, the French always remained near major waterways and did not intrude into the interior of New France.

4. For a more thorough discussion of this issue, see Cumming and Mickenberg, 1972.

5. Two additional factors contributed to the relatively peaceful relations between the French and the Indians: the military alliance of the Huron, the Algonkian and the French; and the fact that the French settled in an area occupied by the Algonkian Indians, who were migratory hunters (Jenness, 1967), who had no real tribal organization, and who were themselves recent arrivals in the area (Cumming, 1969).

6. See I.G. Shea, Charlevoix's *History of New France*, Vol. 2, 1879, p. 39.

7. Manifest destiny, though it varied considerably, was the belief that Whites should control the world, or at least large parts of its. The Hamlite rationalization was the belief, taken from the Bible, that Ham was cursed by God and turned into a non-White person so that "he and his descendants should remain cursed and be subservient to Whites from then on." To the British, the Indians were clearly descendants of Ham.

8. The two parties agreed in 1988 that a 246 square kilometre reserve with full mineral rights would be established.

CHAPTER 2

WHO IS A NATIVE?

INTRODUCTION

Before we can discuss Native issues or Native-White relations, we must first identify who is a Native. Before we continue, it is important that the reader appreciates the plethora of terms now used in identifying the original inhabitants of North America. The indigenous population has undergone name changes which are not universally accepted—either by the indigenous population or the nonindigenous peoples. For example, Eskimos are now referred to as Inuit in Canada, while in the U.S.A. they are still referred to as Eskimo. Indian people have been referred to as Aboriginal or, in a more generic sense, Natives. Today, the term "First Nations" has been used by a segment of the indigenous population, and generally by treaty Indians. This chapter will define the various terms used to identify the growing number of indigenous sub-groups in our society.

The importance of the terms used to identify various indigenous groups goes unnoticed by the general public. Newspapers talk about Indians or Natives, terms that conjure up a stereotypical image that is useful to convey a message to the reading audience. However, we shall see that as the labels take on legal significance, their importance and implications grow. Thus it is essential for the reader to have a clear understanding of the terms used to identify indigenous groups. To achieve this, we must begin with a brief historical overview of how the concept of the "Native" came into existence. This will also provide a clue as to how the concept has changed over time and to the meaning it now has for Canadians.

At the time when Europeans made first contact with the peoples of what is now Canada, they met Aboriginals from a variety of cultural backgrounds; e.g., Beothuk of Newfoundland, Micmac of Nova Scotia, as well as a large number of peoples from the eastern regions of Québec. There was a kaleidoscope of ethnic groups, each one was unique as a result of its economic organization as well as its language, religion and values. Incoming Europeans found this ethnic diversity hard to deal with, and they quickly found a way to resolve the dilemma. Because of ignorance and a tendency to put all Aboriginals into one category, Europeans quickly labelled all Aboriginals as Indians. There would be some recognition of the different tribes, usually because of linguistic difference, but there was no real attempt to view Aboriginals as distinct from each other, except for minor cultural differences. These differences were considered minor attributes and were subsumed under the master trait of Indian, which was a more meaningful and universal term from the Europeans' point of view.

Having noted the extreme diversity among Native people, it must be pointed out that in a number of other ways there was some commonality. Native people interpreted life from a certain common perspective which was at variance from that of Europeans. For example, Europeans in the sixteenth and seventeenth century viewed science and religion as closely linked. They envisioned a rigid vertical hierarchal order of life with God on top; below God was a complex order of angels; below the angels, all other forms of life were ordered according to their descending levels of importance. These "natural" inequalities were fixed and ordained by God. Thus, poor people were not equal to rich people, and, it followed, ethical considerations appropriate for rich people did not need to be applied to the poor. Native people's view of their reality was quite different. They viewed all things (living and non-living) as having souls with a spiritual essence. Humans were no different than the trees, the lakes or the bears. Humans did not have any predestined significance in the world; and while humans were different from other elements on earth, they were basically the same—having a spirit that gave them life. There were many other differences between Natives and Europeans, such as attitudes towards animals, views of their environment and approaches to time.

DEFINING A NATIVE

For the first three hundred years after sustained contact was made with Canadian Aboriginals, there was no difficulty in determining who was or was not an Aboriginal. Nor was there any real need to achieve a legal definition. Residents living in a small community were aware of who was Aboriginal or not. Ancestry and way of life became the determining factors. This is not to say that the question never arose, but rather, when it did arise, the answer was clear from the local residents' perspective. It would not be until 1850 that the first statutory definition of who was an Indian was enacted. This definition stated that an Indian was:

- First—All persons of Indian blood, reputed to belong to the particular Body or Tribe of Indians interested in such lands, and their descendants;

- Secondly—All persons intermarried with any such Indians and residing amongst them, and the descendants of all such persons;

- Thirdly—All persons residing among such Indians, whose parents on either side were or are Indians of such Body or Tribe, or entitled to be considered as such; and

- Fourthly—All persons adopted in infancy by any such Indian, and residing in the Village or upon the lands of such Tribe or Body of Indians, and their descendants.

It is clear that at this time the concept of Indian was a mixture of biology and culture. At this time, and for some years to come, people of mixed ancestry were assigned either to Indian or White society and did not constitute a separate category: only Indians and non-Indians existed.

Changes to the definition of who is an Indian have been made over time, and one of the first changes was to drop the blood quantum factor; that is, having a certain proportion of Indian blood. While this is not part of a Canadian definition of who is an Indian, this has been one of the major attributes used in the United States to distinguish Indians from non-Indians. The blood quantum theory also has been and continues to be used in defining who is or is not Black in many of the American states.

After contact was sustained for some time, cultural and linguistic attributes became the master traits associated with "Indianness" and "Whiteness." Thus, if a person evidenced a certain way of life, he/she was designated Indian or White, although in everyday life having evidence of visible phenotypical traits of an Indian made it difficult to pass oneself off as a non-Indian. Nevertheless, if the individual gave evidence of being "White," he/she would normally have been treated as one. For example, if the individual lived in a house rather than a tipi, wore cotton or wool clothes rather than clothes made out of animal hides, and cut their hair, they were likely to be treated as non-Native, i.e., because they followed a White lifestyle. The result was that our ethnic system was divided into two categories—Indians and non-Indians.

As the treaties were being established in the late 1800s, mixed ancestry people often took treaty and became Indians under the *Indian Act*. However, they could have declared themselves as non-Indian and been treated accordingly. Both before and after Confederation, it was possible to treat people of mixed ancestry, either individually or in groups, as Indians.

British and Canadian law did not distinguish Métis from Indians as representing two different people; as we have seen, mixed races were forced to assimilate into White society or become Indian. At the time of treaty signing, negotiators made it clear that Métis could become Indians, and thus participate in the benefits granted status Indians under the treaty, or live as non-Indians on the reserve—if the Indians agreed. However, they would not be acknowledged as a separate legal entity.

With the establishment of the *Indian Act (1876)* and the subsequent establishment of a roll, i.e., a list of all status (legal) Indians, it became possible to track and identify who was or was not Indian. And, as new legislation was passed, one could evaluate each person listed on the roll according to any new criteria that were enacted. Those who met the criteria remained on the roll, and they retained their Indian status. However, those who did not measure up to the new criteria were then dropped from the roll and by definition were no longer Indian. Whether their offspring retained their listing on the roll also varied according to the existing legislation. Nevertheless, it is important to remember that those struck from the roll were not necessarily considered Métis, although a large number began to define themselves by that term. If people struck from the roll were not Métis, how did they see themselves and how did others relate to them? Formally, they were classified as non-status Indians, which meant they were neither Indian nor Métis. On the other hand, they were not White.

It would not be until the *Manitoba Act*, 1870, that Métis were first given statutory recognition. One motive behind this recognition was the search for peace—and the establishment of government control—in the Red River area.

> And whereas, it is expedient, towards the extinguishment of the Indian Title to the lands in the Province, to appropriate a portion of such ungranted lands, to the extent of one million four hundred thousand acres thereof, for the benefit of the families of the half-breed residents, it is hereby enacted, that, under regulations to be from time to time made by the Governor General in council, the Lieutenant-Governor shall select such lots or tracts in such parts of the Province as he may deem expedient, to the extent aforesaid, and divide the same among the children of the half-breed heads of families residing in the Province at the time of the said transfer to Canada, and the same shall be granted to the said children respectively, in such mode and on such conditions as to settlement and otherwise, as the Governor General in Council may from time to time determine.

Thus, since the late nineteenth century, there have been three major Native subgroups—legal or status Indians, non-status Indians and Métis. However, these three groups are not recognized in all parts of Canada. The legal status of each of these categories also varies as one goes across the country; e.g., in Québec, Métis are not recognized, while in Alberta, there are formal Métis colonies with official rolls denoting the membership. Nevertheless, there has been a social, if not legal, recognition of the three groups since the late nineteenth century. The category of non-status Indians became diffuse as we moved into the twentieth century, although these people have long lobbied for some official recognition and legal rights. As the twentieth century unfolded, more and more attention was given to the legal category of Indian. The label Métis also began to recede in importance with regard to the federal and provincial governments.

In the census before 1941, ethnic origin was traced through the mother. Since eastern Indian tribes were matrilineal and matrilocal, this seemed a satisfactory means of distinguishing Indians from other ethnic groups. Before 1941, children whose mother was Indian were also defined as Indian. However, this was only true for those people who had been previously defined as Indian under the *British North America Act*.[1] Before 1941, Statistics Canada still made a distinction between Indian and "mixed origin."

In 1941, the definition was changed so that, for off-reserve Indians, the father's ethnic status determined that of his children. For those who lived on the reserve, both the mother's and father's lineages were used to classify a person as Indian (Romaniuk and Piche, 1972).

In 1951 a more complex legal definition was introduced, stating that only those individuals who fell under the *Indian Act* would be classified as Indians. Today, while the federal government only recognizes any legal obligation to registered Indians, it nominally recognizes the ethnic group referred to as Métis. On the other hand, certain provinces such as Alberta and British Columbia, have formally recognized the Métis and have established Métis colonies.

Culture and race no longer affect the definition of an Indian: today's definition is a legal one. If someone who exhibits all the racial and cultural attributes traditionally associated with "Indianness" does not come under the terms of the *Indian Act*, that person is not an Indian in the eyes of the federal and provincial governments. The following sections explain the categories in the government typology.

REGISTERED INDIAN

The terms "legal," "registered," and "status" are generally used interchangeably to denote an Indian who is of federal concern. Registered Indians are defined in a legal manner, as opposed to other types of Indians who lack special legal status. Because the original *Indian Act (1876)* has continually been changed by the federal government since Confederation, the legal definition of an Indian has been continually revised. In short, "Indian" refers to a person who, pursuant to the *Indian Act*, is registered as an Indian or is entitled to be registered as an Indian. Because of the complexity of such a definition, we reproduce sections 11, 12 and 13 of the 1978 *Indian Act* in their entirety. We present this definition because it represents the federal government's thinking for nearly a century. It also allows us to make a comparison to the more recent changes which have been made to the *Indian Act*.

11. (1) Subject to Section 12, a person is entitled to be registered if that person

(a) on the 26th day of May 1874 was, for the purposes of *An Act providing for the organization of the Department of the Secretary of State of Canada, and for the management of Indian and Ordnance Lands*, being chapter 42 of the Statutes of Canada, 1868, as amended by section 6 of the Statutes of Canada, 1869, and section 8 of chapter 21 of the Statutes of Canada, 1874, considered to be entitled to hold, use or enjoy the lands and other immovable property belonging to or appropriated to the use of the various tribes, bands or bodies of Indians in Canada;

(b) is a member of a band

   (i) for whose use and benefit, in common, lands have been set apart or, since the 26th day of May 1874, have been agreed by treaty to be set apart, or

   (ii) that has been declared by the Governor in Council to be a band for the purpose of this Act.

(c) is a male person who is a direct descendant in the male line of a male person described in paragraph (a) or (b);

(d) is the legitimate child of

   (i) a male person described in paragraph (a) or (b), or

   (ii) a male person described in paragraph (c);

(e) is the illegitimate child of a female person described in paragraph (a), (b), or (d); or

(f) is the wife or widow of a person who is entitled to be registered by virtue of paragraph (a), (b), (c), (d), or (e).

(2) Paragraph (1)(c) applies only to persons born after the 13th day of August, 1956. R.S., c. 149, s. 11; 1956, c. 40, s. 3.

12. (1) The following persons are not entitled to be registered, namely,

   (a) a person who

      (i)   has received or has been allotted half-breed lands or money scrip,

      (ii) is a descendant of a person described in sub-paragraph (i)

      (iii) is enfranchised, or

      (iv) is a person born of a marriage entered into after the 4th day of September 1951 and has attained the age of twenty-one years, whose mother and whose father's mother are not persons described in paragraph 11(1)(a), (b), or (d) or entitled to be registered by virtue of paragraph 11(1)(e), unless, being a woman, that person is the wife or widow of a person described in Section 11, and

   (b) a woman who married a person who is not an Indian, unless that woman is subsequently the wife or widow of a person described in Section 11.

(2) The addition to the Band List of the name of an illegitimate child described in paragraph 11(1)(3) may be protested at any time within twelve months after the addition, and if upon the protest it is decided that the father of the child was not an Indian, the child is not entitled to be registered under that paragraph.

(3) The Minister may issue to any Indian to whom this Act ceases to apply, a certificate to that effect.

(4) Subparagraphs (1)(a)(i) and (ii) do not apply to a person who

(a) pursuant to this Act is registered as an Indian on the 13th day of August 1958, or

(b) is a descendant of a person described in paragraph (a) of this subsection.

(5) Subsection (2) applies only to persons born after the 13th day of August 1956, R.S., c, 149, s. 12; 1956, c, 40, ss, 3, 4; 1958, c, 19, s, 1.

13. Subject to the approval of the Minister and, if the Minister so directs, to the consent of the admitting band,

(a) a person whose name appears on a General List may be admitted into membership of a band with the consent of the council of the band, and,

(b) a member of a band may be admitted into membership of another band with the consent of the council of the latter band, (1956, c, 40, s, 5).[2]

Registered Indians are under the legislative and administrative competence of the federal government, as spelled out in the *British North America* (BNA) *Act*, and are regulated by the contents of the *Indian Act*. Slightly more than 450 000 Canadians are considered registered Indians. Being registered means that, with some exceptions, a Native is attached to a band and on the "roll" in Ottawa. Over the years, a number of different criteria have been used by the federal government to decide who is and who isn't an Indian. For example, at one time in history an Indian who achieved a certain educational attainment was automatically taken off the roll and was no longer a registered Indian. The descendants of this person usually lost their status also.

As identified in Figure 2.1, there are subtypes of legal Indians. First of all, legal Indians can be categorized according to whether or not they have "taken treaty"; that is, whether or not their ancestors signed a treaty with the federal government. As Figure 2.2 shows, Indians in British Columbia (with the exception of Vancouver Island), the Yukon, Québec, and the Atlantic provinces did not sign any treaties. Other groups, like the Iroquois of Brantford and Tyendingaga, who emigrated from the United States, are also considered non-treaty registered Indians.

Regardless of whether or not their ancestors signed a treaty, Indians are further subdivided into reserve and non-reserve, according to whether or not their ancestors were provided with reserve lands. For example, although a treaty (No. 11) was signed by Indians in the Northwest Territories, virtually no reserves exist. On the other hand, although British Columbian Indians have not taken treaty, most of them live on reserves.

In summary, the classification of a group of people as Indian arises from a legal definition. The concept "Indian" today does not solely reflect social, culture or racial attributes. The distinction between an Indian and a non-Indian is strictly a legal one.

FIGURE 2.1   Social-Legal Categories of Natives Residing in Canada

Indians					
Registered					Non-Registered[a]
Band Membership				No Band Membership	Band Membership
Treaty		Non-Treaty			
Reserve	Non-Reserve	Reserve	Non-Reserve		
250 000	100 000	75 000	10 000	20 000	10 000

a. Estimated number through *Bill C-31* reinstatements.

Inuit		Métis		Indian ancestry
With disc number	Without disc number	Off-colony	On-colony	over 1 000 000
20 000	15 000	over 100 000	4000	

FIGURE 2.2   INDIAN LAND SURRENDERED FOR TREATIES

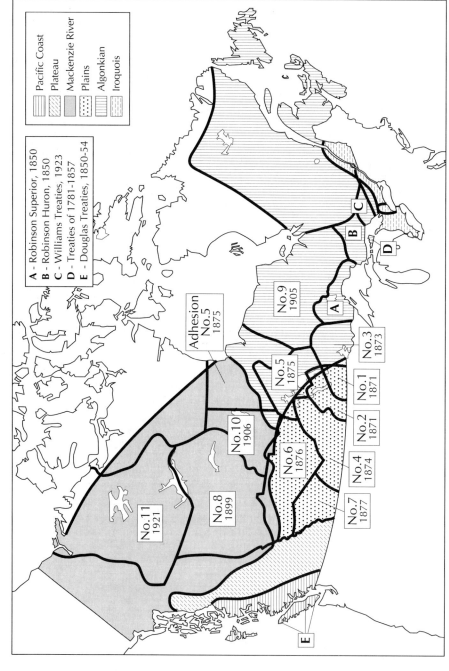

Legend:
- Pacific Coast
- Plateau
- Mackenzie River
- Plains
- Algonkian
- Iroquois

A - Robinson Superior, 1850
B - Robinson Huron, 1850
C - Williams Treaties, 1923
D - Treaties of 1781–1857
E - Douglas Treaties, 1850-54

No.9 1905
No.3 1873
Adhesion No.5 1875
No.5 1875
No.1 1871
No.2 1871
No.10 1906
No.6 1876
No.4 1874
No.11 1921
No.8 1899
No.7 1877

INDIAN ANCESTRY

Although people in this group—i.e., people described as having Indian ancestry—may exhibit all the social, cultural and racial attributes of "Indianness," they are not defined as Indians in the legal sense. Members of this group are not considered registered Indians because their ancestors refused—or were not allowed—to make agreements with the Crown. Included in this category are those Indians who have undergone "enfranchisement"; that is, who have lost their Indian status.

Enfranchisement can occur in several ways. For example, until 1960 an Indian had to give up legal status in order to vote in a federal election. An Indian may choose to give up Indian status by applying formally to Ottawa. In so doing, that person also surrenders status for all heirs (see Table 2.1).

One of the most common ways of losing Indian status was through intermarriage. Under section 12.(1)(b) of the *Indian Act*, any legally Indian female who married a non-Indian male lost Indian status for herself and for her children. On the other hand, if an Indian male married a non-Indian female, the female became legally Indian as did any offspring that may have resulted.[3]

In general, a move from Indian to non-Indian status is made on the basis of legal criteria that are set forth by the *Indian Act*. However, informal changes to the *Act* also affect movement between categories; e.g., the Minister of Indian Affairs announced that, at the request of band councils, the government would suspend certain sections of the *Indian Act* that discriminated against Indian women who married non-Indians, as well as against their children. The Department of Indian Affairs has also empowered the government to declare that any portion of the *Act* does not apply to any Indian individuals, groups or bands. These powers under section 4.(2) were recently invoked for members of certain bands in Québec.

TABLE 2.1 ACCUMULATED ENFRANCHISEMENTS (1876-1985)*

1876-1918	102
1918-1948	4000
1948-1968	13 670
1968-1969	785
1969-1970	714
1970-1971	652
1971-1972	304
1972-1975	467
1976-1985	94

* These figures include adult Indians enfranchised upon application together with their minor unmarried children as well as Indian women enfranchised following marriage to a non-Indian. Approximately 30 percent of the cases fall into the first category. The concept of enfranchisement is no longer considered operative since 1986, when further changes were made to the *Indian Act*.

SOURCE: Department of Indian Affairs, 1980, 1987.

INDIAN STATUS TODAY

In 1985, *Bill C-31 (An Act to Amend the Indian Act)* created new legislation which redefined who is and is not Indian. The bill was passed so that sexual discrimination would be eliminated, bringing the *Indian Act* into line with the *Canadian Charter of Rights and Freedoms* (sections 15 and 28). It also abolished the concept of enfranchisement and provided for the partial reinstatement of those people who had lost their Indian status. Moreover the bill defined eligibility for various benefits that the federal government has provided for registered Indians.

The new *Act* has introduced four types of Indian: 1) status with band membership; 2) status with no band membership; 3) non-status, but with band membership; and 4) non-status, non-band. As a result, one may hold legal status but not be a member of a band. Previously no such distinction was made. In addition, those people who had lost their Indian status through marriage or enfranchisement may now reapply for status as a legal Indian, and some may also apply for band membership. Those individuals whose ancestors (more than one generation removed) lost their status are not eligible. Indian status is reviewed by the Department of Indian and Northern Affairs, and a decision is made as to whether or not the individual has a legal right to claim Indian status. On the other hand, band membership is determined by the band council. There is one exception to this rule. The approximately 20 000 women who lost their status through intermarriage automatically become band members if they are reinstated by the federal government through DIAND.

Others who are reinstated must wait for two years to come under section 6(1) and 6(2) of the new *Indian Act*. Because acceptance into a band means that resources such as housing will have to be shared, many band councils are refusing to accept reinstated Indians into their band membership lists. Bands were given until the middle of 1987 to enact a membership code. If they failed to do so, then all individuals who had been reinstated as Indians and had some historical basis for claiming membership to a particular band were automatically given band status. As a result, a new group of Indians (legal Indians with no band status) has been created.

At the time the *Bill* was passed, it was estimated that about 20 000 women would be eligible for reinstatement. In addition, somewhere between 60 000 and 100 000 children and enfranchised individuals would be eligible for reinstatement. Most of those who applied early have been reinstated. However, these were the easiest cases to document, and preliminary results suggest that later applicants will have much greater difficulty in "proving" their case. The *Bill* also addresses the issue of transmitting one's status (section 6).

> 6. (1) Subject to Section 7, a person is entitled to be registered if
>
> > (a) that person was registered or entitled to be registered immediately prior to April 17, 1985.

(b) that person is a member of a body of persons that has been declared by the Governor in Council on or after April 17, 1985 to be a band for the purposes of this Act.

(c) the name of that person was omitted or deleted from the Indian Register, or from a band list prior to September 4, 1951, under subparagraph 12(2)(a)(iv), paragraph 12(2)(b) or subsections 22(2) or under subparagraph 22(2)(a)(iii) pursuant to an order made under subsection 109(2), as each provision read immediately prior to April 17, 1985, or under any former provision of this Act relating to the same subject-matter as any of those provisions.

(d) the name of that person was omitted or deleted from the Indian Register, or from a band list prior to September 4, 1951, under subparagraph 12(1)(a)(888) pursuant to an order made under subsection 109(1), as each provision read immediately prior to April 17, 1985, or under any former provision of this Act relating to the same subject-matter as any of those provisions.

(e) the name of that person was omitted or deleted from the Indian Register, or from a band list prior to September 4, 1951.

   (i) under section 13, as it read immediately prior to September 4, 1951, or under any former provision of this Act relating to the same subject-matter as that section or

   (ii) under section 111, as it read immediately prior to July 1, 1920 or under any former provision of this Act relating to the same subject matter as that section: or

(f) that person is a person both of whose parents are or, if no longer living, were at the time of death entitled to be registered under this section.

(2) Subject to Section 7, a person is entitled to be registered if that person is a person one of whose parents is or, if no longer living, was at the time of death entitled to be registered under subsection (1).

(3) For the purposes of paragraph (1)(f) and subsection (2).

(a) a person who was no longer living immediately prior to April 17, 1985 but who was at the time of death entitled to be registered shall be deemed to be entitled to be registered under paragraph (1)(a); and

(b) a person described in paragraph (1)(c), (d) or (e) who was no longer living on April 17, 1985 shall be deemed to be entitled to be registered under that paragraph.

7. (1) The following persons are entitled to be registered:

(a) a person who was registered under paragraph 11(1)(f), as it read immediately prior to April 17, 1985, or under any former provision of this Act relating to the same subject-matter as that paragraph, and whose name was subsequently omitted or deleted from the Indian Register under this Act; or

(b) a person who is the child of a person who was registered or entitled to be registered under paragraph 11(1)(f), as it read immediately prior to April 17, 1985, or under any former provision of this Act relating to the same subject-matter as that paragraph, and is also the child of a person who is not entitled to be registered.

(2) Paragraph (1)(a) does not apply in respect of a female person who was, at any time prior to being registered under paragraph 11(1)(f) entitled to be registered under any other provision of this Act.

(3) Paragraph (1)(b) does not apply in respect of a child of a female person who was, at any time prior to being registered under paragraph 11(1)(f), entitled to be registered under any other provision of this Act.

Individuals who have obtained status through section 6(2) and then marry a non-Indian will then have children who are non-Indians. However, if they marry an Indian, then the children will be Indian. If those individuals who are registered under the conditions of section 6(1) marry Indians, their children will be Indian. However, if they marry a non-Indian, the children will become Indians under section 6(2) but will be unable to pass Indian status to their children. One final possibility would be to have two Indians under section 6(2) marry. In this case, the children would be Indian under the provisions of section 6(1). All children born "out of wedlock" will automatically be registered as Indians under section 6(2) unless the mother can prove that the father was a status Indian, in which case they would be registered under section 6.1.

Finally, the *Indian Act* also forces any enfranchised Indian who received more than $1000 of band funds (at the time of enfranchisement) to repay this money with interest before he or she can receive any band-fund disbursement or other band benefits.

By 1985, 42 000 people had applied for reinstatement of their Indian status. By the first year, fewer than 2000 had been accepted. By 1989, nearly 67 000 had been reinstated. Between 1985 and 1990, the Indian Registration Unit received over 75 000 applications representing about 135 000 people, of whom over 60 percent are female. Estimates are that by 1992, most of the nearly 200 000 applications will have been processed and about 92 000 registrants and their offspring will have been added to the Indian Register, representing nearly one-fifth of the total registered Indian population (see Table 2.2). Of these registrants, it is estimated that nearly 40 percent will have their band membership restored under section 11(1) of the *Indian Act* (Joseph, 1991; Paul, 1990).

The addition of *Bill C-31* people to the Indian roll has created substantial social and political problems for reserve Indians as well as financial problems for the federal government. A serious rift now exists between Indians who have their roots on the reserve versus those who were enfranchised and forced to live in urban areas.

The return of urban Indians to the reserves has brought about bitterness, jealousy and factions within the reserve community. In many areas, such as in educational institutions, a great deal of animosity exists between "traditional" Indians and "*Bill C-31*" Indians.

Because enfranchisement meant that Indians had to leave the reserve, most migrated to urban areas. Thus, most *Bill C-31* Indians have lived and raised their children in urban areas, and, over a generation of absence from the reserve, have been somewhat assimilated, taking on the attributes of non-Native culture. Under the new legislation, these Natives are allowed to be reinstated, to claim their Indian identity (or, what they had retained of it), and to benefit from the social and economic programs that are available to Indians. In some cases, this means access to a reserve and possible resettlement. Land allocation can be applied for and a share of the band profits will have to be allocated to these new Indians. In other cases, it means access to financial support to go to school. In still other cases, it provides an individual his/her birthright as an Indian. In these latter cases, the financial benefit is not at issue but rather the right to identify oneself with the group—Indians.

There are a number of complex problems involved in the implementation of *Bill C-31*. First of all, at a family level, it means that brothers and sisters may have dif-

TABLE 2.2   NON-NATIVE APPLICATION FOR BAND AND STATUS MEMBERSHIP UNDER *BILL C-31*, 1987.

	Band Membership Restored	Indian Status Restored	Applications for Indian Status
Ontario	1932	5520	27 600
Alberta	1012	2668	9200
Québec	942	3131	14 720
B.C.	928	1931	13 800
Saskatchewan	794	1753	7360
Manitoba	622	1506	8280
Maritimes	476	1521	4600
North	312	836	5520
Unknown	—	—	100
Canada	7018	18 866	91 180

Source: Department of Indian Affairs, 1989.

ferent legal status. A second problem concerns band membership. Although some children (dependent—6.2) have a right to reside on the reserve, it is not certain that independent 6.2 children and their non-Indian fathers are allowed to reside on the reserve. A further problem of *Bill C-31* centres on band membership for reinstated women and their children. Because bands have been given control over their membership, some of these bands have adopted the old *Indian Act* band membership system and thus are able to exclude reinstated Indians from their membership.

The impact of *Bill C-31* has been divisive and counter-productive for Natives on and off the reserve. The inability (or, at least, the perceived inability) of urban Indians to appreciate the traditional way of life has been one focal point of discontent. The sharing of meagre resources has also brought about considerable factionalization within the Native community. Thus far, there has not been a serious attempt by any of the Native groups to deal with this problem.

MÉTIS AND NON-STATUS INDIANS

On the plains of Western Canada in the late eighteenth century, the Métis emerged. They developed economic and social institutions and became a dominant economic force after 1750. By the 1820s, many Métis had taken up residence at Red River, and thus it became the economic and social centre of the Métis. It was at this time they began to develop their own form of self-government. As Charlebois (1975) points out, the Métis developed a separate culture and took on the characteristics of a separate nation. Living in distinct communities, they developed their own local laws and attempted to implement their own form of government.

The Métis' sense of cohesiveness and political solidarity was evident by the late 1800s when they objected to the Hudson's Bay Company's decision to sell Western Canada. Chartier (1988) notes that this same political consciousness was displayed in 1885 when the Métis fought the Canadian government. By the turn of the century, the Métis of Alberta began organizing, and two decades later they were recognized by the provincial government. They were provided with land settlements (colonies). In contrast to the situation in Alberta, Métis in Saskatchewan and Manitoba were not successful in negotiating their legal standing with their respective provincial governments. However, the federal government has dealt with the Métis as a specific and identifiable group.

The Métis are a unique people in Canadian society. Originally they grew out of the symbiotic relationship that existed between Natives and the European immigrants to the New World. Yet it was the later government implementation of a complex set of social and political acts that ultimately determined their status as a separate ethnic group. Figure 2.3 locates the major belts of Métis and non-status Indians in Canada.

FIGURE 2.3   MAJOR POPULATION BELTS OF MÉTIS AND NON-STATUS INDIANS

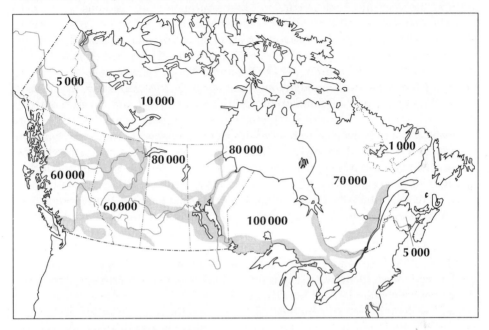

SOURCE: Indian Record Vol. 43 No. 1 (Winter), 7.

Estimates of the number of Métis range from less than 500 000 to more than 1 000 000, depending upon the source. The lack of accurate information resulted, in 1941, in the deletion of "Métis" from the census. By 1980 the *Report of the Native Citizen Directorate of the Secretary of State* showed the following figures:

- Métis and non-status Indian (core population)—300 000 to 435 000

- Métis and non-status Indian (self-identifying population)—400 000 to 600 000

- Métis and non-status Indian (noncore and nonself-identifying population)—1 to 2.5 million

However, the 1981 census, after a lapse of several decades, once again included Métis as a category of ethnic identification. The results were startling, since less than 100 000 people identified themselves as Métis. Only Alberta has kept official records and only for its Métis colonies. In 1980, approximately 4000 Métis resided on those colonies; estimates of Alberta's off-colony Métis population range from 8000 to 15 000. Within the last decade, a number of government agencies have tried to determine more accurately the number of Métis and non-status Indians.

The Métis have argued for many years that, as a special people, they are entitled to Aboriginal rights. The federal government has maintained that those Métis whose ancestors signed treaties or received scrip and land have had their Aboriginal rights extinguished (Cumming, 1973). Presumably, others have not.

Over the years, the federal government has often recognized the existence of Métis claims. Under the *Dominion Act* and the *Manitoba Act*, the government provided scrip and land to Métis to extinguish their Aboriginal rights. The 1889 Treaty Commission was instructed to treaty with the Indians and to investigate and extinguish any half-breed titles (Cumming, 1973). In the 1930s, the Ewing (Halfbreed) Commission asserted the existence of Métis claims. As late as 1969, the Indian Claims Commissioner also argued for the Aboriginal rights of Métis, stating that these were well established in Canadian law. According to the Commissioner, various actions of the federal government such as scrip allocation in Western Canada and the Adhesions to Treaty No. 3 have granted special status to the Métis, both morally and legally.

Even while recognizing Métis claims, the federal and provincial governments have tried to wish them away. The rights of the Métis in the Northwest Territories were ignored until rebellion was threatened in 1885. In the 1940s, as was mentioned, the federal government deleted Métis from the census as a separate ethnic category. In 1944, Indian Affairs removed the names of nearly 1000 Indians from the roll, arguing that they were really Métis. Although a subsequent judicial inquiry forced the department to replace most of the names, clearly, the government was hoping that the Métis would simply assimilate into White society and disappear, along with their claims.

In their attempts to retain their ethnic status and to receive compensation for Aboriginal rights, the Métis, like the Indians and Inuit, have created complex and highly political organizations. The Métis argue that those whose ancestors did not take treaty or receive scrip or land still have Aboriginal rights.

At present, the relationship between the Métis and the federal and provincial governments varies from province to province.[4] In the Yukon, Métis demands have gone relatively unnoticed, or at least are treated with less legitimacy than the Inuit or Dene demands (Coates and Morrison, 1986). On the other hand, in the Northwest Territories, the Métis are working alongside status Indians and Inuit to negotiate an agreement with the federal government. In British Columbia, the provincial government has consistently refused to recognize the special rights of any Aboriginal people in the province, including the Métis.

In Alberta, the provincial government's *Métis Betterment Act*, 1938, outlines its relationships with the Métis. The Alberta government does not acknowledge the legal existence of Métis off the colonies. Therefore, all Métis individuals who do not reside on the colony are considered regular Albertans with no Aboriginal or special rights. Like Alberta, Saskatchewan excludes Métis from any land claim registration now taking place with status Indians. In Saskatchewan, "farms" have been established for Métis, with land bases of less than four square kilometres each. Although Manitoba has historically recognized the Métis, it has recently refused to acknowledge their existence officially. The few monies that the Métis Association had been receiving from the provincial government for special education and cultural activities were cut off in 1982.

In Ontario, the Métis are recognized and are eligible to receive funds from a Native Community Branch. However, the Ontario government is reviewing this policy because of its high cost. Although Québec claims to define Métis and non-status Indians as Indians, it refuses to fund or implement programs for these special groups. In order to be officially recognized by the Québec government, the Métis would have to reject the *Indian Act* and accept new terms outlined by the provincial government.

In the Atlantic provinces, most governments simply refuse to acknowledge the existence of the Métis. Although Prince Edward Island recognizes them, it has no special policy because there are so few of them.

At the federal level, the Métis have only recently received formal, legal and constitutional recognition beyond that established in the *Manitoba Act* of 1870. The Métis argue that, under this act, they were recognized as a separate people with certain rights. Furthermore, because the act cannot be changed without Britain's consent, the Métis and non-status Indians continue to have separate legal status. The federal government has established a cabinet committee on Métis and non-status Indians to investigate more fully the claims and issues put forward by them.

In early 1981, the federal government recognized and affirmed the Aboriginal and treaty rights of Indians, Inuit and Métis. These rights have now been affirmed in the Constitution, with the proviso that only "existing rights" are to be recognized. The Métis argue that their rights are a special case of Aboriginal rights, that they stem from the self-perception of the Métis people as an indigenous national minority (Daniels, 1981) and are derived from their Aboriginal ancestry and title—both of which constitute the national identity of the Métis.

In 1983, members of the Métis Nation created the Métis National Council whose goal was to achieve a clear definition and defence of Métis rights. By the time the First Ministers Conference on Aboriginal Affairs convened that same year, a separate invitation had been issued to the Métis National Council, thereby severing the formal relationship with the Native Council of Canada which had previously represented the Métis.

The Métis National Council has published material which identifies their criteria for determining whether a person is Métis:

The Métis are:

• an Aboriginal people distinct from Indian and Inuit

• descendants of the historic Métis who evolved in what is now Western Canada as a people with a common political will

• descendants of those Aboriginal peoples who have been absorbed by the historic Métis.

They go on to point out that the Métis community comprises members of the above who share a common cultural identity and political will (Métis National Council, 1983). This is not to say that everyone accepts this definition. Gaffney *et al.* (1984) argue that there is no one exclusive Métis people in Canada. They claim that eastern Canadian Métis are different from Red River Métis. At a provincial level, the issue of who is or isn't Métis varies. In Alberta, recent changes to the *Métis Settlement Act* and the criteria set out by the Alberta Métis Nation Association have clarified the definition of Métis. Both government and the Association agree that a Métis is someone who declares him/herself as a Métis, has traditionally held her/himself as Métis and is accepted by the Métis community as Métis.

In Manitoba, the Federation definition of a Métis remains a racial one which enables non-status Indians to join. The Saskatchewan Association of Métis and non-status Indians split in 1987 so that the Métis Society of Saskatchewan defines a Métis in a manner similar to Alberta.

Today, the term Métis has widespread usage. However, two different meanings have been given to the term. As the Métis National Council (1984) pointed out, written with a small "m," "métis" is a racial term for anyone of mixed Indian and European ancestry. Nevertheless, the Métis National Council has objected to this distinction and argues that the acceptance of the latter definition (racial) undermines the rights of Métis people. In the end, there is no one single definition of the concept. There will always be some group who will object to the characterization, no matter what it is. However, for purposes of this book, we will use the more general definition, rather than the narrowly racial one. As Peters, *et al.* (1989) point out, the term is widespread in usage. It appears to have a well accepted general meaning, reflecting the social aspect of Métis identity, and it reflects a reality that cannot be denied.

Today there is a distinction between the historical Métis and the Pan-Métis. (See Figure 2.4). Pan-Métis is a more inclusive term which includes historic Métis, people of mixed Indian-European ancestry and non-status Indians. As Lussier (1979) points out, they gain their identity from a multitude of national roots.

The federal government has taken the position that Métis are a provincial responsibility even though there are federal departments which provide funding for them, e.g., the Secretary of State. Their position is based on the argument that Métis are not included in Section 91(24) of the *Constitution Act, 1867*. Provinces (except Alberta) argue that Métis are included under Section 91(24). The Métis National

FIGURE 2-4   EVOLUTION OF THE MÉTIS

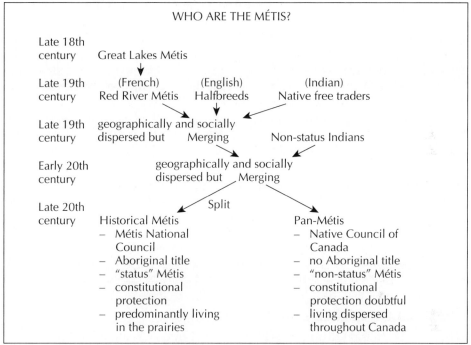

WHO ARE THE MÉTIS?

Late 18th century	Great Lakes Métis		
Late 19th century	(French) Red River Métis	(English) Halfbreeds	(Indian) Native free traders
Late 19th century	geographically and socially dispersed but	Merging	Non-status Indians
Early 20th century		geographically and socially dispersed but Merging	
Late 20th century	Split Historical Métis – Métis National Council – Aboriginal title – "status" Métis – constitutional protection – predominantly living in the prairies		Pan-Métis – Native Council of Canada – no Aboriginal title – "non-status" Métis – constitutional protection doubtful – living dispersed throughout Canada

SOURCE: L.E. Krosenbrink-Gelissen, "The Métis National Council," *Native American Studies,* 3:1 (1989), 39.

Council also argues with the provinces that Métis are a federal responsibility. Chartier (1988) claims that in 1984 the federal minister argued that even if the Supreme Court ruled that Métis were a federal responsibility, the government could refuse to exercise its responsibility. He also argues that Métis are also covered within the term "Indian" (as were the Inuit) in section 91(24). Others, such as Schwartz (1985), view Métis as a people distinct from Indians and thus side with the federal government. However, he does offer a compromise in suggesting that small-*m* Métis would be covered by section 91(24) while capital-*M* Métis would not. What is suggested is that Métis may be entitled to be governed by some federal laws; however, even if this were the case, there would need to be substantial coopera-tion among all the provinces so that a uniform regime of Métis control resulted.

While the federal government treats Métis as a provincial responsibility, certain interpretations of general programs provided to Canadians have allowed the Métis to benefit. In other areas of concern, e.g., constitutional negotiations, an informal agreement has been made whereby the Minister of Justice is to act in a way that en-sures that Métis interests are addressed and that the Métis have someone to listen to their concerns.

INUIT

The category of "Inuit" has also undergone a number of redefinitions. Until confederation, there was no legal definition of Inuit. At that time, there was no real need to make a distinction. And, since the issue was limited to local concerns, the government did not see fit to enter the debate. Immediately after Confederation, the Inuit were placed under the control of the *Indian Act*. However, after a short time they were, and continue to be, placed under the direct jurisdiction of the federal government under the BNA *Act*.[5]

When Canada began to think of developing the North in the early twentieth century, the government decided that a census was needed to establish the actual number of Inuit. As a result, a "disc" number was allotted to each Inuk; for a time, only those with numbers were officially defined as Inuit.[6] However, other definitions of Inuit have developed since and will continue to be used. For example, in the 1978 agreement between the Government of Canada and the Committee for Original Peoples Entitlement (COPE), an Inuk was defined as a member of those people known as Inuit, Eskimo, or Inuivialuit who claim traditional use and occupancy of the land. In the case of the 1975 James Bay Agreement, an Inuk was defined as any individual who possesses a disc number, or has one-quarter Inuit blood, or is considered an Inuk by the local community, and such other persons as may be agreed upon.

RESULTS OF LEGAL DISTINCTIONS

Why have these legal distinctions been inflicted upon Canadian Natives? Those in power have surely been aware that such nominal distinctions have a "divide and conquer" effect. Natives became easier to control as they began to fight among themselves. The distinctions between the non-treaty and the treaty Indians are particularly divisive; the two groups received different privileges, different amounts of money from different sources, and different rights.

Red Power advocates are now attempting to point out the divisive effects of legal distinctions and to suggest ways of counteracting their influence. According to these advocates, legal status is irrelevant in the face of discrimination. Because the distinction between registered and nonregistered Indians cannot be made visually, White Canadians cannot and do not distinguish between the two in daily interactions. All those who "look Indian" fall prey to the same stereotypes, and find themselves treated as though they were lazy, drunk or happy-go-lucky. Moreover, Natives who fall under separate legal categories often lead similar life-styles. Thus, the similarities among Natives frequently overshadow the legal differences.

Dyck (1980) has pointed out that the term "Native" is becoming increasingly popular with academics, laypersons and politicians. This terms, he argues, serves to cognitively combine peoples who, from a White Canadian perspective, are similar. Yet the various categories into which the Native population is divided are not irrelevant; indeed, under specific circumstances, these "internal" differences can be very important. As Dyck suggests, these differences can be exaggerated or they can be ignored by the dominant group at will to suit its purpose. Distinctions can be emphasized to divide the Native population, or they can be ignored through stereotypes and generalizations that avoid individual issues.

CONCLUSION

The organization of Indians into their present-day bands can be understood as a response to the Draconian steps taken against Natives by government. The government, in a sense, forced Natives to deal with them as a band, and, over time, this has become the basis upon which Natives and non-Natives operate. Over time, Natives have accepted the band as the focus of their identity and organization. The indigenous institutional basis of the band is no longer evident. In other words, traditional forms of organization that were an integral part of Native culture have been replaced by a type of administrative structure designed primarily to serve the convenience of the federal/provincial governments. As Cornell (1988) points out, "Structures of authority and decision making, once embedded in the fabric of aboriginal society, are now attacked from the outside, institutionally separate from the culture of Natives" (pp. 101-102). Today the band no longer exhibits a sense of peoplehood but rather is a political-legal construct which has some legal relationship with other structures in our society.

Native identity has become complex and fragmented. For example, many people identify themselves as Bloods or Ojibwa, but this masks a multitude of meanings. For some it may mean a connection with the tradition of Bloods or Ojibwa, and for these people, maintenance of culture is of paramount importance. Others will identify with the local group experiences. Finally, some view their identity in terms of the legal definition of band membership. As a result, we find today that a sense of peoplehood is diverse, yet Natives are forced to act as a single political unit.

Increasingly, for a large number of Aboriginals, Native identity is becoming an important basis for action and thought. The number of Native organizations reflect the importance of such an identity. This Native consciousness has allowed for pan-Indianism to emerge along with the social and political organizations. This pan-Indianism is a kind of cultural synthesis of a number of different but related cultures. The resultant new identity (Indian consciousness) has created a linkage among groups which previously were viewed by others (and themselves) as distinct. While Natives are beginning to develop a consciousness of band and group solidarity, the process of establishing themselves as an ethnic entity is not yet complete. There are still major divisions between the various groups (e.g., Indians, Métis, Inuit) but it is clear that the process of Native self-definition and identification has occurred.

From the turn of the century to World War II, a collective Native identity began to emerge. The development of this identity was gradual and intermittent, varying from region to region. At the same time, however, government actions reduced the amount of intertribal interaction as well as political action. As a result, networks (small at first) among various groups of Natives focused on social and cultural affairs. Nevertheless, these activities promoted a sense of shared Nativism. For example, pow wows began to become public and they drew Natives from other areas of the country for several days of socializing and learning cultural traditions.

NOTES

1. In 1982 the *British North America Act* was changed to the *Constitution Act, 1867*. An attempt is made in this book to distinguish between the two names by using the *British North America Act* when citing legislation passed under the act or references made to it before 1982, and by using the *Constitution Act, 1867* for any references thereafter.

2. Indian Act, R.A., c. 1-6, amended by c. 10(2nd Supp.) 1974-75-76, c.1/8. 1978 (Hull: Minister of Supply and Services Canada: 6-8).

3. One of the major concerns that DIAND had with regard to the changes in Section 12(1)(b) of the *Indian Act* was the financial cost. In a once-secret document of DIAND entitled "Amendments to remove discriminatory sections of the *Indian Act*," the estimates ran from $312 to $557 million. These figures were based on estimates of the number of women who would be reinstated as Indian and the percentage who would return to the reserves; the low estimate allowed for a 30 percent reinstatement and a 30 percent return while the high estimate predicted a 100 percent reinstatement and a 70 percent return rate. In addition, approximately 57 000 children would be eligible for reinstatement.

   A federal-Cabinet discussion paper released in 1982 showed that settling land claims in the next 15 years could cost the government as much as $4.1 billion. About $1.8 billion of these claims concern land in British Columbia, where the fewest treaties were signed; most of the rest would be divided between Natives in the two Territories. The $4.1 billion includes reparation for hunting and fishing rights, payment for land, and the implementation of various programs and other benefits. In addition, another $500 million could be spent by the government in the next 20 years to settle specific claims, (*Indian News*, Vol. 22, No. 7, October 1981:7).

4. For a more thorough statement regarding the status of the Métis in Canada, the reader should consult "Native Rights: Policy and Practices," *Perception*, Vol. 4, 2 (November/December 1981). Much of the present information comes from this source.

5. In 1939 Duplessis was able to get northern Québec Inuit redefined as Indians so that they came under federal, instead of provincial, control (Richardson, 1972).

6. Numbers were stamped on small metal discs which Inuit could carry with them for identification.

INDIAN TREATIES AND MÉTIS SCRIP

INTRODUCTION

The significance in government policy of the post-Confederation treaties has long been the subject of investigation. However, all agree they were intended to give recognition to Indian interests in the land, to provide compensation and to establish an orderly transition of land ownership from one group to another. The treaties also established the rules of relationship between the two parties (Indians and the federal government) after the transfer of land (Daniel, 1980).

While the land rights of Native peoples in Canada have by no means been treated uniformly, there did develop in British North America a consistent body of precedent and tradition which was utilized on new frontiers where fairly rapid settlement or resource exploitation was being promoted. This involved the making of treaties under which Native peoples surrendered most of their territorial rights and gained various forms of compensation. Although numerous land surrender treaties had already been made in the Thirteen Colonies, it was not until after the American Revolution that the system was first systematically used in Canada.

ORIGIN OF THE TREATIES[1]

The initial agreements between the Indians and government have been called "Friendship and Peace" treaties and were carried out in the Maritime area. These pre-Confederation treaties generally dealt with military and political relations and did not involve specific land transfers, annuities, or compensation for rights taken away (Sanders, 1983).

In 1713, by the *Treaty of Utrecht*, France ceded Acadia (excepting Cape Breton Island) to Great Britain, recognized the British sovereign's suzerainty over the Iroquois people, relinquished all claims to Newfoundland, and recognized British rights to Rupert's Land. When the charter for exploitation of Rupert's Land was granted by Charles II to the Hudson's Bay Company in 1670, it is doubtful that even the claimants were aware of the vast territory involved—all the land draining into Hudson Bay from Baffin Island on the northeast to the headwaters of the Saskatchewan in the southwest. For the next century and a quarter, the western boundaries of Rupert's Land were to remain the firmest delineation of British America's western extent.

By the Peace of Paris, 1763, France ceded all its North American possessions to Great Britain, with the exception of St. Pierre and Miquelon Islands (which it retained) and Louisiana (which it ceded to Spain). In the spring of that year the crystallization of Indian misgivings gained expression through the activities of Chief Pontiac, although particular provisions in the *Royal Proclamation* concerning the protection of Indian-occupied lands were designed to allay such fears. The *Royal Proclamation* of 1763 did indeed define lands which were to remain, at the sovereign's pleasure, with the Indians as their hunting grounds, but Rupert's Land and the old colony of Québec were specifically exempted. In what was to become Canada, the hunting grounds in the east comprised a relatively narrow strip between the northern bounds of Québec and Rupert's Land, along with all of what was to become Upper Canada; in the northwest, an amorphous area bounded by Rupert's Land, the Beaufort Sea, and the Russian and Spanish claims to the west and south.

In 1769, St. John's Island (renamed Prince Edward Island in 1798) became a separate government.

By the *Quebec Act*, 1774, in what has been described as a statutory repudiation of *Royal Proclamation* policy, Québec's boundaries were extended to encompass all the land described in the preceding paragraph as the eastern Indian hunting grounds.

With the Revolutionary War of 1775 to 1783, the emphasis in the colonies of Nova Scotia and Québec changed irrevocably to settlement, development, lumbering, fishing and trade; dissolution of the two hundred-year-old partnership between Indian and fur trader was well on the way. The most immediate effect was a 50 percent increase in population in the two colonies occasioned by the influx of United Empire Loyalists, who were, primarily, interested in farming, homesteading and business. These were followed, particularly in Upper Canada after 1791, by a steady stream of settlers with like interests from the south. They brought with them the desire for peace, law, good order and the other concomitants of settled living.

The Treaty of Paris, 1783, signed between Great Britain and the U.S.A., established the boundary from the Atlantic to the Lake of the Woods. At one stroke Canada lost the entire southwestern half of the vast inland domain which French and British adventurers had discovered, explored and exploited with the help of the Indian people. Along with it went that portion of the Indian hunting grounds, established in 1763, bounded by the Great Lakes and the Ohio and Mississippi Rivers. A natural point of departure for the future boundary at the 49th parallel of latitude was also ensured. The inevitable dissension with the Indian people which followed, however, was reaped by the United States rather than Great Britain.

In 1784, as a result of the large-scale influx of United Empire Loyalists into the St. John River area the year before, New Brunswick was separated from Nova Scotia. Cape Breton Island also became a separate entity.

By the *Constitutional* (or *Canada*) *Act* of 1791, the Imperial Parliament divided Québec into the provinces of Upper Canada and Lower Canada, abolished the conciliar form of government which had existed in Québec for two centuries, and established representative government in both provinces. Land was to be granted in freehold tenure in Upper Canada and could be so granted in Lower Canada, if desired.

In 1796, by the Jay Treaty, the fur-trading posts of Niagara, Detroit, Michilimackinac, and Grand Portage—which were still in British hands—were handed over to the United States in accordance with the boundary provisions agreed to in 1783. In order to facilitate what remained of the fur trade, an article in the Jay Treaty provided for the free passage of Indian trappers back and forth across the boundary with "their ordinary goods and peltries"; it is on the basis of this provision that the present Iroquois claim duty-free passage across the international boundary.

In 1803, by the Louisiana Purchase, the United States acquired that vast, vaguely-defined territory west of the Mississippi which had been ceded back to France by Spain in 1800. The consequent push westward, and the inevitable rivalries arising, would once again raise the contentious question of the boundary between British America and the United States.

On the Pacific coast, the leading protagonists changed over the course of time from Russia, Britain and Spain to Russia, Britain and the United States, but it was not from the sea that this contest was to be settled. Indeed, Captain Cook had made his landfall at Nootka Sound in 1778, but the traders who followed him lost their vessels and furs to the Spanish who were engaged in a last endeavour to enforce their claims to the northwest coast. In 1791, Captain George Vancouver arrived to acknowledge, officially, restoration of British rights after the Nootka Convention; concurrently, the Russians were pushing down from the north, following the seal and the sea otter.

The only firm and lasting links with the Pacific coast, however, would have to be established by land, and these were provided through Alexander Mackenzie in 1793, by way of the Peace River canyon to Dean Channel; Simon Fraser in 1808, by the tumultuous river which bears his name; David Thompson in 1811, down the Columbia to its mouth. These Canadian Scots were all members of the North-West Company, and they were rivals, not only of the Spanish, Russians and Americans, but also of the Hudson's Bay Company. With their exploits, the chain of discovery and exploration, whose initial links were forged in the quest for furs along the Atlantic coast over the preceding two centuries, was complete from ocean to ocean—all in the name of the fur trade. In each instance, the ubiquitous Scot was accompanied, guided and sustained by Indian companions.

For the United States, Lewis and Clarke had, of course, paced the Canadians, reaching the Columbia River in 1805. John Jacob Astor established the western headquarters of his fur company at the mouth of the Columbia in 1810.

In 1809, by the *Labrador Act*, Anticosti Island and the coast of Labrador from the St. Jean River to Hudson Strait were transferred from Lower Canada to Newfoundland. Not even the eastern provinces, however, were to be allowed to engage in such peaceful organizational exercises much longer. The improvement in relations which the Jay Treaty appeared to herald had not resolved the border ambiguities at the centre of the continent, and the animosities of the American Revolution were by no means exhausted.

The outbreak of war in 1812 saw 500 000 British Americans (of whom less than 5000 were regular troops) confronted by a population of 8 million in the United States. Great Britain was not only at war with the United States, but had her strength committed to the struggle with Napoléon. Through a combination of dogged determination on the part of the British Americans (aided by several hundred Indians under Chief Tecumseh) in throwing back invasion forces and ineffective planning on the part of the enemy, Canada managed to hold out until the defeat of Napoléon in 1814 allowed Britain to bring all her forces to bear in America. Having thus gained the initiative in no uncertain manner, it is hard to understand why the British did not seek more equitable boundary terms by the Treaty of Ghent in 1814, but both parties appeared content to settle the controversy through a mutual return of conquered territories. Thus were Canadian interests sacrificed to ensure American cordiality.

The United States considered the Jay Treaty of 1796 to be abrogated by the War of 1812-14; but the Convention of 1818 settled the outstanding boundary matters by confirming the border to the Lake of the Woods and extending it along the 49th parallel to the Rocky Mountains. The Treaty of Ghent reinstated the provisions of the Jay Treaty affecting Indian people, but, as the conditions of the former were not considered to be self-executing, it became the individual responsibility of each of the governments concerned to give effect to the relevant provisions by appropriate legislation.

In terminating the international boundary at the Rocky Mountains, the Convention of 1818 left one major area subject to contention with the growing neighbour to the south—the so-called Oregon Territory jointly occupied by Britain and the United States. The first large-scale movement of American settlers into Oregon in 1842 naturally created a clamour for annexation to the United States. Fortunately, the contention was resolved through the Treaty of Washington in 1846, by which the boundary was continued to the sea along the 49th parallel and Vancouver Island confirmed as a British possession. With the agreement of 1825 between Britain and Russia on a description of the Alaska boundary, to all intents and purposes Canada's external boundaries now were fixed and its attention could be concentrated on consolidation.

THE PERIOD FOLLOWING CONFEDERATION

The pre-Confederation treaties were made with the Crown through representatives of the British government. Later, after Confederation, the treaties would be made through the Canadian government. All the terms of the pre-Confederation treaties were turned over to the Canadian government, either at the time of Confederation or since then. When the *Royal Proclamation* of 1763 was issued, Indian rights were, for the first time in Canadian history, specifically referred to. The *Royal Proclamation* confirmed that Aboriginal rights existed. However, the question still remains as to how much of what is now Canada is covered by the *Proclamation*. Driben (1983), for one, points out that it is difficult today to determine the boundaries of what the *Proclamation* referred to as "Indian territory."

When the Hudson's Bay Company (HBC) surrendered Rupert's Land in 1869, Canada inherited the responsibility for negotiating with the resident Native tribes. Prior to the transfer, the *Royal Proclamation* had established the "equitable principles" governing the purchase and surrender of Native lands. The *Imperial Order in Council* that transferred this responsibility is stipulated in Article 14:

> Any claim of Indians to compensation for lands required for the purposes of settlement shall be disposed of by the Canadian government in communications with the Imperial government; and the Company shall be relieved of all responsibility in respect of them.

The administrators subsequently appointed to negotiate federal treaties with the Indians were inexperienced and unfamiliar with Native customs. Lacking first-hand knowledge, these administrators fell back on the legacy of the HBC's treatment of Natives as well as on some sketchy reports of the negotiations behind the Robinson Treaties of 1850 and 1862 and the Manitoulin Island Treaty, also in 1862.

Preliminary negotiations between the Indians in Manitoba and the representatives of the government began in 1870. By 1871, Treaties Nos. 1 and 2 were signed, and in 1873 the lands between Manitoba and Lake Superior were ceded in Treaty

No. 3. Northern Manitoba and the remainder of the southern prairies were surrendered by the Natives between 1874 and 1877 in Treaties Nos. 4, 5, 6 and 7.

The land taken by the Canadian government under Treaties Nos. 1 through 7 provided sufficient land for the mass settlement of immigrants entering Canada. However, by 1899, the pressures of settlement and mineral development again caused the government to negotiate for new lands from the Natives. Although these later treaties, Nos. 8 through 11, differed in many respects from the earlier ones, they were clearly modelled upon earlier treaties.

The federal government decided to negotiate with the Natives largely because its own agents foresaw violence against White settlers if treaties were not established. However, this was not based on particular threats or claims on the part of the Natives, who simply wished to carry out direct negotiations with the government to recompense them for the lands they occupied prior to White settlement. After the first treaty was signed, neither the government nor the Natives attempted to find alternative means to deal with "Indian claims." Government officials based future treaties on prior ones and Indians insisted on similar treatment to that received by those who had signed earlier treaties.

Despite specific differences, the contents of all the treaties are remarkably similar. Treaties Nos. 1 and 2 set the stage. They created reserve lands granting 160 acres per family of 5. Annuities of $3 per person, a gratuity of $3 per person, and a school on each reserve were agreed upon. Other promises were also made orally during the negotiations; some of these were later given formal recognition by an order in council.[3] Treaty No. 3 contained the same provisions as Treaties Nos. 1 and 2, except that its reserve allotment was increased to 640 acres per family of 5.[4]

The federal government desired treaties that were brief, simple and uniform in content. Nonetheless, although constrained by these government limitations, negotiators were often forced to make minor additions to a treaty; sometimes these took the form of verbal promises, presumably to avoid deviations from the standard written form. For example, the government negotiators for Treaty No. 6 were forced to add several benefits such as medicine chests and provisions for relief in times of famine.

In general, however, the government negotiators had by far the best of the bargaining. Indeed, most treaties were written by the government and simply presented to the Indians for signing. The terms, for example, of Treaty No. 9 were determined by the Ontario and Canadian governments well in advance of discussions with Indians. Moreover, there is evidence that, in many cases, hard-won oral promises have never been recognized or acted upon by the government.

In their negotiations with the Natives, treaty commissioners always avoided discussing the nature or extent of Aboriginal land rights. Although the commissioners obscured the issue, the Indians clearly surrendered land claims by signing the treaties. In many cases, the commissioners argued that the Indians had no land rights at all; if the Native negotiators objected to this argument, the commissioners would enlist support from missionaries or traders whom the Natives trusted. In the end, however, no Indian treaty was ever brought before Parliament. Instead, the treaties were presented to Cabinet and ratified by an order in council. This suggests that they were accepted by the Government of Canada both as a recognition of Native land claims and as a means of their negotiation and resolution.

British Columbia: A Special Case

British Columbia was a special case in its handling of treaties. Between 1849 and 1854, James Douglas, the governor of the colony, negotiated a series of treaties with the Indians on Vancouver Island. After 1854, this policy was discontinued: although the colonial office in England supported the treaties, it would not provide Douglas with monies to continue them. The White British Columbia settlers refused responsibility for negotiations with the Indians and would not release public funds to settle land claims.

As Berger (1981: 222-23) points out, British Columbia's House of Assembly had initially recognized Aboriginal land titles. However, when told by London that it would have to provide the funds to settle those titles, the House of Assembly withdrew recognition of Indian land claims. This meant that, technically, the Indians were not entitled to any compensation.

No further treaties were ever made in British Columbia, although Treaty No. 8 covers the northeastern part of the province. With the entry of British Columbia into Confederation in 1871, the administration of Indians and Indian lands in the province fell under the jurisdiction of the federal government. However, the federal government's interpretation of this jurisdiction has remained controversial up to the present.

When British Columbia entered Confederation, the actual terms concerning the treatment of Natives were unclear. The terms of union clearly stated that all public lands were to be the property of the provincial government; this meant that the federal government owned no land outright in the province to give to the Natives. Some provision was made, however, for Native lands. The province agreed to relinquish to the federal government "tracts of land of such extent as it had hitherto been the practice of the British Columbian government to appropriate for that purpose" (Berger, 1981: 224).

Unfortunately, the practice of the British Columbian government was to supply considerably less land than did the federal government. When allotting land, the province had simply set aside a number of acres per family. Although White settlers had received 320 acres of land per homestead, Natives had been granted considerably less. In 1887, the federal government asked the province to determine the size of the reserves by relinquishing 80 acres per Indian family. The province set aside only 20 acres per family, a much lower acreage than that set aside for other Natives by the Canadian government. Understandably, Indians in B.C. objected strongly and insisted on their Aboriginal rights.

The British Columbian Natives continued to oppose the establishment of reserves and to argue title to their own lands. The federal government dissolved its commission in 1910 after the provincial government refused to sanction any more reserves. In the early 1900s, Indians sent delegations to Victoria and to England in an attempt to argue their claims for Aboriginal rights. The federal government partly supported these claims and tried unsuccessfully for a hearing before the Supreme Court of Canada. The province refused to comply.

In 1913, a royal commission was established partly to adjust the acreage of the reserves in British Columbia. In 1916, the commission produced a report detailing lands to be added to and removed from existing reserves. The added land was to be twice the size of the land taken away; however, the land to be taken away was, at that time, worth twice as much money.

As the federal government tried to implement this report, it met increased opposition from the provincial government and from the Natives. The province finally confirmed an amended version of the report in 1923. But the Natives never accepted it. The Allied Indian Tribes of British Columbia emerged to become a powerful political force uniting Native opposition to the decision. In 1923, the Allied Indian Tribes of British Columbia presented a list of far-reaching demands to the federal government and agreed to relinquish their Aboriginal title claim only if the demands were met. These demands were remarkably similar to those met by previous treaties in other provinces, namely, 160 acres per capita, hunting rights, and the establishment of reserves.

The Allied Indian Tribes of British Columbia demanded that either a treaty be negotiated or that their Aboriginal title claim be submitted to the judicial committee on the Privy Council. In essence, they argued that, contrary to the beliefs of the federal and provincial governments, there had been no final settlement of their claims. As a result of the Indians' petition, a special joint committee of the House and Senate was convened to hear evidence and make a decision. This committee decided that the Indians had not established any claims to land based on Aboriginal title; however, it did recommend that an annual sum of $100 000 be spent for the good of Indians in British Columbia.

In order to prevent an appeal of this decision, the federal government passed an amendment to the *Indian Act* that prohibited the collection of funds from Natives for the advancement of a land claim. This amendment remained law until the middle of this century. As a result, Natives became powerless to press their claims and were successfully ignored by the federal government throughout the Depression and World II. Of necessity, local issues replaced larger concerns during this time: the Native Brotherhood of British Columbia was established in 1931 and, in 1942, became prominent in its fight against income tax for Native fishermen. But Native land claims did not emerge again as an issue until the 1960s, when they played an important role in the creation of the Indian Land Commission.

Early Ontario Treaties

Algonkian-speaking peoples formed the Indian population of southern Ontario when the European claim to territorial sovereignty passed from the French to the British in 1763, but European settlement did not occur there to any degree until 20 years later. In these post-Revolutionary years, the separation of the Thirteen Colonies from British North America created an urgent need for land on which to settle disbanded soldiers and other Loyalists. The unsettled areas of British North America provided a ready solution to the problem.

About 10 000 United Empire Loyalists moved into the area of the St. Lawrence-Lower Great Lakes. In presiding over this settlement, the Imperial government did not simply grant land to these newcomers without regard for the Indian inhabitants. As has been seen, the *Royal Proclamation* of 1763 declared that Indian land rights could only be alienated at a public meeting or assembly of the Indians called for the purpose, and then only to the Crown. Although often honoured only in the breach, the *Proclamation*'s principles were respected through a complicated series of formal treaties and surrenders in what became southern Ontario.

To the government, treaties were little more than territorial cessions in return for once-for-all grants, usually in goods. However, there is evidence that some of the Indians involved felt that the government was assuming broader trusteeship responsibilities as part of the bargain. Annuities, or annual payments for the ceded land rights, first appeared in a treaty in 1818 and thereafter became routine. At this stage, the provision of land for Indian reserves only occasionally formed part of the surrender terms. Similarly, the right to continue hunting and fishing over ceded territories was very rarely mentioned in the written terms of surrender. Not until 1850, when cessions of land rights were taken by William Robinson along the northern shores of Lakes Huron and Superior, were treaties made that granted to the Indians all four items: once-for-all expenditures, annuities, reserves and guarantees concerning hunting and fishing. It was for this reason that Alexander Morris, most widely known of the government's negotiators, wrote of the Robinson Treaties as constituting the "forerunners of the future treaties" to be made by the recently created Dominion.

The provisions of many of the southern Ontario treaties and surrenders are quite discordant with more recent agreements conveying far greater benefits to Native peoples elsewhere. Most cessions made in Ontario after 1830 were concluded in trust. The government assumed responsibility for disposing of the ceded lands on the Indians' behalf, with the proceeds of sales usually going to the particular Indians involved. As with land cessions made earlier, which were at times outright surrenders with the government as purchaser, there are strong arguments that inadequate compensation was given. Surrenders concluded prior to 1818 provided for a lump-sum payment along with a nominal yearly rent; in one 1816 surrender of Thurlow Township, for instance, the yearly rent was fixed at one peppercorn. In an 1836 surrender, it was considered sufficient to promise the Chippewa claimants agricultural and educational aid in exchange for their surrender of 1.5 million acres south of Owen Sound. The Robinson Huron and Superior Treaties, as well, supplied only minimal payments to the Indians, although they contained provisions for a limited augmentation of annuities in the future. One oversight in the Huron Treaty presumably left Aboriginal rights intact at Temagami.

The Numbered Treaties

Treaties Nos. 1 to 7 were made during the 1870s in the territory between the watershed west of Lake Superior and the Rocky Mountains in what was then Canada's newly acquired Northwest. These treaties utilized many features of the earlier transactions, but were far more comprehensive in their provisions and more uniform and consistent with one another. Their characteristics and relative similarities were not due to a broad policy worked out in advance by the federal government. Indeed, immediately before the first of these treaties was made, the government had little information about the Indians of its new territory, let alone a policy. It proceeded to deal with the Native occupants in an ad hoc fashion as necessity dictated. Almost inevitably the patterns of earlier Canadian experience were adapted to a new time and place. The seven treaties which emerged were partly shaped by the Indians themselves and were indirectly influenced by United States' practice.

The government's purpose in negotiating treaties in the Northwest was to free land for settlement and development. A corollary of this was the urgent desire to satisfy the Indians sufficiently so that they would remain peaceful. The nature and extent of Indian rights to the territory were not discussed at the negotiations, nor were they defined in the treaties themselves. It is evident from the texts, nevertheless, that the government intended that whatever title the Indians might possess should be extinguished, since the opening clauses of all seven agreements deal with land cession. This emphasis was not reflected in the preliminary treaty negotiations. There the stress was on what the Indians would receive rather than on what they were giving up. The commissioners gave them assurances that the Queen understood their problems and was anxious to help them.

The loss of control over land use and the diminishing game supply threatened the traditional Native way of life. While the Indians attempted to retain as much control as possible over their own territory and future, a secondary desire was the attempt to gain sufficient compensation and support to ensure their survival amidst rapidly changing conditions. As a result of hard bargaining, Indians did manage to have some additional provisions included in the treaties beyond those the government had originally intended. These included agricultural aid and certain liberties to hunt and fish.

Indians today make several points in relation to these treaties. The major one is that the treaty texts do not reflect the verbal promises made during the negotiations and accepted by a people accustomed to an oral tradition. They state that their ancestors understood the treaties to be specifically designed to protect them and help them adapt to the new realities by developing an alternative agricultural base to complement their traditional livelihood of hunting and fishing.

Indian associations strongly deny that the treaties obligate the government only to fulfil their terms as they appear in the bare texts. They uniformly insist that the written versions must be taken together with the words spoken by the government's agents during the negotiations. In a submission to the Commissioner on Indian Claims, the federation of Saskatchewan Indians states that:

> In his various addresses to Chiefs and Headmen at treaty meetings, Commissioner Morris had a single message for the Indians: The Queen was not approaching the Indians to barter for their lands, but to help them, to alleviate their distress and assist them in obtaining security for the future. "We are not here as traders, I do not come as to buy or sell horses or goods, I come to you, children of the Queen, to try to help you. The Queen knows that you are poor: the Queen knows that it is hard to find food for yourselves and children: she knows that the winters are cold, and you(r) children are often hungry: she has always cared for her Red children as much as for her White. Out of her generous heart and liberal hand she wants to do something for you...."

> These verbal assurances and statement of Crown intent, and the many others like them given by Morris in his address to Chiefs and Headmen, cannot be separated from treaty documents because they were accepted as truth by the assembled Indians (*Saskatchewan Indian*, 1982: 30).

The nature and extent of the implementation of treaty provisions are another source of grievance in this area. The government's open policy of detribalization, which held as its goal the assimilation of Indian people into the dominant society, motivated a number of specific policies which were destructive of Indian efforts to develop within the context of their own cultures. The field of education is one of the most conspicuous examples of this process, since it is easy to appreciate the effects of isolating children in residential schools where they were taught that their parent's language and culture were inferior, and where they had instilled in them a set of alien customs and values.

In the Indian view, during the late nineteenth and early twentieth centuries, the government failed to provide the expected agricultural assistance and unduly restricted Indian agricultural development. It encouraged the surrender of some of the best agricultural land from the reserves when its efforts failed to turn the Indians into farmers.

All of the Prairie Native organizations, along with the Grand Council of Treaty No. 3 in northern Ontario, think the treaties should be reworded in terms that will embody their original spirit and intent. As in Aboriginal title areas, the results of such settlements could, they say, provide the basis for revolutionizing the future development of Indian peoples and reserves on Native terms. The treaty Indians' organizations have outlined some specific objectives and proposals for an approach to development. A primary characteristic of these is their rejection of the concept of assimilation or detribalization, and, stemming from this, the conviction that the Indian people must initiate and control the development effort themselves.

Only at the turn of the century, when mineral exploitation provided the impetus, were treaties made to the north of the areas surrendered during the 1870s. Treaty No. 8 was concluded in the Athabasca District, Treaty No. 9 in northern Ontario and Treaty No. 10 in northern Saskatchewan. In addition, adhesions to Treaty No. 5 were taken in northern Manitoba to extend the limit of ceded territory to the northern boundary of the province. Finally, in 1921, following the discovery of oil at Norman Wells, Treaty No. 11 was made in the Northwest Territories.

The "contract" treaties between the Indians and the Dominion began in the mid 1800s (in southern Ontario) and moved westward, eventually encompassing all of Manitoba, Saskatchewan and Alberta. The treaty period ended in 1921 with the signing of Treaty No. 11, which encompasses almost all of the Mackenzie Valley of the N.W.T.. Today, only B.C., the Yukon, parts of Québec and Newfoundland have not "treatied" out with the Indians.

CLAIMS REGARDING TREATIES

As we pointed out earlier, the treaties have been the focal point for specific claims that have been pursued by Indians. Their claims with regard to treaties focus on several aspects. First of all, Indians argue that the treaty texts were not the same as the verbal promises made by the government during the negotiation period prior to the actual signing. Hence, they argue that the treaties obligate the government to keep promises made in both verbal and written contexts; for example, Treaties Nos. 8 and 11 (Melville, 1981). Secondly, inequality among the various treaties' land provisions have provoked specific claims, for example, Treaty No. 5 provides for 71 hectares per family while other treaties provide 285 hectares.

One example of a modern settlement involving a treaty concerns the Peter Ballantyne Band in Saskatchewan. To fulfil its remaining outstanding land entitlement claim, the Peter Ballantyne Band has selected approximately 81 000 hectares of land, including the site of the Prince Albert student residence. With the exception of the residence land, the rest is provincial Crown land. Remaining transfer settlements are now to be made between the province and the band. Under the terms of the Saskatchewan Formula of 1976, which is the federal-provincial agreement under which outstanding treaty land entitlements in Saskatchewan are being settled, the

Peter Ballantyne Band's outstanding entitlement is 92 860 hectares. The selection of these lands must deal satisfactorily with the interests of affected third parties. In May 1979, the band selected the 16.61-hectare Prince Albert residential school site as part of its treaty entitlement. The band has a historic connection with the school because many generations of its children have been educated there. The residence is on Crown land, which is currently utilized for Indian educational purposes, and has been under the control and administration of DIAND for many years.

The transfer to reserve status means the land will continue to be federal Crown land; however, it will be set aside as a reserve for the use and benefit of the Peter Ballantyne Band. The minister has approved the band's request that the land be set aside under the authority of section 18(2) of the *Indian Act* for Indian educational use. The band has stated that the current use of the land will not change in the foreseeable future.

Like other Saskatchewan bands, the Peter Ballantyne Band has placed a strong emphasis on education in relation to the economic and social future of its people. The Prince Albert student residence is ideally situated to facilitate contact between Indian students and non-Indian society.

The Prince Albert School is the only parcel of federal Crown land in Saskatchewan within a major urban area that has historically been administered by Canada, through the Department of Indian Affairs, for the benefit of the Indian people. In this respect the selection is unique and its transfer to reserve status is now viewed as a precedent for future land selections.

Another example is the 1991 settlement between the Alberta Stoney Indian tribe and the federal government. This second largest specific claim ever settled in Alberta provides nearly $20 million in compensation to the tribe for loss of mineral rights on land surrendered in 1929 for hydro development.

Treaties have three possible interpretations. In one sense they can be viewed as agreements between two or more nations. Most Native people claim this interpretation when they refer to the various treaties with the federal government. On the other hand, it is clear that the Canadian government (as evidenced through certain legislation and court decisions) does not interpret the treaties in the same manner.

Secondly, treaties have at times been interpreted as contracts. While there is some legal support for this interpretation, the nature of the court cases dealing with this issue are so specific that one must be cautious in interpreting treaties from this perspective. Nevertheless, former Prime Minister Pierre Trudeau publicly stated that treaties are analogous to contracts.

Finally, treaties can be viewed as pieces of legislation. This interpretation is plausible since many Indian treaties were made before such legislation as the *Indian Act*. Hence, any legal means that attempts to establish an orderly relationship between people could be viewed as analogous to legislation.

To date, it is unclear which interpretation will prevail, although it now seems unlikely that it will be the interpretation of a treaty as a contract. In addition, the courts have tended to rule that the provisions of the treaties can be overridden by federal, but not provincial, legislation. Nevertheless, they have also viewed treaties as enforceable obligations and have in the past forced the federal government to live up to those obligations.

MÉTIS SCRIP

Related to the issue of treaties are the concerns Métis people have regarding their Aboriginal and/or land rights. While not called treaties, several acts were passed by the federal government which provided land for Métis, e.g., *Manitoba Act*, *Dominion Lands Act*. The conditions for the transfer of land to Métis are outlined in these various acts. In the case of the Métis, the allocation of land (or money) was through the process of scrip. Scrip is a certificate giving the holder the right to receive payment later in the form of cash, goods or land (Sawchuk, *et al.*, 1981). This process differed from Indian treaties in that it involved grants to individuals as individuals; it did not purport to set up the Métis as a continuing corporate entity. For over 30 years (1885-1923), there was a series of scrip allotments to Métis. Each time that a new part of the prairie provinces or the Mackenzie Valley was ceded by Indians, persons of mixed blood who did not participate were allocated scrip redeemable in land (Flanagan, 1983).

Prior to 1870, Métis had not been dealt with as a separate group. However, expediency or perhaps humanitarian reasons led to a change; under section 31 of the *Manitoba Act*, 1870, a proportion of 623 000 hectares originally calculated as unoccupied land, was set aside for the children of Métis families in Manitoba. This land was reserved for "the benefits of the families of the half-breed residents." It was to be divided "among the children of the half-breed heads of families" residing in the province at the time of its transfer to Canada. Initially, the amount of land set aside was thought to provide each child with 290 acres (116 hectares). However, due to miscalculations, the government also had to issue money scrip in lieu of land. In 1874 the heads of Métis families were also provided with scrip (71 hectares or $160). Under the *Dominion Lands Act* in 1885, all Métis resident in the Northwest Territories outside the limits of Manitoba in 1870 were granted 107 hectares. By this time, the government had allotted 579 264 hectares of land and $509 760 to Métis in Manitoba. Four years later this would be extended to Métis resident in the area ceded by the adhesion to Treaty No. 6 (Taylor, 1983). In 1899, Métis in the Athabasca and Peace River areas were given scrip, and in 1906 all Métis permanently residing in the territory ceded at the time of making Treaty No. 10 were provided with 107 hectares. Finally, in 1921 each Métis of the Mackenzie River district received $240 to extinguish their Aboriginal rights (Sealey and Lussier, 1975). In all, the government handled more than 24 000 Métis claims (14 000 in the Northwest

Territories, Saskatchewan and Alberta, and 10 000 in Manitoba). These claims involved over one million hectares of land and in excess of $3.6 million.

The use of scrip was not confined to Métis. White settlers in 1873 and later (1885) veterans of the Boer War and officers of the North West Mounted Police, were also given land scrip. The scrip were in two forms and looked as follows.[5]

A typical land scrip certificate read:

Dominion of Canada
Department of the Interior

This Scrip note is receivable as payment in full for ONE HUNDRED and SIXTY ACRES of Dominion Lands, open for ordinary Homestead only if presented by _____ at the office of Dominion Lands of the District within which such lands are situated in conformity with Scrip Certificate form _____ granted by the North West Half Breed Commission this _____ day of _____ , 18 _____ .

A typical money scrip certificate read:

Dominion of Canada
Department of the Interior

In conformity with Certificate form No. _____ granted by the North West Half Breed Commission, it is Hereby Certified that under the authority of an order of the Honourable the Privy Council dated _____ day of _____ 18 _____ as amended by the order of _____ of _____ 18 _____ , and in accordance with the provisions of sub-sec. (e), Sec. 81, 46 Vic. Cap. 17 _____ , a Half-Breed is entitled to TWO HUNDRED AND FORTY DOLLARS IN SCRIP. The coupons attached to this will be accepted in payment of Dominion Lands on presentation at the office of Dominion Lands of the District within which such lands are situated.

Issued at the Department of the Interior, Ottawa, this _____ day of _____ , 18 _____ .

After passage of the *Manitoba Act* of 1870, which set aside lands for Métis, the government began a systematic process of amending the *Act* so that land set aside would not actually be allotted. From 1873 to 1884, 11 amendments were passed, referred to as *Manitoba Supplementary Provisions*. Nearly half of these amendments altered substantive portions of the original law. The effect of all of the amendments was the dispersal of the original Métis people in Manitoba. Only about 20 percent of the claimants received and made use of their land allotments. A similar percentage of river-lot occupants obtained patents and remained on the land they occupied in 1870. Over half the potential recipients were denied their land through a number of government manoeuvres.

Perhaps the single most important factor that prevented Métis from reaping the potential benefits of land claim settlements was the 1874 amendment to the 1870 *Act* which restricted eligibility for the initial allotment. It should be noted that even in the original allotment many children were omitted from participating in the benefits of the *Act*. The 1874 amendment, which declared that heads of family were entitled to the same benefits as children, excluded the heads from receiving any part of the original 1.4 million acres set aside. Instead they were awarded $160 in scrip that could be used to purchase Crown Land (Dickason, 1992). As Dickason points out, "Fortunes were made at the expense of the Métis—half-breed scrip millionaires" were created (1992, p. 317). Scrip was sold to land speculators (bankers and wealthy individuals) for as little as half its face value. In some cases, accepting scrip left Métis poorer than before.

Children who received an allotment were not adequately protected. For example, their children's allotments were subject to payment of local taxes from the moment the allotment was drawn. Thus, even if they were minors and had no way of paying the tax, they were expected to do so. Failure of taxes meant the loss of the property. Finally, Métis river-lot claimants were not compensated by the government for railroad or other public expropriation. However, homesteaders were. There are many other ways in which the federal government acted which placed the Métis in a disadvantageous position.

Some writers such as Flanagan (1983) claim that Métis only wanted money scrip and thus were not interested in obtaining land scrip. He also notes that some Métis insisted on receiving their entitlements in as liquid a form as possible. He points to the Métis of Lesser Slave Lake, who refused to accept scrip until it was rewritten "payable to the bearer." He also argues that Métis were good negotiators and that they operated in a "willing buyer—willing seller" market. We would acknowledge that some Métis preferred money scrip and we would concur that some were skilful negotiators. However, the structural conditions under which Métis operated did not allow for the exercise of choice, nor did they fully understand the implications of not having land deeded to them. For example, nearly 60 percent of the Métis were illiterate, a definite liability when dealing with banks and lawyers. The Métis Association of Alberta also pointed out in their study, *Métis Land Rights in Alberta: A Political History* (1981), that the use of land scrip came about because Métis opposed money scrip and wanted land grants. Métis of the Qu'Appelle Lakes refused to accept money scrip. Thus, land scrip was considered a compromise. There is also no doubt that most of the land scrip issues to Métis eventually were owned by banks and financial agents.

Evidence today is clear that when fraud was committed in obtaining these certificates, the government did little or nothing about it. For example, in 1900 two federal commissioners found that many powers of attorney were signed without the forms being completed. In other cases, Métis who anticipated receiving scrip were asked to sign power of attorney to brokers hoping to make money out of scrip settlements (Purich, 1988). Other evidence shows that land owned by minors was not safeguarded and was lost to White land speculators for much less than it was worth. It is clear that large scale land transfer from Métis to land agents and banks took place. What remains to be seen is how the government deals with these fraudulent transfers.

The scrip claims being pursued today by the Métis centre on several charges: 1) that scrip was unjustly and inefficiently administered, 2) that the compensation was inadequate, 3) that Métis in British Columbia, Southern Alberta and the Yukon received no compensation, and 4) that in certain areas most of the scrip issued was in the form of cash, not land (Hatt, 1983). Driben (1983) argues that since the government agreed to make scrip available to Métis in Western Canada, it was a *de facto* admission that they held Aboriginal title. Furthermore, he argues that the legal definition until just after Confederation did not distinguish between Métis and Indians; they were both considered "Native." Finally, he points out that Métis were, on occasion, included in the treaties, and he cites Treaty No. 3 as an example.

CONCLUSION

From the time the first European set foot on what was to become Canada, until the present limits were fixed by the inclusion of Newfoundland in 1949, European sovereignty over the land was essentially a matter of effective occupation. On the East coast, the Vikings barely established a toehold and disappeared almost without a trace; the bitter contests between the French and first the English, then the British after the Union of the Crowns, was finally resolved by force of arms in 1759-69, following three centuries of contention. On the West coast, despite the claim said to have been established by Drake at the 38th parallel in the sixteenth century, Spain held the coast well north of the 40th parallel until pushed out of contention. The Russian claim to all the coast from the 55th parallel north was never seriously contested by Britain, yet Russian America passed rapidly to the United States by purchase in 1867.

With the extension of international rivalries on the North American continent, traditional inter-tribal conflicts were often intensified. Group movements became more frequent and were subject to manipulation by the competing European factions, both in colonial wars and through the fur trade. The fur trader needed the Indian collector, and from this need grew esteem and understanding. As fur resources were depleted and large-scale settlement became a factor, the Indian could not escape the unappreciative attention of the incoming developers and homesteaders.

Indian treaty activity in Canada began with the Maritime "Peace and Friendship" agreements during colonial struggles, in which the principals agreed to aid each other in conflict or remain neutral. There was no mention of land title, and, invariably, the Indian people were assured they would not be disturbed in their traditional pursuits (hunting, fishing and trapping). Between 1725 and 1779 there were as many as eight agreements of this type.

The most significant date in Canadian Indian treaty matters is October 7, 1763, when, by Royal Proclamation, the British Sovereign directed that all endeavours to clear the Indian title must be by Crown purchase. In effect, the *Proclamation*

applied to lands then west of the settled areas, Old Québec and the Maritimes having been passed over as if they had been adequately dealt with. The anticipated
influx of settlers was accelerated by the Revolutionary War (1775-1783) and then by
the War of 1812; hence, the half-century between 1775 and 1825 witnessed a comprehensive land surrender scheme to extinguish Indian title involving most of
what is now southern Ontario. Compensation to the Indian groups deemed to be
in situ was sometimes in cash, sometimes in goods. The land so "cleared" or "ceded"
was considered freed of all encumbrance, with plenty of room for Indians and non-
Indians alike.

Thereafter, the exigencies of Canada's growth westward and northward dictated
the pace and direction of treaty activity. The discovery of minerals north of Lakes
Superior and Huron precipitated the negotiation of the Robinson Treaties in 1850
with the Ojibeway. Plans to settle the region of the Fertile Belt in the Prairies exerted
similar pressures as the Indian peoples and the Crown in right of Canada signed
Treaties Nos. 1 through 7 between 1871 and 1877. Subsequent treaty activity continued ad hoc—the discovery of gold at the Klondike River (1897) led to Treaty
No. 8 in 1899, thus clearing the access route from Edmonton to the Pelly River;
plans for construction of roads and railways precipitated the signing of Treaty No.
9 in 1905; Treaty No. 10 in 1906 immediately followed the attainment of provincial status for Saskatchewan and Alberta; the discovery of oil at Norman Wells in
1920 preceded Treaty No. 11 by one year.

The commissioners saw the treaties in one way; the Indians in quite another. A
reading of the reports of the Commissioners and of Lieutenant-Governor Morris'
book (1880, 1971) shows that the two groups came together with radically different
expectations. The Indians sought to be protected from land-grabbing settlers and
from the evils they sensed. Buffalo herds were diminishing—the railway was projected; they sought wide ranges which they could call their own and over which they
could live much as they had in the past. The Commissioners saw Indian reserves as
places where Indians could learn to be settlers and farmers. Some Indian spokesmen
appeared to accept the idea of farming, but it is unlikely they fully understood all
that was entailed.

There has been no treaty activity in Canada since the 1923 Chippewa and
Mississauga Agreements in Ontario (agreements which involved compensation
for surrender of Indian hunting, fishing and trapping rights).

In the 1970s, loss of "traditional livelihood" through hydro-electric power development (James Bay) and oil-producing schemes (Northern pipelines) has precipitated a strong dialogue between Native groups and government. This time, by
combining a higher degree of research, with consultation and negotiations on both
sides, compensatory agreements have been or are being worked out in many non-
treaty areas of Canada. In those areas already covered by treaties, the federal government has stated that it will honour its "lawful obligations"; to this effect it has

provided research funding for Indian bands and organizations to investigate claims or grievances relating to the fulfilment or interpretation of Indian treaties.

NOTES

1. Portions of this chapter are from *Indian Claims in Canada and Indian Treaties in Historical Perspective* (Ottawa: Minister of Supply and Services, 1981). Permission has been received from the Minister of Supply and Services Canada to reproduce the material.

2. Pontiac was an early leader of a Nativistic movement directed against the intrusion of missionaries in the area. He was also a firm believer in uniting Indian tribes and had led several successful engagements against the English, including such unorthodox Indian war strategies as laying seige to Fort Detroit.

3. In 1981, the Ontario Supreme Court decided that Native peoples who have treaty rights can legally hunt and fish out of season on Crown land in Eastern Ontario. The decision, involving the 1818 treaty with the Mississauga Indians, was partially based upon oral records of the day. The decision states that the minutes of a council meeting between the deputy superintendent of Indian Affairs and the Indians in 1818 recorded the oral portion of the 1818 treaty and are as much a part of the treaty as the written articles of the provincial agreement.

4. The increased allotment of 640 acres (260 hectares) in Treaty No. 3 became standard for all future treaties except for Treaty No. 5, which reverted to the 160 acre (65 hectares) allotment. Other changes that became standard included assurances of continued hunting, fishing and trapping rights, an annual budget for ammunitions, and the provision of agricultural supplies, such as cattle, seed and farm implements.

5. Over time, the specific words were changed, but the overall structure and legal effect remained the same.

CHAPTER 4
....

NATIVE LAND CLAIMS

INTRODUCTION

The reactive stance taken by Native people up until the past two decades has not served their purpose in establishing their presence in Canadian society. It has meant that the agenda was set by others, which gave the "opposition" an edge in terms of establishing programs and implementing policy. However, it has become clear to Natives that they must become more proactive in their attempts to participate in the social and economic activities in Canadian society. If they do not, they will, in a few short years, be entrapped in a position which will not allow them the manoeuvrability to retain the elements of their culture they feel are necessary to maintain their identity.

In the nineteenth century, Indian land fuelled American economic growth. However, dispossession had an opposite effect on the Indian Nations. While it led to Canadian economic development, it contributed to Native underdevelopment. In short, Native people were unable to sustain themselves. Within a century, this process had destroyed the Native economic base. In addition, the land base was unequally distributed: the most fertile land was taken for White settlers, control over water went to the government and the environment was altered to the disadvantage of Natives. As Cornell (1988) points out, Natives struggled to adapt, but their economies were falling apart and they had no way of entering the new emerging capitalist structure. The result was the beginning of economic marginal-ization and dependency.

The reactive stance Natives typically have adopted can be seen in a variety of institutional settings—religious, economic, educational. The inability to coordinate their actions, the lack of funding and the lack of understanding of the political process have led to this failure to control the agenda when dealing with the fed-eral/provincial governments. The emergence of various factions within the Native community has also hindered their planning and political strategies. Attempts to establish any sense of community and/or compromise amongst Native groups have been lacking—a situation ostensibly at odds with the traditional Native "con-sensus" model of decision-making.

This fragmentation has been a result of both differentiation imposed by outside forces and ideological differences working from within. For example, government agencies have dealt with Native subgroups differentially, depending upon their degree of cooperation with federal policies. In other case, internal ideological dif-ferences have produced different solutions to similar problems. The end result has been a lack of concerted "public will" in Native communities.

This lack of consensus has been exploited by agencies and organizations deal-ing with Natives. It has allowed them to act in any way they felt, justifying their ac-tions through the inability of Natives to agree. However, conditions have changed over the past two decades and Native people are beginning to act in a concerted, proactive manner. They have come to realize that if they do not, decisions will be enacted which will seal the fate of Natives as a people relegated to a marginal po-sition in the political economy of Canada.

It is important to remember that when one side initiates behaviour, it also is at-tempting to strategically control subsequent action. The presentation of a policy program can be orchestrated in terms of place and context, thereby giving pro-posals a heightened appearance of legitimacy. Having to react to a proposal also means that time to consider that proposal is lessened—reaction is expected within a brief time after public disclosure of a government initiative, and this limits the care-ful assessment of the short- and long-term impacts. The presentation of a proposal, unless summarily rejected (which has its own problems), sets the stage for further discussion—directing the nature of the discussion and limiting alternative ways of addressing the question.

Native people have begun to think in proactive terms, not constrained by ex-isting bureaucratic rules. However, a century of control and marginalization have had their impact; a dependency mentality has been created, and it is this sense of limited capacity to act that must be dealt with. Nevertheless, Native people are beginning to become proactive in their dealings with provincial and federal gov-ernments. Natives are also establishing a priority of goals they are prepared to pursue. Boundaries are being established in order to determine when and how they will take action—either reaction or proaction. Agendas are clearly being spelled out and strategies planned. Community divisiveness is being dealt with and ranks are being closed to ensure a unified response to government. Finally, fiscal issues are being considered as only one component in the highly complex matrix of decision-making. If decisions are always based on financial considerations, then the process of consultation and negotiation is reduced to economic choices—a substantial handicap for any group trying to advance its agenda.

One issue in which Natives have become more proactive is their concern over land. They have, after many years, realized that they could pursue land claims even though results would not be easily achieved. The early, disappointing outcome of their land claims slowed their initiatives. However, as they become more skilled at legal confrontation, their successes have increased. They have also fully appreciated the connectedness of land and their culture. As Altman and Nieuwenhuysen (1979) point out, the special relationship which Aboriginal people have with the land seems best described by the word "spiritual." Having fully reclaimed this perspective, Native people have now taken on the challenge of reclaiming land which they feel rightly belongs to them.

THE EARLY LAND CONFLICTS

The Native peoples of Canada have come under European influence in various ways, to differing degrees, and at different historical periods. For example, little impact was made on Natives in the Arctic until this century, and most of that has occurred since World War II. On the other hand, the Indians of the Atlantic coast and along the shores of the St. Lawrence River encountered Europeans early in the sixteenth century. As a result of this contact, the Beothuk of Newfoundland were obliterated. Overall, Indians in the more southerly parts of the country have, since contact, moved towards a Euro-Canadian way of life, while in northern areas, more continuity has been preserved with traditional patterns of living. However, nowhere has Native life been entirely unaffected by the advent of the European settlers and the domination of territory that was once the exclusive domain of Native peoples.

Early relationships between Natives and Europeans were both helpful and destructive, sought after and rejected, rewarding and penalizing. However, for Natives, the positive outcomes of contact were outweighed by the negative. The acquisition of metal tools by Natives allowed them to hunt and gather in a more efficient manner, which probably improved the quality of their life. However, at the same time, this acceptance of "modern" technology meant the destruction of their habitat, their way of life and eventually their ideology, i.e., the belief system which structures the relationships among Native people and their relationship with the cosmos. On the other side, as Miller (1989) points out, Europeans benefited from the contact through profit and expansion; the fur trade was the most obvious advantage.

European-Native interaction has taken many forms. As noted above, the fur trade significantly altered the way of life of a large segment of the Indian population, economically, politically and socially. While the fur trade introduced European goods and commercial values, it also brought with it Western moral and religious persuasions. At the same time, social interaction brought into being the people of mixed ancestry often referred to as Métis. The later occupation of land for settlement was further instrumental in modifying the economic and socio-cultural bases of Native societies. Resource exploitation in almost every part of the country also disturbed the lives of Native peoples both directly and indirectly through its environmental effects. Such activity continues today, with similarly disruptive results.

From an early period, the government of the colonizing society made itself specifically responsible for the relationship between the immigrants and the Natives. In law, the Native interest in land and other natural resources could not be acquired directly by the newcomers, but only through the agency of their government. In addition, the government assumed much of the direction of Native societies, particularly those whose traditional way of life was most disrupted. The historical relationship of the government to Native groups accounts for Native insistence on their continuing special status as the original people of Canada. As a result, the federal government has become the target of Native grievances in regard to land, natural resources and the management of Native affairs. These claims are based on Aboriginal rights or on agreements made with the government that were based on the Indians' position as unconquered indigenous occupants of the land.

THE CONCEPT OF "NATIVE"

To implement the policy of treating Native peoples differently from other citizens, it became necessary to determine the membership of the Native societies. Racial mixing and changing patterns of living have in many cases blurred the distinction between the Aboriginal and immigrant peoples. As was discussed in Chapter 2, the solution that has evolved is that people of Indian ancestry in Canada fall into two major classes vis-à-vis government definition. There are those recognized by the federal government as status Indians and those who are termed non-status Indians. There is also a third group known as Métis. Status Indians are registered by the Department of Indian Affairs and Northern Development; they possess certain rights and are subject to the terms set forth in the *Indian Act*. That act and its administrative interpretation determine what Indian status means, in practice, for the people who hold it.

Unless everyone with any Indian ancestry were to be accorded Indian status, a dividing line had to be adopted to differentiate the two groups. Pre-Confederation Indian legislation set down loose definitions based on heredity and social factors, and these criteria were carried over into the Dominion's own early Indian legislation. In Western Canada, inclusion in the treaties came to be the mark of status; hence the term *status Indian* is frequently synonymous with treaty Indian. The list of registered Indians has been built up by ad hoc methods which often seem to have been quite arbitrary. It is only for the persons and bands on this list that the federal Department of Indian Affairs and Northern Development has accepted responsibility under the *Indian Act*.

Non-status Indians and *Métis* are recognized by the government as holding a status no different from that of other Canadians. While the government of Canada has assumed special responsibilities for the education, health, welfare and economic development of status Indians, the non-status Indian and Métis people rely on the same agencies as other Canadians for these services, which usually means that they turn to the provincial governments. The *Canada Constitution Act, 1867* assigned to the Dominion government responsibility for "Indians, and Lands reserved for the Indians," but gave no clearer specification of those terms. Non-status Indians and Métis argue that the government does not have the constitutional authority to limit these responsibilities by restricting the meaning of "Indian" only to those defined in the *Indian Act*. This question of status and membership in the status group is therefore an important element in the consideration of Native claims and grievances.

The *Inuit* or Eskimo are a fourth Native group. Partly because of their location in the far hinterland of northern Canada, they were for long left with an ambiguous status outside these systems of administration. Some social services were provided by missionaries and traders through different levels and departments of government. The northerly extension of Québec in 1912 was taken by the federal government to mean that the province became liable for its Inuit inhabitants. Meanwhile, serious deterioration of the Inuit economy was increasing the costs of providing relief. The question of jurisdiction was resolved in 1939 when the Supreme Court of Canada declared the Inuit to be Indians for the purposes of the *British North America Act (Canada Constitution Act, 1867)*. While they are therefore a federal responsibility, the Indian Act excludes them from its operation and they are dealt with separately by the federal government.

TYPES OF CLAIMS

These, then are the major groupings of Native people from a legal standpoint. Their claims are significantly influenced by these distinctions. There are three general categories of claims: Aboriginal rights, treaty and scrip settlement grievances, and land claims. Chapter 3 focused specifically on treaty and scrip issues, so this chapter will deal specifically with Aboriginal rights and land claims. The notion of Aboriginal rights underlies all Native claims in Canada. Native people assert that their rights to land derive from their original occupancy, and they point out that

Aboriginal title has been recognized by the dominant society through various judicial decrees and actions of the government. It is important to note that no treaties were ever made for about half the territory in Canada where Native people ceded their lands. On this basis alone, both status and non-status Indians, as well as the Inuit, are now developing or negotiating terms.

Treaty Indians have a number of claims that relate to the agreement for the cession of their lands through treaty. Some of these rest on an insistence that specific treaty terms have not been fulfilled and that the broader spirit of the treaties has not been assumed by the government. A frequent claim is that verbal promises made at the time of the negotiations were not included in the written texts. In some areas, Indian people also emphasize in their treaty claims that these transactions constituted inadequate settlements, even if all their terms were fulfilled. These claims involve assertions about the way in which treaties were negotiated, the disparities between the two contracting parties, and the alleged unfairness of the terms.

Most status Indians belong to bands, which have rights to reserve lands held in common. Most bands, whether in treaty or non-treaty areas, usually have specific claims to make. The most numerous and widespread are those stemming from reserve land losses. Reserve lands were sometimes lost through squatting or being resurveyed. Most typically they were lost as a result of formal surrenders and expropriations by the federal or provincial governments. Claims may be based on the specific nature and legality of these occurrences or on the general propriety of such forms of land alienation. Management of band funds and reserve resources and the administration of band affairs, particularly with regard to economic development, are also central features of many potential band claims.

Land is an extremely important element in Native claims in general. As mentioned above, Native peoples are becoming more articulate about their unique relationship to the land, both past and present, and about the meaning it has for them. They also are aware that the material standard of living that has been achieved generally in Canada derives ultimately from the land and its resources. As a consequence, they seek not only a role in determining the way in which the land and other resources are used, but also a just portion of the benefits derived from their exploitation. This theme is basic in the Aboriginal rights claims, but it also appears in treaty claims, where the original land agreements may be in question, and in band claims concerning lost reserve land or other natural resources.

For the Native people, *trusteeship*, a fundamental element in their claims, involves both protection and assistance. When the federal government assumed political control over Native people, it undertook responsibilities for reserve land and band finances, and it imposed special limitations on Indians as a feature of Indian status. It adopted a protective role over Indians and their affairs analogous to that of a guardian or trustee toward a ward or beneficiary. From this relationship flow grievances and claims that pertain to the government's management of Indian resources.

NATIVE-GOVERNMENT RELATIONS

Canadian jurisprudence has taken the position that Canada was acquired by discovery or settlement (Bartlett, 1984), and although the concept of "existing Aboriginal rights" (from which it is assumed that Aboriginal title flows) is now entrenched in the *Canadian Constitution, 1982* (see sections 25, 35 and 37), no one is able to say precisely what those words mean (Henderson, 1983).

One of the first legal rulings on this issue was handed down in 1885 (*St. Catherine's Milling and Lumber Company* v. *the Queen*). This ruling characterized Aboriginal title as a possessory right, a right to use and occupancy, similar to a usufructuary right, i.e., right based on traditional use and occupancy (Thompson, 1982). The Privy Council in 1888 changed this interpretation slightly when they characterized Aboriginal title as a personal usufructuary right, dependent upon the good will of the sovereign. Unfortunately, since that time few legal cases in Canada have pursued this issue and it would not be until nearly a century later when, in 1973, the *Calder et al.* v. *Attorney General of British Columbia* case came before the Supreme Court of Canada, that this concern was reexamined. Even through the Nishga Indians did not win this case, three of the seven Supreme Court justices ruled that Aboriginal title did exist in common law irrespective of any formal recognition, that is, independent of the *Royal Proclamation* of 1763. These justices argued that once Aboriginal title has been established, it is presumed to continue until the contrary is proven, and that the onus is upon the government to prove that it intended to extinguish Indian title through various ordinances. Since no specific legislation was enacted that provided for Indian title to be extinguished, these judges concluded the Indians may indeed be in possession of Aboriginal title.

Prior to the Nishga case, the federal government held that Aboriginal land rights were so general and undefined that it was not realistic to view them as claims capable of remedy through a policy. However, after this Nishga case, the government announced a change in its policy with regard to legal obligations to legitimate claims being pursued by Indians. The government indicated that it was willing to negotiate settlements with Native groups where Native rights based upon usufruct had not been extinguished by treaty or superseded by law (Bankes, 1983).

Other writers such as Driben (1983) and Cumming and Mickenberg (1972) and Clark (1990) have gone beyond the Supreme Court's ruling and have suggested that Native interest rests on a solid legal foundation. They point to the *Royal Proclamation* of 1763, which pledged, in a legal context, that the Natives' Aboriginal title would be respected. Land title extinguishment could only take place if Indians approved of the action at a public meeting with public officials. When the extinguishment took place, the land could only be ceded to the Crown. Today, according to the courts, Aboriginal rights are vested in Native people by virtue of both the *Royal Proclamation* of 1763 and by the fact that they were the sovereign inhabitants in Canada before the land was considered French or English property (Indian Claims Commission, 1975).

Land Claims Before 1969

Prior to the establishment of the Indian Lands Commissioner (1969) and the Office of Native Claims (1974), Indian claims were handled on an individual basis. The processing of a claim was dealt with either by the Department of Indian Affairs and Northern Development or by the Department of Justice. There was a dual filing system utilized by DIAND through which all claims were sorted. One was labelled "petitions and complaints"; the other "claims and disputes." The former label was interpreted by government officials as representing grievances and as such did not require any legal action on their part. However, the claims in the latter file were interpreted as legitimate and as such did require the department to respond (Daniel, 1980).

At the end of World War II, the federal government created a joint committee of the Senate and the House of Commons to consider changes to the *Indian Act* as well as to investigate the administrative and operational structure of the Department of Indian Affairs. One of the areas the committee was to investigate was the issue of Indian land claims. By the late 1950s, a thorough assessment had been completed of the model used in the United States for dealing with Indian claims and the committee rejected this model. However, when the Joint Committee for the Review of Indian Affairs Policy met (1959-1961), Native organizations once again renewed pressure for the government to settle outstanding land claims. (See Daniel, 1980 for the specifics of a number of cases that were being dealt with and discussed in the media at the time.) As a result, the committee recommended that an Indian Land Claims Commission be established, and by 1962 the first draft of the legislation for the creation of the claims commission was brought forward. However, due to change in the government, internal departmental conflict, the need to consult with the Indians, and the Indians' desire to see how this legislation would deal with their claims against the provincial governments, the legislation was never passed. When the Liberal government took over in 1968, it decided to embark upon a new policy direction by eliminating the legal status of "Indian." This, of course, would have solved the issue of Indian claims in that Indians would have, in a legal sense, no basis upon which to bring claims forward.

As Daniel (1980) points out, the 1969 *White Paper on Indian Policies* was vigorously repudiated by Indian leaders. They were joined in their opposition by a number of non-Indian social and political organizations, and the policy soon became the *bête noire* of government-Indian relations. However, one recommendation of the *White Paper* was for the appointment of an Indian Claims Commissioner. In late 1969, Dr. Lloyd Barber was appointed Canada's first and only Indian Claims

Commissioner, a position he would hold until 1977 when the office was terminated. The Commissioner's mandate was to receive and study grievances and to recommend measures to adjudicate any claim. He himself did not have powers of adjudication since his role was only advisory. He did play an important role, however, in educating government officials and the public at large (Morse, 1985). The Indian Claims Commission and the Indian Claims Commissioner's office had divergent aims, and this was partially a result of the government's insistence that Indians had no legal basis on which to make claims. The creation of the Commissioner's office was an interim structure developed by the government that was meant to be phased out once a new policy could be drafted.

The government also established some funding programs to help defray the costs to Natives of researching and presenting their claims. During the period 1970-73, the Privy Council office provided funds; between 1972-73 the Indian Claims Commissioner; and during 1972-76 the Rights and Treaty Research Program (DIAND) was the major funding agency. In 1974 the federal government created the Office of Native Claims (within DIAND) to deal with specific grievances. While the Indian Claims Commissioner and the Office of Native Claims (ONC) overlapped between 1974 and 1977, their roles were very different. The Indian Claims Commission was established to receive and study grievances presented by Indians as well as to suggest the process by which particular claims could be adjudicated. On the other hand, the Office of Native Claims accepted the legitimacy of Aboriginal land rights. Thus, its function was to coordinate federal negotiations regarding claims Indians presented to the federal government.

Land Claims After 1969

Aboriginal land rights were given a serious blow in the recent *Delgamuukw* v. *the Queen* (1991) case when the B.C. Supreme Court judge, A. McEachern, ruled that the 8000 Gitksan and Wet'suwet'en British Columbian Indians do not hold Aboriginal rights to the land. He stated that the *Royal Proclamation*, 1763, has never applied to the province of British Columbia and that Aboriginal interest in the land did not include ownership of or jurisdiction over the territory. He also ruled that pre-Confederation colonial laws, construed in their historic setting, show a clear intention to extinguish Aboriginal interests in order to give unburdened titles to the settlers, and, thus, the Crown extinguished all Aboriginal rights even though no specific extinguishment act was passed, even before the province entered Confederation in 1871. Therefore, he argued, since Confederation the province has had title to the soil of the province and the right to dispose of Crown lands unburdened by Aboriginal title.

However, the judge did acknowledge that the Indians could use vacant Crown land, but this is not an exclusive right. Furthermore, their use is subject to the general laws of the province.

The trial had taken more than four years, during which time communities, forestry and mining companies fought the Native land claims. Their one-billion-dollar investments were at risk until the judgment was made. Uncharacteristically, the judgment ended with a stern lecture from the judge. He urged that only political negotiations could solve the land issue and questioned the focus on legal and constitutional matters such as ownership, sovereignty and rights. He also noted that the issues now facing Native people cannot be solved by continuing the reserve system, which, he argued, has created "fishing footholds and ethnic enclaves." He concluded his judgment by arguing that enlarging the reserves is not in the best interest of anyone and suggested that Indians must leave the reserve and enter the urban centres of Canada so they can participate in the economic activities found there.

The B.C. Supreme Court ruling on the Aboriginal claims of the Gitksan-Wet'suwet'en Nation is unique and perplexing in a number of aspects. First of all, the judge (Alan McEachern) assesses Native society using a very ethnocentric perspective, e.g., since Natives did not use the wheel, have a written language or use domesticated animals for food production, he claims that they did not have an organized, integrated society. In fact, he argues that early Native life was "nasty, brutish and short." He concludes that "many of the badges of civilization, as we of European culture understand them, were indeed absent" (page 31). In short, the judge introduces highly ethnocentric and biased perspectives about what constitutes "civilization" and/or "development" and concludes that since Natives did not have many of the cultural artifacts of Europeans, they can only be considered "primitive."

The findings of McEachern are also puzzling and without precedent. He rejects testimony from certain experts out of hand and without adequate justification, while allowing testimony from others. For example, he rejects anthropological testimony but accepts that from historians and linguists. Furthermore, there are well accepted principles that the judge did not follow. For example, all testimony must be understood by the judge (since he/she must make a ruling); otherwise, the judge must simply accept the conclusions of the experts—unless those are successfully challenged by information from other experts. Nevertheless, the transcripts of the trial show that the judge openly acknowledges that he does not understand the logic or the argument of certain witnesses, yet he accepts their conclusions unquestioningly, even when the illogical and uninterpretable arguments are questioned by others.

The judge's insistence on seeing himself as a social scientist is without precedent. Much of the data presented to him by anthropologists are rejected with no good explanation. He then proceeds to develop his own biased and ethnocentric explanation about Native people—totally devoid of evidence or logic. Nevertheless, the judgment stands, and it remains to be seen if an appeal can be launched. The decision is unique in that it contradicts earlier decisions by other courts, including the Supreme Court of Canada.

In the *Guerin* v. *Regina* (1984) and the more recent *Sparrow* (1990) cases, the Supreme Court acknowledged and reinforced the fiduciary relationship between the Crown and the Indians. The judgments forcefully noted that the government has a responsibility to act in a fiduciary capacity with respect to Native people. They went on to point out that the relationship between the government and Indians is trust-like rather than adversarial, and contemporary recognition and affirmation of Aboriginal rights must be defined in light of this historic relationship.

It is hard to imagine a more adversarial act than when the Canadian forces were deployed against the Mohawk Indians. The federal government has argued that the introduction of the military was due to the insufficiency of the provincial police force to deal with the situation. It also has been argued that the barricades at Kahnawake were on Indian lands and thus not subject to policing by provincial forces. There is also the argument that the crisis emerged because Natives felt threatened over the destruction of traditional lands. This suggests that the federal government had already failed to observe its fiduciary obligation. The fact that the armed forces were operating under the mandate set by the premier of Québec compounds the breach of federal fiduciary duty. As noted, above, the primary duty to protect the rights of Native people falls to the federal government. There was no evidence during the crisis that the federal government owed a special duty to the Mohawks.

Beyond its fiduciary obligation toward Indians, the federal government is also required to guarantee the rights and freedoms found in the Charter. Actions by government toward Native people reveal that there are numerous violations of Native civil liberties. For example, the presentation by the Indigenous Bar Association to the Standing Committee on Aboriginal Affairs regarding the events of Kanesatake and Kahnawake during the summer of 1990 noted that the most serious violation of Native civil liberties was the Minister of Indian Affairs signing an agreement on preconditions to negotiations with Natives!

The *Sparrow* (1990) case in B.C. is a recent case which has attracted the attention of all individuals interested in Native-White affairs. The *Sparrow* case involves an Indian who was fishing at the mouth of the Fraser River with a 38-fathom net when his licence (to the band) was only for 25 fathoms. He was subsequently charged with illegal fishing. The charge resulted from a failed "sting" operation which the Fisheries Department had set up in 1987. Agents acted as individual Canadians who wanted to buy fish illegally from band members. While the sting resulted in 25 Indians being charged, none were convicted of illegally fishing. It was at this time the Fisheries Department implemented another procedure to reduce the number of fish caught by Natives; i.e., they reduced the net to 25 fathoms so that the Indians would not catch many fish.

After the new regulations were in place, Sparrow, an Indian fisherman, was caught fishing with a net over 25 fathoms and subsequently was charged under the new regulations. Even though historical data showed that Indians had fished this area since time immemorial, the provincial court found Sparrow guilty. The court ruled that Indian rights had been extinguished at the beginning of the century. This was appealed to the county court, then to the Court of Appeal and eventually to the Supreme Court of Canada. The Supreme Court ruled that while the provincial regulations were legal and forced Indians out of their fishing activities, the province could not extinguish Aboriginal rights through regulations. The regulations would have to specifically state that Aboriginal rights were to be extinguished. The Supreme Court ruled that in cases where there are ambiguous or vague regulations, the interpretation would be in favour of Aboriginal people.

Comprehensive Claims

There are two major categories of claims now being pursued by Natives in Canada. The first is referred to as a comprehensive claim or Aboriginal rights claims, while the second is called specific and will be discussed later. Table 4.1 shows the status of comprehensive claim settlement.

These claims take two different forms which are, to some extent, regionally based. In the North, the claims focus on a demand for formal legal recognition of Aboriginal land title and all the rights that are derived from it. In the south, comprehensive claims place more emphasis on the cooperation between Natives and the government for the extinguishment of Aboriginal title and the restitution of specific rights, for example, hunting and fishing rights (Government of Canada, n.d.).

The map in Figure 4.1 identifies the major areas in Canada that are under comprehensive claims processing at the present time. As one can see, almost the entire Canadian North is claimed by Natives; and various Native associations are

TABLE 4.1 STATUS OF COMPREHENSIVE CLAIMS

	Up to 1980	1981	1982	1984	1985	1990
Submitted	21	4	4	1	3	3
Accepted for negotiation	15	0	0	8	1	3
Rejected	3	0	0	0	0	1
Agreements	3*	0	0	0	1	3

*Two claims were final agreements, one was an agreement in principle.

Source: Task Force, 1985.

actively pursuing their cases. Areas in the Arctic are being pursued by the Inuit, while the Métis and Indians in the Mackenzie Valley area of the Northwest Territories and in the Yukon have filed several claims.

In 1977, the Inuit Tapirisat of Canada submitted a proposal for creating a new territory in the Northwest Territories called Nunavut. The proposal encompassed both land claims as well as attempts to establish political sovereignty. Because of this intermixture of issues (politics and land), the federal government refused to discuss either issue. By 1980, the Inuit agreed to separate the issues, and tandem negotiations are now taking place. The Inuit Tapirisat has now turned over land negotiations to the Tungavik Federation of Nunavut. In the Western Arctic, the Inuvialuit have now signed a final agreement with the federal government in regard to their land claims (the COPE Agreement) and are now working out the details of their regionally based political structure (Western Arctic Regional Municipality). The Indians and Métis of the Northwest Territories submitted separate land claims in 1976 and 1977 respectively. The federal government refused to act on these claims until, three years later, the Indians and the Métis agreed that the Dene Nation would represent all Native beneficiaries during the negotiation of the claims. New areas in B.C., the Maritimes and Labrador are also being researched by Natives, with the aim of presenting several comprehensive claims to the federal government.

Comprehensive claims are not negotiations about grievances related to previous treaties, their interpretation and their shortcomings. Rather they are land claims which deal with areas of the country where various Native people continue to live and where treaties were never entered into. A partial exception to this is the Dene/Métis claim in the Northwest Territories. The policy of establishing comprehensive land claims began in 1973 and was subsequently revised and updated in 1981 and 1986. More recently (1991) additional changes were made. As Harry Swain, Deputy Minister of Indian Affairs (1988) pointed out, comprehensive claims are a unique arrangement in which Native people can settle land issues.

The process is one through which Native groups agree to exchange of their Aboriginal title over all or most of the land covered in return for land, money, certain rights and other conditions designed to protect and enhance their social, cultural and economic well-being.

The agreements which emerge from these negotiations are formal, legal and binding documents. They have to be ratified by the Native groups concerned and by the federal government, and are enacted into law by Parliament. They now constitute a substantial body of law and have helped redefine the relationship between the Government of Canada and many of its Aboriginal citizens. Since 1982, these agreements have also been protected constitutionally.

The first of these comprehensive land claims agreements was the James Bay and Northern Québec Agreement, which was reached between the federal and

FIGURE 4.1   COMPREHENSIVE CLAIMS: AREAS CLAIMED BY NATIVE ASSOCIATIONS.

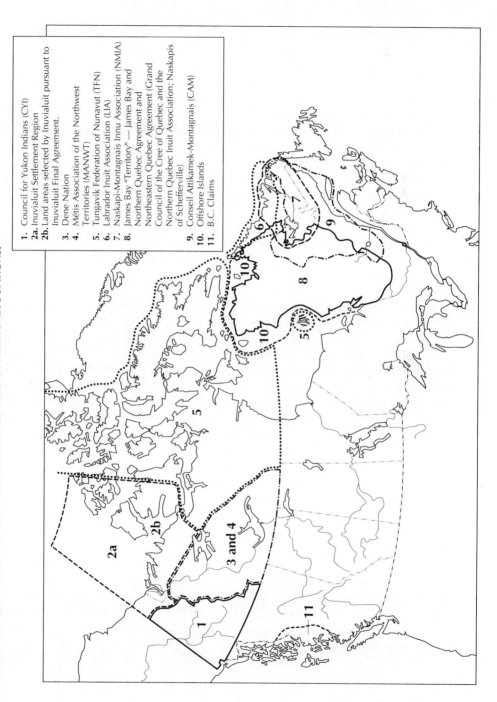

1. Council for Yukon Indians (CYI)
2a. Inuvialuit Settlement Region
2b. Land areas selected by Inuvialuit pursuant to Inuvialuit Final Agreement.
3. Dene Nation
4. Métis Association of the Northwest Territories (MANWT)
5. Tungavik Federation of Nunavut (TFN)
6. Labrador Inuit Association (LIA)
7. Naskapi-Montagnais Innu Association (NMIA)
8. James Bay "Territory" — James Bay and Northern Quebec Agreement and Northeastern Quebec Agreement (Grand Council of the Cree of Quebec and the Northern Quebec Inuit Association; Naskapis of Schefferville)
9. Conseil Attikamek-Montagnais (CAM)
10. Offshore Islands
11. B.C. Claims

provincial governments and the Cree and Inuit communities of Northern Québec in 1975.

This was followed by the Northeastern Québec Agreement in 1978 and by an agreement with the Inuvialuit of the Mackenzie Delta and the Beaufort Sea region in 1984.

More recently, in September of 1988, an agreement in principle was reached with the Dene and Métis of the Mackenzie Valley. A similar agreement with the Council for Yukon Indians was also reached.

Although overall agreement in principle has not yet been reached with the Tungavik Federation of Nunavut, which represents the Inuit of Eastern Arctic, some 18 subagreements (or more than half of the total foreseen) have been reached and initialled by both parties.

Each of these land claims is distinctive and must take into consideration the unique conditions of history, geography, culture and economic circumstances that exist in the particular region and communities concerned. Still, there is a similar pattern to all of these claims—a pattern set initially in 1973 and reinforced in the government's revised comprehensive land claims policy of 1986. As a result, while there are individual differences, a considerable body of precedent has been established in the terms and conditions provided in these settlements.

When faced with the decision to cede in whole or part their Aboriginal title to certain areas, Native Canadians are naturally concerned that in return they receive benefits that will enable them to prosper as distinct and definable groups. The most basic concern is of course for land. All the agreements are, at heart, land settlements. All designate specific lands which the claimant group will own outright, as well as land-related rights in areas where they have certain interests in perpetuity. But Native concerns go beyond mere ownership of land. Essentially they seek, through these agreements, terms and conditions which will allow them to:

- continue to maintain to the greatest degree possible their traditional lifestyle and culture;
- participate in the decision-making process regarding land and resource management within their claim area, and
- receive a fair share of the economic opportunities and economic benefits that may exist in the claim area.

As a result, these comprehensive claims agreements cover a range of issues besides land and basic compensation. The issues include surface and sub-surface resource provisions, guaranteed rights for wildlife harvesting and fishing, resource revenue sharing, participation in renewable resource management, and environmental protection measures.

Land

All agreements confer on the beneficiaries primary interest over extensive areas of land.

Cash

With respect to financial compensation, in consideration for certainty of title over their settlement regions, all signed agreements provide significant financial compensation packages. These are considered payments in exchange for rights.

Wildlife

Wildlife management and Native control over wildlife harvesting are usually negotiated. These are an important part of traditional Native lifestyles. The agreements in principle or subagreements also provide for harvesting rights, priorities and privileges. For instance, some provide for the right to harvest all species up to the full level of economic, social and cultural needs. And, if there are residual surpluses, Native organizations have harvesting priority. Should surpluses still exist, a limited entry system gives preference to local residents in the allocation of commercial licenses.

Various rights and privileges under these agreements include: permit or tax exemptions; the right to sell, barter, exchange and give freely the harvested wildlife; the right of first refusal for new hunting, fishing and tourism lodges over settlement regions; and the right of first refusal for the marketing of wildlife, wildlife parts and products.

Environmental Protection

All agreements have provisions for the protection of the environment and the Native societies in the settlement areas which spell out the terms and conditions of any future development. These regimes subject all developers to specific duties and responsibilities. For instance, before approval of a project, a developer may be required to conduct prior consultation with local communities, offer compensation and negotiate employment of contractual opportunities.[1]

Economic Participation

The agreements recognize the necessity to preserve Native cultural identity and values, in part through enabling Native people to be more equal participants in Canada's economy.

The comprehensive claims policy provides for resource royalty sharing. For example, the Dene/Métis agreement in principle provides that the Native claimants will annually receive 50 percent of the first $2 million and 10 percent of the balance of royalties from the settlement area.

All agreements in principle and subagreements contain various similar provisions to support the beneficiaries and businesses under their control. These cover such items as access to information relating to business ventures and opportunities, tax exemptions; incentive measures, contract splitting and financial and technical support measures.

Interim Protection

The present policy permits the negotiation of interim measures to protect Aboriginal interests while the claim is being negotiated. They are identified in the initial negotiating mandate. These measures operate over the claimed territory and remain in effect until a final agreement has been signed.

They can impose general or specific obligations on the parties which relate to land and its future development, the protection of traditional hunting, fishing and trapping activities and the other rights that are generally negotiated in a comprehensive claim.

The measures enable negotiations to proceed in good faith, thus lessening the need for court intervention which could have the effect of freezing any type of development in a claimed area. It must be said, however, that the agreement on interim measures does not affect the rights of any party to seek judicial recourse should they consider their interests to be endangered.

Other Provisions

There is a whole range of other provisions in the agreements, covering in substantial detail areas such as access to Native lands, establishment of protected areas, fisheries, social protection, and the incorporation and management of local governments. These are positive measures, intended to provide a genuine opportunity for Native economic and cultural progress.

The terms and conditions of the agreements are established in Canadian law and, under the Constitution, cannot be unilaterally changed. They are not subject to override by other existing laws or by any future legislation that may be enacted. The comprehensive claims process has resulted in long-term agreements between Canadian governments and Aboriginal Canadians—agreements that have in fact, redefined in a truly unique way the relationship between Natives, the Canadian government and other Canadians.

In 1990, the government came under attack because of its handling of comprehensive claims. Natives accused the government of pursuing a goal of extinguishing the "burden" of Aboriginal rights and minimizing its legal obligation. A working group composed of Indian leaders representing Native interests across Canada was established to identify problem areas and recommend change. Later in the year, the policy of restructuring the number of comprehensive claims being investigated to six would be removed. Recent amendments to the comprehensive claims policy remove the idea of "blanket extinguishment" of all Aboriginal rights and allows for the retention of Aboriginal land rights provided these rights do not conflict with the negotiated settlement agreement.

Native groups have also been critical of the land management powers accruing to Native communities under comprehensive claims settlements. While the evidence is not clear, it would seem that the management powers provided in settlements exceed the authority under the *Indian Act*, and settlement agreements are constitutionally protected—section 35 of the *Constitution Act*, 1982. In summary, it has been suggested that the powers given to Indians in comprehensive claim settlements supercede limits set by the *Indian Act* (Clark, 1990).

The Assembly of First Nations claims that the existing comprehensive claims policy excludes self-government provisions (1990a). The federal government has argued that this claim is untrue, but, so far, a legal case has not been brought before the courts for resolution. Native negotiators have sought to settle their land claims and to establish the right of self-determination through the process of self-government. The government is prepared to give "advanced" tribes some legal powers similar to those of a municipality but not additional powers.

Specific Claims

A specific claim deals with treaties and scrip (discussed in Chapter 3) and band claims. It is, as the term implies, specific to a particular concern; for example, a clause in a treaty or land withdrawn from a reserve.

Table 4.2 identifies the number of specific claims that have been submitted. As is clear from the paucity of claims that have been settled, the Office of Native Claims was not acting as a "rubber stamp" for substantiating many Native claims.

The 1984-85 year was an extremely active year for the federal government with regard to land claims negotiations. In addition to receiving 36 new cases, the government completed historical analyses on 33 claims and then referred them to the Department of Justice. Twenty-six negotiations were conducted, involving 52 bands. In addition, two "cut-off lands" were resolved. DIAND estimates that between 1500 and 2500 specific claims will be submitted in total. However, since less than 50 are settled each year, it is possible that the next 40 years will be spent trying to settle specific claims.

Band Claims

A special type of specific claim encompassing the multifarious, scattered claims of individual Indian bands are called band claims. Several categories of these can be identified at present, including claims relating to the loss of land and other natural resources from established reserves, as well as issues pertaining to the government's stewardship of various bands' financial assets over the years. Underlying all these claims is the difficult question of trusteeship.

TABLE 4.2 SPECIFIC CLAIMS IN CANADA UP TO 1991[a]

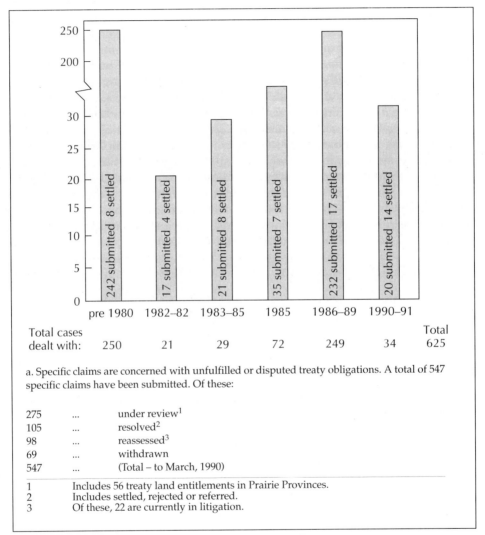

	pre 1980	1982–82	1983–85	1985	1986–89	1990–91	
	242 submitted 8 settled	17 submitted 4 settled	21 submitted 8 settled	35 submitted 7 settled	232 submitted 17 settled	20 submitted 14 settled	
Total cases dealt with:	250	21	29	72	249	34	Total 625

a. Specific claims are concerned with unfulfilled or disputed treaty obligations. A total of 547 specific claims have been submitted. Of these:

275	...	under review[1]
105	...	resolved[2]
98	...	reassessed[3]
69	...	withdrawn
547	...	(Total – to March, 1990)

1	Includes 56 treaty land entitlements in Prairie Provinces.
2	Includes settled, rejected or referred.
3	Of these, 22 are currently in litigation.

SOURCE: *Annual Reports,* Department of Indian and Northern Affairs.

The full story of the government's management of reserve resources and band funds across Canada is only gradually being pieced together from the files of DIAND, from the accounts of missionaries and other White sources, and from the oral testimony of Indian people themselves. Reserve resources include not only land but also minerals, timber and water. Band funds in most cases derive from land and other resource sales.

Where land was surrendered and sold off from reserves, the capital went into band funds, to be administered by the federal government.

Land losses from established Indian reserves account for by far the majority of band claims brought forward to date. Groups of them are probably sufficiently similar to be classified on a regional and historical basis. Grievances arising in New France have certain elements in common, as do Indian claims in the Maritimes, in Ontario, in the southern Prairies, and in British Columbia. The problem of pressure for reserve-land acquisition by speculators and settlers is central to all.

The French, who were the first European power to control the northern half of North America, were the first to establish any sort of Canadian Indian policy. Their approach was dictated by several factors, including geographical distance from the mother country, overwhelming Native military strength, a fur trade economy and negligible White settlement. They sought, if unsuccessfully, the Indian's assimilation into French-Canadian society and saw the converted Natives as equal in civil and legal status to France's European subjects.

There are conflicting interpretations of whether Indian territorial rights were affirmed or extinguished under the French regime; treaties were never concluded for territory either in new France or in Acadia. Land was given to Indians through imperial grace, just as it was to White colonists. However, the Crown, instead of granting such tracts directly to the Native people, handed them in trust to the most efficient civilizing and Christianizing agencies then known, the religious orders. Six Indian reserves were formed in this manner.

At the time of the British takeover in 1760, France's Indian allies had been given land for their exclusive use. By 1851, 230 000 acres (92 000 hectares) were set aside as Indian reserves and a further 330 000 acres (132 000 hectares) were similarly appropriated by the Québec *Lands and Forests Act* of 1922. Additional reserves were created through the transfer of land from the provincial to the federal government by letters patent issued by Québec, through direct purchase by the Dominion from a private party, or through private leases.

The Native peoples of Québec have, over the years, sought increased compensation for land lost from these reserves, settlement of disputes between bands and tribes over reserve ownership, restitution for damages done through logging, fishing and canal construction, and compensation for questionable band-fund management. The existence of these grievances suggests a basic difference in perspective on the part of the Indians and the federal government, which has historically tended to judge the issues solely on their legal merits as determined by the Department of Justice.

In the nineteenth century, for instance, the complaints of the Hurons of Lorette and the Montagnais of Pointe-Bleur against White squatters went unnoticed. Charges that the municipality near the Iroquois' Oka reserve had unjustly taken over land to allow for the construction of three roads were only briefly considered, as was the Caughnawaga claim for land sold as a clergy reserve. The St. Regis

Iroquois' protests against the Québec government's unilateral renewal of leases to, and sale of, islands in the St. Lawrence, along with their claim to compensation for the flooding of additional islands by the Cornwall Canal, were to no avail. Dozens of claims to islands, first voiced in the eighteenth and nineteenth centuries, remained unsettled, and many of the current disputes over expropriation, whether by settlers, clergy or the Crown, go back to these earlier years. At the root of most of this lack of responsiveness is the government's and the court's persistent denial of the Indians' contention that they owned the land initially granted to the religious orders. The denial is based on the grounds that title thereto had been given directly to those orders and not to the Indians themselves.

The arrival of the British in New France, so far as the Indian people were concerned, did not favourably alter the Native's condition. The same could be said for the Maritimes. As British settlement and power increased, large tracts were set apart for Indian use and occupation. Although these lands were called Indian reserves, they were not guaranteed to the Indians through treaties and were subsequently reduced as the land was required for settlement. Further pressures on these reserves in the Maritimes in the early nineteenth century, coupled with problems in dealing with flagrant non-Native squatting, motivated the colonial governments to appoint commissioners to deal with and supervise reserves. These officers apparently had and certainly exercised the right to sell reserve lands without Indian consent. With Confederation, the existing reserves were transferred to the jurisdiction of the federal government, though for a long time the underlying title lay with the respective provinces.

Several claims have been presented to the federal government for past reserve-land losses. Within this category, several main types of claims are emerging. A large number contest the legal status of surrenders of reserve lands. These include submissions on surrenders processed without proper Indian consent, uncompleted sales of surrendered land, sales of lands prior to their being surrendered, lack of letters patent for completed sales, and forged Indian signatures or identifying marks on surrenders. In Nova Scotia, a general claim has also been presented contesting the legality of all land surrenders between 1867 and 1960. This is based on the argument that the Micmac Indians of that province constituted one band; that under the *Indian Act* and its subsequent amendments throughout the period, surrenders could only be obtained at a meeting of a majority of all band members of the requisite sex and age. Another group of Maritime band claims against the federal government arises from the contention that several reserves transferred to the federal government after Confederation were subsequently listed or surveyed by the Department of Indian Affairs as containing smaller areas than the original acreages listed, or were simply never surveyed and registered as reserves at all.

There are also Maritime Indian claims against the federal government's handling of its trusteeship role. The Union of Nova Scotia Indians has put forth a number of claims concerning mismanagement by the government of its obligation to ensure adequate and proper compensation for reserve lands surrendered or expropriated for highway rights-of-way, utility easements and other public purposes.

The sources of Indian claims in southern Ontario are similar to those in Québec and the Maritimes. Probably the bulk of them have not yet been disclosed; at any rate, no formal comprehensive claims statement has emerged. In common with Québec, though, past cases or recorded claims for such losses abound. Some have been rejected by the departments of Indian Affairs and Justice, or by the courts; many, however, lie dormant. It would not be unreasonable to expect these cases, and new contentions based on them, to be advanced in greater numbers in the near future.

Indian people have claimed that unjust cessions and legally questionable government expropriations of reserve lands were common. Government initiatives, along with pressure from White speculators and settlers, were, as usual, dominant factors. The Six Nations' Grand River surrender in 1841, the Mohawks' cession of Ryendinaga Township in 1843, the Moore Township surrender made by the Chippewa later that year, and the 1847 cession by the St. Regis Iroquois of Glengarry County, are prime examples of cases where surrenders were attained under pressure. All these lands were ceded in trust, although there is evidence that the trust provisions were not always upheld. Similar grievances pertain to the government's acquisition of unceded islands. Equally familiar was the variety of expropriation that allowed the sale of individual lots from Indian reserves for clergy and state purposes. Disputes over the status of territory, too, were prevalent. These were generally related to squatter infiltration and occasionally extended into inter-tribal conflicts for reserve lands and, accordingly, for annuities.

The social and economic factors underlying the loss of Indian reserve lands in central and eastern Canada soon found expression on the Prairies. In the years following the making of the treaties and the setting aside of the reserves, the southern prairies were gradually settled. Towns and cities sometimes grew on the very edges of reserves or even around them, and railways ran through them or along their boundaries. As in Ontario, so on the Prairies, reserves located on good farming land were coveted by settlers. For all these reasons, political pressure frequently developed for the surrender of all or a portion of a reserve. In many cases the Indian Department responded by obtaining a surrender of the reserve land in question; proceeds from the sales of such land were credited to the particular band's fund and administered under the terms of the *Indian Act*.

In recent years, the bands and Native associations of the Prairies have clearly articulated several claims arising from previous government policies in relation to land surrenders. At present, they are examining both the justification for these surrenders in general, and the legality and propriety of specific cessions, such as those involving Enoch's Band, near Edmonton. In this case, three surrenders took place. The entire Passpasschase Reserve was ceded shortly after most of the band members left treaty and took Métis scrip. The remaining members moved elsewhere and subsequently the band and its assets were amalgamated with Enoch's Band, residing on the Stony Plain reserve. In 1902 and 1908, political forces largely supported, if not generated, by the minister responsible for Indian Affairs, compelled the surrender of portions of this reserve. In taking the surrenders, government officials used approaches which appear to have been morally and legally dubious. Such questions surround many other surrenders in the Prairie region and also in northern Ontario (Sanders, 1983).

At the heart of many Indian grievances in the northern Prairie provinces is the issue of unfulfilled treaty entitlements to land. Complex in themselves, such claims have been further complicated by the need for provincial assent to any proposed transfer of lands to Indian reserve status. Under the 1930 Natural Resources Transfer agreements, the three Prairie provinces obliged themselves to transfer to the federal government, out of the unoccupied Crown lands, sufficient area to meet unfulfilled treaty obligations. Native people have felt that there has been provincial reluctance to comply with this, and disputes have arisen over the exact nature of the commitments. The Island Lake bands in Manitoba, for instance, have raised the matter of what population base should be utilized in the granting of unfulfilled treaty entitlements. A substantial proportion of the band's allotments under Treaty No. 5 were made in 1924, but the land assigned was approximately 1200 hectares short, if based on the populations at the date and on the Treaty terms. The bands maintain that their total entitlement should be computed using a recent population total, with the 1924 allotment simply subtracted from the new allocation.

In addition, this case points to the inequality among the various treaties' land provisions throughout the West. In common with other treaties in Manitoba, Treaty No. 5 provides for 160 acres (65 hectares) per family of 5, compared with the 640-acre (260-hectare) figure for treaties elsewhere. Since the land in this region of Canada cannot be farmed, an additional inequity is present relative to more southerly fertile regions. The bands contend that a fair solution, satisfying the twin criteria of population data and uniform treaty terms, would be an allocation of almost 120 000 hectares.

In British Columbia, the history of Indian reserves is substantially different from the histories recorded in the other provinces. During the 1850s, when Vancouver Island was still provisionally governed by the Hudson's Bay Company, certain minor surrenders were concluded by the company's chief factor, James Douglas, for several parcels of land there. But these, along with the territory in the northeastern corner of the mainland included in Treaty No. 8, are the only areas covered by treaty. The dual governorship of the two colonies—Vancouver Island and British Columbia—under Douglas in 1858 was soon accompanied by the establishment of comparatively liberal reserves both within and outside the treaty areas. But then, expanding White settlement motivated Douglas's successors to reverse his policy of allowing the tribes as much land as the Indians themselves judged necessary and, accordingly, to reduce the reserves wherever possible. Only with great reluctance did the colonial government allot new reserves in areas opening to settlement.

By 1871, when the colony entered Confederation, Indian complaints concerning the failure to allot adequate reserves and reserve land reductions were already numerous. The Terms of Union that year did nothing to allay these grievances. Fundamentally, the Terms provided for the transfer of responsibility for reserves to the Dominion, and for the conveyance of land for new reserves from the province to the Dominion. Since no amounts were agreed upon, a dispute immediately arose between the two governments over the appropriate acreage to be allotted per family. The province declared 10 acres sufficient; the federal government proposed 80. An agreement establishing an Indian Reserve Commission was concluded in 1875 to review the matter, but there continued to be provincial resistance against attempts to liberalize reserve allotments.

This is just one more source of Indian claims in British Columbia. A recent report by the Union of British Columbia Indian Chiefs, entitled *The Lands We Lost* (1974), details others. They include the by-now-familiar pattern of encroachment by non-Indian people, together with questions about various government surveys and commissions, federal orders in council, and reserve land surrenders. The primary cause of such losses and the major grievance expressed in this regard, was the work of the federal-provincial McKenna-McBride Commission, set up in 1912 to resolve the outstanding differences between the two governments respecting Indian land in British Columbia. The commissioners were appointed to determine the land needs of the Indians and to recommend appropriate alterations to the boundaries of Indian reserves. All reductions were to require the consent of the bands involved, but in practice this stipulation was not followed. The recommendations were subsequently ratified by both governments under legislation that authorized these reductions irrespective of the provisions of the *Indian Act* controlling the surrender of reserve lands. Eventually, some 35 cut-offs totalling 36 000 acres were made, while lands of far less value, although of larger area, were added to the reserves.

In summary, most of the band claims now being dealt with by the federal government have come primarily from the Maritime provinces and the Prairies, with a lesser number from Québec, Ontario and British Columbia. Some of these claims have been submitted to DIAND while others have been channelled through the Claims Commission.

CLAIMS POLICY TODAY

After the 1973 Supreme Court decision with regard to the Nishga Indians in British Columbia, the federal government developed new land claims policy. The new policies on comprehensive and specific claims identified the procedures and limitations of negotiating. The policies also provided the philosophical assumptions (on the part of the government) underlying these policies. These new policies divided land claims into the two types discussed above—comprehensive and specific.

Furthermore, it suggested that the comprehensive claims (British Columbia, Northern Québec, the Yukon and parts of the Northwest Territories) would receive more favourable treatment than comprehensive claims from southern Québec and the Atlantic provinces. However, this policy also specified that Native claims would be dealt with through direct negotiations between DIAND and the Native claimants. The government felt that in southern Québec and in the Atlantic provinces, historical negotiations had taken place between the government and the Indians, however imperfect those negotiations had been. There was some evidence that the government had "taken treaty" with these Indians. However, in British Columbia, northern Québec, the Yukon and in areas of the Northwest Territories, it was clear that no negotiations had ever taken place.

The comprehensive claims policy was adopted in 1981 with the publication of the document *In All Fairness: A Native Claims Policy, Comprehensive Claims*. The policy stated that the federal government was willing "to exchange undefined Aboriginal land rights for concrete rights and benefits" (1981:19). Some of these benefits would entail land, wildlife, subsurface rights and monetary compensation. With regard to land rights, the document stated that lands to be selected by Natives would be limited to traditional lands that they currently use and occupy. It also stated that "third parties" would be fairly dealt with on the issue of subsurface rights and that the government was prepared to grant some subsurface rights in certain areas. Finally, the compensation (in whatever form) was to be "specific and final." However, the policy paper adopted the use of the term Native "interests" rather than "rights."

The process for resolving these comprehensive claims is to follow a negotiating procedure, culminating in a compromise settlement. In summary, Native people are limited in: 1) the scope of what they can negotiate, 2) their standing in relation to other "interests" and 3) the extent of their involvement in trying to settle their claim (Hatt, 1982). The actors involved in the process usually consist of the federal government, the Natives and a provincial/territorial government. Because of the scope of such undertakings, the federal government, until recently, has limited to six the number of negotiations that may proceed at any time. Presently it is negotiating with the council for Yukon Indians, the Dene/Métis of the N.W.T., the Tungavik Federation of Nunavut, the Nishga Tribal Council, the Conseil Attikamek-Montagnais, and the Labrador Inuit Association (Canada, 1985).

In 1982 the government published its policy with regard to specific claims in a document titled *Outstanding Business*. This policy reaffirmed the government's commitment to resolving specific claims and in some respects expanded on the previous role it played in settling claims. As noted previously, specific claims relate to the administration of land or other Indian assets under the Indian Act and to the fulfilment of treaties or other agreements. Under the terms of the policy for specific claims, the process of handling the claims is a combination of adjudication and negotiation. Claims are first submitted to the minister of DIAND, acting on behalf of the Government of Canada. After the claim is submitted, the Office of Native Claims (ONC) reviews the case and analyses the material. The claim and supporting materials (both for or against) are referred to the Department of Justice for advice. On the basis of the Department of Justice's advice, the ONC: 1) negotiates a settlement with the claimant, 2) rejects the claim or 3) returns the claim for additional documentation. If the claim is accepted, the ONC and the claimant negotiate the terms of settlement; for example, land, cash or other benefits. Once the claim has been settled, it represents final redress, and a form release is obtained from the claimant so that it cannot be reopened at some later time.

FIGURE 4.2   CONTRIBUTIONS AND LOANS TO CLAIMANT GROUPS

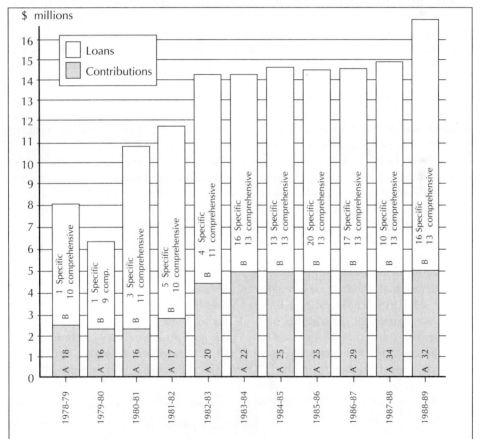

A. The numbers shown in the contributions portion of the chart indicate the number of recipients funded to carry out the necessary research to establish a claim.

B. The numbers in the loans portion of the chart indicate the number of claimants funded that year through loans to carry out research and negotiation on accepted claims.

SOURCE: *Annual Report*, 1987-89, Department of Indian and Northern Affairs, Ottawa, 51.

Because Natives do not have the financial resources to carry out research in order to document their claims, the federal government has made substantial contributions to various Native organizations that are engaged in the research process in order to document their cases. Since 1973, the federal government has spent more than $100 million on negotiations, but has produced only three agreements. More than $22 million (1972-1982) in contributions has been made for research into Native rights, treaties and claims, plus an additional $94 million in loans (1974-1982) (see Figure 4.2). Since the creation of the ONC in 1974, more than $26 million has been spent on the operation and management of the claim process (both specific and comprehensive). If the claim being submitted by the Indians is substantiated and compensation paid, part of the "contribution" portion given to the Indians is repaid. Thus far about $15 million has been repaid by Natives who have signed final agreements. On the other hand, if the claim is dismissed, no repayment is necessary. This infusion of money into Native organizations has enabled them to pursue vigorously many claims which, without the funds, would have never been researched and brought forward.

Figure 4.3 identifies the research contributions and loans provided to Native people between 1984 and 1989 for both specific and comprehensive claims. The graph shows the number of recipients funded to enable them to carry out the necessary research to establish their claim. The graph shows that there has been a steady increase in the number of claimants since the early 1980s. The graph also shows the number of claimants funded through loans to carry out research and negotiation once the claims are accepted as legitimate by the federal government. The data show significant decreases in the funding for specific claims while comprehensive claims funding has remained constant over the past decade.

In 1985, a task force that had been struck to review comprehensive claims policy reported to the Minister of DIAND. The report noted that the negotiating process used up till then to resolve Native claims had tried to incorporate two principles: 1) to encourage the cultural development of Native people and 2) to provide a climate for the overall economic growth of Canada. The government, in dealing with Natives, had argued that Native goals could be best pursued by settling claims through an extinguishment of all Native claims once and for all. Native peoples had not accepted this philosophy. As a result, negotiations had stalled and settlements of various Native claims had been few. The task force recommended that a blanket extinguishment of all Aboriginal rights no longer be an objective. Furthermore, it made the following recommendations.

1. Agreements should recognize and affirm Aboriginal rights.

2. The policy should allow for the negotiation of Aboriginal self government.

3. Agreements should be flexible enough to ensure that their objectives are being achieved. They should provide sufficient certainty to protect the rights of all parties in relation to land and resources, and to facilitate investment and development.

FIGURE 4.3   CONTRIBUTIONS AND LOANS TO CLAIMANT GROUPS: FUNDING FOR COMPREHENSIVE AND SPECIFIC CLAIMS

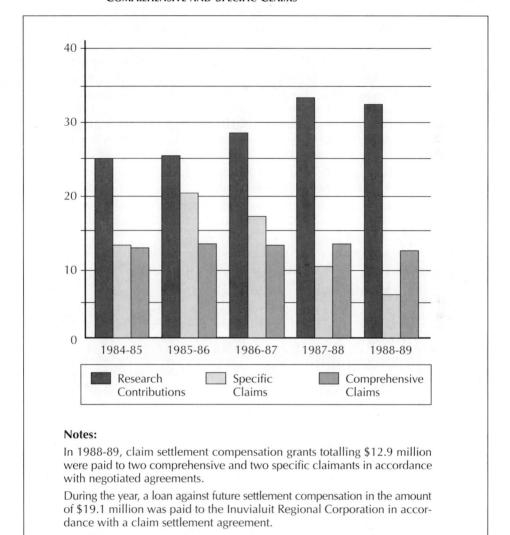

Notes:

In 1988-89, claim settlement compensation grants totalling $12.9 million were paid to two comprehensive and two specific claimants in accordance with negotiated agreements.

During the year, a loan against future settlement compensation in the amount of $19.1 million was paid to the Inuvialuit Regional Corporation in accordance with a claim settlement agreement.

SOURCE: Annual Report, 1989-90, Department of Indian and Northern Affairs, 42.

4. The process should be open to all Aboriginal peoples who continue to use and to occupy traditional lands and whose Aboriginal title to such lands has not been dealt with either by a land-cession treaty or by explicit legislation.

5. The policy should allow for variations between and within regions based on historical, political, economic, and cultural differences.

6. Parity among agreements should not necessarily mean that their contents are identical.

7. Given the comprehensive nature of agreements and the division of powers between governments under the Canadian Constitution, the provincial and territorial governments should be encouraged to participate in negotiations. The participation of the provinces will be necessary in the negotiation of matters directly affecting the exercise of their jurisdiction.

8. The scope of negotiations should include all issues that will facilitate the achievement of the objectives of the claims policy.

9. Agreements should enable Aboriginal peoples and the government to share both the responsibility for the management of land and resources and the benefits from their use.

10. Existing third-party interests should be dealt with equitably.

11. Settlements should be reached through negotiated agreements.

12. The claims process should be fair and expeditious.

13. An authority independent of the negotiating parties should be established to monitor the process for fairness and progress, and to ensure its accountability to the public.

14. The process should be supported by government structures that separate the functions of facilitating the process and negotiating the terms of agreement.

15. The policy should provide for effective implementation of agreements. (DIAND, 1985; 31-32.)

Previous claims were settled through one of two options: 1) by the signing of a final agreement extinguishing all Aboriginal rights or 2) by doing nothing and maintaining the status quo. The proposed policy does not see a settlement as a final agreement but rather as an agreement that will settle immediate issues and define the context for issues that emerge later on. It argues that there is no need to insist on extinguishment of Native rights when a voluntary surrender of rights has been obtained from the Aboriginals. This procedure has been made more acceptable by all parties because of the difficulties that emerged after the signing of the James Bay Agreement, when DIAND found that there were problems of implementation, unresolved disputes, and in some cases a failure to fully implement the agreement in both its spirit and intent (DIAND, 1982a).

The task force suggested several alternatives to the present claims process. Each of the options presented has some shortcomings and will, of course, be subject to interpretation as it is implemented. In addition, the implications of each approach are somewhat unclear at this time. One alternative is to return to the legal technicalities used in pre-Confederation treaties. Specific rights such as land and wildlife harvestry would be subjected to extinguishment or retention. However, the loss or retention of one right would not affect other rights; each would have to be subjected to a court of law.

A second option is to separate land rights from all other rights. Thus land rights could be dealt with by negotiations or through the courts, but would be separate from other Native rights such as culture and religion. Finally, a third option would be to set aside the issue of Aboriginal rights altogether when discussing land rights. Although this would not produce an answer with regard to the existence of Aboriginal rights, it would allow Natives and other parties to carry out economic activities. An example of this approach in another area is that of the federal and Nova Scotia governments' approach to the ownership of offshore rights: the issue of ownership of offshore oil has been set aside so that development of the natural resource could proceed.

Regardless of the option pursued, there will have to be some flexibility in its application, since Aboriginal groups came from different regions, have different interests and operate in different political contexts. The task force has recommended that negotiations continue to be the major mode of settling claims. The force's members felt that litigation fosters an adversarial approach that is not conducive to settling claims and to developing a true social contract between Natives and non-Natives. The task force's report goes on to suggest that prior to negotiations, the process of "scoping" be undertaken. This process, now used in social impact assessments, is that by which important issues and alternatives are dealt with by both parties prior to actual negotiations. The task force also felt that negotiations must deal more expeditiously with Native claims and that Native interests should be protected during the negotiations.

In summary, the task force felt that new approaches to settling Native claims must be undertaken. The policy currently in place has not been effective, either in social or economic terms. If Canada is to continue to develop, these issues must be resolved. At the same time, if Native people are to retain their identity and self worth by developing communities that will actively participate in Canadian society, settlements must be negotiated. As the members of the task force so eloquently stated in their report:

> Much is at stake in working towards consensual settlements with those Aboriginal peoples who have never entered into agreements concerning the destiny of their traditional lands within Canada. In the deepest sense, what is at stake is our identity as a nation that resolves its internal differences not through coercion or domination by the majority, but through agreements based on mutual consent (Task Force, 1985: 101).

In April 1991, the prime minister announced plans to establish a royal commission on Aboriginal affairs. There was also a promise by the federal government to ensure Native participation in the constitutional process and to put more money toward resolving the land claims disputes. Specifically, the government has made a commitment to spend $355 million on resolving land claims over the next five years, four times the amount now spent. The government is also developing "streamlined" procedures to deal with land claims under a half a million dollars. In addition, DIAND will be given complete authority to approve settlements of up to $7 million without having to have the Treasury Board review and accept the proposal. There is a belief that the 250 outstanding claims can be settled by the year 2000.

Defining a Claim

One of the first tasks of the government is to determine the validity of the claim. There must be a determination as to whether the claim is simply a difference of opinion held by one party with regard to another, or whether it is a bona fide claim. A claim is a grievance with a legal basis that is communicated to the second party, either directly or through a third party. When the complaint is communicated to the third party and there is a difference of opinion concerning a right or supposed right, then this is transformed into a *dispute* (Colvin, 1981).

The use of advocates in pursuing a claim and entering into a dispute with the federal government has proven beneficial to the Natives. At times, however, it has been a liability; for example, occasionally the government, rather than attacking the claim, will discredit the advocate and thus weaken both the formal intent of the claim and the willingness of the Indians to continue their case (Daniel, 1980). Nevertheless, advocates have been able to offer Natives a wealth of information (both technical and political) that has helped them in pursuing their claims. At other times, they have even carried the dispute without cost to the Native group. As Daniel (1980) points out:

> ...our research found many instances in which the federal government's disposition towards a claim had the appearance of having been altered to a significant degree by a change in personnel associated with the case... [The] policy with respect to the comprehensive claims of the Chippewas and the Mississaugas seems to have been more liberal after the appointment of R.V. Sinclair, a man known to have been advocate of several claims and an occasional critic of Indian Affairs Policy (216, 146).

There have been a number of other impediments which prevented Indians from proceeding with a claim. For example, the government, until passage of the 1951 *Indian Act*, had to give its approval before another party could take it to court. There also was a time when the government forbade the use of Indian money to support a lawyer to pursue a claims case for them.

The federal government, until recently, held the view that the Department of Indian Affairs alone was responsible for Indians. The idea that Indians have the right to take independent action against the government is a new concept that Indian Affairs officials are only slowly accepting. Because of the impediments mentioned above, we find that Native claims tend to be viewed by most Canadians as a recent activity. However, upon closer inspection, we find the Natives have tried to pursue claims since well before the beginning of the twentieth century. Because of the structure of the bureaucracy and its governing legislation, these claims were either suppressed or simply not defined as bona fide claims. It is only recently that these structural barriers have been lifted to allow the various claims to be presented.

In summary, the federal government, early in the history of Canada, was clear in its policy. The *Royal Proclamation* of 1763 outlined the policy for comprehensive claims, and it codified the process of land surrender. The subsequent treaties, beginning with the Robinson-Huron, 1850, and lasting until the 1920s, suggested that the federal government's policy for dealing with comprehensive claims was well defined. In return for giving up their land rights and pledging to keep the peace, Indians were given compensation, annuities, reserves and "other considerations" even though the contents of the treaties are remarkably similar and generally reflect the fact that they were drafted long before the treaty commissioner was sent into the field to "negotiate" with the Indians. What is contentious at this time is whether or not the terms of the treaties have been upheld and if they haven't been, then what type and amount of compensation should be provided.

Processing Native Claims

Over time, the federal government's strategy for resolving Native claims has changed. In addition, comprehensive and specific claims are dealt with and processed in different manners. Explaining the differences in processing two types of claims means that two variables have to be distinguished in each case: 1) whether or not a third party is involved in the settlement, and 2) the basis of settlement. Figure 4.4 illustrates the various combinations of processing a dispute when the two variables are taken in combination.

Historically, coercion was the major strategy used by the federal government in dealing with Indians and their claims. Later, as treaties were taken with Indians or scrip provided to Métis, elements of negotiation entered into the process, but the central thrust was still that of coercion. As Canada emerged from the turmoil of World War II, the country became a more pluralistic democracy. As Dahl (1967) points out, pluralistic institutions place a high premium on strategies of compromise and conciliation, that is, on a search for consensus. They delay change until there is wide support, thus rendering comprehensive change unlikely. In addition, all parties involved in settling Native claims have come to the realization that legal res-

FIGURE 4.4   Different Methods of Processing Disputes Between Two Parties

| | | Third Party Involvement | |
		yes	no
Basis of settlement	Disputants agree to settle	mediation	negotiation
	Powerful disputant imposes settlement	adjudication/ litigation	coercion

Source: Colvin, 1981.

olutions entail large amounts of time, money and energy—for everyone concerned. Moreover, given the very positivistic orientation of Canadian jurisprudence, Natives have generally found that they have a weak legal case for most of their claims.[2] Finally, as Fudge (1983) points out, Indians are conservative in strategic outlook, emphasizing loss-avoidance rather than risk-taking. As is evident today, comprehensive claims and even some of the larger specific claims have been resolved through negotiation, thereby reflecting this overall philosophy.

Specific claims are generally resolved through the processes of adjudication and litigation. This procedure entails the presentation of evidence from both sides and in the end, the winner takes all. In short, it becomes a "zero-sum game."

Courts and Claims Commissions

Only occasionally have the courts in Canada been asked to adjudicate issues concerning the rights of Indian people. Although there have been exceptions, in general the judicial system has not responded positively or adequately to Native claims issues. In regard to Aboriginal rights, the judiciary decreed that any European colonial power, simply by landing on and laying claim to lands previously undiscovered by European explorers, became automatically the sovereign of this "newly discovered" land. Occupation was taken to confirm that right. The government and the courts both considered Native rights to be matters of prerogative grace rather than obligations that came with the assumption of sovereignty.

Indian people have clearly faced social and cultural obstacles in becoming litigants in a legal system largely foreign to their experience. And even if some might have considered taking action through this forum, they had until very recently little or no capacity to pay the necessary legal fees. As a result, most of the early but significant decisions in the area of fundamental Indian rights have been handed down in cases where the Indian people affected were not directly represented. Many of these cases involved disputes between the federal and provincial governments over questions of land and resources. Indian rights became material to the cases only because the federal government sought to rely upon them to reinforce its own position by citing its exclusive constitutional responsibility for Native people and lands.

As noted previously, what was, until very recently, the only significant case on the question of Aboriginal title in Canada was decided by the Judicial Committee of the Privy Council in 1888. This, the *St. Catherine's Milling* case, involved litigation between the federal government and the province of Ontario over the question of whether the former could issue a timber licence covering land obtained from the Indians and eventually declared to lie within Ontario. The Indians themselves were not represented. The federal government, for its part, argued that it had properly acquired the title to the land from the Indian people; the Judicial Committee of the Privy Council denied that the Native people, at any time, had "ownership" of their land in the sense that Europeans understood the term, and stated "...that the tenure of the Indians, was a personal and usufructuary right, dependent upon the good will of the Sovereign." The Law Lords went on to say that the effect of signing treaties with Indian peoples was to extinguish this "personal and usufructuary right," and to transfer all beneficial interest in the land covered by the treaty immediately to the province. Nearly a century was to pass before the nature of Aboriginal title would receive further consideration by Canada's highest court of appeal.

As has been mentioned, a number of interpretations of the Indian treaties have been put forward by the courts. Some treaties have been regarded as transactions between separate and independent nations; such has been the traditional claim of many Six Nations Indians. Some have been characterized as special protective agreements in which Indian people surrendered their rights to land in return for irrevocable rights conferred upon them by the government. Others have been interpreted as analogous to any commercial contract made at the time with the government. A judgment written by the Judicial Committee in 1867 opted for this last interpretation in a dispute among the attorneys-general of Canada, Ontario and Québec. Indian people thus found themselves constrained by adverse precedent before they could begin to make their own arguments in court.

In addition to the rights at stake, the courts have also dealt with the promise of continued hunting and fishing rights. Their decisions have affirmed the federal government's right to break express promises made by treaty. On occasion, however, the judiciary has questioned the morality of such legislative action. Many of the most fundamental treaty promises regarding social and economic development have not yet reached the courts. It would require a radical departure from established precedent for the courts to give treaties the character granted them by the Indians.

Cases touching the many Native land-loss grievances have, on occasion, come before the courts. Little can be learned about which direction the courts might take in future land-loss claims from a reading of these judgments, since they disclose no clear pattern of judicial thought. Decisions on claims concerning the mishandling of Indian monies have been equally rare and uninstructive. The fundamental question of the relationship between the federal government and Indian people in the areas of land- and monies-management remains legally undefined. Indian people regard this relationship as one of trust, and the federal government has also often referred to it in these terms. This fiduciary obligation places a very heavy burden on the federal government to act in good faith and always to consider the best interests of Indian people as the paramount concern.

As an avenue for Indian claims, the Canadian legal system can only have been seen in Native eyes as an incomprehensible gamble. Only in recent years have the courts responded more favourably to these claims, not by fully and satisfactorily resolving them, but by providing a basis from which the Indian people can negotiate with the government. The realization on the part of both Native and non-Native people in the United States that the ordinary courts were unsuitable forums for the presentation and resolution of Native grievances and claims brought forth a response that has increasingly preoccupied Canadian governmental and Native thought. Efforts that began in the 1930s in the United States to establish a special adjuratory body with powers to hear and determine Indian claims culminated in 1946 with the creation of an Indian Claims Commission. In Canada, the joint committees of the Senate and House of Commons on the *Indian Act* and on Indian affairs, which sat in 1946-48 and 1959-61 respectively, recommended establishing a similar, though more limited, body. As a result, enabling legislation received first reading in the Commons in December 1963, and the draft bill was sent to Indian organizations, band councils and other interested groups for comment. A slightly amended version of the proposal was introduced in June 1965.

The terms of the bill provided for a five-person Indian claims commission, at least one member of which was to be a status Indian, with a chairman who had been a judge or lawyer for at least ten years. The jurisdiction of the commission would have been limited to acts or omissions of the Crown in right of Canada or of the United Kingdom, but not in right of a province. Because of this and because of stipulations about evidence, there was substantial doubt that the commission would have been able to decide on the merits of the Aboriginal title issue in British Columbia, a claim that was one of the main reasons for the creation of the body.

The suggested Canadian commission would have lacked jurisdiction to hear just those classes of cases which, in the United States, formed the bulk of those heard. They included claims for the government's failure to act "fairly or honourably" where land was involved, as well as others requiring that treaties be reopened on grounds such as "unconscionable consideration." The Canadian legislation, on the other hand, would have permitted the commission to consider only failure to fulfil treaty provisions, not the general question of reopening treaties. The bill also ignored the Native organizations that were emerging as a force at that time. Instead, the proposed commission was to be authorized to hear claims only on behalf of bands as defined by the *Indian Act*. Regional Native organizations, however, might not have been recognized as claimants. Furthermore, the commission would have been given authority only to make money awards, not to restore land.

Because of these and other inadequacies, this proposal for an adjudicatory commission met with Indian opposition. On second reading, it was referred to a joint committee of both houses of Parliament, but was allowed to die following the dissolution of Parliament later in 1965. Nothing further was done towards establishing a commission, although the government's intention to do so appeared to be unchanged. In September 1968, the Minister of Indian Affairs stated that he proposed to introduce a bill "in the weeks to come" to establish an Indian claims commission, and he reaffirmed his intention the following December. On this occasion, though, he remarked that the bill had been referred to amendment to the Cabinet committee on Health, Welfare and Social Affairs. This appears to have been the government's last public discussion of the projected commission before the announcement of a new Indian policy in June 1969. This demise was attributed to consultations with Indian representatives and the review of Indian policy which preceded the drafting of the new *White Paper*.

The White Paper and the Indian Claims Commissioner

The first of a series of contemporary responses to Indian claims started with the 1969 White Paper on Indian Policy. This event marked the beginning of new era of unprecedented claims activity. The government proposed an approach that it said would lead to equality of opportunity. This was described as "...an equality which preserves and enriches Indian identity and distinction; an equality which stresses Indian participation in its creation and which manifests itself in all aspects of Indian life" (Canadian, 1969). To this end, the *British North America Act* would be amended to terminate the legal distinction between Indians and other Canadians, the *Indian Act* would be repealed, and Indians would gradually take control of their lands. The operations of the Indian Affairs Branch would be discontinued, and services which had previously been provided on a special basis would be taken over by the federal or provincial agencies which serve other Canadians. Economic development funds would be provided as an interim measure. In short, Indians would come to be treated like all other Canadians: special status would cease.

In laying out these proposals, the government continued to recognize the existence of Indian claims and proposed the establishment of an Indian claims commission, but solely as an advisory body. It was made clear that the government was not prepared to accept Aboriginal rights claims: "These," the paper said, "are so general and undefined that it is not realistic to think of them as specific claims capable of remedy except through a policy and program that will end injustice to Indians as members of the Canadian community. This is the policy that the government is proposing for discussion." Treaty claims, while acknowledged, were also placed in a dubious light:

> The terms and effects of the treaties between Indian people and the government are widely misunderstood. A plain reading of the words used in the treaties reveals the limited and minimal promises which were included in them....The significance of the treaties in meeting the economic, educational, health, and welfare needs of the Indian people has always been limited and will continue to decline...Once Indian lands are securely within Indian control, the anomaly of treaties between groups within society and the government of that society will require that these treaties be reviewed to see how they can be equitably ended.

The government apparently felt that while the central Aboriginal and treaty claims had little virtue and were directly at odds with the proposed policy, there were instances where claims might be accepted. Lawful obligations would be recognized.

Rather than proceeding with the kind of commission discussed in the 1960s, it was decided that further study and research were required by both the Indians and the federal government. Accordingly, the present form of commission was established under the *Public Inquires Act* to consult with the Indian people and to inquire into claims arising out of treaties, formal agreements and legislation. The commissioner would then indicate to the government what classes of claims were judged worthy of special treatment and would recommend means for their resolution.

Given the nature of Indian views on their rights and claims as we understand them, it is not surprising that their reaction to the 1969 White Paper was strongly negative. The National Indian Brotherhood (NIB) immediately issued a statement declaring that,

> ...the policy proposals put forward by the Minister of Indian Affairs are not acceptable to the Indian people of Canada....We view this as a policy designed to divest us of our Aboriginal, residual and statutory rights. If we accept this policy, and in the process lose our rights and our lands, we become willing partners in cultural genocide. This we cannot do.

In the following months, Native groups across the country forcefully and repeatedly echoed this response. When the commissioner, Dr. Lloyd Barber, was appointed in December 1969, the National Brotherhood rejected his office as an out-growth of the unacceptable White Paper, viewing it as an attempt to force the policy on Native people. Indians saw the White Paper as the new articulation of a long-resisted policy of assimilation. The proposal was denounced as a powerful, threatening extension of traditional Indian policy in Canada.

In rallying to oppose this apparent challenge to their rights, the Native peoples in turn produced extensive statements of their own positions. While difficulties were encountered in arranging for research funding, sufficient government monies were made available to finance some of this work. The resulting statements, together with concerted legal and political action on the part of Indians, led to significant changes in the government's approach.

An early response occurred in August 1971, when, in reply to submissions from the Commissioner and Indian leaders, then Prime Minister Trudeau agreed that the Commissioner would not be exceeding his terms of reference if he were to "hear such arguments as the Indians may wish to bring forward on these matters in order that the government may consider whether there is any course that should be adopted or any procedure suggested that was not considered previously." The Commissioner took this to mean that he was free to look at all types of grievances and claims, including Aboriginal rights issues.

In August 1973, the government made a substantial change in its position on Aboriginal rights by announcing that it was prepared to negotiate settlements in many areas where these had not been dealt with. Then in April 1975, on the basis of proposals developed through consultations between Indian leaders and the Commissioner, the government accepted an approach to the resolution of Indian claims based upon negotiation.

This new policy would take the issue of land claims out of the legal arena and provide an alternative forum to solve problems. This also meant that there could be greater flexibility in introducing and using certain documents—for example, historical and anthropological ones—in the negotiating process. In addition, the government felt that this process would also provide a forum which would take into account the interests of nonclaimant groups who reside (or have an interest) in an area that could be affected by a settlement. Finally, and perhaps most importantly, it was believed that the process would allow for transforming the Aboriginal-rights concept into concrete and lasting benefits. In addition, the process would be final and not subject to being reopened at some later time.

This procedure had been attempted in 1890-91 when a three-person board of arbitrators was appointed to settle disputes between the Dominion and the provinces of Ontario and Québec. Claims were presented by the Department of Indian Affairs on behalf of the Indians. Twenty cases were heard by the board, but few were resolved since the cases generally became embedded in federal-provincial conflicts. In addition, because the board had no final adjudicator, its power, by the turn of the century, waned into insignificance. With few exceptions, the Indians derived no benefit from this board of arbitrators.

To facilitate the process of negotiation and to stem the tide of Native opposition to DIAND, the government formed a joint NIB-Cabinet committee in 1974. Its role was to identify and address issues that Indian people felt had to be resolved. As Morse (1985) explains, in order to facilitate this, the Canadian Indian Rights Council was established as an independent body to act as a secretariat for the joint committee. Four years later, the joint committee was dissolved because of lack of progress.

Not all Indians, however, were prepared to give up this process. The four Ontario Indian associations approached DIAND with a proposal to create a new structure that would be applicable to Ontario. As a result, new tripartite councils have been created. The Indian Commission of Ontario, for example, assists the three parties (federal, provincial, Indians) in resolving Indian claims. As Daniel (1980) points out, the functions of the commissioner include arranging mediation to resolve issues that have been authorized by the tripartite councils. However, the commission lacks the institutional structure that could facilitate the processing of a large number of claims, for example, it does not have the authority to bring legal pressure to bear on recalcitrant parties, nor the legal powers necessary to provide an incentive for compromise.

While coercion was widely used in the late eighteenth and nineteenth centuries, the process of resolution of Native claims has changed over time. Negotiation has become the accepted strategy, even though it presupposes that the two disputants are of equal power. But since Natives are not equal in power to the government, it has become clear that this important precondition for negotiation has not been met (Dyck, 1981). In certain cases, the government has tried to equalize that power, for example, through the provision of loans to Native groups so that they can research their claims. Nevertheless, a new strategy for resolving Native claims, one of mediation, is slowly emerging. Modern-day claims, therefore, are not to be viewed solely in a legal context. Many legal experts and politicians are beginning to agree the issues are more of a political than a legal nature. As former Justice Minister Otto Lang stated:

> We have legal questions raised about (claims) and non-lawyers particularly love the legal questions; love to think that the caveat of the court will decide the issue. But probably it is not so. The important questions are political ones (From personal correspondence with the author, 1974).

As Watson (1979, 1981) points out, each group (non-Native and Native) attributes to the other a failure to redeem debts. Native tradition states unequivocally that non-Natives owe them for the land they provided, which permitted White settlement to proceed unhindered. Non-Natives, on the other hand, view treaties as a thing of the past and of small consequence. As a result, they do not acknowledge a debt to Natives. However, these positions are not inflexible, and they are modified and abandoned when opportune. The negotiating of claims, then, is not carried out by a strictly reasoned legal argument, but by public bargaining over symbolic provisions.

Differing Perceptions

We have identified the changes which have taken place over time in the way Native claims are regarded and approached. And we have described the process by which claims are dealt with. It is clear that even when the procedures are carefully identified, substantial differences between the two parties—the government and the Natives—remain. It is important to identify the perception and definition of treaty claims (both comprehensive and specific) held by the Crown, on the one hand, and First Nations, on the other. The Crown views comprehensive claims as a strategy which addresses Aboriginal rights claims. They feel that this policy will sort out land and resource rights among the various stakeholders in Canada and ensure that Aboriginal claims are upheld. To achieve these goals, they have outlined a process by which the claim is prepared, data collected to support the claim and a format established by which the claim is reviewed.

From a First Nations perspective, the policy on claims does not provide any recognition or affirmation of Aboriginal rights, a position they find untenable. They feel that the sole objective of the policy is to extinguish Aboriginal rights for all time. They note that the process for submitting a claim has become increasingly complex and requires extensive research, time and financial resources. There is the feeling that because of these factors, they are becoming less and less involved in the process. Furthermore, they feel that the final settlements established thus far have been biased in the interests of the federal government, developers and multinational companies, while Native peoples' benefits are minimized.

The process of settling a claim is also seen differently by the two parties. The federal government has adapted, for all practical purposes, the criteria outlined in the *Baker Lake* case. More recent developments in case law—i.e., *Sparrow, Sioui, Simon*—which bear directly upon Aboriginal rights, are not accounted for in the current policy. This lacuna is the focus of a major dispute between the Crown and First Nations. Furthermore, the process of settling claims has, until recently, been limited to six comprehensive cases. This means that there continues to be a large backlog of claimants (as of 1991 it is estimated that the number is 26). These claimants have no protection of their interests as they wait for the negotiations to proceed or the courts to hear their case. This has meant, in some cases, that the Native interests were prejudiced before the negotiations began.

Once the process begins, the Crown requires both a detailed agenda which negotiations will follow and a statement limiting the issues to be negotiated. Natives claim that these frameworks are imposed unilaterally by the federal government and limit the scope of issues to be negotiated as well as the substantive issues to be included in the negotiation process. While the federal government takes the position that Native people do not have to negotiate, if they do not, their only recourse is through the courts. Alternatively, the federal government may unilaterally take action. Furthermore, Native people feel that, although they are not forced to negotiate, many pressure tactics—such as funding allocations—are used by the federal government to ensure they do negotiate. The scope of negotiations is also perceived very differently by the two parties. The Crown, in carrying out negotiations, argues that it is prepared to give Natives rights and benefits on such issues as land ownership, participation on management boards, resource revenue sharing, hunting and trapping, as well as financial compensation. Aboriginals argue that their rights regarding the issues identified by the federal government are exchanged for legislated benefits.

They further point out that not only are their rights redefined as benefits, the nature and scope of those "benefits" are limited. For example, under current negotiations, there is no recognition of Aboriginal ownership of subsurface resources; also, participation on management boards is restricted and subject to ministerial veto. This redefinition of issues also means that Native concern with self-government is not negotiated because it is simply defined as being outside the scope of the negotiations.

The process of settling comprehensive claims is viewed by the federal government as Aboriginal extinguishment of all land rights. Although the federal government correctly points out that the current policy does not require surrender of all lands, in practice the policy does not allow retention of Aboriginal title and does not confirm it. Natives are also concerned that provisions in the claims may prejudice the future clarification of other Aboriginal rights.

There is also concern by Natives that when a settlement is made, the cost of carrying out the extended process means that payments must be made to the Crown for loans and interest on those loans. Their concern is at two levels. First when negotiations are being carried out, the federal government monitors the loan funds to ensure the funds be used only as they (the federal government) say. Any attempts to use the funds in a manner not prescribed by the federal government will result in the funds being withdrawn. Secondly, Natives find the principle of loan funding offensive. They are expected to pay from their compensation the costs of negotiation which was brought about by the illegal actions of the Crown. Furthermore, in the settlements, the federal and provincial governments benefit.

This last point is also a source of dissatisfaction on the part of Natives. The federal government has allowed the provinces to enter the negotiation process when they think it is necessary. Native people, on the other hand, argue that provincial involvement is a violation of federal fiduciary responsibility. Furthermore, provincial governments are often a major obstruction in the negotiation process and have, in many cases, vetoed negotiated settlements.

Specific claims are also seen differently by the two parties. Differences between the two stakeholders begin with the historical bases of the claim: the Crown chooses to talk about "assuming responsibility for Indians and lands reserved for Indians" at the time of Confederation; Indians argue that the First Nation-Crown relationship was confirmed by the *Royal Proclamation* of 1763. And, Natives argue, the federal government's responsibility toward Aboriginal people goes well beyond the *Indian Act*; a claim that has support in several decisions by the Supreme Court. Finally, Natives are concerned that many issues such as taxation, fishing and water rights cannot be dealt with under the process of specific claims.

Funding is another source of friction between the two parties. The federal government notes that bands are funded to research their specific claims. Indians acknowledge this but point out that the funding is inadequate, and too many restrictions are placed on how the funds can be used. In other words, because the funds can only be used the way the federal government dictates, many claims are inadequately researched and therefore are not accepted by the Crown as legitimate.

Once the claims are researched, documentation is submitted to the federal government and analyzed by the Specific Claims Branch of DIAND. While this description of the procedure is correct, it is also deceptive, claim the Native people: the description hides (or, at least, fails to make clear) the protracted debate over the potential legal merit of the case—what is referred to as the clarification process. This process usually takes years and requires time, money and effort on behalf of the claimants. Usually the Specific Claims Branch simply refuses to submit the claim to the Justice Department (which rules on the claim) until the Native group submitting the claim agrees to make the claim conform to the government's policy. In short, justice is obtained, but only under the rules as defined by the federal government. Perhaps even more disconcerting is the federal government's use of "discounting" in negotiating with the specific group that has submitted the claim. Discounting is the process by which one party offers compensation to another party on the basis of the degree of probability that the case could be successfully fought in the court system. In other words, if the Specific Claims office feels that the Native claim has a good chance of winning in the courts, the offer of compensation is high. Conversely, if they feel that the case does not stand a good chance in the courts, offered compensation is low. This, of course, runs counter to the generally accepted practices of law, and forces Natives to accept something less than justice.

Natives also point out that in the negotiation process, the definition of the claim itself undergoes changes. Thus, Natives might submit one type of claim, but by the time the Specific Claims Branch and the Justice Department review and accept the case the specifics of the claim may be very different than when first submitted.

The Department of Justice then rules on the claim and takes action accordingly. Natives point out that the Minister of Indian and Northern Affairs has the right to deal with claims in ways that go beyond strict legal obligations. However, thus far the minister has never done so. Furthermore, when a claim is rejected, Native people are not allowed to see the legal opinion which rejected their claim. They only receive a notice which rejects their claim and a vague, general rationale as to why the claim was not accepted. Once the rejection has taken place, there is no mechanism for appeal. Natives have long argued that some sort of independent mediation or arbitration process should be put in place to deal with claims that are rejected on questionable criteria.

The Assembly of First Nations has argued that there should be an elimination of the distinction between the two types of claims—comprehensive and specific. In their submission to the Coolican Task Force, they called for a First Nations rights policy. This new policy would take away the artificial distinction of claims and allow for other issues to be dealt with.

RECENT CLAIMS

There are four modern comprehensive Native claims that have been settled in recent times. The first, in Alaska (1971), became the model for Canadian settlements in James Bay (1975), the Western Arctic (1984), and more recently for proceedings in the Yukon, where an agreement has not yet been signed. These settlements involve three major components: land cession to the Natives, financial payment for cession, and the creation of corporate structures to deal with land, money or environmental issues. For example, the James Bay Agreement created land settlements for the Cree and Inuit in the area. It also provided for the payment (over 20 years) of $225 million, as well as indirect financial compensation in the form of a "guaranteed annual income." In addition, Native corporate and political structures were established.

In the Western Arctic (under the COPE Agreement), the Inuvialuit will be given $45 million (1977 dollars), 11 000 square kilometres of land, and will develop an Inuvialuit corporate structure. The third settlement, involving Yukon Indians, will involve the payment (over 20 years) of $190 million (1983 dollars) in exchange for "extinguishment of Aboriginal rights." In addition, the Indians will be given legal title to and mineral rights for 20 000 square kilometres. A smaller, yet significant, agreement took place in 1991 when the Gwichin of the MacKenzie Delta ratified a land claim agreement with the federal government. The agreement provides ownership of over 4000 square kilometres of land, including subsurface rights to some of this land, as well as a financial payment of $75 million over 15 years. The Yukon Agreement is somewhat different from the others in that it could be characterized as a "one government" model, under which the Indians will participate as full partners in the mainstream of Yukon society rather than operating separately within the more traditional reserve system. In addition, both status and non-status Indians will be treated alike—sharing equally all settlement benefits (Frideres, 1986).

In British Columbia, direct action by Natives in the 1970s and '80s prompted the federal government to reevaluate its policy and programs. Although the provincial government has continued to deny the existence of Aboriginal title, by the late 1980s it became more responsive to Aboriginal concerns. The Ministry of Native Affairs and The Premier's Council on Native Affairs were created to meet with Native groups regarding a range of Aboriginal issues. In 1990, the British Columbia government agreed to establish a process by which Aboriginal land claims could be received and placed on the negotiating table. In August, 1990, the province of British Columbia agreed to join Natives and the federal government in negotiating land claims settlements. This meeting resulted in the creation of a tripartite task force to develop a process for negotiations. By late 1990 this task force was created, and in June, 1991, it submitted its report. The report recommends that a British Columbia Treaty Commission be established, and outlines a six-stage process for negotiating treaties. At present, all parties to the process are beginning to evaluate the Task Force's Report (1991) and prepare for the first round of negotiations.

Specific and band claims are also being resolved. For example, in the mid-1980s the Long Lake No. 58 Indian band of Northern Ontario received nearly $200 000 in settlement of their outstanding claims, which centred on the transfer of 43 hectares of reserve land for the construction of Highway 11 in 1941. A negotiating process involving the Indian Commission of Ontario, the band and DIAND led to the settlement. Other examples of specific claims settlements include the Wagmatcook Indians of Cape Breton Island, who, in 1982, nearly a decade after making their claim, received $1.2 million for compensation of original reserve lands taken without proper authority. However, no responsibility was accepted by the federal government for lands alienated by Nova Scotia before Confederation. In B.C., the Penticton band received over $14 million and 5300 hectares of land in 1985 in compensation for reserve lands lost in 1916. A tripartite agreement was reached in 1991 when the Nuwitti Band accepted 17 hectares to be returned to the Hope Island Indian Reserve. Also in 1985, the Whitedog Indian Band of northwestern Ontario, after 20 years of seeking compensation for the flooding of reserve land, signed an agreement with Ontario for $3.8 million, 1700 hectares of land and additional compensation to resolve economic and health problems.

In 1983, the Ormocto Indian band of New Brunswick received $2.5 million under the specific claims policy. The claim was based on evidence suggesting that the surrender of 29 hectares of land by the band in 1953 was improperly conducted. This settlement also required that the band repay $43 000 in loans received from the government. Finally, it allowed the band to purchase rural land (up to a value of $.5 million), which will be granted reserve status.

In 1984, the Chemainus band in British Columbia settled their cutoff claim against the province and the federal government. The band will receive $700 000 plus the return of nearly 24 hectares of land. In Saskatchewan, the White Bear claim in 1984 was the first major specific claim to be settled. The band received over $16 million and a large parcel of land to be added to the reserve. The claim was based on the argument that the lands of the Ocean Man and Pheasant Rump reserves were wrongfully sold in 1901, when those two bands were amalgamated with the White Bear band.

Even in Québec, which has not treatied with Indians, specific claims are being settled. The Desert River band in western Québec has been offered a $2.5 million settlement for land that missionaries took illegally about 100 years ago. In Ontario, in 1984 the Grassy Narrows Indian band ended the claim it filed in 1977 by accepting $4.4 million. In addition, the federal settlement will alleviate various social and economic problems that have beset band members after mercury was dumped into the Wabigon/English river system from a paper mill in Dryden, Ontario. The monies received from the federal government will be used by the band's economic development corporation ($2.9 million) and social service development and planning corporation ($1.5 million). In addition, the federal government has agreed to help promote a settlement of outstanding issues between the band and the companies involved, the provincial government, and various provincial agencies. In 1985, the Minister appointed Emmet Hall as his personal representative to facilitate negotiations between the band and the private companies—Great Lake Forest Products Ltd. and Reed Inc.—and the Ontario government.

In 1991, the Stoney Indian Band signed the second largest specific claim ever settled in Alberta. The historic settlement agreement provides $19.6 million in compensation to the tribe for loss of mineral rights on land surrendered in 1929 for hydro development. In Saskatchewan, the specific land claim of the Kawacatoose Band was accepted for negotiation in 1991; and a land claim settlement was signed by the Island Lake (Ministikwan) Band, the federal and provincial governments resolving a claim dating back to 1914. Finally, in 1991 an agreement was reached between the Mohawks of the Bay of Quinte and the federal government whereby lands held under the 1835 Turton Penn lease agreement will gradually be returned to Indian control.

The outcomes of these modern-day settlements, like the treaties of the past, are now coming under serious question. For example, operational and funding procedures of the James Bay Agreement are not functioning properly, and the Natives are not obtaining what they expected to get out of it. A more serious question has arisen in Alaska—nearly two decades after an agreement was signed. In that settlement, 12 regional and 225 village corporations were established to regulate and monitor the land and money distribution (18 million hectares of land and $1 billion). Over the past decade, through mismanagement of funds, poor business invest- ments, and a general "bust" in the economy of Alaska, many of the regional cor- porations have fallen heavily in debt. Should the debt continue to increase, in 1993, when shares of these corporations can be sold to non-Natives, payments will be demanded by creditors. Having already expended their cash resources, the only means of repaying the debt will be to sell shares in the corporations and thus shares in the land. The end result might be that the Natives of Alaska will have settled their claim, received their compensation, spent the cash settlement and then have had to sell their land. In the end, they will be worse off than they were before the settlement was made (Berger, 1985).

For Canadian Natives, this recent revelation has called into serious question the wisdom of pursuing the Alaska model for settling comprehensive land claims. This is one reason for the impasse in negotiations presently taking place in the Yukon. Alaska Natives are asking that the federal government reopen the agreement (a process possible under American law but not under Canadian law) and return to a system of reserves, reestablish a trustee-ward relationship, and dispense with the corporate-model structure.

A similar argument to reopen the treaties might be made for Canada. The White Paper introduced by the government in 1969 brought to the collective at- tention of Canadians the problems of Natives and their claims. This was but- tressed by the Supreme Court decision in 1973 (Nishga case) and the Berger Commission (1974), which both gave some credence to Native claims.[3] However, over the past decade, the public interest and support have waned (Ponting, 1987). The issue of land claims has been overshadowed by other concerns such as cruise missiles, acid rain, constitutional reform, health care, energy policies and French-language issues. Settling land claims is an issue that is slowly fading into the background, and this will mean reduced interest in and support of Native claims on the part of White Canadians. National surveys carried out in 1990 show that less than five percent of the people questioned felt that Native- White problems should be the first in our national priorities. The environment, senior-citizen issues, "independence" and women's issues were cited as having higher priority than Native issues. It would seem, then, that the government's commitment to settling claims is a one-time deal, and Natives, consequently, are well aware that failure to achieve a settlement now may mean that the issue will be shifted to a lower priority and require a heavier investment of time, money and energy sometime in the future. On the other hand, to settle now, under existing conditions, may mean that by the end of the twentieth century their land and culture will be lost.

COMPREHENSIVE LAND CLAIMS: CASE STUDIES

1. JAMES BAY

The James Bay and Northern Québec Agreement (1975) and the Northeastern Québec Agreement (1978) required the federal and Québec governments to enact special legislation in respect to local government and land administration for Natives in the area. Between 1976 and 1979 a number of bills were passed to enact the agreements. Thirty-one boards, committees, commissions and councils were established in order to deal with the organizational structure that resulted from the agreements; for example, the Cree School Board, the Income Security Board, and the Cree Trappers' Association. (See Figures 4.5 and 4.6). The agreements also required that the traditional financial arrangements between Natives in the area and the federal government be changed as bands began to take on more and more political control and accountability. The new agreements (confirmed in the Cree/Naskapi Act, 1984) provided for:

1. funding for local government, safeguarding of community infrastructure and delivery of essential services;
2. the determination of funding needs;
3. the principle of local autonomy and the elimination of unnecessary central administration;
4. unconditional grant funding; and
5. grants that will be submitted to Parliament annually based on give-year agreements (Indian and Native Program, 1985; 261-262.)

In return for the Cree allowing Phase I to proceed, they received $136 million from the Québec and federal governments. This money was invested in the Cree Regional Economic Enterprises (CREECO) and the Cree Regional Authority Board of Compensation. CREECO dominates the Native economy with $36 million in revenues and through its control of the airways and housing projects. Both companies have expanded and created hundreds of jobs. However, profit is slow to come, and CREECO registered a $5.2 million deficit in 1989. In addition to the above revenues, CREECO obtained over $30 million in Hydro-Québec contracts in 1989 and over $50 million in 1990. This has created permanent jobs for the Cree and changed their lifestyle considerably. With assets of over $140 million, the Cree have invested in Québec government bonds, debentures and blue chip stocks (they were required under the terms of the Agreement), thus generating over $11 million revenue. Other monies received were used by communities to build infrastructure and develop creative investments; e.g., Waskaganish Enterprises

Development Corporation entered into a joint venture with Yamaha Motors Canada to build fibreglass freighter canoes.

Proponents of Hydro-Québec's James Bay development, which will divert and store the waters that flow into James Bay and Hudson Bay, feel that the production of 26 000 megawatts of power is reason enough for its existence. The original project altered the flow of several rivers in the region. When the water from the

FIGURE 4.5   AREAS AFFECTED BY THE JAMES BAY HYDRO-ELECTRIC PROJECTS

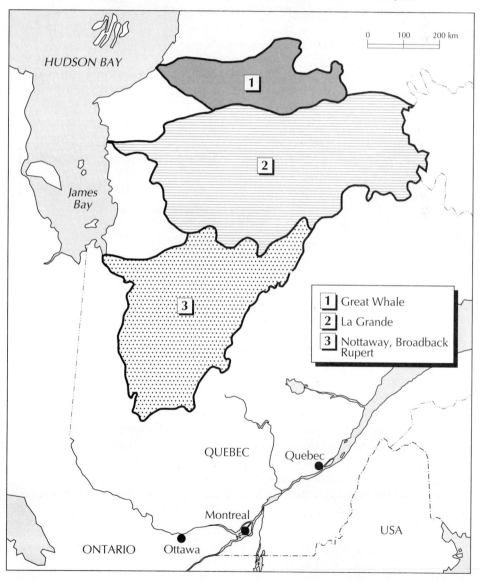

FIGURE 4.6 THE JAMES BAY HYDRO-ELECTRIC PROJECT

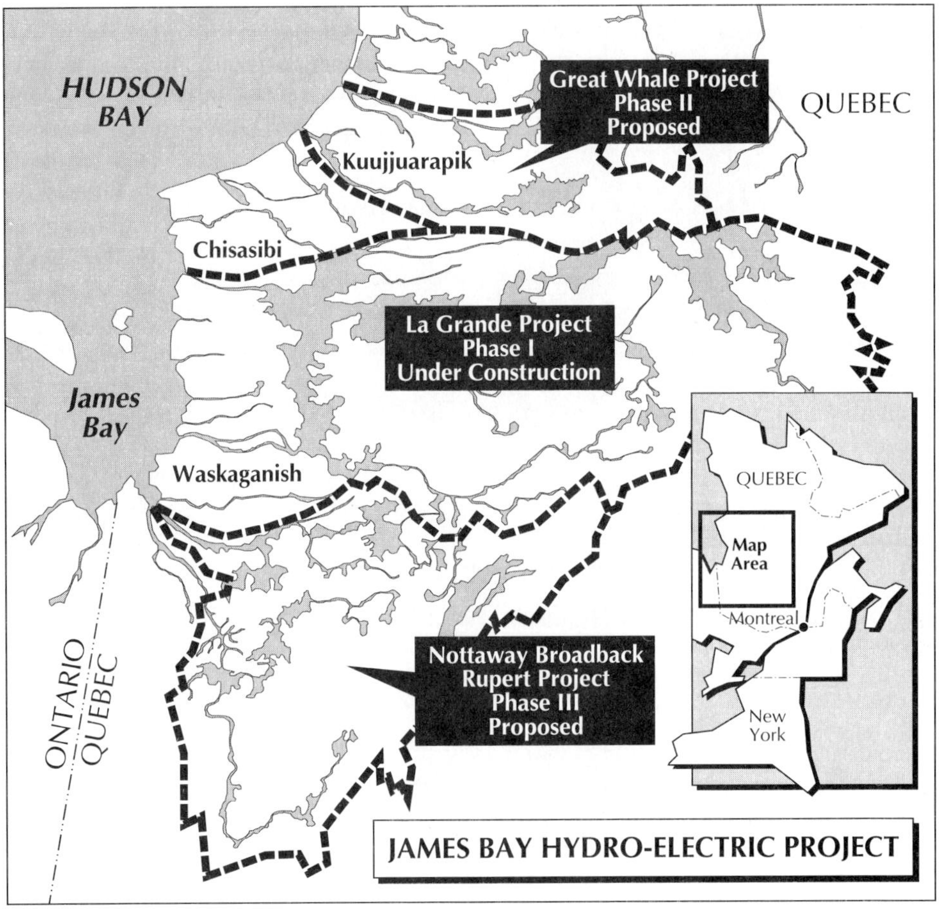

Caniapiscau River was first diverted to a reservoir, the volume (19 billion cubic metres) was so great, a minor tremor was felt.

The battle over this $50-billion project has once again come to the foreground, now that the first phase has been completed (in 1984) and the provincial government is moving into the second stage. Nineteen years ago, the Cree (10 000 of them) fought against development but eventually agreed to allow the project to proceed after the provincial and federal governments agreed to compensate them.

Today, as Phase II begins, the Cree have asked the court to declare the original settlement "null and void" because the agreement was based upon the assumption that hydro-electric power development was compatible with the Cree way of life—this, the Cree argue, is not true. In Phase I, Hydro-Québec erected 215 dams and dikes and more than 10 000 square kilometres of new lake was created. Some consequences were not anticipated; for example, flooding released mercury from the bedrock and thus contaminated certain fish. But the more dramatic and significant consequences are the social impacts. The sudden modernization and urbanization of a previously nomadic society will have immediate and long-term effects.

The Québec government is now beginning to assess La Grande Phase II (to be completed in 1995), Great Whale (to be completed in 1998) and the Nottaway-Broadback-Rupert project (slated for completion in 2007). Estimated construction costs for these three projects is over $35 billion (1991 dollars). However, there has been substantial Native resistance to the proposed project, as Phase II will involve five claims and will affect an additional 10 000 square kilometres of land (almost two percent of the total area of Québec). At present, preliminary negotiations are going on with the Inuit, who are the major group to be affected by Phase II (unlike Phase I which affected the Cree).

Today 50 percent of the people in Northern Québec are unemployed. The tradition of community food is no longer part of the customs. Alcoholism, substance abuse and wife beating are rampant, as are suicide attempts. On the other hand, the villages established now have water, sewage, electricity and schools. Children no longer have to be sent to southern schools to be educated in English.

2. COUNCIL FOR YUKON INDIANS (CYI) CLAIM

The CYI, representing all people of Yukon Native ancestry (approximately 6500), was formed in 1973. It united the Yukon Native Brotherhood and the Yukon Association for Non-Status Indians for the purpose of negotiating their claim, originally entitled "Together Today for Our Children Tomorrow" and submitted to the federal government on February 14, 1973. Between 1974 and 1979, a number of attempts were made to reach negotiated settlement of the claim, but in each case they failed to achieve agreement.

Renewed and intensive negotiations, begun in 1980 with the appointment of a chief government negotiator, led to the initialling by the negotiators for Canada, the Yukon Territorial government and the CYI of an overall Agreement-in-Principle in January 1984 covering all major settlement issues, including the selection of land and local government for most of the Yukon bands. The Agreement-in-Principle was formally approved by the federal government in April 1984 and was ratified by a majority of Yukon bands by July 1984.

However, at general assemblies in August and October 1984, the CYI passed resolutions calling for the renegotiation of major elements of the Agreement-in-Principle. It also called into question the support of those bands that had already ratified it.

After the announcement of the new federal Comprehensive Claims Policy in 1986, a new mandate for the CYI claim was developed. Negotiations resumed in 1987 and an Agreement-in-Principle, which was ratified by all parties, was signed in May 1989. It provided for cash compensation, land ownership including the subsurface, and self-government arrangements. An umbrella final agreement and individual agreements with each of the 13 Yukon Indian bands were signed in late 1991.

The Yukon First Nations Self-Government Agreement allows for the First Nations to integrate traditional decision-making structures with contemporary forms of government.

The institutions and structures of government will be defined by the First Nations themselves through constitutions which will not be subject to approval by other levels of government, but will be subject to the *Charter of Rights and Freedoms*. There also will be a general requirement in the self-government legislation to ensure that mechanisms for political and financial accountability are in place. The specific mechanisms will be defined by the First Nations in accordance with their traditions and values.

One key feature of these arrangements is that First Nation governments will be directly accountable to their citizens.

First Nations will have law-making powers of a local and private nature on settlement lands. Examples of these powers are:

- use, management, control and protection of settlement lands;
- planning, zoning and land development;
- control or prevention of pollution and protection of the environment; and
- licensing and regulating of any person carrying on any business, trade, profession or other occupation.

First Nations will also have selected powers over their citizens on and off settlement lands. Examples of these powers are:

- provision of health, social and welfare services to citizens;
- provision of programs and services related to First Nations language;
- guardianship, custody, care and placement of First Nations children, except licensing and regulation of facility-based services off settlement land; and
- provision of services for resolution of disputes outside the courts.

Exercising these powers will require coordination with the government of the Yukon. The agreement makes provision for the Yukon and First Nation governments to take action to protect individuals in situations of actual or imminent danger irrespective of the jurisdictional arrangements.

First Nation governments will also take on the responsibilities outlined in the Umbrella Final Agreement. Examples of these responsibilities include participation in decision-making bodies such as the Renewable Resource Councils, Development Assessment Board and the Surface Rights Board. Federal laws will continue to apply, and the laws of the Yukon government will continue to apply until the First Nation passes its own laws to replace them (to the extent it is empowered to do so by the provisions of the agreement).

Funding for First Nations governments will be provided through multi-year funding agreements from the federal government that will enable First Nations to determine their own priorities and allocate resources accordingly.

The principles of the Yukon First Nations Agreement were put to the test when the Na-Cho Ny'a'k Dun Natives completed their negotiations with the Yukon government. This agreement was attached to the 1990 Umbrella Final Agreement and became, to a certain extent, the model for future negotiations with other Natives in the Yukon; e.g., Teslin Tlingit Council, Champagne and Aishihik. The overall Agreement with Natives in the Yukon provided for $257 million (1988 dollars) in cash compensation and over 40 000 square kilometres of land—approximately 9 percent of the Yukon. More than half of this will include Native subsurface ownership. In the Na-Cho Ny'a'k Dun agreement, Natives will control nearly 900 square kilometres of settlement land and own the subsurface rights to about half. Other wildlife agreements are also part of the settlement.

3. DENE/MÉTIS CLAIM

This claim has been under active negotiation since 1981. Following almost three years of intensive negotiations, the prime minister and Dene/Métis leaders of the Mackenzie Valley formally signed the Dene/Métis Comprehensive Land Claim Agreement-in-Principle on September 5, 1988, in Fort Rae.

Approximately 11 000 Indians and 2000 Métis, constituting approximately 40 percent of the population of the area, inhabit 27 communities in the Mackenzie Basin of the N.W.T. The Agreement provided certainty of rights and title to the use of land and resources for the Dene and Métis, the government, and the people of Canada. It was to provide the Dene and Métis with ownership of 181 299 square kilometres of land, including 10 101 square kilometres of subsurface ownership; financial compensation of about $500 million; and a share of any resource royalties the government collects in the future. Participation in public government management boards was guaranteed to the Dene/Métis for land use planning, environmental impact assessment, land and water management, and wildlife management.

The agreement was rejected by the Dene/Métis annual assembly in 1990. It was then agreed that the five Dene/Métis regions would have the option of pursuing regional settlements based on the Agreement. Community self-government will be under discussion in a forum completely separate from that of the land claim.

4. INUVIALUIT (WESTERN ARCTIC) FINAL AGREEMENT

The Committee for Original Peoples' Entitlement (COPE) representing approximately 4500 Inuvialuit living in six communities in the Western Arctic Region and originally part of the general Inuit claim, submitted a separate claim in May 1977 in the light of anticipated pipeline construction in their area. An Agreement-in-Principle was signed by COPE and the federal government on October 31, 1978. It dealt with land, wildlife, financial compensation, eligibility, corporate structures, and economic and other measures. In May 1979, agreement was reached on 85 percent of the remaining lands over which the Inuvialuit would have surface rights. In 1982 a series of meetings culminated in the preparation of an aide memoire which identified the agreed-upon major elements remaining to be negotiated.

At that time, there was extensive discussion of contentious issues arising from the Agreement-in-Principle. The Final Agreement was approved in May 1984. Parliament subsequently passed the *Western Arctic (Inuvialuit) Claims Settlement Act* on June 16, 1984. A secretariat, established within the Northern Program of Indian and Northern Affairs Canada (INAC), oversees implementation of the Act.

Under the settlement, the Inuvialuit received specific rights and benefits in exchange for relinquishing their interests based upon traditional use and occupancy. These rights and benefits include title to 91 000 square kilometres of land, (13 000 square kilometres with full surface and subsurface title; 78 000 square kilometres excluding oil, gas and specified mineral rights), cash compensation ($45 million in 1977 dollars), wildlife harvesting and management, economic measures (including a $10 million Economic Enhancement Fund) and Inuvialuit participation on advisory boards dealing with land use planning and environmental management. The Inuvialuit have also signed bilateral agreements with the Council for Yukon Indians, the Dene/Métis and the Tungavik Federation of Nunavut resolving their overlapping interests in the Inuvialuit Settlement Region.

With reference to the relationship of the Western Arctic Agreement to territorial interests as a whole, laws of general application apply to all Inuvialuit lands as they do to all other private property. The government continues to regulate development activities and remains ultimately responsible for environmental management.

Inuvialuit lands remain subject to easements and rights of way which existed as of July 13, 1978. The public has a right of general access along navigable rivers and the right to cross Inuvialuit lands to reach other lands. While Inuvialuit lands may be leased, they cannot be sold except to other Inuvialuit or to the Crown. In the event Inuvialuit lands are needed for public purposes, they can be so acquired subject to the provision of alternative lands or financial compensation. Inuvialuit lands are except from property tax but improvements, as well as proceeds from development of Inuvialuit lands, are taxable in accordance with the laws of general application.

5. TUNGAVIK FEDERATION OF NUNAVUT (TFN) CLAIM

The Tungavik Federation of Nunavut (TFN), formed in summer 1982 to take over the claims negotiation role of the Inuit Tapirisat of Canada (ITC), represents over 17 000 Inuit in central and eastern N.W.T. The Inuit claim to the area was first presented by ITC in February 1976 and has since undergone a number of revisions.

Early negotiations resulted in little progress because of debate over establishment of a new territory—Nunavut. Following meetings with the Minister of Indian and Northern Affairs in 1980, the Inuit agreed to proceed with land claims negotiations on the understanding that their aspirations for Nunavut would be dealt with outside land claims. Intensive negotiations got underway in late 1980 resulting in the initialling of wildlife provisions of an Agreement-in-Principle in October 1981, subject to review by the government and by the Inuit. Following this review, the amended provisions were reinitialled by the government and TFN in May 1986.

A government decision in November 1982 approving the principle of division of the N.W.T., (and consequently the possible establishment of Nunavut) created a favourable climate for further progress towards a land claim settlement.

The Cabinet approved a mandate in December 1987 to complete an Agreement-in-Principle with TFN. Through 1988 and 1989, subagreements covering most of the main elements of a claim settlement were concluded. The main elements of the AIP include a total of approximately 350 000 square kilometres of land, which includes 36 257 square kilometres with sub-surface rights, and financial compensation of $580 million.

The general provisions of the agreement are:

- the Final Agreement will be a land claims agreement within the meaning of section 35 of the Constitution Act, 1982;

- close consultation between the government and the Inuit shall take place in the preparation and/or amendment of legislation proposed to ratify or implement the Final Agreement;

- that in exchange for the rights and benefits in the Final Agreement, the Inuit of the Nunavut Settlement Area as represented by the Tungavik Federation of Nunavut will cede any Aboriginal claims and title they may have to lands and waters in Canada;

- that any other existing or future constitutional rights that the Inuit may have are not affected, and the ability of Inuit to benefit from government programs is not affected; and

- that the devolution or transfer of jurisdiction or powers from Canada to the territorial government will not be restricted, provided Inuit rights delineated in the Final Agreement are abrogated.

In 1991, Nunavut (our land) was created and covers over 300 000 square kilometres—a fifth of the land area of Canada. After 15 years of negotiation, a settlement was finally established. The boundaries were approved by the people in the Northwest Territories in a 1992 plebiscite and will need to be ratified by Parliament. This new territory will be self-governing, but will not have the full powers of a province. In addition to receiving money from any mining or oil development in the area, the Inuit will receive 50 percent of the first $2 million in royalties received by the federal government and 5 percent of the remaining royalties. A wildlife management board will also be established to govern hunting and trapping activities. To facilitate the political transition, the federal government has set aside over $13 million to help the Inuit develop their territorial government.

NOTES

1. The Canada-U.S. free trade agreement does not change the negotiated rights of Indian and Inuit people. The responsibility for determining the pace and conditions of exploration and development remains in Canada.

2. Judges taking this stance narrowly define concepts and words. For example, a positivistic judge would interpret the term "medicine chest" (as used in a treaty) as a "small wooden box with an assortment of medicines and bandages for injuries." A more liberal interpretation would be to define the term in the context in which it was being used as well as within that of the twentieth century. As a result, some judges have defined the concept as "universal health care" because Indians were trading their land for health services available at that time. Now that health services have expanded and become more comprehensive, it does not mean that Indians are not eligible because they agreed to a "medicine chest."

3. In 1974, the federal government appointed Mr. Justice Thomas Berger to conduct a social and environmental impact assessment on the proposed pipelines which would cut across the Mackenzie Valley, where they would eventually connect with the existing pipeline system. Soon after his appointment, Berger de-

clared that he would visit all communities in the North that were likely to be affected and solicit their assessments and recommendations. He also held hearings in major urban areas in southern Canada. After more than two years of hearings, he submitted the first of two volumes of his report to the minister of DIAND—*Northern Frontier, Northern Homeland.*

His recommendations were straightforward. He did not recommend against building the pipeline but rather concluded that a ten-year moratorium be placed on its construction in order for the Native people to prepare themselves for such a project, to settle the land claims they had with the federal government and to allow further testing of some "state of the art" technology being proposed in the construction of the pipeline.

In the end, the federal government accepted Justice Berger's recommendation not to build the pipeline at that time and chose an alternative route. However, due to hydrocarbon finds in British Columbia and Alberta, the decline in the price of oil and gas, as well as other social, economic and political factors, the entire idea of transporting hydrocarbons from the North to the South was dropped.

CONCLUSION TO PART I

The historical relations between Natives and non-Natives have set the stage for today's negotiations between them. Natives are convinced that their treaties represented international agreements and confirmed their status as a sovereign group. They are also convinced that they were cheated by government officials. Buttressing their position is their sense of moral outrage when they look at their position in Canadian society compared to that of the newcomers, the non-Natives. Government officials on the other hand, take the position that the treaties were not agreements between sovereign states, but that they were legal and binding and that Natives got a "good deal" when one assesses the costs over the past century. Neither believes the other and each is convinced that they have been, and continue to be, taken advantage of by the other. Natives, relying on the questionable procedures used in the treaty "negotiations" by government officials, feel they were cheated and deserve compensation well in excess of that which was given. They use a twentieth-century mindset and economic sense to evaluate what were, for the most part, nineteenth-century deals. Government officials, using a legal approach to assess the Canadian government dealings with Natives, point to the written agreements. The courts have also taken this approach, although more recently they have begun to broaden their approach in interpreting the legal agreements and assessing the historical contexts in which they occurred.

Which of the two positions is correct? The answer, unfortunately, is locked away in history and we will never really know. It is difficult to interpret events that took place well over a century ago. To rely on the written records gives credence to only one position. We are only too painfully aware today of how non-Whites, Aboriginals, and other minority groups were abused in Canada in the past (Berger, 1981).

On balance, history would seem to support the position that non-Natives and their elected officials took both a philosophical and practical approach in dealing with Natives that would not be acceptable today. First, they viewed Aboriginal peoples as less than human and incapable of having any kind of civilization. Concurrent with this view was the pressure being placed on government officials to expand the country's land base so that immigrants could settle the land and farm it. The economy developed by Native peoples was not conducive to population concentrations nor was it compatible with large-scale agricultural activities. The conflict began in the seventeenth century and it has not yet subsided. The Canadian government took an expedient approach to solving the problem of developing Canada and handling Natives. The wisdom of such a policy is still being debated.

The reaction of Native peoples to the various treaties, to the creation of reserves and to other government legislation was initially one of disinterest. They had thought they were signing peace treaties, and they found that life was not much different after signing the treaties than it was before. Changes were slow to materialize, and it would not be for many years that Natives would begin to understand the implications of signing the treaties. However, by that time, the social fabric of mainstream Canadian society had changed. The two solitudes had been created and it was difficult for Native peoples to consider from their vantage point that things could change. They looked around at the conditions in their own community, at those in other native communities, and they concluded that this was simply the way life was. By the end of the nineteenth century, this passive acceptance of a way of life was established, and it would not be for another half century that Natives would be stirred into action and attempt to change their position in Canadian society.

The strategy utilized by Natives to reassert themselves has been an interesting choice. Having had some success in forcing the government to settle "land claims," the Natives chose this path to follow. Since land was considered an integral part of Native culture, it provided a moral, philosophical and even religious significance that could be used to justify this strategy. Their early claims were met with hostility and disbelief, and those that made it into the legal arena were usually unsuccessful. But there was the occasional victory and it became clear that the government could not ignore a legal challenge. This particular strategy also succeeded in promoting solidarity among the different Native groups.

Since the end of World War II, a new moral ethic has emerged which gives legitimacy to the Native cause. Indian organizations have emerged and created a leadership that understands the legal and bureaucratic structures of various forms of government. This leadership came out of the cohort that had been educated in mainstream Canadian society; consequently, they understood the rules of the dominant group and were able to adapt them to their own goals and strategies. This was perhaps an unintended consequence of the push in the late 1960s to assimilate Natives into the mainstream of Canadian society.

Aboriginal land claims are based upon the premise that under the *Royal Proclamation* of 1763, all lands not having been ceded or purchased by the Europeans, remained part of the reserves set aside for Indians. In a sense then, all of Canada was, at one time, a reserve. Only those lands ceded, by treaties or otherwise, to the Europeans are not part of the "Indian Reserve"; hence all nontreatied lands are Indian lands.

Native people do not view their rights solely in terms of legal claims. They view the claims process as a vehicle by which they can establish their constitutional rights. Because only the courts exist as an alternative, many Native groups have little choice but to use the claims process as a way of proceeding with their attempt to assert their Aboriginal rights. Native people (along with some support by Canadians) argue that experience shows that attempts to deal with Native claims through the existing process have been a failure. Nevertheless, the *Sparrow* (1990) case clearly noted that Section 35 of the *Constitution Act, 1982* is a solemn commitment to Aboriginal peoples which must be given meaningful content by the government's legislation, practice and policy.

PART 2

Native people comprise numerous sub-groups, each reflecting its own goals and objectives. Whether the divisions between groups reflect language, cultural or legal differences, Native people nevertheless all have a bond formed by their subjective feelings of Nativeness or by objective conditions of living a marginalized life. We begin Part II with a detailed statistical profile of Native people to illustrate their socio-economic position in Canadian society. Our statistics also reveal developments or trends over time as well as presenting a "comparison group," so the reader is better able to interpret the information.

The reader should be advised that the statistical information presented in this book emanates from a number of different sources; as a result, the "totals" from various tables may not always agree. These discrepancies are a results of different definitions of the concepts under investigation. Despite these minor discrepancies, however, statistical information is essential to assess and determine the success of federal policies and programs developed to help people. However, the continuation, change or elimination of these programs is not solely a result of the statistical evaluation. Political decisions are quite different from academic ones, and this must be borne in mind by the reader.

As the government began to view the "Indian Problem" as being within its purview, it created a special organization to deal with its "wards." The result has been the emergence of a federal mega-department, unable to solve the problems it confronts. Nevertheless, this organization has developed a myriad of programs and projects across the country in its attempt to improve the quality of life for Native people. Thus far, it has had little success. This complex, highly mobile organization is currently undergoing changes never before experienced. The acceptance of self-government for Natives has had a profound influence on the department's operations and its members.

The role of Native women in both their own culture and that of Canadian society has been sorely neglected. Colonization had a tremendous impact on the role and function they have played within their own community. Nevertheless, through time, Native women have continued to play an important political role. This role may not be readily visible to non-Natives; but within the Native community, their actions are taking on increasing importance. Their actions coalesced when they began to fight against discriminatory sections of the *Indian Act*, e.g., section 6(1)(2). Their successful fight against this provision led them to realize that concerted political action could bring about change. The active role of the Native Women's Association of Canada in recent unity discussions underscores their resolve to bring "women's" issues to the political forefront.

While Canadians have flocked to urban areas over the past thirty years, Native people have resisted this allure. While about one third of the total Native population could be classified as urban, most have retained their rural ties. Nevertheless, Natives are influenced by the growing metropolis. The influence of cities on the countryside has been pervasive, and the structures of Native society have been profoundly altered because of this influence. At the individual level, Natives, at some point in their life, come face to face with entering the urban milieu, either temporarily or permanently. Their adaptation to city life has not been a successful one and most return to the reserves or rural communities where they were born.

The last chapter in Part II focuses on the Native organizations that have emerged over the past two decades. Native organizations have changed in both structure and focus. They have evolved from small, local issue-oriented organizations to organizations that are national, complex and highly institutionalized. Many are capable of implementing programs supported by the Canadian government but are unable to implement their own. Today, Native organizations are being forced to form alliances both with other Native organizations and with "mainstream" Canadian institutions in order to provide their clients with the skills and support necessary.

The interplay of the bureaucratic structure of government and the organizations of Native people has gained national attention when major issues are being discussed. For example, the role of the Native Council of Canada or the Assembly of First Nations has received considerable press over the past five years as these organizations have been involved with constitutional issues and the question of unity. At the same time, local organizations have not received the attention they require. More emphasis will need to be placed on helping the grass-roots organizations if Natives are to effectively bring about change.

CHAPTER 5

DEMOGRAPHIC AND SOCIAL CHARACTERISTICS

INTRODUCTION

The demographic and social attributes of any people must be known if meaningful policies and programs are to be established. Every five years the federal government undertakes a national survey in order to collect information about Canadians. Every ten years a census is undertaken which collects data from every Canadian. This systematic collection of data allows government (federal, provincial, municipal) to assess its current programs and policies as well as project into the future what will be required. It is for that reason that DIAND also collects information on Native people.

Statistical information about Native people is collected by both Statistics Canada and the Department of Indian Affairs and Northern Development. There are other agencies which also collect data on Native people; however, the three major national agencies collecting information on Native people are the Vital Statistics Section of the Health Division of Statistics Canada, the Decennial Censuses of Canada and DIAND. Unfortunately all three differ widely in their terms of reference and in their method of enumeration; as a result, statistics coming from one agency are not strictly comparable with statistics from the others. At present, no attempt has been made to reconcile the statistics produced by these major sources.

Needless to say, the lack of standardized data severely limits the accuracy of short-term trend analyses and makes future projections difficult. Moreover, because the definition of an Indian has changed over time, statistics reported by different agencies show wide discrepancies; in some cases, revised definitions of Indian status have meant that statistics related to a certain group are no longer appropriate.

Our socio-demographic profile of Natives in Canada will begin with a discussion of population growth, including births, deaths and migration. It is a mark of the confusion brought about by unclear and inconsistent definitions that the meaning of migration has been expanded to include those who have been redefined either as Indian or non-Indian.

POPULATION GROWTH

It is crucial for policy and program analysts to have information regarding the size of the population they are dealing with. They must also be clear about the growth rate. The figures in Table 5.1 show a five-fold increase in the absolute size of the registered Indian population over the past century. During the same time period, however, the Indian population has come to constitute a smaller and smaller portion of the total population, decreasing from 2.5 percent in 1881 to 1.2 percent in 1990. During the 1950s the rate of increase for registered Indians was 3 percent. While this

TABLE 5.1 Population of Native people in Canada, 1881-1984

Year	Registered Indian population
1881	108 547
1901	127 941
1929	108 012
1939	118 378
1949	136 407
1954	151 558
1961	191 709
1966	224 164
1971	257 619
1974	276 436
1981	323 782
1984	349 000
1986	403 042
1991	521 461
1992	531 981

SOURCES: Information Canada, *Perspective Canada I* (Ottawa: Queen's Printer, 1974), 240; *Perspective Canada II* (Ottawa: Queen's Printer, 1977), 282; Siggner (1986), 3; *Native Agenda News*, March, 1992.

TABLE 5.2   ABORIGINAL POPULATION BY PROVINCE; SINGLE/MULTIPLE ORIGIN,[a]
1986.

	Inuit		Métis		Indian	
	Single	Multiple	Single	Multiple	Single	Multiple
Canada	27 285	9180	59 745	91 865	286 230	262 730
Nfld.	1810	2315	265	1170	1745	2955
P.E.I.	—	30	40	125	375	740
Nova Scotia	135	180	225	850	5570	7485
N.B.	15	180	185	560	3685	5015
Québec	6470	890	5700	5740	37 150	26 440
Ontario	680	2285	3715	14 560	51 160	99 560
Manitoba	185	515	14 205	19 015	40 965	14 990
Sask.	45	155	12 215	13 475	43 385	11 830
Alberta	300	830	16 880	23 250	34 490	34 475
B.C.	240	790	3930	11 360	56 955	55 835
Yukon	35	30	80	140	3165	1605
N.W.T.	17 380	975	2205	1610	7585	1785

a. Ethnic origin is determined by individuals claiming identification with one (single) or
more (multiple) ethnic group.

Source: Statistics Canada, "Population by Ethnic Origin and Sex, Showing Single and Multiple
Origins, for Canada," 1986 Census—20% Sample Data, Catalogue 93-109, 2.21-2.25.

increased to 3.4 percent by the late 60s, it once again decreased to 2.8 percent in
the early 1970s, where it remained until the mid 1980s (see Table 5.3). With the introduction of *Bill C-31*, the registered Indian growth rate increased to over 7 percent
and averaged well in excess of 6 percent until the 90s when it decreased to about 2
percent. These growth rates must be compared to the general Canadian growth
rate of about one percent over the past decade.

The overall Aboriginal population (Indian, Métis, Inuit) is growing very fast. It
is estimated that by the twenty-first century, the Aboriginal population will be in
excess of 1 million. Figure 5.1 shows the proportion of the Canadian population-
constituted by Natives for 1981 to 2001. Projections show that from 1981 to 1991,
on-reserve Indians have increased their population by one-third. During this same
period, off-reserve Indians will have more than doubled. Inuit increased their population by one third during this time also (see Figure 5.2). In summary, status
Indians and Inuit will continue to have higher growth rates than the Canadian
population for several decades.

TABLE 5.3 POPULATION GROWTH OF STATUS INDIANS: TOTAL, ON AND OFF RESERVE, 1981-2001

Year	Total status Indians, both sexes		On-reserve Indians both sexes		Off-reserve Indians both sexes	
	Total population	Growth rate	Total population	Growth rate	Total population	Growth rate
1981	336 900	—	237 600	—	99 300	—
1982	345 400	2.52	245 900	3.49	99 500	0.20
1983	354 400	2.61	253 300	3.01	101 100	1.61
1984	364 700	2.91	261 000	3.04	103 700	2.57
1985	376 400	3.21	268 000	2.68	108 400	4.53
1986	403 042	7.08	275 891	2.94	127 151	17.30
1987	431 439	7.05	282 671	2.46	148 768	17.00
1988	458 807	6.34	291 485	3.12	167 322	12.47
1989	485 186	5.75	299 869	2.88	185 317	10.75
1990	510 905	5.30	308 727	2.95	202 178	9.10
1991	521 461	2.07	316 273	2.44	205 188	1.49
1992	531 981	2.02	323 855	2.40	208 126	1.43
1993	542 426	1.96	331 457	2.35	210 970	1.37
1994	552 799	1.91	339 070	2.30	213 729	1.31
1995	563 082	1.86	346 711	2.25	216 371	1.24
1996	573 269	1.81	354 379	2.21	218 890	1.16
1997	583 356	1.76	360 599	1.76	222 757	1.77
1998	593 346	1.71	366 808	1.72	226 538	1.70
1999	603 271	1.67	373 027	1.70	230 245	1.64
2000	613 117	1.63	379 258	1.67	233 860	1.57
2001	622 901	1.60	385 514	1.65	237 387	1.51

SOURCE: Indian and Northern Affairs Canada, *Highlights of Aboriginal Conditions, 1981-2001, Part I: Demographic Trends*, 1989, 21.

In 1990, registered Indians made up nearly 2 percent (1.8) of the total Canadian population. They are generally affiliated with one of the 596 bands in the country, and approximately three-fifths resided on the 2284 reserves and Crown land. Table 5.2 identifies the Aboriginal population by province and ethnicity.

Table 5.3 identifies the registered Indian population and average annual growth rates for both on- and off-reserves. Other data show that the growth rates are extremely high, as the population more than doubled in size since 1966. The estimated Indian population by the end of the twentieth century will be over 600 000. These data also show that in 1966, 80 percent of the Indians lived on a reserve; by 1990, this had decreased to 60 percent.

FIGURE 5.1   ABORIGINAL GROUPS: PROPORTION OF CANADIAN POPULATION, 1981, 1991, 2001

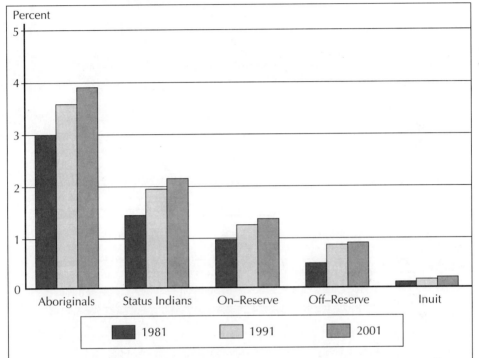

- Canada's aboriginal populations are growing rapidly. Most aboriginal groups will increase their proportion of the Canadian population by 2001, except non-status Indians.

- The percentage of all aboriginal peoples in the Canadian population will have increased by one-fifth in the short-term, from 3.0 percent in 1981 to 3.6 percent, in 1991. The long-term increase will be more gradual, to 3.9 percent by 2001.

- The proportion of Canadians who are status Indians was 1.4 percent in 1981. This will have increased substantially by 1991. The long-term increase will be more gradual, to 3.9 percent by 2001.

- Growth in the proportion of Indians on-reserve is expect to be from 1.0 percent in 1981 to 1.2 percent in 1991 and 1.3 percent in 2001.

- The off-reserve Indian population will have doubled its share of the Canadians population by 1991, from 0.41 percent in 1981 to 0.77 percent. It will increase only marginally in the long-term, to 0.81 percent by 2001.

- Population projections for the Inuit forecast that their percentage share of the Canadian population will not change substantially due to their small population size, from 0.11 percent in 1981 to 0.12 percent in 1991 and 0.14 percent in 2001.

SOURCE: Highlights of Aboriginal Conditions, 1981-2001, Part I, Demographic Trends, INAC, 1989, 5.

FIGURE 5.2 CANADA'S ABORIGINAL POPULATIONS, 1981-2001

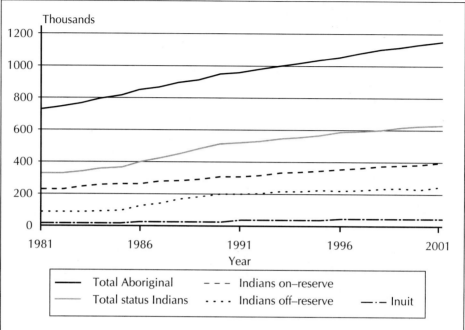

- By 1991, the estimated population of Canadians with aboriginal origins will increase nearly one-third, from 735 500 in 1981 to 958 500. In the long-term, a further one-fifth increase to 1 145 100 is projected by 2001.
- The total status Indian population will have grown by one-half by 1991 to 521 500, up from 336 900 in 1981. By 2001, the number of status Indians will increase another one-fifth to 622 900, almost double the 1981 figure.
- By 1991, the number of Indians on-reserve will have increased one-third to 316 300, up from 237 600 in 1981. In the long term, the projections estimate a population of another one-fifth, to 385 500 in 2001.
- The number of Indians off-reserve will have more than doubled by 1991, from 99 300 in 1981 to 205 200. There will be little population growth between 1991 and 2001, when the off-reserve population is projected to be 237 400.
- The Inuit population has a projected growth to 1991 of nearly one-third, from 25 900 in 1981 to 33 400. By 2001, another one-fifth increase is project, to 40 900, over one and a half times the 1981 figure.

Source: Highlights of Aboriginal Conditions, 1981-2001, Part I, Demographic Trends, INAC, 1989, 4.

TABLE 5.4   REGISTERED INDIANS AND INDIANS REGISTERED UNDER *BILL C-31*: AVERAGE ANNUAL GROWTH RATES, CANADA, 1981-2001

Year	Registered Indians			Average annual growth	
	Excluding *Bill C-31*	*Bill C-31* population	Total	Excluding *Bill C-31*	Including *Bill C-31*
1981	323 782	0	323 782		
				2.59	0.00
1982	332 178	0	332 178		
				2.95	0.00
1983	341 968	0	341 968		
				2.00	0.00
1984	348 809	0	348 809		
				2.82	3.28
1985[1]	358 636	1605	360 241		
				3.16	7.66
1986	369 972	17 857	387 829		
				2.40	7.24
1987	378 842	37 056	415 898		
				2.71	6.73
1988	389 110	54 774	443 884		
				2.65	5.06
1989[2]	399 433	66 904	466 337		
				3.66[r]	5.75[r]
1991	429 178	92 282	521 461		
				1.99	1.91
1996	473 559	99 710	573 269		
				1.78	1.67
2001	517 226	105 675	622 901		

1. In 1985, the *Indian Act* was amended to allow, through *Bill C-31*, the restoration of Indian status to those who had lost it due to discriminatory clauses in the *Indian Act*. The reinstatement process was expected to be largely completed in 1990/91.

2. The high annual growth rate between 1989 and 1991 is due in part to the upward adjustments of the Indian Register for the purposes of the projections and to the Department's estimate of 86 000 *Bill C-31* registrations in 1990/91 plus the growth due to natural increase.

3. Totals may not add up due to rounding.

r. Datum revised.

SOURCES: Indian and Northern Affairs Canada, *Basic Departmental Data*, 1990, 7; 1981-1989: Indian Register, DIAND; 1985-1989: Membership and Entitlement Directorate, DIAND; 1991-2001: *Population Projections of Registered Indians, 1986-2011*, DIAND, 1990.

In June 1985, amendments were made to the *Indian Act* (*Bill C-31*) which restored Indian status and membership rights to individuals and their children who lost them because of discriminatory clauses—e.g., 12-1(6)—in the previous *Indian Act*. Table 5.4 reveals the Indian population changes with and without *Bill C-31* additions. At the outset, fewer than 2000 people were reinstated. However, by 1989 these new registrants represented nearly 15 percent of the total registered Indian population, and it is estimated that by 1991 they will make up nearly one fifth of the Indian population. Table 5.4 shows that the annual growth rate has consistently exceeded 2 percent. However, when *Bill C-31* Indians are added to the figures, the growth rate increases to an astounding 6 percent.

Three factors affect the overall growth rate of the Native population: the birth rate, the death rate and the rate at which people lose or gain Indian status. It is important that decisions-makers have a clear picture of the impacts of each of these factors with a view to predicting long-term changes.

The natural increase (births minus deaths) for the Native population has been declining over the past 30 years because of a rapidly declining birth rate. For example, in 1921, the crude birth rate for Natives was over 50 per 1000 population. By the 1970s this rate had decreased to 28.5, and by 1991 was reduced further to 22.2; still nearly double the national average.

Romaniuc (1984) has noted that the decline in the birth rate can be deduced from looking at the child/population ratio. The ratio of children under five years of age to the total Indian population fell from 19 percent in 1961 to 13 percent in 1981. Further evidence of fertility decline can be inferred from the average number of children born to ever-married women 20-24 years of age. This was 2.3 in 1961 but fell to less than 1.5 in 1991. At the same time, the childless ever-married women in the age category 20-24 went up from 11 percent in 1961 to 28 percent in 1991.

The birth rate is significantly influenced by the average age of marriage. Although, overall, the proportion of married Indians is lower than the national average, the proportion of married Indians in the highest-fertility age group of 20 to 24 exceeds that of non-Indians. Moreover, the fertility of Indians between 20 and 24 appears to be twice the Canadian average.

The average number of children by age group also reflects changes that have taken place in Native communities. In 1986 Native women had an average of 3.8 children compared to 2.5 for non-Native women. When controlling for age, we find that the older Native women (65 and over) had 6.3 children during their child-bearing years (3.2 for non-Native); 6.1 children for Native women 45-64 (3.3 for non-Native women of this age). There are, however, considerable regional variations in Native birth rates. Native women living in Eastern Canada have similar fertility rates to those of non-Native women, while Native women in the Prairies have much higher rates.

The second factor in determining the growth rate of a population is the mortality rate. Traditionally, the mortality rates for Native people have been very high, with

FIGURE 5.3   LIFE EXPECTANCY AT BIRTH, STATUS INDIANS AND ALL CANADIANS, 1981, 1991, 2001

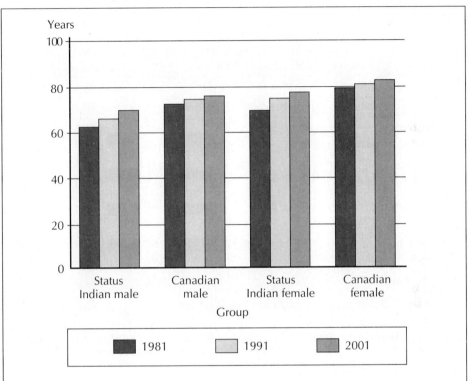

- Life expectancy at birth for status Indians is increasing and will continue to increase. Between 1981 and 2001, the life expectancy at birth for status Indians is expected to increase by 8 years for both sexes.

- Nonetheless, non-Indians live longer than status Indians. In 1981, the life expectancy at birth for status Indians was approximately 10 years less than that of the national population, the same as it had been 20 years earlier.

- While the life expectancy at birth will continue to increase for both status Indians and Canadians, there will still be a gap. The gap is narrowing, however. By 2001, it is projected that the life expectancy for status Indians will be 6 years less than that for Canadians, 70 versus 76 for men and 77 versus 83 for women.

- Nonetheless, the projected life expectancy for status Indians in 2001 will still be less than the 1981 Canadians figures for both sexes.

SOURCE: Highlights of Aboriginal Conditions, 1981-2001, Part I, Demographic Trends, INAC, 1989, 5.

TABLE 5.5 Specific Measures of Mortality Among Registered Canadian Indians and Among Canadians as a Whole*

		A Crude death rate	B Infant mortality rate	C Average age at death	D Male life expectancy	E Female life expectancy
1960	Indians	10.9	79.0	—	59.7	63.5
	All Canadians	8.0	27.3		68.5	74.3
1965	Indians	8.7	52.6	36.0	60.5	65.6
	All Canadians	7.5	23.6	64.0	68.8	75.2
1970	Indians	7.5	43.2**	42.0	60.2	66.2
	All Canadians	7.5	18.8	66.0	69.3	76.4
1976	Indians	7.5	32.1	43.0	—	—
	All Canadians	7.4	16.0	67.0		
1981	Indians	9.5†	22.0	45.2	62.0	69.0
	All Canadians	6.1†	10.0	69.0	72.0	78.0
1991	Indians	9.2†	13.0	54.0	68.0	73.1
	All Canadians	6.0†	8.0	72.1	74.0	80.0

* Due to the difficulty of obtaining data, the data in any given cell may be for a different year than for that shown. The difference is never more than two years and usually only one, and in any such cases of discrepancy the data are more recent than the date shown.

** This figure is an average of the rates for 1969 and 1971, since the 1970 data are unreliable due to incomplete reporting that year.

A Death per 1000 population.

B Deaths of children in first year of life per 1000 live births.

C Sum of the age at death of all persons dying in a given year divided by the number of people dying that year.

D & E Age to which a person can be expected to live, calculated at time of birth.

† These figures are standardized death rates.

Sources: Medical Services Branch, *Health Data Book* (Ottawa: Department of National Health and Mortality Projections of Registered Indians, 1987 to 1996, INAC 1985); *Indian and Canadian Mortality Trends*, 1991, Ottawa, Health and Welfare Canada.

life expectancy almost half that for a non-Native person. By 1960, a Native's expected life span had increased to 60 years (while for Whites it was 69) and it remained there until the 1980s. Figure 5.3 shows the life expectancies at birth for Indians and all Canadians by gender. It shows that the general trend of increasing life expectancy continues. By the turn of the century, it is estimated that Indians will increase their life expectancy by eight years. Nevertheless, the data show that non-Indians still live longer than Indians. While the gap remains, it is narrowing; by the twenty-first century, it is predicted that the life expectancy for Indians will be 70 versus 76 for non-Native men and, for women, 77 versus 83. The average age at death is markedly lower for Natives than the national average. As Table 5.5 shows, for Natives the average age at death is 54 and for non-Natives, 72. Recent data show that while Natives' life expectancy has increased to 68 for males and 73 for females, it still remains nearly 10 years less than that for the average Canadian. Overall standardized death rates in 1981 show that for Indians it was 9.2 per 1000 compared to just 6 among the total Canadian population. Infant mortality (deaths of babies before the age of one) is perhaps an even more important factor in determining the growth rate of the population. The number of Indian deaths per 1000 live births was nearly 80 in 1960. However, this decreased to 17.0 in 1991.

The above discussion shows that Natives, since the turn of the century, have gone through three stages of birth-death trends. During the first half of the century, the Native population was characterized by extremely high birth and death rates. Then, after World War II, the death rate decreased substantially (because of medical advances and increased sanitation and housing), although the birth rate remained high. Today we see the third phase, which is a decline in both the fertility and mortality rates (Siggner, 1986).

The in-out migration pattern refers to the number of Indians added to or deleted from the federal roll of registered Indians. Table 5.6 shows the number of Indians who were enfranchised between 1955 and 1982, when enfranchisement was phased out. Unfortunately, the number of individuals who gained Indian status other than through birth cannot be determined. The number of non-Indian females marryingIndian men was estimated at 300 in 1969 and over 600 in 1977. However, figures are unavailableconcerning whether these women had children prior to their marriage and how many children they had after marriage.

Based on information in Table 5.6, the annual enfranchisement rate per 1000 Indians has varied between 6.3 and 1.1. Despite this apparently low rate, however, over 13 000 Indians lost their status between 1955 and 1975. Moreover, the offspring of these 13 000, now old enough to have their own children, also surrendered their Indian status.

TABLE 5.6   ENFRANCHISEMENTS* OF REGISTERED INDIANS, 1955-82

	Enfranchisements upon application		Enfranchisements following marriage to a non-Indian		
	Adults	Children	Women	Children	Total enfranchisements
1955-56 to 1959-60	912	724	2078	484	4198
1960-61 to 1965-65	401	239	2198	694	3532
1965-66 to 1969-70	207	107	2440	655	3409
1970-71 to 1974-75	54	20	1823	117**	2014
1975-76 to 1977-78	10	15	309†	—	334
1978-79 to 1981-82	12	13	—††	—	15

* On enfranchisement, an Indian permanently gives up all rights under the *Indian Act*. Enfranchisement in this sense has nothing to do with the possession of voting rights, which were guaranteed to all Indians in 1960.

** Prior to 1972-73, minor, unmarried children were automatically enfranchised with their parent(s). Since 1972-73, minor, unmarried children have been enfranchised only when it is requested by the parent(s) and when the application is approved by the Department of Indian Affairs and Northern Development.

† Includes both women and minor children.

†† Changes in the *Indian Act* no longer required women to enfranchise.

SOURCE: Information Canada, *Perspective Canada II*, (Ottawa: Queen's Printer, 1977), 285; Membership Division, Membership and Statutory Requirements, Reserves and Trusts, IIAP, 1982, Table 25, document #06445.

As Table 5.6 shows, over 80 percent of enfranchised Indians lost their status through marriage to a non-Indian. Indeed, a close analysis of the data suggests that voluntary applications for enfranchisement have virtually ceased. The mostrecent statistics on enfranchisement show that nearly all Indians who surrendered their status did so involuntarily as a result of the "marriage rule" then enforced by the *Indian Act*. However, the most recent changes to the *Indian Act* represent an end to legislative discrimination on the grounds of sex. Consequently, involuntary enfranchisement will no longer be an issue.

Both the enfranchisement rules and the "double mother" rule in the *Indian Act* have now been changed. As early as 1980, DIAND allowed bands that wanted to opt out of the conditions of 12(1)(b) and 12(1)(a)(iv) to do so. By 1984, 103 bands had opted out of the former section while 309 acted on the latter. When *Bill C-31* was passed in 1985, new rules prevailed. This bill was introduced in order to comply with section 15(1) of the *Canadian Charter of Rights and Freedoms*. In short, any individual who was registered as an Indian and subsequently lost status due to discriminatory sections of the *Indian Act* could be reinstated. This included women who were deleted from the register upon marriage to a non-Indian (sections 12(1)(b) and 14); individuals deleted at the age of majority because their mothers and paternal grandmothers were not Canadian Indian by birth (sections 12(i)(a)(iv)); individuals deleted due to husbands'/fathers' enfranchisement (sections 10 and 109); and any illegitimate children of Indian women who were deleted from the register upon proof of non-Indian paternity (subsection 12(2)).

However, under this new change, only the first generation of those listed above are eligible for registration. Applications will be accepted (you must apply) until the year 2003. This means that minors of today can achieve the age of majority and then apply. However, first-time registration is limited to first-generation children of a reinstated individual. If these children are themselves parents at the time of registration, their children cannot be registered. Once registered, however, these children have the capacity to transmit status to any children they have thereafter.

AGE

Figures 5.4, 5.5 and 5.6 show the distribution of Native Canadians by age relative to the total Canadian population. The data reveal a very young population: well over one third of the Native population is younger than 15 and over half are younger than 25. Of the total Canadian population, only about one fifth of the population is under 15 and about one third are under 25 years of age. When on-reserve Indians and Inuit are singled out of the status Indian population, greater discrepancies are evident. Thirty-seven percent of on-reserve Indians and Inuit are under age 15, while nearly two thirds of them are under the age of 25.

Thus far the evidence reveals that the proportion of young people in the overall Native population is growing. However, the growth is slowing down as the Native population ages. For example, in 1981, the median age for Natives was 19 while for the overall population it was 32. Today we find the Native median age is 23 while the overall population has only increased to 33. Nonetheless, the proportion of Natives in the ages between 15-44 is similar to that found in the non-Native population. In the 45-65 category there are nearly twice as many non-Natives than Natives. A similar profile is evident in the age category 65 and over.

FIGURE 5.4 **AGE STRUCTURE OF THE POPULATIONS: CANADA AND INDIANS OFF-RESERVE**

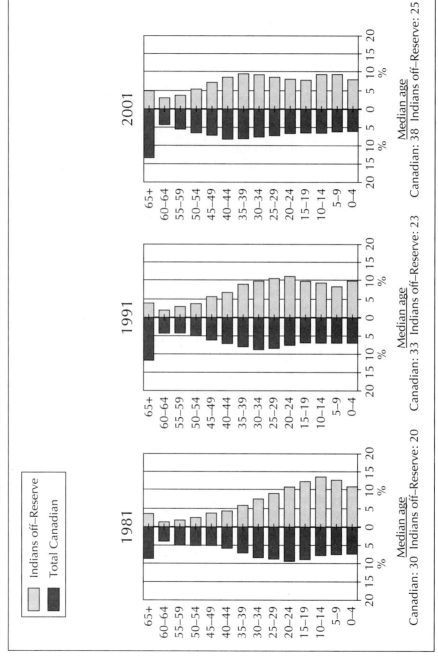

SOURCE: Highlights of Aboriginal Conditions, 1981–2001, Part I, Demographic Trends, INAC, 1989, 12.

FIGURE 5.5 **AGE STRUCTURE OF THE POPULATIONS: CANADA AND INUIT**

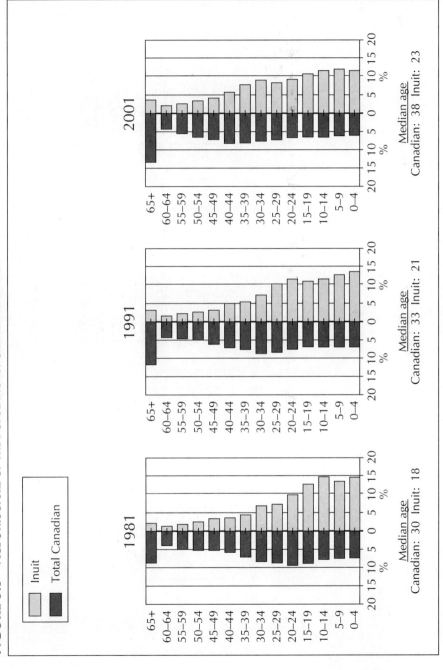

Source: Highlights of Aboriginal Conditions, 1981-2001, Part I, Demographic Trends, INAC, 1989, 14.

FIGURE 5.6   AGE STRUCTURE OF THE POPULATIONS: CANADA AND TOTAL STATUS INDIANS

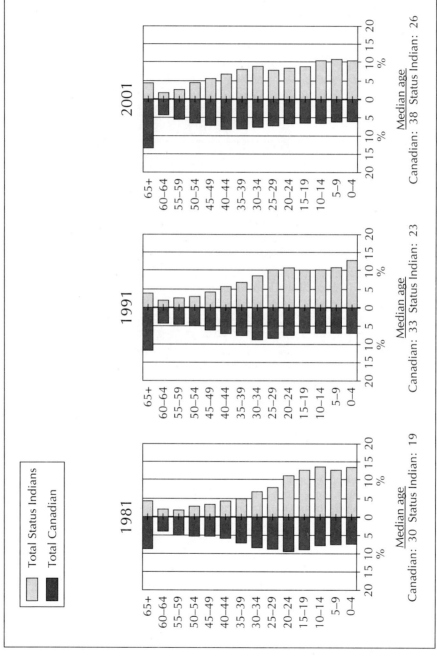

SOURCE: *Highlights of Aboriginal Conditions, 1981–2001, Part I, Demographic Trends*, INAC, 1989, 8.

The dependency ratios are outlined in Table 5.7. They show that, again, while the Native young dependency ratio is falling, it is substantially larger than that of non-Natives. At the same time, the aged dependency ratios have remained the same over the past decade. The overall dependency ratio for the Canadian population has remained stable over the past decade and will continue at this level (.47) into the twenty-first century. On the other hand, the dependency ratio for Natives is expected to decline from .77 (1981) to .56 in 2001. In the case of Inuit, the overall dependency ratio will decline from .84 (1981) to .61 in 2001.

As both the Native and Canadian populations continue to age, the starting points are different: in the case of the general population, they are aging into retirement, while Natives are aging from youth to the working age group. The aging patterns of Inuit mirror that of status Indians.

The above figures carry a number of implications. Clearly, there is a stable Native population-growth rate, meaning continued high growth, as well as a decreasing death rate. Unless birth rates also decrease, more and more Natives will belong to the prime employment category of 15 to 40, and the demand for jobs will increase. As Table 5.7 shows, the dependency ratios are already over twice as high for Natives as for the general population; this means that the working-age population must support a large number of non-productive people. Unemployment is already rampant among Native Canadians, and, as more and more Natives move into the prime employment category, fewer and fewer jobs are likely to become available. The data from Census Canada show that the number of people in the labour-force age (15-64) has been increasing—from 46 percent in 1966 to nearly 65 percent by 2001. This is likely to add more than 75 000 Native people to the labour force.

RESIDENTIAL PATTERNS

Where do these people live? Indians reside in all parts of Canada, although they are not evenly distributed. Tables 5.8, 5.9 and 5.10 reveal the regional dispersion of Indian people over time. The data show that while the overall Indian population has increased all over Canada, the biggest gains were in Saskatchewan and Alberta. Approximately one fourth live in Ontario, and another 16 percent in each of Saskatchewan and B.C. Western provinces show similar numbers, while much smaller numbers reside in Québec and Atlantic Canada. Tables 5.9 and 5.10 identify the on- and off-reserve Indian population by region. In 1988, nearly 65 percent of status Indians lived on the reserve. While the number on the reserve has decreased over the years, nearly two thirds of the population remain on lands set aside for Indians and held in trust by Ottawa. Less than half the Yukon Indians live on reserves, Crown lands or settlements, while in the N.W.T. over 80 percent are "on reserve." Within the provinces, Saskatchewan reveals the lowest percentage,

TABLE 5.7 **AGE DISTRIBUTION AND DEPENDENCY RATIO OF NATIVE AND NON-NATIVE POPULATION**

	Age Group				Population	Dependency Ratio*			
						Young		Aged	
	0-14 years	15-64 years	65 years and over	No age given		Indian	Non-Indian**	Indian	Non-Indian**
	percent								
1924	32.2	51.2	5.9	10.7	104 894	62.9	56.5	11.5	7.9
1934	34.7	55.4	6.2	3.7	112 510	62.7	50.3	11.1	8.8
1944	37.5	55.9	6.6	—	125 686	67.0	42.4	11.8	10.2
1954	41.7	53.2	5.1	—	151 558	78.5	49.0	9.6	12.5
1964	46.7	49.1	4.2	—	211 389	95.0	58.1	8.6	13.1
1974	43.2	52.4	4.2	0.2	276 436	82.4	47.5	8.1	13.0
1981	39.0	57.0	4.0	—	323 000	68.4	48.8	7.0	12.8
1991	35.0	60.0	4.0	—	521 500	65.2	46.3	7.0	13.6

* The dependency ratios reflect the relationship between the groups least likely to be involved in the work force (i.e. the young and the elderly), and the working-age population.

** Data were not available for the corresponding year; the years represented are: 1921, 1931, 1941, 1951, 1961, 1971.

SOURCE: Information Canada, *Perspective Canada II*, (Ottawa: Queen's Printer, 1977), 287; *Census of Canada*, 1981; Indian and Northern Affairs Canada, Quantitative Analysis and Socio-demographic Research, 1992.

while Québec shows nearly three fourths of its Indian population on reserve. By the end of the twentieth century, it is estimated that there will be substantial increases in the on-reserve population for the prairie region. When we focus on the off-reserve population, we see that all regions have experienced increases. However, the largest increases were in Saskatchewan and Alberta, with Québec having the lowest. As we predict the future, the data suggest that Alberta as well as Manitoba will continue to have substantial increases in off-reserve Indians.

Indian Bands

Until 1985, nearly all Indians were affiliated with a band. A band is a group of Indians who share a common interest in land and money and whose historical connection is defined by the federal government. However, it is important to point out that the term "band" is also a political term; it is often arbitrarily imposed on Native groups, regardless of cultural differences, for the government's administrative purposes. The ministry of Indian Affairs can create and do away with band designations, so that the number of bands often varies from year to year.

When the federal government first divided various Indian tribes into bands, it showed very little concern about the impact of these divisions on Indian culture. For example, some tribes were matrilineal, tracing descent through the mother's side, while others were patrilineal. Yet, when the band system was established, tribes were arbitrarily thrown together, and all were treated as patrilineal. This produced serious social disorganization and a wide-ranging disruption of tribal culture.

Under the 1951 *Indian Act*, section 2(1), "band" means simply a body of Indians. At present, over 200 000 Indians live on reserves and belong to 592 different bands; the largest of these is the Six Nations band, near Brantford, Ontario, with a population of 8200. Each band is administered by one of 87 agencies across Canada; the Caughnawaga agency handles only one band, and the New Westminster agency handles 32.

The average size of Indian bands in Canada has increased to approximately 500 people; in 1950, the average was 200. Most Indians currently live in bands of less than 500; the modal category (a single category with the greatest frequency) containing 43 percent, is 100-499 (see Table 5.11). Another 36 percent have a population of less than 100. Only 11 bands are very large, with over 2000 members; most of these are located in Ontario and Alberta.

Band designations are not the only means of differentiating Indian peoples. Two further criteria are language and cultural lifestyle. Indians have been divided into ten traditional linguistic groups: Algonkian, Iroquois, Sioux, Athapaska, Kootenay, Salish, Wakash, Tsimish, Haida and Tlingit. Six major cultural areas have also been established: Algonkian, Iroquois, Plains, Plateaus, Pacific Coast and Mackenzie River. There is, of course, a considerable overlap between the two categories (see Figure 5.7).

TABLE 5.8   REGISTERED INDIAN POPULATION BY REGION, 1966-2001

Region	1966		1976		1986		1988		1989		1996		2001	
	No.	%	No.	%	No.	%	No.	%	No.	%	No.	%	No.	%
Atlantic	8494	3.8	10 891	3.8	15 636	4.0	17 711	4.0	18 433	4.0	21 835	3.8	23 398	3.8
Québec	23 186	10.3	29 580	10.2	38 962	10.0	44 111	9.9	45 742	9.8	53 280	9.3	56 125	9.0
Ontario	52 408	23.4	64 690	22.4	86 544	22.3	101 612	22.9	107 862	23.1	126 755	22.1	134 372	21.6
Manitoba	31 000	13.8	42 311	14.6	57 488	14.8	64 315	14.5	67 092	14.4	84 684	14.8	93 020	14.9
Saskatchewan	31 362	14.0	43 404	15.0	60 545	15.6	68 246	15.4	72 111	15.5	93 250	16.3	105 830	17.0
Alberta	25 432	11.3	34 130	11.8	48 706	12.6	55 290	12.5	57 590	12.3	75 954	13.2	84 684	13.6
B.C.	46 543	20.8	53 342	18.5	66 604	17.2	77 153	17.4	80 742	17.3	96 472	16.8	102 552	16.5
Yukon	} 5 739	} 2.6	3181	1.1	4249	1.1	5510	1.2	5973	1.3	7133	1.2	7602	1.2
N.W.T.			7409	2.6	9095	2.3	9936	2.2	10 792	2.3	13 906	2.4	15 318	2.5
Canada	224 164	100	288 938	100	387 829	100	443 884	100	466 337	100	573 269	100	622 901	100

SOURCES: 1966-1989: Indian Register, DIAND; 1996-2001: Population Projections of Registered Indians, 1986-2011, DIAND, 1990.

TABLE 5.9 REGISTERED INDIAN POPULATION ON-RESERVE[1] BY REGION, 1966-2001

Region	1966		1976		1986		1988		1989		1996		2001	
	No.	%[2]	No.	%[2]	No.	%[2]	No.	%[2]	No.	%[2]	No.	%[2]	No.	%[2]
Atlantic	6444	75.9	8066	74.1	11 132	71.2	11 989	67.7	12 398	67.3	13 905	63.7	14 775	63.1
Québec	18 720	80.7	24 198	81.8	31 043	79.7	32 765	74.3	33 029	72.2	38 238	71.8	40 223	71.7
Ontario	36 508	69.7	44 227	68.4	55 289	63.9	57 058	56.2	58 934	54.6	72 229	57.0	76 339	56.8
Manitoba	26 752	86.3	31 723	75.0	41 211	71.7	43 864	68.2	44 646	66.5	55 115	65.1	60 648	65.2
Saskatchewan	26 920	85.8	30 746	70.8	38 744	64.0	36 775	53.9	37 795	52.4	56 442	60.5	64 162	60.6
Alberta	22 573	88.8	26 841	78.6	35 030	71.9	36 863	66.7	38 144	66.2	48 656	64.1	54 630	64.5
B.C.	37 019	79.5	34 073	63.9	40 876	61.4	42 785	55.5	43 054	53.3	54 327	56.3	57 805	56.4
Yukon }	5482*	95.5*	2620	82.4	2463	58.0	3042	55.2	2948	49.4	3905	54.7	4182	55.0
N.W.T. }			7143	96.4	8399	92.3	8625	86.8	8723	80.8	11 562	83.1	12 750	83.2
Canada	180 418	80.5	209 637	72.6	264 187	68.1	273 766	61.7	279 671	60.0	354 379	61.8	385 514	61.9

*Yukon and N.W.T. combined for 1966.

1. On reserve includes Crown lands and settlements.
2. Percentages are based on regional totals shown in Table 5.8.

SOURCES: 1966-1989: Indian Register, DIAND; 1996-2001: Population Projections of Registered Indians, 1986-2011, DIAND, 1990.

TABLE 5.10   REGISTERED INDIAN POPULATION OFF-RESERVE BY REGION, 1966-2001

Region	1966[1] No.	%[2]	1976 No.	%[2]	1986 No.	%[2]	1988 No.	%[2]	1989 No.	%[2]	1996 No.	%[2]	2001 No.	%[2]
Atlantic	2050	24.1	2825	25.9	4504	28.8	5722	32.3	6035	32.7	7930	36.3	8623	36.9
Québec	4466	19.3	5382	18.2	7919	20.3	11 346	25.7	12 713	27.8	15 041	28.2	15 902	28.3
Ontario	15 900	30.3	20 463	31.6	31 255	36.1	44 554	43.8	48 928	45.4	54 526	43.0	58 032	43.2
Manitoba	4248	13.7	10 588	25.0	16 277	28.3	20 451	31.8	22 446	33.5	29 570	34.9	32 372	34.8
Saskatchewan	4442	14.2	12 658	29.2	21 801	36.0	31 471	46.1	34 316	47.6	36 809	39.5	41 669	39.4
Alberta	2859	11.2	7289	21.4	13 676	28.1	18 427	33.3	19 446	33.8	27 298	35.9	30 054	35.5
B.C.	9524	20.5	19 269	36.1	25 728	38.6	34 368	44.5	37 688	46.7	42 145	43.7	44 747	43.6
Yukon }	257	4.5	561	17.6	1786	42.0	2468	44.8	3025	50.6	3228	45.3	3420	45.0
N.W.T }			266	3.6	696	7.7	1311	13.2	2069	19.2	2343	16.8	2568	16.8
Canada	43 746	19.5	79 301	27.4	123 642	31.9	170 118	38.3	186 666	40.0	218 890	38.2	237 387	38.1

1. In 1966, numbers include 274 individuals with unstated places of residence distributed as follows: Atlantic 5, Québec 24, Ontario 51, Manitoba 12, Saskatchewan 33, Alberta 69, B.C. 56, Yukon and N.W.T. 24.

2. Percentages are based on regional totals shown in Table 5.8.

SOURCES: 1966-1989: Indian Register, DIAND; 1996-2001: Population Projections of Registered Indians, 1986-2011, DIAND, 1990.

Over time, White Canada has systematically obliterated many Native cultural and linguistic distinctions. The forced migration of some groups from one area to another has caused cultural and linguistic mixing. For example, the Ojibeway were originally from southwest Québec and eastern Ontario. By 1750, they had moved into the area of the Great Lakes, and by 1805, they were established in Saskatchewan. Other groups, such as the Assiniboine and Chipewyan, have been split through migration, with some group members moving north, and others, south.

Urban Migration

The recent trend in the residential patterns of Canadian Indians indicates that an increasing number of them are moving to urban areas. Of these, over half are relocating in large metropolitan areas of more than 100 000 people. There are two explanations for the migration to large cities. First, unskilled employment is easier to obtain in large cities than in small towns. Second, Native ghettos are developing in various cities such as Winnipeg, Toronto and Edmonton; once a sizable population of an ethnic group resides in a given area, other members of that group find it easier to move there.

Siggner (1980) has looked at the migration patterns of registered Indians by comparing census data from 1966 to 1971. He found that only 20 percent of the Indian population moved one or more times during this period as compared to 25 percent of the national population. More than half (52 percent) of the Indian migrants were headed toward an urban area. Siggner also found that nearly one fourth of all Indian migrants had moved more than three times during this five-year period. A recent analysis by the author using 1981 and 1991 data confirms Siggner's results and suggests the pattern has continued. Even though the migrant population is a very young group, between 20 and 25, it is not made up solely of single adults, as might be expected. Indeed, evidence suggests that many Indian migrants are parents with small children.

Reserves

Canada has some 2241 reserves, though this number, like the number of bands, varies over time according to the policy of the federal government. Reserves can vary in size. Although there is no minimum area, 71.5 hectares per person is the maximum; some reserves in British Columbia cover only a few hectares, while the largest is in Alberta—900 square kilometres. In Eastern Canada, each band is generally limited to one reserve. In the West, one band may hold several reserves; British Columbia has over 1600 reserves, but less than 200 bands (Allan, 1943).

Clearly, the reserve still provides security and roots for most Indian people. The reserve is where the majority of Indians have grown up among family and friends. Even for those who leave, it continues to provide a haven from the pressures

TABLE 5.11   NUMERICAL AND PERCENTAGE DISTRIBUTION OF INDIAN BANDS BY SIZE AND GEOGRAPHIC LOCATION, FOR REGIONS.

| Region | Distribution of bands by population size | | | | | | Distribution of bands by geographic location | | | | | | | |
	100	100-499	500-999	1000-1999	12000	Total	Remote No.	Remote %	Rural No.	Rural %	Semi-Urban No.	Semi-Urban %	Urban No.	Urban %
Atlantic	8	16	3	2	—	29	—	—	13	45	10	34	6	21
Québec	12	14	5	7	1	39	14	36	5	13	15	38	5	13
Ontario	35	52	20	5	3	115	34	30	52	45	21	18	8	7
Manitoba	10	25	12	11	1	59	25	44	26	46	5	9	1	2
Saskatchewan	5	44	16	2	1	68	10	15	43	63	13	19	2	3
Alberta	9	13	11	3	5	41	7	17	19	46	12	29	3	7
B.C.	96	83	14	2	—	195	53	27	77	40	41	21	23	12
N.W.T.	17	—	—	—	—	17	8	—	7	—	1	—	—	—
Yukon	14	—	—	—	—	14	13	—	—	—	—	—	1	—
Canada	206	247	81	32	11	577	164	29	242	42	118	21	49	9

SOURCES: Statistics Division, *Registered Indian Population by Sex and Residence, 1977* (Ottawa: Program Reference Centre, IIAP, 1979); Ponting and Gibbins, 1980, 35; Perreault, J., L. Paquette and M. George, *Population of Registered Indians, 1981-1986* (Ottawa: INAC, 1985).

FIGURE 5.11   NATIVE LANGUAGE AND CULTURAL DIVISIONS

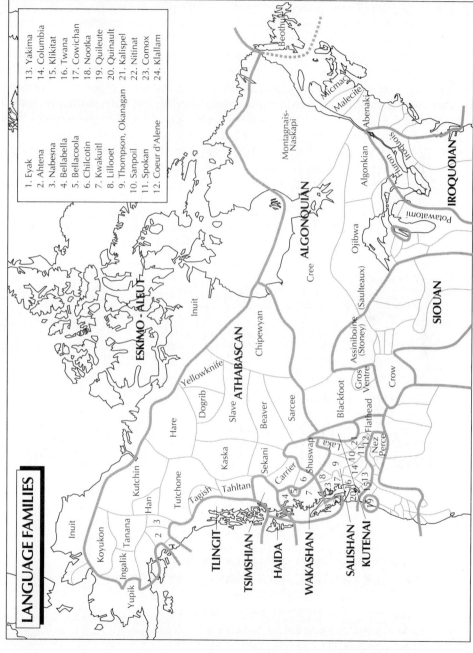

LANGUAGE FAMILIES

1. Eyak
2. Ahtena
3. Nabesna
4. Bellabella
5. Bellacoola
6. Chilcotin
7. Kwakuitl
8. Lillooet
9. Thompson, Okanagan
10. Sanpoil
11. Spokan
12. Coeur d'Alene
13. Yakima
14. Columbia
15. Klikitat
16. Twana
17. Cowichan
18. Nootka
19. Quileute
20. Quinault
21. Kalispel
22. Nitinat
23. Comox
24. Klallam

SOURCE: R. Bruce Morrison and C. Roderick Wilson (eds.) *Native Peoples.* Toronto: McClelland and Stewart, 1986, p.27.

of White society. These factors, combined with the prejudicial attitudes of White culture, create a strong internal pull and external push toward remaining on the reserve.

Even if an increasing number of Indians leave the reserve, the absolute population of those who remain will still show a sizable increase. This could pose a number of problems for Canada. Reserves are potential hotbeds of political and social discontent. In addition, if Indians on reserves become economically developed, they could pose a competitive threat to some Canadian corporate structures. Already, in British Columbia and Alberta, Indians have angered local businessmen by building housing developments on reserve lands close to major cities.

Reserves are situated in a variety of geographical contexts which have significant implications regarding development potential, population mobility and transportation routes. DIAND has characterized the reserves in four ways: urban, rural,

TABLE 5.12 REGISTERED INDIAN POPULATION LIVING ON-RESERVE[1] BY DIAND GEOGRAPHICAL ZONE, CANADA, 1971-1989

Geographical Zone	1971	1976	1981	1986	1989
Urban					
Number	67 414	76 485	86 816	98 474	103 572
Percent	35.8	36.5	38.2	37.3	37.0
Rural					
Number	77 314	83 392	86 574	102 289	108 511
Percent	41.0	39.8	38.1	38.7	38.8
Remote					
Number	11 108	10 947	13 167	14 224	15 494
Percent	5.9	5.2	5.8	5.4	5.5
Special Access					
Number	32 677	38 813	40 935	49 200	52 096
Percent	17.3	18.5	18.0	18.6	18.6
Total					
Number	188 513	209 637	227 492	264 187	279 663[2]
Percent	100	100	100	100	100

1. On-reserve includes Crown lands and settlements.
2. Excludes eight individuals living on reserve or Crown lands from the General Lists with unspecified geographical zones.

SOURCES: Indian and Northern Affairs Canada, *Basic Departmental Data*, 1990, 15; 1971-1989: Indian Register, DIAND; *Classification and Housing Economic Categorization of Indian Bands by Zone, 1987*, Band Support and Capital Management Branch, DIAND.

remote and special access. Reserves within 50 kilometres of a service centre are considered urban. Rural is a zone where the reserve is located between 50 and 350 kilometres from a service centre. Remote is when a reserve is beyond the 350-kilometre limit but is accessible by a year-round road. The special access designation is for any reserve where no year-round road connects the reserve to a service centre.

Table 5.12 shows the distribution and proportion of Natives in each of the designated zones. While a majority of Natives live in urban and rural zones, considerable numbers live in remote and special access reserves. Table 5.11 shows that over one third of the Natives in Québec and Manitoba and over one quarter in Ontario and B.C. live in reserves that have no road access to a service centre. A substantial number in Québec and British Columbia reside in special access areas. On the other hand, fewer than 20 percent of Natives in Alberta and Saskatchewan live in either remote or special access areas.

Approximately 2240 separate parcels of reserve land make up a little less than 3 million hectares of land (more than 6 million acres). The total area of reserve lands per capita has decreased over the past 20 years. This per capita decrease has resulted despite the total increase in Indian lands over the past five years. One way in which Indian lands have increased recently is that, as a result of a number of court and other legal decisions, land has been given back to the Crown to be held in trust for Indians. For example, in 1991, the Department of Justice has forced the Minister of Indian Affairs to return nearly 300 hectares of the Riding Mountain National Park in Manitoba to the Crown to hold in trust for the Keeseekoowenin Indian Band. Many other smaller land claims have been settled, and additional lands added to the existing inventory. However, because of the high population growth, per capita allocations are less today than they were previously. In 1959, across Canada, there was 13 hectares per capita; but by 1991, there was only 11.9 hectares per capita (see also Table 5.13). The exception to this is in the North where Natives have signed agreements with the federal government which give them control over vast areas of land. For example, the Gwichin of the Mackenzie Delta have ratified an agreement with the federal government which provides them ownership of 8622 square miles of land in the Mackenzie Delta.

The nature of the reserve system is a major source of the recent growth in Indian identity. Because the reserve is a closed spatial area, it fosters an ease of communication among Natives and renders communication with outsiders difficult. When communication takes place only within a group, contrast conceptions of other groups emerge: one's own groups is seen as "good," while the other group is seen as "bad." If outside communication is discouraged, internal communications become susceptible to group censorship; that is, members cannot criticize their own group or praise the other group without inviting negative sanctions. For example, an Indian who suggests that the federal government's position might contain some legitimate points becomes open to accusations of complicity or gullibility. As a result, information that might change their group's stereotypic, negative evaluation of government action cannot be processed. Through this dynamic, the reserve can easily become a centre for radical, militant activities. This is clearly a major reason for the federal government's desire to abolish them.

LANGUAGE USE AND RETENTION

The language of any group is the repository of concepts, images and history which allows individuals to organize their social environment. As such, language shapes the thoughts of those who use it. Reitz (1974) has argued that languages are an expression of collective identity and an important element in the survival of an ethnic group. Thus it is important to know the extent to which Native people use and retain their Aboriginal languages. Price (1981) has investigated the potential for the survival of Native languages in Canada. He found that long-term future viability has been secured for at least nine Native languages by a minimum of 1000 speakers. An additional 26 languages are spoken by an estimated 100 to 1000 Natives.

While Natives still maintain a relatively high degree of adherence to their mother tongue,[1] this is slowly diminishing. In 1941, fewer than 10 percent of Natives claimed English as their mother tongue. The figure reached 15 percent in 1951 and over 25 percent in 1961; another 2 percent claimed French. By 1991, 60.4 percent claimed English; fewer than 5 percent were bilingual (i.e., spoke a Native language as well as either English or French). Of those who claimed Native dialects as their mother tongues, more than 40 percent were "somewhat" bilingual.

In reviewing various surveys from the 1970s, Price (1981) found that the percentage of Native-language speakers within different Native populations varied from a low of 62 percent in Toronto and Vancouver, to 73 percent in Winnipeg, and up to 100 percent on many reserves. He also found Saskatchewan to be most conservative in the retention of Native languages. However, Stanbury and Siegel (1975) found that only 18 percent of Vancouver Indians used their Native languages in their homes.

Overall, 22 percent of the nearly 1.5 million Natives speak an Aboriginal language at home. Of those who listed an Aboriginal language as their first language, 22 percent speak Cree, 6 percent speak another Algonkian language, 3 percent speak Athapaskan and 1 percent Sioux. Of those claiming to speak an Aboriginal language, we find that the average age is well in excess of 40. This suggests that it is the older segment of the population that still retains the language and not the younger portion (Siggner, 1986).

The overall diminishing of Native-language use is somewhat mediated by special schools and language instruction programs. Almost 34 000 students (or 42 percent of Native enrolment) received some Native language instruction in school during the year. In addition, the number of students taking courses in which an Aboriginal

TABLE 5.13 REGISTERED INDIAN POPULATION AND INDIAN LANDS, BY REGION, 1989

	Atlantic Provinces	Québec	Ontario	Manitoba	Sask.	Alberta	B.C.	N.W.T.	Yukon	Canada
Total Indian population	15 636	38 962	86 544	57 488	60 545	48 706	66 604	9095	4249	387 829
% of total Indian population	4.0	10.0	22.3	14.8	15.6	12.6	17.2	2.3	1.1	100.0
% of total provincial/ territorial population	0.6	0.5	0.9	4.9	5.4	1.9	2.2	17.2	16.5	1.4
% living off reserve	28.8	20.3	36.1	28.3	36.0	28.1	38.6	7.7	42.0	31.9
Number of Indian bands	31	39	126	60	68	41	196	14	17	592
% of Indian bands	5.2	6.6	21.3	10.1	11.5	6.9	33.1	2.4	2.9	100.0
Number of reserves and settlements	67	33	185	103	142	90	1610	29	25	2284
% of reserves and settlements	2.9	1.4	8.1	4.5	6.2	3.9	70.5	1.3	1.1	100.0
Approximate area of reserves (hectares)	31 800	85 450	736 210	235 120	645 010	725 010	372 300	—	—	2 830 900

SOURCES: INAC Program Reference Centre, *Registered Indian Population by Sex and Residence*; Siggner, 1986, 3.

language is the medium of instruction over half the time has increased more than 60 percent during the 1980-84 period. However, like other ethnic minorities, Natives have learned that, to integrate into the larger society, they must learn to speak English or French. Thus, to a certain extent, the decreasing number of Native-language speakers reflects an increasing move away from the reserves and an increasing contact with non-Natives. Of course, the educational process had also increased the number of English/French-language speakers, though the high Native drop-out rate at elementary levels has minimalized its impact on English/French-language retention and use. However, as Natives increasingly recognize the value of English/French-language education, their languages and dialects may disappear even more rapidly.

Jarvis and Heaton (1989) use census data to examine Aboriginal language shifts for all the provinces and territories of Canada with the exception of P.E.I.. They found that nearly all Natives who change language shift to English (96.8 percent). They also found that fewer than 30 percent of Native persons began with an Aboriginal mother tongue. However, of those individuals, nearly three fourths are still using their Aboriginal language as their principal language in the home. Natives living in the north of Canada were reluctant to change languages, while Métis were most likely and Inuit were least likely to do so. The authors found that gender had little to do with linguistic shifts. When age was investigated as a possible determinant of linguistic changes, the authors found that the young (under 14) and the old (65+) were least likely to take on English as their operating language. Younger children will, as they grow older, be more fully exposed to the larger society and begin the process of linguistic shift. Thus, the fact that young people still retain their Aboriginal tongue is no indication that they will be fluent in that language as they enter the labour force. The lack of shift in the older generation is due to the fact that they have spent their lives speaking an Aboriginal language and have been least exposed to the modern industrial society outside their community (Jarvis and Heaton, 1989).

RELIGION

According to present statistics, 56 percent of Indians in Canada are Catholics. This, of course, reflects the early Jesuit and Oblate missionary work among the Natives. The second largest Indian religious group is Anglican, with 25 percent. Another 12 percent of Indians belong to the United Church, and the remaining 7 percent are evenly distributed between the other Christian churches in Canada.

This information is based on official government statistics. However, no information has been gathered regarding the extent to which Native people still adhere to pre-Christian religious beliefs. Apparently, a significant percentage of Natives have retained their indigenous religious beliefs.

Nonetheless, Christianity has had a definite impact on Native culture during the past few centuries. Its ideology of acceptance and obedience has contributed significantly to a widespread conservatism and fatalism among Native peoples.

MARITAL STATUS

Figures on the marital status of Natives do not support the stereotype of the broken Native family. The percentage of divorced Natives is very similar to that of the general Canadian population. There are, however, a number of explanations for this statistic. Because Native people are frequently poor, they often avoid the court costs and alimony payments that accompany formal divorces by simply separating from or deserting their families. Moreover, many women, even though they live with a man and bear children, never officially get married. Instead, they live common-law or marry according to tribal ritual, which has not been recognized by the federal government since 1957. Native women may choose not to marry for various reasons. Unmarried women with children receive a fairly substantial income through the baby-bonus scheme: an unmarried Native woman with three children received greater financial compensation than a married-but-separated woman with three children. Unmarried Indian women are also eligible for various educational and vocational-training programs not available to married women. Finally, unmarried women, until recently, did not risk losing their Indian status.

The low official divorce rate of Natives, then, should not be used as an indicator of family stability. In addition, some anthropologists have argued convincingly that White North American standards of family stability should be used only for the White population and not for members of other cultures. The definition of stability is so open to various culturally-based interpretations that no attempt to apply it to another culture can be free of ethnocentric bias.

Other statistics suggest that Native family patterns depart from White norms. About 60 percent of the Native population are officially married as compared to 67 percent of the overall Canadian population. Husband-wife families make up about 76 percent of the Native families, with 20 percent consisting of female lone parent families. Non-Native families have respective figures of 89 and 9 percent. Young Natives between 15 and 19 are much more likely to marry than are other Canadian teenagers (Anderson, 1978). Both of these statistics have implications for the high illegitimacy rate characteristic of the Native population.

Related to marital status is the number and growth rate of families. In 1991, there were 114 600 Indian families; an increase of 28 percent from 1986. There is no question that *Bill C-31* had significant impact on this growth rate; in 1987, the growth rate for Indian families was 9 percent, six times that of the general Canadian family. However, even when the impact of this legislation is removed, the growth rate of Indian families continues to be considerably higher than for the general Canadian.

Figure 5.8 compares the average family size for Natives and other Canadians. The results show that the Native family is larger than the Canadian family, although there has been a decrease in family size from 1981 to 1986. Aboriginal family size decreased by nearly one-half person. Inuit and on-reserve Indians had the largest family size (4.3 and 4.2 respectively), which is one person larger than the average Canadian family, while off-reserve families were nearly the same size as Canadian families.

When examining the number of single-parent families, Natives reveal different profiles than the Canadian population (see Figure 5.9). The data show that the number of Native single-parent families is twice that of the Canadian average. Single-parent families were most common for off-reserve Indians (30 percent), while such families were least common among the Inuit, 20 percent. Almost 60 percent of Indian single parents who are female live off-reserve, while 77 percent of the male Indian single parents live on-reserve. For all groups, single-parent families are generally headed by females; the 1986 ratio was 5:1. For off-reserve single-female families, the ratio was 9:1

FIGURE 5.8   Average Census Family[a] Size, Aboriginals and all Canadians, 1981, 1986

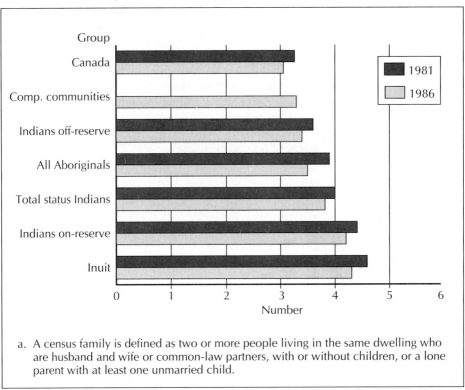

a. A census family is defined as two or more people living in the same dwelling who are husband and wife or common-law partners, with or without children, or a lone parent with at least one unmarried child.

Source: *Highlights of Aboriginal Conditions, 1981-2001, Part II, Social Conditions*, INAC, 1989, 11.

FIGURE 5.9   Sᴵɴɢʟᴇ-Pᴀʀᴇɴᴛ Fᴀᴍɪʟɪᴇs, Aʙᴏʀɪɢɪɴᴀʟs ᴀɴᴅ ᴀʟʟ Cᴀɴᴀᴅɪᴀɴs, 1986

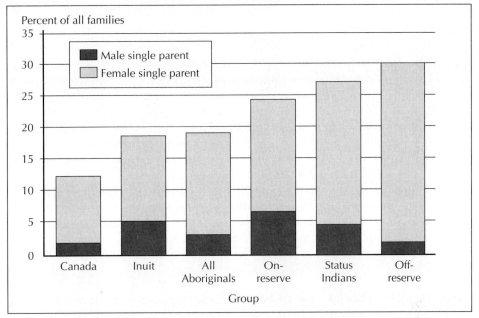

Sᴏᴜʀᴄᴇ: Highlights of Aboriginal Conditions, 1981-2001, Part II, Social Conditions, INAC, 1989, 12.

SOCIO-ECONOMIC STATUS

The quality of life experienced by Canadians is a function of their position in the stratified social system. Those who rank high are able to enjoy the benefits of a modern, industrial society. They are able to enjoy the enhanced educational, medical and leisure activities that are available. On the other hand, those who place low in our hierarchial system, will not be able to benefit from the increased technological innovations and will not be able to enhance their quality of life. In our social system, four factors influence one's ability to participate in the modern, industrial society: income, labour force participation, occupational status and education.

Income

In 1966 Hawthorn, *et al.*, established that the per capita income per year for Natives was about $300, and for other Canadians, about $1400. On a yearly earnings basis, Native workers received $1361 while Canadian workers received $4000. By 1986, the average Native income, for those in the labour force, had increased to over $9000. While these figures represent a substantial increase in income, the overall average Canadian income had increased to nearly $20 000; representing twice the income received by Native people.

Before discussing income further, it is important that the reader fully appreciate that income can be generated from a number of sources. The most general categories employed in this review are those of wage (earned) and non-wage (unearned or transfer).

We begin by reviewing Figure 5.10. It illustrates the major sources of employment (earned) income for 1980 and 1985. First, it should be noted that all groups identified show a drop in employment as their major source of income. However, while the decrease is 4 percent for Canadians, it is 13 percent for status Indians. The data also show that about half of the Indians obtained most of their income from employment. This percentage is increased when all Aboriginal groups are included.

The question of source of income is reversed when we review Figure 5.11, which shows unearned income. According to the census, between 1980 and 1985, every Aboriginal group reported an increase in the number of Natives receiving government transfer payments (non-wage income) as a major source of income. The increase was 16 percent higher for off-reserves and 12 percent higher for the total

FIGURE 5.10 MAJOR SOURCE OF INCOME: EMPLOYMENT, ABORIGINALS AND ALL CANADIANS, 1980, 1985

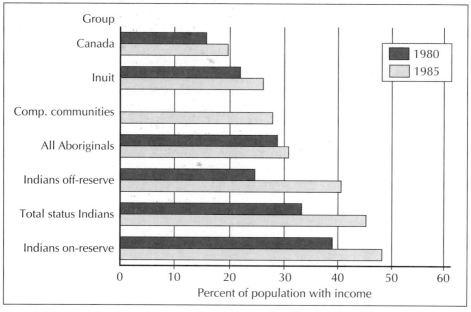

SOURCE: *Highlights of Aboriginal Conditions, 1981-2001, Part III, Economic Conditions*, INAC, 1989, 15.

Indian population. At the same time, there was only a 4 percent increase for the general Canadian population.

We now move to the question of how many Native and non-Native people have an income. Figure 5.12 shows the percentage of individuals over 15 years of age who have an income. At least 75 percent of the total Canadian population have some income. However, nearly one fourth of the Native population reported no income while nearly 90 percent of the Canadian population reported income. In all cases, the data show that between 1980 and 1985, more Canadians reported receiving an income than did Natives. Within the Native community, Inuit have the lowest proportion with an income.

Individual and family incomes are reported in Figures 5.13 and 5.14. The data show that the disparity between Canadian and Native individual income increased during the 1980-85 period; in 1980 the average income for Indians was 59 percent

FIGURE 5.11   MAJOR SOURCE OF INCOME: GOVERNMENT TRANSFER PAYMENTS, ABORIGINALS AND ALL CANADIANS, 1980, 1985

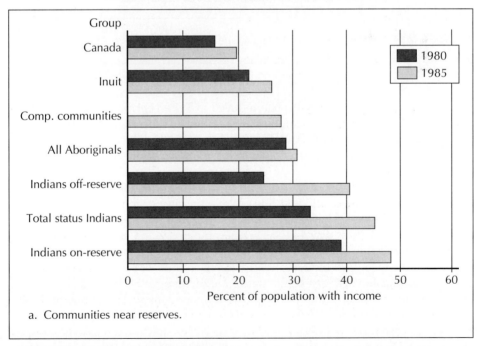

SOURCE: Highlights of Aboriginal Conditions, 1981-2001, Part III, Economic Conditions, INAC, 1989, 15.

FIGURE 5.12 PERSONS WITH INCOME, ABORIGINALS AND ALL CANADIANS, 1980, 1985

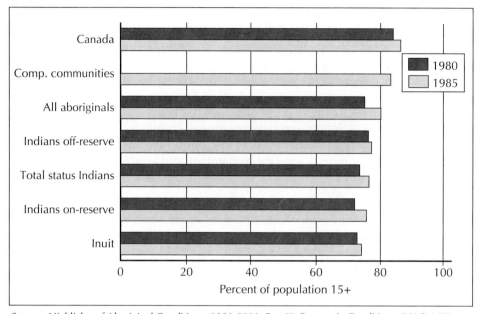

Source: Highlights of Aboriginal Conditions, 1981-2001, Part III, Economic Conditions, INAC, 1989,

of that for Canadians; by 1986 this had reduced to 54 percent. Family incomes show a similar pattern. Status Indian families have an average income of $21 800, which is about half that of the average Canadian family of $38 000. Like individual incomes, family income disparity has increased and recent information suggests the increase continues.

According to the 1986 census, over half the Indian population had incomes of less than $20 000 (see Figures 5.13 and 5.14). While the proportion of families with incomes of $20 000 to $40 000 is similar for all groups, four times as many Natives have incomes under $20 000 as over $40 000. When compared with Canadians, we find that twice as many Canadian families had incomes over $40 000 than under $20 000. Table 5.14 shows the income of Indians and Canadians in units of $5000. The table shows a strong relationship between ethnic status and income.

In summary, we find that the disparity of income between Natives and non-Natives noted by Hawthorn in the 60s still exists. In addition, the data suggest that the gap between the two groups is getting larger. This startling fact emerges despite the large and complex structure we have put in place to help Native people find a niche in our society.

FIGURE 5.13   AVERAGE INDIVIDUAL INCOME, ABORIGINALS AND ALL CANADIANS, 1980, 1985

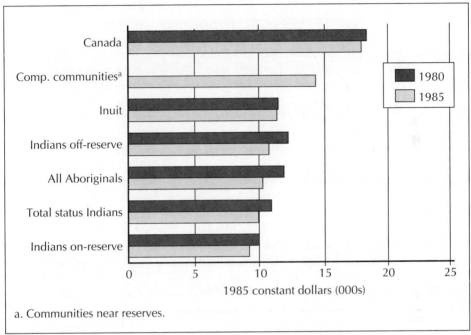

SOURCE: *Highlights of Aboriginal Conditions, 1981-2001, Part III, Economic Conditions,* INAC, 1989, 16.

Labour Force Participation

The extent to which Natives have been over- or under-represented in various occupational categories has been well established.[2] To make the data more meaningful through comparison, similar "over-under" statistics will be noted for British Canadians. The data show that there has been an increasing under-representation of Natives in professional and financial occupations; that is, a smaller proportion of Natives are in these occupations. Simultaneously, there has been an increasing over-representation over time in the primary and unskilled jobs. Statistics for the British "charter" group show an opposite trend. British under-representation between 1931 an 1961 increased only for low-prestige jobs. Moreover, British over-representation in the professional and financial category increased from 1931 to 1991.

Darroch (1980) has examined the over-under occupational representations of various ethnic groups. Using an index to measure the discrepancy between an ethnic group's occupational distribution and that of the entire labour force, Darroch determined the ethnic job distribution for 1971, and compared his findings with previous data. He found that, for most ethnic categories, occupational differentiation has been substantially reduced. However, for Native people, comparison of the 1951 index (23.9) with the 1971 index (29.0) shows a considerable increase. More recent data suggest this disparity is continuing to increase.

The participation in the labour force, we will quickly see, is highly differentiated as we look at comparisons between Canadians and Natives. Figure 5.15 reveals the labour force activity for 1981 and 1986. The data show that Native Canadians are twice as likely to be unemployed as other Canadians. In 1971, Native labour force participation was about 35 percent. This has increased 10 percent since that time. This is a substantial difference from the 62 percent participation rate evidenced for Canadians.

The participation rate varies by region of the country. As Figure 5.16 shows, all Natives have increased their participation rate since 1971. It also shows that in Prince Edward Island, Natives have a higher labour force participation rate than the Canadian average. On the other hand, Saskatchewan reveals extremely low participation rates.

Indians living on the reserve have the highest proportion of their population not in the labour force (57 percent). On the other hand, off-reserve people have the highest percentage of unemployed (17 percent). While more Natives entered the

FIGURE 5.14   AVERAGE FAMILY INCOME, ABORIGINALS AND ALL CANADIANS, **1980, 1985**

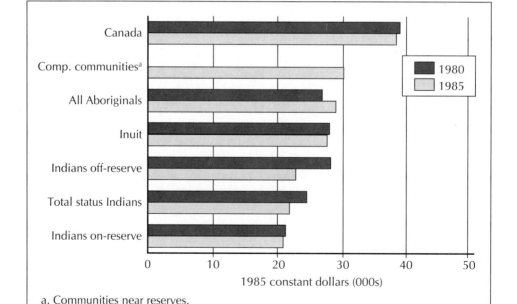

a. Communities near reserves.

SOURCE: *Highlights of Aboriginal Conditions, 1981-2001, Part III, Economic Conditions,* INAC, 1989, 17.

TABLE 5.14   Family Income by Income Group, Aboriginals and all
Canadians, 1985

Income Bracket	Inuit	All Aboriginals	Canada	Comparable communities[a]
No Income	0.41	0.27	0.24	0.21
Under $5000	6.56	6.80	3.06	4.14
$5000-$9999	11.74	10.18	4.47	6.31
$10 000-$14 999	11.46	12.16	7.78	13.07
$15 000-$19 999	11.67	10.21	8.88	13.80
$20 000-$29 999	19.61	18.20	17.64	21.45
$30 000-$39 999	16.37	16.44	18.29	17.10
$40 000-$49 999	9.46	11.43	14.77	10.83
$50 000-$59 999	5.87	6.91	9.84	5.83
$60 000 and over	6.84	7.35	15.02	7.27

a. Communities near reserves.

SOURCE: *Highlights of Aboriginal Conditions 1981-2001, Part III*, Indian and Northern Affairs, 1989, 40.

labour force between 1981 and 1986, the percentage of unemployed doubled, while for Canadians, the increase was minor.

For those natives employed, they are more likely to be employed full-time than are other Canadians; over 80 percent of status Indian are employed full-time, compared to 79 percent for Canadians (see Figure 5.17). However, during the 1981-91 decade, the percentage of people working full-time has decreased for all Canadians, although the rate of decrease was greater for Natives than for non-Natives.

The occupational distribution of Natives and Canadians are shown in Figure 5.18. The primary category includes mostly unskilled jobs which require little education and have low incomes. Manufacturing (or secondary) jobs are those which require some skills (semi-skills) and a modest educational background. Finally, tertiary activities are those occupations in service, clerical and managerial positions, including social service, teaching and medical health. These types of jobs are skilled and require educational backgrounds. The data show that most Canadians (Natives included) work in the tertiary sector. However, Natives have a lower proportion of these jobs than other Canadians (68.6 versus 74.9 percent). In addition, Natives are more likely to be found in primary activities than other Canadians. On-reserve Indians, for example, have the highest proportion of people working in primary industries—nearly 16 percent—a figure which is more than three times the proportion of the total Canadian population with primary jobs.

FIGURE 5.15   **LABOUR FORCE ACTIVITY, ABORIGINALS AND ALL CANADIANS, 1981, 1986**

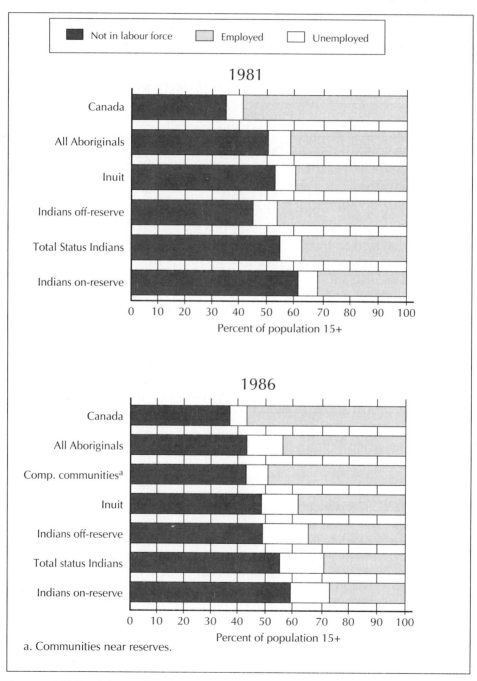

SOURCE: Highlights of Aboriginal Conditions, 1981-2001, Part III, Economic Conditions, INAC, 1989, 10.

FIGURE 5.16   **PROPORTION OF ON-RESERVE POPULATION IN THE LABOUR FORCE BY PROVINCE**

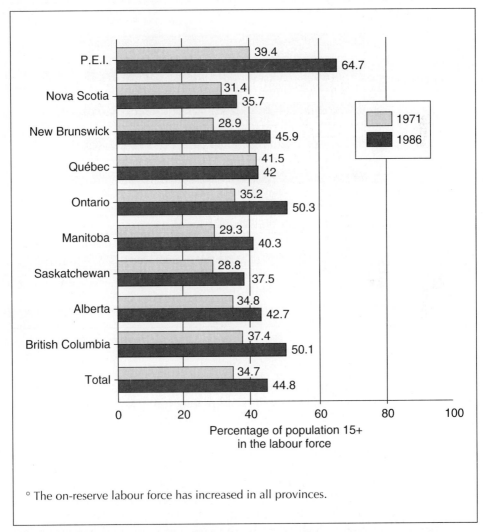

° The on-reserve labour force has increased in all provinces.

SOURCE: Highlights of Aboriginal Conditions, 1981-2001, Part III, Economic Conditions, INAC, 1989, 88.

FIGURE 5.17   FULL-TIME EMPLOYMENT, ABORIGINALS AND ALL CANADIANS, 1981, 19086

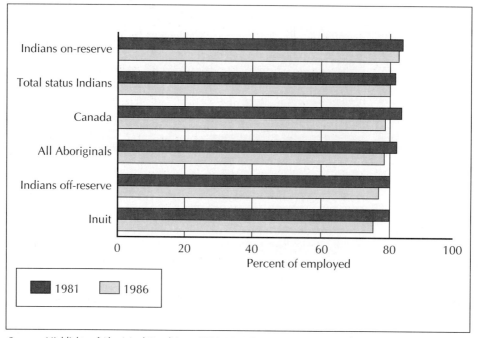

SOURCE: *Highlights of Aboriginal Conditions, 1981-2001, Part III, Economic Conditions*, INAC, 1989, 12.

A more detailed view of the specific occupations held by Natives is identified in Table 5.15. Seven percent of Natives hold managerial positions in the labour force. On the other hand, 15 to 17 percent are involved in professional, clerical and service industries. Nearly 40 percent of the Aboriginal labour force work in occupations at the primary level or lower.

In summary, Native people are participating more in the labour force over time. However, their participation is marginal and is not representative of the jobs which characterize a post-modern industrial society. In an attempt to further integrate Native people into the labour force, the federal government has introduced a number of programs to help Natives find jobs and relocate if necessary. For example, relocation programs have now exceeded $1.3 million since 1974. Off-reserve housing subsidies have helped Natives enter urban areas with high job-potential. In other cities, outreach programs have been established to help Natives find jobs in urban centres.

FIGURE 5.18   Occupational Distribution, Aboriginals and all
Canadians, 1986

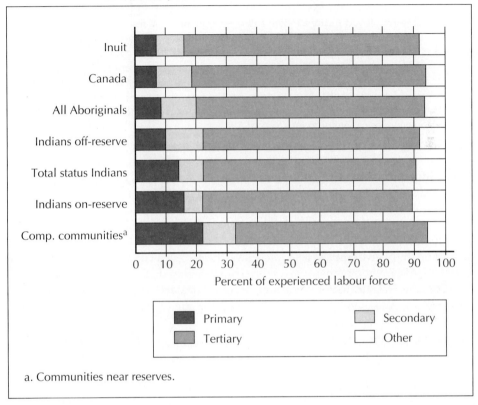

a. Communities near reserves.

Source: Highlights of Aboriginal Conditions, 1981-2001, Part III, Economic Conditions, INAC, 1989, 13.

These federal programs are attempting to raise Natives to the average Canadian standard of living. Unfortunately, the programs offer too little to be more than band-aid measures; they also operate only for short periods of time as pilot projects. In addition, the programs are generally designed only to meet the needs of middle-class Natives. Finally, the independent structure of programs reflects a lack of wide-ranging, integrated federal policy.

DIAND summarizes the bleak employment outlook for Indians as follows:

> The increase in working-age population of 50 000 to 60 000 over the next ten to fifteen years will far exceed recent rates of non-reserve job creation and will occur in an off-reserve employment market already saturated by the earlier national "baby-boom."

The low levels of labour-force participation reflect a continuing reliance on traditional pursuits as well as dependence on social support.

In the absence of successful job creation, social support for increasing numbers of unemployed Indians may double over the next ten to fifteen years.

Despite improvements in education and shifts toward more active involvement in professional pursuits, Indian earnings are still below national levels.

Both expanded on-reserve economic development and improved access to off-reserve labour and commodity markets cannot be achieved in time to provide sufficient job opportunities on reserves for the rapid increase in the working-age population over the next ten years, without an immediate and massive focus on Indian economic development. (*Survey*, 1980, pp. 6-7).

Native participation rate in the labour force is about 20 percent lower than the national rate. And it has been estimated that of those who do participate over 12 percent will remain permanently unemployed. However, these figures should be approached warily. The criteria that determine the active labour force are largely based upon White middle-class values and include only those Natives who have worked or looked for work during the past week. Moreover, because primary and unskilled jobs are extremely susceptible to seasonal factors, the time of year has a disproportionate impact on the Native employment rate. Nevertheless, even taking these factors into account, Native unemployment is still three times higher than the national average.

Because Natives usually work at seasonal or part-time jobs, they have little job security. And even in seasonal jobs, Natives are often discriminated against.

TABLE 5.15 OCCUPATIONAL DISTRIBUTION FOR NATIVE PEOPLE, 1986

	Aboriginal	Indian[a]	Métis[a]	Inuit[a]
Managerial/ Administrative	18 345	14 635	3490	835
Professional	36 030	28 895	6975	1750
Clerical	39 540	30 855	8345	1745
Sales	15 890	12 410	3650	485
Service	43 080	32 010	10 595	2035
Primary	21 220	16 210	5215	630
Processing	14 160	11 205	2950	420
Product Assembly	14 085	11 135	2840	620
Construction	23 405	17 220	6065	1125
Other	28 215	21 185	6465	1705
Total	253 980	195 750	56 590	11 355

a. Includes both single and multiple origins.

SOURCE: *1986 Census Highlights on Registered Indians: Annotated Tables*, DIAND, 1989.

La Rusic (1968) found that highly skilled Indian men employed by mining-exploration companies as line-cutters and stakers never received the same high pay or good working conditions that Whites received. Thus, the low income of Natives reflects both the seasonal nature of their jobs and discrimination. The results show that once Natives are able to enter the labour force, they do quite well, although less so than the general population. For example, nearly half of the Natives in the experienced labour force were engaged in white-collar jobs (the comparable figure for the general population was 64 percent). Twelve percent of the Natives (compared to nine percent for the general population) were engaged in occupations in the primary industries (Siggner, 1986).

EDUCATION

Canadian culture places a great emphasis on the value of education. Education is generally seen as essential to success; young people who do not show academic potential are usually regarded as early failures. Certainly, education has a great impact on lifestyle and life chances. Yet, for a variety of reasons, not all Canadians are able to use the educational system as effectively as possible. Natives, in particular, are excluded by several factors from the benefits of White education. The *Indian Act* allows the minister to provide educational services to Indian students from ages six to eighteen who are living on reserve or Crown land. In addition, post-secondary education is encouraged through grants made to eligible Natives.

The federal government does appear to have fulfilled its responsibility to Natives in the area of financing for education (Frideres, 1972). Federal expenditures for Native education were $13.5 million in 1956 and $52 million in 1967; by 1980 they reached well over $270 million, or 39 percent of the total Indian-Inuit Affairs budget. The total education budget in 1986 was estimated to be nearly $600 million. However, less than one percent of this money has gone directly to Native communities to be administered by Natives themselves. Most has been spent on the creation of various federal administrative and bureaucratic positions or on capital grants to provincial and local governments to purchase "seats" in non-Native schools. Natives themselves have had little control over the money allotted for their education and have had little input into the educational process. In each province, the curriculum used in Native schools is regulated by the provincial government and is the same as that designed for White, middle-class students in all the other public schools (Waubasgeshig, 1970). This process is now undergoing scrutiny.

People see and make sense of the world in many different ways; they also see their relationship to the environment in different ways. Since this is so, they approach problems looking for different solutions, and they may process information differently in arriving at those solutions. Hence the educational process has an important impact on people exposed to it. For those who accept and are able to utilize the process to its fullest, the results are positive. However, there are others who do not accept it or are otherwise unable to take maximum advantage of conventional educational methods.

This suggests that some people who are exposed to our particular type of educational system may be mismatched with the teaching process. Any discrepancy between learning style and instructional methods will lead to inefficiency and possibly to failure on the student's part. Researchers (Pask and Scott, 1971; Cohen, 1969) have identified two main styles of thinking—field dependent (relational) and field independent (analytical). The analytical type of thinkers tend to solve problems using spoken language, and they think in words rather than by meaning. They examine ideas by dividing them into their separate elements and then by evaluating and integrating all the aspects of the problem before drawing a conclusion. On the other hand, relational thinking is a style that solves problems through incorporating visual-spatial and holistic strategies. The relational thinker deals with the tangible world and perceives that all things exist in a vast relationship with all others. While there are certainly variations of these types of thinking, they characterize the opposite poles of our experience.

The present school system has been established on the premise that all members of our society are field-independent thinkers. To some extent, this may indeed be the predominant mode of thinking in our culture. However, some cultural groups do not promote this type of thinking and consequently find the present school system useless. Our best evidence suggests that Indian culture promotes the relational type of thinking (Weitz, 1971). If such a statement is true, then the dismal educational record of Indian people should not come as a surprise.

Other experts in the field feel that the poor performance of Natives in formal education settings is a result of substandard schools and lack of reinforcement of education in the families. In addition, the Native community does not place a high value on obtaining an education. Thus, these structural conditions make it extremely difficult for many Native people to achieve success in the educational system.

History of Native Education

For many years after Britain took control of Canada, Native education was controlled by the military, acting for the Crown. Then legislation was passed in 1830 transferring the responsibility to the provincial or local governments.

> Several legislatures had made provisions for the attendance of Indians at schools serving non-Indian children, including the payment to local authorities in both Upper and Lower Canada for the incorporation of Indian reserves into established school districts or school sections, and some provision had been made in the statutes for the financing of Indian education. (*Special Senate Hearings on Poverty*, 1970: 14, 59)

In general, White settlers were indifferent to Native education: a public fund was not established for this purpose until 1848. In some cases, Whites encouraged the school enrolment of Native children to pressure the province to establish more schools. As the density of the White population increased, however, Native education was increasingly ignored. Later, the federal government was reluctant to operate schools for Indians, and passed the responsibility to other, mainly religious, agencies.

With the passage of the *British North America Act*, Canada's Parliament was given the power to administer Native affairs, including education. In 1876, the *Indian Act* was passed, providing the legal basis for federal administration of Native education. In addition, most treaties signed after 1871 contained an educational commitment:

> To maintain schools for instruction on the reserve and whenever the Indians of the reserve shall desire it or to make such provision as may from time to time be deemed advisable for the education of Indian children.

Federal and provincial government policy on Native education can be considered in two phases. The first, from 1867 to 1945, has been labelled the "paternalistic ideology," while the second, from 1945 to the present, has been called the "democratic ideology" (Hawthorn *et al.*, 1967). The second phase simply refers to the "open door policy" that enabled Natives to attend school off the reserve.

The paternalistic policy, by which Natives were considered backward children, was adopted and perpetuated by various religious orders in Canada. After Confederation, the first schools for Natives were quasi-educational institutions set up by religious orders. Under sections 113 to 122 of the *Indian Act*, the federal government could legally arrange for provincial governments and religious organizations to provide Native education. Four churches—Roman Catholic, Anglican, United and Presbyterian—began to educate Natives in denominational or residential schools. Of these, the Catholics and Anglicans have had the greatest impact on Natives in Canada, and continue to do so.

Education has traditionally been viewed by churches as the best way to acculturate Native people. The religious missionaries who, up until recently, controlled Native education, were far more concerned with teaching useful practical knowledge and skills. Because they felt that Natives would always live in isolation, the missionaries made no attempt to prepare them for successful careers in modern Canadian society. Instead, they concentrated on eradicating all traces of Native languages, traditions and beliefs.

> Paying little attention to the multitude of linguistic and other cultural differences among the tribes, and the varied traditions of child-rearing in preparation for adulthood in the tribal communities, the government entered the school business with

a vigour that caused consternation among the Indians. The package deal that accompanied literacy included continuing efforts to "civilize the natives."... Children were removed—sometimes forcibly—long distances from their homes, the use of Indian languages by children was forbidden under threat of corporal punishment, students were boarded out to White families during vacation times, the Native religions were suppressed (Fuch, 1970: 55).

Because religious ideologies are fundamentally conservative, they discouraged protest and revolt on the part of the Natives. For example, Roman Catholicism holds that poverty is not a social evil, but is God's will. Instead of struggling against God's will, Catholics are encouraged to humbly accept their fates to ensure a place in heaven. Thus Roman Catholicism discourages social change, particularly that which involves force: in heaven "the first shall be last and the last shall be first" (Matt.19:30).

Churches that operated schools were given land, per capita grants and other material rewards for their efforts.[4] Often, these grants resulted in the material exploitation of the Natives as churches pursued property and profits (McCullum and McCullum, 1975). Even today, the churches' continuing opposition to integrated joint schools, Native teachers, Native language use, and so on, suggests a greater concern for their vested financial interests than for the quality of Native education. As Hawthorn *et al.* point out:

> We note that the greater the educational resources possessed by a church or the greater its investment in Indian education, the greater its anxiety to maintain the status quo. On the contrary, the faiths having the least material interests in Indian education are much more open to innovation (1967: 61).

Well over half of Canada's Natives today are Roman Catholic. A special joint Senate-House of Commons committee (1946-48) interpreted Sections 113 to 122 of the *Indian Act* to stipulate that, when the majority of Native band members belong to a given religion, members of that religion must be in charge of education in that school. This suggests that religious groups will continue to control many Native schools, despite their proven antipathy to Native independence.

> Until 1945, Native schooling was "education in isolation." During this period, schools and hostels for Indian children were established, but scant attention was paid to developing a curriculum geared to either their language difficulties or their sociological needs. A few Indian bands established schools for their children on the reserves, but the majority of them had neither the financial resources nor the leadership to establish and operate their own schools. Provincial governments were too preoccupied with their own priorities to become involved in Indian education. Missionaries provided a modicum of services, but their "noble savage" philosophy effectively insulated the Indians from the mainstream of society (*Special Senate Hearing on Poverty*, 1970: 14, 59).

Residential schools were almost all built in the country, far from White settlements. Contact between Native children and their parents was minimized. The schools were highly regimented and insisted on strict conformity. There were few adults and most of these were non-Natives; as a result, normal adult-child relations could not develop. Few of the teachers were well qualified; they neither stimulated the children nor acted as positive role models. The average annual staff turnover was never less than 21 percent and often more, particularly in later years.

In 1945, the "open door policy" was introduced that allowed students to travel off the reserve to receive an education. This was a radical departure from the earlier policy of isolation, and residential schools began to decline in enrolment. Particularly since the early 1960s, the number of Native children attending residential schools has been drastically reduced. The unpopularity of these schools should come as a surprise to no one.[5]

TABLE 5.16   ENROLMENT BY SCHOOL TYPE, ON-RESERVE POPULATION, CANADA, 1975/76-1989/90

Year	Federal	Provincial	Band-Operated	Private	Total
1975/76	29 581	38 079	2842	1315	71 817
1976/77	30 012	36 884	3340	1481	71 717
1977/78	29 412	41 358	5639	1679	78 088
1978/79	28 605	45 438	5796	1520	81 359
1979/80	27 742	45 742	6311	1442	81 237
1980/81	26 578	46 852	7879	1492	82 801
1981/82	22 525	43 652	13 133	1156	80 466
1982/83	21 825	38 511	15 912	1164	77 412
1983/84	21 893	39 474	16 715	n/a	78 082
1984/85	21 669	40 080	18 372	n/a	80 121
1985/86	19 943	39 712	20 968	n/a	80 623
1986/87	18 811	40 053	23 407	n/a	82 271
1987/88	17 322	40 520	26 429	n/a	84 271
1988/89	13 783	40 954	30 845	n/a	85 582
1989/90	11 764	41 720	34 674	n/a	88 158

SOURCES: Indian and Northern Affairs Canada, *Basic Departmental Data*, 1990, 43; 1975-1978: Nominal Roll, Statistics Section (Management Services), DIAND; 1979-1989: Nominal Roll, Education Branch, DIAND.

Types of Indian Schools

Today, Natives can attend either federal schools or integrated joint schools. There are four types of federal schools: day schools; denominational (also called residential or religious) schools; boarding and hospital schools; and band schools.

Federal

Day schools form the largest group under federal control. They are located on the reserve and provide education only for those who live there, including the non-Native children of teachers.

Denominational schools are those operated by religious groups. Since the late 1930s, DIAND has also operated residential schools, at first through the churches and, more recently, directly. When day schools were established in 1950 for elementary education, residential schools began to provide secondary education only. Since the late 1960s, the residential schools have been systematically shut down; as of 1987, there were only two operating in Canada.

Hospital schools provide classes for Natives in government hospitals from the pre-school level through to adult education.

Boarding schools are for Native orphans or children from broken homes, and may or may not be on the reserve. All boarding schools are presently under government-financed church control, mainly Roman Catholic. Although these schools are technically integrated, they have a majority of Native students.

The creation of band schools emerged out of the political lobbying that Natives participated in during the late 1960s and early 1970s. By 1973 the National Indian Brotherhood produced a document, *Indian Control of Indian Education*, which was later accepted by the federal government and adopted as official educational policy for Native education. This policy explicitly incorporated the principles of parental responsibility and local control. It was, for Indians, a time when they believed that they would become active participants in affecting their own educational experiences. The educational branch of Indian Affairs established guidelines and procedures for school transfers to bands and introduced a national formula-funding system for the allocation of resources for the band-operated schools.

By 1980, well over one hundred band-operated schools were educating students. By 1990, the number had increased to three hundred. On average, the number of band-operated schools has increased by 15 each year. Out of the 379 federal schools, 80 percent are now band-controlled schools. Band-operated schools make up an increasingly larger portion of the total Native student enrolment. Figure 5.19 shows that their share of Native students increased from less than 5 percent in 1976 to over 25 percent by 1986. Table 5.16 shows the number of registered Indians enrolled in Kindergarten to Grades 12/13 by type of school. The data also show that there has been a steady increase (8 percent) in the number of students attending school. The figures also show that a steady increase in the number of students

FIGURE 5.19   Registered Indian Population, Enrolment by School Type

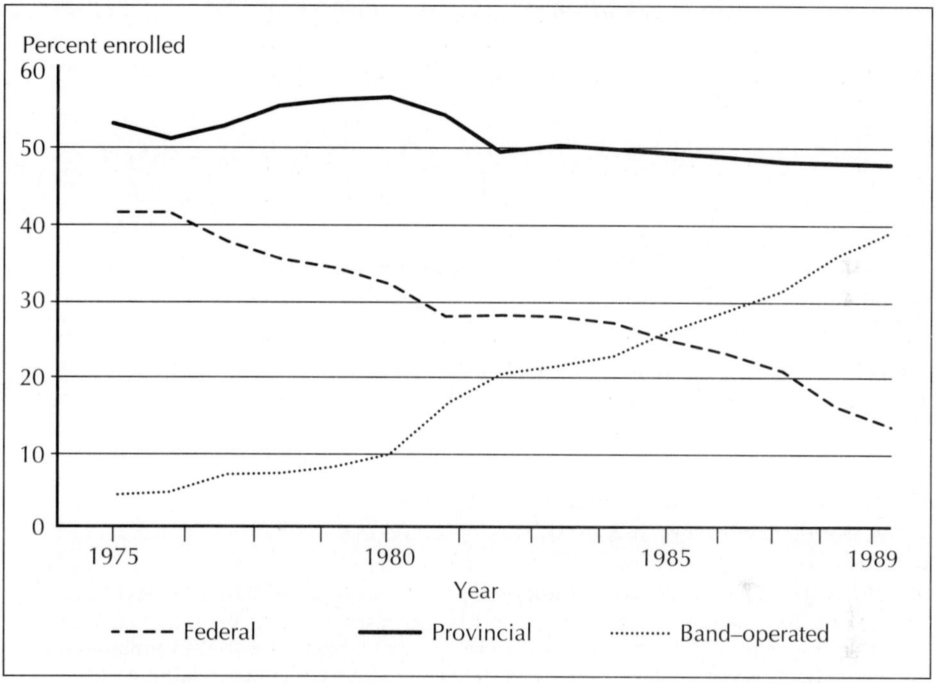

Source: *Basic Departmental Data, 1990* INAC, 1990, 42.

attending provincial schools was evident until 1980 when band operated schools began to significantly increase their student population. As a result, provincial school registrations have remained stable over the past five years.

Provincial

Integrated joint schools are not controlled by the federal government. Essentially, these are provincial schools that allow Natives to attend. The structure and curricula of these schools are not significantly different than in those controlled by the federal government. The difference lies with the administration and financing. Although education is a provincial responsibility, the federal government pays each local school board a per diem fee for each Native child enrolled there.[7]

In 1963-64, approximately 55 000 Indians were enrolled in elementary and secondary schools. Of these, 59 percent were in federal day schools, 13 percent were in residential schools, and one percent were in hospital schools. The remaining 27 percent were attending integrated joint schools.

TABLE 5.17   ENROLMENT IN KINDERGARTEN, ELEMENTARY AND SECONDARY SCHOOLS ON-RESERVE,[1] CANADA, 1960/61-1989/90

Year	Enrolment[2]	Population 4-18 Years	Enrolment Rate
1960/61[3]	41 671	57 550	72.4%
1965/66[3]	54 670	73 632	74.2%
1970/71	68 449	81 531	84.0%
1975/76	71 817	88 660	81.0%
1980/81	82 801	88 581	93.5%
1985/86	80 623	92 080	87.6%
1986/87	82 271	94 169	87.4%
1987/88	84 271	95 336	88.4%
1988/89	85 582	96 606	88.6%
1989/90	88 158	97 751	90.2%

1. On reserve includes Crown lands and settlements.
2. Total enrolment include registered, non-registered Indians and Inuit in Kindergarten to Grade 13.
3. A breakdown of on/off-reserve Indian population was not available in 1960/61 and 1965/66. Based on 1975 Indian Register data, off-reserve was estimated to be 26 percent of the total population. Data were also not available for the 4-18 population for 1960/61 and was estimated to be 42 percent of the total Indian population.

SOURCES: Indian and Northern Affairs Canada, *Basic Departmental Data*, 1990, 35.
Enrolment: 1960-1975: Nominal Roll, Statistics Division, DIAND. 1980-1985: Nominal Roll, Education Branch, DIAND. 1986-1989: Year End Status Report on Performance Indicators, National, DIAND. Population: Indian Register, DIAND.

Data from the Indian-Inuit Affairs Program (IIAP) show that from 1964 to 1981, over 800 agreements were made between local school boards and the Department of Indian Affairs in order to secure positions for Native children in provincial schools. Figure 5.19 shows the relative trends for Native enrolment by type of school.

The data provided in Table 5.16 show that total Indian enrolment has steadily increased from 1961. In 1961, over two thirds of the Indian elementary and high school students went to federal schools. By 1966 this had dwindled to 52 percent. By 1980 the figure had decreased to 44 percent. However, since that time, the number of students attending federal schools (band and non-band controlled) has increased. However, the increase is due to the tremendous increase in the number of students attending band-operated federal schools. Today 52 percent of Native students attend federal schools although three quarters of these students attend band-operated federal schools.

Table 5.17 shows that the percentage of school age children attending school has also increased. In the early 1960s, less than three quarters of the potential student population was attending school. This increased to a high of 93.5 percent in 1980/81, but has since decreased to 90.2 percent today. The decrease noted from 1980 to 1989 was a result of the government's change in policy regarding the funding of off-reserve Indians and the elimination of funds for off-reserve urban students to buy books and supplies.

School Attendance: Primary and Secondary

Most Indian children attend federal schools until Grade 6 and then switch to provincial schools for their secondary education. Fewer than 10 percent continue in the federal school system; this is partially due to a lack of federal secondary schools. In the 1950s and 1960s the federal government embarked upon a policy to phase out federal schools, and they began by closing federal secondary institutions. While this policy has been discontinued, there are few federal secondary schools which Indian students can attend.

The switch from one school system to another has a serious disruptive influence on the educational and social development of Native children. The change of social milieu has the greatest negative impact. Initially, Native children enter federal schools as a distinct cultural group with a minimal knowledge of English or French. However, because they all share a similar social status, no one is at a disadvantage. When these students transfer as a group, the group is usually broken up and the individuals are sent to different provincial schools where they become outsiders among White students who have spoken English or French from birth.

Native students at provincial schools face considerable discrimination. On the reserve these students have already met indirect, institutionalized racism; however, as Lyon *et al.* (1970) have shown, Native students in integrated schools are exposed daily to direct discrimination from teachers and other students. In the long term, racism results in a serious and permanent distortion of the Native children's self-image. The more short-term effects of discrimination include lower marks and a tendency to drop out at an early age.

Elliot (1970) draws attention to age differences as a disruptive factor for Native students in provincial schools. The competition for achievement is greater in integrated schools than in federal schools. Native children, not used to the intense competition that exists among White, middle-class students, may become psychologically uncomfortable and begin to lose academic ground. Usually, they do not receive adequate counselling prior to or following placement in integrated schools. Not surprisingly, these social disruptions eventually result in a high drop-out rate among Native students.

The rate of Natives attending school has shown a general increase over the past two decades. This is particularly true for the younger ages. For example, in the late 1960s, only about 43 percent of Native children aged four to five went to

FIGURE 5.20 ON-RESERVE STUDENTS REMAINING UNTIL GRADE 12 OR 13 FOR CONSECUTIVE YEARS OF SCHOOLING

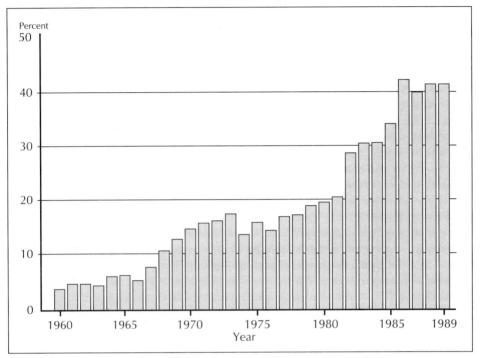

SOURCE: Basic Departmental Data, INAC, 1990, 36.

kindergarten. By the early 1990s, this figure had increased to nearly 70 percent. Similar increases are evident for older groups, but not at nearly so dramatic a rate. Over all, about 33 percent of Indians aged 15 to 24 are attending school full time, while over 40 percent of the general population is doing so. Looking at the issue from another perspective, the differences are clearer. More than half the Natives 15 years and older with less than a Grade 9 education are not attending school. The corresponding figure for the general population is 22 percent.

Successful school completion to Grades 12 or 13 is still much lower among Native students than among Canadians as a whole. In 1966, fewer than 5 percent of Indian students remained in school throughout the 12 or 13 years. Although dramatic increases have since occurred, Figure 5.20 shows that the rate for Indians remains less than one half of the national rate.

TABLE 5.18 **O**N**-R**ESERVE **S**TUDENTS **R**EMAINING **U**NTIL **G**RADE **12** OR **13** FOR **C**ONSECUTIVE **Y**EARS OF **S**CHOOLING, **C**ANADA, **1960/61-1989/90**

Year	Percentage	Year	Percentage
1960/61	3.4	1975/76	15.8
1961/62	4.3	1976/77	14.3
1962/63	4.3	1977/78	17.0
1963/64	4.1	1978/79	17.2
1964/65	5.8	1979/80	18.9
1965/66	6.0	1980/81	19.6
1966/67	5.1	1981/82	20.7
1967/68	7.5	1982/83	28.6
1968/69	10.6	1983/84	30.5
1969/70	12.6	1984/85	30.6
1970/71	14.6	1985/86	33.9
1971/72	15.6	1986/87	42.2
1972/73	16.2	1987/88	40.2
1973/74	17.4	1988/89	41.4[r]
1974/75	13.6	1989/90	41.6[1]

1. Preliminary. The percentage for 1989/90 was obtained by dividing the number of students in Grades 12 and 13 in 1989/90 by the number of students in Grade 1 in 1978/79. These percentages are under-estimated since Québec students graduate in Grade 11.

r. Datum revised.

SOURCES: Indian and Northern Affairs Canada, *Basic Departmental Data*, 1990, 37; 1960/61 - 1977/78: Statistics Division, Program Services Branch, DIAND; 1978/79-1989/90: Nominal Roll, Education Branch, DIAND.

Table 5.18 shows the retention rate of Indian students for the past 30 years. The trend shows a steady increase in the number of Indian students remaining in school, although in the past 10 years (when large numbers of band schools were established) the retention rate has doubled. While these figures reflect a positive impact of education, the data do not provide information on the number of successful graduates. Furthermore, there is some information which casts doubts on the above figures. While Indian students remain in school, they do not receive a diploma or matriculation degree. The province of Alberta, for example, has had few Indian graduates from the regular provincial school system over the past decade. Nevertheless, as Table 5.19 shows, an increasing number of students are attending high school.

TABLE 5.19   Enrolment of Registered Indians in Kindergarten, High School and University, 1949-1985

	Kindergarten enrolment	University enrolment	High school enrolment as a % of total school enrolment[*]
1949-50	—	9[**]	3.0
1953-54	—	—	4.6
1957-58	2562	27	5.9
1961-62	3560	50	8.1
1965-66	3583	131	10.2
1969-70	6807	321	13.3
1973-74	8666	1055	16.5
1974-75	9273	2047	16.2
1975-76	8582	2071	17.1
1976-77	8668	—	17.3
1978-79	—	4000	17.6
1981-82	—	5500	18.4
1984-85	—	7100	20.1

[*]   Students in grades 9-13 as a percentage of all students enrolled in grades 9-13.
[**]   Figure is for 1948-49.

Sources: Departmental Statistics Division, DIAND; Information Canada, *Perspectives Canada III* (Ottawa: Queen's Printer, 1980), 178; Indian and Northern Affairs Canada, *Basic Departmental Data*, 1990.

Quality of Native Education

The quality of Native education is determined by a variety of factors, including operation and maintenance costs, pupil-teacher ratios, the proportion of Native teachers, educational expenditures, and overall per-student education costs.

The pupil-teacher ratio provides some evidence as to the amount of time teachers can spend with individual students. Teachers in charge of a class of 27 have less time to deal with students than those operating in a class of 17. Federal schools have pupil-teacher ratios which are higher than in provincial schools. In addition, the educational qualifications of teachers in federal schools are less than those evidenced in provincial schools. This partially reflects an unwillingness of teachers to teach on reserves and the ability of outstanding teachers to move to large urban areas. In the end, while all teachers have to meet minimal standards, most teachers on the reserves are considered unable to secure jobs elsewhere in the school system.

Operation and maintenance costs for Natives in federal and provincial schools have escalated rapidly, rising from approximately $65 million in 1970 to $164 million in 1980. By 1990, the costs had escalated to $736 million. These increases appear to be keeping pace with increasing Native student enrolments and with the general increase in all educational costs. As noted previously, between 1970 and 1980, the total educational expenditures for Natives decreased relative to the total DIAND budget from nearly 50 percent to 39 percent. In current-dollar terms, expenditures per student have doubled since 1970, matching the national average. In constant-dollar terms, this represents a modest three percent decline. In 1979, for each Native student, $2600 was spent in federal schools and $2250 in provincial schools; the national average is $1900.

In the fiscal year 1984-85, $7 million was used to deliver special education programs to those Indian students identified as "hard to serve." This group of students includes those with some form of disability, including physical handicaps and perceptual difficulties. These funds enabled Indian and federal education authorities to develop and provide more appropriate programs for these students. This is an area which has been identified as a high priority for Indian communities. Five million dollars will also be spent over each of the next two years to carry out urgently needed renovations to ensure that school facilities meet recognized health, safety and energy conservation standards.

The proportion of Native administrators and teachers in federal schools more than tripled between 1966 and 1981 to over 36 percent. However, even though 90 percent of the teachers in Native schools have formal teaching credentials, only about 23 percent are university graduates. In addition, reserve schools do not have the professional backup resources, for example, curriculum development specialists and language consultants, that are part of most provincial schools.

Educational Attainment

In terms of financial aid, DIAND appears to be providing adequate educational opportunities to Native students. Yet most Natives attain only a low level of educational achievement. The following section presents data on the educational attainments of Native Canadians.

Figures 5.21 and 5.22 illustrate specific educational attainments usually associated with the achievement of literacy. Figure 5.21 shows that the rate of functional illiteracy is declining, although we can see that it is considerably higher for Aboriginal people. The results show that nearly 40 percent of Indians have less than a Grade 9 education, which is twice the national rate. Inuit have the highest proportion of adults who are functionally illiterate. Figure 5.22 shows that Aboriginal people are increasing their educational qualifications, which will allow them to take on better jobs and receive higher incomes. The data show that nearly 40 percent of all Aboriginals have at least a high school education; a substantial increase since 1981

FIGURE 5.21 LESS THAN GRADE 9 EDUCATION, ABORIGINALS AND ALL CANADIANS, 1981, 1986

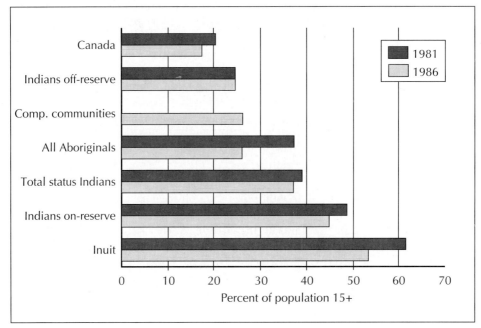

SOURCE: Highlights of Aboriginal Conditions, 1981-2001, Part III, Economic Conditions, INAC, 1989, 5.

TABLE 5.20 HIGHEST LEVEL OF SCHOOLING FOR POPULATION 15 AND OVER, 1986 (ALL ORIGINS)

	Métis	Indian	Aboriginal	Inuit
Less than Grade 9	23 870	85 255	117 190	10 995
Grades 9-13	43 350	147 930	191 930	6700
Trade certificate/diploma	2345	8320	10 680	425
Other non-university	19 005	69 800	87 325	2860
Some university	5685	24 135	29 210	805
University degree	2780	13 530	15 620	300
Total population 15+	97 035	348 970	451 955	22 085

SOURCE: 1986 Census Highlights on Registered Indians: Annotated Tables, DIAND, 1989.

FIGURE 5.22   AT LEAST HIGH SCHOOL EDUCATION, ABORIGINALS AND ALL CANADIANS, 1981, 1986

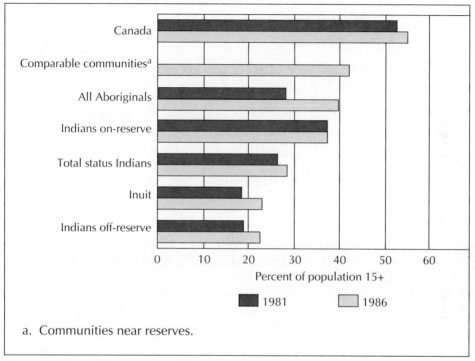

a. Communities near reserves.

SOURCE: Highlights of Aboriginal Conditions, 1981-2001, Part III, Economic Conditions, INAC, 1989, 6.

when only 28 percent had this level of education. However, on-reserve Indians show the lowest educational achievements with only approximately one fifth of the population having achieved a high school education.

Table 5.20 identifies specific categories of educational attainment for Native people. Overall, approximately one fourth of the Native population has less than a Grade 9 level of education. On the other hand, over 40 percent of the Aboriginal population has between 9 and 13 years of education. An additional 20 percent have some other form of secondary (non-university) educational training. Approximately 5 percent of Aboriginals have attended university, while slightly more than 3 percent have successfully completed their university degree.

The reasons for the high drop-out rate among Native students are at the same time complex and straightforward. According to Castellano:

...the distorted reflection of himself which is presented to the Indian child is not even the chief source of the sense of incongruity which most Indian children experience in the White school system. Far more significant and handicapping is the fact that the verbal symbols and the theoretical constructions which the Indian child is [being asked] to manipulate bear little or no relation to the social environment with which he is most familiar (1970:53).

The Canadian educational system has been developed and refined by and for a White, urban, middle-class culture. This system becomes alien and meaningless in the context of life on a reserve (Fisher, 1969). The subject matter is largely irrelevant to the Native child's everyday life. And the curriculum is set firmly within a White, middle-class system of values, bearing little relation to local Native concerns. Classes are taught by teachers who are almost always White and who seldom become involved with the local Native community. Furthermore, the competitive hierarchical structure of the schools is foreign to Native values. Not surprisingly, Native students are alienated from their educational system at a very young age.

Native students also have to contend with the poor image of themselves projected by the mass media, including films and books used in the schools. A recent study of social studies texts for Grades 1 through 8 revealed that Natives were generally portrayed, if at all, as nonentities, evil-doers, or savages (Vanderburgh, 1968). These portraits have a serious impact on the personal development of Native children. As Kardiner and Ovesey (1951) have pointed out, people to whom negative traits are continually assigned will eventually begin to incorporate them into their identities. Someone who is continually called inferior will eventually believe it to be true.

Hawthorn *et al*. (1967), Elliott (1970), and others have argued that lack of parental support is an additional factor in the drop-out rate. However, there are many structural reasons for this. Not surprisingly, because Native parents have had no control over curriculum, textbooks or staff, they have come to regard the educational system as an "outside," racist institution, to be tolerated but not supported. In some provinces, Indians still cannot be school board members.[8]

Active adult community support for education will only develop when Natives who live on the reserve are allowed to hold teaching and administrative positions. To blame parental neglect for the high drop-out rate is naïve: when all the structural variables are considered, the reaction of Native parents to the educational system is not apathetic, but actively and understandably hostile.

Post Secondary School Attendance

IIAP also promotes post secondary education for Natives. It provides financial assistance and instructional support services. All Indians and Inuit who have been accepted in a post-secondary school qualify for financial support that covers tuition, tutorial assistance, books, supplies and transportation. The cost of providing these services is just below $8000 per student.

Since the mid-seventies, the Native post-secondary enrolment has increased nation-wide from 2500 to over 15 000. This reflects an increase from less than one percent to about 9 percent in the past two decades (for those in the 18 to 24 age group). Nevertheless, this is still considerably lower than the overall national rate of over 20 percent.

The data (Table 5.21) show that there has been a steady increase in the number of Native students attending post-secondary institutions. The 1985-86 year shows a substantial increase because this was the first year *Bill C-31* Natives were redefined as Indians. These major increases provided the impetus for change in education policy regarding Natives, as well as for budgetary increases. With regards to expenditures, the data given in Table 5.22 show the enormous increase in funding (operating grants and contributions). The operating items are

TABLE 5.21   NUMBER OF STUDENTS UTILIZING FEDERAL POST-SECONDARY SUPPORT PROGRAM, 1975-1989

Year	Number of full- and part-time students	Percent increase
1975-76	2500	7
1976-77	2684	7
1977-78	3599	34
1978-79	4148	15
1979-80	4502	11
1980-81	4999	9
1981-82	5467	25
1982-83	6810	23
1983-84	8062	18
1984-85	8617	7
1985-86	11 170[a]	30
1986-87	13 196[a]	18
1987-88	14 242[a]	8
1988-89	15 572[a]	9

a. Figures for these years include the number of *Bill C-31* students.

Sources: DIAND 1988, 4; Standing Committee on Aboriginal Affairs, 1989b, 39; *Basic Departmental Data*, INAC, 1989; Standing Committee on Aboriginal Affairs, 1990, 27:33; DIAND 1987-88 Estimates Part III, 2-67.Part III, 2-67.

TABLE 5.22 Expenditures for Post-Secondary Education

Year	Operating	Grants	Contributions	Total
1984-85	2 313 100	28 855 451[b]	22 590 449	53 759 000
1985-86	2 063 034	26 766 509	44 867 230	73 696 773
1986-87	1 516 336	31 352 345	64 999 106	97 867 787
1987-88	[a]	34 375 127	75 867 853	109 078 000
1988-89	1 718 415[a]	32 113 292	88 610 293	122 442 000
1989-90	1 418 400[a]	35 206 570	110 522 053	147 147 000

a. Actual amount not cited; figure obtained by subtracting grants and contributions from total No amount is given for operating expenditures in 1987-88 since subtracting grants and contributions from the total results in a negative number. The discrepancy is related to the use of two separate sources, *Public Accounts* and *Main Estimates Part III*, the latter being the source of actual total expenditure for 1987-88.

b. Actual amount not reported in *Public Accounts*; figure obtained by subtracting operating and contributions from the total.

Sources: Totals for 1984-85 and 1987-90 are from Indian and Northern Affairs Canada. *Estimates. Part III. Expenditure Plan; Public Accounts*, 1986-1990.

expenditures which are used for DIAND program administration. Grants are funds given to regional or district offices and that are then given directly to Native students attending post-secondary schools. The second-last column (contributions) are funds that cover the basic costs of operating educational institutions and that are set aside for Native students. Between the early 1980s and today, program funds have increased well over 200 percent, while the percentage of total post-secondary support-programs funding administered by Natives increased to 25 percent.

Indian post-secondary students are older than the national average—the median age for Indians is 25; for the national group it is 20. This suggests that many of the Native students are mature students who are returning to school after an interruption.

Beyond the elementary school level, and particularly beyond the secondary level, the pattern of Native student enrolment diverges sharply from the Canadian norm. In 1981, fewer than one percent of Natives attended university, as compared with nearly seven percent of the general population. Of all Native students involved in any form of post-secondary education, 60 percent are enrolled in vocational training; this refers to programs in such areas as carpentry, sheet-metal work, motor mechanics and farming. Another 30 percent of Native post-secondary students are enrolled in "upgrading" courses; although these can range from courses on canning preserves to courses in advanced mathematics, they are most often of the former type. It seems clear that nearly all Natives who enrol in post-secondary training are being prepared for jobs at the semi-skilled level or lower (DIAND, *1978-79 Annual Report*).

Figures 5.23 and 5.24 show a dramatic increase since the early 1960s in the number of Natives attending college and/or university. A number of universities have tailored special programs to meet the interests and needs of Native students, while others have provided remedial services to assist Natives who are entering university. However, even though the increase in Native enrolment has been rapid, the Native participation rate is still less than one-half the national level. For example, in 1975, 20 percent of the Canadian population between the ages of 18 and 24 were enrolled in universities, and only 8 percent of the Native population.

Even more dismal than the enrolment figures are the statistics that reflect the rate of graduation from universities. In the 1967-68 academic year, 156 Native students were enrolled in universities in Canada. Of these, 17 percent withdrew voluntarily during the year, and 15 percent failed one or more courses, generally resulting in automatic exclusion under the terms of their special-entry program. The rest passed all their courses but, at the end of the program, only 6 percent remained to graduate. These figures remained constant for the next decade. In 1970, 432 students were enrolled in universities and only 12 percent graduated. Today, over 14 000 Natives are enrolled in post-secondary educational institutions. Of these, about 7 percent graduate, compared to a graduation rate of well over 16 percent for non-Natives. Clearly, a Native student's chances of finishing university are still quite small. For individuals having attended university, non-Indians are about 2.4 times as likely as Indians to earn a degree. However, while the success rate for Indians is lower than that of the general population, it is increasing. Language and cultural differences, as well as the effects of discrimination, have not been adequately addressed and continue to place Native students at a serious disadvantage in the university system.

The challenge facing Native communities today is to take control over the formal education process; however, there is nothing in the *Indian Act* that would give them any leverage in doing this. The minister of DIAND has complete control over which schools students attend and over the nature of contents of any education agreement. Natives have no right of appeal or review. Any change to the *Indian Act* would require action by Parliament, and the federal government has taken the position that it will not amend the *Act* piecemeal, even though there might admittedly be some need for change. Hence, it is unlikely that the *Act* will be changed in the near future to allow for greater Indian control in matters of education (Barman, Hebert, McCaskill, 1987).

Even if the *Act* were changed, it is unlikely that Natives could take control of the education process. In the first place, the federal government has more trust in provincial school authorities (with regard to finances) than in Native people. Second,

FIGURE 5.23   **U**NIVERSITY AND **C**OLLEGE **E**NROLMENT OF **I**NDIANS **B**ETWEEN **1957**
                   AND **1987**

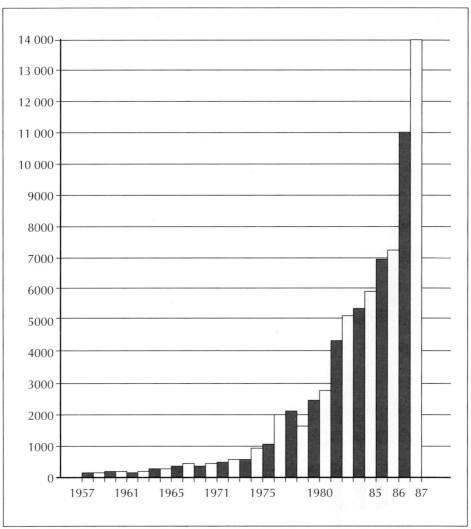

SOURCE: Employment and Related Services Division, DIAND, 1978; Indian and Northern Affairs
Canada, 1986, *Basic Departmental Data*, 1988, INAC, 37.

FIGURE 5.24   Uᴺɪᴠᴇʀsɪᴛʏ Eɴʀᴏʟᴍᴇɴᴛ: Pᴇʀᴄᴇɴᴛᴀɢᴇ ᴏꜰ Pᴏᴘᴜʟᴀᴛɪᴏɴ 18-24 Yᴇᴀʀs;
Iɴᴅɪᴀɴ ᴀɴᴅ Nᴀᴛɪᴏɴᴀʟ, 1945-1988.

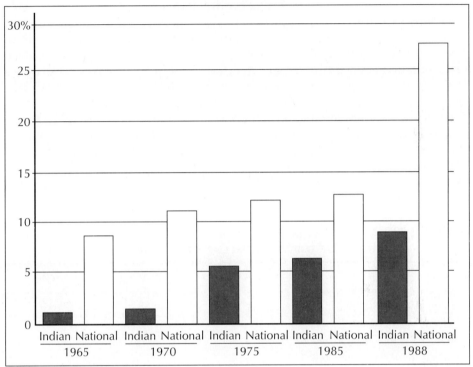

Sᴏᴜʀᴄᴇs: Education in Canada, Cat. no. 81-229, Statistics Canada; *Post-Secondary Courses for Indian Students*, 1965, 1975, DIAND; *Registered Indian Population by Age, Sex and Residence for Canada*, 1965, 1970, 1975, DIAND; INAC Customized Data, Research Branch, Corporate Policy, 1985, *Basic*

because the federal government does not operate an educational system, it relies on the provincial curricula and standards. Thus is it not interested in developing new approaches to education that would be appropriate or relevant to the diversity of Native communities (Longboat, 1987). Finally, policy within DIAND in regard to education, is developed and carried out by department officials; it is not a cooperative effort between Natives and the government. For example, even though the government adopted a stance acknowledging Indians' right to control education in the early 1970s, they added an important condition. Any agreement that had been signed with provincial officials would be honoured until its term expired. In other words, local control of education would not be discussed until the terms of the agreement had concluded. Because most of the capital agreements (an agreement to pay a percentage of the school board's capital and building costs) are 20- to 25-year contracts, Native communities will have to wait an entire generation before they can begin to discuss local control of their schools (Longboat, 1987).

From 1980 until today, there were some major policy developments. Changes were made to the E-12 guidelines in 1987,[9] and the publication in 1988 of the Assembly of First Nations' *National Review of First Nations Education* brought about substantial changes in government programs. Earlier changes (1983) made it possible for Native students to obtain preparatory study prior to full time entry into university. Native studies programs were created in the 1980s at various universities which allowed Natives to gain entrance to the school under conditions different from those of non-Native students. However, these programs are small (usually there are about five to ten Native students) and they are currently under attack as universities are looking for ways to cut expenses.

TABLE 5.23   UNIVERSITY PARTICIPATION RATES, AGED 15+, FIRST NATIONS CITIZENS COMPARED WITH CANADIANS, 1986

	First Nations	Canadians	Ratio
Crude participation rate[a]	6.2	18.5	3.0
Eligible participation[b]	22.6	33.2	1.5
Crude university success rate	1.3	9.6	7.4
Eligible university success rate	4.8	17.3	3.6
Attempted university success rate	21.3	52.0	2.4
1981 adjusted success rate	24.7	56.5	2.3

a.   Proportion of the adult population (aged 15+) that has ever attended university.

b.   Proportion of the adult population (aged 15+) having at least a high school diploma that has ever attended university.

Crude University Success Rate = Percentage of adult population (aged 15+) having a university degree.

Eligible University Success Rate = Percentage of adult population (aged 15+) that has at least a high school diploma who have achieved a university degree.

Attempted University Success Rate = Percentage of adult population (age 15+) who attempted university and achieved a university degree.

Adjusted Success Rate = Percentage of adult population (age 15+) who attempted university and achieved a university degree, adjusting for those students still in university attendance.

SOURCE: Indian and Northern Affairs Canada, 1990, 41.

The participation rate of Natives over the age of 15 remains well below that of Canadians in general. Non-Natives are one and one-half times more likely to attend university as Natives (see Table 5.23). Nevertheless, the data presented have unambiguously pointed out that there have been dramatic increases in Native participation in educational institutions. This has been made apparent by both Natives and government policy analysts.

LIVING CONDITIONS AND QUALITY OF LIFE

"Living conditions" refers to specific objective factors that affect a Native's ability to maintain a quality of life commensurate with that of other Canadians. This includes such considerations as the availability and quality of housing and the provision of community services such as health care and welfare. As pointed out previously, the life expectancy of Natives is still much lower than the national average. Other indicators, such as the rates of suicide, violent death and alcohol abuse, demonstrate a general increase in social problems and a lowering of the quality of life, especially among reserve Indians.

Housing

The federal government has no legal or treaty obligation to provide housing units or to repair existing ones for Natives. However, it does have an historical commitment to provide housing for Indians, which, so far, it has chosen to continue.

Because of the geographical isolation and limited natural resources on reserves, most of them do not have the economic ability to meet the cost of various capital facilities. Therefore, funding by DIAND is critical for these communities. One of the more important types of community facility that is being subsidized by DIAND is housing. Support to individuals and bands to provide adequate housing takes place through subsidies for the construction and renovation of houses on reserves. The subsidy levels for new construction vary from $19 000 to $50 000. Today, about 46 000 housing units have been built on reserves under the Indian and Inuit Housing Program, at a cost of well over $100 million in 1984-85. In addition to this, rural and Native housing programs have provided an additional $88 million to subsidize housing for Inuit, Métis and non-status Indians.

Over the past 25 years, the number of dwellings on the reserves has increased from just over 25 000 to over double that number. Table 5.24 shows the growth rate of the number of dwellings in relation to the growth rate of the population. Between 1983-84 and 1989-90, an average of 3263 new dwelling units per year were built on reserves. In 1991, the number was slightly above 4000. In terms of renovations,

TABLE 5.24   Number of Dwellings and Persons per House On-Reserve, Canada, 1963-1986

Year	Total Population	Growth Rate	Number of Dwellings	Growth Rate	Number o Persons per House
1963	151 966		25 206		6.05.5
		5.2		5.2	
1965	160 274		26 515		6.0
		9.2		3.5	
1967	174 958		27 429		6.4
		2.2		4.0	
1969	178 760		28 517		6.3
		2.0		5.0	
1971	182 362		29 934		6.1
		2.6		4.2	
1973	187 123		31 200		6.0
		6.2		5.9	
1975	198 775		33 636		7.8
		4.1		1.6	
1977	206 947		34 189		6.1
		6.3		28.2	
1981	219 996		43 817		5.0
		9.5		2.5	
1984	240 791		44 908		5.4
		6.2		19.5	
1986	255 788		53 686		4.8

Sources: Indian and Northern Affairs, *Basic Departmental Data*, 1988, 71.

Population:

1963-1965: Summary of Biennial Indian Housing Survey Reports: 1958-1973 by Region and District, Departmental Statistics Division, DIAND.

1967-1986: Indian Register, DIAND, 1967-1986.

Number of Dwellings:

1963-1973: *Summary of Biennial Indian Housing Survey Reports: 1958-1973 by Region and District*, Departmental Statistics Division, DIAND.

1975: *Indian Housing Survey 1975*, Departmental Statistics Division, DIAND.

1977: *Statistical Report, Listing of Information Related to the Housing-Needs Analysis*, Program Support Group, DIAND, 1977.

nearly 4000 homes per year since 1983 have been renovated, with an average subsidy of $8000 to $10 000.

The above figures must be interpreted in the context of public housing standards. Native housing units, because of the standards employed by DIAND, have a life span of 15 to 20 years, less than half the national average life span. Thus, even though there has been an increased number of housing units built on reserves, the poor quality of the houses and the increase of people living on the reserves through *Bill C-31* intensifies the competition for good housing.

A more recent evaluation of the on-reserve housing program estimated that about three-quarters of all existing housing were inadequate in that they failed to meet some of the basic standards of safe and decent living. For example, while only two percent of the Canadian population live in crowded conditions, more than one third of the Natives' houses were found to be overcrowded. (The average Canadian house had 2.1 people living in it; Natives have dropped from 6 in 1963 to 4.8 today). In addition, the number of Native houses requiring major repairs nearly doubled between 1985 and 1991. By rating housing conditions as good, fair or poor, government officials determine the state of Native housing stock and provide an overview of housing conditions on reserves. Generally, slightly less than half the houses are in good condition.

Almost all of the housing on reserves is provided by the federal government, and because individual title is severely limited, most homes are not owned by individuals but by the band. The band councils "rent" the houses at a breakeven point to keep the costs down. As a result, the absence of individual ownership reduces the chances the occupant will maintain the unit in good repair. Houses on the reserves are also single-family units.

The above-mentioned program and philosophy have been unnecessarily restrictive and have partially contributed to the lack of Native housing. Some reserves in Ontario and Québec have tried to combat the official rules and methods by investigating the feasibility of providing multi-unit buildings. A recent study carried out by DIAND shows that nearly $1 billion would be needed to bring the housing of Natives up to average Canadian standards.

Infrastructure Services

The number and extent of government services available to Natives have a considerable impact on their quality of life. A major factor in the provision of services is accessibility by road or rail; without good transportation access, services are difficult and costly to provide. Yet only about a third of the reserves even have year-round road access. Nearly half of all reserves and settlements are accessible only by water. And only 18 percent are accessible by both rail and road.

Figure 5.25 shows the average percentage of housing on Indian reserves with central heating, with a sewer (or septic tank), and with running water. The data show that, on the average, 90 percent of reserve houses have electricity, and 75 percent have running water. Recent statistics show that the picture has continued to improve. For example, about 50 percent of the Indian reserve population had adequate water supply and sewage disposal in 1977. By 1989/90, this had increased to 86 and 77 percent respectively.

The percentage of reserves with adequate fire protection equipment has increased since 1970, but is still only about 35 percent. In Manitoba, less that 10 percent of reserves have sufficient equipment, but in the Yukon and the Atlantic provinces nearly 70 percent have adequate fire protection.

While these data show improvements, there can be little doubt that housing for Native people is inferior to that for the non-Native population. Less than three quarters of Natives' homes have central heating in contrast to over 90 percent of non-Native homes. As we have seen, crowding is also a problem for Natives. One in 43 non-Native homes was crowded compared to the one-in-six proportion of Native homes. More than 15 percent of Native homes require major repairs. Overall, Natives have the least favourable housing conditions of any ethnic group in Canada.

SOCIAL ASSISTANCE

Native people rely upon social assistance more than any other ethno-cultural group in Canada. Participation in social assistance programs is just one indicator of poverty. The data examined show that this reliance is increasing even though a variety of economic development projects have been implemented. The extent of social assistance indicates both the quality of life of Native people and how well the economic programs are working. Table 5.25 shows the total social assistance expenditures for Indians from 1973 to 1990. The results show that the amount of expenditures has doubled over the past two decades. However, even though the budget has doubled, the expenditures per recipient has remained constant at slightly more than $4000. The average annual number of recipients per month has increased by nearly 50 percent over the past eight years, and is now about 60 000. When dependents of these recipients are added to the figures, we find that over 130 000 Indian people are receiving social assistance. The data in Table 5.25 show that the cost of this is nearly $400 million per year.

In addition to the above, over 500 adult Indians are in residential care, with a cost of over $13 million per year. This represents a ratio of 3.2 per 1000 which has only slight decreased from 1971 when the ratio was 3.7 per 1000.

Since the mid-1970s, when the number of Indian children in care peaked at 6.5 percent of the total child population (16 and under), there has been a steady decrease. Today there are just under four percent of the children under care. As Table 5.26 shows, this represents about four thousand children in care facilities. Figure 5.26 shows that the cost of child care has risen from just under $2 million in the mid-sixties to well over $100 million today—a seven-fold increase.

TABLE 5.25   SOCIAL ASSISTANCE EXPENDITURES, REGISTERED INDIAN POPULATION, CANADA, 1973/74-1989/90

Fiscal year	Number of recipients[1] (current $)	Total expenditures (current $)	Per recipient current	Tota expenditures[2] (81 constant $)	Per recipients (81 constant $)
1973/74	n/a	53 319 000	n/a	112 014 706	n/a
1974/75	n/a	64 105 000	n/a	121 410 985	n/a
1975/76	n/a	73 023 000	n/a	124 825 641	n/a
1976/77	n/a	78 660 000	n/a	125 055 644	n/a
1977/78	n/a	85 753 000	n/a	126 293 078	n/a
1978/79	n/a	105 983 000	n/a	143 414 073	n/a
1979/80	n/a	122 004 400	n/a	151 182 652	n/a
1980/81	n/a	141 985 300	n/a	159 713 498	n/a
1981/82	39 146	165 030 100	4216	165 030 100	4216
1982/83	42 101	196 241 700	4661	177 113 448	4207
1983/84	43 750	216 157 600	4941	184 434 812	4216
1984/85	45 408	235 433 500	5185	192 504 906	4239
1985/86	48 494	255 288 200	5264	200 698 270	4139
1986/87	50 879	278 070 900	5465	210 023 338	4128
1987/88	54 170	314 446 000	5805	227 529 667	4200
1988/89	56 573	351 706 500	6217	244 580 320[r]	4323[r]
1989/90	59 680	390 017 600	6535	258 289 801	4328

1. Excludes Indians residing in N.W.T. and Newfoundland.
2. The expenditures in constant dollars have been calculated using the Consumer Price Index based on the year 1981 from Statistics Canada.
r. Datum revised.

SOURCE: Indian and Northern Affairs Canada, *Basic Departmental Data*, 1990, 57; Social Development Branch, DIAND.

Since the mid-1970s, when the number of Indian children in care peaked at 6.5 percent of the total child population (16 and under), there has been a steady decrease. Today there are just under four percent of the children under care. As Table 5.26 shows, this represents about four thousand children in care facilities. Figure 5.26 shows that the cost of child care has risen from just under $2 million in the mid-sixties to well over $100 million today—a seven-fold increase.

TABLE 5.26   ON-RESERVE CHILDREN IN CARE, REGISTERED INDIAN POPULATION, CANADA, 1966/67 - 1989/90

Fiscal Year	Children in care[1]	Children aged 16 and under	Percent	Fiscal Year	Children in care[1]	Children aged 16 and under	Percent
1966/67	3201	93 101	3.4%	1978/79	6177	94 866	6.5%
1967/68	3946	93 484	4.2%	1979/80	5820	94 414	6.2%
1968/69	4310	94 616	4.6%	1980/81	5716	94 916	6.0%
1969/70	4861	94 698	5.1%	1981/82	5144	94 608	5.4%
1970/71	5156	95 048	5.4%	1982/83	4577	96 105	4.8%
1971/72	5336	94 777	5.6%	1983/84	4105	98 379	4.2%
1972/73	5336	94 906	5.6%	1984/85	3887	97 586	4.0%
1973/74	5582	94 634	5.9%	1985/86	4000	99 213	4.0%
1974/75	5817	96 960	6.0%	1986/87	3603	101 841	3.5%
1975/76	6078	96 493	6.3%	1987/88	3836	101 537	3.8%
1976/77	6247	96 417	6.5%	1988/89	3989	102 529	3.9%
1977/78	6017	96 780	6.2%	1989/90	4178	105 992	3.9%

1. The total number of children in care calculated by Social Development Branch is obtained by dividing the total number of case-days by 365. Child care cases do not include preventive and alternate approaches to child and family services (e.g., homemakers). Excludes Indians residing in the N.W.T. and Newfoundland.

SOURCES: Indian and Northern Affairs Canada, *Basic Departmental Data*, 1990, 47.

Children in Care:

1966/67-1980/81: Statistics Canada, *Social Security, National Programs*, 1978, Cat. No. 86-511; 1981/82-1989/90: Social Development Branch, DIAND.

Children aged 16 and under:

Indian Register, DIAND.

FIGURE 5.25   Reserve Housing: Running Water, Sewer/Septic Tank, Central Heating

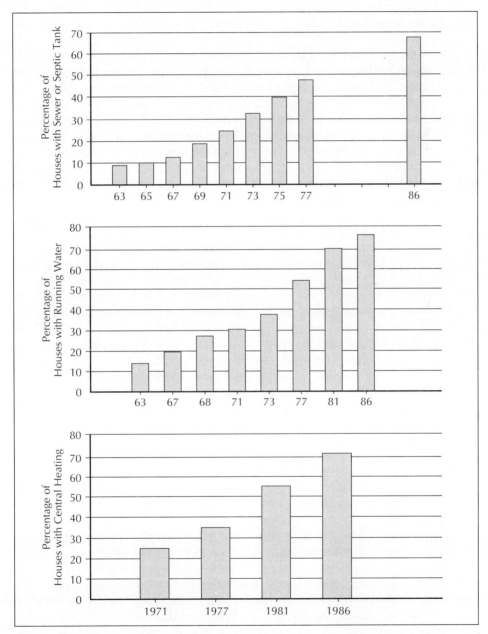

Source: Basic Departmental Data, INAC, 1988, 69.

The number of Indians receiving social assistance has increased since the early 1980s. While the increase between 1981 and 1986 was from 16.5 to 17.8 percent, a similar increase for non-Natives was revealed, 6.2 to 7.9 percent. Nevertheless, these figures show that the rate of poverty for Indians is twice as high as for the general population.

The funds provided through social assistance enable Native people to maintain basic levels of health, safety and family unity. It provides Native recipients with food, clothing and shelter as well as counselling to enable them to achieve independence and self-sufficiency. In addition to the social assistance program, Indian Affairs also offers welfare services to ensure that Natives who need protection from neglect or who need help with personal problems have access to a variety of services.

Over all, over half of the total Native population received social assistance or welfare payments in 1991. An even more astounding fact is that nearly 90 percent of Indians, at one time in their life, have received social assistance/social support. These figures compare with 12 percent for non-Natives in 1991 and a lifetime non-Native experience with social assistance of 22 percent. There are regional variations in the numbers of social-assistance recipients. Both Natives and non-Natives in the Maritimes have required social assistance and social welfare at much higher rates than elsewhere in Canada. Finally, it should be pointed out that most of the Natives who have received welfare payments were employable. These facts suggest that social assistance to Native people is offered as an alternative to employment, not as a measure to help them enter the labour force and obtain wage labour. As the data show, there is an increasing number of Natives who seek social assistance and social welfare. These conditions have not reversed, which suggests that economic dependency will continue well into the twenty-first century.

Unemployment creates a need for social assistance that goes beyond simply providing funds for food and housing. A considerable number of studies have shown that an indirect effect of unemployment is its negative impact upon interpersonal relationships. Unemployment places considerable strain on individual relationships, including relations within the family. These interpersonal problems do not appear immediately, but develop slowly and come into full play when a person feels emotionally battered and unable to cope with other stresses (Lauer, 1984).

In summary, social assistance is a far more serious problem for Native people than for other social groups in our society. Structural factors have produced the problems which have forced Native people to become dependent on social assistance; yet most Canadians engage in a form of the fallacy of personal attack, implying or asserting that Natives themselves are the cause of their need for social assistance. Maintaining that Native people, as a group, have brought on their own problems draws our attention away from dealing with the structural problems preventing Native people from fully participating in Canadian society. At the same time, Canadians appear to be largely in agreement that our "social charter" requires that we provide assistance to people unable to attain an adequate quality of life. Yet we provide that assistance grudgingly and not without comment, while, at the same time, failing to try to solve the underlying conditions that brought about the problem.

HEALTH

The federal government believes that, with certain exceptions, they do not have any legal or fiduciary obligations with regard to health care for Native people. Natives disagree and claim the right to special treatment. Disputes between First Nations and the federal government revolve around three issues. First is the conflict in definitions of health. Second is how health policy is implemented for Native people. Third is the funding of First Nations health services, including the statutory, constitutional or fiduciary obligations of the federal government regarding the provision of health services to Natives (Speck, 1989). Nevertheless, the federal government has accepted some responsibility with regard to Native health. Under Health and Welfare Canada, approximately $500 million are spent on six major health programs: Community Health Services, Environmental Health and Surveillance, Non-Insured Health Benefits, National Native Alcohol and Drug Abuse Program, Hospital Services, and Capital Construction. While there is no direct federal government legislation for the provision of these services, custom and historical commitment provide the basis and rationale for covering the cost of these programs. There are some exceptions, such as the references to the provision of a "Medicine Chest" in Treaty No. 6.

Until 1945, the Department of Indian Affairs solely provided health care services to Indians on the reserve. However, in that year, these services were transferred to the Department of Health and Welfare, and they have remained there since that time. In 1962, Indian Health Services (a division in Health and Welfare) was merged with six other federal health programs to form a specific branch, Medical Services. In 1964, Treaty Indians were defined as insured persons under provincial medicare. By 1970, the present structure of Indian Health Services was in place, although the 1974 *Lalonde Report* for the federal government first set the stage for the transfer of health care away from the federal government. By 1981, a proposal to transfer responsibility for health care services to Indian communities was approved. In 1982, Indian Health Services standards were developed and introduced as a way of measuring the extent to which Indian health needs were being met. The *Neilsen Report* was leaked in 1985 and focused on duplication of services as well as on determining the legal basis of federal government involvement with Natives.

In 1986, Health and Welfare (Medical Services Branch) announced a new policy initiative: The Indian Health Transfer Policy. This new policy was to facilitate a developmental approach to transferring health care and services to Native communities, centred on the concept of self-determination. It was hoped that it would lead to First Nations autonomy and community control of health care services

FIGURE 5.26 **R**EGISTERED **I**NDIAN **P**OPULATION **O**N-**R**ESERVE, **C**HILDREN **I**N **C**ARE

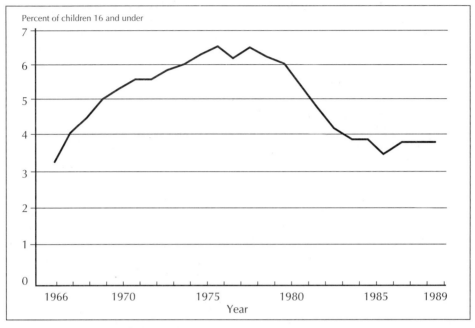

Percent of children 16 and under

Year

SOURCE: Basic Departmental Data, 1990, INAC, 46.

(Speck, 1989). The Transfer Policy in health care is a continuation of the "devolution policy" developed by Indian and Northern Affairs Canada a decade earlier in that it proposes that a larger share of the responsibility now allocated to the federal government be taken on by First Nations.

There is considerable conflict between the two parties with regard to this transfer. Speck (1989) points out that First Nations are denied self-determination which, in turn, denies them the opportunity to create conditions whereby Native health could be improved. For example, she notes that the federal government continues to administer health services as an isolated "thing" which is separate from the political, social and economic dimensions of life; a fact Natives and others have consistently identified as one of the major problems in health care for Natives.

Today, in all but three of the provinces, insurance premiums are paid for everyone by provincial governments, who take payments from tax revenue. A variety of arrangements exists in these provinces for payment of premiums by registered Indians, ranging from bulk payments to general means tests. As Speck (1989) points out, the specific features which differentiate Native from non-Native health services are the payment of medical and hospital insurance premiums by the federal government for three provinces, the provision of public health services by the federal government rather than the provincial, and the federal funding of additional non-insured services for Indians (p.193). Regardless of the source of funding, a full range of medical services is provided to Indians, although these vary from one province to another, depending upon the standards set by each province.

Programs of Medical Services

The federal government has assumed jurisdiction over the health of Indians. While the *Indian Act* itself says little about the specifics (see Section 73[1]) and its main focus is on the prevention of the spread of infectious diseases, there remains a strong financial commitment to Native health care through a variety of programs (Woodward, 1989). Health and Welfare Canada operate a number of programs which also provide health care to Native people throughout Canada. The first major program is Community Health Services, which focuses on communicable disease control, health education, mental health, nursing, and the provision of medical advice and assistance. The second is the non-insured health benefits program. Through this program, Native people are provided general health care through access to the provincial medicare systems and supplemental programs. In addition, the program includes the transportation of patients, dental services and other medical appliances and services. The third major program is one in which funding is provided to train and employ local health care workers, under the aegis of the Community Health Services. Also, in 1983, the National Native Alcohol and Drug Abuse Program was put in place. This experimental program still exists and has expanded its role as it deals with treatment, rehabilitation and education.

The provision of services for Native people is carried out through all three levels of government. Those services provided by provincial and municipal agencies are generally fully reimbursed by the federal government. At the federal level, Medical Services has over two hundred doctors (less than one percent are Native) and over 1000 nurses (about 10 percent are Native). Over 500 community health workers are also contracted by Medical services to provide health care for Native people. Nearly all of the community health workers are Natives. On a per capita basis, Medical Services Branch spends about $400 per year per Native, approximately the same spent on non-Native people (Grescoe, 1981).

Health services are also provided through contributions and contract arrangements with Native organizations, bands and post secondary educational institutions. Community Health Services carry out this program through four main activities: (a) health care and treatment services, (b) public health services, (c) involvement of Indians in the health care system, and (d) the provision of physical facilities (DIAND, 1984).

The overall structure for providing medical and health services to Native people is complex. At the national level, several government agencies interact to set policies, determine programs and establish funding levels, e.g., Deputy Minister of Health and Welfare; Director General: Policy and Evaluation, Treasury Board; and the directors of Indian/Inuit Policy, Planning and Evaluation. At the provincial level, the regional director oversees implementation of the programs for each health zone, which involves doctors, nurses and environmental health officers. At the local level, for those bands involved in health care delivery, band councils make decisions regarding training programs and determining who will be admitted to various health programs.

Health Conditions of Native People

Many of the statistics about disease and illness among Native people have been published and are well known. Illnesses resulting from poverty, overcrowding and poor housing have led to chronic and acute respiratory diseases, which take a heavy toll among Native people. The standardized death rate for the Native

FIGURE 5.27   DEATH RATES 1978-88, INDIAN AND CANADIAN POPULATIONS

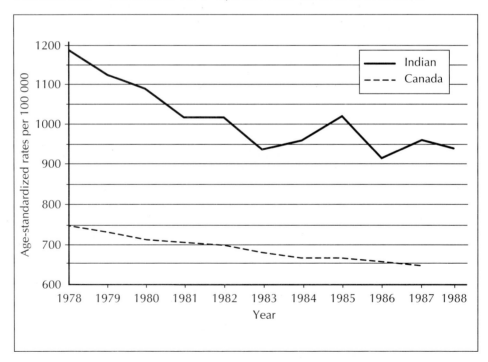

SOURCE: Ellen Bobet, *Inequalities in Health: A Comparison of Indian and Canadian Mortality Trends,* Health and Welfare Canada, 1990.

population is more than double the general Canadian population—15.9 versus 6.6 deaths per 1000 population (Nuttall, 1982; Brady, 1983; INAC, 1988) with an average age of death more than 20 years below that of the average non-Native Canadian.

The overall trend in Native mortality shows that it has improved substantially over the past decade. Nevertheless, there is still a considerable gap between Natives and the general Canadian population (see Figure 5.27). The data reveal that the overall death rate among Native people has decreased by nearly one third since 1978. However, it is still higher than the national rate. The gap between Natives and the general Canadian population is particularly wide for ages 15 to 44. Natives in this age group are more than three times likelier to die than the average Canadian.

Infant mortality has tremendous impact upon the population of all societies since infants will (if they live) contribute to the growth of the population when they reach childbearing age. Over the years (see Figure 5.28), there has been a substantial

FIGURE 5.28   **INFANT MORTALITY, INDIAN AND CANADA, 1960-1988**

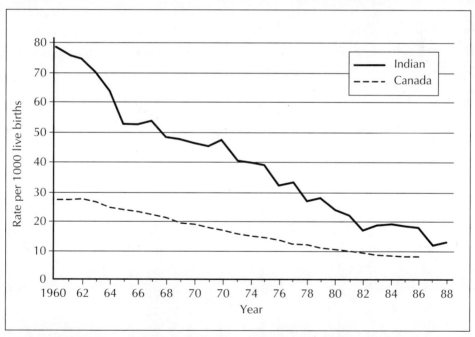

SOURCE: Ellen Bobet, *Inequalities in Health: A Comparison of Indian and Canadian Mortality Trends,* Health and Welfare Canada, 1990.

TABLE 5.27 MORTALITY RATES BY CAUSE, REGISTERED INDIAN POPULATION, CANADA, 1982 - 1988 (REVISED)

Classification of Diseases	1982	1983	1984	1985	1986	1987[1]	1988[1]
				Rates per 100 000			
1. Infectious & parasitic	9.2	6.5	11.9	8.9	13.8	9.6	6.0
2. Neoplasms	62.0	54.8	57.9	54.4	58.0	69.8	65.1
3. Endocrine, metabolic & immunity disorders	15.2	10.3	7.5	16.4	12.6	20.0	12.7
4. Blood and blood-forming organs	0.4	2.1	1.4	0.8	2.4	1.2	3.0
5. Mental disorders	9.2	8.9	4.4	5.5	6.1	4.0	7.1
6. Nervous system & sense organs	4.6	4.4	6.5	6.7	5.7	9.2	10.0
7. Circulatory system	159.2	139.7	140.7	156.4	122.0	128.5	133.2
8. Respiratory system	44.3	51.3	47.3	46.4	40.5	43.5	44.7
9. Digestive system	34.4	28.1	22.1	24.5	23.5	18.4	16.4
10. Genito-urinary system	9.9	9.6	9.2	7.6	6.5	8.8	8.9
11. Complications of pregnancy, childbirth, etc.	0.0	0.0	0.0	0.8	0.0	0.4	1.1
12. Skin & subcutaneous tissues	1.1	0.7	1.0	0.0	0.0	0.0	0.4
13. Musculoskeletal system	1.4	0.7	3.1	2.1	0.8	1.6	1.5
14. Congenital anomalies	7.4	14.7	10.6	9.3	12.6	9.6	7.4
15. Conditions from perinatal period	17.7	11.0	11.2	14.8	12.6	9.2	10.0
16. Symptoms, signs & ill-defined conditions	25.2	24.3	20.1	25.7	33.6	25.5	27.2
17. Injury and poisoning	205.3	178.0	192.4	203.6	164.6	187.9	166.7
Others	10.3	22.6	22.8	19.8	42.6	12.8	12.7
TOTAL	616.9	567.5	570.2	603.8	557.8	559.8	534.1

1. Rates for 1987 and 1988 no longer include N.W.T. Indians because of the transfer of health services to the government of the Northwest Territories.

2. Population served by Health and Welfare Canada.

SOURCE: Demographics and Statistics Division, Medical Services Branch, Health and Welfare Canada, 1990.

decrease in infant mortality rates. The data show that the infant mortality rate among Indian people is now less than one sixth of what it was in 1960. However, it should be noted that it is double that of the general Canadian population: the Canadian infant mortality rate is 7.9 per 1000 while Natives' rate is 17.5 per 1000. A closer look at the infant mortality rate shows that Native perinatal (still births and under one week) deaths are twice as high as the general population. On the other hand, neonatal (birth to one month) death rates for the two groups are very similar. Post-neonatal (one month to one year) death rates are more than three times higher for Indians. These rates reflect the poor housing and other environmental conditions Native children are born into.

The effectiveness of the Native Health Care system is related as much to the environmental conditions in which Natives live as to the treatment and facilities provided. Health care provided is sometimes countered by social and economic problems such as overcrowding, poor nutrition, chronic unemployment, and community and family violence. Thus, a Native, after receiving effective medical treatment, finds him/herself returning to social conditions which created the problem in the first place. In short, the worst causes of poor mental and physical health are not dealt with.

What are the specific causes of death? For the past decade, over one third of all Indian deaths (compared to eight percent in the general population) are due to accidents and violence (see Table 5.27). For all age groups up to 63, Native people are four times as likely as other Canadians to die from these causes. The most frequent are motor vehicle accidents, drowning and fire. Although these rates are extremely high, they have been reduced by over 40 percent since 1980.

The other major causes of death (in order) are: diseases of the circulatory system, respiratory system, cancer, suicide, and chronic conditions; e.g., tuberculosis, diabetes. A comparison of life tables (length of life) between the Native and non-Native populations over the past 20 years shows that there has been little improvement for Native people and even a deterioration in the past decade (Nuttall, 1982). Today, the life expectancy of a Native person is 30 years less than that of a non-Native.

Bobet (1990) shows that in Native society, compared to the rest of the population, suicide and self-inflicted injuries are three times higher (six times higher for the 15 to 24 age group), homicide rates are twice as high, congenital anomalies are 1.5 times higher, tuberculosis is over nine times higher, and pneumonia over three times higher. Native people have five times the rate of child welfare, four times the death rate, three times the violent death, juvenile delinquency, and suicide rate, and twice the rate of hospital admissions of the average Canadian population. Native people are also exposed to severe environmental hazards: industrial and resource development have polluted water and disrupted fish and game stock for many reserve communities, seriously affecting quality of life. For example, residents of the White Dog and Grassy Narrows reserves in Ontario were found to have 40 to 150 times more mercury in their blood than the average Canadian (Bolaria, 1979). Various environmental disturbances have upset other Native communities such as Cluff Lake (uranium pollution), Serpent River (acid discharge), and St. Regis (fluoride pollution). Obviously, the Native lifestyles vary considerably from those of non-Natives.

In summary, statistics show that the quality of life experienced by Native people is far inferior to that of non-Natives. How have they found themselves in this position? These conditions have come about as a result of the cultural imperialism of the Canadian government and the racist philosophy that promoted the dominant society's insistence on the inferiority of Native people.

NATIVES AND THE LAW

With regard to criminal procedures under federal and provincial legislation, Native people are subject to the same laws that other Canadians are. Our legal system has taken the position that the Criminal Code will be applied equally to all Canadians. People come into contact with the justice system at various junctures. Starting with police contact, the individual may or may not move to the next stage, which is the courts, and then on to incarceration and finally release. Do Native people find their experience with the justice system different than non-Natives? We begin our discussion with the first contact, the police.

Less than one percent of the police force is Native. While a small program to encourage Natives to join the Royal Canadian Mounted Police was implemented, by the late 1980s it was phased out (see Figure 5.29). When Natives come into contact with the police, are they treated differently than non-Natives? Unfortunately data on this aspect of policing are not available. However, there is considerable evidence to suggest that Native people are more likely to be charged with an offence than non-Native people in similar situations. Thus, when police are able to exercise their discretion in charging an individual or not, Native people are more likely to receive a formal charge. Yerxa (1990) found that nearly 80 percent of the Indian men he surveyed had been arrested at some time in their lives (see Table 5.28). These data confirm that Native people are at a much higher risk of entering the second level of contact with the justice system—the courts. Barkwell, *et al.* (1989) found that once Métis adults moved into the court system, they were differentially dealt with; e.g., Native people charged are less likely to receive bail. They are also more likely to be placed in jail and less likely to be placed on probation (see Figure 5.30).

Canadian courts are highly professional, standardized and centralized. Only individuals who have completed a rigorous education and internship are allowed to enter the courts; lay judges and community involvement are not allowed.

FIGURE 5.29   **THE EMPLOYMENT OF ABORIGINAL PEOPLE IN THE CRIMINAL JUSTICE SYSTEM IN ALBERTA, 1990**

Criminal Justice System Component	Total Number of Employees	Number of Aboriginal Employees	Aboriginal Employees as a % of Total Employees
Police			
•R.C.M.P.	2052	50-55	2.4-2.7%
•Municipal Police	2583	27	1.0%
•All Police	4635	77-82	1.7-1.8%
Alberta Solicitor General[a]			
•Corrections	2000	54[b]	2.7%
Correctional Services of Canada			
•Prairie Region	2071[c]	93	4.5%
•Alberta	894	31	3.5%
National Parole Board		6	
Alberta Attorney General			
•Crown Prosecutors	125	Not known	
•Justices of the Peace	398	4	1.0%
Provincial Court Judges	111[d]	0	0%
Court of Queen's Bench Judges	64	0	0%
Appeal Judges	8[e]	0	0%
Legal Aid Lawyers Roster	2647[f]	28	0.9%

a. Includes salaried staff in Corrections and Law Enforcement.

b. Does not include 37 non-salaried Aboriginal staff wage positions, for example, in the Summer Temporary Employment Program.

c. Number of employees.

d. Excludes two supernumerary and one vacant position.

e. Excludes one vacant position.

f. From an alphabetical listing of lawyers willing to accept Legal Aid cases, provided by Legal Aid Society. Ethnic status was not defined.

g. The number of members of the Indigenous Bar Association has been used as an indicator of the potential number of Aboriginal lawyers. However, not all members of the Indigenous Bar Association provide Legal Aid services. Therefore, the percentage of Legal Aid lawyers of Aboriginal ancestry is very likely to be lower than 0.9%.

SOURCE: Report on the Task Force on the Criminal Justice System and Its Impact on the Indian and Métis People of Alberta, March 1991, 8-42.

TABLE 5.28 Percent Having Previous Sentence to Federal Jails by Gender and Ethnic Status, 1989

Number of Previous Commitments	Aboriginal		Non-Aboriginal	
	Male	Female	Male	Female
0	41%	47%	51%	74%
1	24%	27%	20%	18%
2	14%	27%	13%	6%
3	9%	0%	7%	0%
4	6%	0%	3%	0%
5+	6%	0%	6%	6%
Total	338	15	626	19

Source: Canadian Centre for Justice Statistics, Statistics Canada, *Adult Correctional Services in Canada,* 1989-90.

FIGURE 5.30 Adult Corrections Referrals, 1987, % Native v. % Non-Native

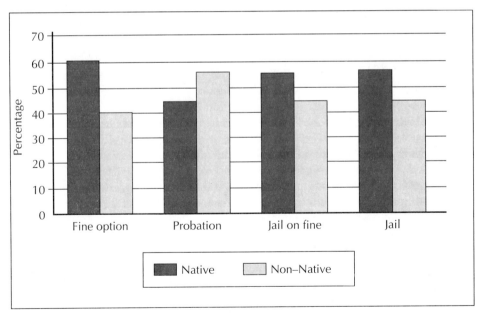

Source: Manitoba Métis Federation Justice Committee, 1989.

While most people hold the court system in high regard, Aboriginal people tend to see the courts as a tool of oppression. There are few individuals of Native ancestry in the judicial system. Natives do not experience the courts as being accountable to their communities, nor do they see them as resolving disputes between parties.

For Natives, justice can only be obtained through the establishment of day courts and justices of the peace. These would be staffed by Natives and would be a suitable compromise, allowing justice to be more equitably distributed. This arrangement would allow Native people to become more involved in the system. It is argued that in the adjudication of criminal offenses, the involvement of elders and laypersons (as members of the Aboriginal community) would lend greater legitimacy to the process. And, in the end, their involvement would be more effective in resolving problems in the community (Indigenous Bar Association, 1990).

As noted above, the Canadian criminal justice system is viewed by Aboriginals as a foreign system not compatible with their way of life. Because of the difference in world view, the Aboriginal cannot fully comprehend our dominant society's court process, nor can the courts fully understand the Native. For example, the difficulties of language incompatibility have been noted in many Aboriginal claims that the court system does not adequately represent Aboriginals. As the Alexander Tribal Government (1990) pointed out in their submission to the Task Force on the Criminal Justice System and Its Impact on the Indian and Métis People of Alberta, some members of the courts suffer from "cultural blindness." They are unable to see and hear accurately the Aboriginal victims, accused, and witnesses who appear before them.

Furthermore, because of the isolation of many Native communities, Aboriginals have pointed out that the provision of justice by our courts is viewed by Natives as serving the convenience of the judges and lawyers while community people are inconvenienced. Native people have argued that in isolated communities, the courts rush the process of justice so they can return to their homes. Postponements of courts are also based upon convenience to the courts, not the community. In short, few court hearings are held in Native communities, which supports the Native view that courts are foreign institutions.

The right to counsel upon arrest is another issue of concern for Aboriginal people. For many Natives in remote communities, this right is meaningless because counsel is not easily available. And, although police have the duty to advise people of their rights to silence and to consult a lawyer, they do not have to make counsel available. A 1989 study in an urban Canadian centre noted that over 60 percent of the Native defendants were with legal counsel. Thus, in urban areas, access and use of legal counsel is widely used while in rural areas it is almost nonexistent. And, when legal aid is available for Natives in these isolated communities, it doesn't begin until the actual court appearance. Our research has also found that, regardless of his/her criminal record or the type of offence with which the person was charged, an Aboriginal was more likely to be held in custody than to be released with a summons to appear.

Barkwell *et al.* (1989) investigate specifically how Métis in Manitoba are treated in our legal system. Their data show that Métis people are differently affected by the operation of the justice system. Looking first at Métis youth, the authors found that Métis children are committed to youth institutions at twice the rate they are diverted from court. (This is true for Native youths in general.) The Manitoba Métis Federation Justice Committee (1989) found that alternative measures are less frequently used for Métis youth than for others. They also noted that, although the Young Offenders Act (section 3(d)) provides for police to exercise their discretion in taking no measures against youth for minor infractions, this is differentially applied (a situation also noted by Barwell *et al.*). Métis youth also have high custody rates.

Once in the court system, Native people are more likely to enter guilty pleas simply to get the process over with. Natives do not want to remain in custody because time in the remand centre is considered "dead time." The Native Counselling Services of Alberta Courtwatch determined that 90 percent of Aboriginals plead guilty compared to 75 percent of non-Natives; 96 percent of the Natives were found guilty compared to just over 80 percent for non-Natives (see Table 5.29).

The lack of alternatives to incarceration is problematic for Canadian courts. Nearly one third of Native males sentenced to jail and two thirds of Native females sentenced to jail were so because of fine defaults. In view of the high unemployment rate and the high rate of Natives on welfare, the above statistics should not surprise us. And, as the Canadian *Cawsey Report* notes, the incarceration of fine defaulters does not meet the general principles which guide sentencing, which are the protection of the public, the deterrent effect, and the rehabilitation of the offender.

An individual charged with an offence, under the *Canadian Charter of Rights and Freedoms* is not to be denied reasonable bail without just cause, within 24 hours of the charge. Judges can release individuals charged in a number of ways: on their own recognizance (with or without surety), on cash bail, on an order to appear with conditions. Nearly one third of non-Natives are released on their own recognizance, while only six percent of Natives are so released. Furthermore, if a cash bail is ordered, most Natives do not have the funds to post such a bond. Finally, it is important to note that the denial of bail has a significant effect on both the likelihood of a conviction and on the severity of any sentence that is ultimately meted out (Griffiths and Verdun-Jones, 1989).

The personnel involved in our court system know surprisingly little about Aboriginal culture or the people. Not surprisingly, many Native people are contemptuous of court personnel. Native people clearly see that the Canadian court system does not arrive at a real resolution of disputes. Horowitz (1989) points out that

TABLE 5.29   **PERCENT OF NATIVES IN TOTAL ADMISSIONS TO JAILS BY YEAR AND PROVINCE**

	1985-86		1986-87		1987-88		1988-89		1989-90	
	P¹	F¹	P	F	P	F	P	F	P	F
Nfld/Labrador	4%	1%	5%	1%	4%	4%	5%	6%	4%	2%
P.E.I.	4	—	3	7	3	—	3	6	3	—
Nova Scotia	4	1	4	3	4	1	5	1	4	1
New Brunswick	4	3	4	2	4	2	4	2	5	5
Québec	—	—	2	1	—	—	2	2	2	1
Ontario	9	2	9	4	9	4	10	5	8	5
Saskatchewan	64	61	64	56	66	51	65	52	66	54
Manitoba	54	34	56	39	55	36	44	35	47	40
Alberta	10	22	10	20	11	22	11	11	11	23
B.C.	16	13	18	14	19	12	18	17	19	14
Yukon	57	33	60	33	60	54	63	50	65	44
N.W.T.	85	76	90	73	88	63	88	96	88	75
Canada (Total)	20	10	18	10	22	11	19	13	18	11

1.   P = Provincial jail, F = Federal jail

SOURCE: Adult Correctional Services in Canada, 1989-90, *Preliminary Data Report*, Canadian Centre for Justice Statistics, Ottawa, Statistics Canada.

courts are well suited to dealing with historical facts (events that have transpired between the parties to a lawsuit) but not with social facts (the recurrent patterns of behaviour on which policy must be based). He also points out that Canadian judges take a more "textually-oriented" type of reasoning that is poorly grounded in socio-economic facts.

In summary, the courts and personnel have little understanding of Native culture. Their actions result in perceptions and charges by Native people that they are racist. The Native lack of respect for Canadian criminal justice has resulted in a lack of respect for our court system and a desire to replace it with tribal courts. The *Cawsey Report* (1991) also points out that the mechanistic, procedural, impersonal and methodical way of dealing with people in courts further contributes to this lack of respect.

Correctional Institutions

In its submission, the Task Force on the Criminal Justice System and Its Impact on the Indian and Métis People of Alberta noted that "no correctional system in Canada ... is presently situated or equipped to deal with those underlying or causative factors which result in a disproportionate number of Natives entering the system." A look at the recidivism rates of Natives confirms that the existing system has had little impact on the level of crime in Aboriginal communities. In short, incarceration has not been a deterrent, nor has it led to rehabilitation.

Extensive documentation exists which shows that there is an over-representation of Native people in our jails. Over a five-year period (1985-90), nearly 20 percent of the provincial jail population has been Native (with wide variations—see Table 5.29), while at the federal level Natives have counted for about 8 percent. Given that the total Native population makes up about 5 percent of the Canadian population, this over-representation is substantial. As the Alberta Task Force pointed out, nearly 14 percent of charged persons were Aboriginal, yet 30 percent of those in the provincial jails were Aboriginal. The data for the province of Alberta show that in 1989, the rate of offender admissions for Natives was just over 90 per 1000 population, while the rate for non-Natives was one ninth! (see Table 5.30). They conclude that the courts appear to contribute to the over-representation of Aboriginal people in prison in a direct and significant manner. Furthermore, Aboriginals are less likely to receive a probation release than they are to be admitted to a correctional centre.

As Natives proceed through the justice system, they are more likely to receive a sentence leading to admission to a federal jail. For example, between 1985 and 1989 in Alberta, the increase in federal jail sentences was 19 percent for non-Aboriginals; the increase was twice as large for Aboriginals. Table 5.31 shows the percentage of Native offenders for five major categories. It shows that male Native offenders are more highly involved in person offenses (which generally bring about harsher sentence) than property offenses.

TABLE 5.30 RATE OF OFFENDER ADMISSIONS PER 1000 OF THE POPULATION FOR ALBERTA, 1989 AND 2011

Age Structure (Years)	1989						2011					
	Native			Non-Native			Native			Non-Native		
	No. of offenders	Native Pop.	Rate /1000 pop.	No. of offenders	Non-Native Pop.	Rate /1000 pop.	No. of offenders	Native Pop.	Rate /1000 pop.	No. of offenders	Pop.	Rate /1000 pop.
12-18[a]	1893	26 680	71.0	3899	322 520	12.1	2766	38 988	71.0	4137	342 212	12.1
19-24[b]	3273	12 450	262.9	8159	168 850	48.3	4741	18 033	262.9	10 339	213 967	48.3
25-34	3724	23 148	160.9	9188	461 152	19.9	5751	35 745	160.9	8634	433 355	19.9
35-44	1527	12 873	118.6	3411	362 927	9.4	3647	30 742	118.6	3547	377 358	9.4
45+	551	12 577	43.8	1529	613 923	2.5	1647	37 600	43.8	3019	1 212 100	2.5
Total population (0-45+ years)	10 968	120 239	91.2	26 186	2 298 061	11.4	18 552	203 333	91.2	29 676	2 904 367	10.2

a. For this age category the admission data are for the 12 to 18-year age group and the population data are for the 10 to 19-year age group.
b. For this age category the admission data are for the 19 to 24-year age group and the population data are for the 20 to 24-year age group.

SOURCE: Government of Alberta, *Justice on Trial*, 1991, vol. I, 8-16.

TABLE 5.31 MAJOR OFFENCE OF INMATES IN FEDERAL JAILS FOR CANADA BY GENDER, 1990

	Percent Native		Total number	
	Male	Female	Male	Female
Murder[1]	14%	8%	1540	52
Manslaughter[2]	20%	33%	864	49
Sex offenses[3]	15%	20%	1591	5
Robbery	9%	16%	3095	55
Break and entry	11%	0%	2013	7
Other	7%	37%	4164	143

1. Includes murder 1, 2, capital and noncapital murder.
2. Includes attempted manslaughter.
3. Includes rape and other sexual offences.

SOURCE: Adult Correctional Services in Canada, 1989-90, *Preliminary Data Report*, Canadian Centre for Justice Statistics, Ottawa.

Female offenders, because of their small numbers, tend to be overlooked in federal statistics. Nevertheless, nearly half of the female provincial jail admissions are Native.

Robertson (1988) focuses on the incarceration of Native women. Within Manitoba, a majority of admissions to the provincial jail for women are Native (68.4 percent). One hundred percent of the women transferred to the federal jail were Aboriginal. This incarceration rate for Aboriginal women mirrors their arrest rate; as Barkwell *et al.* (1989) report, over the past decade, Winnipeg police indicate that about 70 percent of the women arrested are Native. Within the overall provincial correctional institutions for women in Manitoba, about one third of the population is Native. In federal correctional facilities, Native women make up about 14 percent.

Once in jail, the length of sentence and release data also reveal that Aboriginals are disadvantaged. Table 5.32 shows that a larger percentage of Natives are sentenced to two to ten years than non-Natives. Release data also show that the most desirable release (full parole) favours non-Aboriginals (32 percent for Aboriginals, 54 percent for non-Aboriginals) and that the reverse is true for the least desirable release, mandatory supervision (29 percent for non-Aboriginals, 48 percent for Aboriginals). Even after Natives are released, they are discriminated against. As the Alberta Task Force pointed out, when a post-release decision is required of a parole board, Aboriginals receive more negative decisions than non-Aboriginals. In short, this means that when Natives receive a parole (day or full), they are more likely to be sent back to prison.

TABLE 5.32 LENGTH OF SENTENCE FOR FEDERAL INMATES FOR NATIVES AND NON-NATIVES

Years	Native		Non-Native	
	Male	Female	Male	Female
<2	9%	9%	4%	3%
2-3	22%	30%	20%	23%
3-4	17%	22%	16%	16%
4-5	11%	11%	10%	10%
5-6	8%	7%	7%	6%
6-10	15%	7%	15%	15%
10-15	4%	5%	8%	7%
15-20	<1%	0%	3%	<1%
20+	<1%	0%	2%	<1%
Life	12%	11%	14%	19%
Indefinite	1%	0%	1%	<1%
Total[a]	46	11 902	264	1425

a. Total inmate population for each category.

Source: Adult Correctional Services in Canada, 1989-90, *Preliminary Data Report*, Canadian Centre for Justice Statistics, Ottawa.

Incarceration is based on the concept of control through the deprivation of various rights and privileges. Secondly, incarceration is used to rehabilitate the offender. For many offenders serving custodial sentences, incarceration has done little to deter any further involvement in crime. Nor has it helped change either the attitudes or behaviours of offenders; in other words, they are not helped in dealing with the forces—internal and external—which have shaped their perceptions of self and of society at large. Rather, through ineffective and archaic policy and methods of administration, the negative behaviour of the individual is exacerbated, resulting in further tension between the inmate and custodial staff. Indeed, as mentioned previously, the ingrained suspicion and resentment that Aboriginals have had toward non-Aboriginal bureaucracies (especially prison services and other levels of criminal justice) has been created to a large degree by the historical and contemporary relationships they have experienced with all levels of the broader dominant society. These same relationships have inadvertently, in many cases, forced Aboriginals to resort to negative or aggressive behaviour as a way of dealing with the situation.

CONCLUSION

As we have seen, Native people in Canada reside in scattered communities and are divided by geographical boundaries, cultural differences and legal distinctions. However, Native Canadians do share one common feature: across Canada, they lead marginal lives, characterized by poverty and dependence. Indeed, many people argue that Natives are members of a culture of poverty. Not only are they alienated from middle-class Canadian society through White racism, but also through the destructive mechanisms by which one class profits at the expense of another.

The position of Natives in today's society is not the result of any single factor, but of complex historical and contemporary events. The alienation of Native Canadians began with historical subjugation and subsequent economic displacement. This was followed by a failure to recognize and guarantee certain inalienable Native rights.

The subjugation and control of Native Canadians has been continued through a process of individual and institutional racism. The federal government has neglected to consult with Natives concerning their welfare, has failed to develop and finance effective programs to assist Natives, and, at times, has actively prevented Natives from becoming organized in pursuit of their rights. The political organization of Natives has also been hindered by the factionalism that has developed within different segments of Native society. All these factors, and others, have led to the marginality of Natives in Canada.

Both Natives and government officials decry the poverty and associated ills that currently face Native people. Sine 1960, considerable efforts have been made to raise the social and economic status of Natives. DIAND has substantially increased its expenditures and attempted to develop a new philosophical perspective through which to solve the "Indian Problem." But, as the data presented in this chapter have illustrated, the efforts of DIAND have not been successful. Although Natives have achieved some absolute gains in income, education and occupational level, they continue to fall further and further behind other ethnic groups in Canada.

Despite the statistics provided above, little seems to have been done to redress or correct the problem in any significant manner. It should not come as a surprise then, that Natives feel hostile toward our justice system. Native people's contact with the legal system has brought about an experience that not only denies them their self-esteem, but also contributes to their dysfunctional state, leaving them unable to cope with the legal system in particular and with mainstream Canadian society in general.

NOTES

1. Statistics Canada defines "mother tongue" as the language a person first learns in childhood and still understands.

2. The data show how many percentage points each group is over or under its representation in the general labour force. That is, if ethnicity were not a factor in occupational placement, the proportion of each ethnic group in every occupational category would be the same proportion of that group to the total population. For example, if Natives made up 1.2 percent of the total population, they would make up a similar percentage in each occupational category. Ideally, the over-under representation should hover around zero.

3. Denominational schools are founded and operated by a particular religious group. Residential schools are also denominational.

4. Religious schools receive a fixed amount, proportional to the number of pupils, for the administration, maintenance and repair of their buildings.

5. See Caldwell (1967) and the Canadian Superintendent (1965).

6. All of these schools were funded by the federal government but operated by religious orders.

7. In certain provinces, such as Nova Scotia, the Department of Indian Affairs has a master agreement with the province concerning payment for Native students in provincial schools.

8. This policy of exclusion is now under review. Natives now use school committees to communicate their desires and objections. These committees are set up by the band council and authorized to act on behalf of the Native community, but under regulations drawn up by Indian Affairs.

9. These are written documents produced by the government of Canada outlining the policy and programs designed to deal with Indian educational issues such as funding, building of schools, eligibility of students, etc. (for kindergarten to grade 12/13).

CHAPTER 6

INDIAN AFFAIRS AND GOVERNMENT POLICY

INTRODUCTION

The British Indian Department, the first department set up by the Crown in America, was established in 1755. However, 1830 is considered the beginning of an ordered system of Indian administration in Canada. In 1860, responsibility for Indian affairs was transferred by the British government to the government of the Province of Canada. At the time of Confederation, the *Constitution Act, 1867*, gave the new federal government legislative authority over "Indians and lands reserved for Indians." In 1939, a Supreme Court decision extended this to cover Inuit. Over the years, Indian affairs have been under the control of many different government departments, such as Agriculture and Citizenship; and it would not be until the 1960s that the current structure was put in place.

DIAND comprises a number of programs, sectors, branches, directorates and secretariats. Three major programs make up the department activities—Indian and Inuit Affairs, Northern Affairs, and Administration. Within the Indian and Inuit Affairs Program, which is the central focus of this book, four sectors have been created to deal specifically with Native people. All of these organizations will be identified below in an attempt to illustrate the size and complexity of DIAND.

And, it should be noted at the outset, the size and complexity of the organization's structure have certain implications in terms of how it operates. Furthermore, these branches, directorates and secretariats are not the only federal agencies which deal with Native people. The Secretary of State, Justice and the Medical Division all have organizations within their departments which have Native people as part of their mandate. In addition, there are many other branches of both federal and provincial government which deal with Native people. Hence, the scope and complexity of the structure of government involvement in Native life should be clear to the reader. The attendant problems of coordination and delivery are great indeed. It should come as no surprise, then, that there is a great deal of overlap, confusion and conflict among and between the many organizations which deal with Native people. Likewise, it should be clear that Native people find this complex web of uncoordinated organizations difficult to understand and to deal with.

The Department of Indian Affairs and Northern Development (also now known as Indian and Northern Affairs Canada) was created in 1966 and is responsible for all federal policy and programs concerning Canadian Indians and Inuit; it also administers the Northwest Territories and the Yukon. DIAND administers 36 separate acts, including the *Department of Indian Affairs and Northern Development Act*.[1] The department's mandate includes:

- fulfil the obligations of the federal government arising from treaties, the *Indian Act* and other legislation;
- provide for the delivery of basic services to status Indian and Inuit communities;
- support Indian and Inuit economic development and community economic self-sufficiency;
- negotiate community-based arrangements that result in enhanced decision-making and authority for Indian communities;
- support constitutional discussions regarding the definition of the rights of Aboriginal peoples and related matters;
- negotiate settlements in respect of claims to Aboriginal rights;
- provide transfer payments to the governments of the Yukon and Northwest Territories;
- support the economic development of the North and protect the northern environment, including Arctic seas;
- foster the political development of the northern territories and coordinate federal policies and programs in the North; and
- administer lands and resources in the North (Annual Report, 1990).

The Department of Indian and Northern Affairs has been in an organizational flux for over two decades. More recently, it began to substantially reorganize in 1985 and completed this reorganization by 1987. In general terms, the major change was the Department's redefinition of itself as an "enabler" and an advocate for initiatives launched by Native people. This new identity stands in stark contrast to the previously held role of controller and regulator of Indian issues. As Weaver (1991) points out,

> ...in contrast to the historic role of DIAND as custodial administrator, new paradigm thinking proposes a smaller, more responsive and more development-oriented administrative role. Its job is to constructively support and advance First Nations political autonomy, and to service the negotiated agreements... (pp. 14-15).

The reorganization was designed to achieve four goals which were identified after intensive meetings had gone on between government and Native people. The four themes were self-government, economic development, quality of community life, and protection of the special relationship between the federal government and the Native people. In an attempt to achieve these goals, the department agreed that it would shift more decision-making to Indian communities; remove barriers to economic growth; develop better housing, education and social services in order to respond to local needs, achieve better management of Indian lands and monies, and protect the special relationship that exists between the federal government and the Indians and Inuit of Canada.

Canada's status Indians and Inuit want the opportunity to deal with their own problems and with their own cultural, social and economic development. Primarily through the Department of Indian Affairs and Northern Development, the federal government is working toward that goal by supporting the development of self-government by Indians and Inuit.

In consultation with Native leadership, programs and policies are being devised to achieve the four main goals described above. The government supports Indian and Inuit self-reliance and is trying to reinforce this support through the following strategies, largely implemented through the Department of Indian Affairs and Northern Development:

- develop new opportunities to build long-term well-being and self-reliance among status Indian and Inuit people;
- vigorously pursue the resolution of outstanding obligations to Indian people, especially with respect to land claims;
- ensure that existing levels of basic programs and services to Indians on reserve are maintained; and
- implement improvements which strengthen the capacity of Indian individuals and communities to become more self-reliant.

There are also long term objectives which the Department of Indian Affairs and Northern Development has outlined. These are:

- negotiate fundamental changes to the legislative relationship between status Indians and the Crown;

- develop the resource and other economic potential of Indian lands;
- provide necessary community and individual services and facilities on reserves;
- satisfy legal obligations to Indians and resolve specific claims;
- encourage the provinces to provide status Indians who choose to live off-reserve with full access to regular provincial programs;
- negotiate and implement comprehensive claims settlements with Inuit; and
- provide necessary community and individual facilities and services for Inuit; and
- meet obligations to Inuit contained in claims settlements.

Central to all federal efforts and initiatives is the desire to have status Indians and Inuit decide their own futures. The government's overriding objective is to nurture the socio-cultural and political development that will ultimately see Canada's first citizens realize their dreams. But this cannot be achieved without sound economic growth. Therefore, the federal government will continue to contribute to economic development opportunities by bolstering Native participation in commercially viable businesses and institutions.

STRUCTURE OF DIAND

The structure of DIAND is outlined in the following Figures 6.1 to 6.10. As presently organized, the department is aligned with its programs.[2] It is also highly decentralized, with approximately 75 percent of its employees delivering more than 500 distinct services in 9 regions consisting of 49 districts (see Figure 6.1).

In addition to the responsibilities noted above, the Department plans to undertake several new initiatives with regard to Native people. Specifically they are:

- To advance self-government initiatives at the community level.
- To coordinate settlement implementation and to continue to promote self-reliance.
- To establish and implement new funding arrangements with bands.
- To review comprehensive claims and the related policy.
- To support the development of a treaty renovation policy.
- To facilitate Indian control of Indian education.
- To assess existing program delivery mechanisms and related organizational structures to establish Indian control and community self-sufficiency (Government of Canada, 1989).

The new organizational structure of DIAND shows that there are seven major sectors in the department (see Figure 6.2): Lands, Revenues and Trusts, Indian Services, Economic Development, Self-Government, Finance and Professional Services, North and Canada Oil and Gas Lands Administration. This structure

FIGURE 6.1   REGIONAL OFFICES OF THE DEPARTMENT OF INDIAN AFFAIRS AND
NORTHERN DEVELOPMENT

■ Regional Office (Northern Affairs Program)
□ Regional Office (Indian and Inuit Affairs Program)
● District Office
▲ Sub-district Office
○ Service Centre
✳ Advisory Centre

Atlantic
1. Amherst

Québec
2. Sept-Îles
3. Québec City

Ontario
4. Brantford
5. Toronto
6. Sudbury
7. Thunder Bay
8. Sioux Lookout

Manitoba
9. Winnipeg
10. Thompson

Saskatchewan
11. Regina
12. Fort Qu'Appelle
13. Prince Albert
14. Meadow Lake

Alberta
15. Edmonton
16. Calgary
17. Lethbridge
18. St. Paul
19. Fort McMurray
20. High Level

British Columbia
21. Vancouver
22. Prince George
23. Nanaimo

Yukon Territory
24. Whitehorse
25. Teslin
26. Watson Lake
27. Haines Junction
28. Ross River
29. Carmacks
30. Beaver Creek
31. Mayo
32. Dawson

Northwest Territories
33. Inuvik
34. Norman Wells
35. Fort Simpson
36. Yellowknife
37. Hay River
38. Fort Smith
39. Rankin Inlet
40. Iqaluit

SOURCE: *Annual Report 1989-90*, INAC, 1990, 40.

FIGURE 6.2   ORGANIZATIONAL STRUCTURE OF THE DEPARTMENT OF INDIAN AFFAIRS AND NORTHERN DEVELOPMENT

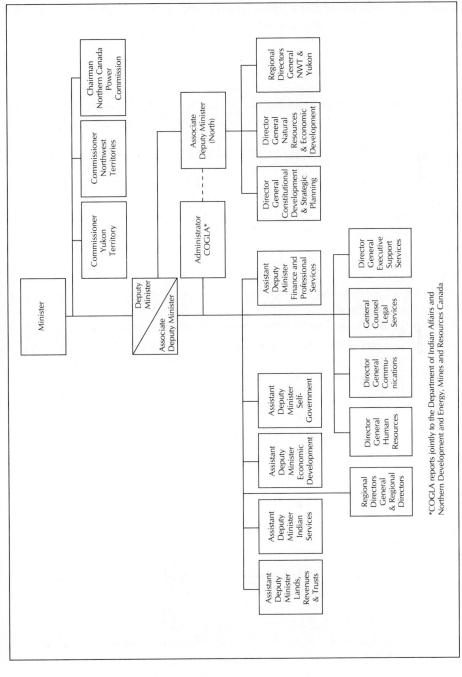

*COGLA reports jointly to the Department of Indian Affairs and Northern Development and Energy, Mines and Resources Canada

Source: Annual Report 1987-88, INAC, 9.

shows that each sector of the department communicates directly to the Deputy Minister while no formal linkages exist among the units. However, informal communication, on a daily basis, goes on among the various units in an attempt to keep each sector informed of other activities being carried out in the department.

Although this chapter will focus upon the Indian and Inuit Affairs Program, all of DIAND's branches and sectors deal directly and indirectly with Native people. A brief statement about the mandate and goals of each of these sections will allow a better understanding of the structure and focus of DIAND as a whole.

INDIAN AND INUIT AFFAIRS

The activities of the Indian and Inuit Affairs Program are directed toward the approximately 450 000 registered Indians in Canada and the 7550 Inuit who live in northern Québec, Labrador, and south of the 60th parallel elsewhere in the country. The structures of the programs are outlined in Figures 6.3 to 6.10.

The program administers the statutory requirements, defined in the *Indian Act*, including the registration of Indian people, the deployment of reserve lands and other resources, and the regulation of band elections. It also attempts to ensure that the federal government's lawful obligations to Indians and Inuit under the *Indian Act* and the treaties are fulfilled.

The Indian and Inuit Affairs Program provides a wide range of services of a federal, provincial and municipal nature to Indians and Inuit. In meeting its responsibilities, the Indian and Inuit Affairs Program works closely with other federal departments and agencies such as National Health and Welfare, the Department of Justice and the Secretary of State. In addition, individuals working for the Indian and Inuit Affairs Program provide training and advice and monitor operations for the delivery of basic services.

In keeping with the principle of self-development, Indian and Inuit Affairs attempts to assist and support Natives in achieving their cultural, educational and social aspirations. In addition, the agency tries to promote the economic and community development needs of Natives and to ensure that Canada's constitutional and statutory obligations and responsibilities to Natives are fulfilled (Government of Canada, 1990).

Self-Government Sector

As government has conceded the legitimacy of Native self-government, it has found that it must put together both an organizational structure to handle requests and procedures to implement such requests (see Figure 6.3). This sector continues to work toward establishing a new relationship with Native people, based upon increased Native community control and self-reliance. As a result, three branches are now part of the Self-Government Sector: 1) Constitution, Legislation and Federal-Provincial Relations, 2) Community Negotiations and Implementation and 3) Policy.

FIGURE 6.3   Self-Government Sector

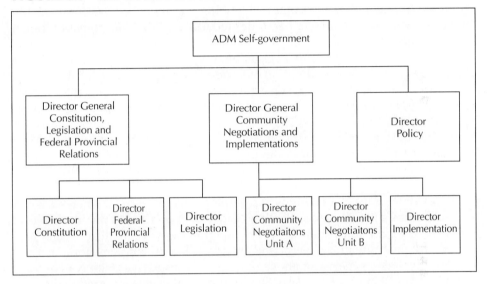

Source: Annual Report 1989-90, INAC, 1990, 6.

The objective of the Self-Government sector of Indian Affairs is to enhance decision-making authority at the community level. Also, there is an attempt to introduce greater flexibility for communities in setting priorities and working out program implementation. In line with this thinking is the goal of strengthening Aboriginal self-government. This goal is being pursued by the Constitution, Legislation, Federal-Provincial Relations Branch in their ongoing activities. All three directorates carry out a wide range of activities. For example, The Constitution Directorate represents DIAND on federal delegations to the United Nations Working Group on Indigenous Populations. It also is currently assessing the result of the International Labour Organization's deliberation over the past decade—*Convention 169 on Indigenous and Tribal Peoples*—in order to determine whether Canada will ratify it. It also continues to work on drafting a universal declaration of indigenous rights. The Constitution Directorate also provides assistance and funding for Aboriginal organizations dealing with constitutional matters which affect Native people.

The Federal-provincial Relations Directorate was created in 1989 because of the need to coordinate federal and provincial activities. For example, in self-government negotiations, it became clear that provincial governments would have to enter the negotiations because of shared jurisdictions with the federal government. The Federal-Provincial Relations Directorate has also supported tripartite negotiations in Ontario and Nova Scotia with the long-term goal of creating tripartite commissions in all the provinces in order to facilitate the achievement of Indian self-government.

Recently, a new directorate, Legislation, was created because of the need for strategic planning and coordination of various federal and provincial pieces of legislation. The activities of this directorate include the development of corporate legislative strategies and the coordination of legislative initiatives, including self-government proposals. The directorate also will review federal legislation to ensure consistency and coherent consideration of the government's Native policies. Because of the recency of this directorate, there is little evidence available to assess its impact on policies emerging out of DIAND or other departments.

The Community Negotiations and Implementation Branch emerged when the federal government agreed to allow Native communities to pursue self-government. Its central role is to help Native communities develop their form of proposed self-government, review it and then facilitate its implementation. They are also involved in the negotiations (initial and substantive) with Native communities. As of March 1990, nearly 80 proposals had been submitted to the government for processing. This Branch also provides technical support to parties involved in negotiations concerning the implementation of land agreements. For example, this group was instrumental in bringing about the James Bay and Northern Québec Agreement, resulting in the final Agreement in Principle between the federal government, Inuit and Naskapi negotiators. This branch also was responsible for securing an agreement between Hydro-Québec and the federal government which led to the transfer of $26 million in self-government operating and capital grants.

As community negotiations continue, the Community Negotiations and Implementation Branch provides technical analysis on a number of issues arising out of the quest for Native self-government. These include such issues as the administration of justice, structure and procedures of government, lands and resources, and political accountability. This group works with the Comprehensive Claims Branch (Northern Program) and has, over the past years, participated directly in self-government negotiations with several bands, providing policy advice to federal negotiators. This group also develops policies for renewable and nonrenewable resources and environmental management, which are introduced when self-government proposals are evaluated.

Economic Development Sector

The Economic Development Sector is responsible for community planning, development and access to resources (see Figure 6.4). Most of the work of this sector is focused on developing and supporting the implementation of these goals with regional economic development staff and Indian and Inuit representatives. Its major focus today is to implement the Canadian Aboriginal Economic Development Strategy.

FIGURE 6.4   ECONOMIC DEVELOPMENT SECTOR

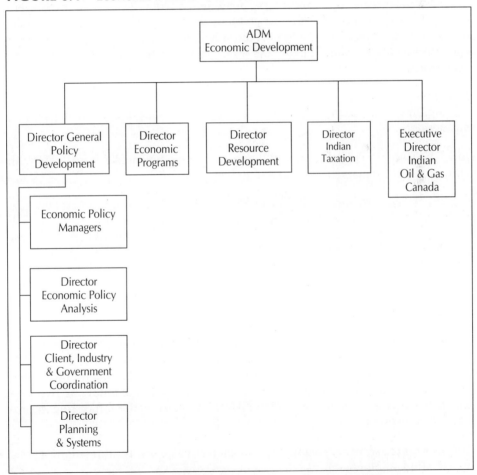

SOURCE: *Annual Report 1989-90*, INAC, 1990, 11.

Recently, the government established the Canadian Aboriginal Economic Development Strategy which focused on helping Aboriginal peoples achieve their goal of economic self-reliance. This partnership among DIAND, Industry, Science and Technology, and Employment and Immigration Canada committed $74 million over a five-year period to ensure achievement of their goal. This approach is different from past attempts of providing economic development services directly to Native people. This new strategy offers support for Native economic development decision-making, priority-setting, and delivery of economic development services though community based organizations and development.

In order to implement this program, close cooperation between Native communities, the private sector and government (federal, provincial, territorial) agencies is necessary in order to promote greater participation by Native people in the mainstream economy. The Canadian Aboriginal Economic Development Strategy comprises eight programs; the first three are spearheaded by Industry, Science and Technology.

Business Development: This program will provide Aboriginal individuals or communities with the capital and support services to start or expand an existing business.

Joint Ventures: This program will help Aboriginal businesses forge links with other firms in the mainstream economy.

Capital Corporations: The goals of these activities are to support and build a network of autonomous Aboriginal financial institutions.

The next set of activities carried out by the Canadian Aboriginal Economic Development Strategy is directed by DIAND.

Community Economic Planning and Development: Aboriginal communities will be assisted in delivering their own business, employment and resource development services.

Access to Resources: This program will assist Aboriginal communities to gain access to and develop renewable and nonrenewable resources.

Canadian Employment and Immigration has also joined the task of helping Native people secure economic self-reliance. Their role in the following two programs has been substantial, although DIAND has also had a minor role in promoting these programs.

Urban Employment: Programs will assist Native people residing in urban areas to find employment.

Skills Development: Because many Native people lack the technical skills that would allow them to enter the labour force, this program is designed to increase those skills.

And there is one more program undertaken by this consortium.

Research and Advocacy: This program which will promote Aboriginal employment and business.

These eight economic programs are the major activities the federal government has undertaken to create economic development on the reserves and to help individual Natives integrate into the mainstream economy.

In addition to the implementation of the Canada Aboriginal Economic Development Strategy, this group also works in the area of Native taxation as well as the administration of the *Indian Oil and Gas Act*. The Indian Oil and Gas Canada mandate is to identify, administer and tender for permit or lease, Indian petroleum and natural gas rights on behalf of Indian bands. This body has also conducted workshops for bands as well as developed a resource information management system for royalties, land finance and oil and gas. This past year it began to transfer to the Indian Resource Council responsibility for enhancing employment and training opportunities for Native people. The Indian Taxation Advisory Board was created in the Economic Development Sector (as a result of the 1988 amendments to the *Indian Act, Bill C-115*) to consider new taxation bylaws. For example, the Board granted bands broad powers to tax interests in Indian lands. This group of ten people (seven Indian leaders) have also published reports on taxation, developed a model bylaw and sponsored an international conference on real property taxation.

The overall strategy employed by this group is to develop an Aboriginal economic development program for the long term which will be designed to support control by Native communities, i.e., community-based decision-making, priority-setting and delivery of services. For example, recently the Blood Tribe was given $2.5 million to buy new equipment and material so that Kainai Industries (a locally operated business) could build 50 modular home units. DIAND's community economic planning and development program has been the key component of this strategy. This component is designed to assist Natives, through Community Economic Development organizations, to create, maintain or strengthen local organizational, advisory and development capacity, which will help Native community members more clearly define and achieve their economic goals. The Good Stoney Band (near Calgary), received nearly $2 million in order to create a conference centre. This centre has created 25 jobs and generated approximately $3 million in wages and other benefits over a five-year period. Nearly $40 million was provided to bands or tribal councils in order to increase Native employability, e.g., academic upgrading, skills training and on-the-job training.

The program has also assisted other activities such as literacy programs, adult basic education and skills development for Indians and participation in the development of pilot Native employment and training centres. There also have been some monies contributed to research on a number of ongoing projects that will allow a better understanding of how reserve economies work and of ways to enhance the economic value of federal programming for Native communities.

The business development activities are handled by the Commercial Development program. Because of the creation of the Canada Aboriginal Economic Development Strategy, direct contributions from DIAND to Native businesses will cease. The contribution of $10 million to the Indian Business Development program, the $1 million provided in direct loans and the nearly $2 million in loan guarantees will be phased out, as will the management and advisory services to Indian businesses. For example, two portions of the direct loan portfolio ($6 million) were sold outright and two others were contracted out to Native lending institutions. In future, decisions will be made by Native people and their corporations, although DIAND will continue to provide loan guarantees to Indian businesses on-reserve.

Lands, Revenues and Trusts Sector

One of the more controversial sub-departments in the Indian and Inuit Affairs Program is the Lands, Revenues and Trusts Sector (see Figure 6.5). Its mandate is to protect the rights and interests of Indians. Its day-to-day operations consist of administering reserve lands, natural resources, band trust funds, and the estates of some individual Indians. In addition, this section registers Indians and identifies band membership. The Indian Land Registry administers about five million hectares of land, and processes some 40 000 transactions per year; for example, birth and death certificates. The trust fund managed over $1.5 billion in 1989, with revenues of $900 million and disbursements of well over $400 million.

In its role of administering Indian land and money, the department has occasionally been found guilty of improper administration. Recently the courts have awarded individuals and bands damages or other redress because DIAND has not carried out proper administrative procedures. For example, the Musquean band of British Columbia (*Guerin* v. *the Queen*, 1984) brought a breach of trust suit against the Crown. The federal government had not carried out the terms of a lease requested by the Indians and did not inform them of this breach. Almost a decade after the suit was launched, the Supreme Court ruled that a breach of trust had indeed occurred and found in favour of the Indians. This ruling overturned a federal Court of Appeal decision which had overturned the original judges' decision. The importance of the ruling lies in the judges' statement that the band had a "preexisting right to its traditional lands" and that the Crown had "breached a fiduciary obligation to the band." This decision has forced the government to clarify its role when

FIGURE 6.5   Lands, Revenues and Trust Sector

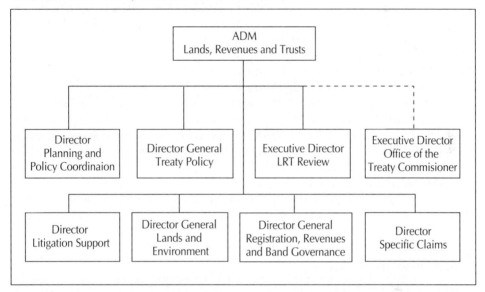

SOURCE: *Annual Report 1989-90*, INAC, 14.

dealing with Indian land as well as obtain informed consent from the band on whose behalf it is acting.

This sector of Indian Affairs is also responsible for the government's legal obligations in matters respecting lands reserved for Indians. This sector, through the Specific Claims Branch, also undertakes the assessment of specific claims submitted by Indian bands and conducts negotiations on behalf of the government. The assessment process entails determining whether the federal government has breached legal obligations to a band and compensating the band if the government has breached this obligation.

This sector administers the 2263 reserves and handles the business affairs of approximately 23 000 individual Indians. The Registration, Revenues and Band Governance Branch (Indian Registration and Band Lists Directorate) is in charge of dealing with the applications for entitlement to Indian status under *Bill C-31*. Thus far, nearly 100 000 people have applied for Indian status after *Bill C-31* removed the sex discrimination clauses from the *Indian Act*, abolished the concept of enfranchisement, restored Indian status and band membership to those who had lost them unfairly and enabled bands to determine their own membership rules. Thus far the branch has reviewed and confirmed the entitlement to Indian status of over

25 000 applicants by 1989. In 1990, 15 000 more applicants were registered. However, at current rates, nearly half of those applying are denied status because they are unable to prove they meet the stipulations of the *Indian Act*. Needless to say, this has precipitated considerable frustration and tension between Natives and government workers. This directorate also facilitates the transferring of membership from Ottawa to band control, bringing the number of bands having control of their membership to 231 or 39 percent of all bands.

The Lands and Environment Branch implemented the *Indian Lands Agreement (1986) Act* which was enacted into law in 1988. This Act permits bands in Ontario to negotiate with the province and the federal government to remove provincial interests in surrendered Indian lands and minerals. Over the past two years, this directorate has added 27 559 hectares of land to the total Canadian existing reserve land base (now at 2 686 996 hectares), an area roughly half the size of Nova Scotia. This branch also provides bands and Indian organizations with advisory, technical and other support to deal with environmental problems facing them. Over $2 million have been given to Indian groups to analyze environmental problems, participate in assessment and regulatory processes and negotiate compensation for environmental damages.

The Treaty Policy Branch focuses on policy development in two related areas— fishing and treaties. DIAND, in conjunction with other federal agencies has developed policies and programs for Natives wanting to enter the fisheries sector of the economy. The second focus of this branch, treaties, centres on the government's commitment to resolving claims of Indian bands. As well as being concerned with the fulfilment of Indian treaties, specific claims relate to the administration of land and other assets under the *Indian Act*. In 1989, the processing of specific claims was changed in an attempt to resolve these cases in shorter time periods. Thus far it is unclear how much of an impact this will have on the resolution of these claims. This directorate works with the Litigation Support Group which administers the Test Case Funding Program. Funding is provided so that Native groups can take their cases to the courts in an attempt to resolve outstanding conflicts which the government believes will set a precedent for other similar remaining cases.

Indian Services Sector

This unit of Indian Affairs supports Native people through the provision of education, social development, housing, community infrastructure and band management (see Figure 6.6). This sector of Indian Affairs was a key component when the Department moved from delivering services directly to Natives to enabling Natives to deliver the services themselves. The five-year transition plan began in 1986 and completed the role-change by 1991. The Alternative Funding Arrangements Program was key to this transition, which permitted bands and tribal councils to negotiate new financial and administrative arrangements in which the primary ac-

FIGURE 6.6   Indian Services Sector

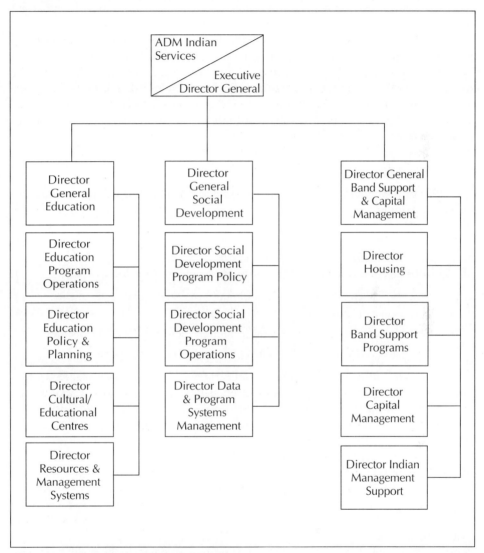

Source: Annual Report 1989-90, INAC, 1990, 18.

countability of Indian leaders is to their own community. The goal of this program is to increase local band control. As a result of these changes, there has been a fundamental change in the relationship between the federal government and Indian people in the nature of services delivered, as well as in how they are delivered.

For example, in 1988, nearly 70 percent of the Indian and Inuit Affairs Program's total expenditures were managed or administered by Indians, compared with about one-third in 1980.

Three major branches make up this sector—1) Education, 2) Social Development and 3) Band Support and Capital Management. The provision of services of the Education and Social Development Branch is discussed in chapter 5. Under the third branch, diverse activities are carried out through four directorates. The overall goal of this branch is to assure funds for Indian groups which are taking over control of the delivery of services. It also administers the funds transferred to Indian regional governments.

Northern Affairs

The Northern Affairs Program assists the social, cultural, political and economic development of the Yukon and the Northwest Territories, and while not specifically directed toward Native people, it does place particular emphasis on the needs of Northern Natives. The program operates directly, as well as indirectly, through the governments of the two territories (see Figure 6.7).

The objectives of the Northern Affairs Program are directed toward:

- the transfer of provincial-type responsibilities to the territorial governments,
- the settlement of land claims,
- establishing cooperative mechanisms to support economic development, and
- the enhancement of Arctic sovereignty and circumpolar cooperation.

The Constitutional Development and Strategic Planning, Natural Resources and Economic Development, and Comprehensive Claims branches make up the focus of this program. The first branch has established the groundwork for transferring programs resembling provincial programs to territorial governments. Its overall goal is to encourage the development of northern political institutions and diversification of the economy, thereby reinforcing Canadians' sovereignty. The Natural Resources and Economic Development Branch has a myriad of functions, ranging from the Biological Division—focusing on the management of wildlife— to carrying out the responsibilities for the North American Air Defense Modernization Project. The third branch, of more importance to this book, is the Comprehensive Claims Branch. This Branch deals with Aboriginal groups which continue to occupy and use lands whose Aboriginal title has not been dealt with by treaty.

Most of the activities of this Branch have been focused on three major claims; the Yukon, Dene/Métis and the Tungavik Federation of Nunavut. In addition to these, this branch continues to carry on negotiations with the Nisga, the Labrador Inuit and the Conseil Attikamket-Montagnais.

The Administration Program

The administrative activities of DIAND provide financial, administrative and management services (see Figures 6.8 to 6.10). These help the department meet its human resources requirements and provide services to enhance productivity. The Human Resources Branch continues to advance its goals of downsizing and improving the representation of Aboriginals and women at the senior management level. Other activities carried out by this branch involve informing Canadians (Natives and non-Natives) about the activities of DIAND. The Human Resources Branch also serves as the central link between the programs and the Ministers' offices on such matters as cabinet submissions and regulatory reform. And they also conduct program evaluations.

The territorial governments, with federal financial support, are now chiefly responsible for providing government services to territorial residents. Therefore, the Northern Affairs Program concentrates on Northern resource development, environmental protection, and political, social and cultural development. The program also helps to coordinate federal government activities in the two territories.

In order to carry out the activities of DIAND, 40 offices in Canada have been established to implement the policies and programs developed (see Figure 6.1). They also provide a linkage between the communities and federal bureaucrats. As such, they have an important role in both the input and output of decisions made regarding Native people.

INDIAN-INUIT AFFAIRS PROGRAMS

The government of Canada operates more than 100 programs that are directed in whole or in part toward Native people in Canada.[3] The direct cost of these programs is well in excess of $3 billion (see Table 6.1). The beneficiaries of these programs—Indians, Inuits, Métis and non-status Indians—make up about 600 000 people.

FIGURE 6.7   NORTHERN AFFAIRS PROGRAM

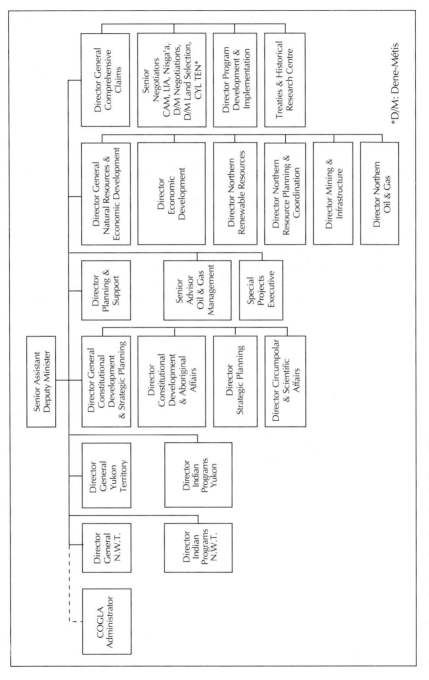

SOURCE: *Annual Report 1989-90,* INAC, 1990, 22

TABLE 6.1   BUDGETARY EXPENDITURES AND REVENUES FOR THE DEPARTMENT OF INDIAN AND NORTHERN AFFAIRS

Expenditures	1988-89	1989-90
Operating Expenditures		
Indian and Inuit Affairs	$245 559 713	$257 721 995
Northern Affairs	100 727 869*	65 102 417
Administration	42 906 585	48 357 800
Capital Expenditures		
Indian and Inuit Affairs	15 454 374	7 714 188
Northern Affairs	18 995 824	19 416 296
Grants, Contributions and Other Transfer Payments		
Indian and Inuit Affairs	1 772 924 660	2 011 957 173
Northern Affairs	38 757 443	41 494 398
Territorial Government	850 890 122	921 073 869
Total	$3 086 216 590	$3 372 838 136

* $43 128 838.42 relates to the Northern Canada Power Commission debt deletion

Revenues		
Indian and Inuit Affairs	$17 403 487	$16 025 039
Northern Affairs	39 281 239	37 598 536
Administration	113 341	47 411
Total	$56 798 067	$53 670 986
Non-Budgetary Expenditures		
Loans, Investments and Advances		
Indian and Inuit Affairs	$34 654 959	4 688 930
Northern Affairs	(97 226 843)	(2 699 105)
Total	$62 571 883	$1 989 825

SOURCE: *Annual Report 1989-90*, INAC, 1990, 67-68.

The actual programs and services delivered to Native people vary by group and location. Some are provided directly from the Indian and Inuit Affairs Program, while others are from territorial governments who are, in turn, reimbursed for their costs. Indians living on reserves deal directly with the federal government. On the other hand, off-reserve Indians face a complicated pattern of eligibility for

FIGURE 6.8   FINANCE AND PROFESSIONAL SERVICES

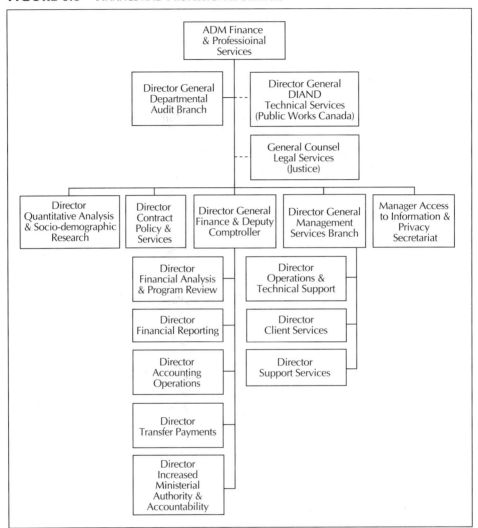

SOURCE: *Annual Report 1989-90*, INAC, 1990, 33.

FIGURE 6.9 **HUMAN RESOURCES BRANCH**

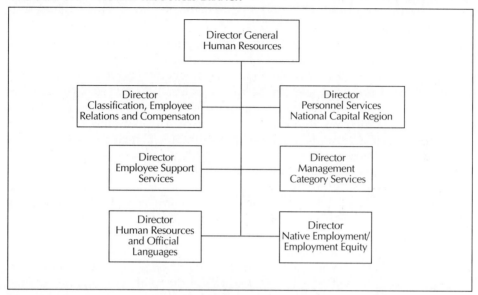

SOURCE: *Annual Report 1989-90*, INAC, 1990, 35.

FIGURE 6.10 **EXECUTIVE SUPPORT SERVICES BRANCH**

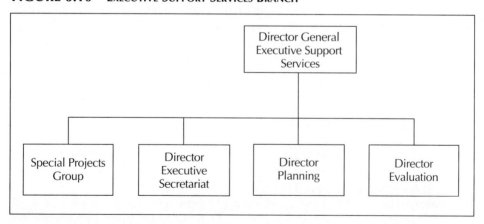

SOURCE: *Annual Report 1989-90*, INAC, 1990, 38.

government services (Government of Canada, 1985). The federal government takes the position that off-reserve Indians should avail themselves of provincial services, while the provinces argue that Indians are a federal responsibility. Sometimes proof of residence is required (for example, proof of having lived 12 months off the reserve) before provinces consider Indians eligible for provincial services.

Services provided to Natives far exceed the federal government's constitutional and legislative responsibility. Many programs and services have been implemented as a strategy to lessen Native poverty and distress. While some programs have produced positive results, most of them have been dismal failures—both in the short and long term. Meanwhile expenditures continue to increase.

In the early 1980s, nearly 60 percent of the Indian and Inuit Affairs Program's expenditures were made through contribution arrangements to Indian bands or various Indian organizations. In turn, these groups provided the specific services as outlined in the contract or agreement. In 1990, Ontario and Manitoba were each allocated about 18 percent of the budget. In addition, 30 percent was equally divided between B.C. and Saskatchewan. Alberta received about 5 percent. The remaining portion of the budget was equally split between headquarters and the Territories. On a per capita basis, Ontario and Alberta have the lowest Indian and Inuit Affairs Program expenditures. These low figures reflect the relatively high rate of employment in Ontario and the resource rich bands in Alberta.

The Indian and Inuit Affairs Program supports Natives in their quest to preserve and develop their culture. Support is channelled through three streams. First, financial assistance is given to bands, councils or nonprofit corporations that support Native heritage. The cultural development program which supports Native artists is the second program. Third, the community social services provide advice and guidance to band councils, their staff, and community service organizations.

The Indian and Inuit Affairs Program traditionally has been highly centralized, with its headquarters in Ottawa. It is responsible for policy development, resource allocation and planning for Indians and Inuit through a variety of methods; for example, direct service delivery, grants and loans. However, since the late 1970s, when decentralization occurred, the nine regional offices—one in each territory, one for the Atlantic provinces and one in each of the remaining provinces—have begun to develop their own programs. These programs emerge from the specific district structures (except in Manitoba). Thus, the districts have become influential, except in Alberta where control is retained in the regional office.

About 15 percent of the total number of employees of the Indian and Inuit Affairs Program are Natives (see Figure 6.11). In addition, Natives have not yet gained access to policy-setting positions; only 2 percent of the Natives employed by the Indian and Inuit Affairs Program are at the senior- and middle-management level. The largest proportion (28 percent) are at the operational level, primarily involved in teaching. Less than 10 percent of its employees have been with the Indian

FIGURE 6.11   **DIAND** Employee Demographics, **1990**

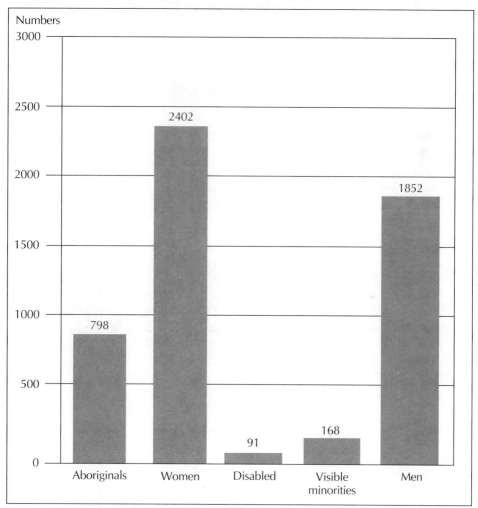

SOURCE: *Annual Report 1989-90*, INAC, 1990, 36.

and Inuit Affairs Program more than 15 years. This latter group is generally called the "old guard" and has almost total control over policy development and implementation. Only one or two of them are Natives.

The Indian and Inuit Affairs Program's policies, objectives, priorities and programs are established by senior executives and then passed down and back up the

TABLE 6.2   INDIAN-INUIT AFFAIRS PROGRAM BUDGET: 1986-87 MAIN ESTIMATES ($000)

	Percent	Budgetary			Total	1985-86 Main Estimates
		Operating	Capital	Transfer Payments		
Reserves and trusts	2.8	28 439	224	15 062	43 725	32 391
Elementary/secondary education	25.8	70 891	—	337 731	408 622	390 144
Post-secondary education	4.5	2 578	—	68 563	71 141	59 169
Social assistance	16.3	8 609	—	249 838	258 447	244 673
Welfare services	4.7	3 409	—	71 880	75 289	64 250
Other education and social services	0.8	637	—	12 262	12 889	11 871
Economic development	4.0	12 713	—	50 184	62 897	56 405
Band management	7.8	10 994	—	113 193	124 187	124 190
Capital facilities and community services	27.9	53 488	68 193	320 807	442 488	432 793
Program management	2.6	41 688	—	—	41 688	43 555
Program administration	2.8	42 222	2 140	—	44 362	45 613
Total		275 668	70 557	1 239 520	1 585 745	1 505 054

SOURCE: Indian and Northern Affairs Canada, *1986-87 Estimates,* 2-10, 2-13, 2-17.

bureaucratic ladder.[4] Budgets must be developed for each program and approved by Parliament. Most of the budget of the Indian and Inuit Affairs Program (74 percent) is nondiscretionary; that is, it is set aside for specific items and is non-transferable. As the year proceeds, the Indian and Inuit Affairs Program often requests more money. Table 6.2 shows the expenditures for 1985-87.

In 1967, the Indian and Inuit Affairs Program accounted for 1.06 percent of the government's total budget. This figure peaked at 1.74 percent in 1972-3 before it was reduced to 1.70 percent in 1980, and in 1987 it stood at about 1.60 percent. It has remained at this level for some time, although indications are that this will decrease in 1992. In 1965, the Indian and Inuit Affairs Program was allocated about one-half of the total DIAND budget. This proportion increased to nearly 75 percent in 1969, but has since steadily declined to a present level of 50 percent. Between 1970 and 1979, actual dollars spent on Natives through DIAND increased threefold. In addition, the Indian and Inuit Affairs Program budget is not the only source of monies directed toward Indians and Inuit. If all the federal programs for Natives were taken into account, the total expenditures for Native peoples would be nearly $3 billion in 1985, with an estimated 1990 budget figure in excess of $5 billion. However, during the 1980-89 period, the proportion of total federal expenditures for Natives declined, with DIAND experiencing a lower expenditure growth rate than other government departments.

Since 1960, considerable shifts have occurred in the distribution of funds among operating expenses, capital costs, and expenditures for grants and contributions. In the early 1960s, over half of the budget was used to meet operating expenses, while the rest was evenly split between the other two categories. In 1980-81, however, operating expenditures only accounted for 37 percent of the budget, while capital expenditures on additions and betterments had decreased to four percent. Expenditures on grants and contributions had increased substantially and comprised nearly 60 percent of the total budget (*Annual Report*, DIAND, 1980-81). This distribution has remained in place and suggests a wide-scale transfer of the administrative costs of Indian and Inuit Affairs programs to provincial governments.

The actual spending patterns of the Indian and Inuit Affairs Program have substantially changed in recent years. In the early 1960s, approximately 45 percent of the budget was spent on education. By 1978, this had decreased to 39 percent and by 1990 was further reduced to 33 percent. Other activities funded by the Indian and Inuit Affairs Program also show changes in fiscal priorities. Community affairs accounted for about 43.1 percent of the budget in 1970 and 1978 but decreased to slightly more than half that in 1990. Economic development, always a low Indian and Inuit Affairs Program priority, has ranged from between 6 and 9 percent of the total budget until 1989 when it was 5 percent.

Those who determine Indian and Inuit Affairs Program policies seldom, if ever, have direct experience with Native issues. Policies are developed by Indian and

Inuit Affairs Program bureaucrats and amended by bureaucrats from other government areas that are likely to be affected by the policies. As Weaver (1980) points out in her analysis of the 1960 White Paper, the Privy Council Office, the Prime Minister's Office, the Treasury Board and the Cabinet wield the most direct influence on federal policy concerning Natives. In the 1960s, the Privy Council Office and Prime Minister's Office were restructured to assert the primacy of the prime minister and Cabinet in setting policy and monitoring programs. This restructuring has allowed the Privy Council Office, Prime Minister's Office, and Cabinet to maintain much closer control of Indian and Inuit Affairs Program activities and to evaluate those activities in the context of other government departments (Poss, 1975). The 1960s also saw a major restructuring of the system of standing committees in the House of Commons. This change has permitted members of Parliament to interact more directly with the staff of the Indian and Inuit Affairs Program, and to expand their roles through a process of open discussion (Weaver, 1980).

These two changes removed policy development and implementation from the total control of particular departments and ensured that policies would be evaluated in the context of policies from other departments. Policy advisory councils were created to report to the Cabinet; in effect, these councils are one step above the Cabinet in power. Information from each department is now filtered through the Privy Council Office and Prime Minister's Office instead of passing directly from senior bureaucrats to cabinet ministers (Ponting and Gibbins, 1980).

These changes have had a direct effect on organized attempts by Natives to influence policy and program development. There is now another entire set of bureaucrats that must be lobbied. Moreover, they can only be lobbied by an intermediary and within the confines of committees with legitimate powers of inquiry (Pross, 1975). As a result, Native groups have reorganized their efforts to influence the politics that affect them. They have also found new ways to counter the increasing input of the Privy Council Office and Prime Minister's Office into general policy recommendations (Preshus, 1974).

GOVERNMENT POLICY

The federal government had previously maintained that, under section 91(24) of the *British North America Act*, it has the constitutional obligation to provide funds and services to registered Indians *on reserves*. It argued that off-reserve Indians were a provincial responsibility. At present, there is ongoing debate between federal and provincial governments concerning which of them should finance and deliver services to Natives both on and off the reserves.

The federal government acknowledges a special relationship between itself and Native Canadians. It agrees that registered Indians and Inuit possess special rights, privileges and entitlements, whether they live on or off the reserves. But although the federal government acknowledges its responsibility to on- and off-reserve Natives, it claims that they should look to other levels of government for certain services. In addition, the federal government regards its responsibility for off-reserve services in a different light than that for on-reserve services. More specifically, under section 91(24) of the *BNA Act*, the government has accepted responsibility for on-reserve services in more program areas than for off-reserve services.

The federal government argues that as Natives move off reserves, they become citizens of a province; as such, they have a basic right to the same services provided by the province to all its other residents. Nevertheless, the federal government has a number of direct off-reserve support programs in such areas as housing and post-secondary education. In addition, it provides transfer and block payments to the provinces based on Native population figures under such programs as Established Program Financing and Equalization. These programs are intended to help provide the same services to Natives as are provided to the general provincial population.

The federal government, then, maintains that each government has its respective responsibilities based on separate, distinct bonds with Native peoples. Natives who live off reserves are residents of provinces and often contribute to provincial tax revenues; in addition, they have often provided indirectly many other resources now available to the provinces, and they are included in the calculation of transfer and block payments to the provinces. The provinces, on the other hand, take the position that Indians are a federal concern and not under the jurisdiction of provincial governments.

In early 1991, Ottawa decided to limit spending on social services for Indians. It decided that it would no longer pay social assistance to Indians for the first year after they leave a reserve. Provinces have reiterated their stance that Indians and the welfare of Indians, whether it be on-reserve or off-reserve, is a responsibility of the federal government. Indians likewise agree with the provinces' stand and argue that the social services question is a federal responsibility and should not be transferred to the provinces. The projected costs and savings of such a move is also debated. Western provinces feel that such a policy move will cost each of them $15 to $20 million per year. The federal government, while giving no specific figures, calculates the cost as much less. In addition, the federal government argues that the savings they accrue through this change will be reinvested in child and family services on the reserve. This program, they argue will reduce long-term costs for Natives and, thus, will save the provinces additional monies in the long term.

The Indian and Inuit Affairs Program has been in the process of decentralization since 1964. Originally, DIAND simply stated that Natives were to become a provincial responsibility. This policy was rejected by Native organizations and provincial governments alike. In the mid-1970s, a new policy emerged involving the transfer of federal responsibility to Native bands rather than to the provinces. At the same time, administrative responsibilities were being shifted from Ottawa to the regional and district offices of DIAND. As a result, Natives have gained a somewhat greater involvement in the policy formations of the Indian and Inuit Affairs Program (Ponting and Gibbins, 1980).

The shift of responsibility to band governments is taking place at three levels. First, funds for program management are being transferred from the Indian and Inuit Affairs Program to the direct control of the bands. This transfer began in 1968; by 1971, bands were managing about 14 percent of a $160 million budget and, by 1978-79, about 35 percent of a $659 million budget. Today they control well over half the budget exceeding $1 billion. Second, core funding grants are provided for the basic administrative costs of chiefs, councils and band managers. In 1978-79, these grants represented 4 percent of the total DIAND budget; by 1989 this had increased to 15 percent. Third, band training and support services are supplied to encourage management skills and to provide technical support.

At present, about 50 percent of the total capital and 60 percent of the school budgets are administered by the bands. Approximately 90 percent of the bands are involved in the core funding program, but these figures show considerable regional disparity. Manitoba bands control a great deal of their operational expenditures, while the Yukon bands control very little. As DIAND explains,

> The varying levels of band-administered funds in each region do not reflect the degree of interest of bands in administering funds but rather:
>
> • The level of social assistance administered by provincial authorities.
> • The number of Indian children attending provincial schools (*Survey*, 1980, 116).

This policy of decentralization was apparently designed to promote the autonomy of Native bands. It marks a shift in federal policy from programs that promote integration and assimilation to those that encourage tribal government and cultural self-sufficiency. Increasingly, band councils are responsible for financial allocations. However, although the Indian and Inuit Affairs Program is relinquishing specific control over expenditures, it still retains control of the overall allocation of funds. In effect, this policy, has shifted critical attention away from the Indian and Inuit Affairs Program to the local chief, council and manager.

This policy has also meant that Natives must be fully involved in discussions on a broad range of program-related and political issues. With the new band autonomy, certain programs can no longer be implemented without first consulting Natives. Moreover, Native associations have been steadily putting pressure on the Indian and Inuit Affairs Program, requesting forums for discussion of a range of issues related to federal and provincial policies.

Again, this attempt to provide a forum for Native participation reflects a shift in federal policy from a desire to assimilate Natives toward an increasing emphasis on tribal government. The tripartite (i.e., federal/provincial/Native) discussion partly arose from a belief by Indian Affairs personnel that Natives had developed enough political leadership skills to articulate their needs. In addition, the provinces became willing to discuss priority issues set forth by Natives, largely to avoid being excluded from any far-reaching negotiations that might take place elsewhere in Canada. However, despite promises to the contrary, Natives are still effectively excluded from much of the negotiation process. Presently, much of the discussion between federal and provincial officials circumvents involvement through the use of personal communications, confidential documents, and so on.

In general, the Indian and Inuit Affairs Program in the 1960s tried to turn Natives into Whites by integrating them into the capitalist system and encouraging them to shed the Natives ways. In a statement at the Federal-Provincial Conference on Poverty in the mid-1960s, the Indian Affairs Department summed up its policy of assimilation as one that enabled Natives "to realize their potential in the economic, social, and cultural sectors of their lives." In the 1970s, this policy shifted to promote the retention of Native culture in accord with a new emphasis on multiculturalism. In addition, the policies of the 1970s began to focus on the urban Native population, although, as yet, no coherent strategy with regard to these Natives has been developed.

The origin of DIAND's changing policy goes back to 1959, when Prime Minister John Diefenbaker was embarrassed during a foreign tour by strong criticism of Canada's Native policy. Upon his return, he established a joint committee of the Senate and the House of Commons to investigate and advise on the administration of Indian Affairs. The context was a favourable one for Native Canadians: Diefenbaker had just won a decisive victory in the 1958 election and Gladstone, a Blood Indian from Alberta, had just been appointed to the Senate. Due to the joint committee's recommendations, the law was changed in 1960 to give Natives the right to vote in federal elections. The committee also recommended that the Indian and Inuit Affairs Program should cease to provide special services to Natives and instead should rely on and share the existing services of other agencies, including those of the provincial governments.

This position was later echoed by the Alberta White Paper on Human Resources Development in 1967, which proposed that the federal and provincial governments should develop a comprehensive program to extend all of their services to Natives. Just such a program, as outlined in the Hunter-Motherwell Agreement, had recently been terminated due to a breakdown in negotiations. Now, in an attempt to get the jump on the federal government, the Alberta White Paper urged the phasing out of federal services and facilities for Natives where provincial and municipal services were already available. Under Alberta's proposals, the federal government was to accept total financial responsibility for all programs and services extended to registered, on-reserve Natives; in turn the provincial government accepted financial responsibility for programs offered to all other Natives. Ten years later, under the Tripartite Agreements, this policy, to a limited extent, was adopted.

In 1976, a new mega-policy was introduced by the minister of DIAND to promote "Indian identity within Canadian society." The definition and evolution of Native identity were to be treated as flexible and dynamic. In general, the policy continues to recognize Native status, treaty rights, and special privileges resulting from land claims settlements. Within Native band and reserve communities, local self-determination and control of Native affairs are to be encouraged. In addition, for the first time, the policy noted that different needs, aspirations, and attitudes among Natives in all parts of Canada rule out a single uniform strategy. As a result, the policy emphasizes joint participation in program development with organized Native leadership at all levels.

Under the new policy, the federal government takes the initiative in defining the aims and general shape of strategies applied to Native issues. If the government chooses, this process can involve Native representatives at various levels. The major goal of the new policy is to transfer the administration of programs and resources to band governments. The rate of transfer is determined by the desire and ability of each to assume control of its own affairs, including the implementation of programs. With experience, band administration is becoming more efficient. In 1977, of the nearly $150 million managed by bands, 74 percent was for operating expenses and 26 percent for capital expenses; this was a substantial improvement from 1972 when 90 percent of the funds were used as operating expenses and only 10 percent for capital expenses.

At present, the 1976 policy changes are being reconsidered. For example, many critics question the value of programs that encourage a strong cultural identity among Natives without raising their socio-economic status. However, these questions have yet to be translated into programs. In Alberta, for example, nearly 75 percent of the service expenditures for off-reserve Natives are spent on community affairs, generally for social assistance; only 14 percent is spent for education and an even smaller percentage for economic development.

Another recent change in philosophy involved the coordination of all existing services in a vast program specifically tailored to the needs of Native people. However, so far there is little to suggest that this philosophy is being put into practice. At present, no complete model of services for Natives has been developed. Several tentative models have been put forth by Indian and Inuit Affairs Program personnel, yet little seems to have come of them.

In general, policies at the Indian and Inuit Affairs Program are developed internally by middle-level administrative personnel who employ data collected by external consultants. Normally, the Indian and Inuit Affairs Program hires 10 to 15 consultants per year to carry out specific research. Although policy development is continuous in the Indian and Inuit Affairs Program, it tends to increase dramatically when a government has been defeated or when an election is in progress. This suggests that policy evaluation and development are not systemized but are, instead, a "filler" activity on the part of the Department (Ponting and Gibbins, 1980).

THE LATENT FUNCTIONS OF THE INDIAN AND INUIT AFFAIRS PROGRAM

Like many other organizations, the Indian and Inuit Affairs Program is a highly structured, rational system that espouses specific policies and pursues specific goals. It has defined Native welfare as its sole concern; overtly, all its activities are geared to improving that welfare. Also like other organizations, however, the Indian and Inuit Affairs Program pursues certain latent goals that are quite independent of its stated formal goals. As Perrow (1980) and several others have observed, organizations often exist not only to serve their stated goals, but rather to serve other interests. In fact, some would even argue that the stated policy and goals of an organization largely function only to legitimize its existence. An organization makes its stated goals explicit through its formal policy statements. Its latent goal structure, however, only becomes apparent through an examination of the services that it provides for interest groups other than those it manifestly serves.

The organizations dealing with Native people all possess a number of latent functions. For the past century, the Indian and Inuit Affairs Program and its forerunners have stated their primary manifest goal as the ultimate participation of Natives as equals in Canadian society. The latent goals of these organizations include such self-referential aims as cost-efficiency and freedom from conflict within their own structures. Another latent function is to provide resources for other organizations. Many other institutions make extensive use of the nearly $700 million and 5000 employees provided to the Indian and Inuit Affairs Program at public expense; examples range from Native organizations to educational institutions to businesses.

Although other latent functions could be documented here, none is so extensive as the latent attempt by federal administrators to control the lives of Natives. Throughout its history, the major latent function of the Indian and Inuit Affairs Program has been the regulation of Native behaviour. Native people have been lured to cities where their dependent status forces them to conform, or they have been segregated on reserves, concealed from the view of middle-class Canadians. They have been arbitrarily dispersed throughout cities or forcibly bused out of town back to the reserve. Often, the control of Natives has been achieved through the behavioural requirements attached to various social services. For example, the off-reserve housing program requires applicants to have steady full-time jobs before they are eligible for loans.

Regardless of the technique, the result is that Natives are manipulated and restricted in their actions. To be sure, some Natives are helped in the process: at least 16 people have received off-reserve housing in one major city over the past 10 years. Many more have obtained educational benefits, training, counselling, and money, but only after conforming to middle class behavioural criteria. Thus, the control factor is the central goal of the majority of organizations dealing with Native people.

The insistence of the federal government upon control over its Native "wards" has characterised federal-Native relations since Confederation. As Whiteside points out:

> Perhaps we should recall the various measures the bureaucrats introduced during this period to ensure "orderly administration": (1) the development of a single piece of legislation in 1876, to govern all the Indian Nations, regardless of varying traditions and history; (2) the systematic destruction of tribal governments and replacement of them with band councils which were really an extension of the Department's [Indian Affairs] structure; (3) the systematic attempt to destroy Indian culture and the outlawing of Indian religious ceremonies; (4) the introduction of

compulsory enfranchisement provisions to control bad Indians; (5) the systematic attempts to harness and discredit Indian leaders who attempt to develop or strengthen Indian political organization (1980:6).

On the reserve, the Indian and Inuit Affairs Program is a "total" institution in that it has a monopoly on the delivery of services to a captive clientele. Its organization is characterized by specialization, hierarchy and regimentation, while its clients are relatively uneducated, unspecialized and varied. By limiting the choices available to its Native clients, the Indian and Inuit Affairs Program shapes and standardizes Native behaviour at minimal cost and risk to itself.

The success of the Indian and Inuit Affairs Program is not assessed on the basis of the assistance it provides to Natives, but rather on the basis of how effectively it has kept Native behaviour under control. The brighter officials at the Indian and Inuit Affairs Program know perfectly well that they will not be fired, transferred or demoted for failing to help Natives receive decent educations, find jobs, mend broken homes and settle into life in the city. Rather, the officials' assessment will be based on the number of Natives they handled, and at what cost per person. Programs that fail to meet their announced goals do not result in fired personnel or radical organizational changes. The upper management of the Indian and Inuit Affairs Program can simply blame failures on a need for organizational restructuring, a lack of adequately trained fieldworkers, a poorly allocated budget, and so on.

All this is not to suggest that the Indian and Inuit Affairs Program does not help Natives. On the contrary, some Natives get bursaries to go to university, some get loans to buy houses in the city, and others get vocational training. Nor is this analysis intended to suggest that Indian and Inuit Affairs Program officials deliberately neglect the needs of Native people. Rather, such neglect is the result of internal and structural forces that cause a reordering of goal priorities.

Certain internal forces acting upon the Indian and Inuit Affairs Program cause it to downplay its stated goal of improving the quality of Native life. Government officials tend to become disproportionately concerned with the number of their employees, the size of their budgets, and the quantity, rather than the quality, of their programs. Because it is difficult, time-consuming, and speculative to assess the effectiveness of an organization, readily quantifiable criteria become the indicators of a successful program. Because these indicators measure cost efficiency rather than program effectiveness, they are simple to tabulate, highly visible and extremely responsive to changes.

A second internal factor is the emphasis on stability within the Indian and Inuit Affairs Program. There is an implicit rule that conflict should not be evident in any federal department. If conflict does exist, it must remain an internal affair. The preoccupation of the Indian and Inuit Affairs Program with remaining conflict-free results, once again, in a downplaying of stated goals and objectives.

In all of the organizations that deal with Native issues, officials accept and promote the existing expectations, norms and mores of a free-enterprise, class-based system. This places severe limitations on the programs offered to Native people. For example, not one organization has suggested that most of the Indian and Inuit Affairs Program's budget should be given directly to Native people or used to organize Natives into an effective political force. Quite the contrary. One of the better-known attempts to organize Natives politically in a western urban centre resulted in the dissolution of one district DIAND office and substantial reassignment of DIAND personnel. A similar response ended the ill-fated Community Development Program, which was phased out within a few years of its inception.

PROVINCIAL-INDIAN RELATIONS IN ALBERTA: A CASE STUDY

After the federal government, the provincial governments have the most extensive relationship with Native people. Tensions between the federal and provincial governments have been apparent for some time concerning Native issues. The following material documents the relationship between the provincial government of Alberta and the Natives within its borders.

An understanding of the overall political climate of Alberta is essential to comprehend its policies, particularly in relation to the federal government. The most seminal document behind Alberta's policy is *The Case for Alberta* (1938). Even though it is nearly 50 years old, this document is still excerpted in the briefs of the present government. It graphically illustrates Alberta's deep frustration with federal policy. Its basic theme is that the federal government has consistently failed to heed the social and economic needs of Albertans.

In 1967, Alberta's Premier Ernest Manning produced a White Paper on Human Resource Development which announced that the development of human resources had become the priority goal of his government. Specifically, he wanted to raise the status of economically and socially deprived Albertans. Manning took the position that all individuals and organizations should have equal access to programs and services, and he promised to remove any discriminatory barriers and phase out separate-but-equal programs based on ethnic distinctions. The White Paper promised to:

1. Endeavour to persuade the Government of Canada to enter into a comprehensive agreement which will allow the Indian people, under federal jurisdiction, to receive wherever possible the same facilities and services as are available to other residents of the province.

2. Assure to Métis and to Indian people under provincial jurisdiction access to services and development programs on the same basis as all other residents in similar social and economic circumstances and encourage them to become self-determining and responsible residents of Alberta on the same legal basis as other citizens (1967: 79-80).

The Alberta government was aware that the federal government planned to turn over the financing and delivery of Native services to the provinces. Tentatively, this plan had already been mapped out in the short-lived Hunter-Motherwell Agreement of 1965-66. Alberta wanted to get the jump on the federal government by defining its policy stance before the federal government could develop a long-term organizational structure.

In the late 1960s, Premier Harry Strom hired several lawyers who were specialists in Native Affairs to investigate and advise on this issue. At the end of the decade, the Alberta government developed a policy that, while not specifically related to Natives, did have implications for them. This policy stated that the provincial government would recognize ethnic differences but would not direct any program toward specific ethnic groups. Specific programs concerning Natives would be carried out exclusively by the federal government.

During 1977, the Alberta government undertook an extensive analysis of provincial programs and services available to treaty Indians. Traditionally, registered Indians had been reluctant to actively pursue provincial services because of a fear they had of eroding their historical relationship with the federal government. The Alberta government wanted to counteract this reluctance by claiming that it wanted to provide all Albertans the maximum opportunity for personal, social and economic advancement (Policy Statement, *Alberta Hansard*, April 25, 1978). As a result, the Alberta government decided to make provincial services and programs officially available to recognized treaty Indian and Native bands on the same basis as to other Alberta residents. Although this policy seemed to focus on reserve Indians, its implications for urban Natives were obvious.

This Alberta policy can be seen as a more current statement of the Hunter-Motherwell Agreement of the mid-1960s. Under this old agreement between the federal and provincial governments, registered Indians who entered the city would be classified in one of two ways: unemployable Indians would remain under federal jurisdiction, while employable Indians would move to provincial jurisdiction. All Indians who were off-reserve for more than one year became the responsibility of the provincial government, even though they remained band members. Under this agreement, the province also promised to provide welfare services to all treaty off-reserve Indians. However, the province later changed its mind and returned many financial responsibilities to the federal government.

Under the new policy, Alberta would assume the full cost of delivering services to off-reserve treaty Indians as long as the federal government agreed to redirect its off-reserve expenditures so that on-reserve services could be brought up to provincial standards. The Alberta government, also wanted to be reimbursed for the on-reserve services it delivered on a 100-percent fee-for-service basis. To date, this policy has not been implemented. Natives reacted negatively to the policy because they wished to remain solely under federal jurisdiction. The federal government has also been reluctant to meet all the terms of the policy.

CONCLUSION

In summary, throughout Canada's history little attention has been paid to developing a long-term policy to deal with Native problems. Moreover, funding of Native programs has always been minimal. Once it became clear that Indians would accept their fate peacefully, the government was allowed to ignore Native issues for more pressing concerns, such as building the railroad and encouraging White settlement. In the history of Native-White relations, government has only acted on Native issues when forced to. And when government has acted, it has invariably done so in White interests.

Our analysis of the Indian and Inuit Affairs Program has shown that its programs have changed considerably over the years, failing to reflect any long-term, consistent policy. In general, however, the Indian and Inuit Affairs Program has taken a wardship approach to Natives. Its budget continues to grow in size, partly as a result of its increased bureaucratic structure; other government departments have also increased their budgets to deal with Native issues, but to little effect.

Recently the federal government has tried to involve provincial governments in Native affairs. Generally it has not had much success. Provincial governments, already hard-pressed for funds, have rejected the costs entailed by direct involvement. For their part, Natives have always tended to distrust the participation of provincial governments, fearing a lessening of federal responsibility. Native Canadians are convinced that the federal government must continue to honour its historical agreements with them, and that any transfer of these agreements is unlikely to be in their best interests.

NOTES

1. Legislation under DIAND'S responsibility includes the following:

- *Alberta Natural Resources Act*
- *Arctic Waters Pollution Prevention Act*
- *British Columbia Indian Cut-off Lands Settlement Act*
- *British Columbia Indian Reserves Mineral Resources Act*
- *Canada Lands Surveys Act*
- *Canada Petroleum Resources Act*
- *Caughnawaga Indian Reserve Act*
- *Condominium Ordinance Validation Act*
- *Cree-Naskapi (of Québec) Act*
- *Department of Indian Affairs and Northern Development Act*
- *Dominion Water Power Act*
- *Fort Nelson Indian Reserve Minerals Revenue Sharing Act*
- *Grassy Narrows and Islington Indian Band Mercury Pollution Claims Settlement Act*
- *Indian Act*

- *Indian Lands Agreement (1986)*
- *Indian Lands, Settlement of Differences Act*
- *Indian Oil and Gas Act*
- *Indian (Soldier Settlement) Act*
- *James Bay and Northern Québec Native Claims Settlement Act*
- *Land Titles Act*
- *Manitoba Natural Resources Act*
- *Manitoba Supplementary Provisions Act*
- *Natural Resources Transfer (School Lands) Amendment Act*
- *New Brunswick Indian Reserves Agreement Act*
- *Northern Canada Power Commission (Share Issuance and Sale Authorization) Act*
- *Northern Canada Power Commission Yukon Assets Disposal Authorization Act*
- *Northern Inland Waters Act*
- *Northwest Territories Act*
- *Nova Scotia Indian Reserves Agreement Act*
- *Oil and Gas Production and Conservation Act*
- *Public Lands Grants Act*
- *Railway Belt Act*
- *Railway Belt and Peace River Block Act*
- *Railway Belt Water Act*
- *St. Peter's Indian Reserve Act*
- *St. Regis Indian Reservation Act*
- *Saskatchewan and Alberta Roads Act*
- *Saskatchewan Natural Resources Act*
- *Sechelt Indian Band Self-Government Act*
- *Songhees Indian Reserve Act*
- *Territorial Lands Act*
- *Waterton Glacier International Peace Park Act*
- *Western Arctic (Inuvialuit) Claims Settlement Act*
- *Yukon Act*
- *Yukon Placer Mining Act*
- *Yukon Quartz Mining Act*

2. The following descriptions of DIAND and the summary of each sub-department's scope and mandate have been taken from the Department's *Annual Report, 1980-81.*

3. Much of the following discussion has been taken from the work of Ponting and Gibbins (1980). Any reader who wishes to investigate either the structure of the Indian and Inuit Affairs Program or the personalities within it should consult this work.

4. Ponting and Gibbins (1980) indicate that "the resultant process is a complicated one which must be launched almost two years prior to the beginning (April 1) of the fiscal year for which the figures are being prepared."

NATIVE URBANIZATION

INTRODUCTION

The effects of urbanization on Native Canadians have not been adequately studied, despite the concern expressed by the various levels of government. Partly this is due to a lack of data to support the claims of Native leaders and municipal and provincial government officials as to the issue's importance. Because urban Natives are highly transient and tend to blend into the general population of the urban poor, statistics are particularly difficult to obtain; politicians, as well as academics, tend to concentrate their efforts elsewhere. However, the issue of urbanization has recently been brought to the attention of municipal, provincial and federal governments by indirectly related issues such as social services, unemployment and urban crime.

When Hawthorn carried out his study of Native people in the 1960s, he predicted a major influx of reserve Indians into major urban centres. He also went on to point out that when this happened, special facilities would be needed to deal with the process of social adjustment. While the migration has not been as massive as Hawthorn predicted, it has been substantial (see Figure 7.1). Nevertheless, this "hyper mobile" population (Comeau and Santin, 1990) has posed considerable problems for city planners and urban programs. However, by the mid 1980s this migration movement began to slow down (Comeau and Santin, 1990). As Siggner (1986) points out, today the mobility patterns of Natives and non-Natives are almost identical; nearly one fifth of both groups lived at a different location than the one they had lived at ten years previously.

FIGURE 7.1 **DISTRIBUTION OF REGISTERED INDIAN POPULATION ON- AND OFF-RESERVE**

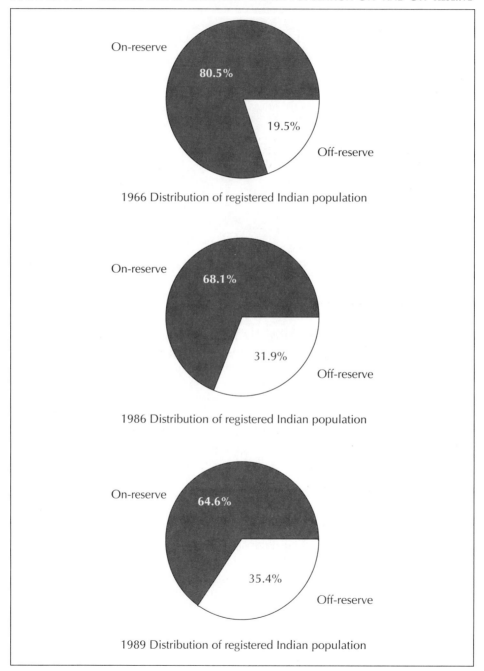

On-reserve
80.5%
19.5%
Off-reserve

1966 Distribution of registered Indian population

On-reserve
68.1%
31.9%
Off-reserve

1986 Distribution of registered Indian population

On-reserve
64.6%
35.4%
Off-reserve

1989 Distribution of registered Indian population

As Natives were forced onto reserves, their social and economic structures were incapable of supporting a growing population. As the Native population continued to increase, greater demands on scarce resources emerged. Nevertheless, lack of job skills and low educational achievement kept Natives on the reserve. Unemployment was high and temporary farm labour was the only alternative form of work they found. However, after World War II, Canada shifted from a rural, agricultural economic system to an industrialized, urban society. As a result of this transition, Natives found themselves migrating to urban centres in larger numbers than before. For example, in Manitoba, the urban Indian population jumped over 300 percent between 1966 and 1986.

Before the War, nearly all Native people lived in rural areas of Canada. However, by 1960, about 15 percent had moved to urban areas. By 1986, this percentage increased to nearly one third (see Figure 7.2). By 1987, well over 35 percent of Indians

FIGURE 7.2   Percentage of Registered Indians Living Off-Reserve by Region

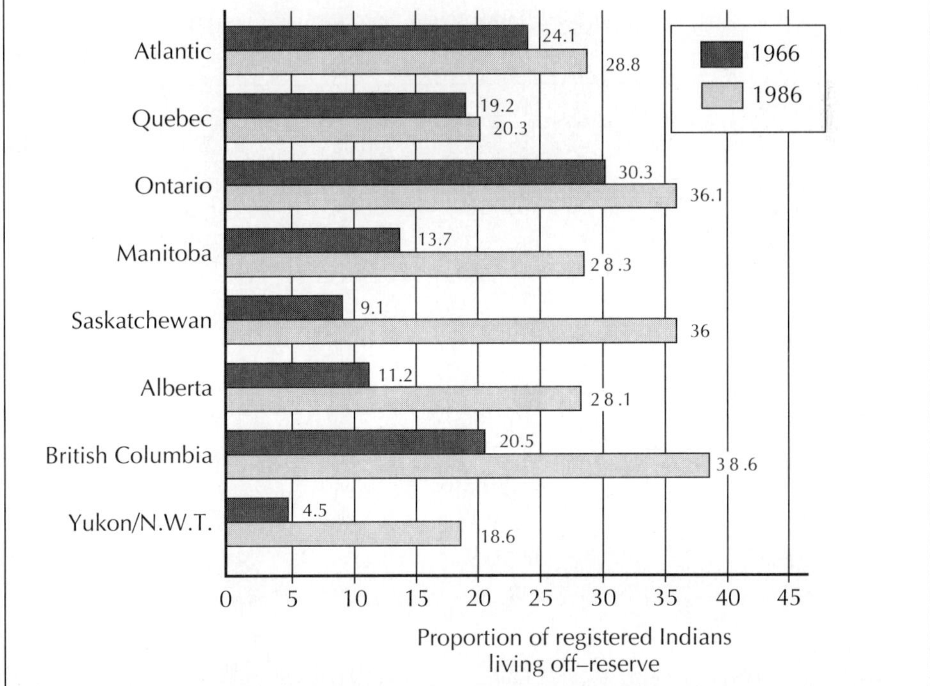

Source: Indian and Northern Affairs Canada, *Basic Departmental Data,* Evaluation Directorate, Minister of Supply and Services, Ottawa, 1988, 9.

in Canada were living off the reserve. While these figures show a dramatic increase in the proportion of Natives living in urban centres, they vary considerably from the statistics for the general population which show 80 percent of the population currently living in urban centres. Table 7.1 reveals the off-reserve population by age group from 1981 to projections in 2001. The results show that the off-reserve population is aging and will continue to get older; e.g., in 1981, about 3.5 percent were in the 45-49 age group, while by 2001, that number will be doubled.

Nearly 80 percent of off-reserve Indians are living in large metropolitan centres. Table 7.2 shows the rate of growth in the Native population for selected cities between 1951 and 1986. Clearly, a rapid growth has taken place in the number of Natives moving to the city. However, Table 7.2 does not reflect the number of Natives who have entered the city as other than full-time residents or whose lifestyles have frustrated the attempts of an enumeration agency to

TABLE 7.1 PopuLATION BY AGE GROUP, INDIANS OFF-RESERVE, 1981, 1991, 2001

Age	1981 Population	% Total pop.	1991 Population	% Total pop.	2001 Population	% Total pop.
0-4	10 908	10.99	19 252	9.38	18 934	7.98
5-9	12 651	12.74	16 535	8.06	22 320	9.40
10-14	13 294	13.39	18 701	9.11	22 116	9.32
15-19	12 205	12.29	19 791	9.65	17 261	7.27
20-24	10 559	10.64	21 395	10.43	17 632	7.43
25-29	8 751	8.81	21 083	10.27	19 399	8.17
30-34	7491	7.55	19 902	9.70	21 827	9.19
35-39	5985	6.03	17 313	8.44	22 282	9.39
40-44	4401	4.43	13 781	6.72	20 079	8.46
45-49	3407	3.43	10 650	5.19	15 997	6.74
50-54	2599	2.62	7994	3.90	12 136	5.11
55-59	2079	2.09	6046	2.95	9042	3.81
60-64	1428	1.44	4373	2.13	6590	2.78
65+	3523	3.55	8373	4.08	11 772	4.96
Total	99 281	100.00	205 188	100.00	237 387	100.00

Source: N. Hagey, G. Larocque and C. McBride, *Highlights of Aboriginal Conditions, 1981-2001, Part I, Demographic Trends* (Ottawa: Indian and Northern Affairs Canada, 1989), 27.

count them. Only a few cities in Canada have tried to gather up-to-date and dependable data, with often surprising results: on the basis of its own figures, Regina predicts that by 1991, over one fourth of its population will be Native. Tables 7.2 and 7.3 illustrate the contrast between the official figures and the estimated actual Native populations in selected urban centres. The discrepancies can be considerable: in 1991, Calgary officially claimed slightly less than 4000 Natives, yet a number of agencies placed the estimated figure at between 5000 and 10 000.

Table 7.2 shows a steady increase in the urban Native population since 1951. Presently there is some debate as to whether the urbanization process has peaked or will continue to increase. So far, the evidence suggests that the rate of Native urbanization has stabilized and will only increase at a slow rate.

TABLE 7.2   Growth of Indian and Métis Population in Urban Centres,*
1951-1986

	1951	1961	1971**	1986
Calgary	62	335	2265	3865
Edmonton	616	995	4260	10 795
Hamilton	493	841	1470	1775
London	133	340	1015	—
Montréal	296	507	3215	7485
Prince Albert	211	225	1045	—
Prince Rupert	—	880	1780	—
Regina	160	539	2860	5175
Saskatoon	48	207	1070	5380
Toronto	805	1196	2990	5595
Vancouver	239	530	3000	11 015
Winnipeg	210	1082	4940	18 000

*   The cities chosen were those which had the largest number of Indian residents.
    The numbers are probably understated since many arrivals in a city are itinerant and
    are, therefore, very difficult to count in a census.
** Does not include Inuit

SOURCE: Information Canada, *Perspective Canada I* (Ottawa: Queen's Printer, 1974), 244; Canadian Metropolitan Areas, *Dimensions*, Statistics Canada, Table 9, 1986.

TABLE 7.3 ᴇꜱᴛɪᴍᴀᴛᴇᴅ ᴜʀʙᴀɴ ᴄᴏɴᴄᴇɴᴛʀᴀᴛɪᴏɴꜱ ᴏꜰ ɴᴀᴛɪᴠᴇꜱ, 1991

Province	Centre	Indians	Indians and Other Natives
British Columbia	Vancouver	6 500	15 000 - 20 000
	Chilliwack	—	865
	Kamloops	—	515
	Victoria	2300	3000 - 4000
	Prince George	1200	2000
	Prince Rupert	2400	3000
Alberta	Calgary	—	5000 - 10 000
	Edmonton	—	10 000 - 15 000
Saskatchewan	Regina	5300	15 150
	Saskatoon	1800 - 2000	5000 - 10 000
	Prince Albert	1600 - 1750	—
	North Battleford	700 - 800	—
Manitoba	Winnipeg	6000 - 16 000	15 000 - 20 000
Ontario	Ottawa-Hull	2500	—
	Toronto	—	15 000 - 20 000
Québec	Montréal	—	700 - 800 permanent 7500 transient
	Québec City	—	3000 - 4000
Atlantic	Halifax	—	1000

Sᴏᴜʀᴄᴇ: City officials for each city identified, 1991.

The number of off-reserve Indians varies widely from province to province. Data from 1966 show that most areas of Canada had surprisingly low numbers (see Figure 7.2). Today, three provinces have over 36 percent of their Native population living off-reserve—British Columbia, Saskatchewan and Ontario. The most dramatic increases from 1966 to 1986 have been in the west and north, where off-reserve rates have doubled, and in one case, Saskatchewan, quadrupled.

Migration is a reciprocal process, referring to the movement of Natives both into and out of the city. In some cases, Natives who move off the reserve settle permanently in the city; others only sojourn in the city, remaining for a while, then moving back to their reserves. Nevertheless, urban areas continue to be the destination of Indian migrants. Even though urban areas are the recipients of large numbers of Natives, they also contribute to the total number of out-migrants among Native people. The end result was that for the period of 1976-81, compared to 1966-71, urban areas showed a 6 percent increase in the influx of Native migrants, but a net loss of 2 percent in the Native population.

Before examining the process of migration in detail, a brief characterization of the Natives who presently live in Canadian cities will be useful.

URBAN INDIAN PROFILE

Table 7.1 shows that, in 1981, more than one fourth of the Indian population between the ages of 25 and 44 lived off the reserve. However, this proportion of off-reserve Indians increased substantially from the early 1950s until the early 1970s when it began to decrease. By 1991, well over one third of the urban Indian population was in this age category. These figures support the observation that urban migration is slowing down as the urban migrants age and fewer immigrants enter the urban setting. When age groups are compared, however, no substantial difference emerges in migration patterns. This suggests that members of all age groups migrate in almost equal numbers to urban centres, although somewhat fewer Natives over 65 migrate. The high proportion of children up to 14 years old shows that many Natives bring their children with them as they enter the city. For example, Vincent (1970) found that in Winnipeg over half the Natives were younger than 30; other studies have since supported this finding, with slightly different figures (Indian Association of Alberta, 1971; Denton, 1972; Nagey *et al.*, 1989). Vincent also found that 60 percent of urban Natives were married, though not necessarily living with their spouses.

According to the male-female ratio, there are about 10 percent more Native women in urban centres than men. This figures does not include women who have been forced off the reserves through marriage to non-Indian men.

Levels of education for off-reserve Indians are significantly lower than the national average (Stanbury and Fields, 1975; Federation of Saskatchewan Indians, 1978). However, when compared to the educational levels of on-reserve Indians, the difference is not significant. In other words, there is no "brain drain" operating on the reserves. A number of surveys over the past two decades have been undertaken to assess the labour force involvement of urban Natives (Stanbury and Fields, 1975; United Native Nations Manpower Survey, 1976; Bob Ward Associates, 1978, DIAND, 1980; Frideres and Ryan, 1980). More recent surveys confirm the earlier findings. All the data show that the unemployment rate for off-reserve Natives is between five to six times higher than for non-Natives living in the urban area. Not only are unemployment rates higher, the length of time Natives have held jobs is also much less than non-Natives. Only about one fifth of the urban Native population have held jobs for more than a month.

The surveys attributed unemployment among off-reserve Natives to a lack of training and a need to attend to family responsibilities. However, Stanbury and

Fields (1975) also found that discrimination in employment contributed significantly. Nevertheless, because of the low labour-force participation rate, high unemployment, and low educational attainment, the income levels of urban Natives are very low. Well over half of the Natives in urban centres had incomes well below the poverty level. This number is to be compared with less than one fourth of the non-Native population. Because of their difficulty in attaining employment and their low incomes, many Natives in urban centres require extensive social assistance; e.g., housing, childcare, food. We find that Natives who live in urban centres are exposed to many more services than those living on the reserve. However, because of legal wranglings, they are not able to gain access to this multitude of services. Their lack of access is also a result of their poor understanding of their rights as Canadians and their unwillingness to press for services they might need. As a result, urban Native people continue to live in poverty, as they did on the reserve.

Decision to Migrate

Most studies of Native migration have focused on the individual, i.e., on the factors which lead individuals to migrate to the urban centres from their reserves. The effects of the reserve community upon migration have seldom been investigated. The work of Gerber (1977, 1980) is an exception to this and merits an extended discussion in any analysis of Native urbanization, since both levels of variables need to be discussed if we are to clearly understand the process of Native urbanization.

The structures of particular reserves have an important influence on Native migration patterns. Gerber found that Prairie reserves are very communally oriented, while Eastern reserves tend to be much more individualistic. For example, Eastern Indians are more likely to hold location tickets (legal document entitling an individual to the right to occupy and use a piece of land), which they can will or sell to other Indians. This cultural variable has considerable impact on an individual's decision to migrate (Reeves and Frideres, 1981).

The specific structural factors of reserves that Gerber found important in affecting Native urbanization were: proximity of the reserve to an urban centre; road access; the size of the band; the degree of community development; and the retained use of Native languages. As Table 7.4 shows, high-migration bands were small, not in the Prairies, and were largely English-speaking. In addition, the sex ratio of high-migration bands was, on average, 141 men to 100 women.

Gerber found that the development of personal resources and group resources were particularly important in determining migration patterns. Table 7.5 shows the typology she developed to indicate potential migration patterns. Bands in Cell 1 are "inert," in that they are not adapting to the larger dominant culture or attempting to develop internally. Those in Cell 2 are "pluralistic." They are high in community development yet low in personal resources; even though considerable economic and social development has taken place, individuals have not partici-

TABLE 7.4   THE CHARACTERISTICS OF HIGH-MIGRATION BANDS

Band Size	Less than 400 members
Employment	Tradition of working off-reserve; poor on-reserve opportunities
Urban proximity	Semi-rural, urban, poor road access to urban centres for daily commuting
Education	Higher than average attainment; high proportion at inte grated schools
Language	English or French spoken on reserve
Band government	Poorly formulated

SOURCE: L.M. Gerber, *Trends in Out-Migration from Indian Communities Across Canada* (Ottawa: Department of the Secretary of State, 1977).

TABLE 7.5   GERBER'S TYPOLOGY FOR MIGRATION PATTERNS

		Level of community development	
		Low	High
Level of personal resources	Low	1[a]	2
	High	3	4

a.Numbers are for identifying the cell, i.e., the type of band.

SOURCE: Gerber, 1979.

pated in the education system or labour force to any great degree. In contrast, the bands in Cell 3 are "integrative." They have prepared individuals, through education and job experience, to enter the dominant culture, but have not created opportunities within the community; as a result, individuals must move to the outside world. Finally, the "municipal" Natives have a high rate of migration, but opportunities exist on the reserve for those who choose to remain.

In short, as one moves counterclockwise from Cell 1 in Table 7.5, the likelihood of urbanization increases. Apparently, the band itself provides the basic structural context that determines the rates of and reasons for urban migration. Those bands with high community development provide opportunities for their members to remain on the reserve. Those communities with high personal-resource development encourage their members to migrate to the city; when, in addition, community development is low, individuals are forced off the reserve but can compete successfully in the urban context. However, as Gerber argues, an increase in off-reserve residence also results when community development stimulates out-migration to compensate for a lack of personal-resource development.

Clearly, the structural conditions that govern life determine, more or less, the decisions of individual Natives to migrate off the reserve. Denton (1972) also points out that, in addition to social factors, cultural factors come into play. According to Denton, reserves are governed by strong "village norms and social control mechanics which encourage work, independence, and earning one's own money" (1972:55). Thus, from an early age, children are socialized into work roles and, as they grow older, make increasing contributions to family maintenance (Honigman, 1967). Often, conflicts result between children and parents; children are taught to be self-reliant and independent, but at the same time must bend to the will of their families.

These structural, social and cultural conditions, then, are instrumental in pushing the young Indian off the reserve and into the urban context. Moreover, a decision to return to the reserve is also influenced by these factors; community development must be such as to easily absorb the returnee.

A number of academics have divided Native city-dwellers into transients, migrants, commuters and residents. The *transient* moves continually from one place to another without establishing full residence in any urban area (Nagler, 1971). The *migrant* simply transfers a social network from a rural base to an urban one, moving to the city but only interacting with other Natives. The *commuter* lives close enough to an urban centre to spend large amounts of time there, yet retains residence on the reserve. The *resident* has been born in the city and spends most of his/her time in an urban context.

Many researchers have assumed that the longer an individual Native resides in an urban area, the more likely integration into the dominant society becomes. This assumption is true only for a certain segment of the urban Native population. Some Natives, in order to become socially and politically integrated into White society, terminate most social and family ties with their band. But most Natives are unable to integrate into the larger society, whether they desire to or not.

Although social factors undoubtedly play a part, most Natives tell investigators that they have come to the city to participate in the labour force. This provides a legitimate explanation to non-Natives and allows Natives to apply for welfare aid more easily. However, Natives are very much aware of the poor opportunities for steady employment in the city. What, then, are the real reasons for urban migration? First of all, as pointed out previously, an increase in population has created overcrowding on the reserve, specifically in the areas of housing and employment. Most reserves are rural-based and can only provide jobs for a limited population. As Deprez and Sigurdson (1969) point out, because the economic base of most reserves is incapable of supporting the existing Native population, out-migration is essential.

Each Native must assess the chances of obtaining work and housing on the reserve. Because both are scarce, a great deal of competition exists among reserve residents. As in most social organizations, access to housing and employment is partially controlled by a relatively affluent social elite. The housing needs of young, single males and females are not considered high priority; young singles are seen as capable of entering the world outside the reserve and generally lack a social network on the reserve, which is required if Indian officials are asked for help. In particular, unmarried females, with or without children, receive low priority in housing allocation. This partly accounts for the high ratio of males to females on certain reserves, as well as for the high proportion of children under 15 who have moved off the reserve.

Migration away from the reserve is much more the result of push factors than of pull factors. The urban setting is attractive only to those who are qualified to participate actively in it; few Natives are able to do so. Most Natives decide to leave the reserve only when they are forced to by an absence of housing and employment opportunities.

Entering the City

In the early stages of urban migration, the first Native institutions to emerge in a city are bars with large Native clienteles. From these first interactions, cliques then emerge and create a social network for Natives to enter and leave at will. Through these cliques, the second stage of urbanization evolves; Native social and cultural centres develop, along with more extended social networks. Price (1979) calls these centres "second-stage institutions." The centres inhibit integration into the city, yet increase the odds for urban survival. In addition, they promote and facilitate a chain migration of Natives to the cities.

The third stage of urbanization, institutional completeness, has not yet been reached. Institutional completeness is the creation and maintenance of a set of institutions, such as schools, churches and employment agencies, that meet most social, cultural and economic needs of the ethnic group. Native institutional completeness has failed to develop in the urban centres for a number of reasons. The leaders of Native bands generally remain on the reserve, even though regional, provincial and national government offices are located in urban areas. Native political organizations continue to focus on rural issues, such as band claims and treaty rights. Due to internal rivalries between Native factions, urban Native leaders have failed to gain political momentum. Moreover, because urban Native organizations, such as friendship centres, are continually preoccupied with crisis situations, they have not been able to address the general social and economic needs of urban Natives.

Clearly, few Natives enjoy the stable and social networks in cities that would permit institutional completeness to develop. Native urbanization will not be complete until agencies are developed and staffed by Natives to provide employment and services to the Native community. At this time, Natives have become heavily involved in social and cultural centres, provincial political associations, and local and Native political organizations. Each urban area is developing somewhat differently, however, and according to varying schedules.

Progressive urbanization is producing more and more urban Natives. What happens after the Native enters the city? What kinds of experience take place? The answers to these questions largely depend on the lifestyle of the individual. For the purposes of this discussion, urban Natives can be divided into transients and residents.

Transients are those individuals who are unable or unwilling to integrate into White society because of their high mobility patterns. Because they retain a rural orientation and possess few skills, transients are not able to participate in the social or economic fabric of Canadian society. As a result, they become more and more dependent on the same social-service organizations that, ironically, encouraged them to migrate in the first place.

Table 7.6 lists some of the value differences that exist between Natives and Whites. Of course, both value systems are in a state of flux and neither is as straightforward as it appears. For example, the introduction of social welfare, combined with the Natives' lack of control over their destiny, has led to a dependency ethos that did not exist before contact with White culture.

A basis for some of the irreconcilable differences that exist between Natives and non-Natives lies in the philosophical assumptions made about human beings and society. The basis of present Western thought can be found in the liberal political philosophy of Rousseau, Locke and Hobbes, which stressed that individual self interest should take precedence over group rights. However, it was argued, individuals must operate in a collective unit so that all individuals can survive. To further this aim, a state apparatus was created in which individuals voluntarily agreed to subordinate their self-interest to the common good. Nevertheless, the individual is considered to be morally prior to any group, and the individuals within a state are to be viewed as acting for themselves, not as members of any collectivity (Boldt and Long, 1985).

Contrary to this Western philosophical position (which emerged out of feudalism), Native people were not grounded in state institutions nor in relationships which supported vertical hierarchical arrangements. Vachon (1982) argues that Natives have a cosmocentric view of the universe (in contrast to homocentric) which focuses not on the individual but on the "whole." Individuals then, are to be subordinate to the whole. Human beings are just part of the whole, which also includes animals, plants and inanimate objects. All of these parts must exist in harmony, and the parts as well as the whole can only survive if each works in harmony with each other. Therefore, all the parts are forced to interact with each other and take the other into consideration. Human beings, in Native culture, are viewed as just another limb in the body of life, but a limb with certain additional responsi-

TABLE 7.6   Cultural Differences Between Whites and Natives

Indian values	White values
Group emphasis	Individual emphasis
Cooperation (group concern)	Competition (self-concern)
Present oriented	Future oriented
Non-awareness of time	Awareness of time
Age	Youth
Harmony with nature	Conquest of nature
Giving	Saving
Practical	Theoretical
Patience	Impatience
Extended family	Immediate family
Non-materialistic	Materialistic
Modest	Overstates (over-confident)
Silent	Noisy
Low self-value	Strong self-value
Respects other religions	Converts others to own religion
Religion a way of life	Religion a segment of life
Land, water, forests and other resources belong to all, and are used reasonably	Land, water, forests and other resources belong to the private domain, and are used in a greedy manner
Equality	Wealth
Face-to-face government	Representative democracy

Source: Tanner, A. (ed.), 1983, 296-297.

bilities. As a result, individual self-interest was defined as group-interest and the group and the individual were seen to share a common identity. Laslett (1963) uses the onion-skin analogy to illustrate the relationship of the individual to the whole. The entire onion represents group-orientation attributes. Each person has more or less of these group attributes as he/she moves through society over time. However, if all oriented attributes are removed, there is no core of self or individual remaining. While not all Natives fully subscribe to this perspective, there are remnants of this philosophy present today in varying degrees.

In summary, White society can be characterized as using "linear and singular" thinking. A good example of this is the concept of time as defined by non-Native Canadians. First, time is conceptualized as a straight line. What is immediate in time is present; what is behind is the past and the future is yet to be achieved. Time can be viewed as a row of similar units which can be divided into separate and different units. Thus, for example, we think in terms of minutes, hours and days. Implicit in this linear thinking is the view that time flows one way and cannot be made up. Linear thinking also lends itself to singular thinking; that is, linear thinking propels individuals toward values which imply "one answer," "one way." Linear thinking can be either horizontal or vertical, but the general principle remains the same. This linear world-view also leads to specialist activity in that one moves toward "one thing." You can only be good at one thing, not a number.

In contrast to the linear world-view, the Native world-view can be characterized as cyclical or holistic. This view begins with the premise that everything is interrelated. It is a generalist perspective rather than the specialist one which characterizes Canadian non-Native culture. As many Natives note, their view of the world is more circular; there is no beginning, no end. There are phases and patterns to the world, but they are repetitive and cyclical. Since all parts are interrelated, each part is equal to all others. The system could not continue with a missing part. In addition, when the world is viewed as a whole, there is a tendency to see the whole or group as more important than the individual. Being part of the group is better than being alone. The interrelated whole results in harmony and balance (Cawsey, 1991).

As Natives enter the city, they find a great deal of discontinuity between life on the reserve and life in the city. As they reach the city, Natives enter a world that is generally alien, frightening, frustrating and hostile. Many Natives express total confusion as to "how Whites work." Of course, the reaction of individual Natives to White society varies: some find it extremely bizarre and hostile, while others quickly adapt to the White ethos. The extent to which Natives can reconcile the "two solitudes" of reserve life and city life depends on early socialization experiences and past interactions with White society. Insofar as the structure of Canadian society plays a large role in socialization experiences, it has a profound effect on the ability of Natives to integrate into urban life. We now turn to examining the processes that affect and influence the Native's foray into urban life. We will show how the various organizations impinge upon the Native's attempts to deal with life in an urban area.

Social Organizations and Native Urbanization

In Europe, state-funded social services have been used to expand the rights of citizenship and to encourage members of the lower classes to participate politically (Bendix, 1964). Mass education has been developed to raise literacy levels and to provide the formal qualifications necessary for employment in urbanized settings. In addition, social welfare organizations have been expanded to ensure an educated population and to provide support for an urbanized labour force. These social services pulled people from peripheral areas into the mainstream of modern economy and, by so doing, played a part in the urbanization of European society.

In Canada, the federal government has tried to repeat this process through the urbanization of Native people, but this policy is highly suspect. The government is trying to encourage Natives to abandon their reserves and treaty rights, mobilizing them as Canadian citizens but not as "citizens plus" (White Paper, 1969; Weaver, 1980). "Citizens plus" refers to the view that, since Indians were the first inhabitants of Canada, they should be afforded special status and rights. By curtailing services on the reserves, most noticeably in the area of housing, the government has tried to push Natives into the city, especially during winter. In addition, by transferring the provision of services from the federal to the provincial system, the federal government has attempted to reduce its treaty obligations.

Unlike in Europe, the federal government does not have jurisdiction over those social services, particularly education and social welfare, that have been used to expand citizens' rights and to urbanize members of the lower classes. In Canada, these services generally are provided by provincial agencies. While the provincial educational system has made some effort to increase the Native levels of literacy and formal certification, the welfare system has not been expanded to incorporate Natives into urban society. Although the number of Natives on welfare has increased in cities, they generally receive only short-term services that relieve temporary problems of urban subsistence (Stymeist, 1975).

The lack of educational qualifications continues to prevent full urban integration for most Natives. As stated earlier, Natives who claim a desire for employment as the primary reason for moving to the city generally do so because of the requirements of the welfare system, rather than because they perceive actual employment opportunities for themselves. For some, such as single mothers with children, provincial welfare services allow a higher standard of life in the city than on a reserve or Métis colony. For most, however, government social services are not sufficient to encourage Natives to remain in cities. As a result, an increasing number of urban Natives can be classed as transient.

More and more young Natives are moving back and forth between urban and rural residences, generally on a seasonal basis. Faced with an inability to secure employment, or even to understand and use various government and private agencies, they commute into the city for short periods of time and then leave, their frustrations intact (Frideres and Ryan, 1980). Even though these Natives may spend large amounts of time in the urban context, they retain their social ties in the rural area.

A second group of Natives has succeeded in establishing residence, if not employment, in the cities. This group is predominantly female with young dependents (Gerber, 1977). In lieu of employment, these Natives rely on the support of relatives and friends in addition to government services. For example, from an Edmonton sample, 76 percent of urban Natives had relatives in the city when they first entered and 65 percent had friends (City of Edmonton, 1976).

A third, much smaller group of Natives appears to have successfully settled into urban society. Members of this group most closely approximate the White, middle-class, urban family: they live in single-family units as married adults with children; they have full-time employment; and they live in acceptable housing. Successful entry into urban society appears to be contingent upon attaining a level of education, health and well-being possessed by the vast majority of non-Native citizens of Canada.

The Transition

Natives move into the urban context in a series of stages.[1] Although these stages are serial, they are not necessarily "step-wise sequential"; that is, all of the steps are not essential in order to achieve the final stage. Also, progression through the stages is usually not completed in one continuous sequence.[2] As Figure 7.3 indicates, Natives are exposed to a funnelling effect: although most have some contact with service organizations, few become independent of the organizations, and even fewer are successfully placed in the city.

Natives move from Stage 1 to Stage 2 largely as a result of the recruitment procedures of service organizations. The type of service organization and its policy plays an important role in determining the rate of rural-to-urban transition. (See Table 7.7.) Service organizations have a great influence on the degree to which Natives can successfully adapt to the urban centre.

FIGURE 7.3 STAGES OF ADVANCEMENT OF NATIVE PEOPLE IN FINAL ADAPTATION TO URBAN MILIEU

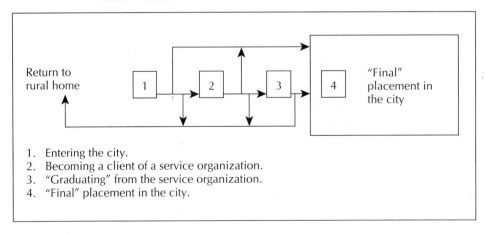

1. Entering the city.
2. Becoming a client of a service organization.
3. "Graduating" from the service organization.
4. "Final" placement in the city.

The issue of whether government or voluntary agencies should deal with Native problems has long been debated in Canada. Although the provincial governments recognize a partnership between the two sectors, they have tried to maintain the primacy of government both in policy formation and in program maintenance. Private agencies do not have the complex network of contacts and services that government programs can provide. Nonetheless, a policy of subsidiarity, by which governments refuse to duplicate the services offered by private citizens, has taken precedence. As a result, the government has become essentially a financier, relying upon the private sector to provide primary services to those in need.

Native Organization Contact

Natives entering the city usually find the process difficult and problematic. Upon entering the urban context, most Natives find that they must utilize the services of a variety of organizations in order to remain. Although some Natives on reserves or Métis colonies find that some form of sponsorship is necessary to remain in an urban centre, most of them are poorly prepared for urban life. Educational standards on the reserves and colonies have been considerably below those in other Canadian schools. The quality of social services, particularly for housing and health, has been well below national norms. Not surprisingly, the lifestyle of the rural Native has adapted to inferior levels of education, work experience, housing and health.

Even disregarding social and cultural factors, the vast majority of Natives entering cities do not have the qualifications necessary to get work, obtain social services, or to succeed in school. Most Natives cannot even qualify for unemployment insurance. Their poverty, combined with their unconventional lifestyles, exposes them to much higher than average levels of detention and arrest by the police. In the end, most Natives are not successful in adapting to city life.

Because of their unique position, urban Natives are much more likely than Whites to come into direct contact with service organizations that regulate and monitor social behaviour. Natives have consistently posed problems to those organizations in their attempts to establish public order and provide various services. Organizations that attempt to deal with native urban problems can be broken down into four categories: public service, acculturating service, accommodating service, and member organizations. Table 7.7 outlines the attributes of each type.

PUBLIC SERVICE ORGANIZATIONS

Public service organizations generally are designed to provide a single, functionally-specific service, such as justice, education or welfare, to the general public. They work within the prevailing Canadian system of values and beliefs and are typically staffed by middle-class executives, clerical workers and members of service-oriented occupations.

TABLE 7.7 ATTRIBUTES OF TYPES OF SERVICE ORGANIZATIONS

Organizational type	Selected attributes of organizations					
	Organizational effectiveness	Value representative	Membership recruitment	Extent of services	Ethnic comp. of staff	Ability to place clients
Public Service	High	Middle-class	Mass*	Singular	Middle-class; White	High
Acculturating Service	High	Middle-class	Very** selective	Multiple; integrated	Middle-class; White	High
Accommodating Service	Low	Native	Mass	Singular	Mixed-Native; middle-class; White	Low
Member	Moderate	Native	Mass; Native	Singular	Native	Low

* Recruitment is selective, yet the services offered are considered the right of all citizens.

** Recruitment is usually based on a sponsorship basis.

SOURCE: J. Frideres and W. Reeves, "Native Urbanization in Canadian Society" (Calgary, Alberta, mimeo, 1984).

From one perspective, public service organizations are designed to provide certain minimum levels of service to the general public. As a citizen, each individual has the right to a basic education, a basic standard of living and equal treatment before the law. In return, the individual guarantees school attendance from ages 6 to 15, the personal maintenance of public health and welfare standards, and submission to the police and the courts in all matters pertaining to public order.

From another perspective, public service organizations, especially education and justice systems, are important mechanisms for encouraging the participation of individuals in society. For example, educational achievement draws individuals out of their immediate locales and moves them into a socio-economic framework through entry into the labour force. Similarly, the basic requirements of public health and order encourage normative social behaviour.

In Alberta, according to available studies, public services have failed to integrate Natives into urban society. Natives who have come into contact with these organizations have tended to become virtually permanent clients, as evidenced by recurrent patterns of detention and arrest, high rates of hospitalization and premature death, and the inability of most Natives to leave the welfare rolls. In the educational system, where permanent subsistence is not permitted, Natives tend to drop out before achieving the minimum standards of attainment for success in the labour force.

Public service organizations do not assist most Natives to live in the city as competent citizens. Indeed, as currently constituted, these organizations more often present a barrier that denies Natives entry into the mainstream of urban Canadian life.

ACCULTURATING SERVICE ORGANIZATIONS

Like the public service, acculturating service organizations draw their staff from the middle class and act to promote or maintain the assimilation of Natives into White culture. Acculturating service organizations include post-secondary institutions, such as colleges and universities, provincial apprenticeship branches, the Central Mortgage and Housing Corporation, and the Alberta Opportunity Fund (a source of credit for small business). The agencies share many characteristics with regard to Natives. They usually obtain many, if not most, of their clients through a system of referrals. Whenever possible, they exercise discretion when accepting prospective clients, taking only those who have a good chance of succeeding in their programs. Once accepted, their clients typically do succeed: formal and informal counselling services, along with other sources of support, minimize the drop-out rates. For example, a few Natives on Indian reserves or Métis colonies who display a potential for academic achievement are maintained through secondary school and then referred to a post-secondary institution, usually a college or a university. Once sponsored, these Natives have a high incidence of success in the system.

Acculturating service agencies are also similar in that their clientele includes very few Natives. Most Natives simply do not have the minimal qualifications necessary to be referred to or accepted into such programs. Furthermore, Natives have found it difficult to obtain services from these organizations because they have difficulty understanding and coping with non-Native rules and procedures.

ACCOMMODATING SERVICE ORGANIZATIONS

Accommodating service organizations attempt to compensate for the lack of preparation revealed by certain visible-minority groups in their contacts with White society. These agencies are often funded by public service organizations to deal with problematic clients. For example, the Special Constables Program of the RCMP, the Courtworkers' Program, and the race relations units of municipal police forces all attempt to handle the problems that have arisen among Natives, the public and the courts. These agencies try to protect the rights of Natives and, at the same time, render the legal system more efficient. Also, several acculturating service organizations support the work of accommodating service organizations; examples include the Native counselling and Native studies programs on the campuses of various universities.

The ability of an accommodating service organization actually to alter the fate of its clients is extremely limited. These agencies support the work of public and acculturating service organizations and generally operate within a White, middle-class value system. They have managed to attract Native clients by hiring a greater proportion of Native staff members and by modifying some operating procedures to reflect their clients' cultural background. However, because funding often depends on enrolment figures, this "accommodation" of Native interests is not entirely altruistic.

Because funding is almost always limited to support for a particular project for a limited time, programs offered by these organizations usually lack scope and continuity. Accommodating agencies are generally expected simply to direct their clients to existing services provided elsewhere. Indeed, accommodating service organizations often are limited simply to registering, screening and referring their clients to other organizations. Moreover, they are unable to offer any real assistance to Natives in their dealings with those other organizations.

MEMBER ORGANIZATIONS

Unlike the other three types of service organizations, member organizations tend to work against the assimilation of Natives into the mainstream of Canadian society. Member organizations represent the interests of Natives as members of a distinct ethnic group. They provide some employment for Natives, promote the revitalization of Native culture, and attempt to provide the broad range of social support necessary to allow people to lead a Native lifestyle. Some organizations, like provincial Indian associations, are working to develop and document a case for entrenched Native economic and political rights. Others, like the Indian friendship centres, are attempting to promote a Native lifestyle in the cities. These organizations also function to encourage the emergence of a Native elite that has not been co-opted into the staff of public service organizations.

Although member organizations successfully provide services to urban Natives, their effectiveness is weakened by a virtual absence of employment for Natives as Natives. Member organizations have tried to promote the institutional completeness needed for ingroup cohesiveness and solidarity. However, this institutional completeness cannot be achieved without the creation of jobs for their members. To remedy this problem, Natives, like Hutterites, need to establish and run their own businesses; at present, there are very few urban Native enterprises. And, like Roman Catholics, Natives should control the beliefs, values and skills taught in government-supported schools.

At present, an inability to establish jobs for their membership stymies the success of Native organizations. Like those who rely on public service organizations, Natives who belong to member organizations continue to be excluded and stigmatized by white, urban society. Unlike the clients of public service organizations, however, Natives in member organizations are less likely to regard themselves and their fellows as failures.

PROBLEMS FACING SERVICE ORGANIZATIONS

As more and more Natives moved to the city in the late 1960s, public and acculturating service organizations came under increasing pressure. In coping with the influx of Natives, public service organizations experienced a disproportionate decrease in effectiveness and a disproportionate increase in costs. Although the schools experienced some problems in assimilating Native children, the brunt of this problem was felt by the police and courts. Young Natives who migrated to the cities lacked the prerequisite skills for employment and were unable to cope in a conventional fashion with the demands of urban society. Frustration and unemployment combined with divergent values to produce a style of life that frequently deviated from the social norms and laws in the cities. While greater expenditures on law enforcement increased the numbers of Natives being processed (and reprocessed) in the system, they did not reduce the threat to public order. This simultaneous decrease of effectiveness and increase in costs was underscored by social scientists, who pointed out that nearly half the inmates in provincial jails were Natives.

Managers of acculturative service programs were also faced with escalating costs accompanied by decreased effectiveness. Their programs were sporadic, unevenly implemented, and made little attempt to find standardized solutions to Native problems. In addition, they were under pressure to debureaucratize existing, legitimate programs.

Acculturating service organizations were also criticized on a different ground. Because Natives as a group were systematically under-certified, exceedingly few Natives enrolled in university, entered unionized occupations, or qualified for credit assistance in purchasing a home or establishing a business. With greater urbanization, Natives became a more visible minority, demonstrably denied access to many of the avenues to success in Canadian society. Native member organizations publicly questioned the legitimacy of training programs and assistance agencies that failed to recruit proportionate numbers of Natives into their publicly funded programs.

Like the public service organizations, then, the acculturative service agencies were faced with a legitimate problem: those Natives most in need of their services were clearly not receiving them. Both in public and acculturative service organizations, middle-level managers, who were responsible for day-to-day internal administration, funding, personnel and clientele, felt that some action was necessary. Although the issue of legitimacy did not actually threaten their budgets, it did increase public scrutiny of funding and internal administration, reducing managerial discretion and hindering the management of day-to-day operations. However, it is important to point out that this legitimacy crisis did not become a political issue; e.g., government did not become involved in determining policy or setting standards.

In order to reach a greater number of Natives, middle-level management in public and acculturating service organizations began to fund new projects proposed by accommodating service organizations.[3] In some cases, existing Native member organizations were co-opted to run these programs; e.g., Plains Indian Cultural Survival School, Native Counseling Services, Native Employment Transitional Services, Native Alcoholism. In other cases, funding was provided for the formation of new Native-oriented service organizations. In yet other cases, such as the Native Outreach Program, existing organizations created a new branch to deal with a specific type of client.[4]

Whatever their origins, accommodating service organizations tend to enhance the legitimacy of existing service organizations. Accommodating service programs essentially dealt with the problem clients of public service organizations, and left other operations intact. For example, Native students unable to complete their secondary education in the public high schools are referred to an "alternative" public school run by Native personnel.

By registering, screening, and referring problematic clients, accommodating organizations could forecast or even regulate the number of clients they deal with, and accommodating agencies could tailor specific projects for particular problematic groups. These special programs justified their high costs and provided a rationale by which public service organizations could offer special treatment to, and acculturating service organizations could relax entry and performance standards for, certain preferred groups such as Natives.

Essentially, by offering a bi-cultural program, the middle-level managers of service organizations shifted some of the responsibility for problem clients onto the shoulders of those operating the accommodating organizations. The bi-cultural program could accommodate both White and Native values. Moreover, accommodating service organizations could attract increasing numbers of clients without seriously affecting either the service standards of acculturating organizations or the cost-effectiveness of public service organizations.

Ironically, the accommodating organizations inherited the same problems of legitimacy that plagued the public and acculturating service organizations. Accommodating organizations are generally small, independent, voluntary associations that undergo major program and staff transformations every few years. Their instability is party due to the nature of their financial support. They face serious problems establishing a permanent source of funding and, therefore, a clearly defined mandate. Usually, their budgets are mostly made up of grants from public service organizations. These grants are generally earmarked for specific projects designed to last for a limited period of time, often one to three years. In addition, they are aimed at protecting the rights of individual clients, and do not attempt to address the general problems of Natives. As a result, accommodating service agencies generally offer services for Natives that are far too restricted in focus to address adequately the low qualifications, marginal living standards, low incomes and high crime rates of Native Canadians.

In summary, the accommodating service organizations have inherited many of the criticisms once aimed at the public service and acculturative service organizations. To get funding, the accommodating organizations orient their programs toward Native culture in hopes of attracting Native clients. However, the placement of these clients then becomes problematic. Because White businesses generally refuse to hire them, Natives become perpetual clients of the agencies and are locked into a limbo between the reserve and the city. As a result, a large number of Natives enter these accommodating organizations, but few graduate. Accommodating service organizations are particularly effective at placing those clients who no longer need their services. Also, because the organizations, to some extent, encourage Native values and lifestyles, they do not prepare Natives for White, middle-class society; at best, they produce marginal Natives.

Because the federal and provincial governments desire to provide social services on an equal basis to individual members of the general public, they have been unwilling to address the problems of particular groups or communities. The current political climate exacerbates this problem. At the constitutional level, the provincial government has refused to accept sole legal responsibility for the social support of status Indians off the reserve. To avoid giving even *de facto* recognition to the collective rights of Natives, these governments have restricted their support of organizations for Natives to narrow-range, small-scale, temporary projects.

The precarious status of accommodating agencies undermines their effectiveness. Overly specific short-term programs discourage the regular, full-time participation of Natives. Moreover, remedial programs are often too narrow to ensure continued Native participation without a broad range of additional social support to counteract the effects of poverty and unemployment. To obtain this support, accommodating organizations must refer their clients to the system of social services offered by public and acculturating organizations, despite the fact that their own projects often run counter to and are not integrated with these social services. Clearly, whatever the efficiency of accommodating organizations under ideal conditions, the absence of wider social support sabotages their effectiveness and undermines what few gains they manage to achieve.

NOTES

1. Some of the material presented has been previously published by Frideres and Reeves in *Canadian Public Policy*, 1981.

2. The lengths of time between each step vary and should not be seen as equal. Movement to the next step is not automatic and several starts may be needed before it takes place.

3. At the same time, Natives on the reserves and in the city lacked an elite to promote a rediscovery and resurgence of Native culture. They also lacked service organizations to encourage participation in the larger society. The end result was the creation of a very passive and apathetic population that remained on the reserve or in rural areas. Those Natives who became "active" were generally coopted and acculturated out of Native culture and into mainstream society.

4. These organizations screen potential clients and sort them into appropriate homogenous streams before providing services. In essence, accommodating service programs stream special problems away from the general program. The bi-cultural program can accommodate White and Native values, thereby rendering acculturating service organizations more effective while increasing the clientele of accommodating service organizations. This new composite organization has allowed an increasing number of Natives to stay in urban areas.

NATIVE ORGANIZATIONS

INTRODUCTION

Organizations have had a long tradition in the culture of Canadian Natives and have been an integral part of Canadian social and political life. Unfortunately, little has been written about these organizations and the role they played in the development of Canada. In the nineteenth century, several efforts were made by Natives to create regional and national political organizations. The demise of these organizations was generally the result of suppression by the federal government and internal discord among the Natives themselves. These problems continued to plague Native political groups well into the twentieth century.

The short-lived and ineffectual structure of Native organizations has been the result of mistakes made by Native leadership, outside interference and the inappropriateness of certain social structures within a larger social system. For example, the burgeoning number of Native organizations, all representing a myriad of goals and objectives, has prevented Native people from pursuing a cohesive and integrated set of objectives. Different tribal and linguistic groups have also prevented cohesive strategies from emerging.

The nature of the goals which the various organizations have set has also been problematic for Native people. Some groups have tried to pursue local objectives, while others have focused more on regional or national matters. Their goals have been political, social, religious or economic, and this diffusion of focus has led to divisions among those pursuing the goals.

The desire of the federal government to suppress political activity can be seen in Figure 8.2, which illustrates government reaction to a circular (Figure 8.1) distributed by Jules Sioui in a 1943 attempt to organize Native chiefs. A far more serious attempt to deny Natives the right to organize and lobby was the *Indian Act* of 1927, which for many years prohibited the political organization of Natives beyond local levels of government.

FIGURE 8.1 JULES SIOUI'S CIRCULAR

PROVINCE DE
OF QUÉBEC
COMITÉ DE PROTECTION DES DROITS INDIENS
Quartiers généraux au Village Huron de Lorette

Grand chef,

La présente communication vous avise de la tenue, à Ottawa, le 19 Octobre prochain, d'une grande convention des chefs de notre nation. Je dois réclamer la présence à l'hôtel Windsor, de deux ou trois délégués pour chaque tribu indienne.

Les heures graves que nous vivons nous forcent à ébaucher à préciser des projets de réformes sérieuses. Nous devrons établir celles-ci sans retard si nous voulons sauvegarder nos droits, et cela, dans un pays qui est bien le nôtre.

Une réponse affirmative de tous est urgente. Votre aide financière sera aussi bienvenue, car le coût de ces travaux de réorganisation nous sont très onéreux.

Sincèrement,

Head chief:—

This letter advises you that a general meeting of the chiefs of our Nation will take place in Ottawa, on the 19th day of October next. I do claim the presence, at Windsor Hotel, of two or three delegates from each one of our reserves.

The impact of these perilous moments compels us to draw-up serious reforms in order to put a betterment in the Indian situation, and this, without delay, if we want the maintenance of our rights in our proper country.

An urgent affirmative answer is requested. A financial help will be welcome as this rally and the works to be performed are very expensive and their cost rests rather heavily on our shoulders.

Sincerely,

JULES SIOUI
chef exécutif du—C.P.— chief executive
Case postale Loretteville P.O.B.,
Comté de Québec County.

FIGURE 8.2   THE GOVERNMENT'S REACTION TO JULES SIOUI'S CIRCULAR

Ottawa, September 23, 1943

G. Swartman, Esq., Indian Agent, Sioux Lookout, Ontario.
Re: Circular letter to Indian Chiefs
      from Jules Sioui

I have to thank you for bringing the circular enclosed with your letter of September 17 to my attention.

For your information I may say that the person who signed the circular is not a Chief of the Jeune Lorette band. He is an agitator and trouble-maker with whom the Department has had a great deal of difficulty over a considerable period. Although he is a member of the band and an Indian under the law, he is physiologically a White man with no perceptible Indian characteristic. In the more settled parts of Eastern Canada, there are many of these legal Indians who retain their status because of the paternal descent, but who actually have lost all trace of Indian blood. They are often the most prominent among the leaders of movements in support of alleged ancient Indian rights and other claims which form the basis of agitation. Needless to say their activities in this respect usually have ulterior motives of self-interest of one kind or another.

In the present case it is thanks to you that the circular in question came to my attention and I appreciate your promptness in advising me of it. I am taking advantage of the information that you have given me to warn the Indians about the proposed meeting, through their respective agents. A copy of the circular letter that I am sending to all Indian Agents on the subject is enclosed herewith. I sincerely hope that none of the Indians of your agency will waste their time and money by travelling to this meeting or becoming involved in the activities of Mr. Sioui's organization.

Dr. H. W. McGill
Director.

Early Native organizations were generally tied to specific concerns, such as particular land claims. These organizations had a single focus, were relatively simple in structure, and were limited to a particular area or group of Natives. Only since the mid-1950s have Native organizations become multifaceted, complex in structure, and representative of Natives from all across Canada (Patterson, 1972).

It has been suggested that the first Indian Association was established about 1540 when the League of Iroquois was formed (Daugherty, 1982). This confederacy, composed of five Indian groups (Seneca, Mohawk, Onondaga, Oneida and Cayuga), had a governing council to decide on important issues that affected all the tribes. In addition, the council acted as an arbitrator for inter-tribal disputes. This organization did not, however, deal with intra-tribal affairs, leaving each tribe to deal with its own internal affairs.

With the emergence of the fur trade, the League began to exert its influence beyond the confines of the Five Nations. Their strategic location, their relative political cohesion and their alliance with the Dutch and English permitted them both to influence the activities of the fur trade (Daugherty, 1982) and to act as middlemen in that trade. This action led to a series of wars with the French and eventually caused the League to sign a treaty of neutrality with the French in 1701. This policy set the stage for relations between the Iroquois and the English after 1760. Furthermore, the League lost its key position as middleman in the fur trade. The encroachment of colonists and the success of the American Revolution brought about the final demise of the League.

In the late 1700s Joseph Brant (a Mohawk) tried to create a united Indian confederacy but with little success. This interest was renewed by Tecumseh (a Shawnee), who also tried to organize the Indians of the Northwest into a united Indian Confederacy. In the early 1800s, however, his plan ended in his death. During the next 75 years, various Indian leaders tried to unite Indians in an attempt to stop the west and northward expansion of European civilization. Although great Indian leaders such as Crowfoot, Piapot, Peguis and Big Bear made serious attempts to develop various organizational structures that would be effective in safeguarding Native interests, all of them were unsuccessful.

It was not until 1870 that the first Indian political organization in Canada was formed—the Grand General Indian Council of Ontario and Québec. It was formed by both Iroquois and Ojibeway. Their major concern was with the government's implementation of Indian policy. A competing organization (League of Indians) was established in the late nineteenth century. The Council, faced with competition from the League, coupled with a lack of operating funds, was forced to disband.

The League was based in the East, although its leaders thought of it as a national organization concerned with Indian rights. After several conferences, the League of Indians in Western Canada emerged, never to unite with its eastern counterpart. This League split in 1933, and two branches (Alberta and Saskatchewan) were created. The Alberta branch renamed itself the Indian Association of Alberta in 1939 and remains active in political causes today. While other organizations such as the Catholic Indian League (1962) and the Calgary Urban Treaty Indian Alliance (1972) have existed in Alberta, they have been very narrowly focused and short-lived.

The Saskatchewan branch phased itself out in 1942, but in 1946 two new provincial organizations (the Protective Association for Indians and the Union of Saskatchewan Indians) united to form the Union of Saskatchewan Indians. By the late 1950s, this group changed its name to the Federation of Saskatchewan Indians. The Federation has taken an active role in promoting the social, political and economic goals of both registered and non-registered Indians in Saskatchewan. More recently, the Saskatchewan Native Alliance (1970) was formed, and continues to be active today.

In British Columbia, the Nishga Indians formed the Nishga Land Committee in the latter part of the nineteenth century. This organization was the genesis of their concern with land claims, in particular, the claim that would culminate with the 1973 Supreme Court decision and the subsequent development of the government's land claims policy. By 1915, a supporting organization, the Allied Tribes of British Columbia, was created to lobby for land claims. It was short-lived and by the 1920s it had been dismantled. In 1931 the Native Brotherhood of British Columbia began and later amalgamated with the Pacific Coast Native Fishermen's Association, which gave it a broader base of both northern and southern coastal Indians. The Brotherhood, still in existence, did not focus on land claims; rather, it was more concerned about social and economic issues.[1]

The members of the Brotherhood were all Protestants; in 1943, a rival Catholic organization, the North America Indian Brotherhood, was also established in British Columbia. Although the two groups did not clash overtly, ill-feeling and discord between them prevented either from accomplishing much. The federal and provincial governments capitalized on the differences between the two groups by using a divide-and-conquer technique. For example, at various hearings, representatives from both Native organizations were asked for briefs. The government representatives then seized on the contradictions between the recommendations of the two groups and used them as an excuse to ignore all the requests from both of them.

By the 1940s Indians from eastern and western Canada formed a new national organization, the Canadian Indian Brotherhood (later to be renamed the North American Indian Brotherhood). This organization had no religious bias and consisted solely of non-treaty Indians. In 1946 the Brotherhood attempted to form a coalition with treaty Indians from Saskatchewan. This proved fruitless partly because of interference by Saskatchewan's CCF government. The NAIB remained active in National political affairs until it was phased out of existence in 1969. Native organizations in Manitoba did not emerge until the late forties when the Manitoba Indian Brotherhood was formed. Since then, the MIB has been disbanded and a new organization (the Four Nations Confederacy) has been formed. Attempts to merge status and non-status organizations have, at times, been successful. Nevertheless, a definite division continues to persist throughout Canada among non-treaty Indians, treaty Indians, and Métis.

Organizations in eastern Canada, particularly since 1960, have not been as vociferous or as organized as their Western counterparts, but they do have a long history. In 1840, missionaries helped the Ojibeway of Ontario to form the General Council of the Ojibeway Nations of Indians; in 1846, this was renamed the General Council of Indian Chiefs. Although the Council originally included only Christians, in 1882, it expanded its base and became the General Council of Ontario. This organization lasted until 1938 and was the beginning of the present Union of Ontario Indians.

The Union of Ontario Indians was formed in 1946 and still actively concerns itself with contemporary Indian issues. Although Québec's Indians are today without a major provincial organization, the Indians of Québec Association was active during the 1960s and 1970s. Finally, in the Maritime provinces, few Native organizations have been formed. While the Grand General Indian Council was active for a few years in the early 1940s, it would not be until 1967 that the Union of New Brunswick Indians was formed. It deals with Indians in both New Brunswick and Prince Edward Island. In 1969, the Union of Nova Scotia Indians was also formed.

Even though more than a quarter of the Indians in Canada live in Ontario, they have not seriously attempted to link up with other provincial or national Native organizations. The independence and aggressiveness of the Iroquois on the Six Nations Reserve have given them a unique position among Indians in Canada.[2] This group was one of the first to develop agricultural practices and establish semipermanent villages. They were also advanced in their political structures in that they developed powerful confederacies that had an impact on the region. This group also became an important link in the trading networks that developed throughout the region. The pivotal role they have played historically has led them to preserve their traditions and culture, and this has placed them in direct conflict with the federal government. They have resisted the implementation of many policies of the government and refused to be guided by the *Indian Act*. Other Natives, for example, Métis in eastern Canada, including those in Québec, are considered non-Indians; as such they are only nominally recognized by federal and provincial governments as legally Indian.

The emergence of a number of Indian organizations since the late 1960s reflects the impact of two events. First, was the ill-fated federal White Paper on Indian Policy in 1969. This policy statement evoked a strong response from Indian people all over the country and acted as a catalyst for Indian cooperation. It also allowed Indians to identify a clear-cut (at least from their perspective) event which plainly marked the federal government as the enemy. Secondly, changes in funding meant that Indian organizations were eligible for federal funds, and these funds could come from sources other than DIAND. One example of the impact of the White Paper was the creation of the Association of Iroquois and Allied Indians to represent various bands when dealing with different levels of government (Daugherty, 1982). The Union of B.C. Indian Chiefs was also formed during this time (1969) as a result of the fusion of the Indian Homemakers Association of B.C., the Southern Vancouver Island Tribal Federation and the North American Indian Brotherhood.

Many other Native organizations have been created or changed over the past century. The Council of Yukon Indians is the result of a merger between the Yukon Native Brotherhood (representing status Indians) and the Yukon Association of Non-Status Indians. Others have undergone some changes in structure; for example, the Indian Brotherhood of the Northwest Territories has emerged as the Dene Nation. Finally, more locally or regionally based Indian organizations have developed because of their dealings with various levels of government; for example, Grand Council Treaty No. 9 and Grand Council Treaty No. 3.

The Métis have also seen a proliferation of organizations. While the first Métis political organization was established in 1937 (Métis of Saskatchewan), it was, until the 1960s the only provincial Métis organization. Then, in rapid succession, Métis associations were formed in Alberta, Manitoba and British Columbia, and the National Canadian Métis Society also emerged. Métis were then represented at both the provincial and federal level. In 1970, the Métis of the Western provinces met and formed a new organization—the Native Council of Canada. Its goal is to promote Aboriginal rights, land claims and various social and economic policies. The Native Council of Canada represents a wide spectrum of Native people including some status Indians, eastern Canadian Métis and Natives without status under the *Indian Act*. The Council claims to represent 1.2 million Natives, while the federal government estimates the number to be about 100 000. Even though the Council has a diverse constituency and does not have a legal basis, such as the *Indian Act*, the federal government has agreed to recognize it as a lobbying group and even provided it with a seat at the First Minister's Conference in 1982.

As the constitutional negotiations continue, Native organizations have actively participated in presenting their case. They have utilized their grass-roots origins and have taken their concerns and demands to the federal negotiators. While all the Native organizations have played a role, the Assembly of First Nations has been afforded the position of unofficial spokesperson for Native people. A kind of truce has been declared among the various Native organizations in an attempt to present a unified front. Thus far, the provinces (except Québec) and the federal government have accepted their demand for self-government as well as a number of other demands.

A new organization, the Métis National Council, was established in 1983, just before the first round of Constitutional talks. Members of this group split from the Native Council of Canada because they felt that it did not reflect Métis aspirations for land and self-government. The 1981 census has identified fewer than 100 000 Métis, but the Métis National Council claims that there are half a million. This council, like the Native Council of Canada, has been afforded some legitimacy by the federal and provincial governments.

The nearly 30 000 Inuit have also become politically involved during the past two decades. The national organization, the Inuit Tapirisat of Canada, was created in 1970. Its first headquarters were in Edmonton, but by 1972 it has been reestablished in Ottawa. Its original goal was to preserve and promote Inuit culture as well as to negotiate land claims. Over the years, it became evident that one single organization could not represent the diversity of Inuit. For this reason, six regional organizations have emerged: the Committee on Original Peoples Entitlement, or COPE, (the Western Arctic), the Kitikmeog Inuit Association (the Central Arctic), the Kewatin Inuit Association (the Eastern Arctic), the Baffin Regional Association

TABLE 8.1   MAJOR NATIVE POLITICAL VOLUNTARY ASSOCIATIONS IN CANADA, BY DATE OF FORMATION

	Prior to 1799	1800-99	1900-19	1920-29	1930-39	1940-49	1950-59	1960-69	1970-73	1974-80	1981-91	Total
National		2	1		2	1	1	4	5	2	2	20
Regional	2		1	4	1	1		1	1	4	3	18
National-regional total	2	2	2	4	3	2	1	5	6	6	5	38
Nfld.-Labrador								1	2	1	1	5
P.E.I.										1		1
New Brunswick								1	3	2	1	7
Nova Scotia						1		2	2	2	2	9
Québec			1	2	1	1		3	5		3	16
Ontario			1	2	1	2	1	6	7	3	2	25
Manitoba						1	1	2	6	2	1	13
Saskatchewan				1	1	5	2	1	4	3	2	19
Alberta	1			1	2	1	1	4	3	3	3	19
B.C.	1		3	1	3	1	4	8	3	4	1	29
N.W.T.								3	4	4	1	12
Yukon								2	3	1	1	7
Provincial Total	2		5	7	8	12	9	33	42	26	18	162
Grand Total	4	2	7	11	11	14	10	38	48	32	23	200

SOURCE: Don Whiteside, *Historical Development of Aboriginal Political Associations in Canada* (Ottawa: National Indian Brotherhood, 1973), 6.

(Baffin Island), the Makivik Corporation (Newfoundland), and the Labrador Inuit Association. The Tungavik Federation of Nunavut, an umbrella organization, was created to represent the Inuit organizations east of the Mackenzie Delta. It has been through the TFN that the issue of Inuit land claims has been discussed.

COPE had its beginnings in the 1960s when the political awareness of Natives was raised. Their political consciousness was first piqued in the late 1950s when a group of Inuit whalers in the Tuktoyaktuk area arrived at an inland lake only to find all the fish dead from pollutants. Their resolve to establish local control came to fruition when, a decade later, COPE was officially formed.

The Northern Québec Inuit Association (NQIA) was also formed to deal with both local and national issues. The Association established two headquarters (one in Fort Chimo, the other in Montréal). Finally, the splinter Inuit group, Tungavinga Nunamimi, emerged in response to the James Bay Settlement set forth by the NQIA; as a result of their refusal to ratify the agreement, three settlements near Povungnituk created their own organization.

Prior to the creation of contemporary Native associations, there were many tribal organizations. These were closely tied to the religious and cultural components of tribal life and were directed inward, toward members of the group, rather than outward toward society as a whole. Few tribal organizations presently exist, and their role for Natives is more symbolic than instrumental; however, in some areas there has been a resurgence of tribal groups, as in the case of pow-wows.

Membership in the Native political organizations today has generally been determined by ascription: one is born into an organization, rather than choosing to join it. Legal factors also often determine membership; for example, membership in the National Indian Brotherhood was restricted to registered Indians. Table 8.1 illustrates the number of Native associations that have been active since 1700. As the table shows, the total number of organizations has recently increased considerably.

Table 8.2 illustrates the primary function of a number of voluntary associations active at some point between 1800 and 1980. These organizations have generally emerged in crisis situations to serve a specific need at a specific time; hence, many of them have been very short-lived. However, in addition to solving a specific problem, other Native organizations have expanded their roles. In urban centres, many of these organizations offer relief from the frustrations felt by Natives who have recently left the reserve. Natives with similar backgrounds, values and experiences can meet to discuss ways of adapting to urban life and to find solutions to specific individual problems.

The contemporary organization structure has largely resulted from increased urbanization. Although the organizations function within an urban context, however, their members are generally rural in orientation and are concerned with rural issues. At present, there are few organizations run by Natives to address urban issues. Today's organizations are imbued with a sense of cultural nationalism, or

TABLE 8.2 Reasons for the Formation of Native Canadian Political Associations, by Time Periods*

Year	Specific: Treaty rights, land rights, social issues		General Administrative policies		Other general protests		Total	
	No.	%	No.	%	No.	%	No.	%
I prior to 1849	4	100	—	—	—	—	4	100
II 1850-1939	10	31	19	59	3	9	32	100
III 1940-1965	4	14	18	62	7	24	29	100
IV 1966-1980	38	32	36	30	46	38	120	100
V 1981-1990	10	35	5	18	13	47	28	100
Total	66	31	78	37	69	32	213	100

* For purposes of this analysis, all national, regional and provincial associations were counted together. As a result, one could argue that nine "extra" provincial associations are included in the table. (Six in "specific protects," two in "administrative policies," and one in "general protests.") No cell, however, is changed by more than three percent because of the inclusion of associations which might be considered as "extras."

SOURCE: Don Whiteside, *Historical Development of Aboriginal Political Associations in Canada* (Ottawa: National Indian Brotherhood, 1973), 10.

what Smith (1981) calls "ethnic revival." The genesis of this lies in the emergence of Native intellectuals graduating from White schools.

These individuals were equipped to research and piece together an account of the past several centuries seen from a Native perspective. And they were able to promote the historical legacy they discovered. This was reinforced when the National Indian Brotherhood reorganized itself under the rubric of the Assembly of First Nations. In addition, in their efforts to achieve their goals, Native organizations are beginning to use new tactics, such as confrontation, protest, demonstrations and lobbying. As Tanner (1983) points out, Natives are also being taken seriously because they are 1) viewed as a threat to the national security and 2) now able to hire lawyers who have an expertise in Canadian law as it pertains to Native and Aboriginal rights. Finally, the new tactics being employed have generated a great deal of publicity—Native issues now receive media attention and have entered everyday discourse. The result has been some additional pressure brought to bear on government officials to make some concessions.

The Canadian government, rather than responding with negative sanctions against Native organizations, chose to pay attention to and reward the more moderate organizations. The result of supporting the more ideologically moderate organizations was to bring the radical Native groups in line.

THREE TYPES OF NATIVE ORGANIZATIONS

There are three broad categories of Native organizations—band, local and pan-Native. These three categories have been used to classify Native constituencies. For example, band organizations, which deal with the federal government, are based on historical precedents and have their authority vested in the *Indian Act.* Relations between Natives and government at this level are formal and regulated by the terms and conditions outlined in federal statutes. Local and pan-Native organizations, in contrast, have no statutory basis for their dealings with the government. Nevertheless, these two types of organization have had extensive dealings with both government and nongovernment agencies over the years.

In a broad sense, the goals of these various Native organizations are similar. However, the individual groups pursue goals widely ranging from specific services to treaty rights to achieving changes in federal Indian policy. In the 1960s, two events occurred simultaneously which had a tremendous effect on Native organizations. First, new programs were introduced into the reserves, which also brought substantial funds to an otherwise poor constituency. Secondly, the urbanization of Indians meant that for the first time a large number of Natives would not be effectively served by a band organization. This meant that urban Natives had to develop their own organizations. However, neither the band nor the local organizations were able to achieve all their goals acting independently of one another, and this situation led to the emergence of pan-Native organizations.

The original Native urban organizations focused on economic and social welfare goals. The central goal of these organizations was to change Native-White relations to accommodate urban Native communities and their interests (Cornell, 1988). The increase in the number of Natives entering the urban areas resulted in a proliferation of organizations, reflecting the varied goals and objectives of each group. After a time of working at cross purposes, some of the organizations began to carry out cooperative efforts. After several successful ventures, new pan-Native organizations began to emerge. More recently, the pan-Native organizations have attempted to reduce federal control and increase their own control over band and tribal affairs.

As noted previously, there are many different types of Native organizations. Cornell (1988) has developed a typology of Native organizations which is based upon goals. The first distinction he makes is between reformative and transformative goals. A "reformative" organization focuses its efforts on changing the role of Natives without changing the structure of Native-White relations. This approach is based on a belief that there must be a redistribution of social power/rewards to allow Native people their share, and that this can take place within the existing system. For example, they feel that more Native people should be hired by Indian Affairs, that more Native people should be in senior management positions, that social services on the reserves need to be expanded. In summary, these organizations accept and endorse the existing structure of Canadian society and feel that only some changes are needed to make the existing system work better.

"Transformative" organizations agree that a redistribution of rewards and power needs to be undertaken, but not within the existing Native-White structure. They feel that a fundamental change is required; for example, phasing out Indian Affairs, allowing Natives to establish their own legal system, reopening treaties. In summary, their goal is to change the existing structures which impinge upon Native people.

The second distinction Cornell makes among Native organizations is in the degree to which each is integrative or segregative. This distinction reflects the degree of acceptance or rejection of dominant institutions. Organizations with an integrative perspective accept the appropriateness of the dominant culture and thus promote the dominant institutions as the way of maximizing Native interests. As a result of their general acceptance of the dominant institutions, they also believe that Native communities should be built on this model.

On the other hand, Native organizations with a segregative ideology argue against accepting the dominant institutional structure as a role model. These organizations promote goals and objectives which are fundamentally anti-assimilationist. This dichotomy is portrayed in Figure 8.3. When the two sets of distinctions are juxtaposed, we find that four basic types of Native organizations operate.

In category 1, we find those Native organizations whose goals both accept the status quo (with some minor changes) and attempt to integrate into the dominant culture. Category 2 organizations attempt to fundamentally change existing Native-White relations so that integration into the larger society can occur. Organizations in category 3, while accepting current Native-White relations, feel that Natives must develop their own institutions and culture. Category 4 represents those organizations which reject current Native-White relations as well as the dominant institutional structure. Conflict is generally precipitated when organizations in this

FIGURE 8.3 Types of Native Organizations

		Native-White Relations	
		Reform	Transform
Orientation to institutions of dominant society	Integrate	1	2
	Segregate	3	4

Source: S. Cornell, *The Return of the Native* (New York: Oxford, 1988), 154.

final category attempt to pursue their goals. Each of the four types of organization has had a substantial impact on Native-White relations since the 1960s.

Reviewing various Native organizations across the country, one is struck by their diversity. This reflects in part, the differential development of Native people. Change is occurring at an uneven pace; for example, urban Native organizations have different philosophies and goals than small organizations operating in isolated, rural reserves. As Table 8.2 shows, most Native organizations play political, social and cultural roles. These organizations often function in cities to ease the loneliness, frustration and alienation that Natives encounter when they leave the reserve. Other organizations provide economic assistance and educational support and develop centres for urban Natives. The four organizational types illustrate the diversity and varying degrees of complexity found among Native organizations.

NATIONAL LOBBYING ORGANIZATIONS

National organizations that represent one ethnic group from diverse geographical areas have taken on many of the attributes that modern non-ethnic organizations have developed. Thus, Natives have adopted modern technologies in their quest for achieving their own goals. Because their members come from varying social backgrounds and geographical regions, national organizations must adopt a hierarchical bureaucratic structure while still trying to retain their informal character and close relations with local personnel. In addition, they must be flexible in adapting to new political conditions. Our first example will focus on the Métis Associations and then on the now defunct National Indian Brotherhood. A third example is the Native Womens' Association of Canada, more fully dealt with in chapter 9.

In 1944, attempts were made to establish the North American Indian Brotherhood. The rather loose structure of this organization collapsed in 1950 due to internal discord. In 1954, the National Indian Council was formed and, in 1961, it became the official organization both for status and for non-status Indians. By 1968, the NIC had split into two organizations: the National Indian Brotherhood for status Indians and the Canadian Métis Society for non-status Natives. In 1970, the Métis Society became the Native Council of Canada. Also in 1970, the National Indian Council, composed of middle-class, urban Indians, formally dissolved; this was due to conflicts among its registered, non-registered, and Métis members.

Métis Associations

The political agenda of the Native Council of Canada was dominated by the non-status Indians, whose major interest was to be reinstated as Indians. On the other hand, Métis people wanted to pursue their goal of asserting Métis rights and developing a Métis identity. They also wanted to settle Métis land claims. These separate goals produced considerable tension between the two groups and led to a great deal of internal conflict and inaction on the part of the Council. When the Métis were defined as an "Aboriginal people" in the 1982 Canadian Constitution, the Métis of Alberta and Manitoba and the Association of Métis and Non-status Indians of Saskatchewan broke away from the Native Council of Canada and established a rival organization—the Métis National Council (Krosenbrink-Gelissen, 1989). A year later the Louis Riel Métis Association of B.C. and the Métis Federation of Ontario joined the new organization; i.e., the Métis National Council. In the spring of 1983, the federal government gave official recognition to this new umbrella group and allowed them to participate in the First Ministers' Conference as representatives of the political interests of the Métis.

Since its inception, the Métis National Council has focused much of its energies on establishing Aboriginal rights and Métis self-government. It has taken the position that Métis have the basic right of self-government, should they decide to embark upon a path of political self-determination. Once the Métis had secured that right, each community would negotiate specific agreements with the federal government—a form of community-based self-government which Indian people are developing.

Today, Métis are attempting to entrench their rights in the Constitution by 1) adding a preamble that would reflect their historical contribution to Canadian society; 2) creating a charter of Native rights to entrench the collective rights of Métis; and 3) introducing an amending formula to guarantee Native participation in future constitutional conferences and amendments (Daniels, 1981:19).

The Métis have created a number of local, provincial and regional political organizations by which they will attempt to influence provincial and federal leaders. Their conflicts with the federal and provincial governments arise from three issues. First, the Métis claim that the distribution of land and scrip, particularly under the *Manitoba Act*, was unjust and inefficient. Second, they claim that the compensation their ancestors received was insufficient to extinguish Métis Aboriginal land titles; indeed, that Western and Northern Métis were never compensated at all. Third, they argue that they are Indians under the terms of the *British North America Act* and therefore are entitled to special consideration from the federal government (Barber, 1977).

These claims take different forms according to particular regional factors. In Manitoba, the Métis Association wants compensation for the loss of 1.4 million acres (566 580 hectares) of land that Louis Riel won on their behalf through negotiations with Ottawa in 1870. They also want outright ownership of other large tracts of land and compensation for land lost to settlers. In Ontario, the Métis and Non-status Indian Association, which claims a membership of 200 000, is trying to obtain a free-trade zone from the government as a means of settling its Aboriginal land claims without costing taxpayers any real money. A free-trade zone is a parcel of land near an international port of entry where goods can be assembled or brought in from other countries without being subject to customs duty while they remain there. Duties apply only when the goods are moved out of the zone into Canadian Customs territory.

Until very recently, the federal government has responded negatively to these claims. Since the Indian Land Commissioner has lately given credence to some Métis claims, however, the government has decided to honour those it deems legitimate. Nonetheless, the federal government remains fully committed to the extinguishing of Métis as an ethnic category. While compensation may be made in the form of money or land, no concessions will be made in the area of political control.

The Métis National Council, along with western provincial Métis associations, is now becoming actively involved in setting social policy affecting Native people. This has required Métis associations to review existing federal and provincial legislation and policy which bear on Native issues.

The long-term goal of the various federal and provincial Métis associations is to develop local community involvement in social, political and economic issues. Members of the local communities, which possess the necessary resources, must begin to take an active part in changing the daily realities of living in debilitating

FIGURE 8.4 MÉTIS LOCALS AND ELECTORAL DISTRICTS

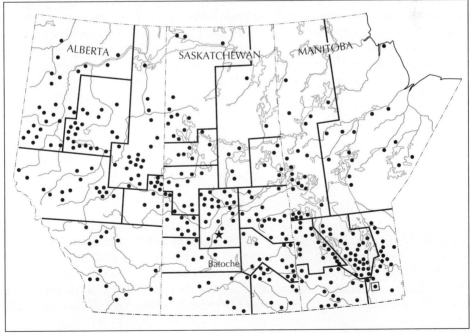

SOURCE: C. Chartier, *In The Best Interest of the Métis Child,* University of Saskatchewan, Native Law Centre, 1988, 106.

socio-economic conditions (Chartier, 1988). However, at the local level, Métis are frequently isolated and feel helpless to address socio-economic issues; therefore, voluntary associations are necessary to bring about interest and action.

Since each of the Prairie Métis organizations is based upon a system of locals (community-based organizations), there is an expectation that each local will create a council which will become the basic administrative unit (see Figure 8.4). These units would link with the provincial Association, but remain accountable to the local community. This bottom-up approach would easily fit into the existing structure and allow for community involvement.

National Indian Brotherhood

The National Indian Brotherhood was originally formed to speak for registered Indians on a number of issues and to help them retain their Native values. However, in 1969, a year after it was formed, the federal government's White Paper forced the NIB into a position of political leadership that it maintained throughout the next decade (Ponting and Gibbins, 1980). During that decade, the NIB became a national organization with its headquarters in Ottawa and about 50 full-time, paid, staff members. It became a relatively influential lobbying agency during this time, and it began to act on behalf of grassroots Native organizations across Canada.

In 1980, the NIB began to turn away from its unsought leadership position and return some of its decision-making powers to regional organizations and local bands. During the early 1980s, the NIB assisted local bands and provincial associations when help was requested. It also took on the new role of lobbying the federal and provincial governments on behalf of local and regional Indian organizations throughout Canada.

In 1981 and 1982, the NIB directed its efforts toward entrenching Native rights in the new Canadian Constitution. In this case, the NIB widened its scope to lobby on an international level. Although the NIB's efforts were not totally successful, the new Constitution does at least address the issue of Aboriginal rights. Due to the expense of these international lobbying efforts, however, the NIB was forced to reduce its staff by nearly 40 percent and to cut back expenditures on other issues. The NIB's position on the Constitution has also created some internal ideological divisions among Indians across Canada.

By 1982, the NIB ceased to exist. The Assembly of First Nations, which met in early 1981, discussed changing the NIB from an association of organizations to emphasize the fact the NIB officials had not been elected on a grassroots basis and did not speak for all Indians. Later in 1982, the Assembly of First Nations emerged as the primary national Indian organization. It represents about 15 affiliated Indian associations and has recently concentrated its efforts on constitutional issues and self-government.

More recently a group of Western Indians have broken away from the Assembly of First Nations because of differences in philosophy and priorities. The Prairie Treaty Nations Alliance represents Indians from Treaties Nos. 1, 4, 5, 6, 7, 8 and 10, covering Alberta, Saskatchewan, southern Manitoba and northeastern British Columbia. Despite more than two years of lobbying and legal action by the Prairie Treaty National Alliance, it has not been able to achieve national recognition or federal legitimacy. Its members are still denied seats at First Ministers' conferences.

Early Indian organizations were generally tied to specific concerns, such as particular land claims or similar issues. These organizations had a single focus, were relatively simple in structure and were limited to particular areas or groups of Indians. Only since the mid-1950s have Indian organizations become multi-faceted, complex in structure, and representative of Indians from across Canada. The National Indian Brotherhood was incorporated as a corporation without share capital (i.e., a non-profit corporation) under Part II of the *Canada Corporations Act* by Letters Patent dated September 29, 1970. The objectives of the Brotherhood, as stated in the application for incorporation and made part of the Letters Patent, were as follows:

(a) to assist Indian people, and to work towards a solution of problems facing Indian people;

(b) to operate as a national body to represent the Indian people and to disseminate information to the Indian people;

(c) to study, in conjunction with Indian representatives from the various parts of Canada, the problems confronting the Indians and to make representation to the government and other organizations on behalf of the Indians;

(d) to assist in retaining the Indian culture and values;

(e) to act as national spokesman for the Indians throughout Canada.

Membership in the National Indian Brotherhood comprised two classes; provincial and national. Provincial membership was open to "every Indian, eighteen years of age of over," who has not been enfranchised and who was resident in a province of Canada, or one of its territories. The term "Indian" was defined as "a person registered as an Indian or entitled to be registered as an Indian."

The national members of the NIB were those Indians elected or appointed as such by the provincial and territorial organizations that make up the National Indian Brotherhood, according to the following formula:

1. Each Provincial Territorial Organization (PTO) was entitled to select two national members for the first 10 000 Indians or portion thereof residing in the province or territory represented by the same PTO, and one national member for every 5000 Indians or portion thereafter. No PTO had less than two national members.

2. The president of each PTO had to be one of the national members selected by each PTO. Where a PTO did not have a president, some member of the executive body of that PTO was selected as one of the national members.

The National Indian Brotherhood continued to represent the Indians of Canada on a wide range of issues without direct accountability to the Chiefs of the First Nations. However, the National Indian Brotherhood, throughout its existence, was continually undergoing a transition and was becoming more representative of Indian people. The Chiefs of the First Nations became more directly involved in 1980 when an Interim Council of Chiefs was established to develop a new structure for the national organization. In the course of restructuring the NIB, the Interim Council of Chiefs agreed to several principles:

1. Any proposed structure should not involve incorporation under the laws of Canada or any province;
2. The National Indian Brotherhood should be restructured, within its present incorporated form, to function as the administrative arm and secretariat of the new, unincorporated First Nations structure;
3. The Indian Chiefs should maintain effective control over the operations and policies of the National Indian Brotherhood;
4. The corporate identity of the National Indian Brotherhood should be retained in order to make use of such a legally constituted body for the purpose of obtaining funds, entering into contracts and, generally, whenever a corporate entity is required.

From this point, it was to be the Chiefs elected by the Indian people who would establish priorities, policies and political direction for the organization. In brief, the National Indian Brotherhood was becoming an organization more representative of Indian people through their elected Chiefs, as opposed to an organization of organizations.

Assembly of First Nations

In 1982, at the 3rd Annual Assembly of First Nations held in Penticton, B.C., a new structure for an Assembly of First Nations was formally adopted by the Chiefs. This new organization was deliberately established outside the corporate structure defined by Canadian law. However, the original charter for the National Indian Brotherhood was maintained primarily as a legal vehicle for liability and funding purposes. As well, the NIB and its staff were to become the secretariat for the Assembly of First Nations. This change was the culmination of two years' work by the Interim Council of Chiefs.

In adopting an organizational structure (see Figure 8.5) for the Assembly of First Nations, the Chiefs were subject to a number of proposed amendments and additions. For example, provisions for an amendment clause, mechanisms for accountability and a process for impeachment were to be included. These changes were to be developed by a subcommittee for presentation to the next Assembly of First Nations for review and acceptance of the Chiefs.

In 1982, a subcommittee called the Confederacy of Nations did meet to review a number of draft amendments which were prepared under their direction by staff of the AFN Secretariat. During their meeting, the Confederacy of Nations adopted a number of items to be included and/or to replace or amend important elements of the Assembly of First Nations' organizational structure.

The Confederacy of Nations is mandated to formulate policy and oversee the direction of the executive and secretariat between sessions of the Assembly. There is no direct comparison between the Assembly of First Nations and any body within government or, likely, within traditional First Nations structures. The intention of the Assembly of First Nations is to represent the needs and wishes of the several Indian nations. Each of these nations has territory and boundaries which reflect both its historical and contemporary geographical realities. Portfolios or standing councils, headed by a chairperson, are intended to develop policy to be recommended to the Confederacy and then to the Assembly and to oversee the implementation of policy laid down by the Assembly.

The Council of Elders develops the rules and procedures of the Assembly for ratification by the entire Assembly. The Council of Elders is a resource for the Assembly of First Nations and its constituents. The members of the Council of Elders are viewed as the custodians of the Assembly's rules and procedures, as they are for other traditional and customary laws. They have the authority to single out and admonish in public those whose behaviour is not in line with these customs and traditions. They educate those in the Assembly who are unfamiliar with their traditions and customs. They have responsibility for the development, implementation and maintenance of a redress system which provides mechanisms for impeachment, discipline and loss of membership. The Council of Elders also investigates and arbitrates any disputes within the Assembly. Finally, the Council of Elders selects and presents the Speaker of the Assembly to the Chiefs. They guide the Speaker in the exercise of his/her duties and in seeking consensus of the Assembly.

At the present time, the on-going political work of the Assembly is carried out by the Office of the National Chief. He is elected by the Chiefs in Assembly, and, for all intents and purposes, he represents the only body or person within the Assembly who can truly be held accountable by the Chiefs. Between Assemblies, the Confederacy tries to function as an Executive Committee and gives its own political mandates and direction to the Office of the National Chief.

Some Vice Chiefs in the past have carried portfolios. At present, all Vice Chiefs provide a means of communication between the National Chief and their regions. But in almost all cases, this function is secondary to their provincially or regionally held position, such as president of a Provincial Indian Association. And those whose vice-chief region is larger than the province or territory where they hold another office frequently find that the task of reporting requires travel outside their primary territory, and this travel is in addition to their frequent trips to Ottawa and to the Confederacy meetings. The result is that many Indian leaders spend considerable time away from their constituencies. This frequent travel also produces "burnout" among leaders and thus turnover in these positions is frequent.

The National Office has historically avoided running programs or providing services. At the same time, there is a desire to have the National Office valued and respected within the First Nations communities. Therefore, a role must be identified for the National Office, one which goes beyond support for the National Executive on major political issues (which have already been fairly well defined).

Since its creation, AFN has established several committees, commissions and portfolios to address the concerns and direction of the First Nations. The current global organizational structure of AFN is presented in Figure 8.5, and the Manpower Chart of the National Office and current list of salaried employees are described in the notes to that Figure.

The Assembly of First Nations is an organization established by Chiefs to respect the sovereignty of First Nations. It can be described as an organization involved in a process of transition from the statutory origins of the National Indian Brotherhood toward a national political institution that derives its existence and direction exclusively and entirely from the First Nations. In some respects, it remains an organization that has not completely divorced itself from its statutory foundations (*Final Report to Assembly of First Nations*, February 18 1985, mimeo).

The AFN takes the position that First Nations have the right to self-government, and that this right exists as an inherent Aboriginal right that has never been surrendered, relinquished or diminished by any formal treaty or agreement or by the Constitution, legislation or policies of non-Indian governments in Canada. One fundamental element of this right to self-government is the sovereignty of First Nations to freely determine their political, socio-economic and cultural institutions, including the capacity to act in collectivities in the formation of regional or national institutions as forms of derivative governments. This power, although it exists, has yet to be exercised by the First Nations. Consequently, no contemporary national institutions exist as a derivative government of First Nations.

The AFN argues that any national institution established to represent or advance the interests of First Nations must reflect the sovereign jurisdiction of First Nations as the source of all that it does on behalf of the citizens of First Nations and, for that matter, on behalf of the governments of First Nations. Therefore, all powers, mandates or responsibilities exercised on behalf of a First Nation are merely delegated, and the passage of time does not alter the nature and quality of the delegated power, mandate or responsibility.

Delegation, according to the AFN, does not result in the transfer of sovereignty, nor does it diminish the jurisdiction of the First Nations. Furthermore, it can never

FIGURE 8.5   CURRENT AFN ORGANIZATIONAL STRUCTURE

Assembly of First Nations &
Aboriginal People

Council of
Elders

Confederacy of Nations

Executive Committee   Political Advisory
(National Chief & Vice Chiefs)   Council[1]

Priorities & Planning Committee[2]

Commission[3]   Commission[3]

Chairperson   Chairperson

Commissioners   Commissioners

Secretariat[4]

1. Political Advisory Council—This Council includes the Chairperson of each
    Commission or Committee. They have been appointed by the National Chief.
2. Priorities & Planning Committee—Set up by resolution of the Confederacy
3. Commissions (15)
    *   Chiefs' Committee on Education
    *   Health and Social Well-Being Political Policy Committee
    *   Social, Cultural and Spiritual Development (includes Youth Council)
    *   Economic Development
    *   First Nations Relations and Communications (includes Housing)
    *   Constitutional Working Group (Task Force)
    *   Treaty Unit
    *   Parliamentary and Partisan Relations, Canadian Public Relations and Media
    *   International
    *   Indian Government Commission
    *   Forestry Committee
    *   Finance Committee
    *   Commission on Structure
    *   Federal Government Relations and DIAND

    There are few differences between a Commission or a Committee. Membership to both
    is informal. Selection of individuals is done on the basis of consultation with the National
    Chief and the Chairperson, Regional input and the person's willingness to be involved in
    a Commission or a Committee. Not all Commission/Committees are set up by resolution;
    e.g., the Forestry Committee, which came about as a reaction to government.
4. Secretariat—The National Chief is the administrative head of the Secretariat and is re-
    sponsible for its day-to-day operation. All secretariat staff are responsible and account-
    able to the National Chief.

result in the creation of an institution or body with inherent sovereignty that has a natural, independent right to act in all matters which concern the First Nations. As well, the AFN claims that all delegated power, mandate or responsibility is a trust. Those individuals or institutions delegated with this trust have a sacred duty to implement or perform in strict compliance with the nature and quality of the delegation. Any variation to the delegated power, mandate or responsibility that may arise as a result of the misinterpretation (deliberate or innocent) of the delegation, or that may derive from unilaterally or arbitrarily adding to, altering or abridging the original delegation is an affront to the First Nations and the usurpation of their sovereignty.

For the AFN, one of the inherent powers of First Nations is the capacity to create temporary or long-term institutions which will be expedient and necessary to accomplish the aspirations and destiny of First Nations. First Nations can:

a) delegate responsibilities and duties and exact the fulfilment and performance of same;

b) delegate power, authority or mandate and exact the fulfilment and performance of same;

c) review, reconsider, alter, remove, transfer, amend or rescind at any time at their absolute discretion, any and all delegated responsibilities, powers, duties, authorities or mandates (*Assembly of First Nations' Report on Structure and Accountability*, nd, mimeo: 33).

It is clear that AFN personnel realize that politics and political relations are not rational processes where reason, truth and justice always prevail. Indian politics and Indian political relations are no exception. However, despite the human frailties of all societies, First Nations, when participating in diplomatic relations with other First Nations in forums such as the Assembly of First Nations, can adopt basic assumptions or ideals to guide their relationship.

First, by virtue of the common heritage, historical experience and contemporary circumstances, the AFN feels that First Nations governments can find sufficient shared interests and aspirations to develop a common struggle based upon mutual trust, confidence and tolerance. Second, there is also a desire to respect the sovereignty of each First Nation. Thus, the fundamental goal of First Nations politics is to facilitate the realization of the freedom and self-determination of each First Nation.

Third, another ideal is for First Nations to recognize their respective, sovereign equality. Thus, a fundamental goal of First Nations' collective politics is to establish a relationship based on diversity rather than on uniformity. Fourth, the relationship between First Nations embraces the ideal of justice. In one sense this would demand that First Nations establish collective, political relations that will not allow a single First Nation to either suffer or benefit as a direct result of privilege, favouritism, preferential treatment or the abuse of power.

In conclusion, the Assembly of First Nations is an organization composed of members from varying backgrounds, cultures, histories and philosophies. Out of respect for diversity and for maintaining solidarity, the Assembly of First Nations is trying to develop some basic principles of organization that are acceptable to all the First Nations.

RED POWER (RADICAL) ORGANIZATIONS

Broadly speaking, Red Power addresses the problem of Natives' inability either to separate from or to integrate with the rest of Canada (Franklin, 1969). While Red Power has so far failed to present a clearcut program, its most important focus seems to be on the control of reserve lands.

Red Power advocates are attempting to unite a number of other moderate and militant groups into a network across Canada. Although there are many important differences, some of their major ideological themes have been derived from the Black Power movements in the United States. In general, Red Power promotes self-supporting, self-directing, and commonly owned Native communities. Red Power members wish to create, develop and carry out their own political, economic and social programs. They also want to improve the Native's image on a personal level by changing both the negative stereotypes of Natives and their own negative thought patterns.

White society often criticizes Natives for being apathetic and unwilling to better their position. Unfortunately, however, one of the most potent forces of colonialism is the way it breaks the spirit and quells the resistance of the colonized minority. Continuing oppression through poverty, poor health conditions, lack of education and job opportunities, stereotyping, and so on, has become ingrained in the very fabric of Native life, and will take more than a few years and a few social programs to overcome. Ironically, when Natives do shake off their apathy and, through Red Power groups, try realistically to better their position, they are again criticized, this time on the grounds of stridency and militancy. Confronted with this Catch-22, Red Power advocates have sensibly decided to progress with their own plans and ignore White reactions.

Those pan-American Indians (Indians who identify with South, Central and North American Natives) who belong to the League of Nations are generally considered the most radical of the Red Power groups. The League is a very loose intertribal organization from which splinter groups, such as the National Alliance for Red Power (NARP), have emerged. More and more militant youths are joining the League or one of its splinter groups.

League members rally around the central issue of treaty and Aboriginal rights. They argue that Native tribes must be viewed as nations, and they want any litigation between Natives and the Canadian government to be referred to the United

Nations. The militance of these groups, exemplified by both peaceful and violent demonstrations since 1970, is continuing to grow.

Waubageshig, a League leader, discussing the possibility of violence in Canada, has stated:

> Violence in our communities, both on and off the reservation, is occurring at this very moment....If this does not stop...then there is going to be a very angry young Indian population which will say, "What the hell! I have nothing to lose." And we may have political violence. If no one listens to what these young people are saying and nothing is done, then violence will erupt (1970:167).

Modern Natives are beginning to view militants like Waubageshig in a far more positive light than they did ten years ago. Recently, the League's activities have included approaching the United Nations to protest the Canadian government's treatment of Indians. Since 1970, the notion of Red Power has been used increasingly by League activists. As Lurie reports:

> In many Canadian reserve towns the White population is relatively small but dominates business and commercial interests. All across Canada there have been hostile, even violent "incidents"—so far without fatalities—and many more are threatened (1971:466).

During the mid-1970s, the American Indian Movements (AIM) gained some support in areas of Canada. AIM views itself as a grassroots organization in touch with the daily needs of Native people. Its general strategy is based on confrontational politics, coercive threats and, occasionally, violence. Its fluid membership and loose structure make it difficult to assess the number of its members. It is also difficult to determine the impact of this group on younger Natives.

AIM and other militant Red Power groups use techniques that are difficult for bureaucrats to deal with. Many Natives feel that recent changes made by DIAND are a direct result of Red Power activities. But Red Power is only in its seminal stages and has so far gained support only from a minority of Natives. Like their White counterparts, most Natives are apathetic in their commitment to social change. Even among the activists, there are many traditionalists who spurn the efforts of Red Power advocates.

As Boldt (1980) and Mackie (1974) have pointed out, many Native leaders are beginning to reject White society entirely and are starting to develop the concept of a Native society—a national, and possibly international, Native community. Boldt states that:

> The pan-Indian concept and the emergent political and cultural movement with which it is associated is serving to identify new boundaries and to create new overarching Indian loyalties at the national level. It is a movement to enhance a sense of commonality and group consciousness which goes beyond mere political organizations to include recognition of a shared history of oppression, cultural attitudes, common interests, and hopes for the future (1980:4).

Boldt (1973) interviewed 69 Indian leaders across Canada to assess the extent of their adherence to militant Red Power ideology. Based on their responses, Boldt was able to identify four basic types of leaders: nationalists, autonomists, adapted departmentalists, and integrationists. Although specific figures were not presented, nearly half the Natives interviewed seemed to hold either a nationalist or an autonomist position.

Nationalists are committed to complete political independence. They want to create a geographically defined nation-state that would provide residence exclusively for a large number of Natives. *Autonomists* also want to establish a national Native federation, but within the existing political structure of Canada. They are interested primarily in controlling the processes that regulate their lives, such as education, police activity and community development. *Departmentalists* want to retain the political and administrative structures that presently relate to Natives, but with some adjustments to allow for Native input into government decision-making. Finally, *Integrationists* want to abolish all political structures, such as DIAND, that grant separate status to Natives. They want to eliminate the category of "Indian" and to assimilate all Natives into White society.

The nationalists see integration as irrelevant. Nationalists are trying to build economic and political institutions that Natives can plan, own and control. On the other hand, the autonomists seek integration of Indians into the system, though they want to remain a distinct ethnic group in the socio-political framework of the country. In addition, they agree with the more traditional Native organizations that social change should be achieved through legitimate means. To date, however, most of the nationalist and autonomist organizations have chosen to act on local community issues rather than on national issues, which suggests that their impact on the total system has been minimal.

No more than three to five percent of today's Natives can be considered Red Power advocates. But this does not mean that militant organizations are not important. As research has shown, only a small percentage of a given population ever takes part in riots, revolutions and urban guerrilla warfare. This small group, however, does need moral, economic and physical support from the wider community, support that Natives increasingly seem willing to give to Red Power activists. It is not surprising that the RCMP has defined discontent among Natives as one of the most serious threats to Canadian unity.

Red Power supporters have shaken off the White liberal humanism that views violence as the worst possible sin. They argue that violence is inevitable in the struggle to combat racism and achieve control over their lives. Although few Whites can agree, more and more Natives are beginning to do so. The recent activities of the Warrior Society at Oka and the supporting individuals who went to Oka or carried out militant activities elsewhere suggest that while these organizations do not have a large membership, the potential number of recruits is high.

LOCAL ORGANIZATIONS

The most common type of Native organization that has emerged over the past two decades has been the locally organized and focused group. These organizations have proliferated in the urban areas, where, over the past quarter century, many Natives have migrated. These organizations have been created by both status and non-status Indians, by newcomers and long-time residents.

Prior to 1970, Native organizations were defined as political entities and therefore were ineligible for funding from such government departments as the Secretary of State. When these organizations were redefined as nonpolitical, they began to receive services and support from various government departments and agencies. Administrative funding for Native organizations is currently managed by the Secretary of State. As a result of this funding, most urban areas in Canada with a sizable Native population have Indian friendship centres. At present there are over 70 centres across Canada, largely because of a $26 million one-time grant by the federal government.

Friendship centres are designed to act both as drop-in centres and as counselling centres. Ideally, Natives who come to the city can use the facilities to help them adapt to urban life. However, a number of problems have plagued the centres since their formation. The federal government funds the centres only on a short-term, year-to-year basis; this prevents long-term planning and development. In addition, the amount of funding is not enough to allow the centres to play their role effectively and ease the process of urban adaptation.

A third problem is a lack of cohesion among the Native administrators and clientele of the centres. There are frequent rifts between political factions concerning goals and strategies; in addition, there are time-honoured differences between status and non-status Natives and among the different linguistic and cultural groups. As a result, each centre is often dominated by one group to the exclusion of others.

Summary

This short review of three types of Native organizations, i.e., national, Red Power and local, has demonstrated several points. All these organizations have become important vehicles for meeting the needs of Native peoples. They have all provided forums for the understanding and discussion of Native issues. Each of these organizations has also had to adapt its structure and objectives to existing conditions or face quickly losing its membership.

Clearly, the use of formal organizations among Natives is likely to increase. They have discovered that formal organizations carry a sense of legitimacy that can be very effective in persuading governments to act in Natives' interest. These organizations have also begun to produce an improvement in Native conditions. They also provide opportunities to develop leadership techniques and other political skills for those who choose to move Native issues into the political arena.

REVITALIZATION MOVEMENTS

Canada is in the midst of an Indian renaissance. New legal decisions, changes in federal policy, and a new generation of educated Indian leaders together have brought about more change in the past decade than in the previous century. Natives are tired of being a people of promise: the promises the treaties made, the promise of new opportunities and, today, the promise of self-government.

Natives today are rediscovering their past and are attempting to sort out their identity. They are trying to develop a positive self-concept, and a group identity that can provide a reference point for them. They, like other minority groups, have developed myths that compensate for their subordinate status in Canadian society. These myths assert Native moral superiority over other Canadians, for example, they show Natives in harmony with Nature, working to conserve the environment. These moral myths give Natives, oppressed for more than a century, a sense of positive self-esteem. In addition, the oppression experienced by Natives and their inability to fight back have produced a perpetual hostility in many of them. Moral superiority can also be one means of expressing their hostility (Fullinwider, 1969).

Today, Natives are developing their sense of history and group identification. Ironically, it has been the White-educated Native intelligentsia that has been instrumental in discovering, packaging and promoting this sense of history and unification. Through a variety of techniques, they are trying to demonstrate their equality with other Canadians on three fronts: 1) through religious statements, 2) through using historical documents, and 3) by the arguments that their culture is a product of the dominant culture's definition.

Because of the segregation and discrimination Natives are continually exposed to, as well as their low position in the social and economic hierarchy of society, they are more or less suspended in a "marginal-man" position. As a result, within the Native communities, a debate is taking place with regard to whether or not Natives should try to adapt to Canadian society. One sector of the community argues that the old traditional culture cannot provide the Native with the skills needed to survive in an urban, industrial culture. Proponents of this view argue that Native culture has been assaulted by the White culture for so long and with such intensity that it cannot be salvaged. While the traditional cultural system may have been adaptive years ago, under today's conditions it no longer addresses Natives' needs. It is useless, they argue, to continue to maintain a dying culture. Hence, their position is that Natives should take on the White industrial-urban culture and allow the traditional culture to fade into the past.

Other leaders argue that the "White man's" culture is not a moral one, nor does it have any relevance to their impoverished position in Canadian society. They feel that it cannot teach Natives how to cope with the kinds of situations which occur in their marginal position. This segment of the Native community argues that they must continue to develop their own culture and reject the White culture or any attempts to integrate.

The rejection of being dominated has been expressed by Natives in many different ways. Cornell (1988) identifies what he calls "lived" resistance movements, movements in which Native communities tenaciously adhere to traditional Native values. These resistance movements are important in opposing social control efforts by the dominant group because they are not based on material interests but rather on a conceptualization of self and community. As a result, they challenge the values of the dominant society and of all of the assumptions held by those adhering to the dominant culture.

These "passive" forms of resistance have given way, in more recent years, to more public forms of Indian activism. The activist movement has resurged and increasing extrainstitutional actions have been carried out—mass protests, civil disobedience, land seizures, occupying buildings and taking up arms. Such forms of activism ensure that the issue under consideration is given a public forum. However, equally important is the symbolism of such an action. Active engagement in overt conflict signifies a fundamental rejection of the formalized, institutional procedures provided for dealing with their grievance (Katznelson, 1976).

A third segment of the community takes a different approach. They point out that oppression over the past century has produced a unique culture—one under siege. As a result, Native people experience numerous personality conflicts, have a reduced self-esteem, and seek relief in the overuse of defense mechanisms. They argue that Natives must be able to resolve their inner conflicts and conquer the inner self. Freedom from within is the first step that Native people must take if they are to resolve their conflicts and remove the self-hatred that characterizes Native behaviour today. The next step is to gain self-knowledge by coming to grips with reality through education.

However, it is a unique type of education that is advocated. To take on a White education would be to ignore the fact that it prepares Natives for a world that is denied to them, that it bears, in other words, little relation to the Native individual's future experiences. Such an education would be neither functional nor adaptive for most Native people. On the other hand, only to engage in traditional education would also be maladaptive in an urban-industrial society. Leaders speaking from this third position argue that Natives' education has to be in the context of the marginal man. Native education must thus be provided at two levels. As Fullinwider points out:

> ...[Each Native] must be educated to function as marginal man...educated in the one he is in, and the broader, dominant culture towards which he, as a member of the race, is headed but, more than that, he should be educated to value the experiences he has in the marginal world and to value himself because of his experiences (1969: 113).

There are many other Native organizations that focus on specific political and economic goals. On a more general level, however, there are two influential social movements that are attempting to promote a wide-ranging return to Native social and cultural values. These revitalization movements have many implications for Native organizations.

The first of these is the pow-wow movement. The pow-wow is a planned inter-tribal affair usually held on neutral ground. There are dancing and social interaction, ritual healings, and serious discussions on the future of Native life. The young are encouraged to learn Native customs from their elders. It is hoped that, eventually, these pow-wows will build community solidarity among Natives everywhere.

As Corrigan (1970) points out, the pow-wow circuit acts as a communications network to promote the social and cultural integration of many Native groups. Other analysts, such as Howard (1951) and Lurie (1971) have also viewed the pow-wow as the current vehicle for achieving pan-Indianism. In an in-depth analysis, Dyck (1979) found that pow-wows constitute an autonomous achievement that summons a large community to celebrate the value and the excellence of Indianness in a manner which is both individually rewarding and collectively uncontroversial (92-93). Furthermore, because pow-wows range over a large geographical area and provide continuity with the past, they can create a larger community out of various separate reserve communities.

The second form of revitalization movement is the resurgence of prophet religions or religious pan-Indianism. Most Native religious movements have resisted assimilation efforts by the larger society. They have developed in the rural areas, and urge their followers to take up a style of life that is in harmony with nature. Humanity is viewed simply as one element of nature, always to be respected. A typical prophet religion is that led by Chief Robert Smallboy of Alberta. In 1968, Smallboy and 150 followers left their reserve for the mountains west of Red Deer, Alberta, to re-establish their former culture. Life in Smallboy's camp is a mixture of traditional and modern technology. Children are taught in a regular school but also learn woodlore, hunting and fishing.

In 1972, the federal government revoked Smallboy's permit to remain on federal forest-reserve land. A year later, almost half of Smallboy's initial followers left and returned to their reserve. However, the movement continually attracts newcomers. Smallboy is presently negotiating with the federal government to remain in a 100-acre tract near Jasper Park. Several European environmentalist groups, such as Survival International, are also trying to have Smallboy's case presented to the international Russell Tribunal, which investigates abuses of Native peoples.

Cultural revitalization movements generally arise when colonized people begin to reject their subjugation. Smallboy's camp may be viewed as an activist movement, although it is too early to analyze its full impact. However, particularly in the West, several other camps have been established by leaders who are beginning to attract small followings of their own.

FUNDING OF NATIVE ORGANIZATIONS

How have Native organizations and social movements improved the quality of Native life? Previously, the Native response to White society has been to incorporate various aspects of White culture (Lurie, 1971). With the growth of various organizations and nationalist ideological movements, however, Natives are becoming more politically, socially and economically aware. Formal organizations have allowed Natives to carry on discussions with the federal government on a legitimized basis. In the past, the government could reject Native claims and recommendations on the grounds that they were speaking as individuals and thus any advice or recommendations that were conflicting or inconsistent could be ignored because they did not represent the demands of Native people as a whole. The creation of rational bureaucratic organizations reflects a collectively determined policy and allows for the presentation of cogent and coherent arguments on a variety of issues.

Although the federal government relaxed its opposition to Native political development after World War II, Native organizations did not really take root until the mid-1960s. Only at that time were Natives able to obtain the funds needed to create formal organizational structures on a regional or national basis. As Whiteside (1980) has shown, money only really became available to Natives around 1966. In 1963, the Centennial Commission provided about $150 000 to Native people to support small projects of their own design. By 1968, the war against poverty was underway, and the Department of Forestry and Rural Development was sending community development workers into reserve areas. As an example, the Federation of Saskatchewan Indians received more than $50 000 to help Natives in a variety of ways, including by the development of organizations through which they could articulate their needs in a systematic fashion.

The Secretary of State also began to fund Native projects. In 1964, it began to provide a small annual grant to the National Indian Council for holding meetings. By 1970, this had escalated so that the Secretary of State was providing nearly $50 000 to Natives for conferences and sustaining grants. When all sources of funding were combined, Natives in 1970 received nearly $1 million for organizational activities.

DIAND originally reacted negatively to the funding of Natives by other government organizations. It considered these other bodies to be in direct violation of the principle, maintained since Confederation, that only DIAND could deal with Native issues. DIAND also began to feel pressure as its decisions and authority came under challenge. Moreover, it felt that the funds Natives were receiving from other government departments and agencies could undermine DIAND's policies. The federal government had, and continues to maintain, a legal distinction of "status Indian" in order to identify a population it is responsible for and to allow the provincial governments to administer to the "nonstatus Native." In an attempt to reassert its sole control, DIAND began to provide each provincial Indian association with a per capita grant of $1 per registered Indian. It also provide $.25 per registered Indian to the newly formed National Indian Brotherhood.

After the federal government released its White Paper in 1969, the Privy Council also approved a grant of $500 000 over five years to Native associations for systematic research on various claims and grievances.

By the 1970s, other federal departments and agencies, such as the Central Mortgage and Housing Corporation and the Department of National Health and Welfare, were also providing monies to Natives. As Whiteside points out:

> The response of the Department of Indian Affairs to this continued "outside" funding was consistent. They fought back and argued that they alone had the responsibility for Indians and it was both irresponsible and unfair for other departments to interfere with this responsibility. The Department argued further, and rightly so, that the monies were being used by the political associations to force the Department to abandon its existing programs in favour of the ones which the associations demanded....Some programs in favour from other departments were transferred to Indian Affairs, where they were allowed to either die or become relatively useless (1980: 11-12).

The impact of Native political organizations has been substantial, both on Natives and on government. For Natives, organizations have granted them input into the federal and provincial policies that affect them, thus providing Natives with instruments needed to bring about social change. But government has also found that dealing with an organization has many benefits. Because the bureaucracies within Native organizations are similar to those in government, both can now interact in an orderly, legitimate fashion. In addition, the government funding of most Native political organizations makes them more vulnerable to government control.

As a consequence, Aboriginal leaders find themselves in the position of having to play by the government's rules in order to achieve their own goals—goals which may be at variance with those of the government. On the other hand, the government's power over Native organizations should not be overestimated. Governments also face a dilemma: without sufficient funds, Native organizations will not be able to negotiate; with too many funds, Native organizations will become too powerful (Krosenbrink-Gelissen, 1991). Weaver (1985) also notes that little evidence exists which demonstrates that the unequal power balance has compromised the positions held by national Aboriginal organizations on political issues.

INDIANS AS AN INTEREST GROUP

The overall aim of Native organizations is to gain sizable input into the government decisions that affect them. In general, Native interest groups have found that appeals to MPs and MLAs are ineffective, except as a last resort. Rather, they have learned to focus on the bureaucratic organizations that affect them most directly, whether at the federal, provincial or municipal level. Interest groups can also influence government in other ways, such as through annual submissions to the federal cabinet on aspects of federal policy. Local and provincial interest groups may deal directly with the government at any level or may channel their appeal through whatever nationwide organizations they possess (Tanner, 1983).

The impact of a Native organization varies in direct proportion to its resources. By resources we mean group assets such as group solidarity, strong organizations, money, that can be directed toward social action which enhances the capacity of the group to achieve its goals. During the first half of the twentieth century, Native resources have been extremely limited. However, since the 1960s there has been a marked increase in Native resources. The nature and extent of resources utilized by Natives have varied over time. Depending on the action taken by Natives, those resources utilized are built up and remain part of the total resources available to them in future. The relative importance of different types of resources may vary from time to time, from situation to situation. For example, economic resources are important, but they may be subordinate to political or legal resources under certain conditions. Furthermore, some resources (primarily economic) are portable, or transferable, while other have limited application (e.g., legal).

Cornell (1988) argues that a useful classification of resources is by function. He identifies two types of resources: direct and mobilizational. Direct resources are those whose influence is directly upon the socio-political structure. Mobilization resources are those used in the process of bringing direct resources to bear on the issues under consideration.

One of the most common direct resources which organizations can use is the number of members and/or supporters. However, because Natives have become both dispersed and factionalized, they have been unable to convert this resource into a force. Commodities that are held by an organization may also be a direct resource. However, the commodity must be one desired by others. In the case of Natives, such commodities are usually in the form of land, services or some other special right. Land and natural resources commanded by various Native organizations have been and continue to be valued bargaining resources. Historically, military assets or, in the case of the fur trade, renewable resources were desired. Nevertheless, over time many of these bargaining resources were lost, and thus Native power has decreased. A third type of direct resource is the extent to which an organization has allied itself with other organizations, particularly those with power. Native organizations' success in the past has been the result of linkages with other non-Native organizations; e.g., religious organizations, human rights groups, conservation groups. Some of these organizations have the aid of Native people as a primary purpose; others have related political agendas and find the alliance with Natives useful for obtaining their own goals and objectives.

As noted above, direct resources may not be useful if they are not mobilized. Having alliances, money and land are of little use if you cannot mobilize them at the time you need to exert power. What are the resources which allow organizations to mobilize and direct their activities? First, if organizations are to engage in sustained, focused activities, they must maintain a structured organization and retain relationships with other organizations. A major explanation for a group's

TABLE 8.3   THE ORGANIZATIONAL STRUCTURE OF INTEREST GROUPS

Institutional	Issue-oriented
Possess organizational continuity and cohesion.	Have limited organization and cohesion.
Are knowledgeable about government sectors which affect them.	Possess poor information about government.
Have a stable membership.	Have a fluid membership.
Have concrete and immediate operational objectives.	Show an inability to formulate long-term goals.
See credibility of the organization as important.	See goal achievement as important.

SOURCES: Adapted from P. Pross, ed., *Pressure Group Behaviour in Canadian Politics*, (Toronto: McGraw-Hill, 1975); P. Pross, "Pressure Groups: Talking Chameleons," in M. Whittington and G. Williams, eds., *Canadian Politics in the 1980s*, (Toronto: Methuen, 1981).

failure or success seems to lie in its basic organizational structure. In Table 8.3, Pross (1975) delineates differences between two types of interest groups. Institutional interest groups can be placed at one end of a structural spectrum, and issue-oriented groups at the other.

Because of their lack of organizational structure, issue-oriented groups are generally less effective in pursuing and achieving their goals. Moreover, their goals are restricted to a narrow focus and can only be pursued one at a time. The highly structured institutional groups, however, are free to pursue a number of broadly defined issues simultaneously. Issue-oriented groups have a small membership and a minimal, usually volunteer, staff to handle communications. Institutional groups, meanwhile can bring extensive financial and human resources to bear on a variety of issues. Clearly, the Native organizations that are more institutional in nature have a greater chance of achieving their goals. Institutional organizations can choose from a variety of persuasive techniques, such as advertising, and can cultivate long-term formal and informal relations with government officials and senior civil servants.

An organization with a strong network forms a basis for recruiting. And, while there will be a sharing of recruits among organizations, that, in turn, leads to a sharing of some of the same ideas. Thus, the linkages of the network are continually strengthened. An institutional type of organization also is in a position to distribute ideas, many more than can an issue-oriented one. Organizations within a network also find that decision-making is facilitated and that coordinated action is more possible.

The ability of a group of Natives to achieve their goals is also a function of the social cohesiveness of the organization to which they belong. The more central membership in an organization becomes to an individual's self-concept (identity), the greater the likelihood that the individual will act for the organization. The strength of the individual's identification with the organization also affects the nature and type of action he/she will take. Finally, leadership plays an important part in any organization's ability to carry out sustained social action. Any organization thus requires a pool of experienced, skilled individuals who are able to simultaneously deal with local community people as well as outsiders.

Certain factors associated with issue-oriented groups can reduce their effectiveness. For example, the emergence of divergent (or different) goals of various sub-interest groups leads to a decrease in ability to achieve goals as well as an increase in the amount of intergroup conflict. In addition, as the organization increases in scope and area, new sub-interest groups emerge; e.g., band affiliation, province, legal status, linguistics, religion, which contribute to the multiple cleavages permeating Native organizations.

The internal leadership structure of a Native organization is also an important determinant of that organization's effectiveness in achieving its goals. Particularly important is the ability of Native leaders to exert strategic control over the goals and objectives of the organization. Organizational leaders must be adept at spanning boundaries at all times. They must monitor and control such factors as their clients' needs, funding opportunities and reserve politics as they attempt to achieve their organization's goals. This requires leaders to be constantly vigilant in promoting their clients' interests while, at the same time, maintaining their legitimacy in the eyes of external power groups.

As Pfeiffer and Salanchik (1978) point out, an organization survives when it is able to quickly adjust to external conditions and also cope with the environment in which it operates. For example, Native organizational leaders invest considerable time and effort in dealing with and attempting to influence such external agencies as DIAND, the Secretary of State, and various economic boards while also attending to the needs of their own constituents (Nielsen, 1991).

Nielsen goes on to note that if an organization is dependent upon two sources for its resources, then the task becomes even more difficult. An effort must be made to balance the relationships. Potential conflicts may rise in areas such as scope, priorities and ideology. For example, funders of Native organizations may object to the organization expanding their services into areas that go beyond the usual range of activities funded by that organization. The funder may request that the organization withdraw that service (reduce its scope) or lose its funding. This may be more problematic if the constituency of the organization (Native people) is pressing the organization to continue its work in this area.

The balancing processes which have to be undertaken by the Native organizations are continuously in flux. Organizations with stable leadership and members are more likely to embark upon strategies which allow the organization to continue its existence. Oliver (1990) identifies several factors which push organizations into a "balancing" mode. Let us take each in turn. *Necessity* is the condition when the organization must take an action in order to meet some legal or regulatory requirement. Non-compliance with this requirement will lead to negative sanctions against the organization; e.g., loss of funding. Thus, when government officials require Native organizations to comply with certain legal standards, the organizations must put themselves into a balancing mode. *Reciprocity* motivates an organization when there is an attempt to collaborate or coordinate its activities with those of another in the hope that there will be a mutually beneficial outcome. There is an anticipation that the benefits of establishing a partnership will outweigh the disadvantages.

A third factor which makes it necessary for an organization's leadership to strive for balance is *efficiency*. All modern organizations are assessed in terms of their ratio of inputs to outputs. The cost-benefit ratios of Native organizations are continually being monitored. The establishment of a *stable* organization (resource flow and exchanges) is important if the Native organization is to remain in existence over time. Finally, the issue of *legitimacy* is significant to organization leaders. The image or reputation of the organization is important if it is to remain credible in the eyes of both its constituents and the broader society.

The evolution, survival or phasing out of an organization is a function of both internal and external forces and how the organizational leadership deals with these forces. There is a need both to deal with the day-to-day issues and to attempt to predict where other organizations will be heading in the future. For if change is to take place and balance is to be achieved, the Native organization must integrate with, cooperate with or support the goals and objectives evidenced by other organizations. If the disjuncture between the Native organization and other organizations is too great, the Native organization will collapse for lack of support. Until recently, issued-oriented Native organizations have not attempted to achieve balance through cooperating with other organizations. They steadfastly retained their original goals and objectives and refused to change their strategies. The outcome has been a rapid demise of the organization.

As noted above, resources are not useful if they cannot be mobilized and brought to bear when needed. Natives have, in the past, mobilized some resources in the form of sporadic, incidental, collective action. However, this mobilization has not been sustained and, within a short time, the resources are in disarray. Natives have lacked the structural organization necessary to carry out political action. An organizational structure, as noted by Cornell (1988), forms a basis for recruiting new members, linking members and providing them with a vehicle to develop shared ideas and mutual respect. Thus, it helps develop a collective consciousness. Organizations also disseminate ideas which can be used to facilitate decisions and carry out concerted action.

To be sure, Native people have always had organizational structures. However, these structures were local (tribal) and focused around kinship. It has only been in recent years that pan-Indian and national Native organizations have emerged. Through this process various Native groups have become linked in their political action. However, while the organizational structures have emerged from the rural-based Natives, organizations are usually located in urban centres, but neither do they act on behalf of urban Natives.

Why haven't Natives become more involved in changing their lives? Why haven't they taken action in the past to provide themselves with the opportunities available to others. The answer seems to lie in their inability to amass the correct resources for the goals they want to achieve. As a rule, the greater the number and variety of resources held by a group, the greater their power. However, it is important to note that the importance of any resource is related to the issue being considered. As Cornell (1988) points out, not all resources are equally valuable, and their relative value depends on a variety of factors. For example, the sizes of a population is an important resource in a democracy but not in a dictatorship. Legal skills are important if decisions are made by a judiciary but are not as important if decisions are made through a political process. Resources can also be assessed in terms of their convertibility, reusability and applicability. For example, education is convertible into jobs, income and power. It also can be used over and over and has a wide applicability to a number of situations. On the other hand, legal skills are limited in terms of applicability but can be used over and over.

PAN-INDIANISM[3]

As stated earlier, the growth of Native organizations and movements is helping Natives to retain their culture and identity and is reinforcing links among Natives all over Canada. The pan-Indian movement emphasizes the values and beliefs central to the culture of Canadian Natives, regardless of local band differences.

The increase in pan-Indianism has led to an upswing in political activities. Because local and/or tribal differences have weakened Native political movements, the development of pan-Indianism has been a political watershed (Cornell, 1988). However, it has not developed to the exclusion of local, regional or tribal organizations. Nevertheless, the development of pan-Indian organizations has been the first step in fostering a spirit of unity and brotherhood among Native people. This political activism also inspired a resurgent nationalism on the reserves, particularly in eastern Canada. While some of the local or band goals were opposed to those of the pan-Indian movement, all were united in opposing Indian Affairs and developing greater self-determination.

Pan-Indianism is largely an urban phenomenon. It not only promotes the traditional values of Native culture, but also tries to facilitate Native involvement in the business and professional life of the city. Its proponents feel that Native culture should be retained as a distinctive jewel in the cultural mosaic of Canadian society (Hertzberg, 1971).

Pan-Indian movements have several ties to White culture. Their emergence has coincided with (although marginal to) the rise of conservation movements throughout North America. The leaders of pan-Indian movements have extensive contacts with White society, while retaining a strong affiliation to a Native tribe. Members of pan-Indian associations are generally part White, bilingual, well-educated, and involved in typically White occupations. In addition, pan-Indian movements were and continue to be widely supported by Whites. However, experience has shown that as the movements become more militant in their demands for structural social changes, White supporters are placed in an increasingly embarrassing position, and eventually withdraw their support.

Pan-Indianism presents a mixture of traditional Native and White values. The emphasis on Native values is all-pervasive, and extends into the decision-making process. For example, Natives feel that, to be valid, resolution of an issue must be reached by consensus, not by majority vote. In past meetings between Native representatives and DIAND, the Ottawa officials often have tired of the Natives' seemingly endless dialogue. Believing the Natives incapable of making a decision, DIAND has simply gone ahead and made it for them. Government officials have still not adequately grasped that, for Natives, all the procedures involved in a dialogue are important in themselves. White officials have also questioned the sincerity of the Natives' consensus approach to group decision-making, claiming that, after a consensus decision has been reached, many Natives still talk against it. Again, the accusation of insincerity reflects a shallow understanding of Native culture.

The resurrection of Native humour and its distinctive style of presentation is another aspect of pan-Indianism. Humour has a high priority in Native culture. Unlike Whites, Natives do not tell jokes as such. Instead they concentrate on stories or anecdotes like the following:

> In a White community, several Indians lived nearby. One day an old Indian's horse died. Since it was winter, he pulled it near to a creek which provided the town with water. Since spring was nearing, the community was concerned with the dead horse polluting its drinking water. A member of the White community was delegated to talk to the old Indian and ask him to move it. He agreed and three days later the delegate from the community saw the old Indian's son move the horse five feet. This, of course, did not solve the problem. The result was that the White delegate moved the horse. Several weeks later, a second horse of the old Indian also died. He pulled his dead horse onto a hill near a Catholic church. Each day the priest would ask the old man to move it and he would agree, but things kept coming up which prevented him from moving the horse. Each week the stench grew greater so that after church service one Sunday, the priest and several White men moved it two miles out of town.

Funny? Not to Whites. Yet, when told to a group of British Columbian Indians, the story produced broad smiles and gales of laughter; an old Indian was able to get White men to do his work for him.

Other cultural traits basic to pan-Indianism include an emphasis on sharing and an absence of emotional attachment to personal possessions. As historical pot-latches show, considerable status can be achieved through the sharing of worldly goods; a refusal to share is interpreted as selfishness. Other Native characteristics that have received less attention from anthropologists include an acceptance of the behaviour of others and a deep respect for basic human rights. These attitudes often serve to alienate Natives from the self-serving, manipulative White society that they find when they leave the reserve. As Lurie (1971) has shown, another Native cultural trait is withdrawal from situations that are anxiety producing.

Although many Natives and Whites see the reserve either as a prison or as a physical and psychological refuge, members of pan-Indian movements regard it as the basis for a viable community. They are not deterred by the fact that reserves are generally poverty-stricken, isolated and lacking in essential services.

Natives have tried, over the years, to build a pan-Indian movement, seeking to unite the various groups such as Métis and non-status Indians. Lussier (1984), however, claims that this movement is not working. He points out that the Métis, once they obtain their own organizations, set their own goals and objectives. To a certain extent, then, Natives are beginning to internalize the distinctions imposed on them by outsiders and to affirm the validity of these distinctions.

LIMITS TO THE ACTIVITIES OF NATIVE ORGANIZATIONS

Every Native organization and movement, formal or informal, is contributing to Native nationalism and providing Natives with a sense of identity. Increasingly, Natives are confronting the despair and disillusion that accompanies rejection by White society. Natives today are angry people: angry at the treatment they receive when they attempt to integrate and angry at the government's attempts to abolish their reserves.

Native organizational efforts are all limited by a relatively small population size, a lack of access to power, and a dependency on the federal government for funding and resources. Although Native organizations have been able to bring some pressure to bear on private companies and local government agencies, their dependency on the federal government is still the most significant limitation to their activities.

As Dosman (1972) has shown, when Natives in Saskatoon organized the Indian and Métis Development Society to be completely independent of the Department of Indian Affairs, it was deliberately discredited and eventually destroyed by DIAND. An even worse example of DIAND interference was its reaction to the Indian Association of Alberta (IAA) in the mid-1970s. When it became evident that the IAA's leader, Harold Cardinal, was moving away from standard DIAND policies, Indian Affairs charged the Association with improperly spending federally allocated money and with failing to account for nearly half of its expenditures. Subsequent events revealed that the Association had spent the money as directed, with written approval from DIAND and the Secretary of State. Then documents were also produced to show that both federal departments had improperly requested that sizable portions of the IAA grant be spent on programs for which money was not allocated.

Another tactic involves forcing the resignation of controversial leaders through sanctions. While this may solve problems in the short term, such government actions unwittingly contribute to the growth of Native nationalism. Nonetheless, the federal government continues to exert control over Native organizations by a variety of means. It can offer or withhold information that is essential for effective planning and operations. It can also co-opt the loyalties of Native leaders or define an organization as radical to reduce the chances of private financing and support.

The growth of pan-Indianism is facilitated by the spreading of information and values relevant to Natives. Until recently, this process was hindered by the absence of today's rapid communication processes, a lack of literacy, and linguistic diversity among the Native population. But as English becomes the working language of Natives, as literacy levels rise, and as greater funding is provided, Native groups are increasingly gaining access to the news media. Table 8.4 shows the distribution of various Native publications in the eight regions of Canada. In 1989, there were 65 Native periodicals, compared to 37 in 1971.

TABLE 8.4   N<small>ATIVE</small> P<small>ERIODICALS AND</small> A<small>SSOCIATIONS IN</small> C<small>ANADA</small>*

	Periodicals	Associations
	Percent	
Atlantic	3	5
Québec	7	6
Ontario	24	19
Manitoba	14	13
Saskatchewan	16	12
Alberta	9	17
British Columbia	10	20
Territories	17	8
Total number	62	392

*   Some periodicals are unilingual (French, English, Native), and others have some combination.

S<small>OURCE</small>: Price, *Native Studies*, 1978, p. 186; Price, mimeo, 1985, p. 1.

Native periodicals tend to be rural in orientation, although over half are published in cities (Price, 1978). As Price (1972) points out, the growth of Native periodicals in a city reflects the increasing development of other institutions.

Periodicals provide information to many Natives throughout Canada and reinforce Native values. Most Native periodicals aim to develop political awareness and Native identity, as well as to promote action on particular issues. In an analysis of three major Indian papers, *The Calumet, Native People* and *The Drum*, Price (1972) found that policies differed quite widely. The northern newspaper (*The Drum*) favoured the assimilation of Natives, while in eastern Canada, the paper (*The Calumet*) aimed for integration. The newspaper for western Natives (*Native People*), however, maintained a basic liberationist, or separatist, ideology. Nevertheless, the three papers did share several themes. For example, each argued that the Indian problem was really a White problem. Other shared topics included the superiority of traditional Native culture, the inability of Whites to understand Natives, and the need for Natives to develop their own resources.

In the North, radio programs in Native dialects not only disseminate information but also provide a platform for Native issues. However, the government still attempts to censor these programs before they are aired. At present, moreover, most programs are controlled by Whites and originate in the South. For example, in 1990 the CBC rejected a Native proposal to give Native broadcasters some access to the new Northern satellite system.

NATIVE POLITICAL ACTIVITY: PRE-1980

From the late sixties until the mid-seventies, much of the activity carried out by Native organizations focused on the federal government White Paper which proposed to do away with Indians, land claims and Aboriginal rights. For over a decade, Native organizations worked to stop this new policy from being implemented. The new focus required Native organizations to reorient themselves and to adopt new strategies in order to influence government officials.

After the federal government published its White Paper in 1969, a number of Native organizations began to play a leadership role in Native-White relations. They adopted offensive strategies and abandoned their previous defensive positions. The White Paper produced a loose coalition of Natives who had previously belonged to separate groups with diverse goals.

Native organizations began their opposition to the White Paper with formal briefs presented to the federal government. These presentations were separate but similar in content; these included the Brown Paper by British Columbia Natives, the Red Paper (*Citizens Plus*) by Alberta Natives, and *Wahbung* by Manitoba Natives. Even those Natives who did not submit formal briefs appeared to be in basic agreement with those who did. The coalition that resulted from the White Paper was an important milestone in Native political organization. Natives had been unable to form strong coalitions against earlier bills, such as *Bill C-130* (1963), which provided for the disposition of Native claims.

The 1969 White Paper to some extent reflected the basic sentiments of White Canada. It assumed that if Canadian Natives were to become fully integrated into Canadian society, they must change radically. It argued that the separate legal status of Natives kept them from fully participating in the larger society. Therefore, the White Paper proposed the following changes, to be implemented over approximately five years:

- Repeal the *Indian Act* to enable Natives to control their lands and acquire title to them.
- Have the provincial governments assume responsibility for Natives as they have for other citizens in their province.
- Make substantial funds available for Native economic development as an interim measure.
- Phase out the Department of Indian Affairs and Northern Development, which deals with Native affairs.
- Appoint a commissioner to consult with Natives and to study and recommend acceptable procedures for the adjudication of claims (*Indian Policy*, 1969:6).

Supporters of the White Paper argued that the creation of reserves and, subsequently, of the *Indian Act* had prevented Natives from participating in the development of Canadian society. They felt that Natives had been legally and administratively discriminated against and therefore had not been given an equal chance of success.

In general, the opponents of the White Paper saw it as a disguised program of cultural extermination (Cardinal, 1969). Opposition particularly focused on the Natives' right to maintain their ethnic identity. Critics felt that Natives should remain legally, administratively and socially separate if they so chose. The *Hawthorn Report* (1966-67), a sort of Royal Commission on the "Indian Problem," recommended that Natives be granted special status as "citizens plus" to ensure the preservation of their separate identity.

Opponents of the White Paper also argued that it would make all outstanding legal suits against the government, especially those concerning land claims, redundant. They also viewed sceptically the government's promise to "make substantial funds available for Indian economic development."

The minister of Indian Affairs, Jean Chrétien, claimed that the White Paper was a response to Native recommendations. Critics have responded that either the Minister acted dishonestly on behalf of White economic interest groups or entirely misrepresented Native attitudes. Whatever the answer, Natives claim they were not consulted before the drafting of the White Paper.[4]

Opponents of the government position want Natives to remain a distinct ethnic group, free to control their own affairs without undue interference by provincial or federal governments. They want to develop Native autonomy through the establishment of inter-provincial Native organizations and the restructuring of present Native social institutions. In other words, they want political organizations to be created by Natives, for Natives and under the control of Natives.

All three of the Native briefs mentioned above presented several arguments against the implementation of the White Paper, along with their own positions and recommendations. Natives have often been criticized for failing make constructive proposals of their own. However, the Brown Paper, the Red Paper, and *Wahbung* each presented several concrete proposals and specific strategies to solve Native problems. The following summaries outline the major recommendations in those Native briefs.

The Red Paper is the best known of the briefs and was the most specific in its proposals concerning education and economic development. The Red Paper argued that the *Indian Act* must be reviewed and amended but not repealed. This argument was echoed by the other briefs, particularly *Wahbung*, which recommended specific changes in such areas as wills, health services and the election of chiefs and councils.

All of the briefs discussed the Department of Indian Affairs. They rejected the White Paper's proposal to abolish it, arguing that it should become a smaller structure more attuned to local and regional Native needs. All the briefs argued that local tribal or band councils must be given more decision-making powers by Indian Affairs so that they can take the initiative in the social, political and economic development needed to tap previously ignored reserve resources. However, only the Brown Paper stated that Indian Affairs personnel should be exclusively Native.

Because treaties have not been established with most British Columbian Natives, land rights are still paramount for them; therefore the Brown Paper explored the land issue in considerable depth. The other two briefs also alluded to land rights, but did not discuss them in detail.

The Brown Paper was the least comprehensive in its treatment of economic development, while the Red Paper was very explicit. The Red Paper proposed that an Alberta Indian Development System (AIDS) be created to upgrade Native socioeconomic status through community economic development. Through AIDS, Natives would arrange to do work needed in the community, and industry-related jobs would be developed. AIDS would be controlled by a dual corporate structure formed by Native and non-Native leaders. Natives would set the goals and priorities of all projects and non-Natives would advise and assist in the development of these goals. A capital fund of $50 million would be needed, $30 million to come from the federal government, $10 million from the Alberta government, and $8.7 million from private industry. Alberta Natives would also invest an initial $1.3 million.

The Red Paper also presented the most extensive recommendations with regard to education. It proposed the creation of an Indian Education Centre (IEC) to be located in the centre of Alberta to provide equal access for Alberta Natives. The IEC would teach Native children how to successfully adapt Native skills and values to life in the larger Canadian context. It would also teach them modern skills to help them achieve success in the job market. In essence, the IEC would be run by Natives to ensure them a secure place in Canadian society.

The federal government initially approved the IEC in principle. In 1971, the Department of the Secretary of State initiated the funding of an educational concept referred to as cultural education centres. These centres were to provide alternatives to existing middle-class White schools. They were designed to render education meaningful to Natives and to stimulate self-worth and self-confidence among Native students. The Department of Indian Affairs opposed the Secretary of State and fought the creation and financing of these centres, ultimately gaining control of most of the funding. Whiteside comments on DIAND's power play:

> In a short time the Department gained control over almost the entire program. Once they controlled the funds, they convinced the existing centres to adopt a very narrow view of education, and to emphasize Indian culture. At the same time, the Department created many small centres which spread the limited funds across more and more centres. Thus, by encouraging small centres and giving the funds to the band councils to do with as they wished, the Department ensured that large centres had to close because of lack of funds (1980:12).

Theoretically, cultural education centres were to be replaced by native studies programs attached to existing post-secondary institutions. In the end, one Native studies program was implemented in Lethbridge and Native counselling services were approved for Alberta's two major universities.

In *Wahbung*, the Manitoba Indian Brotherhood recommended that a joint committee of the Brotherhood and the regional office of DIAND be established, with an equal number of Natives and Whites to handle Native issues. From this committee, several joint boards and commissions covering local government, economic development, welfare, education and policing could be established. *Wahbung* also recommended that a Cabinet committee be formed consisting of Native leaders to advise on cabinet policy decisions concerning Natives.

In 1974, in response to this recommendation, a joint committee of the National Indian Brotherhood (NIB) and DIAND was created. Although it did not take the recommended form, a special cabinet committee was created for the first time to deal specifically with Native concerns. The overall structure consisted of the NIB executive council and federal cabinet ministers. Within this, there was also a joint subcommittee and a joint working group. However, in 1978, the NIB withdrew from the committee and it died a quiet death.

All the briefs argued for immediate recognition of treaty and Aboriginal rights, and the establishment of a commission to interpret the government's treaty obligations. The Brown Paper and *Wahbung* did not make specific recommendations on Native claims. They did, however, recommend that a claims commission be established through consultation with Natives and that it be *able to make binding judgments*. The Red Paper quite explicitly rejected the concept of a claims commissioner. It argued for a full-time minister of Indian Affairs and the creation of a permanent standing committee of the House of Commons and Senate to deal only with registered Indians. The Native briefs also urged Native control over reserve finances, taxation, reconciliation of injustices, housing and health services.

Although the proposals contained in the three briefs were developed independently, there were very few contradictions. The proposals did, however, reflect each group's special needs; for example, British Columbian Natives focused on treaties, Aboriginal rights and the land issue. However, all the briefs agreed on major issues such as economic development, education and the *Indian Act*.

More than two decades after the briefs were presented, little has changed. Some minor recommendations have been implemented in watered-down versions, but basic structural and philosophical changes have not taken place in the government's Native policy.

The basic idea behind the White Paper was the elimination of the reserves. An examination of the reservation termination policy that was implemented in the United States sheds considerable light on this issue. Between 1953 and 1960, over 60 reserves were eliminated in the United States. By 1960, the results were clearly so disastrous that the scheme was halted.

In 1954, the Kalmath Indian reservation of Oregon began to be phased out and, in 1958, termination was completed. Prior to termination, the Indians had developed a thriving business based on reserve forest products. From this resource alone, the average income for each person was about $800 a year and the average family income was $3000 to $4000. Many Indians worked at other jobs on and off the reserve, raising the average income per family to nearly $6000; by 1954 standards, this placed the Indians in about the ninetieth percentile of the American population. By 1985, when the termination was complete, many Klamaths were on welfare and had suffered as a result of extreme social disorganization. Family stability had decayed sharply, crimes of all kinds had risen acutely, and the community social network had broken down. By 1960, a third of the Klamath Indians were on welfare or in mental or penal institutions throughout Oregon. Through termination on White terms, a thriving, self-sustaining community had deteriorated into a social disaster area.

Theoretically, the Klamaths should have succeeded in their transition. As Spencer and Jenning (1965) noted, the Klamaths were much more individualistic than other Indian tribes and, therefore, had more in common with White society. If the results were so disastrous for the Klamaths, then they are bound to be worse for other Natives.

Other terminations of American reserves have produced similar results. However, these findings are consistently ignored by those who favour the phasing out of reserves in Canada.

NATIVE POLITICAL ACTIVITIES: POST-1980

By the 1980s the federal government had decided not to implement the White Paper. However, new issues began to emerge which required the attention of Native people. The debate prior to passage of the *Constitution Act, 1982* required extensive allocation of Native resources to ensure their interests were protected. As a result of their vigilant action, several constitutional amendments were adopted which recognize Aboriginal and treaty rights. These changes recognize and affirm "existing Aboriginal rights" (section 35.1), which then had to be defined. Legal and financial resources had to be devoted to ensure these rights would be properly defined and recognized. The subsequent First Ministers' conferences (1983 to 1987) on Native Affairs also required detailed attention. The introduction of a comprehensive land claims policy (1981), which was subsequently revised in 1986, also meant that Natives had to broaden their resource allocations. The *Penner Report* (1983) was a major all-party parliamentary report on Indian self-government, and while it reflected favourably on Natives' quest for self-government, it meant that Natives would have to promote and lobby Canadians to establish what those rights were.

During the mid-1980s, the *Nielsen Report* was made public, which identified ways in which the federal government might save funds. This report narrowly defined the government's legal obligation toward Natives and identified ways in which DIAND could trim its budget. A major campaign was undertaken by Natives to inform Canadians as to the federal government's legal and moral responsibility toward Natives. Legal challenges emerged, and the Supreme Court of Canada upheld the federal government's fiduciary responsibilities (Guerin, 1985).

At the same time, the federal government reversed its century-long policy on enfranchisement and passed *Bill C-31*. This amendment to the *Indian Act* removed sex discrimination, and allowed for the reinstatement of persons who had lost their Indian status. Furthermore, bands would be given greater control over who was a member. All of these changes required extensive actions on the part of Native people. It also produced a great deal of internal factionalization within the Native community. The divisiveness created by this *Bill* still can be seen on many reserves and in numerous Native organizations (Ponting, 1991).

There were many other activities entered into by Natives during the eighties which have continued on into the nineties. The policy review on land and trusts for Indians has provoked considerable reaction by Indians. While all agree that changes are needed to this section of the *Indian Act*, the mistrust and suspicion of Natives toward the government compel them to monitor the slightest of action by the federal agency. A similar reaction by Native people was noted when the federal government began to develop new policy with regard to comprehensive land claims. When the *Sechelt Indian Band Self Government Act* was passed, the legal resources of Natives were once again put to test. This act removed bands from the jurisdiction of some parts of the *Indian Act*. This change also introduced the policy of self-government by which each community could begin to enter negotiations with the federal government and develop its own community-based government structures. This long, complex process would tax the local communities' resources and force many communities to rethink their desire to achieve self-government—federal government style.

Economic changes also forced Natives to establish priorities as government extended fewer resources to combat social and health issues. Changing educational benefits and shifting health responsibilities onto the bands were just two ways in which government action forced Natives to reallocate their meagre resources. The Kamloops amendment (*Bill C-115*) to the *Indian Act* meant that businesses on the reserve would be taxed. Along with this was the provision for "temporary surrender" of Indian land for economic development.

Natives were required to respond to all of the above initiatives in substantial and meaningful ways. It meant that resources had to be properly allocated and actions had to be monitored over long periods of time. Because of the scarcity of many resources (e.g., money, legal expertise), alliances had to be established. While these linkages enhanced Natives' ability to achieve their goals, it also made the process more complex and intricate. For example, instead of a dual interaction sequence, the introduction of a third party allowed for a triad to be established. This introduction of a third party allowed for coalitions to be formed, but it also meant that one of the coalitions could be against the Natives. The introduction of a fourth (or more) party simply made the process more complex.

An unlikely, independent ally emerged in the 1980s—the courts. Traditionally, the legal system took a very positivistic position in interpreting the law, which generally meant legal rulings against Native people. However, toward the end of the 1980s court decisions were supporting Native claims. The recognition of the Micmac's and B.C. Indians' right to fish, the decision to hear the Manitoba Métis Federation's land claim and the acknowledgement of Canada's fiduciary responsibility to Indians all gave both moral and legal support to the actions taken by Native people.

As a result of the actions taken by both the courts and Native organizations, there have been some federal and provincial policy changes regarding Native people. For example, the possibility of an independent claims commission is being discussed. Other legal changes are being contemplated by the federal government—as Native organizations continue their relentless pursuit of justice in the moral and legal arena. As the new constitution is being written, Aboriginal peoples will continue to make their presence known. They are afraid that otherwise they will be ignored and forgotten by the larger society and the government of Canada. Rather than let that happen, they will continue to unite their forces to achieve their rightful position in Canadian society.

CONCLUSION

The supporters of the White Paper proposal are in essence advocating cultural genocide. They seek the removal of the "citizen plus" policy that grants special status to Natives, arguing that Natives cannot be truly integrated in White society unless special status is removed. Yet, as a charter group of Canada, British Canadians have always claimed special status, as have French Canadians with their entrenched language and religious rights.

Increasingly, Natives are viewed as a threat to the unity of Canada. Ottawa has learned well from its experiences with Québec the problems that will arise if Natives gain power as a distinct cultural group. One solution is to refuse to recognize Natives as distinct, regardless of the problems they would face as a result of this policy. If Natives could be legally defined out of existence, the money now spent on them could be diverted to other, more cost-effective areas.

Removal of the legal status of Natives would not lessen discrimination against them. Natives would occupy the same depressed economic position as they do now, but without any group identification. They would become thoroughly marginal. Moreover, this marginality would not be wiped out in a generation: the stigma of Native birth is not only cultural, but physiological. Because intermarriage between Natives and Whites is only slowing increasing in Canada, the marginal Native will haunt Canadian society for many decades.[5]

Those who want to end the special status of Natives implicitly adhere to the myth of equality. This myth claims that, since everyone is equal, no one should be discriminated for or against. It is easy enough to stop the discrimination that favours Natives by eliminating economic incentives, affirmative action programs, educational advantages and so on. However, out of political expediency and for other reasons, few efforts are made to stop discrimination against Natives.

In a nation that advocates cultural pluralism, the White Paper proposal seems incongruous. Clearly the proposal continues to be supported (as evidenced by the

Nielsen Report) as a response to the recent growth of Native political and economic organizations. There is a recognition by the political elite that if these organizations are allowed to control reserve policies and funds, they will become formidable pressure groups by the twenty-first century. The harsh sanctions imposed by the Minister of Indian Affairs on the Indian Association of Alberta suggest what Native organizations can expect if they continue to challenge DIAND's authority.

At present, more than $1 million a year is provided to Native organizations, with limited results. One problem is simply that Natives are still in the process of developing the skills that most Whites take for granted. Far more serious, however, is the fact that many Native organizations can only take action with federal approval. Only then will the funds be released. Moreover, the federal government seldom agrees with Native organizations on spending priorities. The government is constantly changing it long-range plans and shuffling its bureaucratic slots for allocating monies. Even when an allotment can be clearly perceived as unrealistic at the local level, it seldom can be changed. If DIAND allocates several thousand dollars to be spent on a given project, then no amount of counterargument by local Native organizations can divert this money into another project.

Although substantial amounts of money are given annually to DIAND for Indians, very little of it is spent on meaningful programs that can activate long-range social change. For example, less than 15 percent of the funds given to Indian organizations was used for developing economic projects, notwithstanding the federal government's stated claim that sustainable development strategies have the highest priority. Of DIAND's total budget, 43 percent is consumed by salaries and staff support for its White bureaucrats and never reaches the reserve. If these salaries alone were given to reserve Indians, a sizeable capital base could be established to promote further economic development.

Political skills are vital to the survival of any group of people. In Canada, the cultural awakening of Native people has been preceded and outpaced by the growth of their political awareness. Natives are becoming increasingly sophisticated in their use of organizations to further their goals. This new knowledge will make itself felt more and more in Canada as we move into the twenty-first century.

NOTES

1. For a more complete discussion of the history of British Columbia Native organizations, the reader should consult Drucker, 1958.

2. The Six Nations community is attempting to separate politically from Canada. This may account for their lack of militancy.

3. The term "pan-Indian" is not used by Indians but was invented and is used now by social scientists.

4. See, for example, the work of S. Weaver, *The Hidden Agenda: Indian Policy and the Trudeau Government*, Waterloo, Ontario, University of Waterloo, mimeo., 1980.

5. In 1961, the endogamous rate of Native marriages—Natives marrying Natives— was one of the highest in Canadian history. In fact, it increased from 91 percent in 1951 to over 93 percent in 1961. However, by 1971 the rate had decreased to 77 percent, and by 1981 a further decrease to 67 percent was evident.

Conclusion to Part 2

The statistical data, from whatever source, reveal the disturbing picture—the quality of life for Native people is substandard, by any definition. Inferior housing and lack of employment coupled with high rates of mortality and disease characterize the Native population. Nevertheless, education levels are rising and a generation of university graduates are beginning to enter the labour force (Buckley, 1992). Native communities are losing their isolation due to their connections with the cities and rural Natives are trying to build functional communities that will support their resident population.

The federal government's Department of Indian Affairs has come to intrude in almost every aspect of a Native's life. This strategy of what Dyck (1991) calls coercive tutelage was undertaken to both protect and assimilate Natives. At the same time, the pervasiveness of Indian Affairs and the reluctance of officials to allow Natives to assess the different choices available to them regarding specific issues, has left Native people in a relationship of dependency. Nevertheless, there are signs of change in Indian Affairs. The basic acceptance of self-government of Natives by government has radically changed the operation and the philosophy under which employees operate. This seems to have renewed Native people's belief that Indian Affairs may be able to help them. There has been a steadfast insistence on the part of Natives that control of Indian Affairs remain with the federal government and not be transferred to provincial governments.

The lack of jobs, housing and other social amenities brought about a major urbanization of Natives in the 50s and 60s. While this migration has slowed, the result is that large numbers of Native people now live permanently in urban centres. A host or organizations has emerged in an attempt to help these people adapt and maintain their dignity as they struggle to remain in the city and to deal with urban institutions. As the second generation of urban Natives come of age, they find themselves isolated from their rural origins and lack intimate contact with traditional cultures. This division of the Native population between urban and rural has posed some problems. How do landless urban Natives relate to rural, land-based people? How can the urban population fully appreciate land claims? These issues have produced serious divisions within the Native population but are now being dealt with by the emergence of new pan-Native organizations.

In their attempt to find their roots, Native people have turned to organizations which have facilitated this quest. These new urban, pan-Indian organizations have begun the process of linking the various disparate groups in the city. Other organizations have begun to focus their efforts on issues of importance to Natives— education and jobs. As Natives begin to "take charge" of their lives, they are finding the process of integration easier. One of the most dynamic Native organizations has been the Native Women's Association of Canada. They have been trying to place women's issues on the political agenda of Native-government negotiations for some time. The women claimed it was an infringement on their freedom of expression for Ottawa to fund other, male dominated groups to speak on the Constitution, but not them. Their latest court action to be represented at the unity negotiations was rejected, but it did force the Assembly of First Nations to create a women's circle. This all-women's committee will be made up of Native leaders and will ensure a more focused approach to women's issues. At this time it has been requested by the Assembly to prepare the first draft of the Aboriginal Charter of Rights that will replace the Canadian *Charter* if new constitutional arrangements are approved.

P A R T   3

The role of Native women in contemporary society has been sorely neglected. Compared to traditional activities, Native women now have a very different lifestyle and role to play within their community. Recently, Native women have developed their own political organizations which have provided them with a strategy for obtaining the goals they see as important for themselves, their children and the community. The work of Krosenbrink-Gelissen tackles the role of women and traces the recent political development and impact of the Native Women's Association of Canada. This organization has become a spokesperson for Native women as they deal with being a double minority—a minority as Natives in the larger society and a minority within their own community because of their gender.

The idea that Canada is a peaceful country, sharing its wealth equally with all groups was shattered when the army was sent to Québec to fight the Mohawks. The armed conflict between the Mohawks and the army symbolized a new relation between Indians and the rest of Canada. Perhaps this event has produced a change in the Canadian psyche, and more constructive relations will emerge.

Self-determination and self-government are two ideals Native people have been pursuing for the last century. These are complex issues which not only have philosophical bases but also practical implications. How do they fit into the larger Canadian political structure, which is based upon democracy, equality and justice? How are the concepts defined and what are the boundaries? These thorny questions are currently being discussed, and time will tell whether or not Canadians accept the basic premise and have the will to implement such ideas.

The last chapter tries to provide the reader with a theoretical structure with which to interpret the position of Natives and non-Natives alike. This perspective encompasses both an historical and a contemporary view. We argue that Native society can be viewed as a transfer-payment economy, where almost all the money introduced into the system comes from the federal government (Salisbury, 1986).

Much of the capital flowing into the Native communities is directed toward the provision of a myriad of social services. Regardless of the focus of activity, government officials direct the amount and pace.

As Myers (1914) and Ryerson (1960) have shown, Canada's development can be seen as a series of conflicts between contending groups, beginning with that between European colonizers and Native peoples. Ossenberg (1980) noted this when he pointed out:

> The ascendency of a merchant class through the fur trade was associated with the rapid decline in the power of the Native peoples...as the fur trade was replaced by the wheat economy, the labour of Native peoples became virtually superfluous (1980: 19).

Others have clearly demonstrated that Natives were effectively excluded from the production of agricultural goods even though one of the government's explicit goals was just the opposite—to transform Natives into farmers (and thus assimilate them).

The following section explores issues involved as Natives try to gain control over their lives. It also documents how government wants to shape the nature and extent of their control.

CHAPTER 9

THE NATIVE WOMEN'S ASSOCIATION OF CANADA

BY LILIANNE ERNESTINE KROSENBRINK-GELISSEN*

Aboriginal women have, for the past half-century, found themselves marginalized in their own country and their own community—triple jeopardy. In an attempt to reassert their position in the community, Native women have begun to organize and take action so they might once again control their lives. Over the years, the actions of government have entrenched Native women in the status of second class citizens. The following chapter will illustrate how Native women organized in a concerted strategy by which they would become proactive on a number of government and university issues which would affect their lives.

---

* This chapter was written by Dr. Krosenbrink-Gelissen. It first appeared in *Sexual Equality as an Aboriginal Right: The Native Women's Association of Canada and the Constitutional Process on Aboriginal Matters, 1982-1987* (pp. 74-102 and 116-119), Nijmegen Studies in Cultural Development and Cultural Change, 1991, published by Verlag Breitenbach, Saarbrucken, Germany. Some editorial changes have been made to the text in order to update the material.

Human rights movements, as well as ethnic and women's movements, provided a positive climate in which Aboriginal women could express their concerns. It is important to explain the existence of a separate Aboriginal women's organization with a political mandate that is somewhat distinct from the national male-dominated Aboriginal organizations. The following chapter will identify the context in which the Native Women's Association emerged and the activities which have been carried out by the Association over the past two decades. There will also be an attempt to evaluate the strategies Native women used in order to reach their political goals during the 70s, which is crucial in adequately understanding the change in goals and objectives of the Association after the patriation of the Constitution.

IMPACT OF THE WOMEN'S MOVEMENT

Apart from the human rights movement, the women's movement had the most significant impact on the evolution of the Native Women's Association. The term "women's movement" is used instead of "feminist movement" because the first term is more global and refers to a unifying ideology and to general and common goals; the latter term is always used in combination with a political ideology (for example, liberalism or Marxism), and reflects only a fraction of the women's movement (Delmar, 1986; Jamieson, 1979).

During the 1960s, the concern for equal and just distribution of political power, national income and collective socio-economic provisions grew. Despite legal and political changes that supported the ideology of equality, inequality between men and women in society remained. The second international women's movement after the mid 1960s, therefore, focused on changing norms, values and attitudes as they pertain to women's positions in society (Mitchell, 1986; Steinem, 1983).[1] The movement not only provided new opportunities for women, but also re-defined political issues, making them more pertinent to women in Canadian society (Smith *et al.*, 1985). The women's movement had a significant impact on the awareness of Aboriginal women as well, and to a certain degree effectuated the establishment of the Native Women's Association of Canada. It shaped a climate in which Aboriginal women could voice their griefs and make them relevant to others (Fleming, 1971; Krosenbrink, 1984).

The emergence of an Aboriginal women's movement in Canada during the 1960s had been largely unnoticed by non-Aboriginal people, as well as by Aboriginal men. (Bonney, 1976; Jamieson, 1979). Several Aboriginal women had successful careers and others were seeking leadership positions in political associations, but little publicity was focused on these women as a group. They were considered exceptions to the rule rather than as spokespersons of a developing movement (Goodwill, 1971). Local Aboriginal women's groups, and in particular Indian women's groups, had existed before 1960, but only after that date did they begin to organize themselves on a regional base and become preoccupied with political issues.[2] These regional women's groups organized themselves on the basis of self-identifying Aboriginal identity criteria, rather than on legal criteria such as "status" and "non-status" Indian. Women of Indian and Métis as well as of Inuit ancestry participated in these organizations (Goodwill, 1971). The aspect of self-identification is significant since it stands in contrast to the National Indian Brotherhood's and the Native Council of Canada's membership, which was determined according to legal, external categorizations.

The Royal Commission on the Status of Women was created in 1967 to investigate women's relative inequality with men and to provide the federal government with recommendations; thus providing a forum in which to discuss women's issues (Roosens, 1986). In 1968, the UN's Year of Human Rights, Mary Two-Axe Early, a non-status Mohawk woman from the Kahnawake reserve in Québec, presented her case to the Commission, informing the public for the first time in Canadian history on the issue of sex discrimination in the *Indian Act* and the way it affected Indian women's lives. Mary Two-Axe Early had married a White man and had consequently lost her Indian status. Nevertheless, she and her children returned to the reserve every summer and lived in the house that was willed to her by her parents, which was in accordance with Mohawk traditions. There had been no opposition to her presence on the reserve despite the fact that she and her children were not legally recognized Indians. However, in 1967 she was informed by the band council that, in accordance with the *Indian Act* regulations, she was no longer entitled to property on the reserve.[3] After Mary Two-Axe Early returned to the reserve, she started to organize a women's group, "Equal Rights for Indian Women." She began to receive letters from Indian women across Canada who had heard about her testimony before the Commission and who supported her actions to pursue an *Indian Act* amendment,[4] and she became nationally known for her struggle against sex discrimination against Indian women.

The Royal Commission on the Status of Women heard several other cases of non-status Indian women and appeared impressed with the practical knowledge of these women, who seemed to know what the problems were with the *Indian Act* and how they should be resolved (Goodwill, 1971). In 1970, the Commission released its report and, among the many recommendations, one pertained to Indian women. The Commission condemned sex discrimination in the *Indian Act* and suggested that special status rights be restored to those who had lost them. Furthermore, Indian women should have the same civil rights as other Canadians with respect to marriage and property (Cheda, 1977).

Even though the White Paper on Indian Policy was withdrawn, and recommendation 106 of the Royal Commission on the Status of Women's report in 1970 may have been perceived to be implemented, the socio-political and legal positions of Indian women did not change. First, although the federal government planned a future *Indian Act* revision in which Aboriginal organizations were to have a political voice, the old *Indian Act* remained intact. Second, since national Aboriginal organizations, such as the National Indian Brotherhood and the Native Council of Canada, appeared to be male-dominated, the question remained whether they would be prepared to represent Indian women's concerns regarding sex discrimination in the *Indian Act*. Third, the development of local Indian control on reserves revealed that sex discrimination in the *Indian Act* was not the only problem that affected Indian women's lives; factionalism, favouritism and male chauvinism on reserves played their part as well. Enforced gender asymmetry through the *Indian Act* regulations proved to have had a significant impact on the lives of both status and non-status Indian women, both on-reserve and off-reserve (Krosenbrink, 1983; *The Native People*, 1/4/77; Silman, 1987). It gradually became clear to Indian women that they had to seek a political niche for themselves in order to obtain their rights.

Non-status Indian women were the first to call attention to the issue of sex discrimination in the *Indian Act*, although they were shortly after to be followed by on-reserve status Indian women. Influenced by the women's movement, Indian women realized that they had to take action to deal with their unequal treatment. They began to connect their deprivation with inequality provisions within the *Indian Act* system. It was not only that women experienced the consequences of the *Indian Act* more dramatically than men, but also that both status and non-status Indian women had relatively more off-reserve life experience (Pryor, 1984; White, 1985).[5] Native women noted that one has to leave the reserve in order to learn about the *Indian Act* and its implications. The overall majority of non-status Indian women lived off-reserve. In 1966, 16.4 percent of the status females as against 15.4 percent of the status males were living off-reserve. In 1976, numbers had increased to 29.5 percent against 25.8 percent (Indian and Northern Affairs Canada [INAC], 1983: 5-7).

With more marriages breaking up since the 1960s, more non-status Indian women were separated (or widowed) and went back to the reserve where they found that they were no longer entitled to Indian rights. They wondered why White women who were married, widowed or separated from status Indian men had Indian rights and were entitled to live on the reserve, even though they had no Aboriginal roots (see Table 9.1)(Silman, 1987).

TABLE 9.1 Indian Mixed Marriages[*] in Percentage

Mixed marriages	1966	1972	1973	1974	1975	1976
Status male and non-status female	343	50.0	51.1	48.3	55.0	57.5
Status female and non-status male	65.7	50.0	48.9	51.7	45.0	42.5
Total in percentage	100.0	100.0	100.0	100.0	100.0	100.0

[*] Mixed marriage = marriage between non-status and status Indian persons, based on *Indian Act* regulations. Due to racial connotations, it is presumed that a non-status person is a non-Aboriginal person. However, the opposite may well be the case. Within this table, "Indian" should not be conceived as a social category but as a legal category. Intermarriage = marriage between two Indian persons from different bands or nations. There are no records on intermarriage. Between 1966 and 1976, mixed marriages remained continually around 50 percent of all Indian marriages.

Source: INAC, 1983: 5-12; Jamieson, 1978: 66; Krosenbrink, 1984: 53; Weaver, 1978: 7, 23a.

THE *LAVELL* AND *BEDARD* CASES

Two legal cases from the early 1970s involving the sex-discriminatory status regulations in the *Indian Act* clearly illustrate the complexity of the Aboriginal women's sexual equality problem. The *Lavell* and the *Bedard* cases also had a profound effect on the establishment of the Native Women's Association and the way it manifested itself vis-à-vis national male-dominated Aboriginal organizations.

Jeanette Corbiere Lavell, a status Ojibeway from the Wikwomikong reserve in Ontario who was to marry a white man in December 1970, had already declared before the date of her marriage that she intended to contest sections 12(1)b and 14 of the *Indian Act* in court. Her reason for doing so may be illuminated by the following statement from Mary Two-Axe Early:

> It seems inconceivable that our biological constitution [as women] should be reason enough for our birthright and heritage to be arbitrarily divested at the moment (*The Quil*, 22/10/82).

In a court case involving a liquor infraction in the Northwest Territories in 1967, a precedent had been set. An Indian man, named Drybones, was convicted under section 94(b) of the *Indian Act* for being intoxicated off-reserve. Drybones successfully challenged his conviction before the Supreme Court in 1969 on the basis that this particular section of the *Indian Act* contravened section 1(b) of the *Canadian Bill of Rights* that prohibited racial discrimination. The Drybones case proved that it was possible for the *Indian Act* to be overruled by that *Bill* (Cardinal, 1979; Jamieson, 1978). The *Drybones* case and the report of the Royal Commission on the Status of Women, together with the White Paper withdrawal, resulted in renewed pride in Indian identity.

In June 1971, the Ontario County Court dismissed Lavell's case on grounds that, despite the loss of her Indian status, she had equal rights with all other married Canadian women. As such, it was found that she was not deprived of any human rights or freedoms contemplated in the *Bill of Rights*. The Court did not find her inequality within her own class of people contrary to that bill and, thus, overlooked the fact that the *Indian Act* reinforced an inferior position of Indian women vis-à-vis other Canadian women (Chapman, 1972; INAC 1983; Jamieson, 1978, Krosenbrink, 1984).

In October, 1971, Lavell made an appeal to the Federal Court of Appeals and won. The three judges concluded that the *Indian Act* resulted in different rights for Indian women than those of Indians men when women married non-status males or Indians from different bands. The court decided that section 11(1)f, 12(1)b and 14 of the *Indian Act* contravened the *Bill of Rights* and should therefore be repealed in due course. Right after the decision from the Federal Court of Appeals, the federal government declared that it would bring the *Lavell* case before the Supreme Court of Canada.

The second case concerns Yvonne Bedard, a non-status Iroquois woman from the Brantford reserve in Ontario. She had separated from her White husband and returned to her reserve to live in the house that was willed to her by her parents. A year later, Bedard was evicted from the reserve by the band council, although DIAND had informed the council that on the basis of local control several other bands had decided not to implement that particular section of the *Indian Act*. Bedard successfully presented her case before the Supreme Court of Ontario on the same grounds that Lavell had done (Cheda, 1977; Jamieson, 1978; Weaver, 1978). Together with the *Lavell* case, the *Bedard* case was brought before the Supreme Court of Canada in 1973.

Both Lavell and Bedard received support from various women's groups, which recognized their cases as an opportunity to advance women's rights in general. Duclos argues that it was predominantly White women who were spokespersons for the women's movement in Canada during the 1970s. They created: "an image which constructs gender as the sole basis of women's oppression, cloaked in the privileges and power attached to being white" (1990:38). Hence, feminist groups at that time focused on sex discrimination in the *Indian Act* as an example of the inequality of women, and did not recognize the dual discrimination operating in Indian women's situation. However, feminist groups were able to attract media attention. This way, Indian people across Canada were made aware of the significance of the *Lavell* and *Bedard* cases for the Indian movement.

The *Lavell* and *Bedard* cases created considerable discussions among both Indian and non-Aboriginal people. Lobbying by both groups was complicated by a lack of consensus. Whereas non-Aboriginal groups focused on the matter of sexual equality per se, Aboriginal groups began raising the question whether the federal government should continue determining Indian legal status and band membership. This awkward situation arose from the fact that Indian sexual equality rights were being discussed within the field of women's rights, a field which, as such, had nothing to do with the *Indian Act* (Roosens, 1986).

Over the years, the *Indian Act* created friction between status and non-status Indians which became visible in the political arena. In 1968, the National Indian Council was abolished. Status and non-status Indians, as well as the Métis, had political priorities that were incompatible. Therefore the National Indian Brotherhood was established to represent status Indians politically, and the Native Council of Canada was to represent non-status Indians and the Métis politically (Weaver, 1983; Whiteside, 1973).

"Status" was sometimes linked to biology and culture, meaning that women who had lost their status were not considered real Indians anymore (Krosenbrink, 1983). Furthermore, being legally recognized as an Aboriginal person provided many Indians with a source of pride. And lastly, legal status had gradually become a gauge of "pure" Indian descendance. It is within this framework that the motto "keep the Indian race pure" should be understood. Nevertheless, stigmatization by status persons created problems, in particular, for non-status women.

Both the National Indian Brotherhood and the Native Council of Canada determined their membership in accordance with the status regulations of the *Indian Act*. It should not be forgotten that the *Indian Act* has profoundly affected Indian thinking over time. Other Indians, however, argued that legal status provided a person with official recognition by outsiders and, for that reason, it did not make a status Indian more Indian than a non-status Indian. The same objection was made with respect to Indians living off-reserve, who are for the most part non-status Indians. They argued that not living within an Indian community did not make a person less Indian.

A significant reason for the divisiveness among Indians regarding the legal status issue in the *Indian Act* was that most Indians did not know what the *Indian Act* entailed and could or could not enforce (Silman, 1987). Status Indians found it hard to comprehend the problems that non-status Indians were confronted with.[6] At the same time, a fundamental change of the *Indian Act* seemed inconceivable to many status Indians (Wilson, 1974). A repeal of the *Indian Act*, according to them, would result in the loss of all Indian rights. Hence, those Indian persons who opposed Lavell and Bedard's actions in order to seek an *Indian Act* amendment were not automatically in favour of sexual inequality, but feared the loss of all Indian rights.

In February, 1973, the *Lavell* and *Bedard* cases appeared before the Supreme Court of Canada. The Attorney General of Canada had made the appeal in response to suggestions from government officials who were afraid of the far-reaching implications if previous decisions in the *Lavell* and *Bedard* cases should be upheld. Most important, the appeal was also made in response to pressure from the National Indian Brotherhood.[7] As far as the federal government was concerned, it did not want a revision of the *Indian Act* in view of the previous negative reactions by Indians when change was suggested and because the abolition of sex-discrimination in the *Indian Act* would bring about substantial financial liabilities. The number of status Indians would increase dramatically if non-status Indian persons were to regain status and corresponding government services.

According to the National Indian Brotherhood, sex-discrimination against women in the *Indian Act* was wrong, but the organization was afraid that if previous court decisions were upheld, the federal government would be given the ultimate power to change or even to repeal the *Indian Act* without the consent of Indian people. The White Paper on Indian Policy of 1969 was still fresh in the memories of those involved. The National Indian Brotherhood considered section 12(1)b of the *Indian Act* as a strong lever to force the federal government to negotiate an *Indian Act* revision with the National Indian Brotherhood. It wanted to sidetrack the issue of sexual equality for Indian men and women in the interests of preserving Indian rights either through the *Indian Act* or through other legal guarantees. Therefore, the National Indian Brotherhood wanted Indian women to wait for a redress of their rights in the interest of preserving Indian rights for (status) Indians as a group.

Women, therefore, were requested to subordinate their goal—Indian rights for Indian women—to that of Indian men; they were used as a political vehicle to pursue an *Indian Act* revision the way status Indian males saw fit.

While the National Indian Brotherhood's leading figures were against Lavell and Bedard primarily for political and strategic reasons, it appeared that the majority of its constituency—still not fully aware of the power and limitations of the *Indian Act*—was against these women's actions to regain their Indian rights for other and more far-reaching reasons.[8] The constrained identity boundary mechanisms embedded in the status regulations of the *Indian Act* were largely internalized by Indian people and were therefore conceived of as Indian customary law. A good example of this is provided by the Association of Iroquois and Allied Tribes, of which Bedard's band was a member. The organization stated in a position paper of 1971 that the patrilineal and patrilocal status principles were in agreement with the traditional social organization of the Iroquois (Chapman, 1972). Anthropologists are aware that this claim is false. Furthermore, the National Indian Brotherhood's constituency to a large part feared the influx of White men on reserves if previous decisions in the *Lavell* and *Bedard* cases were upheld. This argument reflected an internalization of White male chauvinism, since it indicated the Indian people's fear that White men would take over political power. The presence of White women on reserves (married, widowed or separated from status Indian men) was not felt to be threatening, despite the increase in this trend (see Table 9.1). This argument also reveals a discrepancy between Indian ideology and practice. Although Indian males and females unanimously acknowledged the Indian women's crucial and continuing roles as mothers in retaining and enhancing cultural patterns, White women were not perceived as a threat to the cultural survival of Indians (Krosenbrink, 1989). Many non-status Indian people argued that sex discrimination in the *Indian Act* is not a women's issue per se. Since Indian women are removed from the centre of life through the *Indian Act* regulations, the survival of Indian communities was actually at stake. They claimed that "Indian motherhood" is vital to the continuation of Indian nationhood (Holmes, 1987; Krosenbrink, 1984; Meadows, 1981, Shkilnyk, 1985). Since the National Indian Brotherhood went so far as to determine Indian band membership in terms of cultural resourcefulness, the devaluation of women was perceived as detrimental to Indian cultural continuity (Weaver, 1978).

The Supreme Court decided, in a 5 to 4 vote, against Lavell and Bedard. The *Canadian Bill of Rights* was not considered effective to overrule the *Indian Act*, and the fact that Indian women were treated differently upon marriage with a non-status man or an Indian from another band was not considered relevant to the cases brought before the Court (Eberts, 1985; Jamieson, 1978; Kerr, 1975). Both the federal government and the National Indian Brotherhood saw the decision as a victory. The National Indian Brotherhood saw it as a victory for Indian rights. That Indian women were denied Indian rights was ignored, since it was not relevant to their political mandate.

The *Lavell* and *Bedard* cases had awakened both the Canadian public and Indian people. The cases presented a moral dilemma over which the women's movement and the Indian movement collided; the Indian ideology of special status was perceived as irreconcilable with the equality ideology of the women's movement. However, to Indian women the issue had never been as described as above. They had never asked for equal rights with other Canadians but for equal rights with other Indians: "We can't begin discussing universal women's rights because at this time we can't even get Indian rights for Indian women" (*Indian Rights for Indian Women*, n.d.: 15). Misinterpretations of Indian women's political goals on the part of both the Indian movement and the women's movement were due to a lack of understanding of the true character of the Indian or Aboriginal women's movement, as the Native Women's Association of Canada argued in the 1980s.

THE NATIVE WOMEN'S ASSOCIATION OF CANADA AND THE NATIONAL COMMITTEE ON INDIAN RIGHTS FOR INDIAN WOMEN

The concept of a distinct national body to represent Aboriginal women's views was given birth in 1971, a few months before the *Lavell* case was before the Federal Court of Appeals. At that time, the National Indian Brotherhood, the Native Council of Canada, and the Inuit Tapirisat of Canada were already established. Through the efforts of the Voice of Alberta Native Women's Society—a provincial non-status and status Indian and Métis women's organization—and with the financial support of the federal government through the Department of the Secretary of State, the first national Aboriginal women's conference was held in Edmonton in 1971. At the conference, the desire was expressed by the delegates from local and regional Aboriginal women's groups across Canada to have a separate national Aboriginal women's organization, in order to have women's issues adequately addressed and to change the images of Aboriginal women held by society at large as well as by their own men. Prevailing gender inequality between Aboriginal men and women had resulted in differing perspectives and political aspirations. Male-dominated national Aboriginal organizations appeared not to be concerned with Aboriginal women's views.

At the Edmonton conference in 1971, a Steering Committee was established with the mandate to draft the basic objectives of the forthcoming Native Women's Association of Canada. It was also resolved to create a commission to discuss the discriminatory status issue in the *Indian Act*. The Steering Committee organized a second national Aboriginal women's conference in Saskatoon in 1972 in order to share social, cultural and political information and to check whether there was enough grass-roots support for the proposed establishment of a Native Women's Association of Canada. Furthermore, a panel of Indian women was featured, including Jeannette Corbiere Lavell, to discuss problems of Indian women that result from the *Indian Act*.[9] During the panel discussions it became clear that Indian women themselves were divided on the 12(1)b issue, which stood as the symbol of sex discrimination against Indian women in Canada. The Voice of Alberta Native Women's Society, which was the only effective provincial Aboriginal women's organization at that time, strongly opposed *Lavell*, despite the fact that its membership consisted of non-status as well as status Indian women. The organization was of the opinion that Indian nations that inhabited Alberta had patrilocal and patrilineal systems of social organization by tradition and that the *Indian Act* status regulations were therefore in agreement with traditional Indian cultures in that province. Several Indians from that area, however, argued that Indian women who opposed Lavell's actions did not fully comprehend the issue at stake and were influenced by their husbands. Furthermore, they were treaty Indians. As such, these women felt that changes in the *Indian Act* would affect treaty rights and that, despite the original patrilineal and patrilocal social organization of the Alberta Indian nations, women were respected and had a political voice, regardless of the *Indian Act*.[10] However, *Indian Act* rights and treaty rights are distinct rights.

During the second national Aboriginal women's conference in Saskatoon in 1972, it appeared that it was not possible to have a single national Aboriginal women's organization if the issue of the status regulations of the *Indian Act* as they pertained to Indian women remained on its political agenda. Indian women themselves were divided between those who based their self-identity on the *Indian Act* and those who based it on other criteria. Therefore, it was decided to create two national Aboriginal women's organizations with distinct political mandates.

The Native Women's Association of Canada (NWAC) held its first national assembly in 1974, but its constitution dates back to July 1973. The Native Women's Association of Canada represents Aboriginal women who base their identity on self-identifying criteria, and includes non-status and status Indian women, Métis and Inuit women. The Native Women's Association of Canada's political mandate promotes Aboriginal women's interests, including their assumption of active roles within their communities. Important issues of concern are women's employment opportunities, economic development of Aboriginal communities, alcohol and drugs abuse, child welfare, environmental issues, and Aboriginal cultures' arts and crafts.[11] Although the Association's aim is to study problems that confront Aboriginal women, no explicit mention is made of the issue of the *Indian Act*. NWAC's organizational structure is divided into three levels. Firstly, the local chapters are affiliated with a provincial or territorial member association, but their goals are flexible according to the needs and interests of those involved. There are some 400 local chapters of the NWAC spread all over Canada, with no less than 100 000 active members. The local chapters are informally organized and are urban- as well as reserve-based. These informal groups are of great importance. They foster networking communications, provide Aboriginal women with an opportunity to develop organizational skills, and establish a career both within and outside the reserve (Keefe, 1976). Secondly, the provincial and territorial member associations each have their own constitution and political mandate and direct the national political agenda. Thirdly, the national office in Ottawa is the base from which the leaders of Native Women's Association of Canada operate politically. However, this office came into being only after 1980 (see Table 9.2).

With respect to determining the political mandate, the Board of Directors is crucially important. The Board comprises two delegates from each provincial and territorial member association, and convenes at least twice a year. The Executive exercises the powers of the Board and is responsible for coordination, planning, administration and public relations. The Association's Executive consists of a national president, two vice-presidents, a secretary and a treasurer. They are elected at the annual meeting of the general assembly and hold office for two years. They are eligible for re-election (NWAC, 1985: 4-5). Hence, 29 persons are the heart of the Aboriginal women's network in Canada.

TABLE 9.2   THE NATIVE WOMEN'S ASSOCIATION OF CANADA **(1974)**

Provincial and territorial member associations (PTMAs)[*]	Year of establishment
British Columbia Native Women's Society	1969
Alberta Native Women's Association	1967
Saskatchewan Native Women's Association (Aboriginal Women's Council of Saskatchewan)	1971
Ontario Native Women's Association	1972
Québec Native Women's Association	1973
Nova Scotia Native Women's Association	1973
Yukon Indian Women's Association	1974
Native Women's Association of N.W.T.	1974
Sheshatshui Native Women's Group of Labrador	1980
New Brunswick Native Indian Women's Council	1973
Aboriginal Women's Association of P.E.I.	1974
The Aboriginal Women of Manitoba (The Indigenous Women's Collective of Manitoba)	1970

[*] Newfoundland has no provincial Aboriginal women's organization.

Source: NWAC, 1985: 4-5; NWAC, 1988.

The National Committee on Indian Rights for Indian Women was established in 1972. It started off as an Alberta non-status Indian women's group in 1971. The National Committee represented both status and non-status Indian women who were committed to combatting the sex-discriminatory status regulations in the *Indian Act*.[12] The organization had provincial and territorial member associations in Québec, the Northwest and Yukon Territories, British Columbia and Alberta. As a matter of fact, Lavell and Bedard were defended before the Supreme Court in 1973 by the Native Council of Canada on behalf of the National Committee on Indian Rights for Indian Women, which was unable to mount the defense itself because it was not formally incorporated until 1974 (Canadian Association in Support of Native Peoples (CASNP), 1978). Furthermore, several feminist groups throughout Canada intervened on behalf of both women (Kerr, 1975; Sanders, 1975; Weaver, 1978).

Despite the fact that the Aboriginal women's movement in Canada manifested itself initially in two separate organizations, informants from both the Native Women's Association of Canada and the National Committee on Indian Rights for Indian Women were unanimous in their statements that without the sex-discriminatory status regulations in the *Indian Act* no separate Aboriginal women's organizations in Canada ever would have existed. Despite their divisiveness on the status issue, they claimed that the patriarchal bias of the *Indian Act* had created vested interests for male Indians and that, irrespective of the legal status of Indian women, they all felt the consequences (Kerr, 1975). Furthermore, it was agreed by female informants that the *Lavell* and *Bedard* cases started Aboriginal women across Canada moving politically. Again, the impact of the women's movement should not be ignored since it stimulated the federal government to pay more attention to women's issues in general.

Although the Native Women's Association of Canada and the National Committee on Indian Rights for Indian Women were considered distinct organizations, the division was not clear-cut at all. The separateness of these organizations, although initially necessary, became more and more a political strategy. This way, the Native Women's Association was able to hold the grass roots together (controversial issues were left to the National Committee on Indian Rights for Indian Women) and tried not to offend the National Indian Brotherhood. Mary Two-Axe Early, who was a prominent member of the Steering Committee of the Native Women's Association of Canada, was also one of the founding members of the National Committee on Indian Rights for Indian Women. Women who held executive positions in the Native Women's Association of Canada appeared to be members of provincial and territorial member associations of both the Association and the National Committee. When the Québec Native Women's Association was established in 1973, members of Indian Rights for Indian Women in that province were voted on to the Board of Directors of the organization (CASNP, 1978). It appeared that women who were actively involved in one or both Aboriginal women's organizations were also involved in other Aboriginal organizations, whether political or nonpolitical, and often had careers that facilitated working with or for Aboriginal people (for example, as teachers, nurses and DIAND employees). To women who were professionally or politically involved in Aboriginal peoples' concerns, their Aboriginal identity became a professional identity as well (Secretary of State [SOS], 1975).

There are several striking differences between national Aboriginal women's organizations and male-dominated Aboriginal organizations. First, the Native Women's Association of Canada and the National Committee on Indian Rights for Indian Women base their membership on self-identifying criteria. Any person of Aboriginal ancestry is included in the membership. The Native Council of Canada and the National Indian Brotherhood, however, base their membership on legal criteria. Furthermore, women's organizations deal specifically with Aboriginal women's issues, and predominantly with Indian women's griefs and goals. The Native Council of Canada and the National Indian Brotherhood politically represent all Aboriginal persons (except the Inuit) but their political agendas are nevertheless male-dominated. This is reflected in their leadership and their decision-making processes as well. And, lastly, the executives of women's organizations do not receive salaries. They do their job on a voluntary basis. Male-dominated organizations' executives receive salaries. For them, political leadership is tied to employment and career-making.

NEGOTIATING INDIAN WOMEN'S RIGHTS DURING THE 1970s

Notwithstanding the fact that the Native Women's Association of Canada's political mandate did not provide for preoccupation with the issue of sex discrimination in the *Indian Act*, right after its formal establishment in October 1974, this became a most urgent and crucial issue for the organization. The upheavals caused by the *Lavell* and *Bedard* cases in 1973 had made it clear to non-status and status Indian women alike that a separate political negotiating position was necessary in order to deal adequately with the legal, political and practical problems confronting Indian women. Thus, the Native Women's Association adopted the National Committee's motto: Indian rights for Indian women. It appeared that both the National Indian Brotherhood and the Native Council for Canada operated in a western, male-dominated political structure and that despite the two groups' different attitudes toward the issue of sex discrimination against Indian women, women had difficulty in seeking leadership positions in either one of these organizations (Green, 1983; Kerr, 1975; Silman, 1987). The higher the organizational level of the National Indian Brotherhood and the Native Council of Canada, the less women were found in political office (Bonney, 1976). Even when Indian women presented their political views separately from male-dominated Aboriginal organizations, they had to take into consideration male views.[13]

The Native Women's Association of Canada's agenda included all issues of interest to its female constituency, but its general theme was that Indian leadership which accepted the *Indian Act* status notions was actively denying the rights and cultural heritages of Indian people. However, since it knew that the *Indian Act* had become a significant frame of reference for many Indian people, it tried to pursue a section 12(1)b amendment rather than promoting a repeal of the whole act (Aggamaway, 1983; CASNP, 1978). In order to reach its goals, it lobbied both the National Indian Brotherhood and the Native Council of Canada, as well as the federal government.

In 1975, the Joint Cabinet-National Indian Brotherhood Committee started working on an *Indian Act* revision. This was in compliance with the federal government's promise, after the White Paper's withdrawal in 1970, and reconfirmed after the Supreme Court decision regarding the *Lavell* and *Bedard* cases in 1973, that nothing in the *Indian Act* would be changed without the consent of the people involved. The National Indian Brotherhood prevented both the Native Women's Association of Canada and the National Committee on Indian Rights for Indian Women from participating in the Joint Committee, and it was not prepared to discuss the issue of sex discrimination in the *Indian Act*. Instead, the National Indian Brotherhood was of the opinion that individual Indian bands should decide on this matter, and it continued to seek self-determining powers for Indian bands within the legal framework of the *Indian Act* (Cardinal, 1977; National Indian Brotherhood, 1977).

As far as the federal government was concerned, the *Lavell* and *Bedard* cases proved that litigation is a useful tool in an overall strategy for change (Eberts, 1985). Ottawa was prepared to work towards a repeal of all sex-discriminatory provisions in the *Indian Act*. However, it took the position that legal status provisions could only be altered after an agreement was reached on a total revision of the *Indian Act*. The *Indian Act* was declared exempt from the *Human Rights Act* of 1977 in order to prevent Indian women from litigating (Holmes, 1987).[14]

In 1978, the Joint Cabinet-National Indian Brotherhood Committee was dissolved since it was clear that it had not accomplished anything. However, in 1976, the federal government had established a Sub-committee of the House of Commons Standing Committee on Indian Affairs and Northern Development in order to prepare an amending formula regarding the sex-discriminatory provisions in the *Indian Act*. Both the Native Women's Association of Canada and the National Committee on Indian Rights for Indian Women were invited to make presentations to the Sub-committee (House of Commons, 1976: 15).

The president of the Native Women's Association declared that priority number one for Indian women had become changing the *Indian Act* in order for women to acquire their rightful place in Indian society. A second representative of the Association commented in her speech to the Sub-committee on Indian Women and the *Indian Act* in the following manner: "Indian Women had much respect and had decision-making powers within their own community. Perhaps it was not as evident to the anthropologist, but within our system it was there" (Respondent from field study). And furthermore, a representative of the National Committee on Indian Rights for Indian Women stated:

> The fundamental role of the Indian mother as a basic link in the cultural and lin-
> guistic continuity must not be underestimated if the preservation and growth of the
> Indian way of life in Canada is indeed a priority (Indian Rights for Indian Women,
> 1979: 14).

Both statements clearly show how the traditional Indian motherhood concept serves to justify the Indian women's claim to equal rights for Indian men and women (Krosenbrink, 1983). Both the Native Women's Association of Canada and the National Committee on Indian Rights for Indian Women were of the opinion that in future women should not lose their Indian rights upon marriage with a non-Indian, and that those who had lost these rights, including both the women and their offspring, should have them restored (*Indian Rights for Indian Women*, 1978; *The Native Perspective*, 2/7/77). When, in 1978, the Joint Cabinet-National Indian Brotherhood Committee was dissolved, the work of the Sub-committee on Indian Women and the *Indian Act* became one of the most important political avenues for Aboriginal organizations to discuss Indian rights.

There are several reasons why, since the mid-1970s, the federal government was prepared to change the sex-discriminatory provisions in the *Indian Act*. First, there were substantial effects of the *Lavell* and *Bedard* cases and pressure from feminist groups. Furthermore, Canada had ratified both the *International Covenant on Civil and Political Rights* and the *Helsinki Human Rights Act* in 1976. The federal government feared that the *Indian Act*'s declared supersession of laws governing the majority in Canada might be overruled (Two-Axe Early *et al.*, 1981: 37). Also, Canada's internationally respected reputation was endangered by political action from another Indian woman.

Because there were no legal resources left for Indian women to combat the *Indian Act*, the UN Human Rights Committee in Geneva accepted the complaint from Sandra Lovelace. She was a Maliseet woman from the Tobique reserve in New Brunswick who had lost her status upon marriage with a White man. When she separated from her husband, she returned with her child to the reserve. There, she was informed by the band council that she was not entitled to Indian rights anymore and could therefore not reside on the reserve. Lovelace was encouraged by status women from the Tobique reserve to take her complaint to the United Nations, since they found her case to be a useful strategy in pressuring the Canadian government to deal with Indian women's issues (Silman, 1987).[15] Due to the international embarrassment inflicted upon the federal government by Sandra Lovelace, it promised the UN Human Rights Committee to offer the necessary information on this case and to seek an *Indian Act* amendment in due course.

During the 1970s, the Native Women's Association of Canada and the National Committee on Indian Rights for Indian Women manifested themselves as separate Aboriginal women's organizations. Active involvement from their constituencies grew, including the number of provincial and territorial member associations. Their existence proved that something was wrong at the level of band politics, as well as with national Aboriginal organizations which claimed to represent the interests of both Aboriginal men and women. Aboriginal women's organizations gave women the opportunity to develop political leadership roles from which they were otherwise excluded. As Gottfriedson argues:

> Some men do reject the idea of women taking leadership roles but we feel that's our responsibility.... We tell our men we want to be involved in all these negotiations [with the federal government] that are taking place since we are the ones who are affected by any policy changes in the future (Secretary of State, 1975: 19).

In particular the Native Women's Association of Canada proved to be an adequate support base on which to develop Aboriginal women's self-confidence, and it reflected a trend towards growing politicization of Aboriginal women's issues. During the 1970s, it became obvious that Indian identity was a negotiable issue. What constituted Indianness was politically negotiated and legally determined through *Indian Act* regulations. It appears that the Native Women's Association of Canada and, particularly, the National Indian Brotherhood differed significantly in their interpretations of Indian identity.

The Native Women's Association of Canada's relationship with the male-dominated National Indian Brotherhood was tense during the 1970s. The National Indian Brotherhood accused the Native Women's Association of Canada of being made up of a group of feminists who were merely interested in women's rights instead of Indian rights. This conflict became obvious during the Native Women's Walk in Ottawa in July 1979. What was initially a local Tobique Indian women's protest against the bad housing situation on the reserve grew into a national Indian women's campaign. Indian women demanded abolishment of section 12(1)b of the *Indian Act*—including reinstatement of the non-status Indian women and their children—and more funding for the Native Women's Association of Canada in order to establish a national political office in Ottawa (Kaye, 1981; Silman, 1987). The National Indian Brotherhood did not support the Native Women's Walk because it did not want any changes in the *Indian Act* until the existence of Indian and Aboriginal rights was fully recognized by the federal government and legal guarantees were given that they would remain, even when the entire *Indian Act* was repealed (Silman, 1987). Noel Starblanket, president of the National Indian Brotherhood at that time, was prepared to make a move in the direction of Aboriginal women's political aspirations, but he was soon replaced by another leader (*Kanai News*, 1/9/79; Starblanket, 1979).

The National Committee on Indian Rights for Indian Women was even more criticized by the National Indian Brotherhood for its lobbying activities in order to seek changes in the *Indian Act*. The Native Council of Canada had a working relationship with the Native Women's Association of Canada, and an even closer one with the National Committee on Indian Rights for Indian Women. The two Aboriginal women's organizations wanted non-status Indian persons to have legal status according to the *Indian Act*. The National Indian Brotherhood represented only the interest of status Indians and appeared not to recognize non-status persons' aspirations, in particular those of women. The Native Women's Association of Canada's position was unique because it wanted ultimately to get rid of the *Indian Act* status regulations, since those regulations defined Aboriginal identity according to narrow legal criteria. However, since it appeared unlikely even in the minds of the Indian people themselves that the *Indian Act* system would ever disappear, the organization pleaded for sexual equality within the *Indian Act* system.

The Native Women's Walk and the *Lovelace* case of 1977 urged the federal government to remove the sex-discriminatory provisions in the *Indian Act*. Ottawa began to operate a political strategy of blaming the National Indian Brotherhood for not having been able to move towards an *Indian Act* amendment earlier. However, in December 1979, the federal government fell. It seemed that Aboriginal women had to start lobbying for Indian women's rights all over again.

WHAT ABOUT MÉTIS AND INUIT WOMEN'S RIGHTS?

Although the Native Women's Association of Canada started off as a national Aboriginal women's organization, the Indian women's rights issue during the 1970s proved that the organization was primarily a status and non-status Indian women's organization. Since 1975, Inuit women had been working towards the establishment of a separate Inuit women's organization, which was to become the seventh associate member of the Federation of the Inuit Tapirisat of Canada a few weeks after the first First Ministers' Conference on Aboriginal Constitutional Matters, in March 1983. Inuit women's problems differed greatly from those of Métis and Indian women, and the Native Women's Association of Canada could barely do justice to their concerns and goals. The Inuit Women's Association and Native Women's Association of Canada today continue to have a close working relationship and to support one another politically (INAC, 1974; IWA, 1985; Krosenbrink, 1987). Inuit women have never been excluded from membership in Inuit councils, or from executive positions in Inuit organizations (Freeman, 1984;

McElroy, 1976). Issues that Inuit women are particularly concerned about are recognized community issues, such as jobs, education and child care. Hence, within Inuit politics there appears to be an integration of women's issues with community issues. On the other hand, women's issues on reserves are not integrated with general community issues. Again, the impact of the *Indian Act* on the socio-political and legal positions of status Indian women is of crucial importance.

Métis women also appeared to be integrated into provincial Métis organizations. There is no national Métis women's organization, and only in Manitoba is there a separate provincial organization. Métis women feel they are politically represented by Métis organizations rather than by the Native Women's Association of Canada. However, they strongly supported Native Women's Association of Canada's actions undertaken to change Indian women's lot (Women of the Métis Nation, 1986). Despite the fact that the Native Women's Association is primarily an Indian women's organization, its political achievements have an impact on the position of all Aboriginal women in Canada.

THE CONSTITUTIONAL PRELUDE AND THE STRUGGLE FOR INDIAN WOMEN'S RIGHTS IN THE EARLY 1980s

Since the late 1970s, there have been two political avenues in Canada open to the Native Women's Association of Canada to discuss Indian women's rights: first, the Constitution repatriation process, which started in 1978; second, the process of revision of Indian women's rights in the *Indian Act*, since 1976. Although these processes are separate from one another, they tended to influence one another strongly. Parliament wanted the sex-discriminatory sections of the *Indian Act* removed before a Canadian charter of human rights, as an element of the Constitution, came into force. The Department of Indian and Northern Affairs commented:

> While the existing membership system may have been in keeping with the mores of the time in which it [the *Indian Act*] was established, it is no longer acceptable in a time which supports equal rights and treatment for everyone, regardless of sex or marital status (INAC, 1982).

When the Liberal government took over political leadership in the spring of 1980, it declared its intent to pursue an *Indian Act* amendment in order to restore Indian women's rights. The issue of sexual equality for Indian women had been intensified since the 1970s and could not be ignored anymore (Romanov, 1985; Sanders, 1985). The sub-committee on Indian women and the *Indian Act* resumed its work in preparing an *Indian Act* amendment and released its report in 1982.

The *Lovelace* Case and the "Option Clause"

While the legislative and the constitutional processes in which equality rights for all women—including those of Aboriginal women—were continuing, the federal government was expecting the UN Human Rights Committee's decision on the *Lovelace* case. It anticipated this decision by considering a moratorium on the sex-discriminatory sections of the *Indian Act* in July 1980 (INAC Communique, 18/7/81). International human rights instruments are not legally binding since they have no sanctioning powers. However, they act as a strong moral imperative, particularly on relatively young democratic nation(s)-states.

The federal government adopted an "option clause" with regard to the *Indian Act*. In the Option Clause it was stated that Indian bands could request the Minister of DIAND to suspend sections 12(1)b and 12(1)aIV, the latter being the double-mother rule.[16] The Option Clause came into force when the United Nations communicated its decision on the *Lovelace* case in 1981. However, the clause was only an interim measure in order to bridge the period until the *Indian Act* was amended. Furthermore, it had no retroactive effect, and the initiative for a suspension of the sex-discriminatory provisions of the *Indian Act* was left entirely with the band councils. In view of the problems women had with band councils, described earlier, the Native Women's Association of Canada did not expect that the Option Clause would likely be used by a majority of Indian band councils, let alone all.[17] Thus, the legal status issue became more and more a political issue at the local community level, and Indian women appeared to be subject to punitive actions by the chiefs and band councillors (Silman, 1987; Two-Axe Early, *et al.*, 1981).

In July 1981, the UN Human Rights Committee informed the Canadian government that it had been found in breach of article 27 of the *International Covenant on Civil and Political Rights* for denying Lovelace Indian band membership and the right to return to the reserve. The committee's decision only dealt with the right of Indian people to determine their own membership, which means Aboriginal self-government, and not with sex discrimination against Indian women in the *Indian Act*, since Lovelace had already lost her Indian status before Canada ratified the Covenant in 1976 (Burrell and Sanders, 1984; INAC Communique, 8/9/82; Kallen, 1982).

For more than a century, the responsibility for initiating sex discrimination against Indian women had been largely the federal government's; however, since the 1970s, Indian women's problems resulting from that discrimination occurred largely on the local level, as well as on the national level of Indian politics. Notwithstanding the existence of mechanisms by means of which they could avoid implementing sex-discriminatory regulations, the majority of Indian bands chose otherwise. And in the political arena, Indian women were seriously hampered in expressing their views through the channels of male-dominated Aboriginal organizations. Thus, prevailing male chauvinist attitudes of Indians themselves became the most urgent problem for Indian women to solve, since legal barriers to women's equality were expected to disappear soon.

The Report of the Sub-committee on Indian Women and the *Indian Act*

In September 1982, the following recommendations with respect to an *Indian Act* amendment were made by the Sub-committee on Indian Women and the *Indian Act*:

1. Children with at least one parent with Indian status, whether born illegitimate or legitimate, were to receive status and band membership (cf. section 11(1)e of the *Indian Act*, 1970).

2. Non-Indian spouses were not to receive status in the future and therefore section 11(1)f should be removed from the *Indian Act*. However, persons who had gained status through this section would not lose it. The Native Women's Association did not agree with this recommendation. It argued that the Sub-committee wanted to continue using legal criteria to determine Indian identity instead of using the *Indian Act* to restore Indian socio-cultural self-identifying criteria.

3. Band councils should be given the right to decide band membership—in particular, with reference to non-Indian spouses—and should receive extensional powers to determine civil and political rights on reserves. How this should be operationalized was not discussed, since this was considered an Aboriginal self-government issue to be discussed in the constitutional process on Aboriginal matters.

4. Section 12 of the *Indian Act* was to be removed. Persons who had lost their status under section 12(1)b or 12(1)aIV (double-mother rule) should have their Indian rights, status and band membership restored, including first generations.

5. Section 14, regarding the involuntary transfer of band membership, should be repealed. Spouses should be allowed to choose band membership in either one of the bands, and their offspring should be able to choose band membership upon majority.

6. Section 109(1), regarding involuntary enfranchisement of wives and minor children should be removed. Persons who had lost their status under this section should be able to regain their status and band membership. Furthermore, sections 109(2) and (3) should be repealed (House of Commons, 1982a, Issue 2: 44-57 and 1982b: 34-40).

At the time when the Sub-committee released its report, the Department of Indian and Northern Affairs had estimated that some 60 000 persons were eligible for reinstatement. This number included over 55 000 "12(1)b women" and their children (INAC, 1982: 18). This number proved to be grossly underestimated once reinstatement legislation was established in 1985.

Before the proposed *Indian Act* changes could be discussed and approved in Parliament, they were overshadowed by the constitutional process on Aboriginal matters which began right after the Constitutional repatriation (April 17, 1982).

Since all legal barriers to women's equality with men in general, and to Indian women's equality with Indian men in particular, were expected to disappear soon with the establishment of a new *Constitution Act*, the Native Women's Association of Canada realized that it should focus on the practice of gender inequality at the community level. As a consequence, it had to redirect its political strategies towards Indian people themselves in order to seek its main goal: Indian rights for Indian women.

By the time that Native Women's Association of Canada was developing new strategies, it had also become the only national Aboriginal women's organization in Canada. The National Committee of Indians Rights for Indian Women stopped being a national political organization in the spring of 1981 and continued its existence the way it began, as an Alberta Indian Women's group, Indian Rights for Indian Women. It appeared that the National Committee on Indian Rights for Indian Women had serious financial problems and that its membership had gradually been amalgamated into the organizational structure of the Native Women's Association of Canada. The latter organization was increasingly accepted by both insiders and outsiders as the representative body of Aboriginal women in Canada (Richardson, 1981). The Association aimed to form a united Aboriginal women's front against the National Indian Brotherhood in the constitutional process on Aboriginal matters. Hence it sought the support of Métis and Inuit women as well. After 1981, the Native Women's Association of Canada's official political mandate became to define constitutional Aboriginal rights as relevant to women and to seek legislative changes of all sex-discriminatory regulations in the *Indian Act* (*Native Women's Association of Canada Newsletter*, 1, 2, 1981: 5).

THE CONSTITUTION REPATRIATION PROCESS[18]

In October 1978, the federal government invited the National Indian Brotherhood, the Native Council of Canada and the Inuit Tapirisat of Canada to attend a First Ministers' meeting on the Constitution. In a proposed amendment of the Constitution, *Bill C-60*, a provision ensured the recognition of Aboriginal rights.

The Aboriginal rights issue created controversy among provincial governments; the majority wanted it to be dropped from the constitutional agenda. The federal government, however, was prepared to establish constitutional guarantees to treaty rights, self-government rights, and Aboriginal peoples' political participation in the parliamentary system. Due to strong lobbying efforts of the three national Aboriginal organizations, Aboriginal rights were included in the constitutional proposal under section 34.[19] However, when no consensus could be reached among the provinces, the federal government offered a new constitutional proposal on November 5, 1981. Previous sections pertaining to equality rights of women (sections 15 and 28) and those pertaining to Aboriginal peoples (section 34) were left out in the new proposal (*Vancouver Sun*, 24/11/81). Section 28 provided for special guarantees that equality rights could not be overruled by the provinces. Section

34 pertained to the Aboriginal rights of the Indians, Inuit and Métis, although these rights were not specified. The two issues brought together a powerful lobbying force and public support. First, the Native groups began to form an alliance, since the issue of Aboriginal rights was important to all three groups. Second, other organizations, such as religious organizations, civil libertarian and women's groups, supported the principle of Aboriginal rights. Because the feminist lobby was too strong to be neglected by provincial governments, the federal government was able to operate a political strategy of "no entrenchment of Aboriginal rights, no sexual equality guarantee" in order to seek a consensus among the provinces on Aboriginal rights and to remove the obstacles to a fast repatriation of the Constitution. Hence, women's issues were used as an instrument to change the Constitution towards an inclusion of Aboriginal rights.

During the Constitution repatriation process, relations between the National Indian Brotherhood and Native Women's Association of Canada became less strained. The National Indian Brotherhood realized that, although it still considered equality rights irrelevant to the Aboriginal or Indian rights issue, it had to deal with them. The federal government intended to pursue *Indian Act* changes in this respect, with or without the consent of the National Indian Brotherhood. Hence, the organization realized that it had to come to better terms with the Native Women's Association. When, in May 1980, Native Women's Association of Canada's national office was established, the National Indian Brotherhood offered office space to the executive.

Despite the fact that their relationship had changed for the better, it remained tense. Sharing of office space lasted only for a year. It was felt that there were still no guarantees that Aboriginal women's views were fully accepted, since male leaders upheld subtle and double standards in their thinking and practices and did not lend credence to the Association's viewpoint. A remark from a National Indian Brotherhood leader in Ontario towards the President of the Ontario Native Women's Association, in 1982, illustrates Indian male leaders' general ignorance of Indian women's political griefs and goals. He declared that he only was prepared to put on the political agenda those Indian women's issues that were "not political" (Ontario Native Women's Association (ONWA), 1983: 27). This remark illustrates the ideological division between Native men and women. First of all, the unwillingness to support political issues concerning women demonstrates a sexist view of the world. Second, the division suggests that only "non-political" women's issues are worth supporting. Finally, the statement reflects a naive position that certain issues are inherently political while others are not.

Separate actions by the national office of Native Women's Association were considered necessary because enforcing changes at the band level, where men still dominated politics, was too hard to do. It was only outside the male-dominated Indian political structures that women could seek political positions (Native Women's Association of Canada, 1985b). While the National Indian Brotherhood conducted separate lobby activities, the Native Council of Canada, Inuit Tapirisat of Canada and the Native Women's Association of Canada formed the Aboriginal

Rights Coalition to conduct their lobbying activities. The three organizations in the Coalition agreed on a sexual-equality guarantee for Aboriginal women. Feminist groups, who lobbied for a restoration of section 28, were organized in the National Action Committee on the Status of Women. The Native Women's Association did not cooperate with the National Action Committee and stated that it was looking for a sexual-equality guarantee in section 34, referring to Aboriginal rights. Despite the disassociation of the Native Women's Association of Canada from the women's movement, the organization was only able to make its political claims because the women's movement had cleared the ground for the promotion of women's issues since the 1960s.

The Canadian public was increasingly prepared to support entrenchment of Aboriginal rights in the Constitution, which proved that Aboriginal organizations were doing a good job (*Globe and Mail*, 24/11/81). Politicians, on the other hand, complained that lobby groups had too much impact on political decisions. On November 23, sections 28 and 34 were drafted in the final constitutional proposal with the consent of the provincial governments. Section 34, however, became section 35, with the addition of the term "existing Aboriginal rights".[20] The new wording was not agreeable to either one of the national Aboriginal organizations. In particular, the Native Women's Association feared that the wording of section 35 of the *Constitution Act* could be interpreted as the continuation of legal discrimination against Aboriginal women. Because of a provision in the *Constitution Act* of 1982, political negotiations between Aboriginal organizations on the one hand and the federal and provincial governments on the other were to continue, but within a new framework: the constitutional process on Aboriginal matters.

WHAT DOES THE NATIVE WOMEN'S ASSOCIATION OF CANADA WANT?

Indian women, as well as Métis and Inuit women, want constitutional protection for Aboriginal women to be clear, unambiguous and adequately secured. This holds particularly for Indian women, given the political sensitivity of the issue of sex discrimination pertaining to them. As a status Indian male stated, equality rights for Aboriginal women is politically a sexy issue.

The Native Women's Association wants sexual equality for Indian women to be guaranteed. Hence, answers to the following questions must be found: what does sexual equality mean to the Native Women's Association of Canada and its constituency; and what criteria are used to measure the degree of equality? The Native Women's Association of Canada is primarily concerned with constitutional protection of Aboriginal women's rights. The Association considers law a valid instrument with which to seek changes in women's positions within their own communities. Constitutional law is considered fundamental since federal legislation and administrative procedures, as set out in the *Indian Act*, cannot be resolved before the constitutional rights of women are resolved. Sexual equality of Aboriginal women vis-à-vis Aboriginal men is not explicitly dealt with in the *Constitution Act* of 1982. As a result of the sex-discriminatory status implications of the *Indian Act*, this presents problems for Indian women. A spokesperson of the Ontario Native Women's Association declared at a conference in June 1982: "No Aboriginal Rights— No Indian Nations" (ONWA, 1983: 23). Implicit, but nevertheless clear, in her de-claration was a reference to the traditional Indian motherhood concept. Without sexual equality rights for Indian women, the primary transmitters of Indian cultures, Indian nationhood will be further endangered.

The Native Women's Association of Canada focused on seeking a sexual equal-ity guarantee in section 25 and/or section 35 of the *Constitution Act*, both sections pertaining to Aboriginal rights.[21] Furthermore, the Association argued that the term "existing Aboriginal rights" should not be so narrowly defined as to deny the rights of non-status Indian persons. As a matter of fact, their Indian rights should be restored first. Otherwise, notwithstanding sexual equality guarantees since 1982, sex discrimination would be perpetuated indirectly. Lastly, the Native Women's Association held the position that the terms "Indians" and "Aboriginal peoples" should reflect all persons who identify themselves as Aboriginal, and not just those who are recognized as legal categories (*Native Women's Association of Canada Newsletter*, 1/8/81: 3).

In the end, the *Constitution Act*, 1982, brought about some fundamental changes to the *Indian Act*, the relationship between Natives and government, and the role of both provincial and federal governments in future negotiations with Natives. Native peoples won recognition of "existing" Aboriginal rights and a provision that such rights could not be adversely affected by anything in the *Charter of Rights and Freedoms*. Subsequent changes to the *Indian Act* removed clauses that were de-fined as discriminatory toward women. This of course led to *Bill C-31* and the re-instatement of thousands of people as Indians. However, the acknowledgement of Indians as having a distinct society and having special status was denied—a recognition that was afforded to Québec in the proposed Meech Lake Accord. It was of special historical interest that Elijah Harper (an Indian MLA in Manitoba) refused to ratify the agreement and thus killed the Accord.

The issue of Aboriginal self-government is recognized as a legitimate goal, both by the Canadian government and by the public. The Native Women's Association of Canada also regards Aboriginal self-government as a political priority. However, the Association has a fundamental prerequisite; the principle of sexual equality for Aboriginal men and women must unambiguously and constitutionally stand above Aboriginal self-government. This guarantee is perceived as necessary and unless it is implemented, Indian women will still be in trouble with band coun-cils under self-government (Silman, 1987). Although Indian men and women are unanimous in their statements on the vital roles of Indian women for the perpetuation of their cultures and community life, the practice of sex discrimination by band councils proved reality to be different from ideology.

With respect to Indian self-government, band membership is of crucial importance. The Assembly of First Nations and the Native Women's Association of Canada agree that band membership should be decided by Indian bands themselves. Nevertheless, under the surface of their common argument important differences of opinions are prevalent. The Native Women's Association claims that Indian women will not accept any proposal, either by the federal government or by the Assembly of First Nations, that will continue to deny Indian women's sexual equality. Indian women do not want to wait until Indian self-government is established on reserves because they fear that some bands will not treat them fairly and will not be willing to restore the rights of Indian women. As already stated, it is primarily for this reason that Native Women's Association of Canada focused on a sexual equality guarantee within sections 25 and 35 of the *Constitution Act*. The Assembly of First Nations holds the position that sexual equality rights for Aboriginal women is not a constitutional issue. This issue should be dealt with by individual bands once self-government is operationalized. There could be two sources outside the Constitution that Indian women might appeal to in cases where self-governing bands have designed sex-discriminatory band membership codes:

1. particular constitutions of Indian bands providing for sexual equality; and
2. recourse to an Indian commission or tribunal set up to hear complaints arising out of the exercise of Indian self-governing powers.

Sexual equality provisions in Indian constitutions, however, can be easily removed, whereas the *Constitution Act* sets certain rights beyond the powers of Parliament and legislatures to override. Furthermore, Indian commissions or tribunals will not guarantee Indian women that decisions will not prejudice them. Besides, the cultural traditions of particular Indian nations may dictate discrimination (Richstone, 1983). Whether sexual inequality is authentically Indian or has historically developed due to the *Indian Act* is not important here. Nowadays, Indian women, as well as Métis and Inuit women, do not wish to be sexually discriminated against either by law or in practice.[22]

The Native Women's Association of Canada was not merely preoccupied with a constitutional amendment but with a legislative amendment as well. As long as the constitutional right of Aboriginal self-government is not entrenched and guaranteed, the *Indian Act* was to remain a regulating force. The Association realized that one cannot do away with the *Indian Act* overnight, because for several generations already many Indian persons have based their identity and existence on the *Indian Act*. As a result, many Indian bands would establish self-government, including band membership, in agreement with *Indian Act* regulations. It was necessary, therefore, to seek sexual equality guarantees both constitutionally, within the framework of Aboriginal self-government, and legislatively, within the framework of an *Indian Act* revision. The Native Women's Association aimed at eventually upgrading, by way of law, the socio-political position of Indian women in particular. Whoever or whatever was going to decide band membership in the future, Indian women did not want sex discrimination anymore.

With respect to section 37 of the *Constitution Act*, referring to the constitutional process on Aboriginal matters, the Native Women's Association of Canada insisted that provincial governments have no power to decide Aboriginal matters and that a constitutional amending formula respecting Aboriginal affairs should require the consent of the Aboriginal peoples. These positions are in agreement with those of the other four national Aboriginal organizations (i.e., Assembly of First Nations, Inuit Tapirisat of Canada, Native Council of Canada, Métis National Council). Based on its political goals, the Native Women's Association of Canada perceived itself to be in the best position to explain the importance of the required amendments for Aboriginal women in general, and for Indian women in particular, during the constitutional process on Aboriginal matters.

The Native Women's Association wanted explicit, legal, sexual equality guarantees for Aboriginal women. In view of the future development of Aboriginal self-government institutions, this was considered of vital importance. To the Native Women's Association of Canada and its constituency, sexual equality comprised a whole range of issues, such as employment, political decision-making, recognition of their women's important roles in communities, political respect by band councils, and, most importantly, the equal right to transmit status and band membership to their families. The main problem for the Association, in view of differences of opinion with, primarily, the Assembly of First Nations, was how to overcome the apparent paradox of claiming Aboriginal self-government on the one hand, while on the other hand requesting an external, legal guarantee of sexual equality pertaining to Aboriginal rights—including self-government.

CONCLUSION

Within the constitutional process on Aboriginal matters, the Native Women's Association of Canada's strategy was more directed towards Aboriginal peoples than to the provincial and federal governments. The Native Women's Association of Canada hoped that with the help of sexual equality guarantees in law, the Indian people's perceptions of women, and their attitudes towards them, might change. The Association was aware that legal sexual equality provisions for Aboriginal women would be established. The federal government was nationally, as well as internationally, held to amending sex-discriminatory regulations. Besides, the women's movement in Canada, which supported Indian women's struggles, was a strong lobbying force, and federal and provincial politicians could not afford conflicts.

Despite the Native Women's Association of Canada not being a formal partic-ipant at the First Ministers' conferences, it was able to play a role. Firstly, the women's organization strongly lobbied to have sexual equality on the constitu-tional agenda. Secondly, it participated in other official delegations, such as those of the Native Council of Canada and the Assembly of First Nations, and those of sev-eral provinces. In the end, sexual equality for Indian women has been established in the amended *Indian Act*. Sexual equality for all Aboriginal women is entrenched within the Aboriginal rights provision of the *Constitution Act* of 1982. Lastly, the Native Women's Association of Canada managed to improve relations with the Assembly of First Nations.

A last significant question posed was: the has Native Women's Association of Canada's strategy been successful in altering gender relations at the Indian band level? The number of protests from bands against the imposition of band mem-bers may be conceived as an indication of unchanged attitudes towards women, de-spite significant legal changes. However, they may just as well not be so, since one can never be sure whether these protests against government's interference in Indian affairs are concerned with self-government issues, rather than being founded on sex discrimination. The issues of reinstatement and band control of its mem-bership within the new *Indian Act*, *Bill C-31*, remain controversial because of the great impact of the old *Indian Act* on the Indian people's self-identity and on commu-nity attitudes toward the sex-discriminatory status regulations.

Discussions on Indian self-government will continue. To bands generally, the old as well as the new *Indian Act* is perceived as a government exercise in re-taining power and setting the parameters of Indian self-control. From this view-point, bands simply do not care that in the old *Indian Act* women were the victims and that the new *Indian Act* is more or less gender-neutral. The issue of sexual equality is not relevant to the issue of true Indian self-government. The inter-woveness of the Indian self-government and sexual equality issues, due to *Bill C-31*, makes the Indian women's position difficult. Nevertheless, if the new *Indian Act* eventually results in changing attitudes towards women at the band level, the Native Women's Association of Canada's primary political goal will have been achieved.

The Native women's groups support, in principle, the concept of inherent self-government. However, they oppose the position that the concept must be en-trenched unconditionally, without a guarantee of gender equality rights. Women's groups feel that the past opposition of males to women's issues does not bode well for them. They have tried, unsuccessfully, to be granted the right to attend Native-government meetings over various issues. As a result, women feel their concerns may not be addressed even if self-government is given to Natives.

NOTES

1. The first international women's movement, between 1860 and 1920, was directed to seeking legal changes, such as women's franchise. Since legislation in most states ensured sexual equality as of the 1960s, the second international women's movement focused on the contradiction between ideology and practice.

2. Since 1937, Indian Homemaker clubs have existed on reserves, on the instigation of the Indian Affairs branch. Gradually, these local clubs were supplanted by other local women's groups whose membership was open to all Aboriginal women and which were community- as well as urban-based. Moreover, due to the impact of the women's movement, Aboriginal women started to decide the purpose of their groups for themselves (Jamieson, 1979).

3. Shortly after the band council had informed her of her eviction, in 1967, her daughter married a status Indian man, and the band council decided that the couple was to have the house that was willed to Mary Two-Axe Early. Although she was not entitled to live on the reserve, it was approved that she lived with her daughter and son-in-law.

4. This Indian women's group was to become a local chapter of the National Committee on Indian Rights for Indian Women in 1972.

5. During a survey that was undertaken by the Ontario Native Women's Association, it appeared that 68 percent of Aboriginal women who lived in urban areas were involved in Aboriginal organizations, whereas 42 percent of the on-reserve status (Indian) respondents were involved (ONWA, 1980: 24-34).

6. During a survey conducted by the Québec Native Women's Association in 1977, it was found that 89 percent of the 435 male and female Indian respondents had only limited knowledge of the *Indian Act*, whereas in Ontario, three years later, 83 percent of the 1101 respondents were reported as not being knowledgeable on the *Indian Act* and its implications (CASNP, 1978: 22-23; ONWA, 1980: 7-13).

7. In particular the Indian Association of Alberta was against Lavell and Bedard and lobbied within the National Indian Brotherhood to gain a majority vote in favour of a Supreme Court case to prevent an *Indian Act* revision by the federal government (Cardinal, 1979: 44-45).

8. In 1872, however, the Grand Council of Ontario and Québec Indians had protested against the sex discrimination of Indian women that was introduced in 1869 (Jamieson, 1978: 30).

9. Lavell was one of the founding members of the Ontario Native Women's Association (ONWA) in 1972.

10. Sanders (1975b: 657) seriously doubts whether the *Indian Act* really codified any particular Indian system of social and political organization. He argues that the *Indian Act* should be perceived as a reflection of the western Victorian type of social organization.

11. According to Roosens (1986: 115) Aboriginal women's arts and crafts groups should be taken seriously since activities that are performed guarantee continuity with cultural histories.

12. In 1972, the Secretary of State created the Aboriginal Women's Programme in order to provide funding for both the Native Women's Association of Canada and the National Committee on Indian Rights for Indian Women. In contrast to the male-dominated national Aboriginal organizations, the Aboriginal women's organizations' executive did not receive salaries as part of the core funding programme. Since 1978, both organizations have received core funding (SOS, 1983: 1-4; Cantryn, n.d.).

13. In 1975, Mary Two-Axe Early and several other non-status Indian women were delegates to the UN Women's Conference in Mexico City. They addressed the issue of sex discrimination against Indian women in Canada, both legally and in practice (particularly, at the band level). The Indian band administrators appeared not to appreciate the Indian women's critical views and non-status Indian women who were still residing on the reserve were informed that they would be evicted in accordance with the *Indian Act* regulations. Mary Two-Axe Early was allowed to remain on the reserve on the condition that she refrained from political activities in the future, which she has never done.

14. Since 1975, equality between men and women has been brought into various Canadian Acts and consolidated in the *Human Rights Act* of 1977.

15. The unfair treatment of the band council, which prejudiced women in the distribution of available houses on the reserve, started women of Tobique moving in 1977. For several months they occupied the band office and requested houses for status and non-status Indian women and their children (Silman, 1987: 11, 93).

16. The Minister could do so, without the approval of the House of Commons and the Senate, on the grounds of section 4(2) of the *Indian Act* of 1970.

17. Numbers and percentages of bands which used the Option Clause vary according to the time frames and sources used. By November 1984, the last time that the Clause was used, some 19 percent of the bands had opted out of section 12(1)b, whereas some 53 percent had opted out of section 12(1)aIV (Holmes, 1987: 6, note 6; *Native Women's Association of Canada Newsletter*, 1/3/82: 18; ONWA, 1982: 35; ONWA 1984).

18. Constitutional negotiations started somewhere in the mid-1970s at a time when Québec separatism and western economic alienation strained Canadian unity,

causing the Trudeau government to realize that a Constitution renewal was imperative (Romanov, 1985: 73).

19. Lobbying efforts included international as well as national actions, such as the Constitution Express; the Indian delegations' visit to the UN office in New York; and the submission of cases to the British Court of Appeals (Sanders, 1985: 178).

20. The inclusion of the term "existing" was the initiative of the Alberta government. However, nobody knew (or still knows) what "existing" meant (Hawkes, 1985: 7).

21. According to Rhode (1986: 155): "Equal rights are, at this historical moment, too restricted in legal content and too divisive in political connotations to serve as an adequate feminist agenda." In contrast to feminist groups in Canada, the Aboriginal women's movement remained preoccupied with legal changes. Feminist groups argue that law is only of limited value, since the consequences of gender difference are not incorporated (p. 157). Note, however, that non-Aboriginal Canadian women have their equality rights already guaranteed, whereas Aboriginal women are still seeking an explicit legal guarantee.

22. One status Indian female expressed doubts whether law can change people's attitudes when she said: "How are you going to legislate attitudes, straighten bands out?"

CONFLICT IN SOCIETY

OKA—MICROCOSM OF INDIAN/WHITE RELATIONS*

For 78 days, the Oka standoff kept Canadians wondering how this armed conflict would be resolved. The events of Oka remain fresh in our minds as we remember the barricades, the tanks, the low-flying aircraft and the nightly interviews with municipal, provincial or federal officials, recounting the events of the day. (See Chronology 1 for an account of the events.) After watching these events, we were convinced that this conflict would produce substantive changes in our treatment of Native people.

Before recounting and explaining these events, it might prove instructive to reflect upon a Native-White conflict which occurred over a decade ago in Alberta. The reader will find the Alberta conflict difficult to remember, vague and unclear in detail. Yet the events which took place ten years ago in Alberta evoked many of the same responses as the Oka dispute. Only now they are faded memories, and the basis of the Cardston blockade remains largely unknown. As we recount the events in Alberta, you will see the similarity of the issues, actors and "final resolution" with those in Oka. While we may have thought the events of the Cardston

---

*   Much of this chapter is from K. Hughes, *The Summer of 1990*, Fifth Report of the Standing Committee on Aboriginal Affairs, 1991. Permission granted from the Government of Canada.

blockade had taught us something, the conflicts which emerged in Oka showed we had learned little.

THE CARDSTON BLOCKADE

In early 1980, young Blood tribe members from Cardston, Alberta, organized a "run" to Ottawa with a sacred bundle containing land-claim documents and soil from the Blood Reserve. They had the full support of the Blood leadership and Elders in carrying out this public event. They carried the sacred bundle from Blackfoot Crossing, the site of the signing of Treaty No. 7, to Ottawa. The run was completed and the documents delivered to the representatives of the federal government on the steps of the Parliament Buildings in Ottawa. The runners demanded a governmental response to the concerns within two and one-half months, not an unreasonable time for the bureaucracy to respond. The federal government did not respond within this period of time, which lapsed on July 19, 1980, during the celebration of Indian Days on the Blood Reserve.

On Sunday night, July 20, 1980, a meeting of the runners was called. The young men attending this meeting became a "council," and by consensus it was agreed that they would blockade the site of land in Cardston which they called the "Little Land Claim." The land in dispute was expropriated by the federal government in 1928 and turned over to the Canadian Pacific Railway for the erection of elevators and other railroad business and commerce. The council decided to deny access to the business establishments in this area. Their purpose was to publicize their claims and force the federal government to deal with their concerns. The blockade began in the early hours of Monday, July 21, 1980, when the police and the Cardston merchants and citizens awoke to find a teepee erected on the access road to the grain elevators and the bulk gas and oil stations adjacent to the Blood Reserve.

The Royal Canadian Mounted Police were alerted and advised by Dennis First Rider that the intent of the blockade was to secure a meeting with the federal Minister of Indian Affairs to discuss their land claims and concerns. The Indians repeatedly advised the RCMP that this was to be a nonviolent demonstration and there were to be no alcohol or weapons on the site.

Negotiations were carried on throughout the day. By the end of the day, the police instructed the protestors to take their blockade down. The Natives did not comply with these instructions, and 17 members of the Blood Tribe were arrested. They were arrested under the appropriate section of the *Criminal Code* for blocking the highway. Barricades were removed by the police and Native vehicles towed away. All prisoners were released later in the day on their own recognizance. Although their release was based upon their agreement not to return to the site of the blockade, almost all of the Natives returned to the site in defiance of this prohibition.

On the morning of July 23, 1980, two large earthmoving machines were brought in by Natives to block access to the business establishments. These vehicles were the property of the Blood Tribe. Once again, negotiations commenced both with the Natives and the Department of Indian Affairs through the Royal Canadian Mounted Police. The RCMP had been trying to get the Natives to abandon their blockade tactics and, at the same time, were trying to keep the growing resentment of the merchants and citizens of Cardston in check. However, they were not intermediaries in the negotiation process. The regional representative of the Department of Indian Affairs was brought to the site and agreed to contact his Ottawa superiors. The RCMP agreed to wait for Ottawa's response before taking any further action.

A day later, the Minister of Indian Affairs contacted the Blood tribe blockaders and agreed to both a meeting and to the topics of discussion. Native protestors felt the response was not detailed enough, nor did it specifically address some of the issues they wanted to discuss with the Minister. At this time, the special tactical unit of the Royal Canadian Mounted Police from Calgary had been alerted and sent to Cardston.

The police officer who had been sent to the scene by the Commanding Officer of the K Division to take charge of the situation was instructed to take the barricades down and, thus, effectively break the blockade. Native protestors refused to leave the site, and there were numerous arrests of Natives as a result of this physical confrontation on July 26, 1980. It was at this time that the scene became ugly and potentially dangerous for all participants in the conflict.

A third confrontation occurred in the early hours of Sunday, July 27, 1980, when the Indians once again left the Cardston jail and returned to the blockade site. This time there was a more violent physical confrontation between Indians and police. The use of dogs to disperse the crowd resulted in Native people leaving the scene. However, this use of force coloured the Natives' perception of the police and changed their relationship with the RCMP for many years following. Native-police relations continue to be strained on the reserve. Neither the Natives nor the community of Cardston have resolved their differences, and neither seems to have forgiven the other for the role they played during the conflict.

The incident at Cardston had a "peaceful resolution." Yet, over a decade later, the land claims of the Blood Indians are not resolved, nor has there been an attempt to deal with the underlying issues. It should not come as a surprise, then, that over ten years later, when a similar event occurred at Oka, Native people from all over Canada empathised with the Mohawks and took a more militant position. The events of Oka also reveal the strategy taken time and time again by the federal government in dealing with Native people—stall, threaten, stall, coerce, stall.... The Oka and Cardston incidents contain all the essential ingredients shared by a society with a colour system. Natives had stepped out of their assigned position in society. Clearly, from the dominant group's perspective, they had to be placed back in their subservient position without disrupting the status quo.

We now turn to a full account of the Oka events to document the process which occurred as well as to provide the reader an understanding of some of the events.

CHRONOLOGY 1 HISTORY OF THE KANESATAKE LAND CLAIM AND THE EVENTS OF 1991

1717
Grant of one half league by three leagues of land at Lac-des-Deux-Montagnes to the Seminary of St. Sulpice by the French Crown, followed by the move of several converted Mohawk families from Sault-aux-Recollets in Montréal.

This created the misconception that the Mohawk settlement at Kanesatake was established at that time. The main reason for relocating the converted Mohawks to this area was the fact that a Mohawk settlement had long been in existence in Kanesatake.

1733
Second concession of land from the French Crown to the Seminary of St. Sulpice.

1763
Census taken at Kanesatake:
307 Mohawks   253 Algonquins
220 Nipissing   76 Other Indians
169 Canadians.

1851
Land set aside at Doncaster for the Iroquois at Kanesatake and Kahnawake for the purpose of removing them from the shores of the main waterways.

1881
Several families of Mohawks moved to Muskoka, north of Toronto, but the majority remain at Kanesatake.

1912
Privy Council rejects appeal of Angus Corinthe, a Mohawk who sued the Seminary of St. Sulpice over land title. This decision does not preclude possible resolution of the "Oka question" through other means.

1945
Crown purchases land then occupied by the Mohawks from the Seminary of St. Sulpice. It is this transaction, among others, that creates the "checkerboard" problem.

1947
Common lands expropriated by private bill in the Québec National Assembly and transferred to the Municipality of Oka—questionable transaction.

1959
Municipality to create golf course on land claims by the Mohawks—construction begins—individual protest action taken, but to no avail.

1961
Ottawa—Emile Colas, lawyer for the Mohawks, spoke to Parliamentary Committee:

> In order that the white man may have more opportunities for recreation, what was once reserved for Indian use and profit is now reserved for golf.

1970

Remnants of pottery and other artifacts found on the beach of Oka park prove that the area was occupied well before 1717 when the King of France made the original grant to the Seminary.

1972 & 1977

Land claim submitted to Crown by Band Council. The Order had sold land to private interests piece by piece, and the Mohawks charge that the land had been granted to the Sulpicians "in trust" for them. Claim is first rejected and then shelved. The reasons given were that the proposals did not meet the claims policies as established by the Crown and that the Mohawks had no legal claim, since their rights had been rejected by the highest courts.

1973

Federal government establishes open door to official Indian land claims.

1974

National Geographic publishes a book entitled *Indians of the Americas*, which includes a map of Aboriginal communities. Aboriginal presence, traced to 1000 BC-1000 AD, recorded at Kanesatake (National Geographic Society-Smithsonian Institution, US; National Archives, Ottawa).

1986

Crown proposes interim measures known as Land Unification proposal. The Band Council, without community consultation, accepts the proposal and commissions a land needs study from the urban planning firm Pluritec Environment (jointly with DIA and, again, without consultation).

1989

Municipality of Oka and Le Club de golf d'Oka Inc. announce plans to expand existing golf course.

April 1

Mohawks hold a protest march through the village of Oka to demonstrate their opposition to the proposed golf course expansion.

August 1

Second demonstration held by the Mohawks at Oka golf club, where a press conference and ceremonial tree cutting were to launch the start of the expansion project. Also in attendance were members of the newly formed Environment Protection group from the village of Oka, as well as an inspector for the provincial Environment Ministry (armed with an injunction which he would serve only if the tree cutting took place). At this same time, Band

Council representatives were in Montréal preparing injunction proceedings. The press conference proceeded but the symbolic tree cutting was stopped.

August 3

The public attention and support for the Mohawk position which resulted from these activities forced the federal government to call a meeting in Dorval. In attendance were representatives of the federal, provincial and municipal governments, as well as the Mohawks, who stated that their participation in any future discussions would be conditional on the imposition of a full moratorium on development in the Kanesatake area.

The first strong opposition to this position came from Frank Vieni, Québec Assistant Deputy Minister of Indian Affairs. After much discussion, Oka village mayor Jean Ouellette agreed to a 15-day moratorium on the golf expansion and Oka parish mayor Yvan Patry also agreed to a limited moratorium on other development.

August 8

The first of a series of initial discussion sessions was held. These meetings were deemed necessary to determine the feasibility of future negotiations, given the history of political friction between the Mohawks and the municipalities. Discussion revolved mainly around the identification of existing problems and possible solutions.

The Mohawks were told by Yves Desilets, the federal representative, that the land claim would not be discussed. His objective through this process was to unify lands for Kanesatake (according to Pluritec recommendations) and create a reserve as defined in the *Indian Act*.

The Mohawk representatives responded that the lands at Kanesatake should be unified, but that establishment of a reserve under the act was not the only solution and that other options must be examined.

The golf course moratorium was subsequently extended; however a condition was attached. The moratorium would remain in effect only for as long as discussions proceeded in a positive direction.

September

In the middle of September the Mohawk representatives decided to ask for a break in order to conduct public consultation workshops in the community. The objectives of the workshops were to fully inform the community on the unification proposal and to ask for a clear negotiations mandate.

The federal government then tabled a proposed framework for negotiations. This document was imposed on the Mohawk representatives and was to form the basis for consultation, along with the land needs report from Pluritec.

Since no commitments had been made by any side at the table, the Mohawk representatives agreed. They did, however, clearly indicate that the community would ultimately determine the direction in which negotiations would proceed and that there was no guarantee that the proposed framework would be accepted.

Attendance at consultation workshops was poor for various reasons. Only 203 out of approximately 650 eligible members participated. Those who did attend unanimously rejected the framework proposal and the Pluritec report. During the course of the consultation process, a position paper was drafted (based on community input), which more accurately outlined the community's desires.

1990
January

The Grand Chief and a councillor were deposed and replaced.This sparked a bitter political dispute which ultimately resulted in an entirely new council being installed.

March 6

New Band Council meets with other parties in negotiations. Prior to this meeting, Band Council meets with Mohawk representative to discuss his role. As the purpose is for all involved to meet the new council, he will not get involved unless specific questions are asked of him.

Band Council advises him that they are considering calling off the talks because they do not agree with the unification proposal.

They are reminded of the fact that the community has also rejected unification according to DIA's terms of reference. They are advised that negotiations should begin, according to the position outlined by the community, and that, should talks break down, it would be because the other parties would not accept the terms.

They are also advised that it would be unwise for the Mohawks to suspend negotiations before they even begin. The Mohawk representative is told that this is his opinion and that of the community, which is not endorsed by Council.

Upon his arrival at the meeting, the Mohawk representative is told he will not be participating.

Band Council asks for indefinite suspension of talks.

Municipal council officially ceases its efforts to maintain the moratorium and states that final decision will be left to golf club membership.

March 9   Mohawks and supporters from various environment groups rally at annual meeting of Oka golf club membership in order to demonstrate opposition directly to members. Golf club executive meets with Mohawks and assures them that the expansion issue is not on the agenda for this meeting. Mohawks later find out that it was in fact the only item of discussion and that unanimous approval was given. Golf club announces that contractors will begin cutting down the forest in the near future.

March 10   Permanent Mohawk surveillance of area in question begins and barricades are later erected on a dirt road leading to the forest.

March 11   A barricade is erected to stop the golf course extension.

March 23   Mayors of six nearby communities write to the federal Minister of Indian Affairs to intervene in the dispute.

April 26   Québec Superior Court grants first injunction to Municipality of Oka against the barricades. The municipality threatens to remove the barricades but does not act. It chooses instead, to call in the Sûreté du Québec (SQ) to enforce the injunction.

May 1   A raid by the Sûreté du Québec is narrowly averted when a meeting is held in the Pines between the province, the municipality, the Band Council and the Longhouse. As the federal government is not present, it is agreed that a second meeting will be held at the Kanesatake longhouse the next day.

May 2   Proposals by the municipal council are rejected because they are not serious and would force the Mohawks to negotiate from a disadvantaged position. It is agreed, however, that meetings will be held between the Mohawks and the Crown.

Meetings resume between the Band Council, the Longhouse and Yves Desilets, who advises that all he is mandated to offer is the unification proposal which has already been rejected. The Mohawks demand a meeting with the federal minister and Mr. Desilets says that a meeting will only be possible under certain pre-conditions. The Mohawks reject the conditions and their persistence results in a meeting in Ottawa on June 21.

The Band Council is told that the most they can achieve would be fee simple title and limited jurisdiction under self-government.

The Longhouse makes a presentation, deplores the fact that the barricades are not being discussed and leaves.

May 3   Several hundred women, children and elderly are evacuated from the Akwesasne-St.-Regis Mohawk Reserve.

June 26   Second injunction served, barricades remain.

July 9   The Québec Minister of Native Affairs, John Ciaccia, urges the mayor of Oka to indefinitely suspend the golf course development, until negotiations proceed.

Tuesday July 10   Oka—Mayor Jean Ouellette asks the Sûreté du Québec to enforce Québec Superior Court order to remove Mohawk barricades.

Wednesday July 11   A force of 100 provincial police officers attacks the blockade with assault rifles, concussion grenades and tear gas.

Corporal Marcel Lemay, 31, is shot and dies in hospital

Provincial police surround the Kanesatake reserve, blocking off all food and medical supplies. Mohawks erect barricades on route 344 using police vehicles abandoned after the failed raid. Mohawks in Kahnawake near Chateauguay block highways leading up to the Mercier Bridge in solidarity, threatening to blow it up if there is a second assault.

Thursday July 12   John Ciaccia meets with Warrior negotiators in Kanesatake.

Sunday July 15   Negotiations break down.

Tuesday July 17   Ottawa—Tom Siddon, Minister of Indian Affairs, announces federal government not involved, because they won't want to jeopardize talks between Mohawks and Québec.

July 18   Premier of Québec makes his first public statement, hinting that the provincial government is prepared for a drawn-out process.

Thursday July 19   Tom Siddon—"We won't talk while there are barricades and we won't talk in circumstances where firearms are used to provoke negotiations."

Siddon announces federal government not involved, but still trying to purchase land in question.

Friday July 20   Kanesatake—Mohawk spokesperson, Ellen Gabriel, issued new conditions to end blockade:

- abandon immediate plan to extend golf course
- withdraw all police forces
- remove police blockades in Kanesatake and Kahnawake
- allow 48 hours after the signing of an agreement for people to leave the two Mohawk territories without being searched.

150 Chiefs from across Canada end three days of meeting at Kahnawake.

Federal Indian Affairs Minister Tom Siddon announces that, even though Ottawa is not involved in negotiations, the federal government is trying to buy the disputed land.

Saturday July 21	Kanesatake—negotiations break off. Québec Human Rights Commission taking statements from residents of the reserves.
July 21/22	United Church of Canada made a pastoral visit to the Mohawk people of Kanesatake and Kahnawake.
Monday July 23	Mohawks ask UN for peace-keeping force to be sent in. United Nations says it cannot comply; only member nations can request peace-keeping force; but working group can look at violations of human rights.

Québec—provincial options:

- negotiations continue away from Oka
- residents of Kanesatake and Kahnawake only involved in negotiations
- observers include Canadian Human Rights groups only—no international groups
- Red Cross continue with taking in supplies.

Ciaccia suggests negotiations start again on neutral territory. Ciaccia's proposal rejected by Kanesatake.

Ottawa—News reports that Deputy Minister Harry Swain makes comments "criminal armed insurrection." Minister Tom Siddon has made no comment.

Tuesday July 24	Kanesatake—Red Cross—second shipment of food and supplies allowed in. Ottawa—Tom Siddon repudiated comments by Deputy Minister Harry Swain.
Wednesday July 25	Kanesatake—Mohawks issue press release: unconfirmed report

that RCMP is getting town residents of Oka ready to evacuate in the event the force attacks Kanesatake.

Oka—Mayor of Oka holding a press conference—negotiations for selling land to federal government. Mayor asked Premier Bourassa to pay for town's expenses. International Human Rights Federation called by Québec Ligue des Droits et Libertés to investigate situation at Kanesatake and Kahnawake.

Ottawa—Ministers Bill McKnight, Kim Campbell, Shirley Martin, Gerard Valcourt and Jake Epp, and M.P. Willie Littlechild meet in Ottawa.

Ottawa—Siddon denies RCMP is ready to attack the blockade at Kanesatake. Negotiations on buying land for the Mohawks continue.

Thursday July 26

Québec—Jean-Claude Fouque, Secretary General of International Human Rights Federation, to investigate abuses by police.

John Ciaccia orders Québec police to allow food and medical supplies to go into Kanesatake and Kahnawake.

Friday July 27

Québec—Ciaccia sends letter to Mohawks.

Ottawa—Federal government offers $1.4 million to purchase 30 acres (will negotiate with Mohawks only if barricades come down).

Ottawa—Assembly of First Nations representative, Ovide Mercredi, goes to Federal Court to force federal intervention in the dispute.

Québec—Sûreté opens hundreds of criminal investigations.

Ottawa—Prime Minister not considering Royal Commission.

Monday July 30

Québec Superior Court—Justice John Gomery heard request by two Mohawks of Kanesatake for temporary injunction forcing the Sûreté to take down barricades—denied.

Kanesatake—Mohawks reject Quebec's proposal to begin negotiations on neutral grounds.

Tuesday July 31

Ottawa—AFN receives invitation by negotiating team to meet at Kanesatake on August 1.

Kanesatake and Kahnawake—International Federation of Human Rights—Jean-Claude Fouque reports 55 cases of rights violations.

Geneva—Ken Deer says UN observers should be sent to monitor the Kanesatake land dispute.

Roger Gagnon, Assistant Deputy Minister, Indian Affairs, says international observers would be welcome at Kanesatake.

Oka town meeting refuses to sell the last parcel of golf course land until the Native barriers are removed.

Wednesday
August 1

Oka—Town Council will only approve sale of 30 acres to federal government provided all barricades and arms are removed by police and Mohawks.

Thursday
August 2

Québec—Robert Bourassa meets with Joe Norton, Konrad Sioui, Lawrence Courtoreille—negotiations may start soon.

Montréal—Police seize all footage of July 11th confrontation from television stations.

Sunday
August 5

Québec and Ottawa reject latest condition by Mohawks that lands be returned to Mohawks and no prosecutions take place.

Robert Bourassa—issues 48-hour ultimatum for Mohawks to accept Quebec's final offer for conditions to negotiate.

Oka council has new offer from federal government to sell 67 acres of municipal land—offer valid until 1 p.m. Wednesday.

Negotiations are off.

Monday
August 6

Mohawks respond to Bourassa's ultimatum—negotiations can start when:
• food, clothing and medical supplies are unimpeded;
• unrestricted access by spiritual leaders, clan mothers, statesmen and legal advisors is guaranteed;
• international team of observers is present.

Tuesday
August 7

Iroquois Confederacy announces plans to name two mediators.

Wednesday
August 8

Ottawa—Prime Minister appoints Allan B. Gold, Chief Justice of Québec Superior Court, as mediator to negotiate an agreement on pre-conditions to full negotiations.

Prime Minister announces the Armed Forces are available at the request of the Québec government.

Bourassa—calls in the army, using section 274 of the National Defence Act.

Geneva—delegates of UN Sub-Commission on Human rights ask Québec for assurances "that non-violent negotiations will continue."

Saturday
August 11

Alan Gold meets behind barricades with Mohawks.

Sunday
August 12

Gold reaches an agreement on pre-conditions involving free access to food and supplies in and out of both communities, free movement of Mohawk advisors, and creation of international team to monitor events while negotiations take place. Signing ceremony in the Pines.

Chateauguay—Québec police use tear gas to disperse white mob. It was the first of three consecutive nights of violence in the Montréal suburb.

Monday **August 13**	Chateauguay—Québec police use tear gas to disperse mob of white Chateauguay residents (and others) protesting the Mercier Bridge blockade and threatening retaliation against the Indians.
Tuesday **August 14**	2500 soldiers and army equipment are deployed to four locations near Oka and Chateauguay.
Thursday **August 16**	First day of formal talks between the Mohawks, provincial and federal governments.
Friday **August 17**	International observers take up places at barricades. Armed Forces announce soldiers and equipment will be deployed to replace Québec police at Oka and Chateauguay.
Monday **August 20**	Army joins Québec police at Oka and Chateauguay. Negotiations are suspended temporarily.
Wednesday **August 22**	Kanesatake—Indian Veterans travel to Oka—Québec police do not allow them to pass.
Thursday **August 23**	Mohawks call off talks with government negotiators.
Sunday **August 26**	Onondaga Territory—Six Nations Confederacy calls for indepedent Oka chief at bargaining table with Warriors. Prime Minister—calls some of Mohawk demands "bizarre."
Monday **August 27**	Québec—Robert Bourassa calls in the army.
Tuesday **August 28**	Kahnawake—residents of the reserve flee—white mob throws rocks at cars. Some Indians are injured.
Wednesday **August 29**	Army and Warriors agree to bring down barricades blocking roads leading to the Mercier Bridge.
Saturday **September 1**	Kanesatake—Army moves into Kanesatake. 100 Mohawks, including women and children, hole up in Treatment Centre.
Tuesday **September 4**	Dorval—Iroquois Confederacy Chiefs travel to Ottawa to try and meet with Prime Minister and ministers of Indian Affairs.

Wednesday
September 5

Ottawa—Iroquois Confederacy Chiefs meet with Tom Siddon.

Thursday
September 6

Kahnawake—Mercier Bridge opens.
    Haudenosaunee—issue first warning.
    Kanesatake—Army offers warriors choice to surrender to them and be held in army compound. Sûreté du Québec will not be involved.

Friday
September 7

Québec—Robert Bourassa urges leaders to persuade Mohawks to accept army offer to surrender.
    Kanesatake—Elijah Harper allowed behind barricades. He travels to Ottawa with two Mohawk children from behind the barricades with letters from children to the Prime Minister and his family.

Saturday
September 8

Kanesatake—army soldiers beat up Mohawk Warrior.
    Ottawa—Elijah Harper presents Haudenosaunee offer proposed army disarmament, custody and prosecution to Tom Siddon—Siddon rejects proposal.
    Ottawa—24 Sussex Drive—Elijah Harper and the two Mohawk children take letters to Prime Minister's residence—Mulroney not home.
    Solicitor General Pierre Cadieux—standoff can only end with Warrior's arrest.

Sunday
September 9

Kanesatake—injured Mohawk Warrior will not be allowed back behind the barricades.
    Minister of Justice, Kim Campbell—Ottawa will not negotiate any form of amnesty.

Monday
September 10

Ottawa—Emergency Chiefs' meeting.
    Kanesatake—injured Mohawk Warrior will be transferred from hospital to military custody.
    Canadian Armed Forces proposal—(1) military custody (2) until charged or 30 days (3) women and children go free.

Tuesday
September 11

Ottawa—Emergency Chiefs' meeting.
    Solicitor General Pierre Cadieux—calls for Mohawks to surrender.
    Québec rejects Iroquois proposal that the land be returned to the Indians and that amnesty be given.

Wednesday
September 12

Ottawa—Emergency Chiefs' meeting.

Tuesday September 18	Soldiers and Mohawks at Kahnawake brawl, with rifle butts, rocks and fists used in the confrontation, during a joint army-provincial police operation to search for hidden weapons. At least 30 are injured.
Monday September 24	American lawyer Stanley Cohen (well known mediator in conflict resolution) leaves Kanesatake carrying a new set of proposals. The proposals are made public and rejected by the Québec government the next day.
Wednesday September 26	Mohawk Warriors, women and children leave the Treatment Centre, ending the 78-day standoff.
November 13	Preliminary court hearings for 47 Warriors and their supporters. Hearings are put off until 1991. Only three remain in custody.
1991 January - March	Public hearings on the Kanesatake and Kahnawake events. Royal Commission on Aboriginal Peoples is announced.
April 23 May	Standing Committee on Aboriginal Affairs publishes *The Summer of 1990*.
October 4	Indian Affairs and Northern Development minister tables the federal response to the report, *The Summer of 1990*.
October 18	Three Natives are brought to trial.

- 47 other Natives have had their cases dealt with by the courts.
- 50 other Natives still waiting for court hearings.

OKA: HISTORY OF THE CLAIM

Few Canadians realize that the Mohawk land claim at Oka is now more than 200 years old. The origin of land disputes between Native and non-Native people in the region of Kanesatake and Oka can be traced to the 1717 land grant by the King of France to the Ecclesiastics of the Seminary of St. Sulpice of Montréal.

In the seventeenth century, the Mohawks were located in the northern part of New York State (from the Adirondacks in the east to the Five Finger Lakes in the west). By the middle of the seventeenth century, following the arrival of the Europeans, a number of Mohawks converted to Catholicism and joined settlements of New France. Later, seigneuries were granted to the Jesuits and the Sulpicians for the benefit of the Indians living in the Montréal area, at Kahnawake and Oka. By the mid-eighteenth century, a portion of the Mohawks of Kahnawake settled in St. Regis, where the Akwesasne reserve was later created.

Around 1721, the Sulpicians established a settlement of religious converts, composed of Iroquois (Mohawk), Nipissing and Algonquin people within the 1717 seigneurial grant at Lac-des-Deux-Montagnes. The original grant was subsequently enlarged by the King of France in 1735. It is generally acknowledged that these tracts of land were granted to the Sulpicians for the purpose of protecting and instructing the indigenous people (a policy reflecting the ethnocentrism and paternalism of that time). However, the precise nature of the obligations of the Sulpicians to the Native people has remained a point of controversy ever since.

Although the *Royal Proclamation* of 1763 recognized that Indian lands had to be purchased by the Crown before settlement could occur, it was not applied in the St. Lawrence Valley or Atlantic colonies. Nevertheless, the Sulpician's claim was accepted, even though the claim made by the Mohawks in neighbouring Kahnawake against the Jesuits of Sault St. Louis had been recognized. After 1787, the Mohawks publicly protested the Sulpicians' claim several times, but to no avail. They continued their protest well after the mid-nineteenth century.

Conflicts between the Native people and the Sulpicians over the land were frequent, particularly over the issue of sale of the land to third parties. In response to petitions from Indians of Oka during the 1800s for title to the land granted to the seminary, the Legislature of Lower Canada enacted a statute confirming the full proprietary title of the Seminary to the disputed land while retaining the somewhat vaguely defined obligations to the Aboriginal population. *An Act respecting the Seminary of St. Sulpice* incorporated the members of the Seminary and provided that the corporation shall have, hold, and possess the "fief and seigniory" of Lac-des-Deux-Montagnes as proprietors in the same manner and to the same extent as the Seminary did under the original land grant. Local Mohawks continued to dispute the right of the Seminary to sell the land and complained about the manner in which the land was managed.

In the early part of this century, the federal government attempted to resolve this issue by initiating a court action on behalf of the indigenous people at Lac-des-Deux-Montagnes to determine the respective legal rights and obligations of the Seminary and the Aboriginal population. In determining the nature of the land rights of the Seminary, its ability to sell the land unencumbered to third parties would also be clarified. This legal action culminated in the 1912 decision of the Judicial Committee of the Privy Council (then the final court of appeal for Canada). The Court stated that the effect of the 1841 legislation "was to place beyond question the title of the respondents [the Seminary] to the Seigniory; and to make it impossible for the appellants to establish an independent title to possession or control in the administration." The Privy Council also said that the Mohawks could not assert title over the land because they had not been in the area from time immemorial. Furthermore, it was accepted that the French had extinguished whatever title the Indians might have had. The Indians had not taken treaty nor had the land been set aside for them in trust. The Privy Council went on to suggest there might be the possibility of a charitable trust, but that the issue was not argued in this case. In essence, the court held that the Mohawk people had a right to occupy and use the land until the Sulpicians exercised their unfettered right to sell it.

The conflict between the Seminary, which continued to sell off parts of the original grant, and the Native people continued. In 1945, in another attempt to end this controversy, the federal government purchased what was left of the Sulpician lands and assumed whatever obligations the Sulpicians had towards the Mohawks, but without consulting the Mohawks about this agreement. This was the beginning of a process that continues today of assembling land under federal jurisdiction for a reserve at Kanesatake.

In the 1960s, further legal action was pursued. However, resistance at the departmental level prevented the claim from being acted upon. One of the obstacles to creating a reserve base under the *Indian Act*, or any future legislation, is that the land purchased in 1945 consists of a series of blocks interspersed with privately held lands within the Municipality of Oka. Both the community of Kanesatake and the Municipality of Oka are faced with the dual problems of making decisions regarding land use and management that may affect the other community and dealing with decisions made by the other community affecting them. The question of coordinating land-use policies has been a source of friction between the two communities for some time.

In 1975, the Mohawks of Kanesatake presented a joint claim under the federal comprehensive land claims policy with the Mohawk people of Kahnawake and Akwesasne, asserting Aboriginal title to lands along the St. Lawrence and Ottawa Rivers in southern Québec. Comprehensive claims, as we have seen, involve claims to an existing Aboriginal title and presume the need to negotiate a range of matters such as land to be held under Aboriginal control, lands to be ceded, compensation and future legislative regimes to be applied to the territory in question (see Figure 10.1). The Mohawk comprehensive claim includes the southwestern part of the Province of Québec, encompassing the area along and adjacent to the St. Lawrence and Ottawa Rivers stretching south and east to the U.S. border and north to a point near the Saguenay River and including areas to the north and west of the St. Lawrence and Ottawa Rivers.

The federal government rejected the Mohawk 1975 comprehensive claim on the following grounds:

1. The Mohawks could not assert Aboriginal title as they had not maintained possession of the land since time immemorial. The land had been alternately and concurrently occupied by the Nipissing, Algonquin and Iroquois.

2. Any Aboriginal title that may have existed had been extinguished first by the Kings of France with respect to the land grants made by them, including the seigneurial grant to the Seminary of St. Sulpice, and by the British Crown through the granting of title to others when lands were opened to settlement.

3. Mohawk presence in the region did not predate European presence, the Mohawks came to settle at Oka only after the Mission was established in 1721.

FIGURE 10.1   Mohawk Reserves in the St. Lawrence Valley

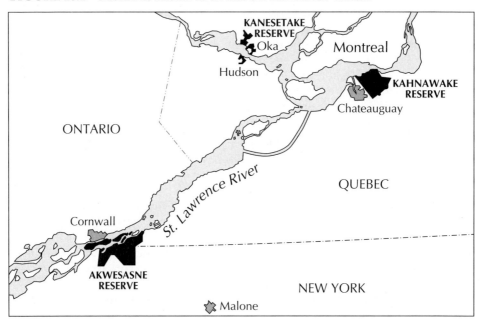

The Department of Indian Affairs restated its view that the fundamental weakness of the Mohawk land claim in the area of Oka is that the historical record, as the Department views it, fails to demonstrate exclusive Mohawk use of the territory since time immemorial—relative to both other Native peoples, and non-Natives people such as the Sulpicians. From the Mohawk perspective, the claims of Canadian governments and non-Native settlers are at least equally flawed.

The Mohawk claim has also been expressed another way. Since the Department has described the Mohawks at Oka as descendants of the Iroquois, Algonquins and Nipissings (Information Sheet, "Mohawk Band Government," July 1990), then the indigenous people of Kanesatake could demonstrate traditional use and occupancy of the land not just as Mohawks but also as descendants of all Aboriginal peoples who used that territory prior to and since the arrival of Europeans.

As an alternative argument to the comprehensive claim, Mohawks say that the Sulpician land grant was intended for the benefit of the indigenous people. Accordingly, the Sulpician Order was not free to sell any of this land without the consent of the Native people concerned. If this argument is used, then this is regarded as a specific claims issue, since specific claims arise from allegations of government mismanagement of particular Indian lands. With respect to any specific claim in this region, the federal government has taken the position that the 1912 Privy Council decision fully answered to the question of any outstanding legal obligation of the federal government. The answer was none.

The Mohawks also submitted a specific claim in June 1977, which was ultimately rejected in October 1986. The Department of Justice advised that a lawful obligation on the part of the federal government did not exist. However, in a letter to the band informing them that no outstanding lawful obligation on the part of Canada existed, then-minister of Indian Affairs, Bill McKnight, undertook a federal willingness to consider proposals for alternative means of redress of the Kanesatake band's grievance.

In summary, Mohawk claims to land have been advanced on a number of grounds, each representing a separate legal argument but also related to one another:

1. territorial sovereignty flowing from status as a sovereign nation;
2. treaty rights;
3. the *Royal Proclamation* of 1763;
4. unextinguished Aboriginal title under common law;
5. land rights flowing from the obligations imposed on the Sulpician Order in the eighteenth century land grants to the Order by the King of France.

From the viewpoints of the federal, provincial and municipal governments, these issues were decided against the Mohawks as a result of the 1912 decision of the Judicial Committee of the Privy Council in *Corinthe* v. *Seminary of St. Sulpice*. However, it is important to note that the issue of Mohawk sovereignty was not directly before that court.

Mohawk land rights issues at Kanesatake are distinct from many other indigenous land rights issues because they are one of a handful of Aboriginal title cases to have reached a final court of appeal (this is not to suggest that there are not other legal issues relating to land that could be litigated); and the Mohawks are one of a few groups to have worked their way through both the specific and comprehensive claims processes. Both claims have been rejected by the federal government. Despite these setbacks, Mohawks continue to argue they have land rights based on all the grounds set out above.

The Mohawk people today argue that, independent of the arrival of Mohawk religious converts in 1721 at the Sulpician Mission at Lac-des-Deux-Montagnes, the Mohawk Nation used and occupied that territory and exercised sovereignty over it long before the land grants by the King of France. The Mohawk people make reference to a number of treaties with European powers (Holland, France and England), which they say acknowledge the sovereign status of the Mohawk people throughout their territory in Canada and the U.S. They also question the legality, under international law, of the land grants. For example, if these lands were unoccupied by non-Native people before 1717 but were occupied and used by indigenous people (whether Mohawk, Nipissing or Algonquin), by what international legal principle could a European power assert sovereignty over the territory in the absence of conquest or cession?

Contrary to this position, the Municipality of Oka, the federal and provincial governments and persons claiming a clear title through the Seminary, argue that the Aboriginal people have no proprietary rights outside of the federally purchased lands and that this issue has been conclusively settled by legislation and litigation. In 1936, the Sulpician order sold nearly all of the land to a Belgian real estate company. The company began to sell the land in parcels for agricultural development. In 1945, the Department of Indian Affairs purchased the seminary's unsold lands plus some additional surrounding land. The seminary retained a small parcel which is used for religious purposes. The land question continued to be important to the Mohawks, but the government felt the issue had been resolved. Lacking funds and legal expertise, the Mohawks were unable to pursue their claims. It would not be until the 1990s, in the face of the Oka affair, that the federal government would act on the claim.

The conflict is over 39 hectares of land. The municipality wanted to use this land to expand an existing nine-hole golf course. This land included a Native cemetery and parts of a pine forest ("the Pines") the Mohawks consider theirs. Ottawa has since purchased the land for $5.2 million and has plans to turn it over to the Mohawks.

CONTEMPORARY EVENTS

The Kanesatake Indian settlement is located west of Montréal, at Lac-des-Deux-Montagnes, where the Ottawa River meets the St. Lawrence. The band's population of over 1000 lives primarily on two main parcels of land at Oka. These lands are made up of roughly 30 small lots within the village of Oka and a checkerboard of various larger blocks of land north and west of Oka Parish. As of 1985, Kanesatake lands totalled 828.1 hectares. In 1986, following the rejection of the specific land claim, the federal government committed itself to a project of land unification by purchasing additional lands in order to create a contiguous land base for Kanesatake Mohawks. Apparently, this project was subject to the conditions and criteria of the Federal Reserve Enlargement Policy. Thus, independent of the existing federal land claims policy, the federal government began a process of land purchase before the Oka conflict. However, it does not appear that any purchases were made between 1985 and the 1990 summer of conflict. Purchases were made, however, during the conflict, including the controversial Pines area.

Nevertheless, the federal government remains intent on assembling a unified land base at Kanesatake. Once this is accomplished, the question arises as to what form of legislative land regime should be applied to it. The Department of Indian Affairs appears to envisage the application of the *Indian Act* on an interim basis but is open to discussion of an alternative legal regime within the parameters of the current federal self-government policy. That is, the current self-government policy could be used to negotiate a local self-government regime over the reserve to displace the *Indian Act*, as the Cree of James Bay, Québec and the Sechelt people in British Columbia have done. However, this raises the complex issues of self-government and indigenous sovereignty and, in turn, the issues of forms of government in the Mohawk community. There are a number of firmly held and conflicting positions within Kanesatake regarding forms of local government, including bitter debates about what values, structure and process embody, or are consistent with, customary Mohawk values. There are different visions not only of traditional Mohawk law but also of what an elective system of government should be.

POLITICAL STRUCTURE OF MOHAWKS

The Mohawks are guided by two groups—the democratically elected chiefs and the traditional chiefs from the Iroquois Confederacy. These two systems were created when Canadians tried to introduce their law into the Iroquois community. Traditionally, five (eventually six) independent Nations (including the Mohawks) were united by a system of government that brought together hereditary chiefs in a confederacy that combined local autonomy with an overall federal control. Further unifying these groups as an agricultural, matriarchal federation was a system of clans cross-cutting through the nations. A powerful confederacy was established and although eventually halted by continued settlement of Canada, it created a stable Indian population capable of governing itself. As a result, the federal government allowed the Confederacy to operate on its own.

Then, after World War I, Ottawa began to press for a democratically elected council. Followers of the Longhouse religion, which favoured the Confederacy, boycotted the elections. The Royal Canadian Mounted Police were used to enforce the election of officers, and, in 1924, they forcibly evicted the Confederacy from the council in order to ensure that an elected council represented the residents. This action split the community, and that division has continued to this day. The Longhouse members refuse to acknowledge the elected council, and the reverse is also true. The recently active warrior society emerged from among the traditionalists, although there is also support for their action by members who vote for elected officers.

The Mohawk Warriors are linked to radical Native leaders who, in the 1970s, forced over 1000 non-Native residents to leave the Kahnawake reserve. In early

1990, conflict between anti-gambling and pro-gambling factions left two people dead on the Akwesasne reserve. However, the Mohawk Warriors do not represented a secret, war-like group bent upon hostile relations with the rest of Canada. Warrior societies are created in response to needs, and a review of Canadian history will demonstrate this. Nevertheless, most of the activities carried out by these various warrior societies are spiritual rather than paramilitary.

MOHAWK BAND GOVERNMENT

Two factors seem clear. First, it would seem that the federal government had resolved the Mohawk claim. Certainly there had been several legal decisions which seem to render the Mohawk claim invalid. Second, the "facts" of the case seems to be based on different interpretations of historical events. However, you will soon see that the federal government's actions toward Native people over the past two centuries has added considerable confusion to the case and that the "facts" are confounded by political issues which are not germane to the case. In particular, both the federal and provincial governments have continually raised concerns about Mohawk government. These concerns are not relevant to either the issue at hand (land claims) or the process by which the claims can be resolved. Thus, before continuing the chronological depiction of the events which led to the Oka confrontation, we first review the historical development of the political structure of the three reserves.

The Iroquois Confederacy originally consisted of five Iroquois nations similar to each other in culture and language. These five were the Mohawk, the Seneca, the Cayuga, the Oneida and the Onondaga. A sixth Iroquois nation, the Tuscarora, was permitted to join in 1710. Today the Confederacy is referred to as the "Six Nations."

All of the Confederacy chiefs were men, but they were chosen and could be removed by women at a council meeting. The office of Confederacy chief was hereditary within clans. Within each such clan, the chief matron, in consultation with other clan women at a council meeting, named the chief from among the clan members. Once elected, a Confederacy chief held office for life, unless he was removed for a serious offence or became too ill to hold office.

While the power to make decisions as chiefs gave men an important role, the power to name and remove Confederacy chiefs gave women an important role in Iroquois political life also. Thus, the political organization took account of men, women, clans and the tribe.

The Confederacy Council consisted of 50 chiefs. There were nine chiefs from the Mohawk tribe: three each from the Turtle Clan, Bear Clan and Wolf Clan. Among the Mohawks, the Turtle Clan was esteemed the most noble, the Bear Clan next and then the Wolf Clan.

There are seven Mohawk communities in Canada, totalling 39 363 persons: Kanesatake, Kahnawake, Akwesasne, Tyendinaga, Wahta, Six Nations at Ohsweken, and Oneida of the Thames. The following discussion will focus on only three of the groups: Kanesatake, Akwesasne and Kahnawake. We limit our discussions to these three communities since they were central to the events at Oka. Other groups in the Six Nations were involved in the resolution of the Oka dispute, but they have played a more supportive (rather than directly active) role in the events.

Kanesatake

The Mohawk community of Kanesatake has a total population of 1591 people, with a resident population of 838. From a historical perspective, as far as it can be ascertained, the Mohawks at Oka are primarily descendants of the Iroquois, Algonquins and Nipissings and have resided there for well over 200 years.

Traditionally, the selection of chiefs was carried out through an hereditary process. The position of chief was handed down from father to son (or some other relative). In 1895, the government made elections mandatory in many bands throughout Ontario, Québec and New Brunswick. By 1899, this regulation was imposed on all bands in Ontario and all provinces east. Elections for chief would be held every three years. In many reserves, struggles emerged between those who adhered to the traditional hereditary system and those who supported elections. In Oka this conflict has not been resolved.

The *Indian Act* of 1951 substantially changed the elective system and its application. As a result, new orders in council were issued. However, the Oka Band was *not* included, probably because there was, and still is, a doubt as to whether the lands at Oka are an Indian reserve within the meaning of the *Indian Act*. Consequently, from 1952, there was a *de facto* heredity system of selection for the Oka Band even though they were supposed to follow an elective procedure. In 1969, after a general meeting, the band decided in favour of an hereditary system of selecting a council of eight chiefs headed by a Grand Chief, in accordance with the traditional method known as the Six Nations hereditary clan system, described above. This traditional system has been revised and modernized to meet the needs of the current members of the community of Kanesatake. But the installation method of choosing a chief and the duties of clan mothers are still the same.

The Hereditary Council of Kanesatake consists of eight council chiefs and a Grand Chief who is from the Turtle Clan. Chiefs and clan mothers can be deposed for a number of reasons including being too ill to carry out the duties of office.

DIAND conducted a house-to-house survey in November 1973 to determine the preference of the voters. The majority of the voting members favoured the clan system. Based on these figures, DIAND confirmed the continued recognition of the traditional chiefs as the governing body. This position was challenged by a faction on the reserve wanting elected officials, and on January 7, 1983, the Federal Court of Canada, Trial Division, ruled that "...custom for elections of Council of a

Band does prevail at Oka until the Minister deems it advisable to alter the proce-dure" under section 74 of the *Indian Act*.

Recently DIAND has participated in negotiations held between three differ-ent groups (the Mohawk Council of Kanesatake, the Committee for Change and the League for Democracy). The purpose of these discussions was to arrive at a con-sensus of the membership regarding the selection of an electoral system.

As noted previously, in 1951 the *Indian Act* was revised and allowed Kanesatake to revert to "band custom" due to the government's failure to issue an order in council specifying that the elective provisions of the 1951 *Act* would apply instead. "Band custom" consisted of what the federal government recognized or under-stood to be traditional activities carried out by the band. The Kanesatake Band, as we have seen, was excluded from the new order in council. One explanation used by the Department of Indian Affairs to explain the reluctance to impose the elective system of the *Act* in 1951 was the government's doubts about whether the lands at Oka are an Indian reserve within the meaning of the *Indian Act*.

The community of Kanesatake is split between those who wish to govern them-selves according to traditional values (and use an hereditary chief system) and those who want an elected band council. As Hughes (1991) points out, even within the latter group there are divisions; those who want elected officials as outlined in the *Indian Act* and those who want elections on the basis of band custom. Fleras and Elliot note that "compounding this factional arrangement was the uneasy jux-taposition of private, municipal, and Mohawk land which, given the lack of any of-ficial status for Kanesatake land under the *Indian Act*, made it doubly difficult to demarcate lines of authority" (1992: 95).

There has also been a difference of opinion among the residents as to how to best solve the land claims problem. Given that the land claims of the past had been re-jected, some felt that only confrontation would bring the issue to a head. Others ar-gued that even though the courts had rejected their land claims, they had implicitly suggested that solutions be found through negotiations. For example, why did Indian Affairs purchase land for the Mohawks as far back as 1945 if their claim was not valid? In 1986 the Minister of Indian Affairs proposed redress for Mohawk grievances by suggesting a federal land reunification package.

In 1989 the federal government offered a land reunification package to the band whereby all band members might live together on nearby federal land. The most recent alternative suggestion made by the federal government in 1992 was the possibility that the government of Canada might buy land at the centre of the dispute between Kanesatake Mohawks and the Oka Village Council.

The community of Kanesatake has experienced intense internal debate over appropriate forms of Mohawk government for the past thirty years and perhaps longer. Until September 1969, the *Indian Act* Band Council at Kanesatake, while technically operating under band custom, modelled its method on the election process of the *Indian Act* and its regulations, according to the Department of Indian Affairs. In October 1969, the Department recognized a change in custom following a request for official recognition by the "Kanesatake traditional Chiefs," who backed their request with a petition from what appeared to be a majority of the resident adult population (158 out of 292). As of October 27, 1969, the "traditional chiefs" were recognized as the body with which the Department would deal in matters relating to band affairs. An internal departmental memo in 1970 described the 1969 change in custom as a change from a process of using an election system similar to that of the *Indian Act* to the hereditary chiefs system. This memo described the challenge to the authority of the hereditary chiefs by a group known as the Kanesatake Indian Committee or Gaspé group (which had originally supported the change in custom to hereditary chiefs). This memo took note of a matter which continues to be an issue today: The *Indian Act* makes reference to custom but there is no explicit responsibility placed on the Department in this regard. Whether or not the Department of Indian Affairs should adjudicate disputes over interpretation of custom is debatable.

The 1970 memo also describes how changes can be made to the composition of the Kanesatake Band Council under the system of custom the Department had recognized up to this point. The (hereditary) Chiefs explained that under custom this may be by death, resignation or, in the case of bad behaviour, a request by the clan mother, after suitable warnings, that the individual resign. Thereupon a band meeting would choose a replacement. In 1970, the Gaspé group challenged the legitimacy of the existing Band Council on the authority of a petition signed by 121 of the 158 people who signed the 1969 petition. The Gaspé group argued that people who signed the petition were not eligible under traditional law. In the end the Department decided it was not knowledgeable enough about custom to adjudicate a dispute over interpretation of custom. If requested by a petition of a majority of electors to recognize a change in custom, the Department decided it would arbitrate only, and this through the process of a majority vote at a meeting or referendum of resident electors clearly setting out the proposed change in custom.

Since 1899, the federal government has tried to govern the Kanesatake community through the provisions of the *Indian Act*. Since at least 1951, this has involved having to cope with a continuous controversy over:

1. whether or not the *Indian Act* Band Council should be selected according to band custom as recognized and monitored by the Department or according to the election provisions of the *Act* and its regulations.
2. what properly constitutes band custom and how to deal with allegations that band custom has not been properly followed in the selection of a given chief or council.

Over the years, the government and some parts of the community have attempted to resolve these controversies by a series of referenda, petitions, court cases, meetings and house-to-house surveys. These initiatives have been limited to determining what system of *Indian Act* governance the community may want. However, an important part of the community-the Longhouse at Kanesatake-regards any initiative related to the *Indian Act* as contrary to Mohawk law.

Akwesasne

The community of Akwesasne is part of the Mohawk Nation and, it follows, part of the Iroquois Confederacy. The reserve straddles the Québec, Ontario and United States borders.

Within Akwesasne, there are now three separate councils of Mohawk people which exercise the functions of government.

1. The Mohawk Nation Council is the national council for Mohawks, i.e., it represents Mohawks throughout Canada and operates under the traditional system as part of the Iroquois Confederacy.
2. The United States side of Akwesasne has three elected tribal chiefs operating under the laws of New York State and the federal laws of the United States.
3. The third council, the Mohawk Council of Akwesasne, was first created as a band council under the *Indian Act* in 1898 and has continued to operate until the present day.

The Mohawks of Akwesasne had been forced to comply with the 1899 regulations which dictated that elections of chiefs would take place under the rules outlined in the *Indian Act*. They, like other Mohawks, resisted this, and, when the 1951 revisions to the *Indian Act* were passed, they found loopholes in the *Act* which suggested they did not have to follow its election regulations. As a result, they began to use a "customary" election procedure. This was used in the 1988 band elections, and it was at that time that the Akwesasne decided to formalize their voting procedures.

On June 6, 1988, the Department of Indian Affairs and Northern Development received a request from the residents to revert to a custom electoral system which had been used in the election earlier in the year.

The request met the criteria of the DIAND policy for reversion to custom, and it was decided to take the necessary action to revoke the application to the band of section 74 of the *Indian Act*.

1990 *Indian Act*—Section 74

Elections of Chiefs and Band Councils
Also see: Indian Band Election Regulations, C.R.C. 1978, c. 952; Indian Band Council Procedure Regulations, C.R.C. 1978, c. 950; Indian Band Council Borrowing

Regulations, C.R.C. 1978, c. 949; Indian Referendum Regulations, C.R.C. 1978, c. 957, all in Chapter 5.

74. (1) Whenever he deems it advisable for the good government of a band, the Minister may declare by order that after a day to be named therein the council of the band, consisting of a chief and councillors, shall be selected by elections to be held in accordance with this Act.

> Sections 74 to 80 [of the *Indian Act*] apply only to councils that choose to be elected in accordance with the Indian Act and not by custom of the band as set out in s. 2(1) ("council") [which states that in the case of a band to which section 74 does not apply, the council chosen according to the customs of the band or where there is no council, the chief of the band, is chosen according to the custom of the band].

(2) Unless otherwise ordered by the Minister, the council of a band in respect of which an order has been made under subsection (1) shall consist of one chief, and one councillor for every one hundred members of the band, but the number of councillors shall not be less than two nor more than twelve and no band shall have more than one chief.

(3) The Governor in Council may, for the purposes of giving effect to subsection (1), make orders or regulations to provide

(a) that the chief of a band shall be elected by
   (i)   a majority of the votes of the electors of the band, or
   (ii) a majority of the votes of the elected councillors of the band from among themselves, but the chief so elected shall remain a councillor, and
(b) that the councillors of a band shall be elected by
   (i) a majority of the votes of the electors of the band, or
   (ii) a majority of the votes of the electors of the band in the electoral sec tion in which the candidate resides and that he proposes to represent on the council of the band.

(4) A reserve shall for voting purposes consist of one electoral section, except that where the majority of the electors of a band who were present and voted at a referendum or a special meeting held and called for the purpose in accordance with the regulations have decided that the reserve should for voting purposes be divided into electoral sections and the Minister so recommends, the Governor in Council may make orders or regulations to provide that the reserve shall for voting purposes be divided into not more than six electoral sections containing as nearly as may be an equal number of Indians eligible to vote and to provide for the manner in which electoral sections so established shall be distinguished or identified.

The regulations with respect to band elections were amended accordingly by deleting the name of the Mohawks of the Akwesasne Band from the schedule listing the bands holding elections under section 74 of the *Indian Act*. The necessary Orders were signed on December 14 and December 21, 1989.

The term of office of the Mohawks of the Akwesasne Band Council elected in 1986 under the *Indian Act* expired on July 7, 1988. The Band Council had met the requirements of departmental policy for reverting to custom, and, under normal circumstances, the required ministerial revocation Order required to accomplish reversion would have been obtained in time for the custom election scheduled for June 25, 1988.

As time passed, band members became less supportive of the custom election process. In 1988, some 200 band members indicated they wanted to follow the electoral provision in the *Indian Act*. A referendum was scheduled. However, controversy over the authority of the minister to call a referendum and over who was the rightful leader of the band led to litigation and a postponement of the referendum.

Kahnawake

The Kahnawake Band is part of the Iroquois Confederacy and participates in the Grand Council of Chiefs, the governing body of the Confederacy. The Kahnawake Band was originally placed under the elective provisions of the *Indian Act* by way of the *Indian Advancement Act* of 1889.

Basically, Kahnawake is a progressive, nationalistic community which presents the government with a unique opportunity to attempt to promote the band's self-government aspirations within the constraints imposed by the governing legislation.

In keeping with the principles of Mohawk traditional government, the Kahnawake Band Council believes the *Indian Act* and its relevant election regulations to be too rigid and restrictive. Consequently, the band has held its last five to six elections according to its own internal custom regulations, rather than under the *Indian Act*. The Kahnawake Band presently consists of one chief and 11 councillors.

For the purpose of formalizing the Kahnawake Band's electoral system, efforts are currently underway to revert the band to a custom system. In this respect, the band's supporting documentation entitled "Regulations Governing the Mohawk Council of Kahnawake Elections" is being reviewed.

Summary

Before the enactment of the first federal Indian legislation in 1869, indigenous communities governed themselves according to their own traditional values and systems of government. In the nineteenth century, the *Indian Act* tolerated some continuation of "band custom" in matters of local government but only as a temporary measure. When certain First Nations refused to adopt the *Act*'s elective system of band councils, the federal government tried various means to force them to do so. Various statutory provisions were enacted giving the minister of Indian Affairs increasing powers to depose traditional leaders, and, on occasion, some traditional leaders were arrested and symbols of office confiscated.

In 1899, the people at Kanesatake were brought under the *Indian Act* elective system—that is, the federal government decided that the *Indian Act* should be applied to First Nations in Ontario, New Brunswick and Québec. There is no indication that this decision was taken as a matter of an expressed choice of the people concerned. In fact the introduction of an elected council was actively but unsuccessfully resisted by the Mohawk people. At St. Regis (Akwesasne), traditional chiefs were arrested in 1899 and five held in prison for one year. This type of repression was repeated at Ohsweken, Ontario in 1924. At Ohsweken, the elected council system was introduced in 1924, when RCMP officers dismissed the traditional chiefs from the Council House, confiscated the Council's Wampum belts (symbols of authority) and organized the election of a Band Council.

THE LONGHOUSE

Mohawks identifying with traditional Mohawk law and customs call themselves "the Haudenosaunee." In English, this means "People of the Longhouse." The Mohawk Nation is a constituent element of the Six Nations Iroquois Confederacy. The Confederacy is sometimes referred to as the Iroquois, the League of Five Nations, the League of Six Nations or the Six Nations Confederacy. The Six Nations Iroquois Confederacy is composed of the following nations from east to west: Kanienkahaka (Mohawk), Oneida, Onondaga, Cayuga, Seneca and Tuscarora.

The Six Nations Iroquois Confederacy has as its Constitution, the Great Law of Peace (Kayanerakowa), considered by some to be the oldest constitution in the world. It is said to be a fundamental tenet of the Great Law that any Haudenosaunee who cease to follow traditional customs in favour of an outside system of government, religion or way of life, alienate themselves from the Confederacy.

Accordingly, Longhouse members will not participate in any initiative connected to an *Indian Act* system of governance, nor do they recognize the possibility of any legitimate form of Mohawk government other than the Longhouse system. In a letter dated June 2, 1967, Chief Samson Gabriel stated: "We recognize no power to establish peacefully, or by the use of force or violence, a competitive political administration. Transactions of such groups in political and international affairs is very disturbing to the Six Nations Iroquois Confederacy Chiefs."

The Longhouse has never been equated with "band custom." This is impossible because adherents of the Longhouse refuse to recognize any federal authority over the Mohawk nation. The Longhouse people would likely view any attempt at incorporating the Longhouse system into an *Indian Act* band custom system as compromising Mohawk sovereignty and the tenets of the Great Law.

The band custom system of Hereditary Chiefs is regarded by Longhouse members as alien, as something created outside of traditional law and, therefore, as illegitimate. While both the Longhouse and the *Indian Act* custom of Hereditary Chiefs rely on a clan system and involve clan mothers in the selection of leaders, the two systems are distinct. The Longhouse people have stated that, contrary to the system of Hereditary Chiefs, the Iroquois Confederacy does not acknowledge a Grand Chief nor Head Clan Mothers, nor do people vote on clan mother decisions. As the events of the summer of 1990 show, the Longhouse continues to exist at Kanesatake, and with this institution, resistance to the *Indian Act* or any form of federally delegated local government also continues. In fact, the refusal of the Longhouse to participate in any federally sanctioned activity affecting local government extends to refusing to participate in referenda and elections. The existence of several competing groups and the refusal of Longhouse members to participate in federally sponsored referenda and elections, has contributed to the difficulty of any one group achieving more than a plurality.

The relationship between the Longhouse people and the Mohawk Warrior Society is tenuous, other than a relationship of mutual support between those identifying themselves as Mohawk Warriors and the Longhouse members present in the Pines on July 11, 1990. The Longhouse and the Warrior Society are most closely associated with Mohawk assertions of sovereignty. The Warrior Society as it is currently known appears to be of relatively recent origin. It is often described as having been inspired by the "Manifesto" of Louis Koroniaktejeh Hall entitled *Rebuilding the Iroquois Confederacy*, written in the early 1970s. However, Mohawk sovereignty claims are at least as old as the institution of the Longhouse. The Mohawk communities of Kanesatake and Kahnawake argued their sovereign status long before the summer of 1990. For example, in 1946, before the Joint Senate and House of Commons Committee on revision to the *Indian Act*, a delegation described as the Iroquois tribe of Lac-des-Deux-Montagnes asked for the abolition of the *Indian Act*; they claimed they were not subject to any federal or provincial laws within their territories by virtue of their treaty rights, saying that "by virtue of our treaty rights we demand of the Canadian Government the recognition and respect of our sovereign rights and privileges as a Nation" (House of Commons, *Minutes of Proceedings and Evidence*, No. 33, p. 1796, Brief dated 24 October 1946).

The Longhouse people assert a sovereign status for the Mohawk Nation. Indigenous people across the country assert a right to recognition as sovereign nations but, with a few exceptions, in a sense falling short of complete independence. The majority of First Nations people seek recognition under the Constitution of Canada of an inherent right to self-government. This seems to mean, in part, recognition under the Constitution of areas of exclusive First Nations jurisdiction which will be exempt from, or beyond the purview of federal and provincial legislation.

ATTEMPTS AT RESOLUTION IN KANESATAKE

The status of Kanesatake with respect to land does not fit within the usual pattern of Indian reserve lands in Canada. The Kanesatake people are in an anomalous situation under Canadian law: members of the Kanesatake "Indian Band" are "Indians" within the meaning of that term under the *Indian Act*, have an *Indian Act* Band Council, live on federal Crown lands (since 1945) reserved for their use (within the meaning of section 91(24) of the *Constitution Act, 1867*), but do not live on lands clearly having status as an *Indian Act* reserve. This means there is no clear legislative regime applicable to provide for local control and administration of these lands.

The question is, whether any organization or mechanism exists within the Mohawk community to continue the important mediating role performed in 1990 by the Six Nations Iroquois Confederacy. Without such a process, there is little hope for resolving any fundamental issues. The matter was to have been heard in the Federal Court of Montréal in January 1991 but has been postponed indefinitely.

In 1990, the issue of fair and accountable representation was raised again. In October 1990, a federal attempt to initiate negotiations for the transfer of land acquired during the Oka crisis failed when none of the factions making representations to the Minister of Indian Affairs and Northern Development to act on behalf of Kanesatake had a clear mandate from the community. The Minister issued a call to the Kanesatake Band Council, the Coalition and the Mohawk Traditional Longhouse to demonstrate the support they had within the community. (The Coalition consists of the Kanesatake League for Democracy, the Committee for Change, the Mohawk Council of Kanesatake, and *C-31* Indians.) On November 6, the Minister informed Jerry Peltier that he was prepared to commence negotiations with the Coalition based on the popular support they were able to secure (some 400 community members signed a petition in support of the Coalition). The Minister also invited the Kanesatake Band Council and the Longhouse to participate in negotiations, an offer which was later declined.

The Coalition assumed the task of preparing for, and carrying out, negotiation sessions with the Government of Canada. Under a Framework Agenda negotiated between the Coalition, the province of Québec and the federal government, they were also charged with conducting community information sessions. These sessions were to lay the groundwork for ratification of the Framework Agenda. Throughout the process, continuing attempts were made to persuade the other Mohawk interest to participate. Ultimately, however, it was clear that no action could be taken until a plebiscite was conducted.

Throughout the winter of 1990 and spring of 1991, the federal government tried to interest all parties to form a coalition and meet with the federal government to resolve the land dispute. After it was clear this would not happen, the federal government determined that the election process for the Mohawk community would take place in June of 1991. The government hired an independent firm to conduct an election of an interim chief and band council. The election took place on June 27, 1991. Once elected, the interim chief and council were responsible for band governance and for the establishment of a Mohawk custom election code. Once the election code is developed and ratified by the community, another "final" election will be held. The plebiscite was defined as important in order to resolve the question of leadership in the Kanesatake community, a question which, in turn, kept the land issue from being resolved (see Chronology 2).

CHRONOLOGY 2   EVENTS LEADING TO KANESATAKE PLEBISCITE

1991 **September 26**	Warriors lay down their arms and end their 78-day siege. The federal minister immediately announced that he had instructed his officials to organize a meeting between himself and the people of Kanesatake.
October 1	Minister meets with various representatives of the Kanesatake community in Ottawa. He reiterates the government's commitment to settling the land question and urges representatives to demonstrate community support for negotiations as soon as possible.
October 15	Federal officials commence preliminary efforts to encourage a healing process in the community.
October 16	Minister holds meetings in Dorval with the Band Council and members of the Coalition (representing the Kanesatake League for Democracy, the Committee for Change, the Mohawk Council of Kanesatake and *C-31* Status Indians), again urging them to demonstrate support within the Kanesatake community.
November 1	Minister is presented with a petition signed by a majority of adult band members urging that the Coalition form the community's negotiating team. Minister promises to give the petition his careful consideration.
November 2	Siddon meets with Québec Native Affairs Minister, John Ciaccia, in Québec City.
November 6	Siddon announces the membership of the Kanesatake negotiating committee.
November 23	Funding arrangement reached between DIAND and the Coalition.

Minister reassured the Coalition that negotiations on all outstanding land issues could commence immediately.

December 6 Bernard Roy, federal negotiator, meets with Québec government officials and representatives of the Coalition to agree on a process for upcoming negotiations of the land issue.

1992
February 8 Federal Minister of Indian Affairs travels to Oka in an attempt to bring various community factions closer together. Over two days, the Minister meets separately with the Mayor of Oka and representatives of the Longhouse, the Band Council and the Coalition.

February 14 Framework Agenda between the federal government and the Kanesatake Mohawk Coalition to guide ongoing negotiations at Oka was referred to the Mohawk community for ratification.

February 20 Federal Court rules the federal government may proceed with a referendum to determine Kanesatake community's preferred form of governance.

March 6 DIAND, Québec and the Coalition agree on the ratification process of Framework Agenda.

March 21 Members of the Band Council, the Traditional Longhouse and the Kanesatake Mohawk Coalition meet with representatives of the Akwesasne Peacemaking Centre, the Kahnawake Outreach Program, Health and Welfare Canada consultants and others to discuss the community healing process.

April 9 A series of workshops to discuss the Framework Agreement with the Mohawk community is held. The need for a referendum is strongly expressed.

May 31 Plebescite held; results issued by Canadian Election Consultants. An election will be held.

June 34 Indians are found not guilty in various charges against them as a result of the Oka affair.

In the meantime, the Kanesatake community remains in a state of legal and political uncertainty with an *Indian Act* Band Council that seems unable to gain majority support. They live on federal Crown land reserved for their use but with no legal regime to provide community control.

RECENT EVENTS LEADING TO THE OKA CONFLICT

The dispute over the golf course expansion involved land sold by the Sulpicians some time ago. At the time of the July 1990 crisis, the land was privately held. The

Municipality of Oka held an option to purchase that land and planned to exercise that option for the purpose of leasing the land to the Oka Golf Club. This land is significant to the Mohawk community because it formed part of "common lands" dating back to the eighteenth century settlement and since used for recreational and other community purposes by the Mohawks. These lands also provided access to a Mohawk cemetery in the pine forest. The pine forest, known as the Pines, itself is significant as one of the earliest reforestation efforts in North America. It is tragically ironic that the trees were planted in a cooperative effort between Native and non-Native people in the late nineteenth century.

The year 1987 is a logical starting point for an examination of contemporary events underlying the Oka conflict. It was in March of that year that the Club de golf d'Oka Inc. sought a renewal of its lease of the existing nine-hole course. This proposal led to friction between the Municipality and the people of Kanesatake, who had always objected to the presence of the golf course and claimed the land as their own. A few months later the Kanesatake Band Council sought to block this proposal. The golf course is situated west of the Municipality, which is surrounded mostly by forested land.

It also appears that in early 1987, the community of Kanesatake was once again experiencing turmoil over the issue of appropriate systems of governance. Some members of the community were seeking a change from band custom, by which the Six Nations Traditional Hereditary Chiefs have been appointed, to some form of elective system. In addition to this debate, the Longhouse objected to the traditionalist claims of the *Indian Act* Band Council.

Subsequently, the Department of Indian Affairs engaged a consulting firm to conduct a survey to determine whether there was community support for a change in local governance. The result of this study and further consultations by the Department was a decision taken by the Department to conduct a referendum on whether the community wished to change the selection of the *Indian Act* Band Council back to an elective system governed by the *Act*. The Six Nations Traditional Hereditary Chiefs launched an action in the Federal Court to block this proposed action. In February 1991, the Federal Court Trial Division held that the federal government has the power to conduct such a referendum as a result of the Minister's discretionary power under the *Act*.

On May 20, 1987 Grand Chief Alex Montour wrote to the office of the Minister of Indian Affairs on behalf of the Six Nations Traditional Hereditary Chiefs, to express the concerns of Kanesatake Mohawks respecting renewal of the golf course lease. Chief Montour stated that the Mohawk people had unjustly lost, and were interested in taking back, their former ancestral land. He stated that the Minister of Indian Affairs had in the past expressed an intention to consider the purchase of additional lands to redress the situation at Kanesatake.

The Honourable Bill McKnight, then minister of Indian Affairs, replied as follows.

Thank you for your letter of May 20, 1987...concerning the land granted by Le club de golf d'Oka Inc.

Please note that the lands acquired in 1945 from the Sulpician Fathers did not include the above land. In fact, the lands which were not occupied by the Indians but known as the "common lands" were sold to the Municipality of Oka in 1947 and converted into a golf course. For your information, the remaining land was used for various development projects. Furthermore, as you know, these lands were part of your land claim which has not been accepted for negotiations, after analysis and review by the Department of Justice.

Consequently, I trust that you will understand that Indian and Northern Affairs Canada cannot intervene in this private matter.

Documentation from the Department reveals further correspondence regarding the Oka golf course in April and June of 1988.[1]

The Municipality of Oka obtained an interlocutory injunction from the Québec Superior Court against the Six Nations Traditional Hereditary Chiefs and the Warrior Society, ordering the Mohawks to abstain from interfering, disturbing, intimidating or threatening municipal employees from performing their work on municipal land.

In May 1988, Le Club de golf d'Oka Inc. submitted a proposal to the Municipality of Oka to expand its golf course from 9 to 18 holes. The Municipality held an option to purchase the land required for the proposed expansion.

Between August and September 1988, the Municipality selected a site for the proposed expansion and made an offer to purchase the privately held land which was adjacent to municipal lands. The Municipality maintained that the proposed golf course expansion did not involve the Pines but rather land owned by Mr. Maurice Rousseau and that it was already the object of a housing development plan. The Municipality seemed to be under the impression that the Pines (the original common lands used by the Mohawks within the Sulpician grant) were restricted to the evenly planted rows of trees, placed in this fashion by Mohawks and Algonquins under the guidance of the Sulpicians, and that the forested land owned by Mr. Rousseau was a natural growth forest.[2]

By March 13, 1989, the Municipality had accepted an offer by Mr. Rousseau to sell approximately 45 acres of land for $70 000, on condition that the land be used for the golf course expansion and provided that the Municipality accepted a subdivision plan for the remainder of the land, amounting to approximately 30 acres. By this time, signs of strain in the relations between Natives and non-Natives were evident.

In April 1989, 300 Mohawk people peacefully marched through the streets of Oka. They invited non-Native residents to join them in opposing the golf course expansion on political, social and environmental grounds and maintained that a moratorium on development would be beneficial to all. The Mohawk people also asserted ownership of the land and stated a wish to maintain its current character as a recreational site. Several public meetings followed. Local environmentalists also organized themselves in opposition to the proposed expansion. In June 1989, Le Club de golf d'Oka and the Municipality reached an agreement in principle on the rental and expansion of the golf course lands. The Municipality viewed the development as beneficial to both itself and the region. At the same time, the Department of Indian Affairs invited the Municipality to participate in tripartite negotiations (provincial-municipal, Mohawk, federal) on the land unification project for Kanesatake.

In September 1989, a tripartite negotiating committee began work on a framework agreement to govern a negotiation process on the issues of land unification for Kanesatake and resolution of jurisdictional issues between the communities of Oka and Kanesatake. There is no evidence such an agreement was at any point actually signed by all three parties. It is clear that Mohawk consent to the framework agreement was to be contingent upon community approval through a process of consultation. From September to December 1989, the moratorium on development was renewed by the Municipality, the Oka golf club and Mr. Rousseau.

In January 1990, a controversial change in the leadership of the Six Nations Traditional Hereditary Chiefs occurred. Clan mothers removed Clarence Simon as Grand Chief and appointed George Martin in his place. Mr. Simon alleged that the clan mothers did not properly follow the band custom in this matter. At the same time, the Band Council was struggling to deal with a budget deficit.

In their evidence before the Standing Committee on Aboriginal Affairs, both the people of the Longhouse at Kanesatake, headed by Samson Gabriel, and the representatives of the *Indian Act* Band Council (Six Nations Traditional Hereditary Chiefs) maintained that the land unification project as conceived by the 1989 proposed framework agreement was rejected by the community because it was not viewed as likely to provide a sufficient quantity of land (80 hectares over 25 years was proposed), nor was it considered likely to address the longstanding problems or unique character of Kanesatake. The discussions continued into early summer. The evidence suggests some form of community endorsement of "occupation" of the disputed territory. Subsequent to the community meeting a small group from within Kanesatake took over the process and decided on the use of arms.[3]

THE OKA CONFLICT

On May 1, 1990 the provincial police (the Sûreté du Québec) were asked to enforce an April 26 injunction against members of the Kanesatake Band. The injunction was the result of the first barricades the Indians had put up on March 11 and refused to take down. Nevertheless, discussions took place in the Pines between the representatives of the province, the Municipality and the Mohawks. The Mohawks eventually concluded that the Municipality had no serious proposal to offer, and it was decided to reconvene the meeting the following day at the Longhouse and to summon the federal representative.

On May 1, 1990, municipal officials went to meet the Mohawks and once again requested the removal of the barricades, but were refused. Instead, the Mohawk people present purportedly refused to lift the barricades and demanded a 15-day moratorium of the golf course expansion work and a resumption of negotiations with the federal government. Soon afterwards, there was a series of meetings between the Mohawks and the federal representative, who assumed responsibility for representing the interests of the province and the Municipality as well.

From the viewpoint of the Municipality, armed and masked outsiders had taken over the situation and were attempting to provoke confrontation. The Municipality felt that the federal government was being taken in by a radical element from outside Kanesatake and that the issues of lifting the barricades and of local land claims had been overtaken by the wider question of Mohawk sovereignty in Canada.

Over the month of May, the Longhouse sought a meeting with the federal Minister of Indian Affairs. In the meantime, the Municipality contacted members of the provincial cabinet. The Municipality stated that on May 7, it requested the assistance of the Sûreté du Québec from the Québec Minister of Public Security, the Honourable Sam Elkas. The Municipality felt this request did not receive the attention it deserved. The Municipality of Oka said that by May 14, there were armed warriors present and the barricades were still in place because of lack of government action. The Municipality adopted a resolution authorizing the purchase of Mr. Rousseau's land for the golf course expansion and further authorizing the signing of the lease with the Oka golf club. At this time it was also decided not to sell any land to the federal government.

However, on June 5, 1990, the Municipality adopted a resolution proposing a moratorium on construction of the golf course and the resumption of negotiations, on condition that the barricades be lifted. The Municipality says this proposal was communicated to the Mohawks at the barricades but was refused.

As noted earlier, some individuals within the Longhouse at Kanesatake made a decision to engage in armed resistance sometime around early July. These people, often known as the "People of the Pines" or the "Longhouse People of the Pines," have carefully insisted they were not and are not a "breakaway" Longhouse. It appears that, while the People of the Pines recognize Samson Gabriel as the legitimate Chief of the Longhouse of Kanesatake, there was a difference of opinion within the Longhouse over the critical issue of armed confrontation. The People of the Pines supported the use of arms, and Chief Samson Gabriel and others did not.

A meeting between the Municipality and the Minister of Indian and Northern Affairs occurred on the 28th of June. Another injunction was obtained by the Municipality on June 29, and the judge, granting the injunction, compared the situation at the barricades to a state of anarchy. By this time many barricades had been erected in the area and encompassed a large area around the disputed lands.

From July 2 to July 6, 1990, there were public announcements by the Municipality and the provincial Minister of Public Security warning the Mohawks to take down the barricades. On July 9, 1990, Mr. Ciaccia (Québec minister of Native Affairs) sent a letter to the mayor, which was publicly released the following day. The letter requested an indefinite suspension of the golf course project to allow the Mohawk people to take down their barricades. The provincial minister tried to explain that the situation involved more than strict questions of legal rights because of the fundamentally different historical perspective of Native people.

On the morning of July 11, 1990, the provincial police tried to dismantle a road block set up by the Mohawks of Kanesatake. An exchange of gunfire occurred between the Sûreté du Québec and armed persons behind the barricade in the Pines. When the exchange stopped, Corporal Lemay of the Sûreté had died from gunshot wounds. A later assessment concluded that he was not killed by a police bullet but by a person or persons unknown.

Four days later, the provincial government of Québec asked the Canadian Armed Forces to move against the Mohawks at Oka. The armed forces moved in and began encircling and dismantling the barricades. By August 14, 1990, more than 2500 soldiers were placed in positions outside Oka and Kahnawake. The armed forces began to engage in extensive psychological warfare such as sending jets at low altitude over the reserve, stationing tanks around the area and displaying a range of heavy weapons; e.g, howitzers, tanks, bulldozers.

The armed standoff at Oka sparked Native blockades on railways, highways and bridges primarily in Ontario, Québec and B.C. For example, the Mount Currie band in B.C. set up a blockade on the B.C. main rail line; likewise, the Pays Plat band in Northern Ontario blocked a rail line. Their actions halted rail traffic for several days.

Within a few days of the blockade, more than two thirds of the people in the vicinity of Oka left their homes, and nearly 2000 more left their homes in nearby Chateauguay. About 800 Natives left their homes in both Kahnawake and Kanesatake.

The Mohawks at Kahnawake set up a blockade on the Mercier Bridge, which links the Island of Montréal to South Shore communities. The result was that many of the residents of Chateauguay had to spend up to three hours commuting to work in Montréal. The bridge was blocked in support of their fellow Mohawks in nearby Oka. The difference between the roadblock at Oka and that at Chateauguay is that the Oka road (which had been blocked for four months before the Mercier

Bridge was blocked) is an unimportant side road. When it was blocked, it inconvenienced no one except the Mohawks. But when the Mercier Bridge was blocked, Whites were inconvenienced, and, thus, action had to be taken.

Demonstrators from the community of Chateauguay nightly approached the barricades to protest the Mohawks' action. Individuals congregated on the bridge to jeer at Mohawks and yell obscene and racist remarks.

The Sûreté du Québec precipitated the conflict when they stormed the blockade west of Montréal which had been erected March 11. The Sûreté directed 100 tactical officers to move in and clear the area. As they moved in to clear the area with trucks and front-end loaders, they fired tear gas into the barricades. By the end of July, 1000 Sûreté officers were in Oka and another 500 at Chateauguay, outside the Kahnawake Mohawk reserve.

It seems that some residents at Kanesatake—albeit, a minority—supported the strategy of armed resistance from the beginning. It is not clear to what extent the community as a whole was involved in the decision to arm the barricade in the Pines. Following the experience of the police raid on July 11, the Native community was suddenly galvanized into a state of unity by the traumatizing effect of an outside threat. For the duration of the armed standoff, the community appeared to be united on central issues of land rights, sovereignty and relations with non-Native society. The continued negative experience with the provincial police and the armed forces seemed only to reinforce the reaction. Allegations of human rights violations against the police and the army have been widespread and persistent.

From the government's viewpoint, the use of the police and the army was essential to the maintenance of law and order in the communities affected by the crisis. From the viewpoint of the Mohawk people and First Nations across the country, the actions of the provincial police on July 11, 1990, and the use of the armed forces at Oka, is very much connected to the issue of Mohawk land rights. (See Chronology 1 for an account of the events over the summer of 1990).

With respect to the negotiation process that followed July 11, each party demonstrated great tenacity in maintaining entrenched positions: statements and proposals were redrafted throughout the summer to say essentially the same things. The only exception was the Six Nations Iroquois Confederacy in its role as intermediary.

After reviewing the Standing Committee on Aboriginal Affairs report on the Kanesatake and Kahnawake events in 1991, the federal government responded in a variety of ways. First, they established a Royal Commission on Aboriginal peoples. The results of this commission are intended to become input for the constitutional reform process and to establish the presence of Native people in Canada's constitution. Second, the federal government has undertaken new steps to deal with land claims. For example, an Indian Specific Claim Commission was created to provide independent dispute resolution. The Commission is also able to provide mediators between the parties when requested. The limit on the number of comprehensive claims has also been lifted and further changes to the comprehensive land claims process are being reviewed. Third, policing and the administration of justice have been given high priority by the federal government. A new policing policy has been established so as to provide expanded police services on Indian reserves. These changes will add over $100 million in policing services over the next five years. There has also been a major initiative in the administration of justice for Native people. Thus far, discussions have focused on developing policies on the administration of justice, justices of the peace and sentencing. There has also been funding provided to Native organizations in order to develop research and pilot projects related to the administration of justice; e.g., a public consultation process was funded which will make the administration of justice more responsive to Aboriginal peoples.

Finally, the government has attempted to address one of the root causes of the Mohawk land dispute. The Department of Indian Affairs and Northern Development has purchased nearly 60 hectares of land and is attempting to negotiate the purchase of additional parcels of land. At the same time, the municipality of Oka received financial compensation from the federal government for loss of income from this land.

In 1992, the Grand Chief of the Mohawk Council of Kahnawake and the Minister of State for Indian Affairs and Northern Development signed a framework agreement to start negotiations on a new relationship between the government and the Kahnawake. In the long term, the Mohawks are proposing to revive the structures, institutions and principles of the Great Law of the Iroquois of Six Nations. In the meantime, they intend to change their existing relationship with the federal government to get recognition of their jurisdiction in a variety of areas; e.g., policing. Negotiations will continue for the next two years and will include the nature and scope of Mohawk government, justice, land management, land control, environment, social services, health, education and cultural matters.

CONCLUSION

The events just described illustrate the process of escalating violence when each side refuses to negotiate. In this case, it was clear that the overwhelming military superiority of the Canadian government would prevail. Nevertheless, it was important, from the Natives' point of view, that they achieve some symbolic victory. They felt that the government was punishing Natives because they had halted the Meech Lake Accord earlier in the year. The province, on the other hand, faced with a politically sensitive issue, chose to turn it over to the federal government for resolution.

It was only at this time that a neutral third party entered into the process. It was the resolute stance the army took regarding the use of firearms which prevented further bloodshed. Instead, they embarked upon a wide-ranging series of psychological strategies against the Natives maintaining the blockade. In the end, it was a strategy which brought about closure of overt conflict without casualties.

The event is over, and yet the issues have not been resolved. The psychological victory achieved by the federal government has not produced a decision which is defined as just. It has prevented Native people from further expressing their concern and frustration over land claims. We are continuously told that Canadians are recognizing that Native people must assume more responsibilities for their own affairs, setting their own priorities and determining their own programs. Unfortunately, the Oka affair gives ample proof we are not yet ready to act.

The Oka confrontation revealed in microcosm a larger issue which has plagued politicians and Native people for the past century. Issues such as "self government," "sovereignty" and "tribal control" all remain vague, not clearly defined. Neither side wishes to clearly explicate or unpack the terms so that meaningful negotiations can take place. The issues have arisen without a clear history; that is, they have not resulted from a goal clearly stated by one or the other parties. Rather, as Campbell and Pal (1991) point out, they have occurred almost accidentally, as a result of accumulated contradiction and tensions. In our clumsy attempt to deal with Native issues, we continue to reject meaningful discussion and the development of realistic goals—for both parties. Rather, there seems to be a belief that "things will work out," and the governments (federal and provincial) refuse to approach the problem systematically. The resolute refusal by the four first ministers' conferences on Native issues to deal substantively with Aboriginal issues is a glaring reminder that the federal and provincial governments do not consider Native issues to be high on their priority list.

Politicians have not exhibited any leadership in the arena of Native policy. To be certain, at Oka there was action (delayed) and a resolution, but as Campbell and Pal (1991) note, no leadership. Action was taken by our political leaders so that the Oka problem seemed resolved. Bridges were opened, barricades were removed and weapons taken from Native people. Through the use of power, governments were able to "resolve" the problem so that they would no longer be part of the daily media show. But the resolution did not solve the problem, nor did it bring the two parties closer to a single reality. Rather, it enlarged the chasm between Native people and other residents. Lingering bitterness and antagonism remains in the area, and there has been precious little effort to heal the wounds.

As both the Cardston and Oka scenarios reveal, Canadians have not convinced elected leaders that they could show vision, creativeness and understanding so that Native issues could be dealt with. These issues will not be solved in a year; but once the vision is set, the goals outlined, then we can begin to develop policies and programs to achieve those goals. Thus far, we have not attempted to discuss with Natives their issues and to develop, jointly, ends which will serve both Canada and its Native people.

NOTES

1. On June 15, 1988, the Minister replied to Chief Gabriel in a similar vein as the 1987 letter to Chief Montour. However, the Minister pointed out that a study had been initiated, with the Band Council's support, to assess land needs at Kanesatake.

2. Mr. Michel Girard, an historian who has studied the history of the Oka forest in some considerable detail, has documented that both the original nine-hole golf course and its proposed expansion involved lands that were once part of the historic "common lands" which are of such importance to the local Mohawk population.

3. The evidence suggests that there was debate within the Longhouse over the issue of armed resistance on or about July 5, 1990.

C H A P T E R 11

SELF-DETERMINATION

INTRODUCTION

Until the late 1960s, the federal government took the position that ethnicity was outmoded both as a form of identity and as a basis for a relationship. This was particularly true in the government's assessment of Native ethnicity. There was a feeling that Nativeness would be superseded by more rational and modern structures. However, the continually widening economic gap between Natives and non-Natives and the consequences of various political events, for example, the Bilingual and Bicultural Commission, the *Hawthorn Report*, and the White Paper on Indian Affairs, have given rise to the resurgence of ethnicity and an increase in class tensions. The importance of both class and ethnicity for Indians has varied over time, according to the context and the issue. Until the late 1960s, the various provincial governments and federal departments dealt with Natives as though they were a separate class and were to be treated as a homogeneous group. Since then, however, the class-based relationship has been dropped and ethnicity, disguised as tribalism, has become the basis for Native interaction with the dominant society and its agencies.

The reluctance of both the provincial and federal governments to support Native self-government stems from both a practical and ideological stance. In terms of practicality, the thought of having to deal with 500 mini-governments stretches the imagination. There is also concern about the financial aspect of such a structure. In terms of ideology, a fourth level of government would mean that the status quo would have to change. Both levels of government would have to give up power and new relations would have to be established with Native people.

The objections to self-government also imply that Natives have not moved sufficiently far along a linear path of development toward "civilization" for them to take on some responsibility for their own affairs. This rejection of the idea of Native development was explicit, until recently, in the *Indian Act*.

Deloria and Lytle (1984) argue that self-government involves recognition by the dominant group. According to them, a minority group can be involved in some measure in decision-making, but this process must be monitored carefully so the goals and policies emanating from the minority group are compatible with those of the dominant group. There is a linkage between responsible self-government and development.

Natives argue that they are trying to achieve self-determination. Self-determination is the right of being recognized as a distinct culture with all the rights afforded to a sovereign nation. Native people view self-determination as a concept which provides greater recognition of the cultural differences of peoples who live within enclaves defined by the dominant culture (Turpel, 1990).

As we moved into the 1970s, assimilation once again became an unacceptable policy. Instead, self-determination became the new vision, which, in turn, gave credence to the idea of Native survival. Natives began to demand programs which would support indigenous institutions, and they wanted the freedom to adopt whatever non-Native institutions they thought were compatible with Native values.

The use of ethnic exclusiveness has become an increasingly important means of differentiating people and of establishing ethnic organizations that are region- or nation-wide (Shaw, 1985). Various ethnic symbols and connections have been created to enhance the social and political positions of Natives. Native party leadership has sought support and solidarity on ethnic grounds. Whether or not Natives will be able to prevent the ethnic mask of solidarity from cracking, remains to be seen. It also remains to be seen if old divisions, for example, treaty—non-treaty, status—non-status, Blood-Blackfeet, can be set aside and issues can be dealt with solely from an ethnic perspective. Since the beginning of the 1980s, the various levels of government have once again characterized Nativeness (ethnicity) as a problem for Canadian society, saying that it undermines the existing political order. This sort of pronouncement was very evident at the last two first ministers' Constitutional conferences on Native affairs. Whether this stance will successfully divide Native people or whether Natives can maintain their ethnicity in the face of modernization, also remains to be seen.

SELF-DETERMINATION

Natives today are trying to shed their colonial status and resist further inroads by non-Natives on their way of life. The cultural resurgence and the defense of territory are but two overt expressions of Native self-determination. Other forms of resistance have included economic and political action, the reinterpretation of historical events, the formation of inter-tribal and international networks, and, on occasion, union with non-Native groups. Regardless of the specific strategy used, their overall goal is to achieve independence and self-determination. The Native quest for sovereignty is based upon their belief in Aboriginal rights.

The concept of self-determination was born during the French Revolution, although it had certainly been developing long before. Our use of the term refers to the right of Native people to determine their political future and freely to pursue their cultural and economic development (Umozurike, 1972). Politically, this idea is expressed through independence, self-government, local autonomy, or some other form of increased participation in the governing process. Native people seek independence to ensure democratic government and the absence of internal or external domination. Unfortunately, the concept of self-determination has been variously defined and interpreted over the last decade. This has exacerbated the problem of cross-cultural communication between Natives and those non-Natives who discuss the issue. Whatever unifying factors are used to define a people, for example, ethnic, national, class or racial ones, they are arbitrary symbols—but they are profoundly meaningful to the people using them. The basis for unifying people may change over time or may contain more than one of the components identified above, and it may lead to different strategies being employed by different Native people to achieve the common goal of self-determination.

Self determination involves a new respect for Native culture and a commitment to its survival. There is a desire to build upon traditional aspects of Native culture as a way of leading Native people to economic prosperity. This, in turn, will enhance self concepts and validate the positive aspects of Native culture. In adapting the Native "ethos" and institutions to the larger society (both Canadian and global), Natives want to proceed at their own pace. They want to ensure that social change occurs at a speed which is not disruptive and which produces minimum instability.

There is also a seemingly contradictory stance which Natives have taken regarding federal trust. Natives feel that the federal government has a "trust relationship" with Native people which must be honoured. As Cornell (1988) points out, the demands for self-determination and a continued relationship of entrustment—i.e., independence and paternalism—seem contradictory. Closer inspection of this ideological position reveals that most Native people feel that they will be better able to achieve self-determination if they deal with the federal government rather than provincial officials. They are clearly aware that linkages with the federal government mean that they are dependent upon the federal government both politically and economically. However, Natives believe that through this linkage with the federal government, they will be able to obtain some long-term base financial support which will allow them to become economically developed.

Native people in Canada, aside from having certain physical traits that allow us to identify them as members of a single group, also have a number of socio-cultural characteristics that set them apart from other Canadians and that could form the basis for their solidarity. These include such "ideal" factors as:

1) utilization of land as a common resource base;

2) cultural attachment to place;

3) a fundamentally ecological world-view;

4) a flexible economy and system of exchange;

5) an extended kinship and reciprocity system; and

6) dependence upon a cooperative system of enterprise.

The actions Native people take in the future will depend upon how they choose to develop a sense of identity and cohesion. For example, if the basis for solidarity were to be solely class-based, then their goal would be to change the political system. On the other hand, if the basis were ethnic, then they would demand a separate state or, at least, a relationship of autonomy within the state (Rohen, 1967).

As the issues confronting Native people have increased in number and scope, policy-making (for both Natives and the government) in regard to these issues has become more and more complex. Many more government departments (besides DIAND) have become active participants in the policy process dealing with Natives. As Weaver (1985) notes, this has led to central government agencies playing the role of referee when different departments disagree over policy creation, change or implementation. Overall, this has reduced the ability of DIAND to carry through with its own policies. In short, Native policy is no longer the exclusive role of one department, but results from a collaboration by a number of departments and agencies.

CONSTITUTIONAL PATRIATION

Before we begin discussing sovereignty and self-determination, we need to place these ideas in their philosophical and political context. The federal government's desire to patriate the Constitution facilitated the efforts of Natives to discuss their concerns and bring several new issues to the foreground. The discussion of constitutional issues provided a national and international forum for Natives to air their concerns about their inability to participate in Canadian society. The average Canadian could no longer claim to be ignorant of the issues, nor could the elected representatives hide behind such a facade. The issues became public and were forcefully articulated by the Native leaders, who also managed to convey a sense of urgency.

Until the late 1970s, the federal government's attempts to patriate our Constitution were vague and episodic. Eventually, however, constitutional reform won national attention because of 1) Québec's threats to secede from Confederation, 2) the increasing alienation of the West, and 3) conflict between the federal and provincial governments (Gibbins, 1986). Constitutional reform was not initiated by Natives' concerns nor by lobbying efforts exerted by Native organizations. Nevertheless, Native people had become interested in the constitutional issue and had been active in the arena since the mid-1970s, when northern Natives had developed and presented the *Dene Declaration*. This was followed by the Inuit's *Nunavut Proposal* and the Federation of Saskatchewan Indians' *Indian Government*. In line with these new political philosophies, Indian organizations adapted to the new realities of the time; for example, the National Indian Brotherhood reorganized during the 1980-82 period and created the Assembly of First Nations. These political activities by Natives were made possible through increased government funding and by the 1973 Supreme Court ruling in the Nishga land-claims case, which acknowledged (albeit indirectly) the existence of Aboriginal rights.

When the first constitutional amendment bill was introduced in 1978, only vague references were made to Native issues. This suggested that Natives were not considered an important element in Canadian society by the federal and provincial governments. It also seemed to imply that the 1969 White Paper (which would have done away with the legal concept of Indian) was being implemented through the back door. Because of pressure brought to bear by a variety of non-Aboriginal groups, the federal government agreed to allow the three major Native organizations to attend the first ministers' meetings as observers. Natives responded by claiming that this was exclusion in disguise. They preferred to sit at the conference as equals and be given voting privileges when matters pertaining to Aboriginal people were discussed.

Late in 1979, the Continuing Committee for Ministers on the Constitution (CCMC) met to decide how to handle further challenges and protests from Aboriginal people. They created a steering committee to meet formally with the three Native organizations representing the status Indians, Inuit, and non-status Indians and Métis—the National Indian Brotherhood (NIB), the Inuit Committee on National Issues (ICNI) and the Native Council of Canada (NCC). The Federal-Provincial Relations Office, the federal body dealing with Natives on this issue, met both formally and informally with Native groups through the remaining months of 1979. But it was not until December of 1979 that the Aboriginal associations and the steering committee of the CCMC formally discussed the Aboriginal position on Canada's Constitution. By 1980, the new Liberal government provided each of the three Aboriginal associations $400 000 to research and cover costs of preparing a brief on constitutional reform and Native people. In addition, two provinces—Ontario and Saskatchewan—also provided Native organizations with substantial sums of money.

When the 1980 First Ministers' Conference was held, Native issues were not on the agenda and Aboriginal peoples were invited only as observers. The Natives, feeling completely left out when issues directly affecting them were being discussed, chose to act in a more visible political manner. First, they held their own mini-conference, and, later, they began to lobby in England. In late 1980, they placed a half-page advertisement in *The Times* of London. Their goal was to generate some sympathy among the British members of Parliament and not to allow patriation of the Constitution unless safeguards for Aboriginal people were inserted. At a more practical level, they hoped the British Parliament would respond by discussing Canadian Native issues, thereby disrupting its already packed schedule. This, in turn, would force the British prime minister to put off dealing with Canada's request to patriate the Constitution, an outcome neither the British nor Canada wanted. Next, the Natives presented their position to the Special Joint Committee of the Senate and House of Commons in Canada and found that committee members were sympathetic to Native concerns. In the end, the actions of Peter Ittinuar (an Inuit), Warren Allmand (Minister of Indian Affairs), and Anthony Kershaw (Chair of the British Foreign and Commonwealth Affairs Committee) forced the government to add a Charter of Rights to its proposals for patriating the Constitution (Sanders, 1983).

By this time, the Union of British Columbia Indian Chiefs had filed a lawsuit against the federal government to establish whether relevant treaty obligations would remain with Great Britain or would become the responsibility of the Canadian government. In October, the Constitution Express (a protest train) was scheduled to travel from Vancouver to Ottawa. From there a delegation was to continue to New York to meet the United Nations. In addition, the Foreign Affairs Committee of the British House of Commons (Kershaw Committee) began hearings concerning British responsibilities for the Canadian Constitution, and this meant that Indians could submit briefs and act as witnesses. Finally, the Russell Tribunal in Amsterdam began looking at the plight of North American Indians, giving Canadian Indians another international forum in which to plead their case. Although the Kershaw Committee found, in November 1980, that Britain no longer had treaty responsibilities for Indians, Natives continued to pursue every available avenue of political action.

This increased international activity on the part of Natives produced some coalitions among the three major Native groups, as well as among non-Native organizations. By early 1981, the federal government relented and added two sections to the constitutional proposals that 1) protected the rights of Aboriginal peoples, and 2) required that future first ministers' meetings be held to deal with

Aboriginal issues. However, further amendments were introduced by the government that would have permitted it and any provincial government to come to a bilateral agreement nullifying the protection of Aboriginal peoples (Zlotkin, 1983). As a result, Natives, with the exception of the Inuit, withdrew their short-lived support of the first constitutional conference.

The Inuit Committee on National Issues (ICNI) continued to support the federal government. Committee members felt that Native people could carry on negotiations about Aboriginal rights with the federal government after patriation had occurred. The ICNI emerged in late 1979 because of the heavy work loads carried by individuals in the Inuit Tapirisat of Canada (ITC). The ICNI was responsible for representing Inuit views on the Constitution and on other issues of national significance. The ITC would then be free to pursue, full-time, its work on land claims. The ICNI had two co-chairpersons and one representative from each of the five Inuit regions: COPE, Western Arctic; Kitikmeot Inuit Association, Central Arctic; Keewatin Inuit Association, Keewatin area; Makivik Corporation; Québec and Labrador Association, Baffin Region Inuit Association, Labrador.

In late 1981, the Supreme court ruled that a unilateral request to amend the Constitution by the federal government was legal but not in keeping with tradition. But since the federal government wanted the provinces' support, it agreed to delete the clause affording protection to Aboriginal people from the final form of the accord.

When it was announced, the *November Accord* of 1982 did not contain any clause recognizing or affirming Aboriginal or treaty rights. The Native groups strongly objected to this and created a Native alliance group—the Aboriginal Rights Coalition. In addition, they began to intensify their international lobbying (Sanders, 1983). It was also at this time that media support began to materialize on behalf of the Natives; for example, *The Globe and Mail* supported the entrenchment of Aboriginal rights. As a result of both domestic and international concern, the premiers agreed to reinstate the Aboriginal-rights clause with one change: "rights" was changed to "existing rights."

After the passage of the *Canada Constitution Act*, 1982, Natives moved their efforts to England in an attempt to stop patriation. The Indian Association of Alberta (with the help of Nova Scotia and New Brunswick Native organizations) filed lawsuits to stop patriation. The Federation of Saskatchewan Indians also initiated legal action. Finally, the Union of British Columbia Indian Chiefs (joined by the Four Nation Confederacy of Manitoba and the Grand Council Treaty No. 9 of Ontario) brought suit to have the *Canada Act* declared *ultra vires*. But by June of 1981, all cases and appeals had been dismissed and it was clear that the *Canada Act* was valid legislation.

Aboriginal rights were entrenched in Section 35 of the *Constitution Act*, 1982, which came into force April 17, 1982. In addition, Section 25 of this act ensures that Aboriginal rights are not adversely affected by the *Charter of Rights and Freedoms*. Finally, Section 32 requires that the federal government convene additional constitutional conferences to deal with Aboriginal peoples. Section 32 also requires that future first ministers' meetings be held to deal with Aboriginal issues. The first conference, held in 1983, resulted in minor changes to Sections 25(b), 35 and 37 of the Constitution. Since then, three additional first ministers' meetings have been held to deal with Native issues. None of these meetings produced any substantive results. (For a thorough review of the first two conferences, see Schwartz, 1986.) The unilateral imposition of *Bill C-31* by the federal government suggests that neither side has been able to establish a sympathetic relation with the other. *Bill C-31* changed the *Indian Act* with regard to band membership. Under this bill, bands will control their own membership, and Indian women will no longer lose their status by marrying non-Indians. In addition, Indians who lost their status because of Section 12, 1(b) of the *Indian Act* can now be reinstated and allowed to return to their reserve (see chapter 1).

Between the first conference in 1983 and the last one in 1987, the *Penner Report* was released, *Bill C-31* was passed, the task force reviewing comprehensive claims policy released its report, and *Bill C-43* (the *Sechelt Indian Band Self-government Act*) was introduced. A new political climate was evident as the participants prepared for the last conference, but internal discord emerged on the Natives' side, and a lack of political will was apparent in the preliminary statements released by the premiers. The talks, therefore, were doomed to failure before they began.

Provincial officials had quietly agreed among themselves to take a stand against the form of Indian self-government being promoted by the Assembly of First Nations. The premiers were not prepared to be innovative in their approach to Native issues, nor were they in any mood to propose new policy directions themselves. In short, their chief concern was to maintain the status quo while still fulfilling the requirement to hold this conference, as set out in the Charter in 1982.

The last meetings turned out to be the least inspiring of all the conferences on Aboriginal issues. Only the federal government was willing to strike a new deal with Natives and attempt to develop new paths for self-determination. Although some provincial officials might have felt that a new deal was in order, their actions did not support one. This last conference, like those before it, ended without the participants agreeing on any substantive issues. It did not even come close to producing an agreement on the role of Natives in Canadian society, nor was there any consensus on a plan for dealing with the issues raised by Native leaders.

Native involvement in the constitutional patriation process was based on several premises. First, Natives saw the Constitution as a symbolic statement about what is important in Canadian society. They also viewed the document as a potential lever for use in future political action. As Gibbins (1986) points out, the inclusion of Natives and Native concerns in such important documents legitimizes the group's interests and claims. In short, Natives felt that if they could be recognized as an important group in Canadian society, they could use this as a stepping stone to further such aspirations as settling land claims. They also wanted to influence the government in regard to Aboriginal and treaty rights. Finally, they hoped that through their involvement in the patriation of the Constitution, they would be able to exert pressure on the federal government to discuss issues of sovereignty and self-government.

The initial involvement in the constitutional talks by Native groups was minimal because of a lack of organization and funds. Also, they did not offer any stance of their own in regard to Aboriginal rights, but merely reacted to the federal and provincial governments' vague pronouncements. It was only after debate had been initiated that Native groups put forth proposals with regard to Aboriginal, treaty and land rights. Federal and provincial officials reacted to these proposals by asking for more information and clarification. The governments did not put forth any new proposals, but simply used this strategy of stalling to maintain a benevolent image by never having to say no (Schwartz, 1986). It was also during this time that Natives began to discuss the issues of sovereignty and self-government. Although their concerns were initially dismissed by government officials, their persistence paid off. Slowly these issues entered the public arena of discussion, and when the *Constitution Act*, 1982, was finally enacted, Aboriginal rights had been entrenched. In addition, other issues such as self-government had by this time come under government scrutiny.

Aboriginal peoples were strongly opposed to the distinct society clause [Section 2(1)(b)] of the 1987 Meech Lake Accord. The Assembly of First Nations argued that it perpetuated the idea of a duality in Canada and strengthened the myth that the French and English peoples are the foundation of Canada. It distorts history in that it makes it seem as though Aboriginal society never existed. Furthermore, this Accord failed to give explicit constitutional recognition to the existence of First Nations as distinct societies.

The preamble to the *Constitutional Act*, 1982, makes a significant statement on the nature of Canadian culture: "Canada is founded upon principles that recognize the supremacy of God and the rule of law." This assumption is insensitive to cultural differences and inaccurate for Aboriginal groups. Furthermore, the Charter does not support a collectivist idea of rights for culturally distinct (non-European) peoples. Turpel notes that the Charter expresses the values of a liberal democracy on the European model. It favours individualism and assumes a highly organized and impersonal industrial society. The paradigm of rights, based on the protypical right of individual ownership of property, is antithetical to the understanding of the individual's relationship to society that is widely shared by First Nations peoples.

SOVEREIGNTY AND ABORIGINAL RIGHTS

The following section of this chapter will treat the specific issue of sovereignty and the concept of Aboriginal rights. We will not be able to discuss all the legal aspects of these issues, rather we will try to provide the reader with the historical context out of which these issues have emerged. In addition, we will try to give a sense of what the various groups mean when they use these terms. The last section of this chapter will focus on Indian self-government and what it means both to Natives and to non-Natives.

When the concept of sovereignty is applied to a particular region or people, it suggests that a political state exists. As Nadeau (1979) points out, in order for a state to exist, three conditions have to be present: population, territory and government. Indians argue that since they possess these three attributes, they should, in turn, have sovereignty.

The concept of sovereignty as defined by Indians implies that their people have the right of self-determination. This right, they argue, arises not only out of the various treaties, the *Constitution Act*, 1867, the *Royal Proclamation* of 1763, and assorted other federal acts, but also (and perhaps more importantly) as a gift from the Creator. This gift has never been, nor can it ever be, surrendered. As Nadeau points out:

> Thus *the Indians assert sovereignty and the right to create their own unique forms of self-government. They will have the right to exercise full internal sovereignty. Indian government is responsible for peace, order and good government within Indian territory and for the maintenance and well-being of Indian people....* They should have exclusive legislative, executive and administrative jurisdiction over Indian lands and resources and people within its territory...and when issues of Indians extend beyond the reserve, Indians will have full control (1979: 6-7).

Natives also argue that there are certain federal statutes (or documents that have the force of statutes), that specify that the federal government has a special trust relationship with them and is responsible for providing the resources that will enable them to achieve their goal of self-sufficiency.

Recently, some Indian organizations have formally established their positions on this issue; but, partially because the various Native groups cannot agree and partially because the issue has not been fully analyzed, no precise statement on sovereignty, self-determination, or self-government has been articulated by the Natives. Indian groups such as the Manitoba Indian Brotherhood (1971), The Grand Council Treaty No. 9, and the Federation of Saskatchewan Indians (1977) have tried to present statements on the issue, but the resultant documents are vague and incomplete.

Historical Context

There is no question that prior to the arrival of the Europeans Indians occupied and controlled the area that is now called Canada. The question of sovereignty, however, remains unresolved and the Government of Canada has taken the position that Indians, Inuit or Métis were never nations in the legal sense and are not now to be treated as such. Needless to say, Natives disagree with this interpretation and argue that they always have been nations and should be accorded all the rights, privileges and responsibilities pertaining to nations.

On the basis of certain historical documents, the Crown, until the twentieth century, recognized the inherent sovereignty of Indians. In this century, however, recognition has been less overt and consistent. More recently, there has been a formal rejection of Natives' claims to sovereignty. How has this come about? The initial relations of the Crown with Natives were heavily influenced by pragmatic factors, and this led directly to the recognition of Native sovereignty. But over time, this necessity passed away, and the Crown could afford to take the position to which it now subscribes. As a result, various political and legislative acts have been put in place which have, at least to the government's satisfaction, phased out any recognition of Native sovereignty. To illustrate this, we will briefly look at some of the major acts that have a bearing on such a claim. Ironically, these acts have been interpreted by both Natives and government officials to substantiate their opposing positions. We will begin by looking at the Native interpretation.

Historically, royal charters (including the Hudson's Bay Company charter of 1670) were used to establish political relationships between peoples. Many of the early charters recognized the autonomous status of Indian peoples and their ownership of land. For example, the HBC charter states that the Company was to make peace or war "...with any Prince or people whatsoever that are not Christians...." Also during the early history of Canada, various royal instructions from the British Crown could be interpreted as being based on the premise that Indians existed as nations. For example, the instructions sent to the governor of Nova Scotia (after the signing of the Treaty of Utrecht, 1713) stated that Indians were a nation. The signing of various treaties in 1725 (after the Seven Years War) by Indians and the British suggest that the agreements were between two independent, sovereign nations. In other words, these actions imply that Indians were viewed as an organized body of people with their own distinct government systems.

Treaties between Indians and Euro-Canadians were made as legalistic, written documents. Natives have viewed these documents as sacred and as representing agreements between two sovereign nations. Euro-Canadians, on the other hand, view them as having a status similar to a contract, although they are not contracts.

In a sense, treaties were procedures used by Euro-Canadians to expedite a political process ensuring economic and military inroads. As Turpel (1990) points out, it is interesting that treaties with Natives are not considered equal to treaties carried out with other sovereign international peoples or nations. If you raise the question why, the answer is that Aboriginal people were not sufficiently "civilized" to qualify as sovereign people, or that they had already lost their sovereignty through some predestined and mysterious process. But both these myths have been challenged successfully. Why then are these arguments perpetuated? Why do we continue to pretend that Native people lack distinct cultures, or have inferior cultures, or had no political structure. The answer is clear. To accept the opposite view would require substantial changes in Native-White relations, with all the attendant costs.

The *Royal Proclamation* of 1763 is further evidence that the Crown explicitly recognized Indians as sovereign nations. In addition to this, and consistent with it, over 80 treaties were concluded between various Indian groups and the Crown. These treaties seem to recognize the sovereignty of Indian nations.

The *Constitution Act, 1867 (British North America Act)* and the Rupert's Land Transfer are two additional pieces of evidence used by Indians to argue their sovereign status. Specifically, they cite Section 109,91(24) and 146 of the 1867 *Act*. The Rupert's Land Transfer stated that the claims of the Indian tribes to compensation for lands required for purposes of settlement would be considered and settled in conformity with the equitable principles which had been used by the British Crown in its past dealings with the Aboriginals. The *Indian Act* also seems to give Indians a measure of self-government which implies that they are sovereign. Finally, the *Constitution Act*, 1982, the Universal Declaration of Human Rights, and the *Declaration Regarding Non Self-Governing Territories* (of which Canada is a signatory) provide some basis for concluding that Indians have sovereignty.

In addition to the various statutes or acts that have been part of our history, the Canadian and British courts have made rulings that would seem to recognize the inherent sovereignty of the Indian people. In the early *Mohegan Indians* v. *Connecticut* (1769) case, the Privy Council made explicit recognition of tribal sovereignty. This view was reinforced in a series of judgements in the United States (1810-1832). In the *Worchester* v. *Georgia* (1832) case, the court affirmed that the Indian nations are recognized as having rights of self-government. The courts also upheld the *Royal Proclamation* of 1763 as confirming the inherent sovereignty of Indian Nations. Canadian court cases that concur with the above include the *R*. v. *White and Bob* (1964); *Calder* v. *Attorney General of British Columbia* (1973); and *The Queen* v. *the Secretary of State for Foreign and Commonwealth Affairs* (1982). A more recent Canadian case (*Hamlet of Baker Lake* v. *Minister of Indian Affairs and Northern Development*, 1980) illustrates that the courts recognize the existence of Aboriginal land-use rights and that these rights belong to the Aboriginal collectivity. Thus, if the collectivity has rights, it must be able to determine (as a collectivity) how it will exercise and dispose of those rights (Schwartz, 1986).

Two additional sources of support for Indian sovereignty have been customary law and the trust responsibility for Section 91(24) of the *Constitution Act, 1867*. In the first case, the question is whether or not Indians had laws that were distinct from Canadian law. If they actually had laws and their laws were different, then those laws can be continued and provide a basis for claiming nationhood. In the second case, the question is how much trust responsibility the federal government owes to Indian nations.

While the cases cited above seem to suggest that Indians are indeed nations and have sovereignty, several arguments have been used by the Crown to refute these claims. First, the Crown cites the doctrine of continuity, which states that in the case of conquest or cession, the rights of a "civilized" original people and their laws remain intact until the colonial government changes them through an act of its own parliament. This, they would argue, has occurred over time with the introduction of British law. They might also argue that since the Aboriginal peoples were not "civilized" at the time of European entry, the laws of the colonizing country took immediate effect. A second argument put forth by the federal government is that, depending on how the *Royal Proclamation* of 1763 is interpreted, sovereignty does or does not exist for Indians. The government has interpreted a key phrase of the *Proclamation* in such a way that suggests that Indians *do not have* sovereignty. This phrase states that restrictions on settlements into Indian country were to be "...for present or until our future pleasure to be known." The courts have interpreted this to mean that Indian tenure under the *Royal Proclamation* of 1763 was a personal usufructuary right dependent upon the good will of the sovereign. This ruling was made explicit in the *St. Catherine's Milling* case and has set a precedent for all later decisions. In some cases it has allowed the courts to set aside the issue of the doctrine of continuity when trying to make a decision on Indian sovereignty.

Finally, the courts (and the government using these court decisions) have argued that treaties with the Indians were not international treaties. The courts have ruled (with no explanation) that while the agreements with the Indians are known as treaties, they are not treaties in the sense of public international law; that is, they are not treaties between sovereign nations. Moreover, judges have argued that where treaties were entered into with Natives, they involved a commitment by Indians to obey the sovereign. Finally, no continuing right to self-government (if it existed prior to the signing of the treaty) is mentioned in any treaty.

Today the issue remains as unclear as it was a century ago. No statute, court decision or political statement has been provided by which the issue might be resolved. Indians still argue they have sovereignty; the government says they don't. The issue has recently moved out of the judicial context and into the political arena. Today the government is trying to address the issues of Aboriginal rights and self-government—two crucial concerns that pertain to the sovereignty issue. It is unlikely that the courts or the government will ever find Aboriginals to have sovereignty. This statement reflects both past judicial decisions handed down on Aboriginal issues and practical concerns. Politically speaking, Native self-government would not be a palatable solution to most Canadians. Pragmatically, it would mean that a substantial realignment of our parliamentary democratic system would need to be undertaken.

In an attempt to address this issue without actually confronting the specific concern of sovereignty, the federal government has chosen to discuss two matters that flow from the sovereignty issue—Aboriginal rights and self-government. Aboriginal rights were dealt with in the *Constitution Act, 1982*, and are still being discussed in an attempt to define and implement them. Self-government, the second concern, was addressed by the government's *Penner Report* and is now (under a variety of guises), being implemented. In the end, the federal government hopes that negotiations toward the resolution of these two areas will pose solutions that are acceptable to both groups so that sovereignty will no longer be an issue of concern to Native people.

Aboriginal Rights

Fundamental questions about the relationship between Native people and other Canadians have been discussed for over two centuries, and special rights for Native people have always been a central issue to these discussions. In more general terms, the questions of responsibility and obligation of parties has occupied centre stage. Until recently, it was felt that while Native people had responsibilities to assimilate and an obligation to uphold Canadian law, the Crown was immune from obligations and did not have a responsibility to provide a special law for Native people.

With the passing of the Constitution in 1982, Aboriginal peoples have had their Aboriginal and treaty rights recognized and affirmed. Section 32 of the Constitution explicitly states that all laws and policies in Canada must be consistent with these rights. While the federal government has accepted, in principle, these guidelines, in practice they continue to develop policy and programs which run counter to the Constitution. This is most clearly seen in the area of land rights. Native people feel that their land rights should be recognized and actions should be taken to reaffirm those rights. On the other hand, the government has taken the position that they want to extinguish the "burden" of Aboriginal rights. The federal government has taken a bureaucratic-legal position with regard to dealing with land issues. Natives feel that a legal-political process should be put in place.

Needless to say, the government's position was found wanting by Native people and was finally called into question by the courts with the 1973 *Calder* v. *Attorney General for B.C.* and the 1974 *Cardinal* v. *The Queen* rulings. Ten years later *Nowegijick* v. *The Queen* (1983) and *Guerin* v. *The Queen* (1984) would reaffirm these earlier decisions and fundamentally alter the relationship between Natives and the government (both federal and provincial). Since these rulings, both parties have continued the process of trying to resolve the question of rights and responsibilities; however, today the assumptions have changed.

The federal government has a fiduciary responsibility toward Natives. However, at the same time, it carries out policies which are in its own best interest. When Native interests and government interests come into conflict, government interests are given a higher priority than those of Native people. This conflict of interest has been pointed out by many Natives, yet the federal government refuses to address the issue.

During the past decade, because of international pressure and domestic concern, the Canadian government has tried to grapple with the issue of Aboriginal rights. Specifically, the patriation of the Constitution led to a sense of urgency in resolving the problem. In the end, the government entrenched Aboriginal rights in the Constitution without knowing or specifying what they entailed. The inclusion of the phrase "existing rights" has done little to clarify the meaning of the concept, although as Flanagan (1983, 1985) points out, it may provide for a legitimate basis for excluding Métis Aboriginal rights claims.

There are two opposed opinions about the existence of Aboriginal rights in Canada. On the one hand, there are number of academics, historians, and some legal advisors who are convinced of their existence. When one considers case law, however, it appears that many of the judges are not of the same opinion. Past and current court decisions suggest that if Aboriginal rights do exist, they take the form of personal usufruct—the right of an individual to occupy and use a piece of land—not collective, group rights. The *Baker Lake* decision (1980) is one notable exception to this rule.

The *Hamlet of Baker Lake* v. *Minister of Indian Affairs and Northern Development* decision arose out of a dispute between the Inuit around Baker Lake and the private corporations that were attempting to exploit the mineral potential in the area. In this case, Justice Mahoney ruled that the original Inuit had an organized society. He stated that they did not have a very elaborate system of institutions, but that theirs was a society organized to exploit the resources available in the area. He also recognized the existence of Aboriginal land use rights *and* that these rights belonged to the Aboriginal collectivity. It follows that, if the collectivity has rights, it must also have the right to determine how it will exercise those rights.

Some people argue that Aboriginal rights are one form of human rights. If this is the case, it might prove instructive to first discuss the issue of Aboriginal rights within an international context. While international law has no specific precedent-setting power for Canadian law, it does exert an educative and persuasive force. For example, the concept of guardianship has been heavily influenced by international law. In addition, it indicates that Aboriginal rights are not a recent issue. As Davies (1985) shows, the theory of Aboriginal rights goes back well into the sixteenth century. The Spanish theologian Francisco de Vitoria is usually called the father of Aboriginal rights. His pronouncements and views, while not accepted by many, had a discernable impact on the ways various countries would view Aboriginal rights. Other international laws have also influenced our thinking about Aboriginal rights. Other issues, such as "discovery" and "occupation," have been less influenced by international law, but international law does reflect concern over these issues, as well.

A Native tribe, however, has no status as a legal entity under international law. It is generally accepted that, even though Indians were "sovereign and independent" societies before Europeans entered North America, this status was lost through the operation of European international law. The British and American claims tribunals have stated that an Indian tribe is not subject to international law and is a legal unit only insofar as the law of the country in which it lives recognizes it as such (Bennett, 1978).

International law has a more direct influence on how Canada deals with its Native people through, first of all, the international treaties which have been signed and ratified by Canada. Breach of these treaties could bring international censure, judgment by the International Court or Justice, or an arbitration tribunal. Again, however, one must remember that Indians have no international standing and thus cannot sue Canada for breach of its obligations toward them. It should also be noted that Canada is not legally bound by many international treaties because it has not signed them. The rationale for not signing them has two bases: 1) many of the matters involved are not under federal competence but provincial, and 2) a concept of written codes of human rights seems to be contrary to common law and to the doctrine of parliamentary sovereignty.

To provide the reader with a sense of the scope of these treaties, we will examine some of the international agreements that involve the Government of Canada and Native people. First of all, as a member of the United Nations, Canada is morally obligated to live up to the UN Charter, which deals with the concepts of equality and the improvement of conditions for all humanity. Secondly, Canada has ratified the *Universal Declaration of Human Rights*, which, in part, states:

> Everyone has the right to an effective remedy by the competent national tribunal for acts violating the fundamental rights granted him by the constitution or by the law.

Although Canada is not legally bound by the *Declaration*, it has some obligations to fulfil this mandate. Such actions as curtailment of Native hunting and fishing rights, failure to fulfill treaty obligations, and the arbitrary deprivation of property would constitute breach of the *Declaration*.

Canada has also ratified the *Convention on the Elimination of all Forms of Racial Discrimination* (1969), which lists specific measures to be taken for the purpose of securing adequate advancement of certain racial or ethnic groups. Unfortunately, Canada has inherited the concept of human rights as individual rights, but the idea of societies and cultures themselves having rights is a relatively new one.

Although international law could be considered integrationist in its perspective, it is also aware of the dangers in such a perspective. For example, the value of minority group culture is affirmed, and methods are outlined for assuring that "adaptable" traits of the minority group will be acknowledged and preserved. In addition, the integrationist programs are considered valid only if the Native groups themselves agree to the measures and are involved in the planning and implementation of them.

Even though Canada seems to agree with the integrationist perspective, it has not been willing to introduce the safeguards. For example, we tend to segregate Natives more and more. We do not involve them in the planning process, they have little influence in the dominant society, and they are rarely consulted on matters that pertain to their way of life. In short, we do not place any significant value on the Native culture. Neither do we provide them with sufficient assistance or enough protection to meet even the minimal standards of international law. In summary, while there is a body of international law relevant to Aboriginal rights, lack of enforcement has limited its role to that of an educating vehicle.

The Concept of Right

One could say that all rights are legal interests but it would not be correct to say that all legal interests are rights. The word "right" seems to mean that one person has an affirmative claim against another, that is, the other person has a legal duty to respect that right. Thus, the concepts of right and duty seem to go hand in hand. However, the concept of right is not to be confused with that of privilege. The difference seems to lie in the fact that it is the absence of duty that identifies a privilege. Thus, the privilege to do a certain act arises where the privileged person has no duty to refrain from doing the privileged act. When people assert that they have a right, it means that they are confirming that they have a legal interest in an object, such as land. But whether or not someone else can change the nature of that legal interest depends on the powers and the immunities associated with that object. Powers are created by statute and involve the ability to change the nature of the interest. Anyone who tries to deny another's interest in an object but does not have the power to do so can be accused of acting *ultra vires*, that is, beyond the scope of the powers granted them by law (Henderson, 1978; Barsh and Henderson, 1982).

Given the above, we should view the concept of Aboriginal rights as having several different meanings depending on the speaker, the context of its use, and the time at which it is evoked (Weaver, 1985). Regardless of how one defines the concept, however, it always embodies the central characterizing notion of a relationship between a dominant and subordinate component of society (Flanagan, 1982).

At one end of the spectrum, the definition of Aboriginal rights includes the view that Aboriginal peoples are Nations and their relationships with other Nations are governed by international law. As noted previously, this position was espoused by de Vitoria in the sixteenth century, and early nineteenth century Indian supporters in the United States also embraced this definition. However, by the mid-nineteenth century, the American and Canadian courts had rendered this interpretation virtually inadmissible in a court of law.

If the courts were not accepting of this definition, what position were they taking? In the courts' eyes Indian peoples were not to be defined as sovereign states. They were viewed as primitive, unorganized groups of people who led nomadic lives and had no formalized legal system. In view of this, civilized powers could intrude into the lands occupied by these primitive peoples and unilaterally assume sovereignty over both the people and the land. Only expediency or humanitarianism would lead to treaties being negotiated. Any Aboriginal rights that might exist emanate from the prerogatives of the Crown.

Throughout the sixteenth and seventeenth centuries, European countries had followed this line of reasoning. Papal bulls, letters patent and the concept of "discovery" were considered sufficient to lay claim to vast areas of land. Later, a provision would be established that if the inhabitants of the "new country" were "civilized," then their existing laws would remain in effect until altered by the colonizing country. However, if the new country was inhabited by "savages," then it was presumed that they had no law and European law would be considered the existing law.

In the end, the best we can offer for a definition of Aboriginal rights is the one suggested by Cumming (1973): "Those property rights which native people retain as a result of their original use and occupancy of lands" (p. 238). This is not to suggest that this is an official or even legal definition used by litigants or governments. It is simply a definition that seems to capture the essence of Aboriginal rights.

What legal or political conditions would be necessary for Natives to convince others that they have Aboriginal rights? Elliott (1985) has noted three ways in which it could be argued that such rights exist. One of the most easily recognized ways is through reference to royal prerogatives. These are statements made by a government with regard to some issue; if local governments have not been established, they have the force of statutes. In Canada, the *Royal Proclamation* (1763) is an example of a royal prerogative. The *Royal Proclamation* was issued by King George III of Britain, and one section of it deals with Indian people. It suggests that Indians had a pre-existing title to lands. Some would argue, therefore, that it supports Natives' claims to Aboriginal rights. The section that deals with Indian people has never been repealed and thus still remains part of our legal system.

A second way in which the existence of Aboriginal rights can be argued in Canada is by reference to the decisions of the courts; that is, common law. As Elliott (1985) points out, two conflicting notions about Aboriginal rights have emerged out of common law. One was that the *Royal Proclamation* of 1763 gave Indians Aboriginal title, and the other was that Aboriginal title was derived from their use and occupancy of the land from time immemorial.

The courts' interpretation that Aboriginal title derives from royal prerogative was based on one of the few court cases dealing with Aboriginal rights. This case, *St. Catherine's Milling and Lumber Company* v. *The Queen*, 1885, influenced the court's interpretations of Aboriginal rights for nearly one hundred years. The key component of the decision, handed down by the Privy Council, was the recognition of the existence in law of an Indian interest in the land in question, and the Council attributed the interest solely to the provisions of the *Royal Proclamation* of 1763 (Elliott, 1985).

In 1973, Canadian common law on the issue of Aboriginal rights would change from an exclusive basis in royal prerogative to include a possible basis in use and occupancy. This new interpretation was based on the *Calder* v. *Attorney General of British Columbia* (1973) case. In this case, the Nishga Indians (represented by Calder) lost their land claims but won judicial recognition of the crucial issue that their claim to the land was based on their ancestors' occupation and use of it from time immemorial.

Today, both arguments are used to support Native claims of Aboriginal rights. However, the question remains as to whether the *Calder* case stands as a general legal recognition of the validity of occupancy-based claims. The answer, unfortunately, is both yes and no. Some courts have recognized and accepted this argument, while others have not. A review of court decisions would suggest that lower Canadian courts have accepted occupancy-based title as a legitimate argument, while higher courts have not yet given clear legal recognition to occupancy-based Aboriginal title (Elliott, 1985: 81; Federation of Saskatchewan Indian Nations, 1985).

The third support for Aboriginal rights comes from the constitutional framework of a country. While there has been no general legislation passed by the Canadian Parliament that explicitly recognizes Aboriginal title, there are some pieces of legislation that implicitly apply to Aboriginal rights, for example, the *Manitoba Act*, 1870; the *Dominion Lands Act*, from 1872 to 1908; land cession treaties; and, more recently, sections 35 and 37(1) and (2) of the *Constitution Act*, 1982.

As noted above, Aboriginal title, until lately, was interpreted as resting solely upon royal prerogative. More recently, occupancy-based arguments are being reevaluated. Finally, issues emerging out of the patriated Canadian Constitution are beginning to come to the foreground. However, because our court system continues to approach law from a positivist framework, there is little chance that the courts will change their interpretation. Henderson (1983) and Elliott (1985) have noted that the Canadian courts have looked at the legal system as a closed system, and have evaluated the laws on procedural or technical issues, rather than undertaking a comprehensive examination of Aboriginal rights.

The second issue arising from the concept of Aboriginal rights is the question of content. In other words, assuming that Aboriginal rights exist, what do they entail? How long do they exist and under what restrictions? Elliott (1985) looks at land rights and provides us with a concrete example. He begins his analysis of these rights by setting fee simple interest in land as a base line. Fee simple, he points out, gives the owner an unlimited right to use and occupy the land for an indefinite period of time. In addition, there are no restrictions on owners who want to alienate the land. Using fee simple as a comparative construct, we can see the variations that are possible. For example, do Aboriginals hold title to the land? How can Indians alienate their land? Although a few of these concerns have been dealt with by lower courts, previous experience suggests that higher courts tend to reverse these decisions. Finally, the very fact that so few cases have come before the courts has also created uncertainty as to the content of Aboriginal rights.

We now move to the issue of changing or extinguishing Aboriginal rights. Here the question is whether or not these rights can be legally terminated or otherwise changed so that they are not as comprehensive as previously thought. The law has provided for this. Again, using Elliott's example of land title, one can point to treaties which were negotiated for the express purpose of obtaining land rights from Indians. The issue becomes more problematic, however, when actions taken by the government seem to extinguish Aboriginal rights (land title) while not explicitly saying so. This was one of the reasons why the Supreme Court justices differed in their decisions with regard to the Nishga in the *Calder* case.

Finally, we address the question of compensation for Aboriginal rights. As Elliott (1985) has noted, although many statutes provide for compensation when property is expropriated, there is no constitutional right to compensation. Even thought the Canadian *Charter of Rights and Freedoms* provides for the right of the individual to life, liberty, security of person, enjoyment of property, and the right not to be deprived of any of these except by due process of law, it does not deal with compensation. In other words, if private property is expropriated, there is no legal statute that forces the government to compensate one for it.

Regardless of the tentativeness, vagueness, and lack of clarity of the above issues, the *Constitution Act*, 1982 recognizes and affirms the *existing* Aboriginal rights. What these rights are is now the subject of debate. Aboriginals argue that they include a number of general concerns; for example, education, self-government, and housing. But others feel that the list needs to be more specific. The task now before the courts and politicians is to define and outline exactly what Aboriginal rights entail.

Recent court cases have supported interpretations long held by Natives but resisted by government officials. For example, the landmark decision of the Supreme Court in 1973 in the Nishga's land claim case forced Canadians to change their views about Native land claims. More recently, the Supreme Court decision in 1990 (*Sparrow* v. *The Queen*) ruled that Indian rights could only be removed if there was explicit legislation. Thus, unless specific legislation was passed to divest Natives of their land claims and right of self-government, the rights remain theirs. The prerogative legislation which confirmed Aboriginal self-government has never been repealed, and thus one has to conclude that other rights also exist. This is more compelling since the inclusion of the term "existing Aboriginal and treaty rights of the Aboriginal peoples of Canada are hereby recognized and affirmed," in Section 35 of the *Constitution Act*, 1982. This means that if these rights existed prior to 1982, it is not possible, unless the Constitution is changed, to do away with Native rights, e.g., land, self-government.

When we discuss Aboriginal rights such as self-government, we mean the power of a people to enact laws which courts will implement and which will be considered paramount when they are in conflict with the laws of other governments (Clark, 1990). As Clark points out, the concept of self-government must be distinguished from self-management/administration. These latter terms refer to managing or administering laws which have been created and put in place by other legal entities.

One of the most important Canadian cases bearing directly upon Aboriginal self-government is *Sheldon* v. *Ramsay* (1852). In this case, it was decided that the Six Nations Tribe could not be recognized as a separate and independent nation governed by laws of their own (Clark, 1990). In reaching this decision, Justice J. Burns accepted the idea that Indians were a distinct race of people rather than a political entity. This perspective would be upheld by Canadian law in 1921 (Sero) and once again in 1974 when the Supreme Court held that there were no enclaves within a province for which provincial law was not applicable (*Cardinal* v. *A.G. Alberta*). This later decision, argues Clark (1990), was based on the fact that the integration ethic had so dominated the psychology of recent jurists, that the existence of enclaves (recognized by the Privy Council of Great Britain on January 15, 1773) had been mentally excluded from their consideration.

If the evidence overwhelmingly points to the existence of Native rights, why have these not been acted upon? First, for a number of years government officials simply refused to acknowledge that Natives had specific claims or rights beyond that of ordinary Canadian citizens. Government officials acted in a unilateral fashion to suspend certain rights through a variety of procedures. For example, it would not be until the second half of the twentieth century that Natives had federal voting rights. In other cases, historical documents were not released or were ignored as not relevant to the case at hand. Still other procedures were implemented to keep Natives from pursuing various claims, e.g., preventing lawyers from accepting monies to act on behalf of Indian peoples. The end result was that Native claims, whatever they were, were defined by Canadians as not of sufficient importance for federal or provincial officials to pursue; Native claims were considered to be a myth perpetuated by Natives.

After the 1973 Supreme Court decision, both levels of government had to face the legitimacy of Native claims. The government's reaction was to demonstrate that these rights had been repealed or rendered inoperative. Still others claimed that Aboriginal rights had been "superseded" by federal and/or provincial legislation. As Clark (1990: 149) points out, this might have been appropriate if Native self-government had been constituted as domestic common law instead of being confirmed by imperial legislation. In other cases, provincial governments claimed that the 1763 *Royal Proclamation* did not apply to them; others suggested that the *Quebec Act, 1774* repealed the *Royal Proclamation* and, thus, it was not operative. Whatever the basis, they argued Native claims had been extinguished, or at least derogated, from the constitutional character of the protection identified by the *Royal Proclamation*. However, a decade later, it would become clear that the number of court rulings in favour of Native peoples' claims supported the Native position. As a result of these court decisions and a concurrent change in the public's attitude toward the rights of Native people, the federal government began to embark upon a new policy for Indian affairs.

The federal government has responded to Native claims for self-determination in a manner not used before. Until today, the federal government rejected claims for self-government and imposed a formal coercive structure on Natives. However, as Natives continually accessed government and their agencies, a new strategy of social control emerged. Given the changing conditions of today, the government has decided that the desire for control has to be harnessed and diverted. In particular, Native efforts to take charge and develop their institutional structures in alignment with the existing dominant institutions, has incorporated Natives into the existing structure. Furthermore, self-government by band creates a decentralizing effect: Native claims are dealt with on a band by band basis, thus allowing power to be dispersed.

The success of this control strategy is under scrutiny. It is not without risks. Bands with greater independence become potentially powerful political actors; thus, they could have greater influence. As a result, there is considerable debate when the issue of self-government is under consideration. Nevertheless, by the 1990s it was clear that new Native-White relations were emerging. The structure of these relations is unclear today, as both sides continually negotiate their position. What is clear is that there is a continuing attempt to incorporate Natives into the larger Canadian economy. However, coercion is no longer the strategy being employed by the federal government. Rather "cooperative" or "partnership" ventures are being pursued. Underlying these attempts is a strategy to integrate the resources of Native people into the larger society. As Cornell (1988) points out, it is not the Indians themselves but rather their resources which are of interest to the dominant society.

One might also ask why Native people have not pursued their claim of Aboriginal rights more vigorously? In other words, if the case is clear that Natives have certain rights (e.g., land, self-government), why have they not directly challenged the federal government? The answer lies in the practical realities of implementing these rights. The federal government envisions the many administrative and financial costs involved in attempting to implement many different Native governments; for example, assuming that each band achieved self-government, there would be nearly 600 different Native governments (Ponting and Gibbins, 1980). Government officials are concerned with the cost of operating such a structure. Finally, there would be the cost of reparation to Natives by government—that is, if the federal government accepted the inherent right to self-government, under the rulings outlined in recent court cases compensation would have to be made to those bands who expressed a desire to achieve self-government in the past but were thwarted by the federal government. As a result, government officials have steadfastly rejected the idea of Aboriginal rights, irrespective of the court decisions. Nevertheless, as legal decisions have reinforced Native claims—e.g., claims to self-government, to land and to the government's fiduciary responsibility to Natives—the federal government has been forced to deal publicly with these ideals, without fundamentally changing its ideology.

The question still remains as to why Natives have not "forced the hand" of government to recognize their specific claims. First of all, this would mean pursuing additional court cases and running the risk of not having their case upheld. For example, the most recent case in B.C. (*Delgamuukw* v. *British Columbia*) supports their suspicions. And, even though that decision may be reversed by a higher court, the claims of Natives remain in suspension until a higher court rules. Second, Natives have always viewed the courts as foreign institutions which they do not fully understand. But perhaps even more important is the issue of money. It is all very well to force the government, through the courts, to admit to the existence of such rights as self-government. However, even if such rights were publicly recognized, the government is not obligated to bear the cost of resulting administrative structures—it would be a pyrrhic victory for Natives.

As a consequence of the above scenario, both the Native people and the federal government have tried to establish a common ground for dealing with Native rights claims from which a compromise acceptable to both parties would result. The federal government developed its first strategy to deal with this problem in the 1973 Indian Affairs Policy Statement. This document noted that the government was determined to find the most effective way of giving Native peoples control over their affairs. It clearly stated that the government was aware of the problem of Native claims and was prepared to do something about them. However, the statement was equally clear in developing a policy that preserved the government's view of reality. For example, while the federal government acknowledges the Native right of self-government, the only form of self-government defined as acceptable is the delegated-municipal style. This position was buttressed by the federal government's concurrent policy that self-government would be dealt with in all comprehensive land claims. This strategy for enticing Native people to accept self-government under these conditions focused on providing Natives with funds if they were willing participants in the process of *negotiating* their claims, whatever they were. The acceptance of negotiations as a mode of decision-making meant that the government would not have to relinquish decision-making to an independent third party; e.g., the courts. And, by not allowing the courts the right to make decisions, the government avoided the possibility of any (in their view) unacceptable decision confirming Native rights; e.g., inherent traditional self-government. Natives caught between the confirmation of rights and the lack of funds to implement them sought to enter the negotiation process in the belief they could achieve both goals. They did so on the basis of past actions they had undertaken with regard to the federal government and the belief they could replicate the results. For example, the gains Québec Cree achieved when they dropped their court case—guaranteed annual income, a land base and funds to operate Native businesses—gave some support to this view. In other cases, bands were able to negotiate specific claims that they felt were in their favour, instead of taking the long, expensive route through the courts.

During the 1960s, the federal government had implemented a number of policies which were based on the ideology of assimilation. The 1969 federal White Paper was the culmination of this policy development. However, the next few years would see Native people engage in an unprecedented political development which included establishing liaisons with non-Native organizations to fight government policy. By the mid-1970s, the political environment in which Natives found themselves operating had radically changed from that of the previous decades. Strong Native organizational structures (both federal and provincial) had emerged and were confronting the federal government's planned policies. Natives had developed a sustained presence in Ottawa and were becoming skilled lobbyists at various international venues. This was also a time in which the federal government was providing Native organizations with generous funding. The subsequent demise of the 1969 White Paper demonstrated the power of Native political organizations through cooperation among the various Native and non-Native groups.

After this period of unprecedented development, the leadership of major Native organizations became further removed from Native communities. For example, the National Indian Brotherhood began to act in much the same manner as any other large political organization that is funded by an outside agency and thus no longer feels responsible to the people it ostensibly represents. Most Native organizations were established in large urban areas where few of the people they represented resided. It was difficult to maintain communications, especially when representatives of Native organizations began to sound like the federal bureaucrats Natives had dealt with for so many years. Natives placed in departments which dealt with Native people (e.g., Indian and Northern Affairs) were subject to the constraints of federal policy. As a result, they found themselves to be ineffectual, and they were increasingly disregarded as agents of change. At this time, the federal government also began to cut back on funding. A call for a decentralization of Native organizations led to the creation of the Assembly of First Nations and the phasing out of the National Indian Brotherhood. However, by this time, the effectiveness of the NIB had been substantially reduced; first by the funding cuts implemented by the federal government, and then by Natives' perception of the organization as ineffective. The inability of Natives either to thwart or to change the content of the *Constitution Act*, 1982, further weakened their effectiveness. The end result was that by the mid-1980s, Native organizations were disorganized, demoralized and without effective leadership. It was at this time that the federal government publicly revealed its new policy regarding Native rights.

It is important to realize that since Europeans set foot onto Canadian soil there has been a lack of understanding between the two cultures. Euro-Canadians have promoted the Protestant ethic and have evaluated other cultures from this narrow perspective. Assessments of cultures (including their own) have been ethnocentric and based upon such ideologies as individualism, progress and material technological development. These ideologies still exist and are very evident in the recent B.C. Supreme Court ruling by A. McEachern. On the other hand, Natives have viewed Euro-Canadian culture as obsessed with change, the individual and attempts to influence nature. Recent documents sent out by the Assembly of First Nations reflect this perspective. In summary, the cultural gaps so evident in the seventeenth and eighteenth centuries have not disappeared as we head into the twenty-first century.

The conflict generated in the past by these cultural misunderstandings has not been dealt with. In the past, the Natives' lack of power prevented them from thwarting the efforts of various economic and political entities. Today, various groups (e.g., religious, environmental) have found some commonality with Native groups and have formed coalitions to support Native demands. The conflict remains, but the question of who wins now has taken on new meaning.

SUMMARY

From early colonization until the present, no government has genuinely recognized Natives as distinct peoples with cultures different from, but not inferior to, its own. Aboriginal cultures have been, and still are, presumed to be primitive, premodern or inferior in the sense of being at a lesser stage of development than the dominant culture. There is an implicit (sometimes explicit) belief that all cultures are fundamentally the same, but differ in the level of civilization attained. This position presupposes that the dominant culture (Euro-Canadian) is the measure of all others.

Therefore, it is understandable why governments consider it important to take jurisdiction over Native people in order to guide them to a more rational or civilized state of being. The church was used for years as an ally of the state in promoting this strategy. Later, the educational system joined the process. This type of thinking, which views difference as a sign of inferiority, has been, and continues to be, the main basis for the denial of the value of cultural differences. The perception that there is a need for government to protect and civilize the Natives is based on this denial.

When governments have dealt with Native people, it has not been on an equal basis. Governments have always dealt with Natives as a means to achieve an economic goal; e.g., settlement, development.

It has been difficult for non-Native Canadians not to view Native people as simply people who are at an earlier stage of cultural development. There is a great deal of reluctance to view Native people as a manifestation of a different collective imagination, a culturally distinct group. As Ruth Benedict noted nearly a half century ago:

> [Aboriginal] cultures are oriented as wholes in different directions. They are travelling along different roads in pursuit of different ends, and these ends and these means are one society and cannot be judged in terms of those of another society because essentially they are incommensurable (1950: 206).

CHAPTER 12
....

INDIAN SELF-GOVERNMENT

INTRODUCTION

Until the late 1970s, the federal and provincial governments' response to demands for Indian self-government was an adamant "no." They took the position that they could not recognize Indian sovereignty because the only sovereignty that existed in Canada was vested in the Crown. Therefore, if any group claimed sovereignty on any other basis—such as use and occupancy from time immemorial—governments were not prepared to discuss or even consider it. It has only been since the constitutional debate of the early 1980s and the first ministers' conferences that the federal government has agreed to act on the issue. The Supreme Court's ruling in the *Musqueim* case (1985) has also persuaded the two levels of government to rethink their previous position. In that case, the Supreme Court recognized that Indian sovereignty and Indians rights are *independent and apart from the Crown*. The court ruled that these rights flowed from Indian title and Indian occupation (Cardinal, 1986). Nevertheless, provincial governments remain highly sceptical of such a change, although they have not overtly contested further discussion of the issue. Their concerns about Native self-government and their willingness to discuss the issues today emerge out of their growing recognition of the increased role they might play in Native affairs. They are also acutely aware of the federal government's thinking on this issue. For example, Indian Affairs published its *Directional Plan of the 1980s*, in which it argued that Indians, instead of using so many federal

433

programs and resources, should take advantage of more provincial programs and resources. Other federal documents such as the *Nielsen Study Team Report* (1986) and the *Indian and Native Sector* (1986), reiterated these strategies.

Although these federal policies have not yet been implemented, they have certainly coloured the provinces' perception of how the federal government plans to act in the future and have forced them to develop strategies to deal with the possible changes in policy. Because there are significant differences in political philosophies among provinces, there are both constitutional and practical implications to consider. As a result, there are several different stances taken by the individual provinces: Alberta insists that Indians are a federal responsibility, while Québec's position is more ambiguous (Calder, 1986).

From the other side, there has never been a single position among Native groups as to what self-government means or how it is to be implemented (Cardinal, 1986). Indians have insisted that their inherent sovereignty defines and formalizes them as a fourth level of government. Inuit, on the other hand, prefer to develop a provincial-type government because they occupy a large land area and make up nearly all of the population of that area. Finally, the non-status Indians and Métis have publicly accepted the fact that any government for them will have to be delegated by either the provincial or the federal government. It is clear that, because of different historical experiences, the evolution of Native-White relationships has not been the same for the three major Native groups.

Nevertheless, there is some agreement on what is embodied in the concept of self-government. In general terms, Natives agree that the concept of self-government (or autonomy) implies that for important national issues they will remain within the territorial jurisdiction of the provincial or federal government, but that they will enjoy the freedom to regulate certain of their own affairs without interference from outside. While no list of issues has been drafted, it would seem that general principles of democracy, justice and equality would be supported. Other rights such as freedom of speech, the right to be judged by one's peers and equal access to educational and economic institutions would also be supported. By granting autonomy to Natives, the government would acknowledge that certain rights are to be given to a specific part of the state's population, which needs protection in view of the way many of its characteristics differ from those of the majority of the population. Autonomy would also allow the people inhabiting an area to exercise direct control over important affairs of special concern to them, while allowing the larger entity, which retains certain powers over that area, to exercise those powers which are in the common interest of both Natives and non-Natives (Umozurike, 1972). In order to preserve Native culture, language and religion, Natives would prefer to have complete control over their own schools, and they are also interested in excluding the federal/provincial governments from interfering with their traditional way of life. Because they perceive that they're different from the majority of Canadians, they insist on different rights.

BAND COUNCILS AND TRIBAL IDENTITY

Indians and Inuit vociferously argue that they had functioning communities with political structures long before the Europeans arrived. For example, the Six Nations Confederacy of the Iroquois had a well-established system of chief selection, as well as a set of procedures that were used to replace representatives from various nations in the confederacy. For this reason, many Indian people still do not accept the political system imposed upon them by the federal government. As far as they are concerned, they have always had self-government; they consider it a right that they wish to practice today. They point to the *Quebec Act* (1774) which restored to the French, under the British monarchy, the right to be governed by their traditional laws in matters of property and civil rights (Lyon, 1985).

Nevertheless, the governmental system now operating for most bands is that which is prescribed under the terms of the *Indian Act*. The *Indian Act* imposed a band council system of local government. Under these terms, Indians form a council of chief and council members, who are usually elected by the membership to carry out various administrative duties. The actual duties and responsibilities of the council are also specified in the *Indian Act*.

How did this policy of band councils come about? As Daugherty and Magill point out:

> The post confederation period was twofold and somewhat contradictory. On the one hand, it continued the protective or guardianship policy of the colonial period; on the other, it proposed to assimilate the Indian (1980: 2).

In an attempt to implement the policy of the day, the government introduced what was considered a progressive step, the elective system. The first system of elections introduced in 1868-69 was for three-year terms. It was followed by a new one-year elective system. This parallel system was not consolidated until 1951.[1] This electoral system was meant to introduce local (self) government to Indian people.

Gulliver (1969) shows that the early colonial governments found that, as they continued their westward expansion, they were continually met by different groups of Natives. Partly to solve this problem, they "froze" the existing cultural pattern of the tribal group by imposing their own form of government. However, within a short period, they also began to introduce new cultural components to the existing system. This brought about tribal identity and distinctiveness by linking each tribe with an administrative area, and this tribal identity was reinforced by the government's continuing process of control. In some cases, either through migration or administrative decree, new tribes and new identities were created.

Over time, this process slowly destroyed the indigenous peoples' culture but it also created a new tribal identity. This tribal identity was initially fostered by the colonial government because it allowed for easy control and manipulation of each tribe. However, today this structure of many distinct tribes, which all claim real or fictive differences between themselves and other tribes, has led to many problems. For example, it is difficult for bureaucrats to formulate new policies because they do not know which tribes to listen to. Policy implementation is made even more difficult by such a structure.

As Dougherty and Magill (1980) point out, the implementation of this policy attempted "to civilize and assimilate" the Indian into White society but, in doing so, destroyed the indigenous peoples' culture and provided a convenient way for the government to deal with a group of Indians. In short, it was legislation that introduced a form of municipal government to Indians.[2] These band councils functioned (and continue to function) as agents of the federal government, exercising a limited range of delegated powers under federal supervision.

The creation of local Indian government was hailed, at the time, as a progressive step. In reality, however, the local band governments had little power. The Superintendent General had acquired considerable discretionary power over Indian bands, and it would not be until after World War II that some of this power would be relinquished to Indians themselves. Further local control would be evident after the 1951 *Indian Act* changes, but Indian/government relations would not substantially change until the early 1970s.

After the 1969 confrontation between Indians and the government over the White Paper, federal officials responded by issuing a series of departmental circulars that dealt with local Indian government. This brought about the process of "devolution" whereby DIAND began to transfer responsibility for the delivery of programs to individual bands. For example, in 1971 bands controlled 16 percent of the total DIAND budget ($34.9 million); by 1976 they controlled 31 percent ($147.6 million); and by 1983, slightly more than 50 percent of the total DIAND budget ($526.6 million). However, the policy for devolution (control over Indians moving from the federal government to the Indians themselves) has transferred only the delivery of services to the band level. The control over the programs, policies and budget still remains with DIAND (Government of Canada, 1983). Nevertheless, in practice the federal government tends not to exercise its legal powers over a band as long as the band is acting within the law.[3] Recently, however, the legal status of band government has been called into question by the courts.

This system of band councils has lasted for well over a century. Recently, Indians have argued that their right to self-government has been violated. They looked to the United States and the right of Indians there to self-government. In the late 1960s, the government's response to "all this nonsense" was to introduce the White Paper, which suggested doing away with the legal status of Indians. Although this policy was rejected by a coalition of Native and non-Native organizations, it would not be until after the 1973 *Calder* case dealing with Nishga land claims that the federal government would give serious consideration to Native self-government.

The ruling on the Nishga case, even though it was a technical defeat for Indians, showed that they had more rights than the government had previously admitted.

As a result, immediately after the case, a period of politicization occurred for Natives all over Canada, as they began to see a crack in the wall erected by the federal government. They pressed hard on Indian issues, and one of the rights they pursued was that of self-government.

In 1982, a further breakthrough occurred when Canada patriated its Constitution, and, for the first time in history, "existing rights" were guaranteed to Aboriginal people. Specifically, sections 25, 27, 35 and 37 dealt with Indian issues. The most explicit is section 35, which states that:

1. Existing aboriginal and treaty rights of the aboriginal peoples of Canada are hereby recognized and affirmed.

2. [for the purposes of] this act, "aboriginal peoples of Canada" includes the Indian, Inuit and Métis people of Canada.

Native people now argue that self-government is one of their Aboriginal rights and is entrenched within the Constitution. Rather than wait for a judicial interpretation of "existing rights," the government mandated that a constitutional conference (section 27) would be established within one year of the proclamation of the *Act*. At this conference, matters dealing directly with the Aboriginal peoples would be discussed. In short, political negotiations would be the forum within which it would be decided what was included in Aboriginal rights. However, while Aboriginal peoples would be invited to this conference, only the provincial first ministers would have voting or vetoing power. Nevertheless, Aboriginals would be provided with a certain amount of money in order to research and lobby on behalf of their cause. Since the first conference in 1983, three more have been held with little in the way of substantive results. In the 1983 conference, the participants agreed to establish a continuing process of defining Native rights and specified that a series of additional constitutional conferences focusing on Native rights would take place within eight years of the enactment of the *Constitution Act, 1982*.

If nothing else, these conferences have propelled Indian issues into the public consciousness. For example, since the first conference, section 12.1b of the *Indian Act* has been repealed. Other concerns, such as self-government, have taken on new life. The government appointed an all-party special committee on Indian self-government, which reported (*Penner Report*) in 1983 that not only was self-government an appropriate move for Indians but also it should be implemented immediately.

Indian leaders would like to have a fourth order of government, one that fits into their notion of Indian sovereignty. Indians see self-government as a means of allowing them to achieve three central goals: 1) to increase local control and decision-making; 2) to recognize the diverse needs and cultures of Indians throughout Canada; and 3) to provide accountability to local electors rather than to a federal bureaucracy. This new order of government would have powers similar to those of the federal and provincial governments. It would, for example, have full jurisdiction over such areas as resources, education, social development and taxation (Nicholson, 1984).

In addition, the federal government is assessing the feasibility of amending the *Indian Act* in order to establish a legislative basis for Indian self-government. This "study" response seems to be a result of the fact that Native spokesmen have not fully articulated the concept of self-government. While the concept has been discussed in a variety of contexts, the full organizational structure and its implications have not been worked out (Weaver, 1984).

THE CURRENT SITUATION

Within our federal system, we have different levels of government. As Rieber (1977) points out, each level of government relates directly to the immediately superior level, from which it receives its enabling organizational act. However, when Indian government is introduced into the argument, a new structure emerges (see Figure 12.1). In this organizational structure, Indians would not only relate to the federal government (in its trust relationship) but also to lower levels of government.

The major problems confronting Natives in attempting to establish self-government are diverse and extensive. For example, the issue of jurisdiction remains a basic problem. The issue of subrogation must also be resolved. This is the process whereby there is, as a consequence of a change of territorial sovereignty, a legal transfer of liabilities or of rights and duties arising from treaties and other international agreements. Added to this problem is the level of government Natives have to deal with on any specific issues. For example, Natives are part of the tri-partite (Native-federal-provincial) structure in which jurisdictional issues can arise

FIGURE 12.1 Different Levels of Government and Their Relationships

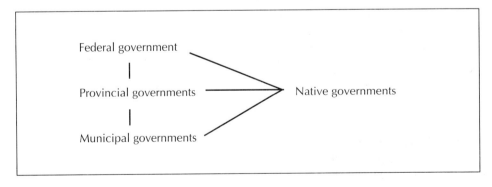

in any one of the three relationships: Native-federal, Native-provincial and provincial-federal. In some cases, issues fall clearly along one of the arms of the triangle noted above. For example, reserves are clearly in the Native-federal arm of the triangle, except under certain circumstances. Other issues that have confronted Native people and that must be dealt with are domain (jurisdictional specification over property), fishing and hunting rights, law enforcement, financing, economic development, community development, and off-reserve Indian rights (Paton, 1982). We also find in the current situation that, according to the *Indian Act*, neither the band nor the band council can be incorporated for the purpose of establishing a band government. Since Aboriginal peoples are pressuring the federal government for local self-government, this problem must be resolved. It must include both the legal and political issues at stake. For example, a municipal government can act in a fashion appropriate to the province, and it may act in a fashion appropriate to itself as a municipality. This means that, in part through social necessity, municipalities, even though created by the province are able to control their own affairs. The federal government would like Native self-government to be modelled on municipal government. Natives, on the other hand, reject this proposal and wish to establish their own form of government which would not be dependent on the provincial government for some issues and on the federal government for others.

FIRST MINISTERS' CONFERENCES ON ABORIGINAL AFFAIRS

There have been four first ministers' conferences to discuss the issue of Aboriginal rights since the passage of the *Constitution Act*, 1982. After the 1983 conference, the issue of Aboriginal self-government became central. Section 37 of the *Act* specified that additional constitutional conferences on Aboriginal issues would be held. As the 1984 first ministers' conference approached, the *Penner Report*, which endorsed Native self-government, was made public. The prime minister opened the conference by proposing a constitutional amendment entrenching Aboriginal self-government and allowing Natives to define what was meant by the term. While three provinces (Ontario, New Brunswick and Manitoba) agreed, the remaining did not. Hawkes (1985) concluded that this conference was a failure of colossal proportions. Nothing was agreed upon, and the meeting ended in suspicion and innuendo.

Although the 1984 meeting produced no tangible policy, the Prime Minister insisted that government "pressure tactics" with Native people would stop and more negotiation would take place (Campbell and Pal, 1991). A year later, when the next first ministers' conference on Aboriginal issues took place, the issue of entrenching Native self-government was introduced by the federal government. There was considerable resistance by both provincial premiers and some Native organizations, and, as a result, the conference was ended before a resolution could emerge.

Subsequent to the conference, the federal government publicly stated it would approach Native communities and organizations to develop procedures to entrench self-government. It was felt that issues could be worked out in time for the next meeting in 1987.

When the 1987 meeting took place, definitions and conditions of self-government had not been resolved. Native people had taken the position that they had an inherent right to self-government and that this right must be entrenched in the Constitution; the exact nature and the process of implementation of this right was to be negotiated later. While some provincial premiers supported this, a number did not. The dissenting premiers argued that Native self-government should be defined up front and must fit within the constitutional structure of Canada. In short, they agreed to Native self-government, but only if it were defined and contingent to certain conditions. As a result, the conference once again ended with no decisions.

However, the federal government began to implement its "bottom-up" process. By 1986, Ottawa introduced its community-based self-government policy and began negotiating with specific Native communities.

The Federal Government's Response: Optional Indian Government Legislation[4]

Natives have long argued that they required an authority base that would allow them, collectively, to advance their own interests. Furthermore, this authority had to derive from their Aboriginal title and not from Parliament (Tennant, 1984). They claim that they originally had a system of self-government that regulated their internal and external relations (Boldt, *et al.*, 1985). As Native organizations lobbied for self-government during the 1970s, DIAND developed a policy (without consulting Natives) to create band government. This devolutionary process was to lead to an entirely new relationship between Natives and the government. Each band would be given the opportunity to choose the form and structure of its self-government. This policy was rejected by Native people because it failed to recognize the Aboriginal source of authority (Tennant, 1984).

The rejection of DIAND's proposed self-government policy led to the creation of a special federal committee that was charged with reviewing all legal and related institutional factors affecting the status, development and responsibilities of band government on Indian reserves (Task Force, 1982). As Tennant (1984) points out, the composition of this committee was crucial both to its functioning and to the recommendations that emerged. He notes that the committee was composed of MPs who came from ridings that had a substantial proportion of Natives and who were very knowledgeable about Indian issues. Weaver (1984) agrees with Tennant's claim and goes on to show that the committee became a vehicle by which Indian interests were articulated to the public. After a cross-country hearing, the committee submitted its report in 1983.

The *Penner Report* listed 58 recommendations designed to integrate Indians into Canadian society. The most relevant for our purposes are the recommendations that Indian people should have self-government and that this should be recognized as an Aboriginal right. As Tennant (1984) observed, the committee recommended that the Indian governments should derive their existence and legitimacy not from Parliament or legislation, not even from the Constitution, but from a pre-existing right. The committee proposed legislation that would have the federal and provincial governments recognize Indian governments, author federal-Indian agreements, and allow Indians to govern themselves (Tennant, 1984). The committee also recommended that DIAND be phased out of existence as its functions were taken over by Indians. This particular recommendation is in line with the average Canadian's thinking about DIAND.[5]

Finally, the committee recommended that the Indian band-government legislation proposed by DIAND be rejected and that new legislation be implemented to clear the way for Indian self-government. It was felt that the proposed legislation simply involved a delegation of power rather than a recognition of the "sovereignty" of Indian First Nations (a term used often in the *Penner Report*).

The committee felt that Indian self-government could be implemented under the existing constitutional structure, and many of its recommendations were set forth within this context. However, committee members were also aware that other changes could take place outside the constitutional structure. To this end, the committee recommended that the government become involved in the creation of new legislation, increased funding and administrative arrangements. In summary, the *Penner Report* called for a new order of government to be established in order to incorporate Natives into Canadian society. The primary unit of self-government would be the band. Thus each Indian governing body would then be related to the other two levels of government through the band government. As Gibbins and Ponting (1986) point out, this may prove to be a fatal mistake, given that much of the political activity in Canada is carried out through intergovernmental relations. Any attempt to deal with nearly 600 Indian governments would be doomed to failure, and, thus, Indians inevitably would be ignored in decision-making processes.

DIAND and the Assembly of First Nations (AFN) quickly responded to the recommendations of the committee. By the end of 1983, a draft policy, *Indian Nations Recognition and Validating Act* was completed by DIAND officials. This proposed act formally recognized Indian First Nations and allowed each nation to enact legislation independently of Canada as long as it did not conflict with the laws of Parliament. The federal government responded in early 1984. It refused to accept self-government *as an Aboriginal right*. Nevertheless, it agreed to drop the band-government legislation and began investigating the possibility of implementing the spirit of the *Penner Report*.

The result was the creation of a new committee consisting of a number of people from the constitutional unit of DIAND and the public-law unit of the Ministry of Justice. Their job was to draft new legislation that would incorporate the rec-ommendations of the *Penner Report* but would also be palatable to Parliament. The first draft was rejected by the Priorities and Planning Committee of the Cabinet. New officials were then added to the committee trying to draft the legislation. In June 1984, *Bill C-52, An Act Relating to Self-Government for Indian Nations*, was introduced. While some of the recommendations of the *Penner Report* were part of this bill, as Tennant (1985) points out, it was little more than the old band-government legislation reformulated. As Parliament dissolved, so did the bill and the policy alliance that had formed between AFN and the government in the workings of the special com-mittee. *Bill C-93* (discussed below), a revision of *C-52*, was then introduced and is the current basis for establishing a negotiating stance with regard to self-government for Indians.

Today, the federal government is busy drafting further legislation that will make self-government an option available to Indian bands in Canada. This legis-lation does not weaken any treaty rights of Indians and it comes into effect only after proper steps have been taken by each band. It is based on the premise that each Indian band government will have decision-making powers for the band itself. The federal government also feels that since there is a diversity of Indian bands in Canada, the policy implementation will be optional. As then minister of Indian Affairs pointed out:

> The system of band government would be created at the local level in which each band would develop its own band charter which could exist between the Indian band government and the band membership. They [bands] could have the power to pass authoritative by-laws, right to enter into agreements with government, de-velop service delivery capabilities, raise additional finances through taxa-tion...(McKnight, 1987).

There are also additional powers that bands could develop and place in their charters. The charter is viewed as the first step to the development of self-govern-ment. The band charter would outline the relationship between the Indian band government and the band membership. Financial issues would also come under the control of band governments.

This legislation would come into effect on a band-by-band basis and only in those bands that wanted it. After each band had established its own charter and had been given approval by the minister of DIAND, the charter would become a legal document and would set the conditions and parameters of the band's self-gov-ernment. The band would then assume all powers available to it under existing legislation (the *Indian Act*), and those powers would be supplemented by the con-tents of the band constitution (charter).

Those bands opting for self-government would then have powers equivalent to those held by other local governments, with some exceptions, for example, they would not control fish and game regulations. In addition, bands could also have some say in the provision of services such as education, health and housing. They could also enter into contractual agreements with other entities, such as other bands, governments and legal corporate bodies.

By proposing the new legislation, the federal government is trying to 1) develop Native self-reliance rather than dependency, 2) develop grassroots programs rather than Ottawa-built programs, and 3) develop community control and participation. To achieve these ends, more local control and decision-making must be possible. The new policy must also be flexible in order to deal with the diverse needs and cultures of Native people. Finally, it is hoped that self-government will make Natives more accountable to their own electors than to the federal government (Rawson, 1986). Structural changes in DIAND are also occurring in order to facilitate these program ends. For example, the department is being regionalized into four new sectors, and the Corporate Policy and Native Claims sectors have been dismantled and absorbed into the new organization.

Six additional issues and methods of dealing with them are outlined in *Bill C-93* (Piepenburg, 1982; Schwartz, 1986). We will briefly identify each in turn and discuss the major elements in each issue.

1. *Land* The reversionary title to lands controlled by a band operating under the legislation would remain within federal jurisdiction until permanently transferred. However, a band would have the necessary legal identity to be a party to actions related to land. A new "Indian land" category would be created to differentiate this land from "reserve land" not identified in the existing *Indian Act*.

2. *Membership* The legislation would give the band authority to determine its own membership as long as the criteria for determining membership were not discriminatory according to the existing *Canadian Charter of Rights and Freedoms*.

3. *Finances* Indian band government would establish a separate trust account into which those trust funds now being held by the federal government would be transferred. This government would also have authority over the levying of taxes, issuing of licenses, borrowing of money, making of loans, establishment of corporations, and the expenditure of tax monies. The Indian band government, as a legal entity, would be tax exempt and so would any board or agency of the band or any economic development corporation that was wholly owned by the band and operating exclusively on the reserve.

4. *Law enforcement* The Indian government could police its own reserves or enter into an agreement with the RCMP or provincial police for the provision of police services. Any offenders against band laws would be dealt with by the band government. Also in the proposed legislation is the "consideration" of the establishment of a tribal court system.

5. *Indian band-government authority* The Indian band-government authority would be an independent, quasi-judicial commission to aid in the establishment and monitoring of the system of Indian band government. It would hear complaints and appeals from band members about the band government. The authority would have seven members, appointed by an order in council and recommended by the minister of DIAND after consulting with local Indian communities.

6. *Appointment of public administration* This last provision deals with the right of the minister to order a special enquiry into the administration of an Indian band government "when it is so warranted."

Self-government for Natives means that they, as First Nations, will govern their own people and their own affairs, including land and its use. Self-government flows from Aboriginal rights which provide for the right of a peoples' cultural survival and self-determination. Specifically, this would exempt them (or at least protect them) from the application of laws of another jurisdiction (Anenakew, 1985; Plain, 1985). The Native proposals for self-government call for a new order of government with powers similar to those of a province. In fact, some proposals have suggested that the Indian First Nations would have the right to sign international treaties and to issue valid passports (Dalon, 1985). These proposals have been summarily rejected by both levels of government. There is a great fear that until all the implications of self-government are clear, it cannot be entrenched in the Constitution or given even tentative support.

At present, the federal government and some of the eastern provinces have taken the approach that they would like to begin with the general principle that self-government is acceptable and then later work out the details. The other provinces want to work the process the other way around; that is, negotiate the specifics and then decide whether to commit themselves to the entrenchment of self-government in the Constitution (Dalon, 1985).

Nevertheless, the federal government's proposal does not suggest that each band's authority will come from its status as a sovereign entity. Rather, the authority is seen to exist because the federal government chose to delegate it to the band.

Natives have objected vociferously to this stance. They are adamant that self-government is an inherent right. They point out that an all-party committee (the Special Committee on Indian Self-Government, 1983) endorsed their constituency's right to self-government. At the same time, as Dyck (1991) points out, there must be no illusions about the difficulties that will be encountered in trying to implement the process. Indians are more adept at resisting authority than they are at exercising it, and that will have to change if self-government is to succeed.

Natives wish to use self-government as a way of taking permanent welfare recipients and allowing them to take control of their lives. Natives have challenged government leaders to address Aboriginal issues with a determination that will result in substantive changes for Native peoples. Ovide Mercredi, Chief of the Assembly of First Nations, has become a dynamic and powerful spokesperson for Native people. He has forged a link among the various Native organizations and presented a unified position before the provincial and federal governments. At this time, the governments have given tentative acceptance to the Natives' right to self-government and are willing to recognize them as a quasi-"distinct" society. Whether this agreement will hold remains to be seen. The question as to whether or not the negotiations this time will prove more fruitful than during the Meech Lake debates is yet to be answered.

Indians are currently involved in a municipal-government form of political system. Each group of Indians comprises a band which elects a leadership to deal with the federal government. In fact, during the 1960s the government was preparing the way for Indian bands to accept municipal status and provincial jurisdiction. However, the 1969 White Paper brought about a major change in Natives' perception of where they fit into Canadian society. Since then, the recognition of Aboriginal self-government has become a *cause célèbre* for Indians. As Weaver (1984) points out, the most explicit demand to date has been the *Dene Declaration* published in 1975. Even though this was rejected by the government, the establishment of the joint Cabinet/National Indian Brotherhood committee in 1974 allowed the ideas in the *Declaration* to be discussed and explored most fully.

This concern came back into the foreground with the debate over the patriated Canadian Constitution (Tennant, 1984). Indians wanted to entrench their rights in the Constitution by establishing a form of Indian government outside the framework of the *Indian Act* (Weaver, 1984). In June 1984, legislation to allow for the recognition of Indian government was introduced in Parliament. The legislation was not meant to displace (or act as a substitute for) constitutional processes and initiatives. It was explicitly noted that it would not detract from existing Aboriginal and treaty rights affirmed in the Constitution.

This proposed legislation (*Bill C-93*) was not what Indian people had in mind when they raised the matter of self-government. (See for example the Assembly of First Nations' *Proposed 1985 Constitutional Accord Relating to the Aboriginal Peoples of Canada*, First Ministers' Conference on Aboriginal Constitutional Matters, 1985). Aboriginal peoples believe that in order to survive as a cultural entity, they must have a land base and self-government. The government, although agreeing with the sentiment that self-government would be helpful, would first like to see the broad parameters as it maps out its response. For example, is it land-based? If so, this might be an appropriate model for Indians and Inuit but not for Métis. In addition, neither the provincial governments nor the federal government are prepared to include in the concept of self-government the notions of full independence or sovereignty. Although Natives do view self-government as an inherent right, they have always pictured its expression as taking place within the Canadian political system (Hawkes, 1985). They also believe that self-government could be attained even without a land base. This could be accomplished by guaranteed representation for Aboriginal peoples in the House of Commons, the provincial legislatures, and the Senate.

Guaranteed representation is an integral part of the Native Council of Canada's proposal for a two-tier government, which they see as best suited to serve the interests of the Native population. The first level would be exclusively Aboriginal, and would include communities in a structure similar to that of band governments. The second level would play an integrating role and provide for Aboriginal participation in non-Aboriginal governing structures through, for example, guaranteed seats in the House of Commons and Senate, provincial legislatures and municipal councils. The NCC supports the idea of guaranteed representation for all Aboriginal people, although it also believes that there should be distinct representation for each group of Aboriginal peoples. The eventual distribution of Aboriginal legislative seats would be determined by establishing a list that Aboriginal people could choose to be on or not. A census would be taken to determine the size of each Aboriginal population, and to determine the proportion of seats to be set aside for each group (Hawkes, 1985).

The Métis Federation and the Inuit Committee on National Issues, have also advocated this model of guaranteed representation. The Métis National Council has put forward the option of having Aboriginal members of both federal Parliament and provincial legislatures selected through indirect election by Métis self-governments. It is noteworthy that the Assembly of First Nations is opposed to guaranteed representation and that the *Report of the House of Commons Special Committee on Indian Self-Government* did not support guaranteed representation in Parliament.

Indian Reaction

How have Native peoples reacted to the legislation dealing with Native self-government? In 1975, the National Indian Brotherhood passed a resolution which in part stated a need for a phased approach to revision of the *Indian Act* and also put forth the principle of optional adoption by bands of any revised provisions of the *Indian Act*. However, Indians today argue that because the political scene is radically different than in 1975, this resolution is no longer applicable and they consider it obsolete. They further argue that if the federal government had consulted with them, they would have long ago realized this was no longer a viable position for Native people to hold.

Nevertheless, the Native people today have some sympathy with the existing legislation, even though it was introduced unilaterally by the federal government. The only consultation held was with provincial governments. Given the suspicious relationship between the two parties, Natives cannot conceive of government legislation acting in their best interest. There is, therefore, a tendency for Natives to react negatively to every new government initiative. They were asked for initial suggestions in regard to *Bill C-52* and then ignored as the process of developing the legislation went on. Thus Native people, while they might agree with certain specific points of *Bill C-93*, feel that they must reject it because of other aspects. Some of the more salient points that need further discussion and classification, according to Native peoples, are as follows.[6]

1. There is a feeling that with the passage and implementation of *Bill C-93* the provincial governments will become more involved in Indian Affairs. This, of course, will weaken the federal trustee role and accelerate provincial jurisdiction over Indian affairs. This would happen by treating the local band governments like provincial municipalities, making them subordinate to provincial legislation.

2. DIAND refuses to acknowledge that Indians have had an Indian government. If any legislation is passed, the judicial powers of Indian chiefs and councils will be weakened. In the end, this will lead to termination of the reserves and total cultural assimilation of the Indian people.

3. No matter what changes are introduced, DIAND still remains the "big brother." The minister still has to approve band charters, still has to approve finances, and still has the right to investigate Indian contracts when he decides that it is warranted. In short, while Indians may take over some local control, DIAND still remains in a position of absolute power over Indian peoples.

4. The provisions dealing with land would, Indians feel, introduce something similar to fee simple in the White world. Each Indian would have his own parcel of land and thus begin the process of assimilation. In addition, certain non-Indians would be allowed to inherit Indian land, but only with a life interest. All levels of government could expropriate Indian land, and, finally, there are no provisions for Indians to acquire lands in addition to their existing reserves.

5. While the legislation identifies the responsibilities and powers of the band government (and treats it as a quasi-judicial body), it does not demonstrate how it would resolve internal conflicts on the reserve. In summary, the legislation does not have enough administrative or financial flexibility to meet the goals of Indian governments.

6. Of immediate interest to Indians is the issue of finances. Although the federal government has developed a funding formula, it is doubtful that it will work. Natives feel that the issue of financing is too complex to fit all reserves into one funding formula. In addition, three-to-five-year funding programs are being developed by DIAND for Indians. This again demonstrates DIAND's control over Indians and the short-term nature of the projects being developed.

Indirectly, the issue of taxation on reserves is also tied into the funding problem. Indians would be expected to tax their residents on the reserves (Aboriginal and treaty rights have exempted them from this) and thus help to fund social and economic programs.

The involvement of provincial governments also plays a part in the financial picture. Since the provincial government receives transfer payments from the federal government, part of the payment is based on the number of Indian people in the province. What does the province do with the money?

7. A number of additional issues have surfaced and are presently being discussed by Native people. These include such diverse issues as Indian governments having absolute control of their capital and revenue funds; bands opting out of the legislation; the role of the federal government in forcing Indians to accept services from provincial, private, and municipal agencies; and the question of who will judge the quality standards for programs developed by Indians.

The end result so far is that Native people feel that they are in a better position to adopt a political strategy of rejecting the entire package than of voicing cautious or tentative support of the legislation. They feel that they will be in a better bargaining position if they reject it outright. Given that premise, negotiations with the federal government may be more fruitful for the Natives.

The general principles of Indian government can be summarized as follows. These principles may not be fully endorsed by all Natives but they would seem to be those that are most consistently advocated. Natives argue that *sovereignty exists in and of its own right*. It is a gift from their Creator, which has never been and can never be surrendered. In the past, Native people formed a variety of political units, with their own government and other institutions. They claim that with colonization, their right to exercise their sovereignty was unjustly abrogated and ignored, and their political institutions were systematically dismantled. But, as in the past, they assert their sovereignty and the right to create their own unique institutions of self-government.

In accordance with the principle of self-determination, Natives want to exercise their right to make and administer decisions on all matters pertaining to themselves and their lands. Native government is the expression of this inherent right of sovereign nations to self-determination. Native people anticipate a new order of government within Confederation, and they are renegotiating the terms of their relationship in the hope that the Constitution will recognize not only federal and provincial governments, but also Indian governments that will exercise full internal sovereignty.

Indian governments will have exclusive legislative, executive and administrative jurisdiction over Indian lands and resources and over the people within their territories. Indian territory will have three components: 1) territory as presently recognized, 2) territory to which there is a valid claim, and 3) those hunting, fishing, trapping and gathering tracts not included in the first two components. Indian governments will have jurisdiction over all persons on Indian land and exclusive jurisdiction in determining Indian citizenship. They will be responsible for peace, order and good government within Indian territory and for the maintenance and well-being of Indian people. Indian jurisdiction will not be limited to Indian territory when matters of social and cultural responsibility for its citizens extend beyond it.

Indian people will develop their own constitutions. They themselves will determine whether they choose to be single units or to amalgamate to pursue common goals as Indian nations. The actual form these political units take will be based on the needs and aspirations of the Indian people involved. Natives feel that the rights confirmed by the *Royal Proclamation*, the *British North America Act*, the treaties, and the trust relationship between Indians and the federal government mean that the Government of Canada is responsible for providing the resources, including land, that will enable Native governments to attain their goal of economic self-sufficiency. This is a necessary complement to their goals of political and self-determination.

SELF-GOVERNMENT: CURRENT STATUS

Aboriginal rights in Canadian law are still somewhat ill-defined, but several basic points are now clear. These rights are collective rights, which derive legal force from common law recognition of the legitimacy of the prior occupancy and use of certain territories. The essence of the common law view of these rights is that they protect whatever it was that the organized society of Aboriginal peoples did before coming into contact with Whites. To date this has focused Native concerns on land use and occupancy (usufruct), but, logically speaking, Aboriginal rights could include many other social activities, such as the determination of descent and family matters. And this, of course, is what is now being discussed under the rubric of self-government.

The *St. Catherine's Milling* case, decided in the late nineteenth century, was regarded as the precedent-setting case with respect to Native rights until 1973. The general import of the decision was that the source of Indian rights in Canada was the *Royal Proclamation* of 1763. However, in 1973, the *Calder* case in British Columbia tentatively ruled that Indian rights were not dependent upon the *Royal Proclamation* but could be viewed as independent rights. However, it was not until 1984, with the *Guerin* case, that the Supreme Court ruled that Aboriginal rights were derived from the original possession of the North American continent; that is, that Indian interest in the land was a pre-existing legal right not created by the *Royal Proclamation*, by statute or by executive order. This ruling set the stage for the federal government's willingness to begin discussions with Native people with regard to self-government.

All forms of Aboriginal self-government will involve a number of common concerns: boundary setting by the group, control over matters that are internal to the group, determination of relationships with external groups, and control over change brought about by external forces. The concept refers to the right of people to determine their political future and to freely pursue their cultural and economic development. Politically, this idea is expressed by independence as well as by self-government, local autonomy, or some other form of participation in government (Peters, 1987).

The reader, having finished the material presented thus far, has probably found it very difficult to ascertain the specifics of what is involved in the notion of Aboriginal self-determination or Aboriginal rights. Our task now is to summarize what the central tenets of self-government are from the perspective of Native peoples. We think that four factors constitute the overall Native thinking on self-government.

1. Greater self-determination and social justice. Protection of and control over one's own destiny, rather than subordination to political and bureaucratic authorities based outside the ethnic group.

2. Economic development to end dependency, poverty and unemployment. Economic justice, in the sense of a fair distribution of wealth between the Aboriginal and non-Aboriginal populations.

3. Protection and retention of Aboriginal culture.

4. Social vitality and development that will overcome such existing social problems as ill health, the housing crisis, irrelevant and demeaning education and alienation.

In order to achieve these aspirations, Aboriginal self-governments would need: 1) political institutions that would be accountable to the Aboriginal electorate, 2) a territorial base, 3) control over group membership, and 4) continuing fiscal support. This would mean control over a number of areas that deal with or affect Native people, for example, citizenship, land, water, forestry, minerals, conservation, environment, economic development, education, health, cultural development and law enforcement.

What is the scene today with regard to Aboriginal self-determination or Aboriginal rights? There are five different forms of Native self-government that now exist in Canadian society. All of these arrangements have focused on Native people with "status." The five current strategies that have been established for achieving self-government for Aboriginal peoples are:

1. Band government under the *Indian Act*, 1876.

2. The *Sechelt Indian Band Self-Government Act*, 1986.

3. The *Cree/Naskapi (of Quebec) Act*.

4. The *Act Concerning Northern Villages and the Kativik Regional Government* (Inuit).

5. Community-based self-government.

We will present a brief outline of the administrative and organizational structure, the powers, and the financial arrangements under the first two of the above strategies. We will then discuss the arrangements made under the new community based self-government.

The *Indian Act*

Critics of band government under the *Indian Act* suggest that this is not a form of self-government, but rather a form of self-administration. Nevertheless, under the *Indian Act*, band councils were created to implement the principles of democracy and to assure the existence of self-government. Under this form of government, a chief and band council are elected; the council has one chief, and one councillor is elected for each 100 band members. The powers held by the band council are wide-ranging; for example, providing for the health of band members, destroying and controlling noxious weeds, removing and punishing persons trespassing on the reserve, providing for entry permits to band lands, and regulating the residence of band members. Certain other by-laws can be passed if the government of Canada feels that the band has the ability to understand and implement the regulations. However, at the same time, the Minister of Indian and Northern Affairs can carry out activities on the reserve without band consent, for example, issuing permits for the use of reserve land and determining the location of roads on the reserve.

Most provincial laws of a general nature are applied to Indian people. Under these regulations, a province, municipality or corporation can expropriate reserve land for public use if it has the consent of the federal government. Certain federal laws take precedence over the *Indian Act*, although the exact relationship between laws in this respect is still under discussion. Each year bands receive money from Indian Affairs for the administration of their own and government programs. Today, over half of the budget allocated to Indians is controlled by band councils.

The above brief summary illustrates that under the *Indian Act*, Indian people do enjoy some elements of self-government. However, they argue at the same time that under these present conditions, almost all actions taken by band councils can be disallowed by the Minister. Furthermore, under these circumstances, Native people can only be reactive, not proactive. Finally, Natives argue that the present structural arrangements between them and the government are paternalistic and contribute to the continuing dependency of Natives.

The *Sechelt Act*

In an attempt to change the existing structural and institutional arrangements between Native people and the government, the *Sechelt Indian Band Self-Government*

Act was passed in 1986. The Sechelt Indian band consists of 33 reserves located approximately 50 kilometres north of Vancouver along the coastline. Through this new legislation, under which Indians are to assume the rights of self-government, the Sechelt band is established as a legal entity. A written band constitution is in place under the *Act*, and the band council becomes the governing body of the band. According to these legal conditions, the band may enter into contracts and agreements; acquire and hold property; and spend, borrow and invest money. The council also has additional powers under the *Sechelt Act*. Not only does it enjoy all the powers identified under the *Indian Act*, it can also carry out actions that were previously entrusted to the Minister, for example, the construction of roads, the granting of access to and residence on Sechelt lands, and the zoning of land.

Currently, the organizational structure created under the *Sechelt Act* is contained within the confines of each of the reserves. However, the possibility exists that if the provincial government gives its approval for a referendum, the federal government could recognize a Sechelt Indian government district, which could then exercise jurisdiction over land outside the Sechelt reserves. If this were to happen, the Sechelt Indian government district council would be the political organization over the entire district. Under the *Sechelt Act*, both federal and provincial laws of general application would be in effect with regard to the band and its members, except those laws which are inconsistent with the *Indian Act* (Peters, 1987). The financing arrangements under the *Sechelt Act* are quite different from those of the *Indian Act*. Under the new *Act*, the band has powers to tax local residents and businesses for maintaining the local infrastructure. Furthermore, the band may seek external financing with regard to any projects they wish to take on. In addition, the band received a single lump sum of money to be held in trust for its own use.

The Emergence of Community Self-Government

In early 1982, *The Alternative of Optional Indian Band Government Legislation* was introduced to pave the way for the implementation of the municipal form of self-government desired by "innovative" bands to negotiate their own specific form of governmental status, which would be incorporated into federal legislation. Those bands which did not want to participate (either then or in the future) could remain under the old *Indian Act*. However, the *Indian Act* would be revised and a new alternative funding arrangement would be implemented for those bands remaining under the jurisdiction of the *Act*. This new alternative would allow Natives to apply to the federal government in order to assume greater control over various facets of reserve life; e.g., management of lands, monies, definitions of who is a member of the band. If, at some future time, the "less advanced" bands wanted to further develop their own form of self-government, they would have the experience of exercising control over financial matters and other concerns.

This new policy is enticing to Native people. It would, on the face of it, lead to greater self-control. It would also make Native leaders accountable to the local population they represent. And, acceptance of this controlled style of self-government would result in the financial support of the federal government. However, it is the unwritten intent of the federal government to channel these new forms of self-government into municipal forms of government, not a fourth level of government. The structure of the new forms of government also ensure that the local Native leaders would provide a buffer between individuals living on the reserves and the federal government. Concern and hostility would be deflected to local leadership, not Indian Affairs personnel. Finally, the acceptance of the municipal style of government by Natives would lead to acceptance of the dominant society's culture and values; thus ensuring the further assimilation of Natives. The implications of this policy have not gone unnoticed by Natives; yet they are in a position in which they must make a decision.

The federal government is very much aware of the control they can exert under the municipal style of government presently being offered to Natives. They are cognizant of the controls that go along with their brand of self-government; a form which makes Native decision-making processes more reviewable by the non-Native system. This, in turn, allows for a greater probability of subjecting Indian political and legal processes to the non-Native processes (Clark, 1990). Natives, on the other hand, prefer a more traditional form of government under which they could develop a measure of cultural and political autonomy.

Native people once again find themselves at the crossroads of their destiny. They are clearly cognizant that they will remain, for some time, economically dependent upon government for the implementation of various programs and services. At the same time, they are determined to develop greater self-control and self-reliance. Their task is to develop a workable system within the context of the Canadian federal system by which they can achieve this goal.

Community-Based Self-Government Policy

Prior to the 1970s, there was still a real belief that Native people would be assimilated and become part of mainstream Canada, albeit marginalized. The massive immigration to the urban areas in the sixties gave further support to this belief. However, court decisions throughout the seventies and into the eighties began to cast doubt on this assumption. Land claims decisions in particular were disturbing to the federal government's long-term goals.

It was in 1978 that federal bureaucrats first embarked on a course with Native municipal government as its goal. This early "pre-policy," unannounced and invisible, was put into action as they forced Natives to separate land claims from self-government. While focusing on land claims, Natives were unaware that there was a new thrust. Natives were flush with victory in winning new sources of funding and seemingly greater influence over the spending of monies earmarked for them. However, the economic recession of the early 1980s dealt a crippling blow to economic development and control by Natives. By the time the recession ended in the mid part of the 1980s, Natives were once again economically dependent. And, by this time, government officials had firmly entrenched the policies and operating procedures for developing municipal style self-government.

In 1985, the federal Cabinet began to discuss constitutional and nonconstitutional initiatives which would enable Natives to take on some form of self-government. After the 1987 First Ministers' Conference, cabinet reaffirmed its commitment to constitutional process and continuation of a community self-government policy. One year later, cabinet authorized up to 15 sets of self-government negotiations with individual bands.

In 1986, the federal government publicly announced its community-based self-government policy. This new policy was intended to circumvent parts of the *Indian Act* and further entrench the municipal style of local government. A community can be individual bands, groups of bands, tribal councils, treaty groupings or other regional entities. As a beginning, the government recognizes that not all bands are the same and a great diversity of Native communities exists. As a result, the policy of self-government can be achieved through a number of avenues, each to be negotiated by the local community.

The policy guidelines delineate the boundaries of the demands it is designed to accommodate, as well as the contents of the negotiations. As noted by the policy:

- negotiations are to be conducted without prejudice to Aboriginal rights, existing or future land claims or future constitutional developments.

- the extent and division of powers between the federal and provincial government will not be changed through self-government negotiations.

- there will be an attempt to accommodate Native governments within the existing constitutional framework.

- the resultant self-government structures must conform with the established principles, jurisdictions and institutions of Canadian jurisprudence.

- all financial arrangements will be consistent with the historic levels provided to that community.

There are many other issues which define the limits of what can be negotiated. For example, any area which the federal government refuses to negotiate with Natives—labour relations, immigration—is not on the bargaining table. Other provisions, such as the government's insistence that criteria for membership be established and retained, limit the nature and type of discussion which takes place. Each of the guidelines has been unilaterally established by the federal government with little consultation with Native people. Furthermore, federal negotiators, thus far, have adhered rigidly to the guidelines, arguing that Cabinet is the only body authorized to change them. At the same time, the government reserves the unilateral right to change the guidelines without prior notice or retroactive enclosures. Native people have pointed out that in negotiations, federal agents have added guidelines which are not part of the written guidelines.

Nevertheless, once a community decides to pursue self-government, it must begin to put together a proposal for self-government. The proposal sets out, in as much detail as possible, the community's overall goals and aspirations in the area of self-government. At this time, departmental officials meet with the community on request to explain the federal government's policy on self-government and the various options which are available. The options range from exercising more of the authorities presently available under the *Indian Act* to new arrangements beyond the current limits of that *Act*. Different parts of the Department of Indian Affairs are responsible for assisting communities in a variety of areas. Hence, once a decision is made by the community to proceed, the proposal is sent to the appropriate departmental officials for action.

The community-based self-government process is divided into four phases: 1) development: the building of community awareness and consensus with regard to goals, 2) framework: design of proposals which are more specific in terms of goals and structure of government, 3) substantive negotiations: negotiations of the two parties over specific issues proposed by the community, 4) implementation: moving the proposal from paper to action in the community.

Development   If the proposal is for new arrangements beyond the present limits of the *Indian Act*, it is referred to the Community Negotiations Branch for further discussions. The proposal must be accompanied by a band council resolution to indicate support for the proposal and for entering the process. There must also be some evidence of community support obtained through workshops, community surveys, meetings or some other community consultation process.

The proposal is assessed by the Community Negotiations Branch on the basis of the following criteria:

- consistency with the department's mandate for community negotiations;
- quality and level of detail provided on community objectives;
- feasibility and achievability, including the practical experience it could provide for other communities;
- extent to which the community exercises authorities now available under the *Indian Act*, and its overall financial and management record;
- extent to which there is evidence of community support for the proposal; and
- the amount of funding requested (if any) to proceed.

Once the preliminary proposal is sent to Ottawa, an assessment is undertaken jointly by the Community Negotiations staff and regional officials. Discussions are then undertaken with the community. Following these consultations, a recommendation on how to respond to the proposal is made to the assistant deputy minister. There are many different recommendations which can be passed on to government. These include

1) proceed with the development of a framework proposal for community-based negotiations;
2) refer the proposal (in whole or in part) to other more suitable departmental processes for action;
3) recommend additional developmental work to clarify what the community wants to achieve through self-government; and/or
4) find that the proposal is outside the general mandate for self-government.

Framework Proposal   Once accepted into the Community Negotiations process on the basis of its initial proposal, the community develops a framework for negotiations. Its purpose is to set out, in detail, what is required to meet the community's objectives (as defined in the initial self-government proposal) and to suggest an agenda and schedule for negotiations. In actual practice, the level of specificity of those proposals varies considerably. Those bands which have achieved economic development may move to this stage with a minimum of detail and structure. Nevertheless, most proposals include the following:

- proposed changes (if any) to the structure or operation of the community's present government, or to the way in which it is selected;
- the specific areas where additional or new authorities beyond the *Indian Act* are desired;
- the type and level of additional or new authority required;
- the areas (if any) where provincial involvement or cooperation is necessary to meet community objectives;
- a community approval and/or ratification process; and
- a proposed schedule of activities in support of negotiations, including a process for community involvement.

Based on the experience to date, the preparation of a framework proposal takes several months to a year. Throughout the community negotiations process, the timing and pace of negotiations is determined by the community. Regional and headquarters officials will assist the community on request. Funding support for this part of the process can be arranged through a contribution agreement.

Once completed, framework proposals are reviewed by community negotiations and regional officials. Meetings are held with the community to ensure that all aspects of the proposal are clearly understood. This process usually involves attempts to co-opt the community into accepting the limits set by government officials. And, while this is referred to as the "response state" of the process, it is in reality part of the negotiating phase. A discussion paper providing a preliminary response to the framework proposal is then prepared. Issues addressed in the paper usually include

- the parameters for negotiations;
- a general description of the current situation with respect to each proposed subject area for negotiation;
- an indication of whether the subject area can be accepted for negotiation and/or what may be required to proceed; and
- an identification of where provincial involvement may be required.

The discussion paper is reviewed in detail with the community and adjusted accordingly to take the community's comments into account. The objective is to arrive at a mutually acceptable document which defines as clearly as possible what will be on the table for negotiations.

During this time, both parties discussing the issues are cognizant of their respective constituents. Native leaders are very much aware of how community members, as well as other Native leaders, will react to their agreement. On the other side of the table, government officials are subject to criticism by their superiors that they have set a dangerous precedent by agreeing to some Native demand or that the agreement proves to be unworkable.

Once general agreement has been reached, the discussion paper, along with recommended action, is sent to senior management in DIAND for approval. If some of the issues involve other federal departments, their approval will be sought on those items. If changes are required as a result of this part of the process, they will be brought back and discussed with the community.

Based on the discussion paper, a draft framework agreement for substantive negotiations is prepared. This document usually includes

- the agenda for negotiations;
- a detailed outline of what the parties will address through substantive negotiations in each subject area;
- an agreed upon process and time frame for completing the negotiations; and
- an identification of the appropriate parties to the negotiations in each subject area (including, where required, other federal government departments and/or provincial governments).

This part of the process does not take a great deal of time since the framework agreement simply reflects the understandings described in the discussion paper. Subsequently, the federal negotiator seeks guidance from senior management and other departments, as required, on items included in the proposed agreement. There is a similar consultation process at the community level by the community negotiator.

Once the draft framework agreement is finalized, it is signed by the Minister of Indian Affairs and Northern Development, but only after interdepartmental consultations have been completed. This signature is a commitment to enter into negotiations on the part of the federal government, not just the Department of Indian Affairs and Northern Development. At the same time, the community will be expected to secure a mandate from its members, preferably through a referendum. However, alternate processes suggested by a community will be considered.

Substantive Negotiations   At the third stage, community and federal negotiators prepare detailed proposals on each subject area which has been accepted for negotiation. The purpose is to determine the specific mechanisms required to achieve the community's objectives. Early in negotiations, the parties will identify areas of agreement and isolate issues in dispute, problem areas, or matters where further Cabinet and/or community direction must be sought.

The length of time required for this work varies, depending on the size of the community, the complexity of the issues, the amount of expert technical advice required, and the degree of consultation with community members required. Funding will be provided to help defray some of the costs to the community, again in the form of a contribution.

Once the contents of the document are agreed upon, the federal and community negotiators initial an Agreement-in-Principle setting out, in whatever detail is appropriate, what has been agreed upon. It will include an implementation plan and a financial arrangements agreement. Final acceptance of the Agreement-in-Principle is conditional on formal ratification by the community and the federal Cabinet. In this instance, a referendum under the *Indian Act* or some other mutually agreed upon ratification process will be required as the indication of community support.

After formal ratification, the Agreement-in-Principle is signed by representatives of the community and the Minister of Indian Affairs and Northern Development on behalf of the government of Canada. However, any legislation required to give the agreement effect has to proceed through the normal legislative process in Parliament, which usually takes several months to complete.

Implementation   Implementation will take place according to the provisions of the implementation plan and can be phased over whatever period of time has been agreed upon. Within the Self-Government Sector, responsibility will be assigned to a specific unit to ensure that all aspects of the new arrangements are implemented on time, in accordance with the Agreement.

STATUS OF SELF-GOVERNMENT

Given the limited options that Native people have regarding self-government and the complexity of the process of applying for community-based self-government, few Native communities have progressed beyond the application stage. Table 12.1 shows that a considerable number of proposals have been developed over a four-year period (1988-1991). However, there is also a noticeable decrease in the number as the process moves from the developmental stage to the framework-proposal stage. Table 12.2 reveals the cost incurred in introducing the community-based self-government policy. One million dollars were directly expended in the first year of operation. However, since 1988, when bands began to develop their applications, this has increased to almost $6 million. (See Table 12.2.) As the process continues and more bands make application, the cost will become increasingly higher.

The reader may wonder why so few arrangements have so far been carried out. If a few arrangements for developing self-government *have* been put in place, why are they not found in more places? Even though the gap between Natives and the government remains large, these few arrangements suggest that there have

TABLE 12.1   NUMBER OF SELF-GOVERNMENT PROPOSALS AND STAGE OF DEVELOPMENT, 1990

	Stage of Proposal						
Stage	Development		Framework Proposal		Substantive Negotiations		Inactive Proposals
Date	Proposals	Bands	Proposals	Bands	Proposals	Bands	
1988	24	72	12	32	0	0	18
1989	60	250	13	23	0	0	22
1990	60	183	10	25	5	11	32
1991	55	169	13	22	9	31	36

TABLE 12.2   FEDERAL GOVERNMENT EXPENDITURES ON THE COMMUNITY-BASED SELF-GOVERNMENT POLICY

Fiscal Year	1986-87	1987-88	1988-89	1989-90	1990-91
Amount ($ millions)	3.985	2.212	4.498	5.754	5.900*

* Denotes approved allocation, rather than actual expenditures.

been some changes in the federal government's policy in this regard. Why not more? To document fully the reasons why more agreements have not been implemented is beyond the scope of this book. However, some major reasons will be identified and discussed.

First of all, there is a difference in approach with regard to how each of the Native groups—for example, Inuit, Métis, Indian—seeks to realize Aboriginal self-government. These groups have diverse histories, languages, cultures, needs and aspirations, and, therefore, they seek different solutions to the problem of self-government. On the other hand, the federal government wishes to provide one solution to the problem. Evidence today suggests that the government is moving away from this approach, but progress so far has been slow.

A second explanation for the lack of progress in the area of self-government is that the Native peoples are approaching the problem from a different perspective than the federal and provincial governments. Natives are asking for constitutional recognition and protection of their rights (self-government) in terms of broad, undefined structures, with details to be worked out later. On the other hand, the governments are not willing to talk about rights in the abstract and want to know what the concepts mean before they are prepared to allow Native self-government. This impasse is referred to as the "empty versus full medicine chest" dilemma. Natives want to begin discussions assuming that the chest is full of rights, while the different levels of government want to assume that the chest is empty and then add to it. Related to this is the charge that neither the government nor the Natives have publicly articulated any clear, comprehensive policy in regard to the specifics of Native self-government.

A third reason for the slow progress is the Native suspicion of government initiatives and policies. The history of poor relations between the two parties has come to influence the interpretation of policies or programs set forth by either party. Natives argue that experiences over time in dealing with the governments have generally shown that any agreements struck worked to the detriment of Natives. They point to the way they were placed in a disadvantageous position by the signing of the treaties, by the 1969 White Paper, and, more recently, by the proposals in the *Nielsen Study Team Report on Native Programs*. As a result, Natives are very suspicious of any proposals set forth by the government.

A fourth factor that has contributed to the lack of arrangements for self-government has to do with the involvement (or lack of it) of the provinces. Status Indians feel that the issue of how they can achieve self-government only concerns the federal government. Once the agreement is in place, then the provincial governments will have to accept the arrangement. The provinces (and to a certain extent the federal government), the Métis and the non-status Indians argue that given the considerable presence of provincial programs and expenditures, the provinces will have to be involved if any meaningful progress is to be made.

Finally, the financial implications of moving to self-government have also tended to draw out the negotiations between Natives and the government. Even when negotiations produce an agreement, the issue of financial responsibility creates major difficulties in implementing the program. If local bands are to provide a variety of services, how will they be operated and funded? Given that existing Native federal programs are already inferior to provincial programs, a considerable amount of additional monies will have to be injected into the programs to bring them up to provincial standards. Native people are aware of this, and linked to their general suspicion of the federal government is the feeling that the government's present movement towards allowing Native self-government might be little more than an attempt to abdicate its financial responsibility.

CONCLUSION

The creation of many tribes has led to the use of tribalism as a tool for Natives negotiating with the federal government and with other special-interest groups. For example, being able to speak for a particular tribe gives leaders some credibility and enhances the leader's ability to achieve specific goals. This has on occasion led to coalitions of several Native groups in their quest for a particular goal. However, the same structure also leads to inter-tribal conflict. As past experience has vividly shown, coalitions are notoriously unstable, and, as a result, they are usually unable to build long-lasting relationships. Rouch (1956) and Rohen (1967) discuss "super tribes" and the process of fission/fusion in attempting to illustrate this process.

One would assume that as Natives in Canada continue their urbanization process, tribalism will lose some of its impact since they will be forced to live in a heterogenous environment. This should weaken tribal identity. However, preliminary evidence suggests that this is not happening. Competition for political power and jobs in the urban areas has tended to increase rather than decrease the incidence of tribalism (Uchendu, 1970).

In their quest for self-government, Natives have created a fiction of statehood—a myth that they traditionally had hierarchically structured governments and a ruling elite. As Boldt (1985) notes, these three factors have not been part of traditional Native society. The basis of Native social order, they maintain, was not built on hierarchical authority wielded by a central political organization. Their analysis of Native culture suggests that these values are irreconcilable with Indian history and experiences.

Nevertheless, Natives are claiming that they have always had some form of statehood and, thus, should also have self-government. The acceptance of this new-model form of European government by Natives has ushered in a new era with regard to Native and non-Native relationships. It also signifies a break with traditional Native culture and may mean that the forced assimilation employed by the Canadian government has been successful.

As Natives continue trying to obtain local control over their lives, they are increasingly using tribalism as a tool to achieve that end. This means that there will be continued inter-tribal conflicts over the important issues of the day. As each tribe seeks to preserve its own interests and obtain maximum power, conflict will become endemic to the situation.

The implementation of this new community-based self-government policy, eventually to become the accepted norm, will require massive ideological and possibly structural changes in the Indian-Inuit Affairs Program. Historically, DIAND was an integrated agent-client organization. During the 1960s, it changed to a highly differentiated, but also highly centralized, organizational structure with a number of divisions delivering programs or services to Indians and Inuit (Paton,1982:20). More recently, both the process of devolution (decentralization) and the concurrent implementation of the policy of band control have adjusted the program's focus. Nevertheless, the administrative and budgetary control held by DIAND has remained highly centralized.[7]

The emergence of the Indian self-government approach is partly a response to dealing with the unwieldy and confused state of affairs that currently prevails in the Indian-Inuit Affairs Program (Paton, 1982: 34). This new policy will give program authority to Indian communities and will establish a system of funding that places bands in a position of direct responsibility to their constituencies.

NOTES

1. Prior to 1951, 400 Indian bands were under a tribal custom system of government, 185 under a three-year system and 9 under a one-year system. By 1975, 384 were under an elective system, while only 169 retained their tribal custom method (Daugherty and Magill, 1980).

2. Our system of local government is made up of four levels: rural municipalities, villages, towns and cities. These municipal units are under the jurisdiction of the provinces. However, Indian reserves (bands) are not included in this structure.

3. Land is an exception. Although the land would be controlled by the band, actual title of the land would remain vested in the Crown. However, Indian band governments would have the abilities to grant interest in land, on behalf of the band.

4. The information that follows is taken from published documents of DIAND, personal correspondence with DIAND officials and from other internal documents produced by DIAND.

5. A series of national surveys showed that Canadians feel that the federal government has become too involved in Indian affairs and that more and more responsibility should be taken over by the Indians themselves. The surveys also revealed that Canadians feel that Indians should become more involved in the national economy and that special rights should not exist for them.

6. For a more complete documentation of Indian objections, the reader should consult Piepenburg (1982).

7. Throughout the country, there are wide variations in the organizational structure of DIAND programs. For example, in British Columbia the program and the budget are almost completely decentralized, while in Manitoba, districts have been abolished.

POLITICAL ECONOMY
OF NATIVES

INTRODUCTION

Since the turn of the century, Native people have been unable to participate fully in the Canadian economy. Even before our economy moved to an agricultural base and then on to one of modern technology, Native people were restricted in their involvement and, as a result, have fallen further behind in their ability to integrate. The result is that Native people find themselves operating in a subsistence or welfare economy parallel to that of the more modern economy. In other words, there are two economies in our society. This dual system emerged over time as changes in the institutional structure and technology took place. Natives were prevented from participating in the economy through a variety of policies and programs established by government. For example, Aboriginal people were prohibited from using resources in direct competition with non-Aboriginal users. Before the turn of the century, Native people were not allowed to take homestead lands, as these lands were only available to immigrants. In other cases, Natives were refused licences to act as commercial big game hunting outfitters in areas where non-Natives had established commercial enterprises. When inland commercial fisheries were created in the Canadian Northwest, regulations were put in place so that Natives could not compete with non-Natives.

The following Table (13.1), created by the Shuswap Nation of British Columbia, indicates the flow of dollars per month by residents of the Kamloops Indian Band. These figures show that about 85 percent of the spending took place off the reserve in nearby White communities. This "economic leakage" is just one more reason that Natives find it difficult to economically develop their communities. This flow of funds also points out how profitable it is for non-Native enterprises to do business with Natives.

As our society moved into an industrial-technological economy, Native people found themselves without the skills and resources necessary to participate. As a result, the two economies emerged—a modern, dynamic sector (industrially and technologically based) and a traditional, subsistence sector. The former sector of the economy creates change, which, in turn, promotes further change, while the latter sector resists change, clings to the old ways and refuses to adopt new technology (Wien, 1986). Native people have discovered that special skills are necessary to participate in the modern economy, and without those skills, they will only be able to participate at the fringes of the industrial economy.

TABLE 13.1 Native Expenditures Per Month On-Off Reserve, 1991

Expenditure	On Reserve	Off Reserve	Total
Groceries	$400 (1.3%)	$29 275 (98.7%)	$29 675
Bank savings	$0 (0%)	$23 590 (100%)	$23 590
Other	$1359 (7.1%)	$17 766 (92.9%)	$19 125
Transportation	$2897 (15.8%)	$15 398 (84.2%)	$18 295
Insurance	$0 (0%)	$16 529 (100%)	$16 529
Gasoline	$14 612 (93.2%)	$1061 (6.8%)	$15 673
Furniture	$100 (0.7%)	$14 222 (99.3%)	$14 322
Clothing	$0 (0%)	$14 303 (100%)	$14 303
Restaurant	$ 3057 (27.7%)	$7993 (72.3%)	$11 050
Entertainment	$300 (2.8%)	$10 450 (97.2%)	$10 750
Vehicle maintenance	$1618 (16.4%)	$8242 (83.6%)	$9680
Appliances	$0 (0%)	$6926 (100%)	$6926
Alcohol	$0 (0%)	$6468 (100%)	$6468
Tobacco	$5192 (97%)	$162 (3%)	$5354
Day care	$2070 (96.1%)	$85 (3.9%)	$2155
Total	$31 605 (15.5%)	$172 470 (84.5%)	$204 075

Source: Shuswap Nation

The analytical model presented here has as its forerunners those offered by Cumming (1967), Carstens (1971) and Patterson (1972). Drawing upon the seminal work of these authors and others, the macro model developed here will view the reserve (or Native enclosure) as an internal colony that is exploited by the dominant group in Canada. Non-Natives will be viewed as the colonizers, while Natives are considered the colonized people.

How did this happen? How did Native people find themselves excluded from the economic activities taking place in the modern sector? To fully answer that question, we need to quickly present an historical perspective. As Mills (1961) argues in *The Sociological Imagination*, an historical perspective is essential when examining inter-group behaviour so that the changing relationships between the structural components of society can be understood. Others have also argued that a knowledge of a nation's history is indispensable to an understanding of its contemporary issues. Certainly, a nonhistorical point of view has no means of evaluating social change. Society is not static. In order to understand the dynamics of change in a social system, its long-range developments must be apparent. As Mills suggested, to have meaning, a social analysis must examine the mechanics behind social trends. In other words, we must ask how the structure of society is changing.

Initially, Natives were regarded as non-human savages to be exterminated or ignored. They were also regarded as lazy, filthy, uninhibited and uncivilized. During the nineteenth century, the Natives fell victim to conscious and unconscious genocide: the expansion of Western civilization that produced this result was viewed as a manifestation of Christianity. White settlers embodied the Protestant ethic of thrift and willingness to work hard. Because Natives did not share this ethic, they were rejected as pagan savages, with no claim to Christian charity (Hunt, 1940).

Eventually, through the proselytizing efforts of various churches, Natives became Christians (Trigger, 1965). As Christians, they came under the rubric of Christian ethics and could no longer be so blatantly exploited. Because prejudice and discrimination were by then solidly entrenched in Canadian society, an ideology of inherent White superiority was introduced to justify White dominance and exploitation. White superiority and dominance were attributed to processes of natural selection, reflecting the Social Darwinism prevalent in the late nineteenth century.[1] By the laws of nature, then, White exploitation and westward expansion were inevitable. As Willhelm has argued:

> In the thoughts of the light-skinned people of early America, no White man ever commands because he "chooses" to do so; it is not by his choice, but by the will of God or the act of Nature that he rises to the fore at the expense of inferior races. To rule is really to submit, in the first instance, as an obedient believer of God's command and, in the second instance, as a helpless pawn abiding by Nature's laws governing the races of men. The White races, in the final analysis, never felt superior in an absolute sense since they yielded to the Christian Bible and to Nature's demand in commanding inferior races.

> When the Indian and Negro were in the animalistic state, they were hea-
> thens; Whites fulfilled obligations to the Almighty in defending racists'
> feelings against the non-believers and would suffer no sense of loss should
> they even exterminate the non-White. Indeed, failure to fulfill Christian
> precepts exposes the right to question Christian descent; to be judged by a
> God on the basis of diligent hard work makes it only proper for man him-
> self to judge others by the identical standard. Consequently, Whites merely
> carried forth their Christian duty to let out extermination and enslavement
> to non-Christians (1969:3-4).

The sciences, particularly biology, were perhaps unwitting contributors to racism in North America. Biologists in the late nineteenth century claimed inferior species could be physiologically distinguished from superior species. Racial attributes were labelled and attributed to various groups to account for their behaviour. The scientists claimed, in fact, that the genetic, racial make-up of individuals caused their social behaviour; the evidence suggests that most White Canadians believed them.

According to racist theory, no amount of effort by Natives or assistance from Whites could compensate for the Natives' natural inferiority. This conviction is evident in the government's decision to establish Native reservations. The reserves were to act as holding-pens for worthless people, inferior children, wards of the nation. In the treaties, when "concessions" were made to Native interests, they generally coincided with White interests (Green, 1969). The Riel Rebellion of 1885, as well as the subsequent execution of Riel, were both the final extension and the climax of Native-White relations in Canada in the nineteenth century, and established the pattern of subjugation that continues to persist today.

Present-day non-Native Canadians have a new strategy in their relationship with Natives—the myth of equality (Willhelm, 1969). This myth's basic premise is that all humans are equal no matter how diverse they appear to be. This acts as a rationale for denying special privileges and affirmative action programs to various minority groups. The federal government's White Paper, which recommended that reserves be terminated and special status revoked, exemplifies this myth. Current legislation also reflects a growing adherence to the myth of equality. Proponents argue that the laws which now express the equality of ethnic groups are sufficient, regardless of the impact of centuries of entrenched discrimination.

Finally, another rationale for racism involved a view of Canada's resources as limited. More for Natives translates as less for Whites. As Dixon has noted with regard to Black-White relations:

> If I am pro-Black, then I must be anti-White. If I am pro-White, then I must be anti-
> Black. Another way of stating the either-or concept is the two-person, zero-sum
> game. According to the strategy of this game, if, for example, a sum of 100 units of
> some commodity is to be distributed between two people, then any changes in a

given distribution means that increasing one side causes a corresponding decrease in the other. Similarly, in the context of...race relations, any gain for Black is viewed as a loss for White and vice versa (1971:29).

The underlying assumption held by most Canadians is that Indians contribute little economic product to the Canadian economy. In addition, non-Natives feel that the larger dominant economy supports the Native economy through governmental subsidies and through the creation of and payment for a variety of health, economic and social services. For example, many people point out that governmental transfers provide between 80 to 100 percent of Native salaries and non-earned income. If Native communities did not receive government subsidies, their local economy would collapse.

However, as Salisbury (1986) points out, this perspective is somewhat erroneous in the implicit assumption that the flow of support is one way. First of all, the flow of money stems from a "contract" agreed upon by the two parties (the federal government and the Natives) and not revised or amended over time. The contents of the agreement were agreed to by both parties at the time of signing and were in the best interests of both parties. The *Royal Proclamation* of 1763 is a good example of an agreement between the two parties that is still legally binding. Under this agreement (we can only assume that the government of the day knew what it was doing), it was understood that in return for the Native's recognition of the sovereignty of the monarch, the monarch would protect Natives and preserve the Native way of life. While some specifics of the agreement have been modified (in favour of the non-Native group), the federal government has accepted the agreement struck with Natives. Hence, the "subsidization" of services to Natives has been and continues to be paid for by Natives through their original transferring of land and allegiance in 1763.

NATIVE DEVELOPMENT: THEORETICAL UNDERPINNINGS

To break the pattern of colonization, Native Canadians must incorporate both the notions of individual entrepreneurship and community ownership with the goal of controlling reserve economies (Dubois, 1940). The problems facing Native people can be addressed through the implementation of strategies which involve both individual and community-based resource development. First, Native people must be provided access to training and employment opportunities. Furthermore, the delivery and control of these training and employment strategies must reside within the Native community. Native communities which have followed this strategy have emerged with some modest success. For example, the Meadow Lake Tribal Council has focused on economic development and currently provides 450 jobs directly, and another 240 indirectly, through a mixture of Indian government, tribal council and band community-based enterprises. Other specific examples would be the Bay of Quinte Band's printing business. The band also manufactures and sells microcomputers through the First Nations Technical Institute. Throughout Canada, Aboriginal communities and their people contribute to the Canadian economy by providing at least 6000 enterprises and an estimated $2 billion in annual expenditures.

Heilbrun and Wellisz (1969) have proposed that the federal government use the International Bank for Reconstruction and Development, the International Finance Corporation, and the International Development Authority as models for its financial dealings with Native communities. These organizations make loans to underdeveloped countries for various projects and provide for economic development. Programs adapted from these models would be of enormous benefit to reserve economies. First, because project workers would not be subject to an annual review for continued funds, they would not have to fear losing their support at the end of the second or third year. Second, projects could be developed that progressed slowly but steadily toward a cumulative goal. Finally, qualified staff would be attracted to the projects by the security that would accompany elimination of the annual funding review.

However, as MacGregor (1961) argues, creative development of any type will not emerge on the reserve until the conscious and unconscious forces opposing the Native administration of reserve lands are significantly reduced. Natives must be given the authority to enact social changes without fear of reprisals from federal and provincial governments.

In general, the federal government has retained control of development schemes by allowing Natives only to implement projects rather than plan them (Hatt, 1969). Moreover, Native programs tend to be short-term experimental or pilot projects, which can be terminated quickly with few problems. According to Hatt, these programs have "therapeutic" value only; because they defuse protest and do not seriously disrupt the status quo, they perform effectively as social control mechanisms. Most government economic development reflects minimal government support, short-term financing, and an unbalanced single-industry approach—in short, the antithesis of Sorenson's and Wolfson's (1969) recommended strategy for economic independence. In all these government programs, there is also a notable absence of any secondary, or processing type, industries on the reserves.

Despite federal resistance, Native people must create viable economic units within the reserve and control them as a community. This view has been expressed by Deprez and Sigurdson:

> There can be no question that it is imperative for Canada's Native population to become involved in more productive economic activities. In strictly economic terms, the continuous dependence of the Indian on government assistance constitutes a serious drain on the financial resources of Canada. Even more significant is the fact that these people comprise a very significant potential labour force and a potential

that today is not being utilized. But by far the most important dimension to the employment problem of the Indians is the humanitarian one, because participation in a viable economic activity is essential if the Indian is to maintain his sense of self-respect (1969:11)

Several basic assumptions underline the need for community development and control, assumptions which the federal government is unwilling to accept. First, all people fundamentally desire to better themselves. When their attempts to do so are blocked, the social and psychological damage is considerable. Second, the major obstacle to improvement is a lack of resources, such as funds, skills, equipment and education. Third, given resources and opportunity, people find their own effective ways to meet their needs and improve their lives. In the past, Natives have been forced to try to solve problems by solutions provided for them by government agencies; procedures not part of the dominant capitalist culture have been attacked and rejected. Fourth, a change in only one component of a group's behaviour seldom produces meaningful, lasting results. A simple influx of money does not solve very much as the social behaviour of humanity has many facets; each component of behaviour stands in a relationship to other components. This must be considered when attempts at change are made (Lagasse, 1962).

Several structural changes need to take place. These changes will not happen overnight, nor will they occur without impact on Native people. The effects of industrialization on a population are well known and have been extensively documented. Industrialization has had a traumatic impact on people in virtually every society that has made the transition from agrarianism. The disruptions of social relationships and related customs and practices are particularly severe. These disruptions were evident when Natives changed from a nomadic to a sedentary society. The interplay of various components of Native life were seriously disrupted. For example, the tipi, which was well suited for nomadic people, provided shelter for Prairie Indians. However, when stationary houses (because of reserve living) were introduced, the system of sanitation did not change accordingly. As a result, stationary homes became a fertile breeding ground for tuberculosis and other infectious diseases. In short, the transition to an industrial economy has always exacted a great deal in human suffering and demoralization from the people going through it. Hence, it should not be expected that Native people will somehow be exempt from this.

Having said so, it does not necessarily follow that Natives must experience the same level of disruption that others have had to undergo. Some structural changes can be introduced to bring about cultural and economic change with minimal impact. For example, movement into the city, a traditionally frustrating and tension-producing activity, can be facilitated through the proper institutional help. The removal of barriers to jobs can be implemented. Other changes such as the settlement of Aboriginal title, and the integration of development plans, can also be undertaken. In addition, development needs to proceed under local control; that is, development should proceed only after plans have been developed which meet the local needs and priorities rather than only meeting the needs of the national or multinational companies. Finally, there must be more integration. Modern and traditional activities need to be developed together rather than allowing one to develop at the expense of the other. The various institutional sectors of Native society also need to be integrated into the dominant society. For example, educational needs have to be integrated with economic needs, and health-care facilities need to be related to the work world (Wien, 1986).

This structural approach to social change necessitates an understanding of the institutional structures that influence Native life. Rather than focusing on the individual as the unit of analysis, such an approach examines the socio-economic role of internal Native institutions and their external relationships (Girvan, 1973). For too long, theorists have viewed Native-White relations as a "Native problem," rather than as a "White problem," and have failed to take external factors into account.

Clearly, the "Native problem" has been created by the economic, cultural and political structure of Canada. Contrary to previous explanations, the position of Native people in Canada is not the result of cultural isolation or particular psychological tendencies of Natives. Nor do individual racial and cultural discrimination provide a sufficient explanation for the low socio-economic position of Natives in Canada. While individual discrimination may have retarded socio-economic upward mobility, it has not eliminated it. Sunkel has shown that a totally marginal group is "deprived of all means of access to a source of income of reasonable level and stability" (1973:141); clearly this is not the case for Natives in Canada (see Figure 13.1).

The marginal position of Natives in Canada can only be explained when various types of discrimination against Natives are considered along with Natives' limited sources of income and their lack of control of the means of production. The manner in which resources are deployed, whether human, capital or technological, determines the level of employment, the extent of industrialization and the distribution of income. As Mariategui (1934) pointed out more than 50 years ago, the roots of the Native problem are economic and lie in the system of land ownership. This clearly implies that the economy is not embedded in social relations, but, rather, that social relations are structures within society's economic institutions (Polyani, 1974).

The federal government argues against the creation of industries and jobs within the reserve. It contends that the reserve is basically a residential area and cannot be converted to industrial or commercial use. For example, recommendation 3 of the *Hawthorn Report* states:

FIGURE 13.1 **LABOUR FORCE PARTICIPATION RATES**

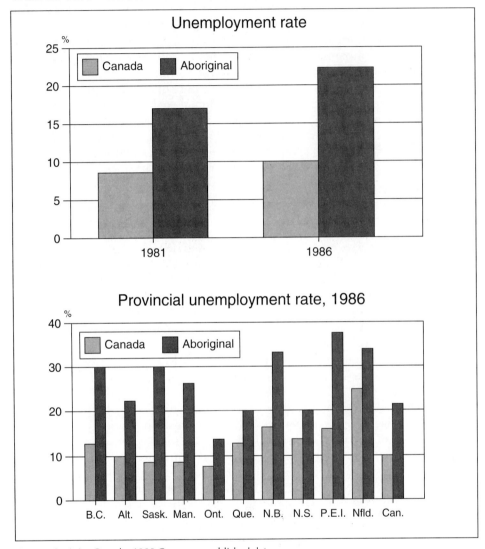

SOURCE: Statistics Canada, 1988 Census, unpublished data.

The main emphasis on economic development should be on education, vocational training, and techniques of mobility to enable Indians to take employment in wage and salaried jobs. Development of locally available resources should be viewed as playing a secondary role for those who do not choose to seek outside employment.

At the same time, the federal government is trying to force the Native population off the reserves and into the cities. The results have been devastating. The most capable and aspiring Natives leave the reserve, which is then managed by a residue of unskilled, low-aspiring individuals. As a result, the reserves are becoming less able to provide their residents with the living standards minimal to survival. Nevertheless, there is now an attempt to reverse this situation.

A far more realistic alternative is to create new industries and upgrade existing ones. The creation of new jobs for Natives would also boost reserve profits, upgrade individual income standards, and provide invaluable experience for the development of Native leaders in community and business affairs. Clearly, Natives themselves want to create and control economically viable ventures on reserves. As Peters stated:

> We want access to development resources which means the right to participate in provincial development activity and the right to direct access to all federal departments without intervention of the Department of Indian Affairs. The Indian Affairs Department is playing a "gate-keeper" role in opening up these resources to Indian communities. There is a tendency for the Department to do all it can on its own and turn over what it chooses to the provinces or other federal departments. In this way, the branch ensures its own future, but, in so doing, is failing to help the Indians to find their place in the provincial and national community (1968:6).

THE EVOLUTION OF NATIVE DEVELOPMENT

After World War II, Native people began to shed their passivity and began to demand an active part in Canadian society. The government (both provincial and federal), having experienced the atrocities of the war, began to implement policies which would forever change the ideological position of Natives. Human rights acts were passed, social assistance programs were put in place and specific actions were taken regarding Native people, e.g., the *Indian Act* underwent its first major revision in almost a century. By the 1960s, the federal government made public their report, *A Survey of the Contemporary Indians of Canada: Economic, Political, Educational Needs and Policies*. This report identified the poor quality of life experienced by Natives and concluded by suggesting extensive changes in government policy and programs. The government did act on the recommendation to set up programs for community development. The strategy was to follow two stages. First, the community would define its own problems and devise ways to achieve its goals. Then, in the second stage, the community would be given resources to implement the program. While Phase One was implemented, Phase Two never was sufficiently funded, and by the late 1960s, the concept of community development died.

After refusing to give local communities the necessary resources to achieve their goals, Indian Affairs implemented the National Indian Advisory Board. However, its ineffectiveness led to its abandonment by the 1970s. By the 1970s, the federal government had settled on a more traditional and orthodox plan for integrating Native people into the economy—modernization. The new approach embodied the principle of assimilation, yet it was hidden behind more opaque beliefs. Modernization meant that if one was to enhance his/her quality of life, then he/she had to move from traditional beliefs, values and behaviour, to more modern ones. This meant that science would be the basis for action, creative rationality would be the underlying mode of operation and new ways of thinking would be embraced. There was (and continues to be) a belief that change was inevitable and preferred. Furthermore, the direction of that change, along with its impact, could be controlled.

The federal government felt that Native people's traditional ways of life would have to end and a cultural replacement would have to be implemented. Specifically, individual values and goals needed to supersede those of groups or communities. Nevertheless, many Native groups rejected this approach. They began to suggest that economic integration of Native people would require more than the drive and motivation of each individual. They began to see the structure of our society as problematic in the poor quality of life for Native people. For example, the Métis Womens' Association of Manitoba saw Native problems as a symptom of larger social and cultural problems. In addition, the Womens' Association argued that, as long as development initiatives were handled solely by outsiders and men, the structural problems would remain.

In the early 1970s, the federal government, in its attempt to implement its modernization policy, established the Indian Economic Development Fund. Native groups felt that while economic development of reserves was important, it could not be run by bureaucrats; the development process had to be operated by Native communities. The National Indian Brotherhood publicly noted its objection to the way the fund was being operated by Ottawa. Natives felt that if economic development was to occur, Natives must have control, and this implies political autonomy (Elias, 1991).

By the mid-1970s, the federal government began to develop community and regional plans for Native economic development. A joint effort of the National Indian Brotherhood and DIAND produced its first report in 1976. Nevertheless, this report made it clear that Native people were not prepared to sacrifice their culture, land or identity in order to develop economically. They wanted to develop in such a way that the two structures were complementary. Native people felt that local self-government could be the structure where both economic development and cultural maintenance could coexist. Under these conditions, Native organizations became involved in economic development. As Elias (1991) points out, by the late 1970s models of change became interdisciplinary. Social and cultural issues become more important and were integrated into these new models of social-economic change.

However, by the mid-1980s, this integrated approach had once more been set aside by Ottawa, and a more singular view of development took precedence—

economic development. The multidisciplinary approach was also rejected by Native organizations. Realizing how few resources they had and the paucity of resources likely to be given to them by Ottawa, they believed that a multi-sector approach to development was doomed to failure. It also needs to be pointed out that Native acceptance of this new thrust was also due to their realization that if full endorsement of the new federal policy was not forthcoming, few funds would be available.

Thus, by the mid-80s, Native organizations accepted economic development as the major thrust of advancement. At the same time, however, they tried to develop new ideologies through different channels. The idea of self-government, sovereignty and Indian rights began to surface and were pursued through other Canadian institutions, e.g., the courts. Nevertheless, they had now accepted a blended (Native/non-Native) course of action by which they would pursue their economic development. Meanwhile, the federal government continued to view its definition of development as the only acceptable one. The Indian Economic Development Fund (established in 1970) was replaced by the Canadian Aboriginal Economic Development Strategy, and, in 1989, the Aboriginal Economic Development Strategy was created. All the development programs established in recent years by the federal government have been explicitly economic and favour individual entrepreneurship and enterprise over any strategies based on community control (Elias, 1991).

In 1989, the federal government earmarked nearly $900 million (over five years) for Native economic development. It also suggested that more Native control would be given with respect to financial resources and decision-making and that the design of the plan was such that Indian Affairs' role in program-delivery would be phased out as local Native control took over. As Gadacz (1991) points out, DIAND's old focus on control, structure, rules and procedures was to be replaced by collaboration, learning, networking and innovation. In short, Indian Affairs would switch roles from a direct supplier of services to an assistant for Native communities.

BAND COUNCIL

Until recently, Native communities have relied upon their internal political-administrative structure to facilitate development. This structure, the band council, has been in place for many years and represents a major force in almost any Native community. It is the community's major strength as well as its major weakness in carrying out development activities.

At the end of the nineteenth century, the federal government introduced the band council structure on reserves. Since then it has functioned as both a political and administrative organization for the reserves. The normal structure for a band council consists of a chief and a certain number of councillors (proportionate to the total population of the reserve), all of whom are elected. The council plays a key role in nearly all the activities of a reserve. It hires a manager and employees to perform administrative duties and to oversee projects and programs operating on the reserve. For example, the council deals with issues related to education, health, social assistance and justice. It also involves itself in the economic activities of the reserve (Bherer, *et al.*, 1990).

In a sense, the council acts like a municipal council. However, what differentiates it from a municipal-style government are its ill-defined and limited powers. Under the terms of the *Indian Act*, the council's powers have never clearly been delineated. Furthermore, the council normally operates with funds from a single source: Indian Affairs. And, Indian Affairs is capable of overriding all decisions made by council. Nevertheless, the linkage between the federal government and the band council is so entrenched that councils may be viewed as the administrative arm of the Department of Indian and Northern Affairs.

It should not come as a surprise, then, that turnover and burnout of council members is frequent. Members of the council are expected to be all things to all people. They are expected to be involved in social, cultural, political and economic ventures undertaken on the reserve. This involvement may be direct, through ownership and/or decision-making, or indirect, through supporting certain activities. Finally, councillors must become experts in each of the areas for which they are given responsibility to oversee. For example, councils are expected to be familiar and deal with over 100 federal programs spread out in 15 sectors and 11 different departments (Bherer, *et al.*, 1990).

Councils find themselves trapped in a dual allegiance; administrative responsibility to both Indian Affairs and to the resident population—their constituency. Tension exists as council members make decisions and are exposed to criticism from both directions. Those who continue to operate within the confines of band council find that their operations become subjected to bureaucratization. Nevertheless, the incentive to remain on council is high because it provides a stable source of income in an environment characterized by high unemployment and it provides status both within the community and outside.

The question remains as to whether or not the band council system is the best way for Native communities to engage in economic development. Or, should a new form of local administration be devised to better create and facilitate community economic development. The band council operates within a larger administrative system which is also fraught with structural inconsistencies. For example, one of the problems faced by Indians today is the fact that the legal status of bands is unclear. It is doubtful whether a band can make legal agreements with other legal entities; e.g., companies. This uncertainty obviously makes it difficult for Native people to carry out economic transactions with other businesses. On the other hand, if Indians create a legally constituted company, then the new entity is no longer "Indian" and, therefore, is not eligible for the benefits available to Indians within the existing legal and administrative structure; e.g., tax exemptions.

STRUCTURAL BARRIERS

Data presented earlier show that Natives possess the lowest economic status in Canada. Those data also suggest that Natives currently serve as a secondary labour pool to provide cheap labour when the supply is scarce and to be quickly laid off when the supply increases. Consequently, Native workers are very useful to White society. Because they ensure that the labour supply consistently meets industry's needs, they keep labour costs and, hence, prices at a minimum. At the same time, they enable White employment to be maintained at a constant level.

As Piore (1968) demonstrates, every nation has a dual labour market. The first market consists of jobs that pay well, offer stable long-term employment, provide good working conditions and include chances of advancement. In the second market, the reverse applies. Research carried out by Buckley, Kew and Hawley (1963) shows that this dual market operates within the economic structure of Canada. In his study of urban Natives, Nagler found that

> ...there are also seasonal commuters [Indians] who come to the city when employment levels are high. These workers usually stay in cities while employment is available in construction and related industries and then return home during the slack periods to which many of these industries are subject (1971:12).

In 1970, a Special Senate Committee Hearing on Poverty cited a large mining firm in northern Manitoba which employed Natives exclusively on a casual basis. Casual workers do not get all the economic benefits, such as health care and insurance, which are given to full-time workers. According to the committee's report, even Natives who had worked at the mine for 20 years were still on the casual payroll. Similarly, La Rusic (1965) showed that no Natives working for mining-exploration companies had ever been on the full-time payroll. Even though these workers were highly skilled, they were denied equal working conditions with Whites. After 12 years, Cree workers were still employed as casual workers and restricted to menial activities.

In a capitalist system, economic development occurs in a series of stages; "precapitalism" gives way to a series of capitalist refinements. As the system develops, it creates certain market forces that affect other regions. "Spread effects" result when growth in one area creates development in other areas, and "backwash effects" occur when growth in one area drains resources out of a hinterland (Dunn, 1975). When urban centres develop, backwash effects create obstacles to development in such peripheral regions as Native reserves.

The early colonizers were primarily interested in Native people as military allies, as a potential market for their manufacturing industries, or as a source of labour for primary industries such as trapping and logging. Natives produced raw materials for White society, but did not participate in any industrial growth. As the colonizers began to bring in capital, technology and skilled labour from Britain and Europe, Natives were increasingly isolated from the mainstream Canadian economy and restricted to employment patterns that were marginal in every respect. Consequently, Natives became increasingly dependent on trade goods and on the capital of foreign-owned companies. This economic cleavage, combined with racial and cultural differences, served to isolate Natives from all aspects of White culture—technological, social and ideological (Stavenhagen, 1963).

It is generally assumed that, as the rate of investment increases in a nation, the production output and the employment opportunities also increase. However, this assumption ignores the distinction between a modern and a subsistence technology. As investments increase in the modern technological sector, automation accelerates; this means that employment opportunities are actually reduced. Therefore, an increase in the rate of investment leads to further under-development of the total employment field and ensures that those in the primitive technology sector (agriculture) will remain unemployed (Sunkel, 1973).

Natives are economically dependent in that they cannot manipulate the operative elements of their economic system (Brewster, 1971). Put another way, Natives are unable to function as an independent economic entity. Because the marginal economy of the reserve is dependent on outside credit, it becomes virtually impossible to amass any savings. And, due to the legal prohibitions of the *Indian Act* and the incursion of capitalist values that encourage entrepreneurship and discourage community ownership, the specialized, dependent economy that has managed to grow on the reserve is controlled by a small Native elite (Dosman, 1972). As a direct result of these factors, Native people have consistently lacked the human and financial capital needed to develop the reserve economy.

The failure rate of Native enterprises is somewhat higher than the Canadian average—40 to 60 percent in the first three years. These failure rates point to the existence of major constraints. First, on the supply side, we find shortages of financial and human capital and the inadequacy of current mechanisms to provide employment-enhancing skills. The lack of financial resources to start up businesses and the limited access to debt financing are major constraints. In some cases, Native communities lack the organizational capacity to develop business projects. In other cases, Natives are culturally ambivalent toward business enterprises. Historical dependency upon government also impacts on Native communities' ability to develop projects which meet their needs and which would integrate with their cultural perspective. Finally, added to the above problems is the fact that, while a plethora of programs is offered to Native communities, the communities are not able to screen programs effectively and decide which would be useful and which are inappropriate.

On the demand side, constraints operate through prejudice and discrimination—at the individual level—which keep Natives from obtaining financial

resources. Legal arrangements, such as the *Indian Act*, also prevent Natives from securing local financing for businesses. National and international companies prefer to transfer their workers from site to site rather than hire local people in rural or
remote areas. In the cities, labour market matching agencies and their services are
not used by Natives. Various programs such as apprenticeship, licensing and union-
ization are not available to Natives because of their limited qualifications. Thus,
Native participation in technical, professional and skilled labour is not possible.
Licensing and contracting practices of government act against Aboriginal businesses. For example, access to resource licensing has been governed by economic
criteria designed for large-scale southern-based commercial enterprises and the
related rates of return or wage levels, rather than by the economic return acceptable
in a low-wage economy.

AVAILABILITY OF CAPITAL

Although the *Hawthorn Report* shows little correlation between the amount of capital income per band and the level of economic development, this finding is somewhat misleading. Few bands are allowed to control their own money. As a result,
when a band does manage to increase its per capita income, the money is not reinvested in the reserve or in the band. Under federal direction, accumulated finances
enter what is commonly called the "trust fund," are invested in government bonds,
or are used to fund one of several welfare projects on the reserve. Although the
money that accumulates is substantial, it is kept out of Native control; in recent
years, DIAND has administered well over $100 million annually in band trusts.

Native groups or individuals who request money from DIAND are generally
turned down. Each request must go through a series of bureaucratic procedures
and be approved by the federal government. It generally takes from one to five
years for a grant or loan request to be approved or rejected. Moreover, the final
terms are never the same as those originally sought: they are modified at each step
along the bureaucratic path. Jean Chrétien, one-time minister of DIAND, vividly detailed the problems in a Toronto speech:

> First the band council decides that they want to do something constructive and
> reasonable with a piece of their land, as many of them do. They pass a council res-
> olution which they hand over to the Department's agency office. It is sent from
> there to the regional office. The regional people, anticipating that their superiors in
> Ottawa will ask questions, ask questions themselves. Back it goes to the agency
> and back to the band. The band gets another meeting organized. They answer the
> questions and put the proposal back into the mill. It goes to the agency, to the region,
> and it finally reaches the head office where the lawyers get at it. They ask more
> questions that the region had not thought of. Back it goes. Eventually all the ques-
> tions are answered and it comes to me (1969:8).

TABLE 13.2 FINANCIAL DATA, EXPENDITURES IN THE NATIVE SECTOR ($ MILLIONS)

	1973-1974	1978-1979	1983-1984	1984-1985
Housing	INAC	23.9	42.9	133.1
	CMHC	*	*	76.1
Infrastructure	INAC	30.6	60.2	194.6
	TC	*	*	7.2
Economic development	INAC	21.9	44.9	39.5
	DRIE	1.1	8.3	18.0
Natural resource	INAC	0.0	0.0	1.1
agreements	F & O	*	*	2.7
Regional development	INAC	85.0	255.7	462.0
agreements	DRIE	0.0	24.7	32.2
Training and mobility	INAC	5.1	8.4	26.1
	EIC	19.2	27.0	118.1
	JUST	*	*	0.2
		*	*	2.6
Major resource development programs	INAC	0.0	0.0	10.5
Health	H & W	1.9	6.8	10.2
		60.1	125.6	273.3
Welfare	INAC	61.5	133.1	278.0
Education	INAC	131.0	252.1	479.0
Culture and	INAC	4.3	7.7	12.1
communications	SEC	9.9	18.1	39.0
Reserves and trusts	INAC	10.9	13.0	21.7
Native claims	INAC	0.0	9.9	50.5
Band management	INAC	25.4	52.5	117.6
Administration of justice	INAC	*	6.1	12.8
	JUST	*	*	3.0
	SGO	*	*	0.4
Total				2 421.6

* Figures not available in this format.

** Estimate of future expenditures, in 1985-1986 dollars, drawn from resource guidelines.

SOURCE: *Nielsen Report*, 1984: 60.

1985-1986	1986-1987**	1987-1988**	1988-1989**	Observations
102.1	101.8	101.8	101.8	$500 million required
88.5	97.3	102.0	106.9	to address backlog
192.1	196.4	202.5	219.5	
26.8	21.7	22.2	*	
34.5	30.4	30.4	30.4	
39.4	144.5	169.8	90.8	
1.8	1.8	2.0	0.3	
2.7	2.7	2.7	2.7	
495.6	578.0	615.0	666.0	
37.3	32.2	31.6	4.4	
20.7	20.1	20.1	20.1	
137.5	114.8	101.3	101.3	
0.2	0.3	0.4	0.4	
5.6	6.8	6.8	6.8	
15.5	18.3	17.2	26.7	
17.9	17.9	17.9	17.9	
358.8	358.8	358.8	358.8	
304.9	312.8	319.7	320.4	
532.5	571.9	577.1	586.5	
12.3	12.6	12.6	12.6	
43.7	47.2	47.7	34.2	
29.3	32.4	32.2	32.3	
170.8	138.9	96.2	64.8	Estimated
121.7	124.2	122.4	122.0	$8 billion
14.1	14.6	14.6	14.6	required to settle
3.8	3.9	3.9	4.1	all outstanding
0.6	1.0	1.0	1.0	claims
2 722.7	3 003.3	3 029.9	2 947.3	

Note:

INAC	Indian and Northern Affairs Canada		F & O	Fisheries and Oceans
			EIC	Employment ImmigrationCommission
CMHC	Canada Mortgage and Housing Corporation		JUST	Department of Justice
			H&W	Health and Welfare
TC	Transportation Canada		SEC	Secretary of State
DRIE	Department of Regional Industrial Expansion		SGO	Solicitor General Office

Once their traditional economy had been destroyed and they had been refused participation in the new emerging industrialization, Native people found themselves increasingly dependent on the government. The degree of poverty on reserves became so serious that social assistance appeared necessary. Table 13.2 reveals the relative expenditures for Indian Affairs. It shows that one half of the Indian Affairs budget is allocated to social assistance; e.g., housing, health. On the other hand, less than five percent of the budget is specifically earmarked for economic development, although the amount increases if other forms of development are taken into account, e.g., regional development agreements. Nevertheless, the large expenditures reveal the ineffectiveness of the programs in that the total department's budget represents an expenditure of about $8000 per Indian.

The relative allocation of funds to various activities has remained stable for some time, although increased expenditures in one category or another will appear occasionally. Table 13.3 identifies the regional expenditures of Indian and Northern Affairs Canada (1984-85), exclusive of such benefits as unemployment insurance and family allowance.

Special funds to help Indians develop were established as far back as 1938. Since then, a number of programs have been developed, the most recent having been created 20 years ago. This program provides for direct loans to Natives and allows INAC to guarantee loans.[2]

In 1989, Employment and Immigration Canada spent more than $139 million to provide training and services to nearly 24 000 Aboriginal people. Even though

TABLE 13.3 REGIONAL DISTRIBUTION OF ON-RESERVE EXPENDITURES BY THE INDIAN AFFAIRS PROGRAM OF INAC IN 1984-1985 FOR GROUPS LIVING ON RESERVES (REGISTERED INDIANS ONLY)

	Millions $	%	Population of reserves	%	Per person
Atlantic	69.0	5.1	9306	4.1	7414
Québec	180.6	13.2	28 263	12.5	6390
Ontario	242.3	17.8	49 487	22.0	4896
Manitoba	243.3	17.8	36 335	16.1	6696
Saskatchewan	221.5	16.2	33 294	14.8	6652
Alberta	170.8	12.5	30 895	13.7	5528
British Columbia	237.2	17.4	37 807	16.8	6274
Total	1 364.7		225 387		

SOURCE: Nielsen Report, 1984: 22.

massive funds have been expended to train Native people, the impact of this program continues to be questioned. Socio-demographic data show that each year over 5000 Native people must enter the paid labour force in order to maintain the current rates of unemployment—a rate double that of the national average (see Figure 13.1). The socio-economic difficulties and resulting social impacts are even more pronounced for Aboriginal women. Jamieson (1989) points out that personal, community and systemic barriers attributed to a lack of self-esteem and lack of support and access, paint a particularly bleak future for Aboriginal people.

Since the early 1970s, successive governments have undertaken programs to redress economic disparities faced by Aboriginal people, particularly in western and northern Canada. In recent years, this has been done through programs specifically targeted at Aboriginal people, with an emphasis on the creation of employment opportunities and on increased access to capital for commercial ventures. Early efforts often resulted in only short-term employment at lower wages than those earned by the mainstream population. The more recent programs focusing on accessing opportunities in the areas of small business development, employment and management training, sectoral and institutional development, and primary resource development have provided more positive results.

In October 1983, the federal government made a significant commitment of resources by launching The Native Economic Development Program, with funding of $345 million to be expended over four years (extended three times, with no increase in funding, expiring in 1989). To fully appreciate the amount of funds committed, the reader should note that $131 000 was loaned to Natives between 1938-48. Not limited to a specific geographic area or Aboriginal group, this program had as its strategic objectives: 1) to increase and strengthen Aboriginal community projects that have a strong economic focus, that increase the self-reliance of Aboriginal people, and that have the potential to be commercially successful; 2) to increase the number of Aboriginally owned and controlled enterprises, including financial and economic institutions and businesses; 3) to increase the access of Aboriginal people to existing economic development resources in the public and private sector; and 4) to increase public awareness of the contribution to the mainstream economy made by Aboriginally owned, managed and directed enterprises. The Native Economic Development Program's mandate covers four areas: Aboriginally controlled and managed financial institutions, community-based business and industrial development activities, Aboriginal enterprise and entrepreneurship development, and coordination of other federal economic development programs.

Under the first objective, capital contributions averaging $4 million had been approved for 26 Aboriginally owned and controlled capital corporations. Seventeen corporations have started operations, and 12 have loan portfolios of more than $1 million each. The corporations concentrate on commercial lending in line with detailed analytical and procedural criteria prescribed in contribution agreements with the program, and together reach more than one-half of the Aboriginal population. The loans tend to be small, between $20 000 and $100 000. Assistance has been given also to economic development corporations both for planning and establishment, and for the start-up and expansion of commercial ventures.

Under the next two objectives, as of March 31, 1989, 436 commercial enterprise projects had been awarded funding totalling $143 million. Half of the projects involved establishment of an enterprise, and one third were for expansion of an existing operation. The Native Economic Development Program equity contribution accounted for an average 50 percent of project cost, with other (mainly federal) government sources contributing another 11 percent. The first 259 projects were concentrated in manufacturing (42 projects), accommodation and restaurants (47), retail trade (40), construction (24) and transportation (24). Twelve percent of the projects were related to tourism (Canada, 1989).

Also under the third objective, $4 million were made available to projects involving innovation, marketing and business studies. Half the funds were awarded to trade shows and other marketing efforts. Finally, under the last objective, 23 scholarships and training programs were supported for $6.4 million, including a national scholarship program through the Association of Canadian Universities for Northern Studies. Under the goal of trying to achieve community-based businesses, the Community Economic Development Program awarded a total $7.1 million for 68 projects. These consisted mainly of studies aimed at assessing the feasibility of economic options for communities, and included a few instances of funding of an on-going economic development secretariat.

In all, more than 5000 projects have been assisted, with the emphasis in the 1980s being placed on commercial undertakings. During 1987-89, for instance, 379 of 625 projects receiving federal assistance were in this class, with funding of $14.9 million. The component in support of primary producing activities was directed at upgrading traditional hunting and gathering and was important in the Northwest Territories and northern Manitoba. Federal assistance to 216 projects totalled $40 million. The provincial and territorial governments fund similar projects, as well as virtually all training-related activities under the Social Adjustment Measures program.

A new National Strategy was adopted in 1989 to help Natives develop economically. This program set aside $873.4 million over five years. The department of Indian Affairs received $430 million, while Industry, Science and Technology received $443.4 million. In addition, the Canada Employment and Immigration Commission continued to expend their current budgeted funds on Native people. This new program structure integrates eight components:

1. Business Development—to continue in a more effective way the commercial enterprise components of various government programs, including the Special Agricultural and Rural Development Agreements, the Native Economic

Development Program, and the Indian Business Development Program so that Aboriginal individuals or communities can obtain the capital and support services to start or expand a business.

2. Joint Ventures—to help Aboriginal businesses forge new and profitable links with other firms in the mainstream economy, thereby providing opportunities for the transfer of management, technical and other business skills to Aboriginal people.

3. Capital Corporations—to support and build the network of autonomous Aboriginal financial institutions established across the country.

4. Community Economic Planning and Development—building on the current initiatives, to assist Aboriginal people living in rural, remote and isolated communities to plan, program, organize and direct their own businesses and employability development services.

5. Access to Resources—to assist Aboriginal communities to develop their economic and employment base by gaining access to commercially relevant renewable and non-renewable resources.

6. Skills Development—to augment managerial, professional and vocational skills among Aboriginal individuals under programs such as the Canadian Jobs Strategy, by greater involvement of Aboriginal people in the planning and implementation of local strategies.

7. Urban Employment—in consultation with local provincial and municipal authorities, to assist Aboriginal people who live in urban areas to find employment through training and work experience initiatives so that they can share fully in the growing prosperity of our cities.

8. Research and Advocacy—to ensure the effective management of the new strategy, to coordinate the programs, and to conduct research and policy analysis. The advocacy role will be played to build support for Aboriginal businesses within the federal government and in all quarters of the Canadian economy (Canada, 1989).

DEVELOPMENT OF NATURAL RESOURCES AND GOVERNMENT POLICY

It is clear that the current levels of development in Native communities are much less than in non-Native communities. Yet it is not difficult to show that potential exists in almost every community, whether it be for development of natural resources or businesses. For example, a growing international demand exists for wild rice. Potential yields are worth more than $100 million annually. Less than 10 percent of all arable Native land of fair to good quality is under cultivation, and, under current conditions, well over 300 additional farm units could be operating. Indian lands contain over 11 000 square kilometres of forests with commercial yield potential, yet only a small amount is presently being harvested. And, while 150 000 Indians live within commuting distance of forestry projects (hiring over 160 000 workers), less than 4 percent of these workers are Native.

There are also opportunities in the commercial, service, transportation and construction sectors, including replacement of services that are currently imported from the dominant economy. Significant potential also exists in tourism and crafts. There are other natural resource developments, e.g., water, which could be undertaken by Native communities to economically develop.[3] However, the tenuous legal status of Native water rights has kept Native people from exercising a strategy of developing water resources; e.g., hydroelectric projects, irrigation. Finally, fishing and mineral exploitation could be undertaken by Native communities.

Each of the above sectors could be developed in a way that involved Native people and improved their quality of life. Bherer, *et al.* (1991) show how three Native communities in Québec (Wendake, Mashteuiatsh and Mingan) were able to establish viable economic enterprises. For purposes of this book, we will take one sector—mineral development—as a case study to show how this one area could contribute to the development of Native people, meet their basic minimum needs and enhance their quality of life.

Only recently has the economic potential of Indian reserves received serious attention (Stillwagon, 1984; Koovos and Brown, 1980). In the United States, the *Miriam Report* in 1928 presented the first comprehensive assessment of Indian lands and became the springboard for the implementation of the *Indian Reorganization Act* of 1934, which dealt with economic development issues for Native people. In Canada, however, no comprehensive assessments have been made with regard to the overall economic potential of reserves.

Recently, two studies, one in the United States, the other in Canada, have been carried out to assess the mineral potentials of reserves.[4] We will begin by assessing the economic potential of minerals on reserves today and the programs that have been developed to facilitate their development. We will also identify the existing federal and provincial policies toward developing Indian natural resources. Next, we will assess the likelihood of natural resource development on the reserves and its implications with regard to Indian economic development.[5] Finally, we will look at the overall economic potential of mineral resource development for Indians and identify various strategies they might pursue to become more economically independent.

For some time there has been a disagreement among federal government agencies over the best way of implementing development programs. On one side, the Department of Regional Industrial Expansion has advocated a strict economic approach, while the Department of National Health and Welfare has argued in favour of a social approach. The former agency argues that jobs have to be created for Natives and that only jobs will enable them to begin the long journey out of poverty. National Health and Welfare counters with the claim that, if Natives are not educated or in good health, jobs will be useless. The philosophical differences between these two positions have never been resolved. What has happened is that, over time, the philosophy of one group or the other has directed the action taken by Indian and Northern Affairs. As a result, programs which focused strictly on economic issues were developed for periods of time, only to lose favour and be replaced by social development programs. Since the 1960s, the pendulum has swung back and forth several times. No one has taken the position that both issues must be addressed simultaneously if Natives are to benefit (Weaver, 1986). In addition, there is a serious ideological split in federal agencies with regard to the role of the provinces in Native affairs. Some agencies argue that the distinction between status and non-status Indians or Métis is invalid. For example, the federal Métis and Non-status Indians Task Force began with the premise that the creation of the different Native categories (for example, Métis and status Indians) was an historical mistake and should not influence government actions. This, of course, meant that they viewed the provinces as playing an important role in helping Natives (in all categories) develop. Other agencies, such as Indian and Northern Affairs, have argued that Indians come under their exclusive purview, and for this reason they do not wish to involve provincial governments.

The second ideological split revolves around the role Natives themselves should play in their development. Some agencies do not support the idea that there should be Native-controlled, government-funded economic development corporations (Weaver, 1986). This position was buttressed by the *Beaver Report* (1979), which suggested that Natives did not have the training or the technical expertise to manage large bureaucratic industrial organizations. The author of the *Report* felt that such development programs should be the government's responsibility to design and deliver. Other agencies disagree with this stance and argue that Natives must learn how to manage them. Again, however, the differences have not been resolved and the debate continues.

Over the years, federal-provincial agreements have been concluded which, while not focusing on Natives or involving them in the discussions, have an effect on Native people. Again, we find that none of these agreements has been targeted specifically for Natives; their impact is noted solely because they apply to regions that have a high proportion of Native people. Most of the programs under these agreements are for a set period of time, thus requiring governments to periodically reassess the program. The programs supported under these agreements are directed at a number of activities, for example, delivering social services, human resource development and natural resource development.

While the federal government has generated a long list of programs designed to help Natives, no significant changes in Native employment or lifestyle have been recorded over the past half century. Economic development ventures undertaken or underwritten by DIAND have a dismal record for many reasons. Most of the funds granted by DIAND are channelled into small businesses in an attempt to maximize help to as many specific individuals as possible with as little money as possible. Secondly, DIAND fails to set clear objectives for its programs and seldom consults with Native people before creating its programs. Thirdly, most projects are marred by DIAND mismanagement; for example, the bringing in of outsiders with no relevant job experience and the hiring of too many workers for the job. The Task Force on Program Review (1985) noted that training programs and make-work projects have become part of Indian life. However, the training of Natives merely for the sake of training, or in skills that are not in demand, has created an artificial economy. Money is brought into the reserve this way, but the economy of the community is not enhanced because the money is not used to develop the infrastructures. In other words, Natives receive money but must spend it outside their community since there are so few businesses owned and operated by Natives. When dealing with Natives, welfare officials have increasing difficulty trying to determine the difference between productive and nonproductive employment.

Overall, the federal government's economic development plans, policies and programs have not been very effective. In the Assembly of First Nations' Brief to the Standing Committee (1984 and 1990), Native leaders identified several barriers to fuller Native participation in economic activities. Specifically, they noted the problems inherent in federal program design and in jurisdictional conflicts between various federal agencies. They also noted that the federal government's Resource Economic and Employment Development Unit was understaffed and underfunded, which meant that it could not handle Indian requests with regard to development.

Natives do recognize the importance of economics in achieving their goal of self-determination. However, they sometimes disagree about the best method for achieving economic independence. As Werhan (1978) points out, there are four major roads to resurgence; some of them have worked well and some still need to be fully tested. One technique that often has been used is to join the economic mainstream as a means of retaining core cultural elements, such as language, intact. A second technique is to work out a compromise with economic competitors in the dominant society so as to secure rights to exploit natural resources alongside the dominant society. A third method consists of pursing alternative routes to large-scale development by encouraging small-scale tribal development enterprises. Finally, a few Native groups have chosen to reject modern economic development and have returned to traditional economic pursuits, that is, they have practiced a subsistence economy. Each of these strategies has benefits and disadvantages. And, given the long-term goal of each group, no one strategy is to be considered the only correct approach. Natives may opt for a certain approach initially and then later switch strategies to better achieve their goals.

Economic Development Policy and Programs

Under existing legislation or within the terms of treaties, there is no requirement that the government develop economic programs for Indians. Nevertheless, because of the extremely low rate of Native involvement in the economy, the federal government has provided some economic development programs. Almost all of them are directed exclusively at status Indians living on reserves, and they take the form of conditional transfers, that is, transfers pertaining to a specific service and from which Indians cannot direct expenditures. Indians living off the reserve are encouraged to take advantage of provincial economic development programs or general programs operated by the Canada Employment and Immigration Commission.

During the past century, the economic development of Native people has been minimal. It would not be until the mid-1960s that DIAND would give serious consideration to developing a policy to enhance the economic position of Natives. Economic development, in this context, refers to a change in the structure of an economy, particularly a change in the direction of less reliance on primary extractive activities such as hunting, mining and agriculture (Rea, 1976). The resultant community development programs that emerged in the 1960s did little in terms of generating economic development for local Natives. Indirectly, however, they became a vehicle for teaching political skills, which would enhance Natives' ability to organize more effectively when dealing with the federal government (Mackie, 1986).

Natural Resources

If economic and political development are to occur on the reserve, it is necessary to establish some sort of proprietary rights for Indians.[6] In short, this right would allow Indians to manage, lease and control access to resource development on their lands, and it would include the right to all revenues and profits generated from the development. However, it is necessary first to determine whether or not natural resources (both renewable and nonrenewable) are indeed prevalent on reserves. Secondly, government policy must be assessed to determine whether or not it is possible to develop these resources.

Other factors also inhibit Native control over reserve lands. Section 20 of the *Indian Act* prohibits Natives from buying land on their own reserves without the approval of the minister. Bands also require special authority to purchase off-reserve lands. For some provinces, section 32(1) of the *Act* only permits products grown on reserves to be sold to other band members, and even this requires written approval from the superintendent. Other economic controls include the *Farm*

Credit Act established by the federal government to help Native farmers. In an astounding bureaucratic paradox, this *Act* gives a Native farmer long-term credit, but only after a first mortgage has been taken on the farm. However, because the Crown owns all the farms on the reserves, Natives cannot get first mortgages; therefore, the *Act* is totally useless to them.

Indian land is also endowed (unevenly) with other natural resources such as timber, water and minerals.[7] Forest lands cover nearly 40 percent of the total reserve acreage and provide an annual income of over $32 million. The production of lumber, pulpwood, fence posts and Christmas trees are the major uses of forest products today. Other reserve lands have potential for maintaining waterfowl and game that could be used in promoting commercial recreation. Still other lands (particularly those near large metropolitan centres) are being developed to provide areas of "exclusive" housing, mainly for non-Indians.

Mineral Development

Minerals are the most recent resource to be developed on reserve lands. The federal government has provided some financial support for Indian bands to develop their natural resources and thereby become further integrated into the mainstream economy.[8] However, the Indian-Inuit Affairs Program budget reflects other priorities, since economic development received only 7 percent of the 1978-79 budget. By 1986-87, the economic development line item showed that it made up less than 4 percent of the total budget (Canada, 1986: 2-10). The lack of formulated policy by the federal government with regard to Indian natural resource development has retarded progress in this field (particularly in Québec and the Maritimes) and has placed Indians who want to develop their natural resources in a very poor position when dealing with outside contractors, who are usually multinational corporations.

Reserves are scattered across Canada and vary in size from a few hectares in Nova Scotia and British Columbia to the huge reserves such as the Blood Reserve in Alberta, which contains 155 000 hectares. However, reserves have yet to be established in the Northwest Territories and the Yukon, even though treaties have been signed in the Northwest Territories, and provisions were made for the establishment of reserves there. The initial selection of land for the placement of the reserves was based on many criteria, although agricultural potential and the presence of fish and game were the most important. The assessment of natural resources on the reserve, with the exception of gold, was never a concern for the placement of reserves. It has recently come to light, however, that a number of reserves are amply endowed with important natural resources. For example, oil and gas development in Canada has become increasingly important. In 1980-81, royalties received from oil and gas development on Indian land totalled approximately $140 million. In addition, rental revenues were approximately $1.2 million.[9] Estimates for 1981-82 were $166 million and $1.4 million respectively, but since the collapse of the world oil prices in 1986, it has been estimated that Native oil and gas revenues have been cut in half.

Government Mineral Policy

The *Constitution Act*, 1867 conferred upon the Canadian government responsibility both for Indians and the lands reserved for them. This *Act* also transferred ownership and control of public lands to the provinces. This, of course, made it difficult for the government to fulfill its responsibility to the Indians. As Bankes (1986) points out, the constitutional division of legislative rights and proprietary interests has created a number of practical difficulties in implementing Indian policy; for example, despite the fact that the provinces were the main beneficiaries of Indian surrenders, they are under no legal or constitutional obligation to transfer land to the federal government for reserves.

During the mid-1960s, the federal government introduced a policy of devolution. The motivating concern behind this policy was that more responsibility should be shifted from the federal government to the Indians themselves.[10] Prior to this, the federal government (under the Indian Affairs Branch) took full responsibility for all Indian matters under the *Indian Act*.

Today, changes are taking place so that Indians themselves now have to make some decisions that deal both directly and indirectly with matters that will affect their way of life. Whether or not they should pursue an aggressive development policy is just one of these matters. The decision whether or not to develop their natural resources must be framed in both a short- and long-term perspective. Often short-term benefits are so attractive that long-term impacts are ignored or minimalized. On the other hand, not to develop existing resources could mean that they will remain (at least in the near future) undeveloped. Indians in the United States have also had to make these decisions, but this has led to the creation of an active inter-tribal organization—The Council of Energy Resource Tribes (CERT). Canadian Indians have not as yet made a move in this direction.

Natural Resource and Mineral Policy

The Department of Indian Affairs and Northern Development first developed mineral regulations with regard to Indian lands in the mid- to late 1950s. Major amendments to the regulations were made in 1966, 1974 and 1977. Under existing law, the Indian Mineral Directorate is responsible for the management and direction of the mineral resources on Indian lands under the authority of the *Indian Act*, the *Indian Oil and Gas Act*, the *Indian Oil and Gas Regulations* and the *Indian Mining Regulations*. The two directorates, Indian Minerals East and West, were created in 1977 and 1956 respectively to act as consultants for Natives. Both directorates are headed by a director who reports to the Director General of the Reserves and Trustee Program in Ottawa. The Governor in Council may make regulations respecting the granting of leases, permits and licences for the exploration of oil and gas on Indian lands. However, all royalties are paid to "Her Majesty in right of Canada," in trust for specific Indian bands.

Before any mineral or hydrocarbon development can take place on Indian lands, the Indian band for whom the land is set aside must make an appropriate surrender to Her Majesty (in right of Canada) of the minerals and the mining rights under the proposed development. The conditions are outlined in sections 37-42 of the *Indian Act*. These sections state that no lands on a reserve shall be sold, alienated, leased or otherwise disposed of until they have been surrendered to Her Majesty by the band for whose benefit in common the reserve was set apart. The surrender made to Her Majesty must be assented to by a majority of the electors of the band and accepted by the Governor in Council.[11] After the Indian band has surrendered its mineral interests (under the conditions of the *Indian Act*), the mineral rights may then be administered under the acts identified above.[12] The word "surrender" is simply the most appropriate legal term to define the consent of the band with respect to mineral exploration and exploitation on the reserve (Blais, 1984). Only minerals hidden from the surface, for example, hydrocarbons and precious metals) require a surrender. Sand, gravel, peat and other such non-metallic minerals do not require a surrender.

The manager of Indian minerals then disposes of oil and gas rights on Indian lands. The manager, through advertisement, calls for tenders on each parcel of land for which a permit or lease is to be granted. Under certain conditions, the manager may, in consultation with the band council, negotiate a lease without going to tender (section 7(5) *Indian Oil and Gas Regulations*).[13] However, under most circumstances, the directorate proceeds with mineral activities on reserves only on receipt of a band council resolution.

Although a mineral surrender by a band gives DIAND full authority to manage the mineral rights, the band council is usually consulted, and its consent is sought, before any final disposition of mineral rights is made. In fact, there is a continuous effort by the Indian mineral department to encourage Indians to become more involved in the management of their mineral resources (Blais, 1984).

Under section 57 of the *Indian Act*, the disposal of the minerals is governed by the *Indian Oil and Gas Regulations* and the *Indian Mining Regulation*. Unless otherwise specified in the call for tenders or in a negotiated agreement, the royalties from mineral development are paid to the Receiver General of Canada. These royalties, as well as rentals (from permits or leases) and bonus monies realized from a sale of mineral rights or a negotiated agreement, are deposited in the band's revenue or capital accounts. This money can be spent only for the benefit of Indians or bands for whose use and benefit it is held in common.[14]

The categories of *capital* and *revenue* monies determine the type of expenditures made. The minister of DIAND can, with or without the consent of council, spend monies for certain expenses. Specifically, the minister may (with council consent) authorize and direct the expenditures of capital money:

> to distribute per capita to the members of the band an amount not exceeding fifty percent of the capital monies of the band derived from the sale of surrendered lands (Section 64.a, *Indian Act*).

Occasionally, individual Indians are entitled to some or all revenues from mineral activity if they are holders of a certificate of possession or a location ticket *and* if the band council agrees.

Beyond the specific federal statutes that control natural resource development on the reserves, there is another level of government influence that enters the scene, that is, the provisions of various federal and provincial agreements in regard to the ownership of natural resources and the subject and amount of benefits from their development. The specific agreements vary considerably across Canada.

The *Constitution Act*, 1867 provided the then existing provinces, Québec, Ontario, New Brunswick and Nova Scotia, with the administration and control of their natural resources (section 109). This act (section 91) also gave to the Crown all legislative powers with respect to Indians and their lands. The provinces of New Brunswick and Nova Scotia agreed (in 1959) that the benefits resulting from mineral development on Indian lands would go to the Indian people for whom the land was set aside as long as the band did not surrender all its interest in the reserve, that is to say, make an absolute surrender. The provinces of Manitoba, Alberta and Saskatchewan were given administration of their natural resources by separate acts in 1930. Under the authority of these acts, all revenues from mineral development on Indian lands have been collected for the benefit of the band. The Alberta government recently changed its tax laws, however, so that companies exploring for gas and oil on reserve lands are ineligible for the tax benefits they would receive for off-reserve exploration.

An agreement with Ontario in 1924 provided that the federal government would collect the monies generated by mineral development on Native lands. These monies were to be divided evenly between the province and the federal government, with the latter's entire share going to the band concerned. The Ontario government waived this provision in several cases, and some Indian reserves (those under Treaty No. 3) were not subject to the 1924 agreement. The 1924 agreement is being reviewed with the intention of providing Indian people with 100 percent of the benefits from mineral development.

In 1943, an agreement with British Columbia was entered into on the assumption that the province owned the precious minerals (gold, silver) and that the Crown owned the base minerals on Indian lands. Under this agreement, the province collected the monies from mineral development, with 50 percent of the monies going to the Crown for the benefit of the Indian band. Since the benefits to the Indians under the agreement have been inconsequential, the Department of Indian Affairs is in the process of renegotiating the agreement to secure improved Indian benefits.

There is no agreement with Québec, which claims all interest to minerals on reserve lands if a band surrenders this interest. Therefore, the bands are not encouraged to consider developing their mineral resources in Québec until they are able to receive some of the benefits from them. There are exceptions to this statement, that is, some Indian reserves are excluded from Quebec's claim depending on how and when the reserve was established. There are no resource agreements with the provinces of Newfoundland and Prince Edward Island.

Indian Natural Resource Base

We now turn to investigate the question of what types of natural resources are found on Indian lands and the magnitude of the deposits. Mineral resources on reserve lands in Canada, with some exceptions, remained underdeveloped until the middle of the twentieth century. With the discovery of the Leduc, Alberta, oil field in 1947, land on nearby reserves such as Stony Plain and Pigeon Lake was also explored and developed. Mining developments on reserves have not been very numerous because of jurisdictional problems, lack of financial incentives and the potential inconvenience to residents on the reserve. As a result, there were fewer than ten mineral leases on Indian land by 1980 (Irwin, 1968; Bankes, 1983).[15] The Indian Mineral Directorate (Reserves and Trust Branch) has recently conducted a survey of most of the reserves in Canada with regard to potential mineral development. The Directorate identified and evaluated the known and potential mineral occurrences on or near Indian reserve lands based on available geological, geophysical and geochemical data.

The reserve-by-reserve evaluation of mineral potential is divided into four categories—metal, non-metal, structural materials, and oil and gas.[16] Data were available to indicate oil and gas leases and permit activity by private-sector industry on specified reserves in each region.

Mineral resources are not evenly divided across tribal lands either by quality or quantity. Table 13.4 identifies the number of reserves for each area of Canada that have potential (and in some cases verified mineral deposits).[17] Using the criteria discussed above, we find that the percentage of reserves having at least the potential of one mineral that could be commercially produced varied from 9 percent (British Columbia) to 63 percent (Alberta). However, the type of mineral on the reserves varied considerably. For example, 45 percent of the reserves in Alberta held exploratory leases or permits, and either depleted or producing wells, while there was no gas/oil exploration or production evident in the Atlantic provinces. Overall, nearly 100 percent of the mineral activity on Indian lands in Alberta was related to oil and gas development. However, this represents less than 2 percent of the

TABLE 13.4   Distribution of Reserves Having Mineral Potential by Region

	Type of mineral								Had at least one resource		Total reserves[a]
	Metal		Non-metal		Structural material		Oil/gas				
	N	%	N	%	N	%	N	%	N	%	
Atlantic	14	20	9	13	8	12	0	0	19	28	64
Québec	8	18	3	7	5	11	0	0	11	24	39
Ontario	28	14	7	4	26	13	8[b]	1	51	26	171
Manitoba	10[c]	8	2	2	3	2	1	1	16	13	103
Sask.	21[d]	15	14[e]	10	10	7	5[f]	3	47	33	124
Alberta	1	1	15[g]	10	29	32	45[h]	49	57	63	91
B.C.	69	4	8	<1	35	2	106	<1	106	9	1629
											2221[i]

a   Total number may not equal actual number of reserves that exist. For some cases, information on the mineral potential of a reserve is unavailable.

b   Three-fourths of these mineral deposits are in the London district.

c   All of these potential minerals are in the Idland Lake District and relate to gold and base metals.

d   All are in the Prince Albert district.

e   Nine of 14 are in Tochwood, File Hills, and the Qu'Appelle district.

f   On the 5 reserves, there are no producing wells, 6 leases (shut-in), 22 exploratory leases, and one permit.

g   Seven of 15 are in Blackfoot, Stoney and the Sarcee district, 8 of 15 in the Edmonton-Hobbema district.

h   On the 45 reserves, 110 leases are producing, 30 leases are for shut-in wells, and 614 leases for exploratory work.

i   According to official statistics, there are 2279 reserves and/or settlements in Canada as of 1985.

total value of marketable production (including synthetic crude oil) for Canada in 1979. Over 90 percent of total Indian oil and gas revenues go to Alberta reserves. In fact, 81 percent go to only 5 reserves in Alberta, 17.7 percent going to the remaining reserves. An additional 2 percent of Indian oil and gas revenues go to British Columbia and Saskatchewan reserves, with 0.5 percent going to all other Canadian reserves.

Using available Statistics Canada data, we were able to calculate the value of the marketable production of non-metals, metals and structural materials by province for the year 1979. Next we calculated the percentage of Indian lands that had a rating of "good" (six or more) in each province. Then, using the assumption that "the quality of Indian lands compares favourably with the national pattern" (DIAND, 1989: 65), we multiplied this percentage by the total provincial value of marketable non-metals, metals and structural materials.

For example, in the Atlantic provinces, Indian lands constitute about 0.0012 percent of the total land area. However, not all reserves were equal in potential, either overall or within one of the three categories—non-metals, metals and structural materials. Hence, the area of those reserves rated six (or more) was calculated and multiplied by the total Atlantic production in that one material area, for example, non-metal. In the case of the Atlantic provinces, total marketable production for the three areas was: non-metals ($1.3 billion), metals ($113 million) and structural materials ($300 million).

Only 13 percent of the reserves had a rating of six (or more) in the area of non-metals, constituting 0.0010 percent of the total land area. This figure was then multiplied by $1.3 billion—the total Atlantic marketable production value. The resultant figure of $1.6 million represents a potential marketable production of non-metals for reserves in the Atlantic provinces. Similar calculations were made for materials for each province. Final calculations show that the yearly total marketable production of non-metals, metals and structural materials for reserve lands in Canada per year would be approximately $15 million.[18]

Comparable figures for gas and oil have not been calculated because of lack of data. However, we could assume that the current ratio of 80 percent of oil and gas production in Canada being in Alberta to 20 percent elsewhere would continue. Hence, excluding Alberta oil and gas revenues, one could add an additional $1 million to the annual income derived from natural resources on Indian lands. Of course, if income generated from Alberta oil and gas revenues are added to the above figures, the annual income would soar well in excess of $100 million per year.

The above figures are, of course, to be viewed as one estimate of potential. This method of calculation used for economic potential has several problems. For example, it does not take into consideration such factors as market conditions or the scale of the economic structure necessary for initiating the development of the resource. Nevertheless, it does give some sense of the potential. Perhaps even more important would be the way in which these resources are developed. Depending upon the strategies used, forward and backward linkages will be developed, thereby adding additional jobs and enhancing development.

Economic Development Strategies

Through the development of natural resources, Natives might be able to generate a modest cash flow and further develop their overall economy. In order to develop the resource, however, a production cost is usually incurred. The actual cost of developing the natural resource is directly related to the type of agreement into which Natives enter with the government or with private industry in order to develop the resource.

Economic development on reserves would not be encumbered with taxes. Indian reserve land has been exempt from taxation since the early nineteenth century. Even though personal property of Indians may not have been exempt at this early time, by 1850 it was specifically noted that property would also be tax exempt as long as its owners resided on Indian lands. These tax exemptions are not part of a treaty but, rather, are embedded in our legislation.

In 1917, the Canadian Parliament passed the *Income War Tax Act*. Although the *Act* made no mention of Indians, the question eventually rose as to whether or not Indians were exempt from it. Although it was clear that income derived from real or personal property on reserves was not taxable, it was thought that income from off-reserve sources might be taxable.

By 1929, an interpretation by the Deputy Minister of Justice led the Indian Affairs Branch to determine that the income of an Indian who resides on a reserve cannot be taxed no matter from what source it is derived. However, by 1931, the Department of National Revenue took a position opposing the Indian Affairs Branch, and confusion reigned until 1939. The tax department seemed to hold that the source of the income, not the residency of the Indians, was the basis on which liability for taxation was to be determined (Daugherty, 1978). After 1939, the departments of Justice and National Revenue began to interpret Indian tax liability in a similar fashion. They both expected that income by Indians from a source off the reserve would be taxable. This position is current today, being reflected in section 82 of the *Indian Act*.

We will now discuss several ways in which Indians could develop their economic base: the concession, the joint venture, comanagement, the service contract, the management agreement, the community development corporation, and local producer's cooperatives. Even though all these activities point to active participation by Natives in developing their mineral resources, the question of the extent of their involvement remains. How deeply do the bands want to be involved, for instance, in projects where the risk factor is high?

The Concession   This strategy has been the traditional way in which Indians (through the federal government) have granted a company mineral production rights. The company makes a direct equity investment for the sole purpose of extracting a resource (Bankes, 1983). As Asante (1979) points out, in many cases the concession amounted to a virtual assumption of sovereignty over the host country's resources by transnational corporations. Under these conditions, the corporation asserted ownership of not only the fixed assets but also of the natural resource itself (Bankes, 1983).

Under a concession agreement, there is very little direct "upfront" cost for the band. Nor are there any operating costs. In addition, these agreements are easy to administer, since the need for supervision, auditing and training is minimal. All of this is provided by the company that agrees to exploit the minerals. In short, the cost to the band is minimal, but the return is also minimal. Natives have also found that this type of agreement does not encourage training of local residents to assume jobs in the industry, thereby introducing them into the wage economy.

The Joint Venture   This means that there are two (or more) parties which pool their money, technical expertise and/or land in order to develop a project. There are two variations of this method. The first is where a separate legal entity is created that will be jointly owned by both parties, that is, the Indians and the development company. The second type does not involve the formation of a separate company, instead, the parties to the venture have a direct, undivided working interest in the project.

The joint venture type of agreement requires that Natives: 1) have the technical expertise, and 2) have some "interest" that is considered valuable by the other part, such as land or mineral rights. There is both a direct and indirect cost with this type of development. The joint venture generally presents an opportunity for the local people to increase their control over the development. It can increase revenues to Indians and it allows for a flexible method of collecting revenues (Bankes, 1983; Asante, 1979).

Comanagement   When renewable resources are involved, Native people generally have opted for a variant of the joint venture strategy. In comanagement strategies, ownership of the resources is not necessary, only that all parties must recognize that each party has a legitimate interest in the resource. For Native people, the use of a comanagement strategy is based on the belief that the orderly use of resources will facilitate the survival and health of their environment. Pinkerton (1989) has argued that comanagement will be most preferred between Natives and non-Natives by Natives as we move into the twenty-first century. There are several reasons for this preference:

1) comanagement creates cooperation among individual workers,

2) comanagement creates a commitment among local workers to share both the costs and benefits of their efforts toward enhancement and conservation, and

3) comanagement creates a higher degree of organization and mutual commitment among Native workers, so they have a better bargaining relationship with external agents.

Comanagement arrangements represent a transfer of decision-making power to Native people, and, therefore, are difficult to negotiate with non-Natives. However, the view that Native people have a legitimate interest in natural resources is one that is slowly being recognized by government and business. The recent *Sparrow* decision by the Supreme Court, which noted that Aboriginal people have a legal and legitimate interest in renewable resources, has gone far to alert government and businesses to accept this perspective and consider comanagement initiatives.

Examples of comanagement can be seen in the Waterhen Moose and Wood Bison agreements between the Waterhen Anishinabe and the Manitoba government. The Teme-Augama Anishinabe in Ontario have used the courts for some time to resolve their land claims, after conflict between the Natives and the government erupted in the late 1980s. In 1990, the two parties agreed to establish a comanagement "stewardship agreement" over forest resources. A final example of comanagement is the creation of the Porcupine Caribou Management Board, which is a massive undertaking involving the federal and both territorial governments as well as four northern Native organizations.

The Service Contract   Under agreements of this type, the status of Indian ownership over the natural resource is reaffirmed. Thus, rather than transferring the title of the resource (as in a concession) to the developing company, the band simply hires the corporation as a contractor or business partner to perform a specific task for a specified amount of money. The disadvantage in using this type of strategy is that bands must have a substantial cash flow in order to pay for the upfront cost of the development, which can be quite high for exploration. Both Zakariya (1976) and Bankes (1983) point out that, under this type of agreement, the band would have no internal control over the project, and there would be few opportunities for Native people to gain employment or technical and administrative skills. Also, the project would have to be carefully monitored by the band to ensure that its members get the maximum benefits from it. The benefits of such an arrangement would include Native ownership and jurisdiction over the natural resource. In addition, other firms would supply the technology (and risk capital) to explore, develop and market the resources.

The Management Agreement   This is a strategy whereby Natives purchase expertise for a specified period of time. The contracted consultants can act as advisors while the Native management retains sole control of the company, or the Natives can choose to relinquish control to the consultants.

The Community Development Corporation   A band can form a corporation and explore for minerals on its reserve. The corporation is granted permits and leases according to terms set by the federal government. These corporations are created to help plan and implement the business development goals of a community or region, and they can be involved either in risking capital or in acting as an advisory body. A variation of this strategy is called a *local producer's cartel*, which involves the formation of a syndicate or trust that is able to take over a business venture from the original developer and carry on all negotiations with developers. When in the mid-1960s, 25 American Indian tribes created CERT (Council of Energy Resource Tribes) in order to control all mineral development on the reserves, they established a cartel.

Some bands have taken this course and have either chosen to remain independent or have entered into joint ventures with other non-Native companies. Two major problems have beset Native groups that have created corporations. First, the corporations tend to benefit from the development more than the band does, and they may become more powerful than the band. This problem has been somewhat alleviated by making all members of the band (including newborns) members of the corporation. The second problem centres on the risk factor and the need for a considerable amount of money up front before the development starts.

The Local Producers' Cooperative   these are usually voluntary, nonprofit societies incorporated to run a business. The members of the cooperative own shares of the business and have one vote at each general meeting. A board of directors is elected to operate the business and carry out day-to-day activities. In effect, a cooperative is a business owned by its customers.

A history of the cooperatives shows that until the 1950s most of the Native trade in Canada (particularly in isolated regions) was carried on through the Hudson's Bay Company. In 1959, the government began to encourage and support a number of locally owned and operated cooperatives. This idea seemed to fit particularly well with one of the elements of Native culture—sharing. The first Native cooperatives were producer-oriented and involved with activities such as art or fishing. Then, consumer cooperatives emerged, where both importing and exporting activities were carried out. In many communities, cooperatives and other private enterprise businesses, such as the Hudson's Bay Company, exist side-by-side, selling and buying many of the same products.

The Native cooperatives have encountered two major problems in their operations. First of all, they lack skilled managers. Secondly, they find it difficult to engage in direct competition with integrated, multinational companies. Nevertheless, they have succeeded in providing employment for Native people. Today they are the largest employer of Natives in the North and register annual sales of $30 million. There are presently about 50 co-ops nationwide, employing about 600 people and generating nearly $10 million in income. There are 13 Native general managers in these local co-ops. However, an infusion of government monies is still required for some co-ops to survive; to date, various government departments have contributed over $10 million to the development of cooperatives. In 1983, the federal government set aside an additional $10 million for a continuation of its Co-op Development Program. Much of this has been put toward training directors, managers and staff. An additional $2 million was set aside to help with new production techniques and marketing strategies.

Each of the strategies identified point to the quest by Natives to gain control over their resources. The variety of strategies being used reflects the differing situations Native people find themselves. Yet the ultimate goal for Native people is to control their land and resources. Nevertheless, establishing the proper administrative structures is only the beginning. Once control has been established, a structure will then have to be devised in order to manage economic development and guarantee an enhancement of quality of life. This will require the necessary skills to operate businesses and participate in a global economy.

To date, the concession has been the most widely employed development strategy used by Natives. Recently, however, the joint venture has become a more attractive alternative for Natives. This strategy has been encouraged by the federal government's involvement. The government has loaned money to Native companies and has guaranteed its backing. But since they allow for no control or ownership of the natural resources, it is unlikely that these joint ventures can be made a viable long-term economic strategy for Native people.

Each of the development strategies discussed above has benefits as well as costs. For this reason the type of agreement that a Native group might wish to make is ultimately determined by the group's goals. For example, if the Native group wanted to maintain a subsistence way of life, like the Cree of James Bay, and still allow development of natural resources, the concession type of agreement might be appropriate. On the other hand, if they wanted to become involved in the project, then a joint venture would seem more appropriate. For example, a joint venture called Shehtah Drilling was formed between Esso (50 percent), the Dene (25 percent) and the Métis (25 percent) development corporations in 1983 to conduct drilling and service-rig operations in the Northwest Territories.[19] The ATCO/EQUTAK drilling venture organized between Atco-Mustang Drilling and the Inuvialuit Development Corporation (with the assistance of Petro Canada), and the Beaufort Food Services, a joint venture between Beau-Tuk Marine and the Inuvialuit Development Corporation, are other examples of joint ventures that have been relatively successful.

In the cases where successful agreements have been made to develop band natural resources, what do Natives do with their increased income? The number of cases is very small, but the Hobbema reserve in Alberta is one good example. There, the Samson Band's energy revenue exceeded $60 million for the 1979-80 year. Besides appropriating one half for individual band members, the band also built and presently operates a 283-hectare grain operation. But the band has also made investments beyond the agricultural domain. In July 1981, the Samson business manager bought the charter of the Edmonton Canadian Insurance Company for slightly more than $1 million. Other Samson Band investments now include rental properties in Edmonton, shares for subdivisions in three nearby towns, shares in a Vancouver condominium project and shares in a housing development in Cold Lake, Alberta. Other oil-rich bands are also investing in land purchases, housing projects and banks. One band has even been trying to work out a deal with a consortium that is seeking a national pay-television licence.

Community Development and Control

Native people have an interest in developing their resource potential, whether it be physical resources, such as coal or gravel, or human resources. Many people expect resource development to transform reserves into self-sufficient utopias and to raise their quality of life to Canadian standards. As Carstens (1991) and the preceding section have pointed out, nothing could be further from the truth. Developing the internal natural-resource base of the reserve will not provide the quick panacea many people are looking for. In fact, there are no quick fixes, although they tend to dominate our thinking when trying to resolve a social problem. It is true that, in the past, reserves have been isolated enclosures. However, today, Native people are part of a wider political and economic system, whose influences are pervasive. If Native people are to meet their basic minimum needs and enhance their quality of life, they will have to begin the process of development of both their natural resources and their human resources.

Native development is the process by which change in the social structure takes place which helps bring about the desired values and goals of Native people. In this process there is an attempt by stakeholders to develop a set of planned activities in order for them to move from one situational state to another. These strategies are planned at the individual, collective or institutional level. Regardless of the level at which planning takes place, thinking about development always involves a progressivistic view. Native people are looking to the future, at which time they hope their quality of life will have changed for the better.

While Native people have tried to evoke change in their lives, they have met formidable obstacles in achieving this goal. External factors, such as the *Indian Act*, discrimination and legal structures, as well as internal factors, such as lack of skills, poor health conditions, factionalism and geographical separation of land bases, have acted as barriers which have kept Native people from developing their potential. Recently there have been changes to the legal structures of our society which have allowed Native people to pursue their goals of development.

In Native communities in areas where existing potential can be clearly assessed, development also has been difficult because of external constraints. As we noted earlier, Québec and British Columbia collect all returns from natural resource development on reserves. Even in Alberta, where Indians receive all of their mineral revenues, changes have been made so as to retard natural resource development on reserves. For example, for the past decade, Alberta has excluded Indian reserves from provincial exploration incentive programs, as well as providing no subsidies to companies drilling on reserves.

Today, Native people's desire for development has become focused because of two necessary, but not sufficient, factors: 1) communication and 2) relative deprivation. Communication was necessary for Native people to obtain knowledge of new alternatives to achieve goals and objectives they desired. This new knowledge led them to the widely held perception that, compared to other Canadians, they were deprived; a feeling that present conditions are inferior to alternatives. Out of these conditions, Native people have changed their social organization and have entered both the domestic and international world.

Native people have also been faced with the need to choose among the various development strategies offered them. Until recently, only one model was offered to Natives because external, individual capitalism was the single model accepted by Ottawa. In other words, if Native communities wanted to develop, the residents would have to obtain funds from off the reserve and operate under the guidelines of individual capitalism within the confines of corporate Canada. Natives themselves have had to make fundamental decisions about how to go about entering the development process while retaining their culture, which they consider important to them. In addition, they must make a decision as to whether or not they will develop their natural resources, if they have any, and, if so, how. This last question is particularly important when addressing renewable resource development. In the case of nonrenewable resources, a question of long-term versus short-term impact is raised. There is increasing evidence and awareness of the impact that development activities can produce. The effects include the change to a wage economy from a subsistence economy, encouraging Native people to relocate in order to follow jobs; the disruption of fish and game populations; and, as has been pointed out, in some cases, serious health threats.

Another concern relates to Indians' view of their reserve communities. Reserves are seen by many Natives as their "homeland." As Pendley and Kolstad point out:

> ...it is impossible to separate tribal attitudes and actions related to their homelands. To tribal members these are part and parcel of the same thing (1980:235).

Natives are well aware that, once a development occurs on their land, they must live with the long-term consequences. Outside developers move on to the next project.

With regard to renewable resource development, Natives have only recently investigated this possibility. Renewable resource development ranges from such varied activities as the pulp and paper industry to tourism. A number of possible projects have been identified by Native people, and it is only now that band councils are investigating the possibility and the consequences of such development. The creation of projects in the area of forestry have been particularly notable for Natives living in northern areas. Other Native communities have investigated the possibility of developing the tourism sector. While these activities look somewhat benign (e.g., tourism) in terms of the physical environment, their impact is much more noticeable in the social structure. For example, the development of tourism results in a number of short- and long-term impacts upon a community. Linkages with transportation companies, advertising agencies, food services and the establishment of housing are just examples of the changes which will take place in a community. Social arrangements among people in the community will also change; for example, some members of the community will become managers, others, wage workers. The normal activities of a Native community are substantially affected when the development of tourism is pursued.

Whether the resource developed is renewable or nonrenewable, Native people are fully aware that the consequences may not be reversible. Furthermore, they are concerned about their ability to negotiate agreements for development with the private sector. At the same time, they are convinced that the federal government cannot be trusted to act on their behalf. For too long the Natives have felt betrayed by government officials in the area of development—as well as in other areas of concern. Native leaders and band councils are caught in a dilemma. On the one hand, they are urged by government officials and residents to develop their resources in order to enhance their quality of life. On the other hand, when pressed to negotiate a specific proposal, band councils are extremely sceptical and nervous about finalizing the deal.

When agreements are brought forth by non-Indians, there is an inherent distrust of the proposal. This means that Native people continually search for hidden motives on the part of the other party. Natives also realize that details must be attended to, a problem for which they have no expertise and over which they have little control. Legal and other "experts," all of whom are non-Indian, must also be party to the development negotiations. Thus, of the four major parties (Natives, government, legal experts, private industry) to any development agreement, three of the four are non-Native. Finally, the cumbersome nature of government bureaucracy and the need to secure grass-roots community approval of a project means that considerable time elapses between project identification and implementation.

As each party evaluates the proposal, changes are made by each party to ensure that it receives the greatest benefit. Further negotiations ensue, and more time passes. Impasse results, and agreements go unsigned; developments linger. As Native people press for development plans, one of the central contentious issues usually on the table involves control. As noted earlier, Native people realize that some external support will be necessary to development. They are prepared to accept that. However, they are not prepared to give up control of that development. In short, Native people seem to be prepared for undertaking development projects, but they want them under their control. Recently, the federal government has reluctantly agreed that perhaps responsibility for community economic development should reside in the Native communities (*Penner Report*, 1983). They have realized that seldom have economic policy solutions originating outside the Native community brought about lasting changes in the available human and natural resources or the quality of life.

Native communities are slowly becoming involved in the process of capacity-building, which allows them to plan and develop their own strategies for development. However, this development must revitalize and strengthen the social, cultural and economic aspects of a way of life which is at the very core of being Native (Hanson, 1985).

CONCLUSION

La Violette (1961) argues that for any ethnic group to survive it must be able to assert control over its fate. Essentially, the struggle for survival is a struggle for identity. The group must view its past positively and maintain strong links with traditional customs and beliefs. It must also achieve political equality and look forward to a promising future. These processes can only be set in motion at the grassroots level. If Natives are going to control their destiny, they must implement some form of community control immediately.

At present, governments are encouraging Natives to develop small businesses on an individual basis. By promoting individual entrepreneurs, White society maintains an indirect control of the reserve. When local businesses are owned by individual Natives, the larger White-dominated economic structure remains intact, and White control is achieved in two ways: first, White society wins the loyalties of the Native businessmen, who are potentially important community leaders; second, the visible ownership of local business by Natives defuses anti-White feelings and reduces the likelihood of violent demonstrations. The community becomes more stable, the leadership potential of White-affiliated Native businessmen is enhanced, and the White domination of the community economy, though less direct, remains intact. In addition, discontent is defused through acceptable channels (Tabb, 1970). Clearly, the strategy of individual entrepreneurship will not change the economic position of Natives substantially in the future.

Although community development must be encouraged, it must *not* be totally financed by the corporate sector of Canadian society. The federal government must not allow the corporate sector to interfere with or influence the development of Native communities. Native economic development is not in the corporations' interests. So far, through close ties with the political elite, corporations have successfully blocked the federal financing that would permit Native development. For example, Saskatchewan Indians hold $150 million in government-backed mortgages and pay almost $1 million a month to mortgage companies. If Indians started paying interest to their own institutions, the profit could be used to build up their own communities. If Natives are allowed to develop and control the reserves, they will eliminate corporate contracts for reserve projects and drain off the un-skilled labour surplus for primary industries.

If the corporate sector were allowed to initiate economic development on re-serves, franchising would result. Under a franchise system, a corporation advances money to an individual Native, who then manages a store which sells the corpo-ration's product exclusively. The corporation also provides certain services and trains staff to ensure proper marketing techniques. In return for setting up the store, providing the loan and training the staff, the company reaps several benefits, including a large percentage of the profits and access to the reserve and nearby communities. Franchising is an efficient and inexpensive way to guarantee White corporate control of the reserve. Again, the presence of a Native staff defuses anti-White sentiments and prevents the organization of a cohesive revolt. Moreover, the development of the reserve by outsiders allows for external control over the speed, extent and nature of that development (Tabb, 1970:58).

Although White institutions are promoting individual entrepreneurship, many Natives have begun to recognize that the result of this policy will be continued subordination. Increasingly, cogent arguments like the following are put forward in support of Native community control and development:

> To accomplish this task, four sets of recommendations are proposed: (i) The es-tablishment of economically viable reserves controlled by the Indians with sufficient natural resources to ensure adequate incomes for the residents. The key element in this recommendation is that the natural resources of expanded Indian lands should be firmly placed in the control of the community and its representative leaders. (ii) The establishment of an Indian corporation which can receive direct grants and long-term low-interest loans to promote economic development on the reserve, to improve and initiate village services, and to in other ways enable Indians to better utilize their natural and economic resources. (iii) A major revamping of the edu-cational system so as to reduce discontinuities in learning, sustain effective ties with parents, strengthen the student's self-image as Indian, and maintain his self-esteem, as well as prepare him to be economically and socially competent in deal-ing with the institutions of the larger Canadian society. (iv) The establishment of an Indian social development program, funded by the federal and/or provincial gov-ernments, which can assist in providing the mechanism for the emergence of new Indian leaders, increase communication with other Indian and non-Indian groups, and promote local and regional community, social, and political infra-structures (Chance, 1970:33-35).

As the process of Native development begins, a balanced approach will be necessary in order to achieve the basic minimum needs of the community. Residents need to have basic educational qualifications, access to adequate health-care facilities, basic housing, and experience in the labour force. Once these minimum balanced conditions have been achieved, an "unbalanced" approach to development must begin. In this approach, one central economic development is pursued. The decision as to what development should be fostered is dependent on the history of the community, its location, and the resources and skills available within it. As these factors are brought together, the central development will lead to other forms of development uniquely suited to the community. Once the key activity is established, money to support social programs will continue to rise without a need for additional specific long-range planning.[20]

Native people are also prepared to negotiate within the existing socio-legal system. In fact, both Natives and private industry as well as government are prepared to negotiate within certain boundaries. The boundaries generally determine the status quo, and all parties are accustomed to operating within it. However, Native people are pressing for change, and, thus, they are posing demands which go beyond the status quo (Lightbody, 1969). As the critical point is approached in the negotiations, tension between the two negotiating parties emerges. Eventually, when Natives force the issue beyond the critical point, tension changes to conflict. As Lightbody explains:

> ...beyond [this critical point] the state must realign its institutional structures about a new ethnic configuration by either physically attempting to suppress the dissident elements into grudging assimilation into the culture, or through accepting the creation of the new...(1969: 334).

Willingness to move beyond the critical point by either party varies with time and conditions, although the history of the negotiations usually is a good clue to whether or not conflict will emerge. For example, the Oldman River (Alberta) conflict, the Oka (Québec) conflict and other Native-White conflicts generally reflect a long history of Natives negotiating for social change which the other party is unwilling to accept. The recent constitutional talks are further evidence that the government is unwilling to change the status quo when it deals with Natives. While it is in favour of establishing conditions for a "distinct Québec society" in the Constitution, there is little evidence that Natives will be given similar consideration.

Currently, Native Canadians find themselves isolated from White society and confronted by discrimination on a daily basis. To counter this position, they have recently begun the long, arduous task of defining their group identity and clarifying their future goals. The recent growth of Native organizations shows that Natives are strengthening their political and cultural position. And, as Boldt has shown, they are increasingly willing to engage in "extra-legal" politics:

> Enlightened Indian leaders reject White society's comfortable notions of slow and steady progress toward the achievement of basic human rights for their people and most are inclined not only to approve of extra-legal activity as a justifiable

means for achieving their conception of the "good society," but are also willing to participate and, if necessary, suffer the consequences of such actions for their cause (1980:33).

Natives have learned over time that externally-directed conflict tends to enhance group solidarity. Group boundaries come into sharp focus as in-group members are differentiated from out-group members. As conflict emerges, the group is also forced to explicitly define its aims and goals. As grievances are defined, adversaries emerge and are identified. In the case of Native groups, the adversaries are White: relations between the two become a zero-sum game.

In a zero-sum game, one player always gains precisely what the other player loses, and vice versa. In other words, relations between the two sides are always competitive and antagonistic. Identification with one's "side" pervades the daily life of each group member. Each participant finds a particular role in the collective action and receives internal and social rewards for behaviour that reinforces group aims. Identification with the group grows, as do linkages with other members. As Pettigrew describes:

> Recruits willingly and eagerly devote themselves to the group's goals. And they find themselves systematically rewarded [by the group]....They are expected to evince strong radical pride, to assert their full rights as citizens, to face jail and police brutality unhesitatingly for the cause. Note that these expected and rewarded actions all publicly commit the member to the group and its aim (1964:195-96).

And, as Himes states, out of organized group conflict grows a strong group identity:

> In the interactive process of organized group conflict, self-involvement is the opposite side of the coin of overt action. Actors become absorbed by ego and emotion into the group and the group is projected through their actions. This linkage of individual and group in ego and action is the substance of identity (1966:10).

With the emergence of Native identity, the sense of alienation experienced by many Natives has been dispelled by a new sense of significance and purpose. The personal ethnic identity of Natives is stronger now than it has been for many decades, as leaders of national and provincial Native organizations have begun to develop a national cohesiveness. As Pitts (1974) points out, ethnic identity is a social product, a result of actions and interpretations in a social context (Paige, 1971). As Brown argues:

> A race conscious group...is a social unit struggling for status in society. It is thus a conflict group and race consciousness itself is a result of conflict. The race of the group, though not intrinsically significant, becomes an identifying symbol, serving to intensify the sense of solidarity (1935: 572).

Native identification is a mixture of internal dynamics and external pressures. At present, that identification is being translated into what Enloe (1981) calls ethnic mobilization—the mobilization of an ethnic group's resources and manpower to better its position. White Canada is bound to respond with such contemporary demobilization techniques as the White Paper in order to remain in a controlling position. Native mobilization in turn will increase, and the accelerating spiral of conflict will be set in motion.

Meaningful changes are desperately needed in the political, social and economic position of Native Canadians. Acting from frustration and helplessness, Native leaders are increasingly abandoning the legal means to effect those changes. If White Canadians do not act quickly and respond effectively to Native demands, the future of Native-White relations in this country may well be written in blood.

NOTES

1. In the middle of the nineteenth century, Charles Darwin published his *The Origin of Species*. His theoretical perspective centred on concepts such as evolution, natural selection, and survival of the fittest. It was an easy step for the layman and the social scientist to apply these biological concepts as evidence that Whites were somehow "more fit" than the groups they had defeated. Similarly, as long as a group continued to successfully exploit and win wars against other nations, it proved itself further evolved.

2. DIAND grants three types of financing: direct loans granted and administered by the department; indirect loans granted by banks and guaranteed by the department and contributions or grants allotted for solving a problem in a community.

3. For example, Elias (1991) points out that the Kaska Dena of northern British Columbia had a total income of nearly $2 million, for a per capita income of just $2000. Half of this income came from domestic production activities. With incomes as low as these, Native people are interested in investments in their local economy. At the same time, domestic production activities have been sorely underfunded by Indian Affairs.

4. In the U.S., the American Indian Policy Review Commission issued its Final Report in 1977; while the Indian Minerals Directorate in Canada carried out a minerals inventory in 1981.

5. We distinguish between the two terms "economic growth" and "economic development." Economic growth is a term used to refer to an increase in the productive capacity of the economy of a region or community. By economic development we mean a change in the "structure" of an economy, for example, less reliance on primary extractive activities (see Rea, 1976).

6. Proprietary (land) rights can vary from the simple (absolute for both surface and sub-surface) to legislative rights. The latter would give Indians the right to regulate matters pertaining to the land. The actual type of proprietary right to be held by Indians will vary by what Indians want to do with the land.

7. Other reserves have specific resources that can be used to promote economic development and generate income for Indians. For example, in Alberta the Peigan band has recently completed negotiations with the provincial government over water rights. In return for its willingness to give access to irrigation head-works and water on the reserve to the province, the band received a cash settlement of over $4 million.

8. Munro (1981) pointed out that the government's fiscal plan for 1985-86 called for an allocation of nearly $345 million to support various types of economic development of Native people.

9. Pendley and Kolstad (1980) show that in 1976 in the U.S. about one quarter of the total uranium production (11 percent of world production) was on tribal lands.

10. DIAND is in the process of developing legislation for increased self-government for Canada's status Indians (see for example the *Penner Report*, 1983). However, this proposed change does not follow the model set forth in the U.S., the 1934 *Indian Reorganization Act*. This *Act* allowed for the establishment of reserve governments based on tribal constitutions. While there may be some similarities between the proposed Canadian legislation and the *IRA*, in the U.S., Indians have the inherent right of "limited internal sovereignty." As Werhan (1978) points out, the United States government recognizes (but does not create) the power of Indian self-government. In Canada, the new proposal would shift ministerial administrative authority to the Indian band, and legislative authority would be given to individual bands over land management, financial affairs, health services and the creation of a band constitution.

    These changes have heightened Indian people's desire to control the developments now impinging upon their lands and culture. Because of the continuing energy crisis and the insistence of the Canadian government in becoming energy self-sufficient, development of the traditional fossil fuels (coal, oil, gas) as well as uranium will become important.

11. The decision can be made at a general band council meeting, a special meeting, or by referendum.

12. The minister may, with the approval of the band council, change the royalties payable. Much of the following technical data is based upon personal communications with the Indian Minerals Directorate, 1981, and the Surveyor General, 1981.

13. *Indian Oil and Gas Act,* 1974; *The Canada Gazette,* Part III, Vols. 1 & 2, 261-263; *Indian Oil and Gas Regulations,* Ch. 963, 1978; *Amendments to the Indian Oil and Gas Regulations,* C.R.C., Ch. 963, 1981; *Indian Mining Regulations,* P.C. 1968-1975; *The Canada Gazette,* Part II, Vol. 102, 79, 1968.

14. The interest on Indian monies held in the Consolidated Revenue Fund varies over time but is set by the Governor in Council.

15. Other industrial activities on Indian land include a producing gypsum mine on the Six Nations Indian Reserve (Ontario) and negotiations for coal development with the Blackfoot (Alberta).

16. The mineral resources listed below in the four categories have been identified on Indian reserve lands in the seven national regions:

    Metals: copper, gold, iron, lead, magnesium magnetite, nickel, platinum group, silver, tungsten, uranium, zinc.

    Non-metals: asbestos, coal, diatomite, feldspar, graphite, gypsum, helium, jade, lignite, limestone, manganese, marl, obsidian, peat, perlite, potash, quartzite, salt, silica, silica sand, sodium carbonate, talc.

Structural materials: clay, sand and gravel, shale, slate, stone, lime, dolomite.

Oil and gas: bitumen, crude petroleum, natural gas.

17. The evaluation of each mineral has been based on a numerical rating of one to ten as follows:

-	=	mineral potential unknown
0	=	no mineral potential
1,2	=	poor mineral potential
3,4	=	fair mineral potential
5	=	moderate mineral potential
6,7	=	good mineral potential
8,9	=	excellent mineral potential
10	=	ongoing production

18. The Indian and Inuit Affairs Program (Economic Development) has given the following figures for metallic mineral resource potential (1974) dollars: B.C., $324 million; Alberta $170 million; Saskatchewan, $418 million; Manitoba, $203 million; Ontario, $2,406 million; Québec, $112 million and Atlantic provinces, $34 million. No criteria were provided for the methods of obtaining these values.

19. The joint venture contract is worth $5 million. The majority of Shehtah drill crews are made up of skilled Native northerners. For further information on this subject see *Arctic Petroleum Operators' Association Review,* Vol. 6, 3, Winter 1983/84, Calgary, Alberta.

20. For a more thorough discussion on the relative merits of the "unbalanced" versus the "balanced" approach, see Rosenstein-Roda, 1943; Nurske, 1953; Scitovsky, 1954; Hirschman, 1958; Lewis, 1956; Perroux, 1953; and Fellner, 1956. The first four authors advocate the balanced approach; the remainder support the unbalanced approach.

CONCLUSION TO PART 3

> It is just and reasonable, and essential to our interest, and the security of our colonies, that the several Nations or tribes of Indians with whom we are connected, and who live under our Protection, should not be molested or disturbed in the Possession of such Parts of our Dominion and Territories as, not having been purchased by Us, are reserved to them....And we do hereby strictly forbid, on Pain of our displeasure, all our loving subjects from making any Purchase or Settlements whatever, or taking possession of any of the Lands above reserved, without our especial leave and License for that Purpose first obtained (*Royal Proclamation*, 1763).

The predictions of Native disappearance made over a century ago have yet to be substantiated. Quite the contrary, Native peoples are perhaps more in the collective conscience of Canadians than ever before. They have survived over the years but have not prospered during this time. The process of dealing with an overwhelming immigrant population has had a substantial impact on many dimensions of their culture. The loss of language is the most obvious effect, but there are many other aspects of their culture that have been eroded or changed.

At the same time, Natives have embarked on a campaign to establish self-determination and to reassert their Nativeness. They are trying to regain the responsibility they once had in running their own affairs. In their attempt to gain control, Natives have established a complex set of organizations. These organizations have tried to outline the assumptions and strategies necessary to achieve self-government. To begin, as a symbolic gesture, they have begun to call themselves First Nations. These First Nations would have full legislative and policy-making powers on issues that directly affect them. In addition, they would take full control over their land and resources. The federal government has failed to accept these premises. However, government has begun, in a quiet way, to question the present system; something that has never been undertaken before. The recently appointed National Task Force on Native Affairs is symbolic of the possible changes that might take place. This blue ribbon group of Canadians may exert influence never expected and produce change at unprecedented speed. Government is ripe for change and the prestige attached to this Task Force may be ample influence to begin the change process.

Over the past century, Native people have been relegated to a peripheral position in Canadian society. During the 1970s, Native people saw some glimmer of hope that this unequal treatment might be rectified. They chose, at that time, to utilize the constitutional route as the vehicle for change. However, by the time the repatriation of the Constitution came, most Native issues had been set aside. Although subsequent conferences on Native affairs were set up in 1983, 1984, 1985 and 1987, little was accomplished. Even the government's *Penner Report*, which recommended the recognition of Native self-government, had little impact.

The militant action of Natives during the past four years has not come without warning. Leaders from various Native organizations cautioned Canadians that they must deal with Native peoples or they would be subject to various kinds of political violence. Thus it was no surprise that confrontational tactics were used by several First Nations across the country; the Innu, the Lonefighters, the Lubicon Lake Cree, the Teme-Auigama Anishinabe, the Barriere Lake Algonquins, the Gitksan-Wet'suwet'an, the Mi'kman, the Lil'owat and the Akwesasu and Mohawks. Other actions have served to unite and mobilize Natives across the country in defiant opposition to government actions. Native people feel they have exhausted other means defending their dwindling interests.

Recently, the consideration of cost has provided the impetus for government to reconsider its position. This has also allowed people to think about the possible benefits of having an independent and prosperous Native population. Government is seriously considering abandoning their subtle forms of tutelage (Dyck, 1991), which, in turn will free up time for Natives who have spent considerable time opposing or negotiating changes to that control. This free time will then be spent working constructively, for the benefit of both Natives and other Canadians.

Self-determination is also related to Aboriginal rights, particularly land rights. For example, many Canadians point out that First Nations did little over the past two centuries to protect their land rights. Natives counter that it is precisely because they have not had self-determination that they have been unable to act in this regard. Natives point out that a spate of federal and provincial legislation, designed to eliminate Indian rights, was passed. As Mathias and Yabsley point out, "These laws are the root of much of the injustice and inequality for Indians and by any standard, they are offensive" (1991: 35). Many of the laws passed by the Canadian government are viewed by Natives as a conspiracy with a conscious intent to eliminate Natives from Canadian society.

The attempt to achieve self-determination by Natives seems contradictory to many non-Natives. Natives want "independence" while at the same time maintaining a trust relation with the federal government. Natives argue that this relationship is temporary. They feel that it is necessary to maintain this trust relationship until they are sufficiently economically independent to "go on their own." They are fearful that if they must rely upon the provinces or private enterprise sufficient safeguards will not be in place to ensure their independence. They are mindful of the devastating cultural impacts of large transnational corporations when they have moved into Third World countries, and they are ill-prepared to deal with such impacts.

Most non-Natives are convinced that there is a "Native problem" and generally have a stock solution to the problem. Unfortunately most non-Natives do not have an adequate understanding of history, nor a\n appreciation of the structural arrangements of our institutions and their impact upon minority groups. In addition, the non-Native generally has as an unshakeable premise the idea that non-Native culture is superior to Native culture. Over the years Canadians have constructed a theory of inferiority which provides the rationale for controlling Native land, resources and way of life. Control has been exerted in order to bring about change in the Native way of life; change that will make Native people more like mainstream Canadians. The control exerted over Indians is viewed as the only way Natives will be able to escape their poverty and marginal existence. The resistance of this control by Natives has been interpreted as further evidence that Natives are unable to change by themselves and has thus enhanced the resolve of the government to increase their control and force change.

Nevertheless, as stated above, the government seems anxious to establish new working arrangements with Aboriginal peoples. However, there are still many philosophical differences between the two groups. The federal government thinks in terms of individual rights, Natives in terms of collective rights; Natives want a distinct fourth order of government, the federal government has proposed a modified municipal-style government; Natives argue that powers inherent in Aboriginal government are through the Creator, government wants to delegate power itself in conformity to Canadian laws. Until some of these basic differences are resolved, little will be accomplished. Change does not come easily, and when it does come, it is small. However, the incremental nature of change suggests that, over time, structural change is possible. As one Native said, "What I do today will have consequences for Native people seven generations later." Natives are also aware that they must work together with government to change the status quo. Natives must give up their reactive stance and begin to develop strategies that are proactive and demonstrate vision.

This process of change requires hard work and compromise and is fraught with potential high costs. Native communities must seize the opportunity now when government is open to new relationships and procedures; to fail to take advantage of this openness now might mean continual stagnation. Old patterns could be perpetuated, ones which continue to relegate Natives to a peripheral position in our society; or a new vision may be presented. As Hall has so eloquently stated, "Aboriginal people have the basic human right to represent their own interests in their own voices.... Aboriginal Societies as peoples with ancient indigenous heritages must be carefully cultivated if the true flowering of Canadian identity is ever to occur" (1991: 17).

BIBLIOGRAPHY

ABERLE, D. 1970 "A Plan for Navaho Economic Development." In *American Indians: Facts and Future, Toward Economic Development for Native American Communities*, Joint Economic Committee. New York: Arno Press.

ABLON, JOAN 1965 ˆ"American Indian Relocation: Problems of Dependency and Management in the City." *Phylon*, 26 (Winter 1965):362-371.

ADAMS, HOWARD 1975 *Prison of Grass*. Toronto: New Press.

AGGAMAWAY-PIERRE, M. 1983 Native Women and the State. In *Perspectives on Women in the 1980's*. Turner, J. & L. Emery (eds.), Winnipeg, The University of Manitoba Press, pp. 66-73.

AHEHAKEW, D. 1985 "Aboriginal Title and Aboriginal Rights. The Impossible and Unnecessary Task of Identification and Definition." In *The Quest for Justice*, M. Boldt, J. Long, and L. Little Bear (eds). Toronto: The University of Toronto Press.

ALBERTA FEDERATION OF METIS SETTLEMENT ASSOCIATIONS 1978 *The Metis People of Canada: A History*. Calgary: Gage Publishing Ltd.

ALBERTA, GOVERNMENT OF 1991 Report of the Task Force on the Criminal Justice System and Its Impact on the Indian and Metis People of Alberta, Volume 1, Main Report, Edmonton.

ALLAN, D.J. 1943 "Indian Land Problems in Canada." In *The North American Indian Today*, C.T. Loram and T.F. McIlwrath (eds). Toronto: University of Toronto Press.

ALTMAN, J. and J. NIEUWENHUYSEN 1979 *The Economic Status of Australian Aborigines*. Cambridge: Cambridge University Press.

ANDERSON, A. 1978 "Linguistic Trends Among Saskatchewan Ethnic Groups." In *Ethnic Canadians*, M. Kovacs (ed). Regina: University of Regina.

ANDERSON, DAVID, and ROBERT WRIGHT 1971 *The Dark and Tangled Patch*. Boston: Houghton Mifflin Co.

ANDRIST, RALPH 1964 *The Long Death*. New York: Macmillan Publishing Co. Inc.

ASANTE, S. 1979 "Restructuring Transnational Mineral Agreements." *American Journal of International Law*, 73, 3:355-371.

ASCH, M. 1984 *Home and Native Land*. Toronto: Methuen.

ASSEMBLY OF FIRST NATIONS 1990a Assembly of First Nations' Critique of Federal Government Land Claims Policy, August 21, Summerstown, Ontario.

_____ **1990b** Doublespeak of the 90s: A Comparison of Federal Government and First Nation Perception of Land Claims Process, August, mimeo.

BANKES, N. 1983 *Resource Leasing Options and the Settlement of Aboriginal Claims*. Ottawa: Canadian Arctic Resources.

_____ **1986** "Indians' Resource Rights and Constitutional Enactments in Western Canada 1871-1930." In *Essays in Western Canadian Legal History*, L. Knafla (ed). Toronto: Carswell :29-164.

BARBER, LLOYD 1977 *Commissioner of Indian Claims: A Report: Statements and Submissions*. Ottawa: Supply and Services Canada.

BARKWELL, L. J. 1988 Observations on discrimination and dehumanization in the criminal justice system. Paper presented to the *Aboriginal Justice Inquiry: Inquiry Proceedings*, (December 15, 1988), Winnipeg: Four Seasons Reporting Services Ltd.

BARKWELL, L., N. CHARTRAND, D. GRAY, L. LONGCLAWS, R. RICHARD 1989 "Devalued People: The Status of the Metis in the Justice System," *The Canadian Journal of Native Studies*, 9.1, 121-150.

BARMAN, J., Y. HEBERT, and D. MCCASKILL (eds) 1987 *Indian Education in Canada*, Vol. II. Vancouver: University of British Columbia Press.

BARNETT, M.L. and D.A. BAERREIS 1965 "Some Problems Involved in the Changing Status of the American Indian." In *The Indian in Modern America*, D.A. Baerreis (ed). Wisconsin State Historical Society :50-70.

BARSH, R. and J. HENDERSON 1982 "Aboriginal Rights, Treaty Rights and Human Rights: Tribe and Constitutional Renewal." *Journal of Canadian Studies*, 2 (1982):55-81.

BARTH, FREDERIK (ed) 1969 *Ethnic Groups and Boundaries: The Social Organization of Culture Difference.* Boston: Little, Brown and Co.

BARTLETT, RICHARD 1980 *Indian Act of Canada.* Saskatoon: Native Law Centre, University of Saskatchewan.

_____ **1984** "Aboriginal Land Claims at Common Law." *Canadian Native Law Reporter*, 1 (1984): 1-63.

BEAR ROBE, ANDREW 1970 *Study Tour of Canadian Friendship Centres*, Vols. 1 & 2. Ottawa: Steering Committee for the National Association of Friendship Centres.

BEAVER, J. 1979 *To Have What is One's Own.* Ottawa: Department of Indian Affairs and Northern Development.

BELCOURT, G.A. 1944 "Buffalo Hunt," translated by J.A. Burgess. *The Beaver* (December 1944): 13-17.

BENDIX, R. 1964 *Native Guilding and Citizenship.* New York: John Wiley.

BENEDICT, R. 1950 *Patterns of Culture.* New York: Mentor Books.

BENNETT, G. 1978 "Aboriginal Title in the Common Law: A Stoney Path Through Feudal Doctrine." *Buffalo Law Review*, 17 (1978):601-623.

BENNETT, J. 1990 "Human Adaptation to the North American Great Plains and Similar Environments." In *The Struggle for the Land*, P. Olson (ed). Lincoln, Nebraska: University of Nebraska Press, pp. 41-80.

BENNETT, JOHN W. 1969 *Northern Plainsmen.* Chicago and New York : Aldine-Atherton.

BERGER, THOMAS 1981 *Fragile Freedoms: Human Rights and Dissent in Canada.* Toronto: Clarke, Irwin and Co. Ltd.

_____ **1985** *Village Journey.* New York: Hill and Wang Co.

_____ **1977** *Northern Frontier, Northern Homeland—The Report of the MacKenzie Valley Pipeline Inquiry*, Vol. 1. Ottawa: Minister of Supply and Services Canada.

BERRY, BREWTON 1963 *Almost White.* New York and London: Macmillan Publishing Co. Inc.

BHERER, H., S. GAGNON, J. ROBERGE 1990 *Wampum and Letters Patent*, Montreal, The Institute for Research on Public Policy.

BIENVENUE, RITA, and A.H. LATIF 1974 "Arrests, Dispositions and Recidivism: Comparison of Indians and Whites." *Canadian Journal ofCriminology and Corrections*, 16 (1974):105-116.

_____ **1975** "The Incidence of Arrests Among Canadians of Indian Ancestry." Paper presented at Canadian Sociology and Anthropology meetings in Kingston, Ontario.

BLAIS, JEAN-LUC 1984 "Mineral Activities and Native Involvement on Indian Reserves." *Native Participation in Mineral Development Activities.* Queen's University, Kingston, Centre for Resource Studies.

BLAUNNER, ROBERT 1969 "Internal Colonialism and Ghetto Revolt." *Social Problems,* 16 (Spring 1969):393-408.

BOBET, E. 1990 *The Inequalities in Health: A Comparison of Indian and Canadian Mortality Trends.* Ottawa: Health and Welfare Canada.

BOEK, W.E. and J.K. BOEK 1959 *The People of Indian Ancestry in Greater Winnipeg. Appendix 1: A Study of the Population of Indian Ancestry Living in Manitoba.* Winnipeg: Manitoba Department of Agriculture and Immigration.

BOLDT, M. 1973 "Indian Leaders in Canada: Attitudes Toward Equality, Identity, and Political Status." Ph.D. disertation. New Haven: Yale University Press.

_____ **1980** "Canadian Native Leadership: Context and Composition." *Canadian Ethnic Studies,* 12, 1 (1980):15-33.

_____ **1980a** "Indian Leaders in Canada: Attitudes Toward Extra-Legal Action." *Journal of Ethnic Studies,* 8, 1 (1980a):71-83.

_____ **1980b** "Canadian Native Indian Leadership: Context and Composition." *Canadian Ethnic Studies Journal,* 12, 1 (1980b):71-83.

_____ **1981** "Philosophy, Politics, and Extralegal Action: Native Indian Leaders in Canada." *Ethnic and Racial Studies,* 4, 2 (1981):205-221.

_____ **1981a** "Social Correlates of Nationalism: A Study of Native Indian Leaders in a Canadian Internal Colony." *Comparative Political Studies,* 14, 2 (1981a):205-231.

_____ **1981b** "Enlightenment Values, Romanticism and Attitudes Toward Political Status: A Study of Native Indian Leaders in Canada." *Canadian Review of Sociology and Anthropology,* 18, 4 (1981b):545 565.

_____ **1981c** "Social Correlates of Romanticism in an Internal Colony: A Study of Native Indian Leaders in Canada." *Ethnic Groups: An International Journal of Ethnic Studies,* 3, 4 (1981c):307-332.

_____ **1982** "Intellectual Orientations and Nationalism Among Leaders in an Internal Colony: A Theoretical and Comparative Perspective." *British Journal of Sociology,* 33, 4 (1982):484-510.

BOLDT, M., and J. LONG 1985 "Tribal Traditions and European-Western Political Ideologies: The Dilemma of Canada's Native Indians." In *The Quest for Justice,* M. Boldt, J. Long and L. Little Bear (eds). Toronto: The University of Toronto Press.

_____ **1985** "Tribal Philosophies and The Canadian Charter of Rights and Freedoms." In *The Quest for Justice,* M. Boldt, J. Long and L. Little Bear (eds). Toronto: The University of Toronto Press.

_____ **1983** "Tribal Traditions and the Canadian Charter of Rights and Freedoms." Lethbridge, Alberta: University of Lethbridge. Mimeographed.

BOLDT, M., J.A. LONG and L. LITTLE BEAR 1983a "The Concept of Sovereignty in the Political Thought of Canada's Native Indians." Mimeographed.

_____ **1985** (eds). *The Quest for Justice.* Toronto: The University of Toronto Press.

BONNEY, R. 1976 "The Role of Women in Indian Activism." In *The Western Canadian Journal of Anthropology*, 6, 3, pp. 243-248.

BOWLES, R. 1979 "Charter Group or Capitalist Class: An Analysis of Faces Shaping Canadian Ethnic Structures." Mimeographed. Peterborough: Trent University.

BOXHILL, WALLY 1984 *1984 Census Data on the Native Peoples of Canada*. Ottawa: Statistics Canada.

BOYES, G.A. 1960 "New Goals for People of Indian Heritage." *Sixth Annual Conference on Indians and Metis*. Winnipeg: Welfare Council for Greater Winnipeg.

BRAROE, N. 1975 *Indian and White: Self-Image and Interaction in a Canadian Plains Community*. Stanford: Stanford University Press.

BRETON, RAYMOND, and GAIL GRANT AKIAN 1979 *Urban Institutions and People of Indian Ancestry*. Montreal: Institute for Research on Public Policy.

BREWSTER, H. 1971 "Economic Dependence." Mimeographed. London: University of London, Institute of Commonwealth Studies.

BRITISH COLUMBIA, GOVERNMENT OF 1991 *The Report of the British Columbia Claims Task Force*, British Columbia Claims Task Force, Vancouver.

BRODY, HUGH 1971 *Indians on Skid Row: The Role of Alcohol and Community in the Adaptive Process of Indian and Urban Migrants*. Ottawa: Northern Science Research Group, Department of Indian Affairs and Northern Development. Information Canada.

BROWN, DEE 1971 *Bury My Heart at Wounded Knee*. New York: Holt, Rinehart & Winston Inc.

BROWN, JENNIFER S.H. 1977 "A Colony of Very Useful Hands." *The Beaver* (Spring 1977):39-45.

_____ **1977a** "Ultimate Respectability: Fur Trade Children in the 'Civilized World'." (Part One of Two Parts.) *The Beaver* (Winter 1977a):4-10.

_____ **1978** "Ultimate Respectability: Fur Trade Children in the 'Civilized World'." (Part Two of Two Parts.) *The Beaver* (Spring 1978):48-55.

_____ **1980** "Linguistics, Solitudes, and Changing Social Categories." In *Old Trails and New Directions: Papers of the Third North American Fur Trade Conference*, Carol M. Judd and Arthur J. Ray (eds). Toronto: University of Toronto Press.

_____ **1980a** *Strangers in Blood*. Vancouver: University of British Columbia Press.

BROWN, W.C. 1935 Racial Conflict Among South African Natives." *American Journal of Sociology*, 40 (1935):569-681.

BUCKLEY, HELEN, J. KEW, and F. HAWLEY 1963 *The Indians and Metis of Northern Saskatchewan*. Saskatoon: Saskatoon Centre for Community Studies, University of Saskatchewan.

BUCKLEY, H. 1992 *From Wooden Ploughs to Welfare*, McGill-Queens University Press, Montreal and Kingston.

BURRELL, G. and D. SANDERS 1984 *Handbook of Case Law on the Indian Act*. Ottawa: DIAND.

CALDER, W. 1986 "The Provinces and Indian Self Government in the Constitutional Forum." In *Indian-Provincial Government Relationship*, M. Boldt, J. Long, and L. Little Bear (eds). Lethbridge: University of Lethbridge.

CALDWELL, GEORGE 1967 *Indian Residential Schools*. Ottawa: Department of Indian Affairs and Northern Development.

CAMPBELL, MARIA 1973 *Halfbreed*. Toronto: McClelland and Stewart.

CAMPBELL, R. and L. PAL 1991 *The Real Worlds of Canadian Politics*, Peterborough, Ontario: Broadview Press.

CANADA, GOVERNMENT OF 1986 *1986-87 Estimates*. Vol. 3, Department of Indian and Northern Affairs Canada. Ottawa: Minister of Supply and Services.

_____ **1986a** *1986-87 Estimates, Part III*, Expenditure Plan, Indian and Northern Affairs Canada. Ottawa: Supply and Services Canada.

_____ **1986b** *1986-87 Estimates, Part II*, Indian and Northern Affairs Canada. Ottawa: Minister of Supply and Services.

_____ **1986c** *Annual Report, 1985-86*. Department of Indian Affairs and Northern Development. Ottawa: Minister of Supply and Services.

_____ **1985** *Living Treaties: Lasting Agreements*. Report of the Task Force to Review Comprehensive Claims Policy. Ottawa: DIAND.

_____ **1982** *Population, Repartition geographique—Terre-Neuve*. Recensement du Canada, 1981. Ottawa: Statistique Canada (Catalogue 93-901).

_____ **1984a** *Les Autochtones au Canada*. Ottawa: Statistique Canada (Catalogue 99-937).

_____ **1983a** *The Report of the House of Commons Special Committee on Indian Self-Government* (The Penner Report). Ottawa: Minister of Supply and Services Canada.

_____ **1982** *Indian News*, 22, 10 (January 1982). Ottawa: Department of Indian Affairs and Northern Development.

_____ **1973** *Report of Task Force: Policing on Reserves*. Edmonton: Department of Indian and Northern Affairs.

_____ **1981** *In All Fairness: A Native Claims Policy*. Ottawa: Minister of Supply and Services.

_____ **1980** *Indian Conditions, A Survey*. Ottawa: Department of Indian Affairs and Northern Development.

_____ **1979** *Perspective Canada III*. Ottawa: Statistics Canada, Supply and Services.

_____ **1979a** *Social Assistance and Related Social Development Programs of the Department of Indian and Northern Affairs*. Ottawa: IIAP, Department of Indian Affairs and Northern Development.

_____ **1978** *A Recommended Plan for Evaluation in Indian Education*. Ottawa: IIAP, Department of Indian Affairs and Northern Development, Program Evaluation Branch.

_____ **1978a** "Evaluation of the RCMP Indian Special Constable Program (Option 3B)." Ottawa: IIAP, Evaluation Branch, Department of Indian Affairs and Northern Development, March 1978a.

_____ **1978b** *Indian Affairs and Northern Development Business Loan Fund: Indian Economic Development Direct Loan Order Policy and Guidelines*. Ottawa: Department of Indian Affairs and Northern Development, Loan Fund Division.

_____ **1979** *Perspective Canada III*. Ottawa: Statistics Canada, Supply and Services.

_____ **1977** *Perspective Canada II*. Ottawa: Statistics Canada, Supply and Services.

_____ **1974** *Perspective Canada I*. Ottawa: Information Canada.

_____ **1966-70** *Annual Reports: 1966-67; 1968-69; 1969-70*. Department of Indian Affairs and Northern Development. Ottawa: Queen's Printer, 1966-70.

_____ **1969** "Canadian Committee on Corrections Report" (Quimet Report). Ottawa: Queen's Printer.

_____ **1969** *Statement of the Government of Canada on Policy, 1969* (White Paper). Ottawa: Queen's Printer.

_____ **1956** *Committee to Inquire into the Principles and Procedures Followed in the Remission Service of the Department of Justice of Canada Report* (Fauteux Report). Ottawa: Queen's Printer.

_____ **1985** *Indian and Native Programs.* A Study Team Report to the Task Force on Program Review. Ottawa: Minister of Supply and Services.

_____ **n.d.** *Indian Claims in Canada/Revendications des Indiens au Canada.* Toronto: Clarke, Irwin and Co. Ltd.

_____ **1984** *Response of the Government to the Report of the Special Committee on Indian Self-Government* (reply to the Penner Report). Ottawa.

_____ **1988** *Census Metropolitan Areas, Dimensions,* Ottawa: Supply and Services.

_____ **1989** *The Canadian Aboriginal Economic Development Strategy,* Ottawa: Indian and Northern Affairs Canada.

_____ **1990** *Annual Report, 1989-90,* Department of Indian Affairs and Northern Development, Ottawa: Minister of Supply and Services.

CANADIAN ASSOCIATION IN SUPPORT OF THE NATIVE PEOPLES 1978 Bulletin on Native Women (special issue, 18,4), Ottawa: CASNP.

CANADIAN SUPERINTENDENT 1965 *The Education of Indian Children in Canada.* Toronto: Ryerson Press.

CANTRYN, M. (n.d.) Evaluation — Native Women's Program, Ottawa: Secretary of State.

CAPUTO, T. and D. BRACKEN 1988 "Custodial Dispositions and the Young Offenders Act", in J. Hudson, B. Burrows, and J. Hornick (Editors): *Justice and the Young Offender in Canada.* Toronto: Wall and Thompson.

CARDINAL, H. 1969 *The Unjust Society.* Edmonton: Hurtig Publishers

_____ **1977** *The Rebirth of Canada's Indians,* Edmonton: Hurtig Publishers.

_____ **1979** "Native Women and the Indian Act." In: Elliott, J. (ed.), *Two Nations, Many Cultures,* Scarborough: Prentice Hall Canada, pp. 44-50.

_____ **1986** "Constitutional Change and the Treaty 8 Renovation." In *Indian-Provincial Relations,* M. Boldt, J.A. Long and L. Little Bear (eds). Lethbridge: The University of Lethbridge.

CARPENTER, JOCK 1977 *Fifty Dollar Bride.* Sidney, B.C.: Gray's Publishing Ltd.

CARTER, S. 1990 *Lost Harvests,* Montreal and Kingston: McGill-Queen's University Press.

CARSTENS, PETER 1971 "Coercion and Change." In *Canadian Society,* Richard Ossenberg (ed). Scarborough, Ontario: Prentice Hall Canada.

CARSTENS, P. 1991 The *Queen's People,* Toronto, University of Toronto Press.

CASTELLANO, MARLENE 1970 "Vocation or Identity: The Dilemma of Indian Youth." In *The Only Good Indian,* Waubageshig (ed). Toronto: New Press.

CAWSEY, R., et al 1991 *Justice on Trial,* Volume 1, Main Report. Edmonton: Government of Alberta.

CAWSEY, JUSTICE R. 1991 *Justice on Trial*, Vol. 1, Task Force on the Criminal Justice System and its Impact on the Indian and Metis People of Alberta, Edmonton: Attorney General of Alberta.

CHANCE, NORMAN 1970 *Development Change Among the Cree Indians of Quebec*. Ottawa: Summary Report, ARDA Project 34002 (Reprint 1970), Department of Regional Economic Expansion.

CHAPMAN, L. 1972 Women's Rights and Special Status for Indians: Some Implications of the Lavell Case, Ottawa, Carleton University, n.p.

CHARLEBOIS, P. 1975 *The Life of Louis Riel*, Toronto: N. C. Press.

CHARTIER, C. 1988 *In the Best Interest of the Metis Child*, Saskatoon, Saskatchewan: Native Law Centre.

CHASE-DUNN, CHRISTOPHER 1975 "The Effects of International Economic Dependence and Inequality: A Cross-National Study." *American Sociological Review*, 40 (1975):720-738.

CHEDA, S. 1977 "Indian Women: An Historical Example and a Contemporary View," In: Stephenson, M. (ed.), *Women in Canada*, Don Mills: General Publishing Co. Ltd., pp. 195-208.

CHRÉTIEN, J. 1969 "Indian Policy... Where Does It Stand?" Speech at Empire Club, Toronto, October 16, 1969.

CLAIRMONT, DONALD H., and DENNIS W. MAGILL 1979 "Nova Scotia Blacks: Marginality in a Depressed Region." In *Canada: A Sociological Profile*, 2nd ed., W.E. Mann (ed). Toronto: Copp Clark Pitman.

CLARKE, ROGER 1972 *In Them Days: The Breakdown of a Traditional Fishing Economy in an English Village on the Gaspe Coast*. Ph.D. dissertation. Montreal: McGill University Press.

COATES, K. and W. MORRISON 1986 "More Than A Matter of Blood: The Federal Government, The Churches and the Mixed Blood Populations of the Yukon and the Mackenzie River Valley, 1890-1950." In *1885 and After*, F. Barron and J. Waldham (eds). Regina: Canadian Plains Research Centre (1986):253-277.

COHEN, F. 1947 "Original Indian Title." *Minnesota Law Review*, 32, 28 (1947):52-57.

COHEN, R. 1977 "Conceptual Styles, Culture Conflict and Nonverbal Tests of Intelligence." *American Anthropologist*, 71 (1977):222-237.

COLE, C. 1939 *Colbert and a Century of French Mercantilism*. 2 Vols., New York.

COLVIN, E. 1981 "Legal Process and the Resolution of Indian Claims." *Studies in Aboriginal Rights*, #3. Saskatoon: Native Law Centre, University of Saskatchewan.

CORNELL, S. 1988 *The Return of the Native*. New York: Oxford University Press.

CORRIGAN, S. 1970 "The Plains Indian Pow-wow: Cultural Integration in Manitoba and Saskatchewan." *Anthropologica*, 12, 2 (1970):253-271.

COTÉ, FRANÇOISE 1984 "Nunavut, la province qui veut naître." *L'actualité* (mars 1984):75-80.

CUMMING, G. GRAHAM 1967 "The Health of the Original Canadians 1867-1967." *Medical Service Journal*, 13 (February 1967):115 166.

CUMMING, P. 1969 *Indian Rights—A Century of Oppression*. Mimeographed. Toronto: Indian-Eskimo Association of Canada, 1969.

_____ 1967   "Public Lands, Native Land Claims and Land Use." In *Canadian Public Land Use in Perspective*, J. Nelson, R. Scace, and R. Kouri (eds). Proceedings of a symposium sponsored by the Social Science Research Council of Canada, Ottawa, (1967):206-238.

_____ 1973   "Our Land—Our People: Native Rights, North of 60." In *Arctic Alternatives*, D. Pimlott, K. Vincent and C. McKnight (eds). Ottawa: Canadian Arctic Resources Committee.

_____ 1973   "Native Rights and Law in an Age of Protest." *Alberta Law Review* (1973):230-245.

CUMMING, P., and N. MICKENBERG 1972   *Native Rights in Canada*, 2nd ed. Toronto: Indian- Eskimo Association of Canada.

DAHL, R. 1967   *Pluralist Democracy in the United States*. Chicago: Rand-McNally.

DALON, R. 1985   "An Alberta Perspective on Aboriginal Peoples and The Constitution." In *The Quest for Justice*, M. Boldt, J.A. Long, and L. Little Bear (eds). Toronto: University of Toronto Press.

DANIEL, R. 1980   *A History of Native Claims Processes in Canada*. Ottawa: Department of Indian Affairs and NortherDevelopment.

_____ 1980   *A History of Native Claims Processes in Canada, 1867-1979*, Research Branch, Department of Indian and Northern Affairs, Ottawa.

DANIELS, H. 1981   *Native People and The Constitution of Canada*. Ottawa: Mutual Press.

DARROCH, A.G. 1980   "Another Look at Ethnicity, Stratification, and Social Mobility in Canada." In *Ethnicity and Ethnic Relations in Canada*, J. Goldstein and R. Bienvenue (eds). Scarborough, Ontario: Butterworth and Co. (Canada) Ltd.

DAUGHTERY, W. 1978   *Discussion Report on Indian Taxation*, Ottawa: Department of Indian and Northern Affairs, Treaties and Historical Research Centre.

_____ 1982   *A Guide to Native Political Associations in Canada*. Treaties and Historical Research, Research Branch, Corporate Policy. Ottawa: Department of Indian and Northern Affairs.

DAUGHERTY, WAYNE, and DENNIS MAGILL 1980   *Indian Government Under Indian Act Legislation, 1868-1951*. Ottawa: Research Branch, Department of Indian and Northern Affairs.

DAVIES, M. 1985   "Aspects of Aboriginal Rights in International Law." In *Aboriginal Peoples and the Law*. B. Morse (ed). Ottawa: Carleton University Press, (1985):16-47.

DAVIS, A.D. 1971   "Canadian Society and History as Hinterland versus Metropolis." In *Canadian Society*, Richard J. Ossenberg (ed). Scarborough, Ontario: Prentice Hall Canada.

DAVIS, ARTHUR K., CECIL L. FRENCH, WILLIAM D. KNILL, and HENRY ZENTNER 1965   *A Northern Dilemma: Reference Papers*, Vol. 2. Calgary and Bellingham, Wash.: Western Washington State College.

DAVIS, ARTHUR 1968   "Urban Indians in Western Canada: Implications for Social Theory and Social Policy." *Transactions of the Royal Society of Canada*, 6, 4 (1968):217-228.

DELMAR, R. 1986   "What is Feminism?" In Mitchell, J. & A. Oakley (eds.), *What is Feminism?* Oxford: Basil Blackwell, pp. 8-33.

DELORIA, V. and C. LYTLE 1984   *The Nations Within: The Past and Future of American Indian Sovereignty*. New York: Pantheon Books.

DEMERS, LINDA 1979   *Évaluation de la qualité des informations ethniques et linguistiques fournies par les recensements canadiens 1901-1976.* Mémoire de maîtrise, Département de démographie, Université de Montréal.

DENTON, T. 1972   "Migration from a Canadian Indian Reserve." *Journal of Canadian Studies,* 7 (1972):54-62.

DEPREZ, PAUL, and GLEN SIGURDSON. 1969   *Economic Status of the Canadian Indian: A Re-Examination.* Winnipeg: Centre for Settlement Studies, University of Manitoba.

DIAND. 1969   *Statement of the Government of Canada on Indian Policy.* Ottawa: Queen's Printer.

_____ **1978**   *Native Claims: Policy, Processes and Perspectives.* Ottawa: Queen's Printer.

_____ **1980**   *Indian Conditions. A Survey.* Ottawa: Minister of Supply and Services.

_____ **1981**   *In All Fairness: A Native Claims Policy.* Ottawa: Queen's Printer.

_____ **1981a**   *Annex III. Indian Band Government Financial Implications.* Revised, November 6. Ottawa: Minister of Supply and Services.

_____ **1982**   *Outstanding Business: A Native Claims Policy.* Ottawa: Minister of Supply and Services.

_____ **1982a**   *James Bay and Northern Quebec Agreement Implementation Review.* Ottawa: Minister of Supply and Services.

_____ **1982b**   *Strengthening Indian Band Government in Canada.* Ottawa: Minister of Indian Affairs and Northern Development. Ottawa, c. 1982b.

_____ **1982c**   *An Optional System of Indian Band Government.* Ottawa: Minister of Indian Affairs and Northern Development. Ottawa, c, 1982c.

_____ **1982d**   "The Legislation Proposals." *Annex I.* Ottawa: Minister of Supply and Services, c. 1982d.

_____ **1982e**   "Financial Considerations—The Funding System." *Annex II.* Ottawa: Minister of Supply and Services, c. 1982e.

_____ **1982f**   "Appendix VI: Pick up of Provincial Program Costs." Ottawa: Mimeographed, c. 1982f.

_____ **1982g**   *The Alternative of Optional Indian Band Government Legislation.* Ottawa: Minister of Indian Affairs and Northern Development.

_____ **1985**   *Living Treaties: Lasting Agreements. Report of the Task Force to Review Comprehensive Claims Policy.* Ottawa: Department of Indian Affairs and Northern Development.

DICKASON, D.P. 1992   *Canada's First Nations,* Toronto: McClelland and Stewart Ltd.

DIXON, VERNON 1971   "Two Approaches to Black-White Relations." In *Beyond Black or White: An Alternative America,* Vernon Dixon and Badmer Foster (eds). Boston: Little, Brown and Co.

DOBBIN, MURRAY 1981   *The One-An-A-Half Men: The Story of Jim Brady and Malcolm Norris, Metis Patriots of the 20th Century.* Vancouver: New Star Books.

DOERR, A.D. 1974   "Indian Policy." In *Issues in Canadian Public Policy.* G.S. Doern and V.S. Wilson (eds). Toronto: Macmillan.

DOSMAN, EDGAR 1972   *Indians: The Urban Dilemma.* Toronto: McClelland and Stewart Ltd.

DRIBEN, PAUL 1983   "The Nature of Metis Claims." *The Canadian Journal of Native Studies,* 3, 1(1983):183-196.

_____ **1975** *We Are Metis*. Ph.D. dissertation. Minneapolis: University of Minnesota.

DRUCKER, P. 1958 *The Native Brotherhoods: Modern Intertribal Organizations on the Northwest Coast*. Bureau of American Ethnology, 168. Washington, D.C.: Smithsonian Institution.

DUBOIS, W. 1940 *Dusk of Dawn*. New York: Harcourt, Brace and Co.

DUCLOS, N. 1990 "Lessons of Difference: Feminist Theory on Cultural Diversity." In *Buffalo Law Review*, 38, 2, pp. 325 381.

DUNNING, R. 1959 Ethnic Relations and the Marginal Man in Canada." *Human Organization*, 18, 3 (1959):117-122.

_____ **1972** "The Indian Situation: A Canadian Government Dilemma." *International Journal of Comparative Sociology*, 12 (June, 1972):128-134.

_____ **1976** "Some Speculations on the Canadian Indian Socio-Political Reality." In *The Patterns of 'Amerindian' Identity*, Marc-Adelard Tremblay (ed). Quebec: Les Presses de l'Université Laval.

DYCK, NOEL 1980 "Indian, Metis, Native: Some Implications of Special Status." *Canadian Ethnic Studies*, 12, 1(1980): 34-36.

_____ **1981** "The Politics of Special Status: Indian Associations and the Administration of Indian Affairs." In *Ethnicity and Politics in Canada*, J. Dahlie and T. Fernando (eds). Agincourt, Ontario: Methuen Publications.

_____ **1983** (ed) *Indigenous People and the Nation State: Fourth World Politics in Canada, Australia and Norway*. Institute of Social and Economic Research, Memorial University of Newfoundland, St. John's, Newfoundland.

_____ **1979** "Pow-wow and the Expression of Community in Western Canada." *Ethnos*, 1-2 (1979):78-79.

_____ **1990** "Cultures, Communities and Claims: Anthropology and Native Studies in Canada, *Canadian Ethnic Studies*, Vol. 22, No. 3, pp. 40-55.

DYCK, N. 1991 *What is the Indian "Problem"?*, Memorial University of Newfoundland, Institute of Social and Economic Research.

EBERTS, M. 1985 "The Use of Litigation Under the Canadian Charter of Rights and Freedoms as a Strategy for Achieving Change," In Nevitte, N. & A. Kornberg (eds.), *Minorities and the Canadian State*. Oakville: Mosaic Press, pp. 53-70.

EDMONTON, CITY OF. 1976 *Native Adjustment to the Urban Environment: A Report on the Problems Encountered by Newly Arrived Natives in Edmonton*. Edmonton: Social Services Department, Social Planning Division.

ELIAS, D. 1976 "Indian Politics in the Canadian Political System." In *The Patterns of 'Amerindian' Identity*, Marc Adelard Tremblay (ed). Quebec: Les Presses de l'Université Laval (1976):35-64.

ELIAS, P. 1991 *Development of Aboriginal People's Communities*, York University, Captus Press.

ELLIOT, J.L. 1970 *Educational and Occupational Aspirations and Expectations: A Comparative Study of Indian and Non-Indian Youth*. Antigonish: St. Francis Xavier University.

_____ **1971** *Minority Canadians: Native Peoples*. Scarborough, Ontario: Prentice Hall Canada.

_____ **1980** "Native People, Power and Politics." *Multiculturalism*, 3, 3 (1980):10-74.

ELLIOTT, D. 1985 "Aboriginal Title." In *Aboriginal Peoples and the Law*, B. Morse (ed). Ottawa: Carleton University Press (1985):48-124.

ENLOE, C. 1981 "The Growth of the State and Ethnic Mobilization: The American Experience." *Ethnic and Racial Studies*, 4, 2 (1981):123-136.

EWING COMMISSION REPORT 1935 *Royal Commission on the Conditions of the Halfbreed Population of the Province of Alberta Report, 1935*. Sessional Paper No. 72.

FEDERATION OF SASKATCHEWAN INDIAN NATIONS 1985 Memo from Chief Sol Sanderson re: Section 122 of the BNA Act and the Bilateral Process, Prince Albert, Saskatchewan.

FEDERATION OF SASKATCHEWAN INDIANS 1978 *Off-Band Members in Saskatchewan*. Mimeographed. Saskatoon.

_____ **1977** *Indian Government: A Position Paper*. Prince Albert, Saskatchewan.

FELLNER, W. 1954 "Long-term Tendencies in Private Capital Formulation." *Long-Range Economic Projections*, Prince, National Bureau of Economic Research.

FERNANDEZ, JUAN 1983 "La loi des Indiens: un instrument de gestion démographique." Association Internationale des Démographes de Langue Française, *Démographie et gestion des sous-populations*, 1 (1983):423-429.

FIDLER, DICK 1970 *Red Power in Canada*. Toronto: Vanguard Publications.

FIELDS, D. and W. STANBURY 1975 *The Economic Impact of the Public Sector Upon the Indian of British Columbia*. Vancouver: University of British Columbia Press.

FINE, SEAN 1989 "Near 1 in 4 Family Murders Among Natives, Study Says." *The Globe and Mail*, October 4. Toronto.

FISHER, A.D. 1969 "White Rites versus Indian Rights." *Transaction*, 7, November (1969):29-33.

FISHER, R. 1977 *Contact and Conflict: Indian-European Relations in British Columbia, 1774-1890*. Vancouver: University of British Columbia Press.

FITZGERALD, P.K. 1956 "Introduction." In *The Indian in Modern America*, D.A. Baerreis (ed). Wisconsin State Historical Society.

FLANAGAN, T. 1983 "The Case Against Metis Aboriginal Rights." *Canadian Public Policy*, 9 (1983):314-315.

_____ **1983** *Riel and the Rebellion: 1885 Reconsidered*, Saskatoon: Western Producer Prairie Books.

_____ **1985** "Metis Aboriginal Rights: Some Historical and Contemporary Problems." In *The Quest for Justice*, M. Boldt, J. Long and L. Little Bear (eds). Toronto: University of Toronto Press.

_____ **1990** "The History of Metis Aboriginal Rights: Politics, Principle and Policy," *Canadian Journal of Law and Society*, 5, pp. 71-94.

FLEMING-MATHUR, M. 1971 "Who Cares That a Woman's Work is Never Done?" In *Indian Historian*, 4, 2, pp. 11-15.

FLERAS, A. and J. L. ELLIOTT 1992 *The Nations Within*, Oxford University Press, Don Mills, Ontario

FOSTER, JOHN E. 1978 "The Metis, the People and the Term." *Prairie Forum*, 3, 1 (Spring 1978):79-91.

_____ **1976** "Mixed Bloods in Western Canada: An Ecological Approach." "The Origins of the Mixed Bloods in the Canadian West." In *Essays on Western History*, Lewis H. Thomas (ed). Edmonton: University of Alberta Press.

FRANK, ANDRÉ GUNDER 1967 *Capitalism and Underdevelopment in Latin America*. New York: Monthly Review Press.

FRANKLIN, RAYMOND 1969 "The Political Economy of Black Power." *Social Problems*, 16 (Winter 1969):286-301.

FREEMAN, M. 1985 "Traditional and Contemporary Roles of Inuit Women." In *Association of Canadian Universities for Northern Studies, Social Science in the North: Communicating Northern Values*. Ottawa: ACUNS, pp. 57-60.

FRENCH, B.F. 1851 *Historical Collections of Louisiana*. Dublin: Arbers Annals, 1851.

FRIDERES, J.S. 1974 *Canada's Indians: Contemporary Conflicts*. Scarborough, Ontario: Prentice Hall Canada.

_____ **1972** "Indians and Education: A Canadian Failure." *Manitoba Journal of Education*, 7 (June 1972):27-30.

_____ **1986** "Native Claims and Settlement in Yukon." In *Arduous Journey*, J.R. Ponting (ed). Toronto: McClelland and Stewart (1986):284-301.

FRIDERES, J. and J. RYAN 1980 *Program Evaluation of the Calgary Native Outreach Office*. Unpublished report. Calgary: University of Calgary.

FUCHS, ESTELLE 1970 "Time to Redeem an Old Promise." *Saturday Review* (January 24, 1970):53-58.

FUDGE, S 1983 "Too Weak to Win, Too Strong to Lose: Indians and Indian Policy in Canada." *B.C. Studies*, 57 (Spring 1983):137-145.

FULLWINDER, S. 1969 *The Mind and Mood of Black America*. Homewood, Illinois: Dorsey Press.

GADACZ, R. 1991 "Socio-Economic Development from a Native Point of View: A Proposed Social Indicator System for Use in Native Communities," Paper presented at the 1991 Learneds (Canadian Sociology and Anthropology Association), Queen's University, Kingston, Ontario.

GAMSON, W. 1969 *Power and Discontent*. Homewood, Illinois: Dorsey Press.

GERBER, L. 1977 "Community Characteristics and Out-Migration from Indian Communities: Regional Trends." Paper presented at Department of Indian Affairs and Northern Development, Ottawa, November 9, 1977.

_____ **1980** "The Development of Canadian Indian Communities: A Two-Dimensional Typology Reflecting Strategies of Adaptation to the Modern World." *The Canadian Review of Sociology and Anthropology*,16, 4 (1980):126-134.

GERBER, LINDA M. 1990 "Multiple Jeopardy: A Socio-Economic Comparison of Men and Women Among the Indian, Metis and Inuit Peoples of Canada," *Canadian Ethnic Studies*, Vol. 22, No. 3, pp. 69-84.

GIBBINS, R. 1986a "Canadian Indians and the Canadian Constitution: A Difficult Passage Toward an Uncertain Destination." In *Arduous Journey*, J.R. Ponting (ed). Toronto: McClelland and Stewart.

_____ **1986b** "Citizenship, Political and Intergovernmental Problems with Indian Self Government." In *Arduous Journey*, J.R. Ponting (ed). Toronto: McClelland and Stewart.

GIBBINS, R. and J.R. PONTING 1986 "An Assessment of the Probable Impact of Aboriginal Self Government in Canada." In *The Politics of Gender, Ethnicity and Language in Canada*, A. Cairns and C. Williams (eds). Vol. 34. Research Studies of the Royal Commission on the Economic Union and Development Prospects for Canada. Toronto: University of Toronto Press.

_____ **1984**   "Prairie Canadians' Orientations Towards Indians." *Prairie Forum*, 2, 1 (1984):57-81.

GIRAUD, MARCEL. 1954   "Metis Settlement in the Northwest Territories." *Saskatchewan History*, 7, 1 (Winter 1954):49-53.

GIRVAN, N. 1973   "The Development of Dependency Economics in the Caribbean and Latin America." *Social and Economic Studies*, 22 (1973):1-33.

GOODWILL, J. 1971   "A New Horizon for Native Women in Canada," In Draper, J. (ed.), *Citizen Participation: Canada, A Book of Readings*. Toronto: Webb Offset Publications Ltd., pp. 362-370.

GOOSSEN, JAYNE N. 1978   "A Wearer of Moccasins." *The Beaver* (Autumn 1978).

GOVERNMENT OF THE NORTHWEST TERRITORIES 1978   *Population Projections, Methodological Report, Northwest Territories 1978 to 1988*. Yellowknife: Statistics Section, Department of Planning and Program Evaluation, 72 pages plus annexes.

GRAND COUNCIL TREATY NO. 9 n.d.   "A Declaration by the Ojibway-Cress Nation of Treaty No. 9 to the People of Canada."

GRAY, JAMES H. 1967   *Men Against the Desert*. Saskatoon: Western Producer Book Service.

_____ **1966**   *The Winter Years*. Toronto: Macmillan of Canada.

GREEN, JEROME 1969   "When Moral Prophecy Fails." *Catalyst*, 4 (Spring 1969):63-79.

GREEN, L. 1983   "Aboriginal Peoples, International Law and the Canadian Charter of Rights and Freedoms." In *The Canadian Bar Review*, 61, pp. 339-353.

GRIFFITHS, C. and S. VERDUN-JONES 1989   *Canadian Criminal Justice*. Toronto: Butterworths.

GUILLEMIN, J. 1975   *Urban Renegades—The Cultural Strategy of American Indians*. New York: Columbia University Press.

GULLIVER, P. 1969   *Tradition and Transition in East Africa*. London: Routledge and Kegan Paul.

HAGAN, J. 1974   "Criminal Justice and Native People: A Study of Incarceration in a Canadian Province." *Canadian Review of Sociology and Anthropology*. Special issue (August 1974):220-236.

HALL, T. 1991 "Aboriginal Futures—Awakening Our Imagination," *Canadian Dimension*, July/August pp. 15-17.

HAMAN, ANDREA 1992 "Periodical Publishing in Canada," *Canadian Social Trends*, Industry, Science and Technology, Supply and Services Canada, Statistics Canada, Ottawa, No. 25, Summer, pp. 29-31.

HARDESTY, DONALD L. 1977   *Ecological Anthropology*. New York: John Wiley & Sons Inc.

HARPER, A. 1947   "Canadian Indian Administration: The Treaty System." *America Indigena*, 7, 2 (1947):129-140.

HARRIS, R. COLE and JOHN WARKENTIN 1974   *Canada Before Confederation*. New York: Oxford University Press.

HARRISON, G.S. 1972   "The Alaska Native Claims Settlement Act: 1971." *Arctic*, 25, 3 (1972):232-233.

HATT, FRED K. 1972   "The Canadian Metis: Recent Interpretations." *Canadian Ethnic Studies*, 3 1 (1972):23-26.

_____ **1969**   "The Metis and Community Development in Northeastern Alberta." In *Perspectives on Regions and Regionalism and Other Papers*, B.Y. Card (ed). Edmonton: University of Alberta, (1969):111-119.

_____ **1982** "On Hold: A Review of 'In All Fairness: A Native Claims Policy'." *The Canadian Journal of Native Studies*, 2, 2 (1982):352-355.

_____ **1983** "The Northwest Scrip Commissions as Federal Policy—Some Initial Findings." *The Canadian Journal o f Native Studies*, 3, 1 (1983):117-130.

HAWKES, D. 1985 *Aboriginal Self-Government*. Kingston, Ontario: Queen's University, Institute of Intergovernmental Relations.

HAWKES, DAVID C. and EVELYN J. PETERS 1987 *Issues in Entrenching Aboriginal Self-Government*. Kingston, Ontario: Queen's University, Institute of Intergovernmental Relations.

HAWLEY, P.L. 1990 *1990 Indian Act*, Toronto: Carswell.

HAWTHORN, H.B. 1966-67 *A Survey of the Contemporary Indians of Canada*, 2 Vols. Indian Affairs Branch. Ottawa: Queen's Printer, 1966-67. Excerpts reproduced by permission of Information Canada.

HAWTHORN, H.B., et al. 1958 *The Indians of British Columbia*. Toronto: University of Toronto Press.

HEILBRUN, JAMES, and STANISLAW WELLISZ 1969 "An Economic Program for the Ghetto." in *Urban Riots*, Robert Conner (ed). New York: Random House Inc.

HENDERSON, J.Y. 1985 "The Doctrine of Aboriginal Rights in Western Legal Tradition." In *The Quest for Justice*, M. Boldt, J. Long and L. Little Bear (eds). Toronto: University of Toronto Press.

HENDERSON, W. 1983 "Canadian Legal and Judicial Philosophies on the Doctrine of Aboriginal Rights." In *Aboriginal Rights: Toward an Understanding*, J. Long, M. Boldt and L. Little Bear, (eds). Lethbridge, Alberta: University of Lethbridge.

HENDERSON, W.B. 1978 *Land Tenure in Indian Reserves*. Ottawa: DIAND.

_____ **1980** "Canada's Indian Reserves: The Usufruct in our Constitution." *Ottawa Law Review*, 12 (1980):160-187.

HERTZBERG, HAZEL 1971 *Search for an American Indian Identity: Modern Pan-Indian Movements*. Syracuse, N.Y.: Syracuse University Press.

HIMES, J. 1966 "The Functions of Racial Conflict." *Social Forces*, 45 (1966):1-10.

HIRSCHMANN, ALBERTA 1971 *The Strategy of Economic Development*. New Haven: Yale University Press.

HODGETTS, J.E. 1955 *Pioneer Public Service—An Administrative History of the United Canadas, 1841-1867*. Toronto: University of Toronto Press.

HOEBEL, E.A. 1956 "To End Their Status." In *The Indian in Modern America*, D.A. Baerreis (ed). Madison: The Wisconsin State Historical Society (1956):1-15.

HOLMES, J. 1987 *Bill C-31, Equality or Disparity? The Effects of the New Indian Act on Native Women*. Ottawa: CACSW.

HONIGMAN, JOHN 1967 *Personality in Culture*. New York: Harper and Row Inc.

HOROWITZ, J. 1989 "Fact Finding in the Courts." In F. L. Morton (ed), *Law, Politics, and the Judicial System in Canada*. Calgary: The University of Calgary.

HOUSE OF COMMONS, 1976 Standing Committee on Indian Affairs and Northern Development, Minutes of the Proceedings and Evidence, Issue No. 53, Ottawa, Queen's Printer for Canada.

HOUSE OF COMMONS 1982 Minutes of Proceedings and Evidence of the Sub-Committee on Indian Women and the Indian Act, Issue No. 2, Ottawa: Minister of Supply and Services Canada.

HOWARD, J. 1951   "Notes on the Dakota Grass Dance." *Southwestern Journal of Anthropology*, 7 (1951):82-85.

HOWARD, JOHN KINSEY 1952   *Strange Empire*. Toronto: Swan Publishing Co.Ltd.

HUGHES, KEN 1991   *The Summer of 1990*. Fifth Report of the Standing Committee on Aboriginal Affairs, Ottawa.

HUNT, GEORGE 1940   *The Wars of the Iroquois: A Study in Intertribal Trade Relations*. Madison: University of Wisconsin Press.

HYTTON, JOHN 1981   "The Native Offender in Saskatchewan, Some Implications for Crime Prevention Planning." In *Selected Papers of the Canadian Congress for the Prevention of Crime*. Winnipeg: Canadian Association for the Prevention of Crime.

INAC 1977   *Arctic Women's Workshop*. Ottawa: DIAND.

———— **1982**   *The Elimination of Sex Discrimination from the Indian Act*. Ottawa: DIAND.

———— **1983**   *A Demographic Profile of Registered Indian Women*. Ottawa: DIAND.

INDIAN ASSOCIATION OF ALBERTA 1983   News Release. "Indian Association of Alberta Steps up Assault Against Indian Government Bill." Edmonton: February 7, 1983.

———— **1971**   *The Native People*. Edmonton.

INDIAN CLAIMS COMMISSION 1975   *Indian Claims in Canada: An Essay and Bibliography*. Ottawa: Supply and Services.

INDIAN MINERALS DIRECTORATE 1981   Personal Communication, Reserves and Trust Branch, Department of Indian and Northern Development, Ottawa.

———— **1981**   Minerals Inventory, Reserve and Trust Branch, Department of Indian and Northern Development, Ottawa.

INDIAN AND NORTHERN AFFAIRS CANADA 1988   *Basic Departmental Data*. Ottawa: Minister of Supply and Services.

INDIAN TRIBES OF MANITOBA 1972   *Wahbung (Our Tomorrows)*. Winnipeg: Manitoba Indian Brotherhood.

INNIS, HAROLD A. 1970   *The Fur Trade in Canada*. Toronto and Buffalo: University of Toronto Press.

IRIW, n.d.   Alberta Committee, The Arbitrary Enfranchisement of Indian Women, Edmonton: IRIW.

———— **1978**   Research Workshop: Resolutions, Edmonton, IRIW, n.p.

———— **1979**   A Study on the Emotional Impact of Arbitrary Enfranchisement on Native Women and on Their Families in Canada, Edmonton: IRIW.

IRONSIDE, R.G. and E. TOMASKY. 1976   "Agriculture and River Lot Settlement in Western Canada: The Case of Pakan." *Prairie Forum*, 1 (April 1976):3-18.

IRWIN, A. 1968   "Management Policy for Indian Owned Minerals: Possible Application to Northern Resources." *Proceedings of a Symposium on the Implications of Northern Mineral Resources Management for Human Development*, No. 5, Edmonton: Boreal Institute, University of Alberta.

IVERSON, P. 1990   "Plains Indians and Australian Aborigines in the Twentieth Century." In P. Olson (ed), *The Struggle for the Land*. Lincoln, Nebraska: University of Nebraska Press, pp. 171-188.

JACK, HENRY 1970   "Native Alliance for Red Power." In *The Only Good Indian*, Waubageshig (ed). Toronto: New Press.

JAMES, BERNARD 1961   "Social Psychological Dimensions of Ojibwa Acculturation." *American Anthropologist*, 63 (August 1961):728-744.

JAMIESON, K. 1978   *Indian Women and the Law in Canada: A Citizens Minus*. Ottawa: Minister of Supply and Services Canada.

————— **1979**   "Multiple Jeopardy: The Evolution of a Native Women's Movement." In *Atlantis* (part 2), 4, 2, pp. 157-178.

JAMIESON, M. 1989   "Aboriginal Women—Barriers to Economic Development," mimeo.

JARVIS, G and T. HEATON 1989   "Language Shift Among Those of Aboriginal Mother Tongue in Canada," *Canadian Studies in Population*, vol. 16(1), pp. 25-42.

JENNESS, DIAMOND n.d.   *The Indian Background of Canadian History*. Bulletin No. 86, Anthropological Series No. 21. Ottawa: Department of Mines and Resources.

————— **1967**   *Indians of Canada*, 7th ed. Ottawa: Queen's Printer.

JHAPPAN, C. RADHA 1990   "Indian Symbolic Politics: The Double-Edged Sword of Publicity," *Canadian Ethnic Studies*, Vol. 22, No. 3, pp. 19-39.

JOHNSON, S. 1976   *Migrating Native Peoples Program*. Ottawa: National Association of Friendship Centres.

JONES, FRANK, and WALLACE LAMBERT 1967   "Some Situational Influences on Attitudes toward Immigrants." *British Journal of Sociology*, 18 (March 1967):408-424.

JOSEPH, S. 1991   "Assimilation Tools: Then and Now," in *In Celebration of Our Survival*, D. Jensen and C. Brooks (eds.), Vancouver, University of British Columbia Press, pp 65-79.

JULL, PETER 1982   Nanvut." *Northern Perspectives*, 10, 2.

KAEGI, GERDA 1972   *The Comprehensive View of Indian Education*. Toronto: Indian-Eskimo Association of Canada.

KALLEN, E. 1982   *Ethnicity and Human Rights in Canada*. Toronto: Gage Publishing Ltd.

KARDINER, ABRAHAM and LIONEL OVESEY 1951   *The Mark of Oppression*. New York: W.W. Norton and Co.

KATZNELSON, I. 1976   "The Crisis of the Capitalist City: Urban Politics and Social Control." in W. Hawley and M. Lipsky (eds), *Theoretical Perspectives in Urban Politics*, Englewood Cliffs: Prentice Hall.

KAYE, L. 1981   "I think I'm Indian ... But others aren't sure." In *Ontario Indian*, 4, 5, p.8, p. 34.

KEEFE, S. 1976   "Sex and Ethnicity in Politics: A Minority Group Model of Political Interaction." *The Western Canadian Journal of Anthropology*, 6, 3, pp. 213-242.

KENNEDY, RAYMOND 1945   The Colonial Crisis and the Future." In *The Science of Man in the World Crisis*. Ralph Linton (ed). New York: Columbia University Press.

KERR, S. 1975   Women's Rights and Two National Native Organizations: The Native Council o Canada and the National Indian Brotherhood, Ottawa: Carleton University, n.p.

KING, CECIL 1972   "Sociological Implications of the Jeannette Corbiere Lavell Case." *The Northian*, 8 (March 1972): 44-45.

KNIGHT, D. 1985   *A Study of Learning Style and its Implication for Education of Indian People*. Mimeo.

KNIGHT, ROLF 1978 *Indians at Work. An Informal History of Native Indian Labour in British Columbia, 1858-1930.* Vancouver: New Star Books.

KOOVOS, A. and E. BROWN 1980 "The Implications of the International Energy Markets for Indian Resources." *The Journal of Energy and Development*, 5, (1980):252-257.

KROSENBRINK-GELISSEN, L. 1983 *Native Women of Manitoba, Canada: Feminism or Ethnicity?* Nijmegen: Catholic University of Nijmegen, n.p.

——————— **1984** "De Canadese Indian Act en de gevolgen daarvan voor Indiaanse vrouwen." In *De Kiva*, 21, 3, pp. 44-45.

——————— **1984** *No Indian Women, No Indian Nation: Canadian Native Women in Search of Their Identity,* Nijmegen: Catholic Univ. of Nijmegen, n.p.

——————— **1991** *Sexual Equality as an Aboriginal Right,* Saarbrucken, Germany: Verlagbreitenbach.

KROSENBRINK-GELISSEN, L. E. 1989 "The Metis National Council: Continuity and Change Among the Canadian Metis," *Native American Studies*, 3.1, pp. 33-41.

KWAN, K.M. and TAMOTSU SHIBUTANI 1965 *Ethnic Stratification.* Toronto: Macmillan of Canada.

LACHANCE-BRULOTTE, GINETTE 1984 "La nuptialité des Indiens du Canada." In *Les populations amerindiennes et inuit du Canada, Aperçu démographique.* Normandeau L. et V. Piche (éditeurs). Montréal: Les Presses de l'Université de Montréal.

LAGASSE, JEAN 1962 "Community Development in Manitoba." *Human Organization*, 20 (Winter 1962):232-237.

——————— **1959** *A Study of the Population of Indian Ancestry Living in Manitoba.* Winnipeg: Department of Agriculture and Immigration.

LAING, A. 1967 *Indians and the Law.* Ottawa: Queen's Printer.

LANG, O. 1974 "Politics of Land Claims Settlements." *Muskox*, 14.

LA PRAIRIE, C. n.d. *Native Juveniles in Court: Some Preliminary Observations.* Mimeo, no date.

LA RUSIC, IGNATIUS 1968 *Hunter to Proletarian.* Research paper for Cree Development Change Project.

LASLETT, P. 1963 "The Face-to-Face Society." In *Philosophy, Politics and Society*, P. Laslett (ed). Oxford: Basil Blackwell,.

LATIMER, C. A. 1986 *Winnipeg Youth Courts and the Young Offenders Act.* Winnipeg: Attorney General, Research, Planning and Evaluation.

LATULIPPE-SKAMOTO, CLAUDETTE 1971 *Estimation de la mortalité des Indiens du Canada 1900-1968.* Mémoire de maîtrise, Département de sociologie, Université d'Ottawa.

LAUER, R. 1989 *Social Problems and the Quality of Life,* Dubuque, Iowa: Wm. C. Brown Pub.

LA VIOLETTE, F.E. 1961 *The Struggle for Survival.* Toronto: University of Toronto Press.

LE DEVOIR. 1985 *16 000 femmes et 46 000 enfants pourront recouvrer leur statu d'Indien* (1 mars, 1985):4.

LEGARE, JACQUES 1981 *La mortalité infantile des Inuit dans l'après-guerre.* Montréal: Université de Montréal, Departement de démographie.

LESTER, G.S. 1981 "The Territorial Rights of the Inuit of the Canadian Northwest Territories: A Legal Argument." Unpublished Ph.D. dissertation. Toronto: York University.

LESLIE, J. and R. MAGUIRE 1978 *The Historical Development of the Indian Act, Treaties, and Historical Research Centres*. Ottawa: Department of Indian Affairs and Northern Development, PRE Group.

LEVINE, S. 1970 "The Survival of Indian Identity." In *The American Indian Today*, S. Levine and N. Lurie (eds). Hardmondsworth: Pelican.

LEWIS, W. 1956 "Economic Development with Unlimited Supplies of Labour." *Manchester School of Economic and Social Studies*, 23 (May 1956):153-160.

LIGHTBODY, J. 1969 "A Note on the Theory of Nationalism as a Function of Ethnic Demands." *Canadian Journal of Political Science*, 2 (1969):327-337.

LINDENSMITH, A., and S. STRAUSS 1968 *Social Psychology*. New York: Holt, Rinehart and Winston.

LITHMAN, YNGVE G. 1978 *The Community Apart: A Case Study of a Canadian Indian Reserve Community*. Stockholm: Department of Social Anthropology, University of Stockholm.

_____ **1983** *The Practice of Underdevelopment and the Theory of Development. The Canadian Indian Case*. Stockholm: Department of Social Anthropology, University of Stockholm.

LONG, J.A., M. BOLDT, and L. LITTLE BEAR. 1982 "Federal Indian Policy and Indian Self-Government in Canada: An Analysis of a Current Proposal." *Canadian Public Policy*, 8, 2 (1982):189-199.

_____ **1983** (eds). *Aboriginal Rights: toward an Understanding*. Lethbridge: Law Foundation.

LONGBOAT, D. 1987 "First Nations Control of Education: The Path to Our Survival as Nations." In *Indian Education in Canada*, J. Barman, Y. Hebert and D. McCaskill (eds), Vol. 2. Vancouver: University of British Columbia Press.

LOWER, A. 1957 *Colony to Nation: A History of Canada*. Toronto: Longman, Green & Co.

LU, CHANG-MEI, et EMERSON MATHURIN 1973 *Projections démographiques des Territoires du Nord-Ouest jusqu'en 1981*. Ottawa: Affairs Indiennes et du Nord, au nord, du 60.

LURIE, N. 1971 "The Contemporary American Indian Scene." In *North American Indians in Historical Perspective*, E. Leacock and N. Lurie (eds). New York: Random House Inc.

LUSSIER, A. 1979 *Louis Riel and the Metis: Riel Mini Conference Papers*, Winnipeg: Pemmican Publisher.

_____ **1984** *The Metis and Non-Status Indians 1967-1984, and the Metis and the Indians 1960-1984*. Ottawa: Treaties and Historical Research Centre, Department of Indian Affairs and Northern Development.

LUSSIER, ANTOINE S. and D. BRUCE SEALEY (eds). 1978 *The Other Natives the—les Metis*. Winnipeg: Manitoba Metis Federation Press.

LYON, L., J. FRIESEN, W.R. UNRUH, and R. HERTOZ 1970 *Intercultural Education*. Calgary: Faculty of Education, University of Calgary.

LYON, N. 1985 "Constitutional Issues in Native Law." In *Aboriginal Peoples and the Law*, B. Morse (ed). Ottawa: Carleton University Press.

MacEWAN, GRANT 1952 *Between the Red and the Rockies*. Toronto and Buffalo: University of Toronto Press.

MACKIE, C. 1986 "Some Reflections on Indian Economic Development." In *Arduous Journey*, J. Ponting (ed). Toronto: McClelland and Stewart (1986):211-227.

MACKIE, MARLENE 1974 "Ethnic Stereotypes and Prejudice: Alberta Indians, Hutterites, and Ukrainians." *Canadian Ethnic Studies*, 6, 1-2 (1974):39-53.

MANITOBA METIS FEDERATION JUSTICE COMMITTEE 1989 *Research and Analysis of the Impact of the Justice System on the Metis: Report to the Aboriginal Justice Inquiry*, November 22, 1989. Winnipeg: Manitoba Metis Federation Inc.

MANUEL, G. and M. POSLUMS 1974 *The Fourth World: An Indian Reality*. Toronto: Collier-Macmillan Canada Ltd.

MARIATEGUI, J.C. 1934 *Siete ensayos de interpretación de la sealidad peruana*, 2nd ed. Lima: Editorial Librariá Peruana.

MANITOBA INDIAN BROTHERHOOD 1971 *Wahbung: Our Tomorrows*. Winnipeg: October, 1971.

MARULE, M.S. 1977 "The Canadian Government's Termination Policy: From 1969 to the Present Day." In *One Century Later*, J. Getty and D Smith (eds). Vancouver: University of British Columbia Press.

MATHIAS, CHIEF JOE and G. YABSLEY 1991 " Conspiracy of Legislation: The Supression of Indian Rights in Canada," in *In Celebration of Our Survival*, D. Jensen and C. Brooks (eds.), University of British Columbia Press, Vancouver, pp. 34-47.

McCASKILL, D. 1981 "The Urbanization of Indians in Winnipeg, Toronto, Edmonton, and Vancouver: A Comparative Analysis." *Culture*, 1 (1981):82-89.

McCULLUM, H. and K. McCULLUM 1975 *This Land is Not for Sale*. Toronto: Anglican Book Centre.

McELROY, A. 1976 "The Negotiation of Sex-Role Identity in Eastern Arctic Culture Change." *The Western Canadian Journal of Anthropology*, 6, 3, pp. 184-200.

McINNIS, E. 1959 *Canada: A Political and Social History*. New York: Holt, Rinehart and Winston Inc.

McKINLEY, PATRICK 1989 "Natives Blamed for Woes." *Winnipeg Free Press*. October 14, 1989.

McKNIGHT, B. 1987 Notes for remarks by the Honourable Bill McKnight.

McLEOD, MARGARET and W.L. MORTON 1974 *Cuthbert Grant of Grantown*. Toronto: McClelland and Stewart.

McNAMARA, ROBERT. 1969 "The Ethics of Violent Dissent." In *Urban Riots*, Robert Connery (ed). New York: Random House.

MEADOW LAKE TRIBAL COUNCIL 1989 A Position Paper on Indian Labour Force Development, submitted to the Canadian Labour Market and Productivity Centre, October.

MEADOWS, M. 1981 Adaption to Urban Life by Native Women. Calgary: University of Calgary Deptartment. of Sociology, n.p.

MELLING, J. 1966 "Recent Developments in Official Policy towards Canadian Indians and Eskimos." *Race*, 7 (1966):382-389.

MELVILLE, B. 1981 *Indian Reserves and Indian Treaty Problems in Northeastern B.C.* Vancouver: B.C. Hydro and Power Authority.

MENDES, E. and P. BENDIN. n.d *The New Canadian Charter of Rights and International Law and Aboriginal Self-determination: A Proposal for a New Direction*. Mimeographed, Saskatoon, Saskatchewan.

METIS NATIONAL COUNCIL 1983 *A Brief to the Standing Senate Committee on Legal and Constitutional Affairs*, Ottawa, September 8.

_____ **1984** *The Metis Natives*. Toronto : Metis National Council.

METIS AND NON-STATUS INDIAN CRIME AND JUSTICE COMMISSION 1977 *Report*. Serpent River Reserve, Cutler, Ontario: Woodland Studio.

MICKENBERG, NEIL. 1971 "Aboriginal Rights in Canada and the United States." *Osgoode Hall Law Journal*, 9 (1971):154.

MILLS, C.W. 1961 *The Sociological Imagination*. New York: Oxford University Press.

MINISTRY OF CULTURE AND RECREATION. 1978 *Metis and Non-Status Indians of Ontario*. Ottawa.

MITCHELL, J. 1986 "Reflections on Twenty Years of Feminism." In *What is Feminism?* Mitchell, J. & A. Oakley (eds.), Oxford: Basil Blackwell, pp. 34-48.

MONTAGU, ASHLEY 1943 "The Myth of Blood." In *Race, Individual, and Collective Behaviour*, Edgar T. Thompson and Everett R. Hughes (eds). Glencoe, Ontario: The Free Press.

MOORE, R. 1978 *The Historical Development of the Indian Act*. Draft Manuscript. Ottawa: Department of Indian Affairs and Northern Development.

MORRIS, ALEXANDER 1880 *The Treaties of Canada with the Indians of Manitoba and the North West Territories*. Toronto: Belfords, Clark & Co.

MORSE, B. (ed). 1985 *Aboriginal Peoples and the Law: Indian Metis and Inuit Rights in Canada*. Ottawa: Carleton University Press.

MORTON, W.L. 1981 "The Historical Phenomenon of Minorities: The Canadian Experience." *Canadian Ethnic Studies*, 13, 3 (1981):1-39.

_____ **1963** *The Kingdom of Canada: A General History from Earliest Times*. Toronto: McClelland and Stewart.

MUNRO, J. 1981 Notes for Remarks by the Honourable John C. Munro, Minister of Indian Affairs and Northern Development to the Standing Committee on Indian Affairs and Northern Development, Ottawa, December 1, 1981.

MURRAY, G. to J. KEMPT 1834 "Correspondence and Other Papers Relating to Aboriginal Tribes in British Possessions," January 25, 1830, *British Parliamentary Papers*, No. 617, 88.

MYERS, G. 1914 *A History of Canadian Wealth*. Chicago: University of Chicago Press.

MYRDAL, G. 1957 *Rich Lands and Poor*. New York: Harper and Row.

NADEAU, RON 1979 *Indian Local Government*. Ottawa: Department of Indian Affairs and Northern Development. Policy Research and Evaluation.

NAGLER, MARK 1971 *Indians in the City*. Ottawa: Canadian Research Centre for Anthropology, St. Paul University.

NAMMACK, GEORGINA 1969 *Fraud, Politics, and the Dispossession of the Indians*. Norman, Oklahoma: University of Oklahoma Press.

NATIONAL INDIAN BROTHERHOOD 1977 Proposed Revisions of the Indian Act. Ottawa: NIB.

NATIVE PROBATION CAUCUS 1989 Submission to the Aboriginal Justice Inquiry. April 4, 1989. *Aboriginal Justice Inquiry Proceedings*. Winnipeg: Four Seasons Reporting Services Ltd.

NEILS, ELAINE 1971 *Reservations to City.* Chicago: University of Chicago Press.

NELSON, J.G. 1973 *The Last Refuge.* Montreal: Harvest House Ltd.

NENRIPIN, JACQUES 1968 *Tendances et facteurs de la fecondité au Canada.* Monographie sur le recensement de 1961. Ottawa: Bureau Fédéral de la Statistique.

NIELSEN, M. 1991 "Balance and Strategy: Native Criminal Justice Organizations, Native Communities and the Canadian State." Kingston: Paper presented at the Annual Meetings of the Canadian Sociology and Anthropology Association.

NEILSEN, MARIANNE O. 1990 "Canadian Correctional Policy and Native Inmates: The Control of Social Dynamite," *Canadian Ethnic Studies*, Vol. 22, No. 3, pp. 110-121.

NURKSE, RAGNAR 1953 *Problems of Capital Formation in Underdeveloped Countries.* New York: Oxford University Press.

NWAC 1981 "Statement by NWAC on Native Women's Rights." In *Women and the Constitution in Canada.* Doerr, A. & M. Carrier (eds.) Ottawa: CACSW, PP. 64-73.

———— **1985** First Nation Citizenship: A Discussion Paper, Ottawa: NWAC.

———— **1985** A Voice of Many Nations: Native Women, Ottawa: NWAC.

O'CALLAGHAN, E. (ed). 1856-57 *Documents Relative to the Colonial History of the State of New York: 1856-1857.*

OLIVER, C. 1990 "Determinants of Interorganizational Relationships: Integrative and Future Directions, *Academy of Management Review*, Vol. 15, No. 2, pp. 241-265.

OLIVER, S.C. 1962 "Ecology and Cultural Continuity as Contributing Factors in the Social Reorganizations of the Plains Indians." *University of California Publications in American Archaeology and Ethnology*, 48, 1 (1962):123-135.

OMBUDSMAN OF MANITOBA 1989 *Nineteenth Annual Report of the Ombudsman.* Winnipeg: Queen's Printer for the Province of Manitoba.

ONWA 1983 *Nations Within a Nation: An Aboriginal Right?* A Report of the Conference Proceedings, November 12, 13 and 14, 1982, Thunder Bay: ONWA.

OSSENBERG, R. (ed). 1980 *Power and Change in Canada.* Toronto: McClelland and Stewart.

PAIGE, J. 1971 "Political Orientation and Riot Participation." *American Sociological Review*, 36 (1971):810-819.

PAQUETTE, LYNE, et JEANNINE PERREAULT 1984 "Un demi-million d'Indiens inscrits au Canada en l'an 2000?" *Cahiers québécois de démographie*, 13, 1 (1984):101-115.

PASK, R. and J. SCOTT 1971 "Learning Strategies and Individual Competence." *International Journal of Man-Machine Studies*, 4 (1971):217-253.

PATON, R. 1982 *New Policies and Old Organizations: Can Indian Affairs Change?* Centre for Policy and Program Assessment, School of Public Administration. Ottawa: Carleton University.

PATTERSON, E. PALMER 1972 *The Canadian Indians: A History Since 1500.* Toronto: Collier-MacMillan Canada Ltd.

PAUL, P. 1990 *Bill C-31: The Trojan Horse: An Analysis of the Social, Economic and Political Reaction of First Nation People as a Result of Bill C-31*, A Thesis, The University of New Brunswick.

PELLETIER, EMILE 1974   *A Social History of the Manitoba Metis.* Winnipeg: Manitoba Metis Federation Press.

_____ **1975**   *Exploitation of Metis Lands.* Winnipeg: Manitoba Metis Federation Press.

PELLETIER, W. 1970   *Two Articles.* Toronto: Neewin Publishing Co., 1970.

PENDLEY, K., and C. KOLSTAD 1980   "American Indians and National Energy Policy." *The Journal of Energy and Development,* 5 (1980): 221-251.

PENNEKEOK, F. 1976   "The Anglican Church and the Disintegration of Red River Society, 1818-1870." In *The West and the Nation,* C. Berger and R. Cook (eds). Toronto: McClelland and Stewart.

PENNER, K., CHAIRMAN (PENNER REPORT) 1983   *Indian Self-Government in Canada: Report of the Special Committee.* Ottawa: Minister of Supply and Services.

PENNOCK, J.R. 1950   *Liberal Democracy: Its Merits and Prospects.* New York: Holt Rinehart.

PERREAULT, JEANNINE, LYNE PAQUETTE, et M.V. GEORGE 1985   *Projections de la population indienne inscrite, 1982-1996.* Ottawa: Affaires indiennes et du Nord Canada.

PERROUX, F. 1953   "Not su la notion de 'pole de croissance'." *Économic appliquée,* 8, (janvier 1953):307-320.

PERROW, C. 1961   "Goals in Complex Organizations." *American Sociological Review,* 26, (1961):854-865.

PETERS, E. 1987   *Aboriginal Self Government Arrangements in Canada: An Overview.* Kingston, Ontario: Queen's University, Institute of Intergovernmental Relations.

PETERS, E., M. ROSENBERG and G. HALSETH 1989   *The Ontario Metis: A People Without an Identity.* Mimeo.

PETERS, OMAR 1968   "Canada's Indians and Eskimos and Human Rights." Paper presented to the Thinkers' Conference on Cultural Rights. Mimeographed.

PETERSON, JACQUELINE and JENNIFER S.H. BROWN (eds). 1985   *The New Peoples: Being and Becoming Metis in North America.* Winnipeg: The University of Manitoba Press.

PETTIGREW, T. 1964   *A Profile of the Negro American.* Princeton: D. Van Nostrand Co.

PFEIFFER, J. and G. SALANCHIK 1978   *The External Control of Organizations: A Resource Dependence Perspective.* New York: Harper and Row.

PICHE, VICTOR, and M.V. GEORGE 1973   "Estimates of vital rates for the Canadian Indians, 1960-1970." *Demography,* 10(1973):367-382.

PIEPENBURG, ROY 1982   "Most important concerns about the optional Indian government legislation." Indian Association of Alberta, Communications Department, Edmonton, December 23, 1982.

PINKERTON, E. 1989   *Co-operative Management of Local Fisheries: New Directions for Improved Management and Community Development,* Vancouver: University of British Columbia Press.

PIORE, MICHAEL 1968   *Public and Private Responsibility in On-the-Job Training of Disadvantaged Workers.* Department of Economics Working Paper. Massachussetts: MIT Press.

PITTS, J. 1974   "The Study of Race Consciousness: Comments on New Directions." *American Journal of Sociology,* 80 (1974):665-687.

PLAIN, F. 1985   "A Treaty on the Rights of the Aboriginal Peoples of the Continent of North America." In *The Quest for Justice,* M. Boldt, J. Long, and L. Little Bear (eds). Toronto: The University of Toronto Press.

POLANYI, KARL 1974   *The Great Transformation*. Boston: Beacon Press Inc

PONTING, J.R. 1984   "Conflict and Change in Indian/Non-Indian Relations in Canada: Comparison of 1976 and 1979 National Attitude Surveys." *Canadian Journal of Sociology*, 9, 2 (1984):137-158.

_____ 1987   *Profiles of Public Opinion on Canadian Natives and Native Issues: Special Status and Self Government*. Calgary: Research Unit for Public Policy Studies, The University of Calgary.

PONTING, J. 1991   "An Indian Policy for Canada in the 21st Century" in C. Remie and J. Lacroix (eds), *Canada on the Threshold of the 21st Century*, Amsterdam: John Benjamis Pub. Co.

PONTING, J.R. and R. GIBBINS 1980   *Out of Irrelevance: A Socio-political introduction to Indian Affairs of Canada*. Toronto: Butterworth & Co. (Canada) Ltd.

PONTING, J. RICK 1990   "Internalization: Perspectives on an Emerging Direction in Aboriginal Affairs," *Canadian Ethnic Studies*, Vol. 22, No. 3, pp. 85-109.

PRESTHUS, R. 1974   *Elites in Policy Process*. London: Cambridge University Press.

PRICE, J. 1982   "Historical Theory and the Applied Anthropology of U.S. and Canadian Indians." *Human Organization*, 41, 2 (1982):42-53.

_____ 1979   *Indians of Canada: Cultural Dynamics*. Scarborough, Ontario; Prentice Hall Canada.

_____ 1978   *Native Studies*. Toronto: McGraw-Hill Ryerson Ltd.

_____ 1972   "U.S. and Canadian Indian Periodicals." *Canadian Review of Sociology and Anthropology*, 9, May (1972):150-162.

_____ 1981   "The Viability of Indian Languages in Canada." *Canadian Journal of Native Studies*, 1, 2 (1981): 349-361.

PRICE, R. (ed). 1979   *The Spirit of the Alberta Indian Treaties*. Montreal: Institute for Research on Public Policy.

PRIEST, G. 1984   *Aboriginal Languages in Canada*. Ottawa: Minister of Supply and Services.

PRITCHETT, J.P. 1942   *The Red River Valley, 1811-1849: A Regional Study*. Toronto: Ryerson Press.

PROGRAMME DES AFFAIRES INDIENNES ET INUIT 1979   *Profil démographique des Indiennes inscrites*. Ottawa: Direction de la recherche.

PROSS, P. 1975   *Pressure Group Behaviour in Canadian Politics*. Scarborough, Ontario: McGraw-Hill Ryerson Inc.

PRYOR, E. 1984   *Profile of Native Women: 1981 Census of Canada*. Ottawa: Minister of Supply and Services Canada.

PUBLIC AFFAIRS, EMPLOYMENT AND IMMIGRATION and ABORIGINAL EMPLOYMENT AND TRAINING GROUP 1990   *Pathways to Success: Aboriginal Employment and Training Strategy*, mimeo.

PURICH, D. 1988   *The Metis*. Toronto: James Lorimer and Co.

RAM, BALL et A. ROMANIUC 1984   *Fertility Projections of Registered Indians*. Ottawa: Statistique Canada (inedit.).

RAY, ARTHUR J. 1974   *Indians in the Fur Trade*. Toronto and Buffalo: University of Toronto Press.

RAUNET, D. 1984 *Without Surrender Without Consent.* Vancouver: Douglas and McIntyre.

REA, K. 1976 The Political Economy Northern Development, No. 36. Ottawa: Science Council of Canada Background Study, Information Canada.

REEVES, W. and J. FRIDERES 1981 "Government Policy and Indian Urbanization: The Alberta Case." *Canadian Public Policy,* 7, 4 (Autumn 1981):584-595.

REITZ, J. 1974 "Language and Ethnic Community Survival;" *The Canadian Review of Sociology and Anthropology,* Special Issue, pp. 104-122.

REPORT OF THE AFFAIRS OF THE INDIANS IN CANADA 1844 "History of the Relations between the Government and the Indians." *Journals,* Section 1. Ottawa: Queen's Printer, 1844.

RHODE, D. 1986 "Feminist Perspectives on Legal Ideology," in J. Mitchell and A, Oakley (eds.) *What is Feminism?,* Oxford: Basil Blackwell, pp. 151-160

RICHARDSON, B. 1972 *James Bay.* San Francisco: Sierra Club.

RICHSTONE, J. 1983 Native Women, the Charter and Constitutional Equality Rights in Canada. Discussion Paper Prepared for NWAC, Ottawa: NWAC, n.p.

RIEBER, J. 1977 *Fundamental Concerns Regarding Indian Local Government: A Discussion Paper of Potential Problem and Research Areas.* Ottawa: Department of Indian Affairs and Northern Development.

ROBERTSON, ELEANOR 1988 *Native Women in Conflict with the Law.* Winnipeg: Unpublished.

ROBITAILLE, NORBERT et ROBERT COINIERE 1984 *Aperçu de la situation démographique et socio-économique des Inuit du Canada.* Ottawa: Direction de la recherche, Orientations générales, Affaires indiennes et du Nord Canada.

ROE, GILBERT FRANK 1955 *The North American Buffalo.* Toronto and Buffalo: University of Toronto Press.

ROHEN, D. 1967 *The Quest for Self-Determination.* New York: Yale University Press.

ROMANIUK, A. and V. PICHE 1972 "Natality Estimates for the Canadian Indians by Stable Population Models, 1900-1969." *The Canadian Review of Sociology and Anthropology,* 9, 1 (1972):1-20.

ROMANOV, R. 1985 "Aboriginal Rights in the Constitutional Process," in M. Boldt and J. Long (eds.), *The Quest for Justice: Aboriginal Peoples and Aboriginal Rights,* Toronto: University of Toronto Press, pp. 23-82

ROMANOW, R. 1985 "Aboriginal Rights in the Constitutional Process." In Boldt, M. & J. Long (eds.), *The Quest for Justice: Aboriginal Peoples and Aboriginal Rights,* Toronto: University of Toronto Press, pp. 73-82.

ROOSENS, E. 1986 Micronationalisme; een antropologie van het etnische reveil, Leuven: Uitgeverij Acco.

ROSENSTEIN-RODAN, P.N. 1943 "Problems of Industrialization of Eastern and South-eastern Europe." *Economic Journal,* 53 (June September 1943):128-156.

ROSS, ALEXANDER 1972 *The Red River Settlement.* Edmonton: Hurtig Publishers.

ROUCH, J. 1956 "Migration au Ghana." Fo. de la Société des Africanistus, 17, 1956.

ROWE, G. et M. J. NORRIS 1984 *Mortality Projections for Registered Indians.* Ottawa: Statistique Canada (inedit.).

RYAN, J. 1978 *Wall of Words: The Betrayal of the Urban Indian.* Toronto: Peter Martin Associates.

RYANT, J., and C. HEINRICH 1988 "Youth Court Committees in Manitoba," in *Justice and the Young Offender in Canada.* J. Hudson, J. Hornick, and B. Burrows (Eds) Toronto: Wall and Thompson.

RYERSON, S. 1960 *The Founding of Canada: Beginning to 1815.* Toronto: McClelland and Stewart.

SALISBURY, R. 1986 *A Homeland for The Cree.* Kingston and Montreal: McGill-Queen's University Press.

SANDERS, D. 1983 The Rights of the Aboriginal Peoples of Canada." *Canadian Bar Review,* 6, 1 (1983):314-338.

_____ **1975** "Indian Women: A Brief History of Their Roles and Rights," *McGill Law Journal,* 21, 4, pp. 656-672.

_____ **1985** "The Indian Lobby and the Canadian Constitution, 1978-1982," In *Indigenous Peoples and the Nation-State: 'Fourth World' Politics in Canada, Australia and Norway,* Dyck, N. (ed.), St. John's: Memorial University of Newfoundland, Institute of Social and Economic Research, pp. 151-189.

_____ **1983a** "Prior Claims: Aboriginal People in the Constitution of Canada." In *Canada and the New Constitution: The Unfinished Business,* S. Beck and I. Bernier (eds). Montreal: Institute for Research on Public Policy.

_____ **1983b** "The Indian Lobby." In *And No One Cheered,* K. Banting and R. Simeon (eds). Toronto: Methuen.

_____ **1985** "Aboriginal Rights: The Search for Recognition in International Law." In *The Quest for Justice,* M. Boldt, J. Long, and L. Little Bear (eds). Toronto: University of Toronto Press.

SANDERS, DOUGLAS 1990 "The Supreme Court of Canada and the 'Legal and Political Struggle' Over Indigenous Rights," *Canadian Ethnic Studies,* Vol. 22, No. 3, pp. 122-129.

SARKADI, L. 1992 "Nunavut: Carving Out a New Territory in the North," *Calgary Herald,* January 4, A5.

SAWCHUK, JOE 1978 *The Metis of Manitoba: Reformulation of an Ethnic Identity.* Toronto: Peter Martin Associates.

SAWCHUK, J., P. SAWCHUK and T. FERGUSON 1981 *Metis Land Rights in Alberta: A Political History.* Edmonton: The Metis Association of Alberta.

SCHMEISER, D. 1974 *The Native Offender and the Law.* Ottawa: Information Canada.

SCHWARTZ, B. 1985 *First Principle: Constitutional Reform with Respect to the Aboriginal Peoples of Canada, 1982-84.* Kingston: Institute of Intergovernmental Relations, Queen's University.

_____ **1986** *First Principles, Second Thoughts.* Montreal: The Institute for Research on Public Policy.

SCITOVSKY, T. 1954 "Two Concepts of External Economics." *Journal of Political Economy,* 62 (April 1954):143-152.

SEALEY, D. BRUCE 1975 "One Plus One Equals One." In *The Other Natives: the Metis.* Antoine S. Lussier and D. Bruce Sealey (eds). Winnipeg: Manitoba Metis Federation Press.

SEALEY, D. BRUCE, and ANTOINE S. LUSSIER 1975 *The Metis—Canada's Forgotten People.* Winnipeg: Manitoba Metis Federation Press.

SHAW, T. 1985 "Ethnicity as the resilient paradigm: From 1960's to the 1980's." Mimeographed, Dalhousie University, Halifax, Nova Scotia.

SHEA, I.G. 1879 *Charlevoix's History of New France*. New York: Colonial Documents, Vol. 2, 1879.

SHKILNYK, A. 1985 *A Poison Stronger Than Love: The Destruction of an Ojibwa Community*. New Haven and London: Yale University Press.

SIGGNER, A. 1980 "A Socio-demographic Profile of Indians in Canada." In *Out of Irrelevance*, J.R. Ponting and R. Gibbins (eds). Toronto: Butterworth and Co. (Canada) Ltd.

_____ **1986** "The Socio-demographic Conditions of Registered Indians." *Canadian Social Trends* (Winter 1986):2-9.

SIGGNER, ANDREW J. 1979 *Aperçu de la situation démographique, sociale et économique de la population indienne inscrite du Canada*. Ottawa: Direction de la recherche, programme des Affaires Indiennes et Inuit.

SIGGNER, A. and C. LOCATELLI 1980 *Regional Population Projections by Age, Sex, and Residence for Canada's Registered Indian Population,1976-1991*. Ottawa: Research Branch, Department of Indian Affairs and Northern Development.

SILMAN, J. 1987 *Enough is Enough: Aboriginal Women Speak Out*. Toronto: The Women's Press.

SILVER, ARTHUR 1976 "French Quebec and the Metis Question, 1869-1885." In *The West and the Nation*. Carl Berger and Ramsay Cook (eds). Toronto: McClelland and Stewart.

SLATTERY, B. 1985 "The Hidden Constitution: Aboriginal Rights in Canada." In *The Quest for Justice*, M. Boldt, J. Long, and L. Little Bear (eds). Toronto: The University of Toronto Press.

SMITH, A. 1981 *The Ethnic Revival*. New York: Cambridge University Press.

SMITH, J. *et al.* 1985 "The Changing Political Situation of Women in Canada." *In Minorities and the Canadian State*, Nevitte, N. & A. Kornberg (eds.). Oakville: Mosaic Press, pp. 221-238.

SLOBODIN, RICHARD 1966 *Metis of the Mackenzie District*. Ottawa: Research Centre for Anthropology, St. Paul University.

SOLICTOR GENERAL OF CANADA 1985 *Native and Non-Native Admissions to Federal, Provincial and Territorial Correctional Institutions*. Ottawa: Solicitor General of Canada.

_____ **1989** *Task Force on Aboriginal Peoples in Federal Corrections: Final Report*. Ottawa: Solicitor General of Canada.

SORENSON, GARY and MURRAY WOLFSON 1969 "Black Economic Independence: Some Preliminary Thoughts." *The Annals of Regional Science*, 3 (December 1969):168-178.

SOS 1975 *Speaking Together: Canada's Native Women*. Toronto: Hunter Rose Company.

SOUTHESK, THE EARL OF 1968 *Saskatchewan and the Rocky Mountains*. Edmonton: Hurtig Publishers.

SPECIAL SENATE COMMITTEE HEARING ON POVERTY 1970 *Proceedings*, Vols. 13-14. Ottawa: Supply and Services Canada.

SPECK, D. C. 1989 "The Indian Health Transfer Policy: A Step in the Right Direction, A Revenge of the Hidden Policy?" *Native Studies Review*, Vol. 5, No. 1, pp. 187-214.

SPENCER, R. and J. JENNINGS 1965 *The Native Americans*. New York: Harper and Row.

SPRENGER, G. HERMAN 1972 "The Metis Nation: Buffalo Hunting versus Agriculture in the Red River Settlement." *Western Canadian Journal of Anthropology*, 3, 1 (1972):158-178.

SPRY, IRENE 1976 "The Great Transformation: The Disappearance of the Commons in Western Canada." In *Man and Nature on the Prairies*, Richard Allen (ed). Regina: Canadian Plains Research Centre.

STANBURY, W. and J. SIEGAL 1975 *Success and Failure: Indians in Urban Society*. Vancouver: University of British Columbia Press.

STANLEY, GEORGE 1952 "The Indian Background of Canadian History." *Canadian Historical Association Annual Report*. Canadian Historical Society.

STANLEY, GEORGE F.G. 1961 *The Birth of Western Canada: A History of the Riel Rebellions*. New York: Longman, Green and Co.

STARBLANKET, N. 1979 *On the Rights of Indian Women and Children Under the Indian Act*. Ottawa: NIB.

STATISTICS CANADA 1989 *Canadian Social Trends: Violence in the Family*. Ottawa: Statistics Canada.

STAVENHAGEN, R. 1963 "Seven Fallacies about Latin America." In *Latin America: Reform or Revolution?*, J. Petras and M. Zeitling (eds). New York: Greenwich Press.

STEA, D. and B. WISNER n.d. "The Fourth World: Introduction." *Antipode*, 16, 2 3-12.

STEINEM, G. 1983 *"Perspectives on Women in the 1980s: The Baird Poskanzer Memorial Lecture."* In *Perspectives on Women in the 1980s*, Turner, J. & L. Emery (eds.). Winnipeg: The University of Manitoba Press, pp. 14-27.

STEWART, WALTER. 1974 "Red Power." In *Canada's Indians: Contemporary Conflicts*, J.S. Frideres (ed). Scarborough, Ontario: Prentice Hall Canada.

STILLWAGGON, E. 1984 "Native American Economic Studies: A Bibliographic Essay," *Sage Race Relations Abstracts*, 9, 1 (February 1984):1-16.

STYMEIST, DAVID H. 1975 *Ethnics and Indians: Social Relations in a Northwestern Ontario Town*. Toronto: Peter Martin Associates.

SUNKEL, OSWALDO 1973 "Transitional Capitalism and National Disintegration in Latin America." *Social and Economic Studies*, 22 (1973):132-176.

SURTEES, R.J. 1969 "The Development of an Indian Reserve Policy in Canada." *Ontario History*, LCI, 2 (June 1969):87-98.

SURVEY 1980 *Indian Conditions*. Ottawa: Department of Indian Affairs and Northern Development.

SURVEYOR GENERAL 1981 Personal Communication, Legal Surveys Division, Surveys and Mapping Branch, Energy, Mines and Resources, Ottawa.

SWAIN, H. 1988 "Comprehensive Claims," *Transition*, 1, 6 (December 1988):7-9.

SYMONS, T.H.B. 1970 "The Obligations of History: A Review of Native Rights in Canada." *Indian-Eskimo Association of Canada Bulletin*, 2, 3 (1970):5-7.

TABB, WILLIAM 1970 *The Political Economy of the Black Ghetto*. New York: W.W. Norton and Co.

TANNER, A. (ed) 1983 *The Politics of Indianness*. Institute of Social and Economic Research, Memorial University of Newfoundland, St. John's, Newfoundland.

TAQRALIK 1984 *Native Women's Association Offers Help to Inuit Women*. Mimeo.

TAYLOR, J. 1983 "An Historical Introduction to Metis Claims in Canada." *The Canadian Journal of Native Studies*, 3 (1983):151-181.

TENNANT, P. 1985 "Aboriginal Rights and the Penner Report on Indian Self Government" In *The Quest for Justice*, M. Boldt, J. Long, and L. Little Bear (eds). Toronto: The University of Toronto Press.

_____ **1984** "Indian Self Government: Progress or Stalemate." *Canadian Public Policy*, 10, 2 (1984):211-215.

THOMAS, CYRUS 1896 "Indian Land Cessions in the United States." In *18th Annual Report of the Bureau of American Ethnology*, Vol. 2, Washington, D.C.: Smithsonian Institution.

THOMAS, D.H. 1972 "Western Shoshoni Ecology Settlement Patterns and Beyond." In *Great Basin Cultural Ecology: A Symposium*. D.D. Fowler (ed). Desert Research Institute, Publications in the Social Sciences, 8.

THOMAS, ROBERT K. 1985 "Afterward." In *The New Peoples: Being and Becoming Metis in North America*, Jacqueline Peterson and Jennifer S.H. Brown (eds). Winnipeg: The University of Manitoba Press (1985):243-251.

THOMPSON, R. 1982 "Aboriginal Title and Mining Legislation in the Northwest Territories." *Studies in Aboriginal Rights No. 6*. Saskatoon, Saskatchewan: University of Saskatchewan Native Law Centre.

TITLEY, B. 1983 "W.M. Graham: Indian Agent Extraordinaire." *Prairie Forum*, 8, (1983):26-28.

_____ **1986** *A Narrow Vision*. Vancouver: University of British Columbia Press.

TOBIAS, J. 1976 "Protection, Civilization, Assimilation: An Outline of Canada's Indian Policy." *Western Canadian Journal of Anthropology*, 6, 2 (1976):13-30.

TRIGGER, B. 1985 *Natives and Newcomers*. Kingston and Montreal: McGill-Queen's University Press.

_____ **1965** "The Jesuits and the Fur Trade." *Ethnohistory*, 12 (Winter 1965):30-53.

TRUDEL, MARCEL and GENEVIEVE JAIN 1970 "Canadian History Textbooks." *Studies of the Royal Commission on Bilingualism and Biculturalism*, No. 5. Ottawa: Queen's Printer.

TURPEL, MARY 1990 "Aboriginal Peoples and the Canadian Charter: Interpretive Monopolies, Cultural Differences," *Canadian Human Rights Year Book*, Ottawa: University of Ottawa, Human Rights Research and Education Centre, 1989-90, pp. 3-45.

TWO-AXE EARLY, M. *et al.* 1981 "Ethnicity and Femininity as Determinants of Life Experience," *Canadian Ethnic Studies*, 13, 1, pp. 37-42.

UCHENDU, U. 1970 "The Passing of Tribal Man: A West African Experience." In *The Passing of Tribal Man in Africa*, P. Gutlaind (ed). Leiden: E.J. Brill (1970):51-56.

UMORZURIKE, U. 1972 *Self-Determination in International Law*. Hamden, Ct.: Anchor Books.

UNIVERSITY OF MANITOBA RESEARCH LTD. 1988 *Manitoba Metis Federation: Survey of Members*. Winnipeg.

VACHON, R. 1982 "Traditional Legal Ways of Native Peoples and the Struggle for Native Rights." *Inter-Culture*, 15 (1982):1-18.

VALENTINE, V. 1978 "Canadian Indians." In *Ethnicity, Language, and the Cohesion of Canadian Society*, R. Breton, J. Reitz, and V. Valentine (eds). Montreal: Institute for Research in Public Policy.

VANDERBURGH, R. 1968 *The Canadian Indians in Ontario's School Texts: A Study of Social Studies Textbooks, Grades 1 through 8*.Report prepared for the University Women's Club of Port Credit, Ontario.

VAN KIRK, SYLVIA 1980 *Many Tender Ties.* Winnipeg: Watson & Dwyer Publishing.

VERDUN-JONES, S. and G. MUIRHEAD 1979-80 "Natives in the Criminal Justice System: An Overview." *Crime and Justice,* 7/8, 1 (1979-80):3-21.

VINCENT, DAVID 1970 *An Evaluation of the Indian-Metis Urban Problem.* Winnipeg: University of Winnipeg Press.

WADDELL, JACK and O.M. WATSON 1971 *The American Indian in Urban Society.* Boston: Little, Brown and Co.

WALDHAM, J. 1986 "The 'Other Side': Ethnostatus Distinctions in Western Subarctic Native Communities." In *1885 and After,* F. Barron and J. Waldham (eds). Regina: Canadian Plains Research Centre.

WALKER, JAMES 1971 "The Indians in Canadian Historical Writing." Paper delivered at Canadian Historical Association Meetings.

WALSH, GERALD 1971 *Indians in Transition.* Toronto: McClelland and Stewart.

WARD, M. 1988 *Indian Education in Canada,* MA Thesis, College of Education, University of Saskatchewan, Saskatoon.

WASHBURN, WILCOMB 1965 "Indian Removal Policy: Administrative, Historical, and Moral Criteria for Judging Its Success or Failure." *Ethno-History,* 12 (Winter 1965):274-278.

WATSON, G. 1979 "On Getting Nothing Back: Managing the Meaning of Ethnicity in Canada's Northwest Territories." *Ethnos,* 1-2 (1979):99-118.

_____ **1981** "The Reification of Ethnicity and its Political Consequences in the North." *Canadian Review of Sociology and Anthropology.* 18, 40 (1981):453-469.

WAUBAGESHIG 1970 *The Only Good Indian.* Toronto: New Press.

WEAVER, S. 1978 Indian Women, Marriage and Legal Status, Waterloo: University of Waterloo, n.p.

_____ **1981** *Making Canadian Indian Policy. The Hidden Agenda 1968-1970.* Toronto: University of Toronto Press.

_____ **1983** "Federal Difficulties with Aboriginal Rights Demands." In J. Long *et al.* (eds.), *Aboriginal Rights: Toward an Understanding,* Aboriginal Rights Conference, January 18-21, 1983, Lethbridge, University of Lethbridge.

_____ **1983** "Federal Difficulties with Aboriginal Rights Demands." In *Aboriginal Rights: Towards an Understanding,* J.A. Long, M. Boldt, and L. Little Bear (eds). Lethbridge: University of Lethbridge, (1983):87-98.

_____ **1985** "Political Representivity and Indigenous Minorities in Canada and Australia," in N. Dyck (ed.), *Indigenous Peoples and the Nation State: 'Fourth World' Politics in Canada, Australia and Norway,* St. John's: Memorial University of Newfoundland.

_____ **1986** "Indian Policy in the New Conservative Government, Part II: The Nielsen Task Force in the Context of Recent Policy Initiatives." *Native Studies Review,* 2, 2 (1986):1-47.

_____ **1980** *The Hidden Agenda.* Unpublished manuscript. Waterloo, Ontario: University of Waterloo, 1980.

_____ **1981** *Making Canadian Indian Policy.* Toronto: University of Toronto Press.

_____ **1984** "A Commentary on the Penner Report," *Canadian Public Policy*, 10, 2 (1984):215-221.

WEIN, F. 1986 *Rebuilding the Economic Base of Indian Communities: The MicMac in Nova Scotia*. Montreal: Institute for Research on Public Policy.

WEITZ, J. 1971 *Cultural Change and Field Dependence in Two Native Canadian Linguistic Families*. Unpublished Ph.D., University of Ottawa, 1971.

WELLS, E. L. 1989 "Self-enhancement through delinquency: A conditional test of self-derogation theory." *Journal of Research in Crime and Delinquency*. 26(3): 226-252.

WERHAN, K. 1978 "The Sovereignty of Indian Tribes: A Reaffirmation and Strengthening in the 1970's." *Notre Dame Lawyer*, 54 (1978):20-36.

WERTMAN, P. 1983 "Planning and Development After the James Bay Agreement." *The Canadian Journal of Native Studies*, 2, 3 (1983):48-56.

WHITE, P. 1985 *Native Women: A Statistical Overview*. Ottawa: SOS.

WHITESIDE, D. 1973 *Historical Development of Aboriginal Political Associations in Canada*. Ottawa: NIB.

_____ **1980** "Bullets, Bibles, Bureaucrats, and Businessmen: Indian Administration in Upper Canada, 1746-1980." Address to the Indian Historical Conference, Walpole Island Reserve, November 15, 1980.

_____ **1972** "A Good Blanket Has Four Corners: An Initial Comparison of the Colonial Administration of Aboriginals in Canada and the United States." Paper presented at the Western Association of Sociology and Anthropology, Calgary.

_____ **1973** "Historical Development of Aboriginal Associations in Canada: Documentation." Ottawa: National Indian Brotherhood.

WHITESIDE, DON (SIN A PAW), and SCOTT DOUGLAS WHITESIDE 1979 "Indians in UpperCanada through 1845, with Special Reference to Half-breed Indians." *The Circle Being Threatened*. Ottawa: Aboriginal Institute of Canada.

WILDSMITH, B. 1985 "Pre Confederation Treaties." In *Aboriginal Peoples and the Law*, B. Morse (ed). Ottawa: Carleton University Press, (1985):122-271.

WILLHELM, SIDNEY M. 1969 "Red Man, Black Man, and White America: The Constitutional Approach to Genocide." *Catalyst*, 4 (Spring 1969):3-4.

WILSON, J. 1974 *Canada's Indians*. London: Minority Rights Group Ltd.,Report No. 21.

WILSON, RICHARD W. 1992 *Compliance Ideologies: Rethinking Political Culture*, Cambridge University Press.

WOHLFELD, MONIKA J. and NEIL NEVITTE 1990 "Postindustrial Value Change and Support for Native Issues, *Canadian Ethnic Studies*, Vol. 22, No. 3, pp. 56-68.

WOMEN OF THE METIS NATION - WORKING COMMITTEE 1986 Metis Women Participate: First Ministers' Conference, 1987, A Proposal for Funding. Edmonton: Metis Association of Alberta.

WOODCOCK, GEORGE 1975 *Gabriel Dumont: The Metis Chief and His Lost World*. Edmonton: Hurtig Publishers.

WOODWARD, J. 1989 *Native Law*. Toronto: Carswell.

WUTTUNEE, W. 1972 *Ruffled Feathers.* Calgary: Bell Books Ltd.

YERXA, J. 1990 "Report on the Survey of the First Nations of Alberta." Edmonton: John Yerxa Research Incorporated.

YOUNG, K. 1984 "Indian Health Services in Canada: A Sociohistorical Perspective," *Social Science and Medicine*, Vol. 18, No. 3, pp. 257-264.

ZAKARIYA, H. 1976 "New Directions in the Search for and Development of Petroleum Resources in the Developing Countries." *Vanderbilt Journal of Transnational Law*, 9 (Summer 1976):545-577.

ZLOTKIN, N. 1983 *Unfinished Business: Aboriginal Peoples and The 1983 Constitutional Conference.* Kingston: Institute of Intergovernmental Relations, Queens University.

_____ **1985** "Post-Confederation Treaties." In *Aboriginal Peoples and the Law*, B. Morse (ed). Ottawa: Carleton University Press.

NEWSPAPER AND MAGAZINE ARTICLES, and PRESS CLIPPINGS

GLOBE AND MAIL, **10/11/81**, p. 9: "Pawley wants entrenched native women's rights"

INAC Communique, 28/7/81, title unknown

INAC Communique, 8/9/82, title unknown

KANAI NEWS, **1/9/79**, page unknown: "On NIB agenda: Indian women's status and Canadian Constitution"

THE NATIVE PEOPLE, **1/4/77**, page unknown: "Native women's rights"

THE NATIVE PERSPECTIVE, **2, 7, 1977**, pp. 43-44: "Starblanket agrees to meet with non-status Indian women's group"

NWAC NEWSLETTER, **1, 2, 1981**, p. 5: "NWAC's 7th annual convention, Regina"

THE QUIL, **Brandon University Newspaper, 22/10/82**, p. 12: "Native women in Canada: The least members of society"

VANCOUVER SUN, **24/11/81**, p. D6: "Vigorous lobby against Charter rights"

INDEX